This book is due for return on or before the last date shown below.

Tests in education

Tests in education
A book of critical reviews

COMPILED BY

Philip Levy

Department of Psychology,
University of Lancaster

Harvey Goldstein

Department of Statistics and Computing,
University of London Institute of Education

1984

ACADEMIC PRESS

(Harcourt Brace Jovanovich, Publishers)

London   Orlando   San Diego   San Francisco   New York
Toronto   Montreal   Sydney   Tokyo   São Paulo

ACADEMIC PRESS INC. (LONDON) LTD.
24–28 Oval Road,
London NW1

United States Edition Published by
ACADEMIC PRESS INC.
(Harcourt Brace Jovanovich, Inc.)
Orlando, Florida 32887

British Library Cataloguing in Publication Data

Tests in education.
  1. Grading and marking (Students)
  I. Levy, Philip   II. Goldstein, Harvey
  371.2′64   LB3060.37

  ISBN 0-12-445880-7
  LCCCN 83-73142

Photoset by Paston Press, Norwich and printed in Great Britain
by St Edmundsbury Press, Bury St Edmunds

Reviewers

J. K. BACKHOUSE   Department of Educational Studies, University of Oxford

S. N. BENNETT   Department of Educational Research, University of Lancaster

S. F. BLINKHORN   School of Natural Sciences, Hatfield Polytechnic

B. L. M. CHAPMAN   School of Education Research Unit, University of Bristol

P. CLIFT   Faculty of Educational Studies, Open University

P. COXHEAD   Department of Educational Enquiry, University of Aston in Birmingham

R. A. DAVIES   formerly of Department of Education, Manchester College of Education

C. W. DESFORGES   School of Education, University of East Anglia

R. DRIVER   Centre for Studies in Science Education, School of Education, University of Leeds

E. P. DUGGAN   formerly of Faculty of Educational Studies, Open University

C. D. ELLIOTT   Department of Education, University of Manchester

A. FORRESTER   Schools Psychological Services, Tameside

C. GIPPS   Institute of Education, University of London

D. R. GOOCH   Ealing, London

N. C. GRAHAM   Department of Educational Enquiry, University of Aston in Birmingham

J. GRAY   Division and Institute of Education, University of Sheffield

J. R. HARTLEY   School of Education, University of Leeds

A. S. HAWKINS   Institute of Education, University of London

J. HEWISON   Health Care Research Unit, University of Newcastle-upon-Tyne

D. ST JOHN JESSON   Institute of Education, University of Sheffield

S. JOHNSON   Centre for Studies in Science Education, School of Education, University of Leeds

D. LABON   Department of Education, University of Southampton

D. H. LEE   Schools Psychological Service, Stockport

A. P. LONTON   Department of Education, University of Manchester

K. LOVELL   formerly of School of Education, University of Leeds

C. MABEY   Research and Statistics Division, Inner London Education Authority

R. MURPHY   Department of Education, University of Southampton

J. NISBET   Department of Education, University of Aberdeen

D. L. NUTTALL   Faculty of Educational Studies, Open University

D. P. A. O'HARE   Department of Psychology, University of Otago

C. F. OWEN   Institute of Education, University of London

C. J. PHILLIPS   Faculty of Education, University of Birmingham

I. PLEWIS   Institute of Education, University of London

P. D. PUMFREY   Department of Education, University of Manchester

H. QUIGLEY   Research Unit, National Union of Teachers

R. REASON   Schools Psychological Service, Stockport

J. RIDGWAY   Department of Psychology, University of Lancaster

R. J. RIDING   Department of Educational Psychology, University of Birmingham

T. ROBERTS   Department of Education, University of Manchester

J. P. RYAN   Department of Education, University of Manchester

D. J. SATTERLY   School of Education, University of Bristol

S. SHARP   Scottish Examination Board, Dalkeith

M. SHIPMAN   Department of Education, University of Warwick

J. SLOBODA   Department of Psychology, University of Keele

A. STIBBS   School of Education, University of Leeds

Preface

The purpose of the test reviews in this volume is to inform and guide a wide range of professionals. One large category includes normal classroom teachers in primary and secondary schools and many teachers who in schools, colleges, universities and other institutions have taken on roles such as remedial specialist, counsellor, training officer, special education teacher or careers tutor. A second group comprises higher administrative staff and educational advisers in local authorities who determine research programmes or advise head teachers. A third group consists of the many professionals who service the education system—educational psychologists, medical officers, speech therapists, paediatricians, psychiatrists and social workers—who use tests or may be required to understand test results in the evaluation of individual cases.

In addition, colleges and schools of education normally accept some responsibility for introducing trainee teachers and advanced course students to tests and testing. Finally, and not least, researchers employ large numbers of tests upon school children and students. We believe that the interests of all these professional groups can be served by access to a single authoritative source of descriptive and evaluative test reviews.

The progenitor of this volume is the series of "Mental Measurements Yearbooks", edited since 1938 by the late Oscar Buros and now in its 8th edition (New Jersey, Gryphon, 1978). However, as its British users will know, while it provides a comprehensive guide to North American tests, its coverage of British tests is inadequate. "Tests in Education" sets out to fill this gap for those who wish to use tests in educational settings—principally at the nursery, primary and secondary school levels, where most guidance about their quality seems to be needed.

Like the Buros "Yearbooks" we rely on independent test reviews by those experienced in test design and use. Our reviewers were selected primarily from education departments of British higher education institutions, from personal knowledge and declared interests. Nearly all of those approached agreed to review, without payment, up to six tests each. Overall guidelines were supplied and the reviewers approached their task with great willingness and often considerable enthusiasm—which we believe are reflected in the high quality of the resulting reviews. We wish to thank them most sincerely.

Copies of all the tests reviewed were supplied free by the publishers and we are most grateful for their co-operation.

We owe a great debt to Academic Press for their continued support for this project. In particular Jim Ricks and Roger Farrand helped to formulate the original idea for this book and sustain its initial progress, and Rosemary Altoft and Julia Maidment at different times have lent their help and expertise.

We are especially grateful to Sylvia Sumner who typed and prepared the final versions for publication.

Every effort has been made to ensure accuracy and a high level of coverage in this first attempt to service British interests in tests. We apologize for any shortcomings which may be discovered—ours is the responsibility—and we would be grateful to hear from readers if errors have crept in or if we have overlooked something of importance.

The use of tests in education is often a controversial activity. Part of this controversy is concerned with the way in which thoughtless or excessive use of tests can narrow or divert the educational curriculum. While we do not wish to minimize such concerns this book deals with the tests themselves, their educational claims, and their technical competence. Our reviewers were not asked to exceed this brief and the reader should bear this in mind.

Finally, we strongly urge that the introduction is read. It provides a background and overview to this particular collection of reviews and also, for those not familiar with test theory, a brief untechnical introduction to that subject.

January, 1984   *Philip Levy*

                                                       Harvey Goldstein

Contents

Reviewers v

Preface ix

Introduction xiii
Aims—range of tests reviewed—availability—types of tests—the
reviewers' task—target populations and ages—publication data—
content—purposes—item preparation—administration—
standardization—sex differences—reliability—validity—score
interpretation—test use—concluding remarks

Abbreviations xxix

Test reviews 1
Early development 3
Language 115
Mathematics 331
Composite attainments 434
General abilities 460
Personality and counselling 611
Other topics 669

Glossary 705

Publishers and distributors 709

Indexes 713
Reviewers 715
Tests 716

Introduction

Aims

Our aim in this book is twofold. First, to inform those who may wish to use tests or to know which tests are available. Secondly, we hope that the presentation of this material, in a format which not only describes the tests, their content and technical support but also provides a critical commentary, will encourage a discriminating use of tests and ultimately a general improvement in test design and service to the user, whether teacher, adviser or researcher. Our experience is that it is in the school system where most tests are used. Test use seems to be increasing in this area (Gipps and Wood, 1981), and the Government's Assessment of Performance Unit has done much to awaken interest in new kinds of test content and administration (Gipps and Goldstein, 1983).

In this overview, first, we introduce the tests reviewed, their range, their accessibility and their availability. Secondly, we introduce the issues which our reviewers were prompted to consider in the preparation of their reviews and we reflect upon some of the reports they have made. Thirdly, we offer an informal commentary on some of the desiderata for published tests, because these are sold, in the main, to users who may sometimes be overawed by the more technically based claims of test developers. We cannot pretend to present a complete account of educational measurement and test theory. Rather, we emphasize the principles and issues frequently referred to by the reviewers. For the reader who requires a fuller account, the books by Cronbach (1970), Lord and Novick (1968) and Thorndike (1971) exhibit a variety of styles and levels of technical discussion.

The range of tests reviewed

In general, the British educational testing scene is not as broadly developed as in the USA. The basic skills in language and mathematics are well represented among the largely British products which we review, as are 'intelligence tests', especially for the age groups formerly within the age range of the once ubiquitous '11+' examinations. Tests of other aspects of the school curriculum are poorly represented, although the work of the Government's Assessment of

Performance Unit has extended test development for mathematics, language, science and foreign language into the secondary age range as well as pioneering new approaches, in an attempt to monitor national achievements in these subjects areas (Gipps and Goldstein, 1983). As yet, however, these test materials are not generally available. Multiple aptitude tests, personality questionnaires, vocational interest blanks, and the like are more rarely published in Britain, yet in the USA personality and vocational tests made up over one-third of the number of tests reviewed in *The Eighth Mental Measurements Yearbook* (Buros, 1978). We have attempted to represent this area where such tests are in use within the British educational system. Nevertheless, the tests reviewed are those made available by British publishers and distributors. USA and other tests have been included only where they appear in British catalogues or are available from British addresses.

We have chosen to review those tests which are the more theoretically based or the more technically developed. Typically, these tests are those which make some claim either to have been 'standardized', or to have been developed on the basis of some research data, or shaped by some theoretical analysis. Here 'tests' not only include the formal examination type of task but also diagnostic instruments, observation schedules and the like, which promise some formal basis for assessment.

By contrast, some other 'tests' on offer are truly class tests, designed for informal use by teachers as classroom exercises, most often in English or mathematics; and there can be found several unstandardized practice tests (e.g. 'reasoning tests') probably left over from the years of the 11+ selection examination. These have been excluded from our remit, but should not thereby be ignored by the class teacher. Such 'tests' produced, for example, by Evans Brothers (e.g. *Evans Attainment Tests, Maths Challenge, Queensway Intelligence Tests*), by Macmillan Education (e.g. *Check Ups* in various topics) and no doubt those by other publishers, sometimes exhibit a richer variety of problem and depth of syllabus than is typically the case for many of the more technically developed tests which we review. Similarly the Careers Research and Advisory Centre (CRAC) has recently published computer-managed careers guides (*Careers on Computer Series*) to assist career choice, and these are excluded.

Also excluded from the reviews are tests such as the USA multi-scale intelligence tests developed primarily for use in individual cases by educational and clinical psychologists, or by others specially trained in their administration and interpretation. For example, the Wechsler series of intelligence scales (e.g. *WISC, WIPPSI*) and the *Stanford-Binet Intelligence Test*—whether in British editions or not—are tightly restricted in their availability and have, in any case, been widely reviewed elsewhere over the many years of their development and use. There are several other restricted tests, British and American, which will be well known to the professionals for whom they are designed, but will have limited interest for a wider readership and are not reviewed.

We have included, however, a special review of *The British Ability Scales* (NFER-Nelson) which have been developed over recent years by teams working at the University of Manchester with research funding provided by the Department of Education and Science, and with advice from the British Psychological Society. These scales are likely to be used in the educational system and it seems appropriate therefore to provide an early evaluation of them, despite their restricted availability.

We have also included a few tests that have been developed out of a local initiative. In late 1981, we wrote to all LEAs asking if they had developed tests which might be regarded as published and therefore made available to a wider range of users. The response was limited. The small number of tests sent to us were sent out for review in the normal way and it will be seen that they emerge with credit (see, for example, Phillips' review of the *Walsall Infant Screening Procedure* and Gipps' review of ILEA's *Classroom Observation Procedure*). Indeed one or two of them are now formally published and distributed by major publishers, e.g. *Infant Screening* (Humberside LEA, Macmillan Education).

Lastly, we have given brief reports, containing basic information rather than a full review, on a few tests which either arrived too late for review or where a reviewer failed to complete the review on time. These are marked (*) in the section indexes and in the main test index.

Availability

A test which is satisfactorily 'published' should have a well identified source for potential purchasers and the test materials should be available upon request. It is reasonable to expect a test publisher to act responsibly towards consumers not only with regard to supplies but also in relation to such things as the claims made for a test and user support generally. To a lesser extent these remarks apply to test distributors also.

For the most part, the tests which appear in the current publishers' catalogues are available quickly upon request. In our experience, this was true especially of those publishers who distributed their own limited range of tests. The National Foundation for Educational Research (NFER) is now, for the purpose of test development and publishing, formally part of a new joint company, NFER-Nelson. This company is by far the largest of the publishers and distributors but it does not have a good reputation for efficiency. The NFER legacy, the large number of items offered for sale, the lack of a fully developed 'house style' in presentation and packaging, and the several agency functions which have been acquired would seem partly to be responsible. It remains to be seen how successful the new company will be in changing this.

The term 'availability' also raises the issue of the restrictions that may be placed upon access to, and use of, test materials by various classes of test users, whether they wish to purchase, administer or interpret tests. This is a complicated issue and diverse practices exist. Some tests were originally developed exclusively for use by LEAs for selection purposes or for monitoring performance. Those LEAs which engage in monitoring their schools' achievements probably attempt to maintain some security over the tests they have developed for this purpose. For example, some of the *Moray House Tests* (Hodder and Stoughton) and the *Senior English and Mathematics Tests* (NFER-Nelson) may require special permission for their purchase and use.

Some tests, as we have already noted, are employed by educational psychologists or other specialists, generally with individual children. In such cases limited access and confidentiality (although surely not secrecy) may be justified in order to retain a greater certainty about the meaning of the test results which might otherwise merely refer to over-practised and specific skills.

Other tests—perhaps because of the rigour and complexity of their administration or because specialist knowledge is desirable for their interpretation—may require some training or supervised experience. Publishers may also exhibit a conflict of interests between wide and open sale and the protection of the test (and children!) from its misuse. There is no easy way systematically to indicate the various interests involved in any test. Our own view is that the normal presumption should be that a test will be 'open' and that the burden of argument should be with those who wish to make a test 'closed'. In consequence, we have devoted this book largely to 'open' tests, that is, those which can readily be purchased for use by teachers and others concerned with education. A few exceptions to this are some British tests for which it is merely suggested (and reasonably enough) that some experience or special knowledge is desirable. Where such tests are reviewed the nature of the restriction in their sale or use is clearly indicated. Interestingly, the 1983 NFER-Nelson *Educational Guidance and Assessment Catalogue* offers training courses in the use of some of the more restricted tests.

Types of tests

It is tempting to offer a fine-grain classification of tests according to their purpose, but—as ever—the complex realities of human competencies resist simple categorization. Thus tests of reading skills, spelling, English usage and comprehension overlap in function, as do tests of number, arithmetic and mathematics. The first group, therefore, is loosely gathered together under 'Language' and the second group under 'Mathematics'.

A third large group of tests is termed 'General Abilities', and includes those called 'intelligence tests', 'verbal tests', 'non-verbal tests' and 'aptitude tests'. These are various kinds of 'reasoning' tests using verbal, numerical, perceptual and other modes of task presentation. (The term 'non-verbal' is a curiously British one, which ill-defines the content of a test; see, for example, the comments of Wood in his review of the *AH2/AH3* tests.) The category of 'Composite Attainments' is self-explanatory and cross-references are given in other sections to their component parts. For example, the 'Mathematics' section refers to the mathematics test of the composite *Bristol Achievement Tests*.

The tests of early development which are included are either composite assessment procedures or special tests for young children up to the infant school age range. These too are cross-referenced where mathematics or language is the central theme. The collection of personality and counselling tests is perhaps the least representative. Despite the large number of USA tests and inventories shown to be available in Buros, these are rarely imported and British development and use—the Eysenck personality tests apart—is rare.

The reviewers' task

The reviewers' basic task was to extract standard information from a study of the test and its manual and to present it under predefined headings. In addition, reviewers were prompted to look for certain features under each heading, for example, the origins of the test items, the adequacy of instructions for discretionary scoring of alternative answers, and the size and representativeness of standardization samples. Secondly, in their general evaluation reviewers were invited to bring together the key points provoked by their analysis of the standard package supplied by the publishers for review.

The reviews are both descriptive and evaluative. By their nature, some reviews will contain unique or idiosyncratic points. This does not mean that they are unjustified. Nevertheless these are individual judgements so that, for example, some tests receive critical comments that other tests might also seem to deserve. We would encourage the reader to study the reviews of the several similar or related tests of interest to them and so develop a broad and critical appreciation before choosing any single test*.

In the following sections we outline briefly the features of a test, general and technical, about which the potential user needs to be informed, and offer some general remarks about the state of the art which is apparent from this collection of reviews. The order of the headings used below follows the sequence of information given in the reviews themselves.

---

* In the course of commissioning reviews some tests were reviewed independently by two reviewers and we have included two of these pairs.

Target populations and ages

Tests are most typically developed within, and designed for, particular year groups. In providing summary data about each test at the head of the review, there is some conflict between naming the year group (e.g. 'second-year juniors'), the age range used in the standardization groups, and the ages for which age-norms or standardized scores are provided in the conversion tables. Ideally, all three bases might have been reported, but test manuals typically were uninformative on one or more of these points. Given the central importance of the standardization procedure the ages of the standardization group are given wherever possible; failing this, the ages for which conversion tables are provided; failing these we merely report what the authors suggest. All available data are, however, listed on the leading page for each group of tests.

Publication data

Many test manuals lack a clear account of the origins of a test and its various revisions. The history of a test has some interest for a potential user, especially given the paucity of information about the purpose or likely value of many tests. In some cases our reviewers can only surmise or infer from their own knowledge that the test is, say, a revamped version of a test produced 20, 30 or even 40 years ago and possibly not restandardized since.

The heading given at the start of each review records all that we can infer from the test and the manual(s) supplied. Thus, a typical heading might be as follows:

1957
1972(M,T); S not stated
No revisions apparent
1981(M); 1982(T) printings reviewed

The year '1957' indicates either the year of first publication or the date when the items were first assembled for preliminary trials. The year '1972' is most probably a copyright date which, in the example given above, is found from the current printing of both the manual (M) and the test form (T). Again in the example, the date of standardization (S) is not stated, nor are any revisions apparent from a reading of the manual. Finally, since some tests may have in fact undergone revision, for example decimalization and metrication or change of cover format or print colour, the dates of printing of the copies reviewed are given.

Content

The contents of a test—the nature of the tasks set, their variety, the symbols used, the knowledge assumed, the responses required, and so on—are of fundamental importance to a user. It is useful to know that what purports, say, to be an 'arithmetic' test is no more than a speed test of addition sums using only one and two digit numbers. The review of the test should allow the reader to determine whether or not it assesses 'arithmetic' sufficiently for their purposes. Test titles especially, can be misleading; see, for example, Shipman's comments on 'the obscure nature of "verbal tests"' in his review of *Verbal Test EF*; or Stibbs' doubts about the definition of 'reading' implied by the *Schonell Reading Tests*; or Stibbs again on the meaning of 'English Progress' in his review of *English Progress Test C3*. The potential list is a long one.

Purposes

The purpose of a test is of primary importance and two classes of test can be distinguished by the way they 'scale' individuals. In the one case, the test assumes a continuum of ability or attainment and provides a score which estimates a testees' position on that continuum, and in the other the test seeks to divide the individuals into two (or occasionally more) distinct groups which are supposed to correspond to recognizably useful or theoretically appropriate categories. Examples of the first kind of test are most intelligence tests and tests used in 'monitoring' educational attainment. Examples of the second type of test are screening tests, mastery tests, diagnostic instruments and criterion referenced tests. Of course, insofar as a test score is usually available for all these types, any of them can be used for any purpose. Thus, for example, a screening test can be used by an LEA for general monitoring purposes, perhaps quoting mean scores for each of its schools, rather than for identifying, say, 'at risk' individuals. Its use for this purpose, however, may not be very efficient if there is a strong 'ceiling' effect where most children are receiving the same, maximum or near maximum, mark, since it discriminates poorly between most individuals and hence between schools. On the other hand, it might be a useful test for comparing the *proportion* of backward children in different schools, and thus provide a more relevant comparison for this purpose than a 'monitoring' test. Similarly, a test designed to produce estimates of average performance, say in arithmetic, may well lack diagnostic finesse for a teacher who wishes to identify what might be done to help low-scoring children. It is important, therefore, to appreciate the distinction between the purpose of a test in terms of the way it scales individuals and the resulting use of the test in an educational context.

While test manuals normally distinguish between the more general purposes of the test—say, screening or monitoring—very few have any clearly useful statement of educational rationale. For example, the *Verbal Test D* claims to 'measure those aspects of intelligent behaviour relevant to a verbally biased education'. For a user who wishes to choose a test for children with a particular curriculum and linguistic background we suspect that such a statement is of little help (see review by Wood). On the other hand, the *London Reading Test* contains a useful discussion of the reading taxonomy used, a method of calculating the readability of test passages and references to further work (see review by Bennett). Further, it is remarkable how often tests which claim 'diagnostic' powers ultimately trust that someone, such as 'the experienced teacher' will be able to make some sense of the signs. As Sharp says in his comment on the *Language Imitation Test* '. . . until further work is carried out to relate LIT results to remedial teaching programmes, much of the test's potential will remain unfulfilled and the value will rest with the teacher's ability rather than its own merit'.

Item preparation

Whatever the general purpose of the test it would be helpful to the user if the test manual contained some description of how the test items were identified, prepared and culled. Ideally, the test constructor should identify some of the defining characteristics of what many have come to term the 'universe' or the 'domain' of the items. Failing this the test constructor might attempt to state some of the principles and aims which guided item generation. In educational tests it might be expected that some formal notion of 'syllabus' or perhaps a 'skills analysis' would guide item preparation. Some items may be rejected or modified after casual classroom trials. Some items may be rejected on the basis of a formal item analysis procedure. Some may be rejected because of scoring difficulties. Item format, instructions, multi-choice alternatives may be modified and so on. At each of these stages the test constructor will presumably gain further insight into the nature of what is being measured and hence ought to be in a position to offer more precise information to the user about the test's purpose and the item domain or universe employed, and hence illuminate its interpretation. Sadly, such discussion is rarely found and we hope that test publishers will give some attention to this in the future. It is our impression, incidentally, that some of the USA tests which are reviewed here are rather more informative on this point, and the new USA (draft) standards for educational and psychological testing★ give emphasis to this issue.

Administration

The less experienced test user, for whom many of the tests reviewed are designed, needs to be told clearly what to do and what to say when the test is to

---

★ "Draft Joint Technical Standards for Educational and Psychological Testing", prepared by a joint committee of the American Educational Research Association, the American Psychological Association and the National Council on Measurement in Education, February 1983.

be administered. The vast majority of tests are well supported by their manuals in this respect, although of course some tests require more preparation and practice ahead of a testing session than others. Nevertheless, even with the most careful description, it is of limited use if the tester does not follow the instructions. There is evidence that in practical testing situations this may often happen (see Gipps *et al.*, 1983), in which case the test norms strictly may not be applicable. Furthermore, if administration practice varies widely then the actual test reliabilities will be lower than those quoted on the basis of strictly controlled conditions. It would be optimistic to expect, however, that the administration of a test during its standardization followed the manual instructions closely, and it would be useful in future if test publishers were to accept the difficulties and provide relevant and realistic information in the manuals.

Standardization

The method used for sampling a defined population and the procedures used for constructing and presenting norms and standard scores are crucial matters. Since, in general, different groups of children will perform differently on a given test, and since, perhaps because of curriculum differences, a test will not necessarily be appropriate for all groups, a clear specification of the intended population is desirable. A clearly defined sampling procedure should be used, preferably random, so that valid norms can be constructed. The sampling design, for example the degree of stratification and clustering used, as well as sample sizes and some objective evaluation of the sample's representativeness, should be available to the user. In general, diagnostic tests do not rely on norms based on probability samples, although some element of norm-referenced judgement inevitably will be present.

The tests in this volume, even where details are given, use standardization samples which are usually non-random and unrepresentative of the whole population. A typical case is *Verbal Test G* which was given 'to a fully representative sample of children . . . *in a selected area*' (unspecified, our italics), there being no further specification or justification of the procedure. Knowledge of the year of standardization is also important. For far too many of the tests reviewed the years of standardization are not mentioned.

To construct age-related norms from the raw test scores, two methods are in common use. The one provides an estimate of 'test-age' (e.g. reading age) for each score for a specified age range; and the other provides a standardized score for each age and score combination, usually having a normal distribution with a mean of 100 and standard deviation of 15. As an alternative to standardized scores, equivalent percentiles are sometimes provided. The test-age method does not, in general, allow a particular child to be assigned a percentile ranking, only an equivalent age (usually the age at which the mean or median score has the specified value). The standardized score method is strictly equivalent to a percentile ranking; both can be used to derive age equivalent scores, and so are in general to be preferred, but sample sizes need to be large if the extreme percentile positions are to be estimated with sufficient accuracy.

Another issue in the derivation of age-related norms is whether these are appropriate for 'adjusting' individuals of different ages all measured at the same time or for adjusting, say, the scores of a group of individuals with the same birth date measured at different ages. There is evidence that different standardizations may be required in these two cases (Goldstein and Fogelman, 1974). It appears that none of the tests reviewed here take account of this. In a few cases, separate norms are provided for different year groups. The *London Reading Test*, for example, provides separate age norms for top primary and bottom secondary children and it is clear that, in the range of overlap, the age adjustments are different in each case. In none of the tests reviewed however, are there any attempts to adjust for 'seasonal' fluctuations although, as with the *London Reading Test*, it is often implied that testing should be carried out only at the time of year when the test was standardized. Indeed, many manuals quote a method of test standardization suggested by Lawley (1950) which ignores both the possibility of seasonal effects and different types of age adjustment, as well as assuming a linear relationship between test score and age. A further discussion of the shortcomings of this procedure can be found in the review of *Verbal Test D* by Wood.

The difference between the age range used for standardization and that for which conversion tables are provided is often a matter for a minor note in the reviews. At first sight all that is involved is a little extrapolation—probably linear—to give additional norms for an extra few months at both ends of the range actually present in the standardization group. Moreover, manuals often advise caution in the use of extrapolated values. However, the danger lies not so much in doubts about the statistical probity of the extrapolated values—e.g. the risks of non-linearity—but rather in the practical implications. If, for example, standardization were performed on 3rd-year juniors in November–December when the observed age range might be 9:03–10:04, then the tables may be extrapolated to 9:00–10:10 to cater for children of any age during the school year. The problem here is as mentioned above, namely that the average difference in score per month of age within the standardizing group is not necessarily the same as the average change in score per month of progress through the school year. Moreover this rate of progress may not be steady and there may be seasonal fluctuations. Extrapolation in these circumstances can be hazardous. To simplify the point, when educational achievements of children are assessed it is important to know at what point during the school year this happens, as well as their age relative to their year group. Ideally then, scores should be standardized by both age and time of year for each year group. The tests reviewed do not do this, and in general therefore it will be prudent only to use the tests at the same time of the year, and over the same age range as in the standardization sample, if this information is available.

Sex differences

In the light of the Sex Discrimination Act (1975), the Equal Opportunities Commission (EOC, 1982) considers it unlawful for tests to have separate sex norms. This advice is given in the context of tests used for streaming or selection and it is argued quite reasonably that 'Any allocation made should be solely on the ground of ability'. The assumption here seems to be that a test user should have sufficient faith in the educational soundness of a test to accept that decisions based on test scores are non-discriminating. Unfortunately, life is not so simple. In the area of reading, for example, some tests appear to show larger sex differences than others and we suspect that it is not beyond the wit of test publishers to tailor tests to provide small or large differences as required. Thus, it is clear that there is room for 'manipulation' which could effectively nullify the EOC guidelines. Moreover, it could be said that a consideration of sex differences is indeed relevant to the *educational* soundness of a test and this leads directly into the area of positive discrimination for particular groups. In our view this issue is far from resolved and merits further attention.

Several of our reviewers refer to sex differences which are noted in the test manuals. Such information may be useful. Indeed, for some purposes referring children to their own sex norms may be useful for diagnostic purposes, just as the use of regional or LEA norms may be used to obtain more precise information. We do not have space here to elaborate further on this complex issue (but see Goldstein and Tanner, 1980, for a related discussion). Indiscriminate advice on this issue, however, is less than helpful. *Reading Test BD*, for example, says 'For most uses of the test it will be necessary to consider boys and girls separately'! A few tests still present separate standardization tables, and other tests which provide data on mean differences advise that the sex difference should 'be taken into account' without stating how.

Reliability

The technical literature on test reliability and validity is extensive and employs a large amount of specialized terminology. In the Glossary, we give a description of the more common types of reliability and validity coefficients. Some general remarks are offered here.

Reliability can be defined and evaluated in a number of ways. All procedures used depend on assumptions of one kind or another. The general assumption—the central model—in all cases is that an observed test score is composed of a 'true score' and 'measurement error', and that the measurement errors occur at random and are independent of the true scores. The reliability is then defined as the proportion of the between-individual variance associated with the true score. The nearer this is to 1.0 the less important is the measurement error.

This model has various operational expressions. The most common methods for estimating reliability uses measures of the *internal consistency* of a test. For these, additional assumptions about the equivalence of items and 'local independence' need to be met in order to obtain satisfactory estimates. In practical terms, all the indices of reliability which are derived from a single administration of a test do not apply to *speed tests*. In the extreme case of such a test, testees would be able to pass all the items were it not for the imposition of a time limit, and every item would have zero difficulty. By contrast, a *power test* is one in which the items are ordered by their difficulty and each testee will have a point beyond which he will tend systematically to fail items. It is to the latter type of test that the Kuder-Richardson formulae (signified KR-20 and KR-21 in this volume), coefficient alpha and split-half methods validly may be applied. Insofar as a test is speeded, that is when many testees are restricted in their score more by the imposition of a time limit rather than by reaching items which place a ceiling on their ability or knowledge, KR-20 is largely meaningless with respect to its intended purpose. There appears to be little or no awareness of this point in the test manuals. It can be shown readily that KR-20 approaches or takes the value 1.0, quite spuriously, as a test becomes more purely a speeded one. The ritual reporting of (suspiciously high) values of KR-20 may thus be grossly misleading. Split-half correlations and coefficient alpha attract similar remarks because of their close relationship to KR-20 (see Glossary). Note particularly the comments of Wood on *Verbal Test D* and of Elliott on *Verbal Test C*. Many more tests deserve similar comments.

On more general grounds, it would also be wise not to judge educational tests too strongly by their internal consistency coefficients (and correspondingly low standard errors of measurement). High internal consistency may be achieved at the expense of breadth of representative content among the items. At the limit, what we measure with high reliability may have low content validity for the class teacher.

Measures of reliability which employ whole tests, such as parallel forms or a test-retest procedure, exhibit other and well known problems in their interpretation. There is the difficulty of ensuring proper parallelism and the existence of memory effects or differential learning between test-retest administrations.

One further caution is needed on the interpretation of quoted reliabilities. The reliability coefficient estimate can be 'artificially' increased simply by using a standardization sample spanning a wide age range over which the average score changes markedly. Ideally, a 'fixed age' estimate is required, for example, by the use of age-standardized scores rather than raw scores. The

Manual for the *Moray House English Test (Advanced) 2* shows clear awareness that use of a wide age range can inflate a reliability coefficient. The *Basic Number Screening Test*, on the other hand, quotes a reliability coefficient based upon unadjusted scores from an age range of over four years.

Validity

A clear distinction needs to be made between validity based on substantive considerations applied to test content (content and construct validity) and validity which is based on the strength of an association with other similar tests or assessment procedures (for example, concurrent or predictive validity). Thus, content validity may be established in terms of items being related to a sampling of an educational curriculum, or construct validity may be suggested by theoretical notions concerning, say, reading ability. Ideally, the test manual should make it clear just how any content or construct validity may have been established and the reader should be able to appreciate the extent to which validity can be assumed.

Associative validity presents certain difficulties. For example, a new test may be constructed to have only moderate correlation with one or more existing tests on the quite reasonable grounds that it is not intended to measure the same characteristics and therefore should exhibit low concurrent validity with them. Such evidence, however, tends to be supportive rather than conclusive. The reviews have augmented the use of the term 'validity', where possible, with a description of the procedures used and their outcomes.

For both reliability and validity measures, the accuracy with which they are estimated is important. Estimates based on small samples will have wide confidence intervals associated with them, and will not only require caution when used, for example to correct for attenuation, but will also affect such things as standard errors of regression coefficients (see Goldstein, 1979, for a discussion). The *Basic Mathematics Test A*, for example, uses a sample of 261 and quotes a reliability of 0.91. The 95 per cent confidence interval for this is approximately 0.887 to 0.928. The sample moreover, spans a two-year age range and so also overestimates the true reliability.

Score interpretation

Tests vary considerably in the extent to which they attempt to help the user interpret results. In some cases manuals are very careful to point out dangers of misuse and emphasize the limitations of the test scores (see review of *Verbal Test D*). In other cases the manual provides little guidance (see review of *Verbal Test C*). It would be very helpful if manuals were to give examples of interpretations which could be made on the basis of particular test results—

discussing both the numerical and the qualitative strengths and limitations. Very few attempt this.

Test use

The original advice to reviewers suggested that they might care to comment on such uses of each test under review as are reported in the literature. To this end 12 major British educational journals were examined for the 15 years up to 1981. Of course, not all test use is reported in the research journals. Some reviewers were able to supplement the references supplied from their own knowledge of the literature. Most, however, found that many of the references supplied reported only somewhat banal uses—for example, large and rather pointless correlational uses in surveys employing some *ad hoc* collection of tests. Thus, one might learn that some tests correlate moderately highly with one or two other tests, but there was little that was distinctly informative about the educational merits of the test. We have not, therefore, listed all the published uses of each test and not all reviews employ the heading *Test use*. Rather it was left to each reviewer (or in some cases ourselves) to evaluate the worth of a reference.

Concluding remarks

It should be obvious by now to the reader of this introduction that there is much to be improved in the world of British test publishing, and an intended consequence of this test guide is an improvement in the quality of the products. Apart from test content itself, perhaps the most serious weakness is the lack of good supporting material.

It has struck us forcibly that the most important gaps in information are to do with the aims and purposes of the test and the technical side of sampling and standardization.

When such details as the date of standardization, the origin of the items and the nature of the sampling frame (if any) are absent from the test manual (and perhaps not even available any longer), it is time to revamp the test. In a few cases a duplicated form of a 'provisional manual' still serves as the sole guide to use a decade or so after the first issue.

Tests often claim representativeness of standardization samples but rather few provide convincing arguments that it exists. It is no doubt more expensive and time-consuming to obtain good up-to-date samples, yet it is crucial to the adequacy of the test norms, and we make no apology for labouring this point.

We have also been struck by the widespread lack of rationale or purpose behind the tests. Very few manuals say how items were selected or what educational philosophy guided the test construction. This will often, perhaps justifiably, imply that very little conscious systematic effort has been devoted to providing an educational rationale for a test's contents. In our view the user of a test has a right of access to such information.

Finally, on the subject of tests which are not norm-referenced, these cannot escape strictures about purpose or rationale. Nor can they ignore questions of reliability and validity; and some indicators of normative standards, even if only expressed in terms of age-related expectations about skill mastery, are still relevant. For these tests too, therefore, there is much room for improvement.

References

Buros, O. K. (Ed.) (1978). "The Eighth Mental Measurements Yearbook". New Jersey: Gryphon.

Cronbach, L. J. (1970). "Essentials of Psychological Testing" (3rd edn). New York: Harper.

EOC (1982). "Do you Provide Equal Educational Opportunities?". Manchester: Equal Opportunities Commission.

Gipps, C. and Goldstein, H. (1983). "Monitoring Children: An Evaluation of The Assessment of Performance Unit". London: Heinemann.

Gipps, C., Steadman, S. D., Blackstone, T. and Steirer, B. S. (1983). "Testing Children". London: Heinemann.

Gipps, C. and Wood, R. (1981). The testing of reading in LEAs: the Bullock Report seven years on. *Educational Studies* 7, 133–143.

Goldstein, H. (1979). Some models for analysing longitudinal data on educational attainment (with discussion). *Journal of the Royal Stastistical Society, Series A (General)* 142, 407–442.

Goldstein, H. (1981). The effects of age grouping on the estimate of a correlation coefficient. *Annals of Human Biology* 8, 181–183.

Goldstein, H. and Fogelman, K. (1974). Age standardisation and seasonal effects in mental testing. *British Journal of Educational Psychology* 44, 109–115.

Goldstein, H. and Tanner, J. M. (1980). Ecological considerations in the creation and the use of child growth standards. *Lancet* 1, 582–585.

Lawley, F. N. (1950). A method of standardising group tests. *British Journal of Psychology (Statistical Section)* 3, 86–89.

Lord, F. N. and Novick, M. R. (1968). "Statistical Theories of Mental Test Scores". Reading, Mass.: Addison-Wesley.

Moser, C. and Kalton, G. (1971). "Survey Methods in Social Investigation". London: Heinemann.

Thorndike, R. L. (Ed.) (1971). "Educational Measurement" (2nd edn). Washington: American Council for Education.

Abbreviations

Publication data

M—Manual: year of publication
S—Standardization: year in which testing of standardization groups took place
T—Test booklet: year of publication of test
T:A—Test booklet, Form A (e.g.)

Test
reviews

Early development

List of reviews

Assessment in Nursery Education   5
Basic Number Diagnostic Test   8
The Boder Test of Reading-spelling Patterns   11
Boehm Test of Basic Concepts   19
Classroom Observation Procedure   26
Domain Phonic Test   30
Early Learning: Assessment and Development   34
Early Mathematical Language   37
First Grade Screening Test   41
The Frostig Developmental Test of Visual Perception   44
Griffiths Mental Development Scales   49
The Harrison-Stroud Reading Readiness Profiles★   53
Infant Rating Scale   54
The Infant Reading Tests   59
Infant Screening Test   66
Keele Pre-school Assessment Guide   70
Language Imitation Test   72
Look: Visual Perception   77
Peabody Individual Achievement Test★   80
The Pupil Rating Scale Revised   81
Reading Readiness Inventory   85
Reynell-Zinkin Developmental Scales   88
Sentence Comprehension Test   89
The Visual Pattern Recognition Test and Diagnostic Schedule   96
Walsall Infant Screening Procedure   100
Woodcock Reading Mastery Tests★   110
Word Order Comprehension Test   111

See also:

Deeside Picture Test   506
English Picture Vocabulary Test   517

★ Brief report only

Essential Mathematics   356
Gates McKillop Reading Diagnostic Tests   181
The Listening for Meaning Test   528
MacMillan Diagnostic Reading Pack   219
Neale Analysis of Reading Ability   230
Non-Readers Intelligence Test   542
Rutter's Behaviour Questionnaires   650
Williams Intelligence Test for Children with Defective Vision   604

Assessment in Nursery Education

Reviewed by P. S. Clift

Authors: Margaret Bate and Marjorie Smith
Publishers: NFER-Nelson
Distributors: NFER-Nelson
Age range: 3:00–5:00
1978 (M, T)
Group test

Test content

This is a whole range of assessment materials rather than a single test. It comprises five main areas:

social skills and social thinking;
talking and listening;
thinking and doing;
manual and tool skills;
physical skills.

Two methods are used. Social skills are assessed on six scales from observation of children during normal everyday nursery activities:

independence—attending to own needs and choosing activities;
conversation skills;
relationships and play with other children;
relationships with nursery staff;
concentration;
behaviour in an adult directed group.

Each scale consists of a number of descriptions of behaviour which might be observed, ordered in terms of development and maturity. The other areas are assessed by asking the children to perform specific tasks. These tasks are grouped in four progressive stages, each identified by a different colour strip on the edges of the pages of the Manual. Descriptions of typical children's performances on these tasks (as indicated during trials) are included, marking out several stages of development in respect of most of the tasks.

Purpose

The purpose of this 'compendium' of nursery assessment is to enable nursery staff to '. . . become more precisely aware of the details of each child's development . . .' in order to see '. . . where a child may benefit from more help and encouragement, and to plan suitable activities aimed at strengthening particular aspects of performance' (Manual, p. 10). Periodic appraisals will enable nursery staff to measure progress and thus the effectiveness of their nursery programme.

Item preparation

The items included were derived in the first instance from a survey of relevant literature, a review of tests and kits already devised for assessment of nursery children, and systematic observations in a sample of nurseries 'throughout the country' (Manual, p. 169). Nursery advisers, and other researchers in the nursery field, were consulted with a view to selecting which aspects of children's performance should be assessed. Descriptors of typical performance were then prepared and independently ranked by researchers and nursery teachers '. . . into the order which they felt constituted a scale towards mature behaviour in the nursery' (Manual, p. 170). These scales then went through three stages of trial and modification in about 80 nurseries altogether.

Incidentally, there is a slight tendency to sexism in some of the items, e.g. a post*man*, a doctor and a dentist (men), a nurse (woman). This sex-role casting is probably justifiable in terms of children's common experience. Less justifiable is the portrayal in the *Street Scene* item of a hapless *female* driver contemplating her broken down car with evident dismay, a dismay equally evidently shared by her own small *daughter*, watched by five other persons, all male, whose reactions range from amusement to exasperation.

Administration

The assessment using observation may be carried out over a period of time, thus forming an extension of the daily observation which takes place as a matter of course in the nursery. The assessment using specific tasks should, as far as possible, arise out of a spontaneous interest in the activities by an individual, or group small enough to be closely observed.

Standardization

Standardization of test scores was not deemed to be appropriate, and hence was not undertaken. There is insufficient information about the nurseries and individual children involved in item preparation and trials to evaluate the claim that the descriptors are of typical behaviour.

Reliability

The measure of reliability offered is the percentage of agreement between two psychologists. This averaged at a somewhat disappointing 54 per cent for complete agreement, but when ±1 points of scale were allowed it rose to an average of 84 per cent. The authors note that if this level of accuracy is acceptable (and for assessment of this type, it probably is), then the items may be judged acceptably reliable. That only two testers were involved and psychologists rather than teachers, is most surprising, and inevitably weakens any claim that the reliability of these scales has been established empirically.

Validity

The concurrent validity of a subset only of the assessment scales was established in relation to an appropriate set of the McCarthy Scales of Children's Abilities (no reference for the latter as given in the Manual). Cramer's V is the statistic of association used, together with a percentage of agreement between scales. Cramer's V varied between 0.2 (one item) and 0.8 (two items), with ten items falling into the range 0.41 to 0.60. It is noted that a Cramer's V of 0.45 equated with a 63 per cent complete agreement, and a 93 per cent agreement allowing ±1 scale points as in the reliability study. This evidence of *concurrent* validity is scant to say the least, but examination of items and indeed the process by which they were prepared suggests that their *content* validity is good.

Interpretation

Only the vaguest and most general hints at how the results of these assessment procedures might be interpreted are given, scattered here and there in the text. It is thus for the nursery teacher, *qua* professional, to decide on what the results signify in relation to purpose, both that of the authors, and her own in using the scales.

General evaluation

If nursery education is to be judged, or worse justified, by its *outcomes*, then clearly some valid and reliable measures of these are needed, both to establish '*standards*' and measure '*progress*'. The format chosen for these outcome measures is compatible with the prevailing nursery ethos, but it is doubtful whether evaluation by outcome is! However, if that is your need, then this compendium should serve you well enough despite its lack of technical sophistication. But just how the planning of nursery programmes ought to be *guided* by outcome measures remains an open question, the answer to which is barely hinted at in the Manual. Herein lie the dangers of teaching to the tests: making them '. . . a syllabus of . . . prescriptions for a nursery programme' as specifically warned against (Manual, p. 11). Just what should our *normative* expectations of nursery children be: ought we to have any? These tests imply we should.

Basic Number Diagnostic Test

Reviewed by Helen Quigley

Author: W. E. C. Gillham
Publishers: Hodder and Stoughton
Distributors: Hodder and Stoughton
Age range: 5:00–7:00
1979 (S); 1980 (M, T)
Individual test

Test content

This test is arranged in the following six sections:
(1) Reciting and naming numbers: Here, the child is asked to count up to 25 and to name the digits printed on the page as the examiner points to them.
(2) Copying figures: The child has to trace over 'dotted' figures and then to copy printed figures.
(3) Writing figures without copying: The child is asked to write the numbers up to 25 in sequence and then random numbers up to 39 as requested by the tester.
(4) Counting and selecting bricks: 30 bricks are placed out in three rows of 10 and the child is asked to count them, then she/he is asked to select groups of 2, 7, 11, etc., bricks.
(5) Addition: The child is asked to perform addition sums, first using pictures of tennis balls then with digits. The balls are not arranged in any coherent fashion so for most children the first items will involve not addition but counting. The instructions say: 'You can use bricks to help you if you like'. Many children would find the use of bricks confusing rather than helpful.

(6) Subtraction: The child is required to perform similar tasks with subtraction as the expected operation.

Purpose

The publishers claim that the test covers the basic number skills that a child could reasonably be expected to have mastered by the age of seven years. They say that its main purpose, however, is to show what the child can and cannot do so that 'specific teaching objectives for that individual child can be determined'.

Item preparation

The sole information given on this in the Manual is that 'the "commonsense" nature of the test was not easily achieved and is the outcome of 18 months' continuous revision'. There is no reference to any theory of mathematical development, nor any outline of the way in which the items relate to the development of number concepts.

Administration

The test is designed to be used by teachers or educational psychologists. The only materials required for the test are an ordinary pencil, a red pencil, a rubber and thirty small plastic bricks. The test is untimed but it is anticipated that no child will take more than 35 minutes. The instructions are contained in the child's Manual which the tester reads to the child. They are clear.

Standardization

The test was standardized in 1979, in 'a representative sample of primary and infants' schools in the City of Nottingham and the Rutland area of Leicestershire'. A total of 24 schools, providing 292 children covering the age-range 5 years–7 years, were involved. Children were selected who would be within six weeks of the following age levels at the time of standardization: 7:00, 6:06, 6:00, 5:06 and 5:00. The Manual continues 'A range of scores obtained by approximately the median 20 per cent of children at each age level was taken for the purpose of determining number age levels'. Miraculously, none of these small distributions overlapped but they combined to cover the whole score range of the test. This process is unsatisfactory.

Scoring

One point is awarded for each correct answer and the total converted to a Number Age by the process described above. However, the authors do state that the test is 'mainly intended to determine what a child needs to be taught rather than to assign a number age to him'.

Reliability

The test contains items which can be used for a retest, in order to assess the progress of the child. A total of 32 children were given the retest items as well as the test items. The authors then say 'using these alternative items (and taking alternative items in the rest of the test) a split-half correlation coefficient of 0.93 was obtained, showing that the test is satisfactorily reliable'. This mixture of methods does not constitute an adequate measure of reliability.

Validity

There is no mention of any validity studies in the Manual.

Interpretation

Three pages in the Manual are devoted to comments on the items. These comments consist of indications of the most likely way in which children fail the items. There are few indications about remedial procedures and no guide as to the diagnosis of the problems that are causing these failures.

General evaluation

There are some technical flaws in the design of this test. The standardization sample is small and there is no indication of the extent to which it represents the target population of 5:00–7:06. No validity studies have been carried out, nor is there adequate indication of the reliability of the test.

Although the purpose of the test is diagnostic and some common errors are cited, no insight is given into the cause of these errors nor of ways they may be remedied. This is a reflection of the fact that there appears to be no appreciation of the development of number concepts underlying the test. The items do not test stages in this development but call only for counting and writing skills and, even for these skills, the prescribed remediation is inadequate.

The Boder Test of Reading-spelling Patterns*

Reviewed by Rea Reason

Authors: Elena Boder and Sylvia Jarrico
Publisher: Grune and Stratton
Distributor: Academic Press
1982
Ages: **
Individual test

Test contest

The test consists of an oral word reading test, derived from a series of graded word lists, and a written spelling test, based on the results of the reading test.

The test has been constructed by a paediatric neurologist and a research psychologist in Los Angeles, and is aimed at an American market. For this reason, the word lists have been calibrated according to the 'grade' levels of reading vocabularies used in American schools.

The contents of the test are as follows:

(1) The Manual.
(2) A test booklet containing 13 graded word lists of 20 words each. Half the words are phonetic and half are non-phonetic. The lists have been graded for both reading and spelling, and start at the pre-primer level (in Britain age 5 to 6) and go on to adult level.
(3) Examiner's record forms for the reading test.
(4) Spelling test forms for the pupil.
(5) Pre-reading forms to check whether the pupil can name or sound out the letters of the alphabet and recite or write the alphabet.
(6) Diagnostic summary forms.
(7) A booklet containing sentences which illustrate the meanings of the words dictated in the spelling test.

Purpose

'The diagnostic purposes of the Boder Test are (1) to differentiate specific reading disability, or developmental dyslexia, from non-specific reading disability through reading and spelling performance alone; (2) to classify dyslexic

---

* Subtitle: 'A diagnostic screening test for subtypes of reading disability'.
** Children with reading difficulties; differential diagnosis of childhood dyslexia.

readers into one of three subtypes on the basis of their reading-spelling patterns, each of which has its own prognostic and remedial implications; and (3) to provide guidelines for the remediation of all four reading disability subtypes identified by the test—the non-specific subtype and the three dyslexic ones' (Manual, p. 5).

The rationale of the test is taken from a reading disability typology introduced by Boder (1968); the dysphonetic, the dyseidetic, the mixed dysphonetic-dyseidetic and non-specific reading disability.

'Group I, the dysphonetic group, is by far the largest. Dysphonetic readers have difficulty integrating written symbols with their sounds, with resulting disability in developing phonic word-analysis, or decoding, skills. They have no gross deficit, however, in visual Gestalt function' (Manual, pp. 6–7).

'Readers in Group II, the dyseidetic group, manifest weaknesses in visual perception and memory for letters and whole-word configurations, or Gestalts, with resulting disability in developing a sight vocabulary, although they have no disability in developing phonic skills' (Manual, p. 7).

'Dyslexics in Group III, the mixed dysphonetic-dyseidetic group, combine the cognitive deficits of the first two subtypes, with resulting disability in developing both sight vocabulary and phonic skills; some are virtually nonreaders and nonspellers' (Manual, p. 7).

Non-specific reading disability refers to reading retardation which does not seem the result of weakness in either visual perception or phonic word analysis.

Other studies that have introduced typologies of reading disability are mentioned in the Manual. Although the subtypes vary according to the criteria used to delineate them, there is apparently considerable overlap and it is argued that most of the subtypes have cognitive deficits primarily in the visual or auditory areas. It seems a pity that the test designers have chosen obscure terminology, of a Greek origin, to describe this dichotomy which is also well known to remedial teachers, i.e. difficulties with the whole word approach or difficulties with sound/symbol correspondence.

Item preparation

The original test was described by Boder (1968, 1971, 1973). It consisted of an informal word recognition inventory used in the Los Angeles school district. This inventory was made up of standard graded word lists, drawn from reading schemes used in the schools. Word presentations were both 'flashed' (for approximately one second) and untimed. Boder's procedural innovation was to follow the word inventory with a written, two-part spelling test based on the reading performance. A spelling test of 'known words' was chosen from words read 'flash'. A list of 'unknown words' was chosen from words read untimed or not at all. Whilst the 'flash' and untimed presentations made it possible to assess respectively visual memory for whole words and phonic skills in reading, the two-part spelling test assessed visual memory and phonic skills in spelling.

It should be noted that the joint reading-spelling pattern is based on the assumption that the same cognitive processes underlie reading and spelling. Readers of this review may feel that this is an oversimplification in that the psycholinguistic processes involved in reading (e.g. Smith, 1973) are not mirrored in the spelling performance. The Boder test is clearly only concerned with certain limited automatic perceptual aspects of reading and spelling and does not take account of reading strategies such as the use of context and meaning.

The present version of the Boder test has word lists which are half phonetic and half non-phonetic at each grade level. The reading levels of the words are taken from the reading vocabularies developed by Harris and Jacobson (1972) and Taylor and Frankenpohl (1960) and the spelling levels are based on the graded spelling lists developed by Plunkett (1960) and Forbes (1968). With few exceptions, the reading and spelling levels of the words in the Boder test are said to coincide. The test designers also mention sources which were consulted in confirming the general applicability of the sequence of phonic skills embodied in the graded lists. There is no mention of systematic trials of the present word lists.

Administration

'As is widely recognized (however), a formal diagnosis of dyslexia should be made with great caution in children between 5 and 8 years of age. The mild and transient forms of developmental dyslexia found in young children may represent a normal variation in reading readiness, a maturational lag that may be spontaneously overcome by the age of 8' (Manual, p. 9).

The earliest age for administering the test is not specified more clearly than this. Presumably, a child has to have a chronological age of at least seven years to obtain a reading quotient low enough to qualify for the subtypes mentioned in the diagnostic flow chart on p. 39 of the Manual. The person tested would also need to have a certain minimum level of reading ability before a spelling test based on the words read 'flash' could be constructed.

The pupil is required to read individual words from the word lists, first within one second ('flash') or, if he/she fails that, within 10 seconds ('untimed') until he/she can read less than 6 words 'flash' of a given list. For the spelling test of known words, 5 phonetic and 5 non-phonetic words are selected from those read 'flash' at reading level, which is the highest level at which the child can read at least 50 per cent of the word list 'flash'. The spelling list of unknown words, 5 phonetic and 5 non-phonetic, is selected from words not read or read 'untimed' at grade level if the pupil's reading level is below the grade level. This is the essence of the procedure but, depending on the pupil's performance, further procedural instructions are given.

The Manual gives very detailed instructions, even to the point of the exact wording to be used in the verbal instructions. Although the Manual contains appendices which summarize the administrative procedure, it is not easy to understand precisely what is required. It would have been more helpful if the procedure had been described with the aid of flow diagrams.

The examiner records all errors and makes decisions about how to proceed on the basis of the child's reading performance. The choice of items for the spelling test and judgements of which responses are 'good phonetic equivalents' may cause confusion despite the guidelines provided. It can be seen that the test is not easy to administer and interpret, and that it cannot be used without practice. Some experience of teaching phonics and adequate theoretical knowledge of the assumed processes involved in reading and spelling would seem essential for test users. The authors mention that all examiners were trained to administer the test when studies of reliability and validity were conducted. There is no mention of whether 'untrained' people can obtain the same results. Given adequate familiarity with materials and procedure, the test takes less than 30 minutes to complete.

Standardization

The differential diagnosis of reading-spelling patterns into reading disability subtypes is based on certain critical cut-off points of performance on the reading and the spelling tests. For example, the Mixed Dysphonetic-dyseidetic reader is described as follows: 'Of the Known Words, 50 per cent or fewer are spelled correctly. Of the Unknown Words, 50 per cent or fewer are spelled as Good Phonetic Equivalents. The reading quotient is less than 67' (Manual, p. 38).

The Manual states that the cut-off points for reading and spelling performance were empirically derived, but only passing reference, with no numerical data, is made to Boder's early clinical work (op. cit.). It is claimed that the reading-spelling discrepancy is the most constant single diagnostic sign of the three dyslexic sub-types and that when the percentage of correctly spelt Known Words (words read within one second) is less than 50 per cent, the reading-spelling pattern is regarded as dyslexic. In view of the crucial nature of this observation in discriminating between the reading retarded and the reading 'disabled', it is most surprising that no quantitative data are offered in the Manual to indicate the basis for this claim. Although the Manual does describe recent studies of validity which use the complete test battery, lack of information about Boder's original work remains an irritating puzzle. In the opinion of the reviewer, *post-hoc* studies of validity which suggest that the cut-off points seem reasonable, do not remove the need for initial investigation of whether those cut-off points exist, and if they do, whether they are the best ones.

The authors report a study by Whiting and Jarrico (1980) which supports the Boder spelling test criteria. Test data for 104 normal readers aged 8–11 years showed that none of these children had less than 65 per cent correct spelling responses for words in their sight vocabulary, and the percentage of good phonetic equivalents among their misspellings ranged from 75 to 90 per cent. Despite the small sample size and the limited age range of the subjects, this study did offer support for the global 50 per cent cut-off point on the Boder spelling test. However, we also need to examine the spelling levels of retarded readers. Presumably this was done by Boder in her clinical work but, as mentioned, the data are not reported in the Manual. In the experience of the reviewer, poor readers who have received remedial help with an emphasis on spelling, may not necessarily show such marked discrepancy between reading and spelling levels.

Scoring

Record forms and summary sheets are clearly presented and easy to use. Inaccuracies can result from inappropriate selection of words for the spelling test and faulty judgements of which responses are good phonetic equivalents. Despite the guidelines provided, it would seem necessary for the examiner to possess prior knowledge of the principles involved.

The summary sheets include sections which require the examiner to make qualitative judgements of the child's performance. These are backed by descriptions and case studies in the Manual. The qualitative aspects of the Boder test are valuable in substantiating the bare bones of the quantitative data.

The reading quotient is calculated as a function of mental age. As word recognition skills can be considered independent of level of intelligence, the procedure does not seem appropriate to the reviewer.

Reliability

Inter-rater reliability for identifying good phonetic equivalents is reported by Ginn (1979). After careful study of the test guidelines, four raters rated the results of 30 'disabled readers' achieving an intraclass correlation coefficient as high as 0.99.

Examination of test-retest reliability for 50 children seen by Boder resulted in correlation coefficients ranging from 0.56 to 0.99 for reading level, correctly spelt known words, good phonetic equivalents and subtype classification. The children were tested twice within approximately two months but the age range of the sample was from 6 years–15 years (see Introduction).

Internal consistency was determined by examining the results of 46 children selected at random from Boder's current private patient files, presumably covering a wide age range also. The correlation coefficients were 0.99 and 0.97 respectively for 'flash' presentation and reading level when the scores of the first and second half of the reading test were compared. High correlation coefficients are also reported for the spelling test, both for the known and unknown lists of words.

These reliabilities, moreover, are based on the use of expert testers, and it is likely that they would be lower in the hands of those who are less proficient or experienced.

Validity

The Manual contains a lengthy section describing a number of studies including four doctoral dissertations. Only a brief resume of selected studies is presented here.

The distribution of the three Boder subtypes was examined in four separate studies for a total of 420 subjects. With a fourth category, the 'undetermined', there was no statistically significant difference between the proportions of individuals in the four categories for the four studies. Whilst dysphonetic children comprised more than half the readers, the 'undetermined' category contained the fewest children. It was argued that the agreement of the four studies supported the notion that the decision rules adopted consistently separated individuals into discernible subtypes. Whether a different classification system and different cut-off points could have produced different groupings with equal agreement is not discussed in the Manual.

Evidence for construct validity is provided by Smith (1970) and Ginn (1979) who compared patterns of responses in the Wechsler Intelligence Scales for Children (WISC-R) with the Boder sub-types. In Ginn's study, for example, 85 per cent of the dysphonetic were classified as WISC-R pattern I with strength in spatial ability, and deficit in symbol manipulation and sequencing ability. Readers of this review may consider that the hypothetical constructs of an intelligence test do not offer support to a typology of reading disability.

Aaron (1978) studied a group of 42 children made up of dysphonetic, dyseidetic and normal readers identified through the Boder diagnostic procedure. The main finding was that the dysphonetic group identified significantly more faces on a test of memory for faces than did the dyseidetic but that the dysphonetic readers recalled significantly fewer digits in sequence than did the normal readers. Aaron concluded that the Boder diagnostic screening procedure was a valid means of differentiating between the two clinical subtypes.

The Boder test has proved useful as an initial screening device for the many studies mentioned in the Manual, in particular, electrophysiological investigations. The value of the test as a research instrument may be demonstrated by its popularity; but this does not necessarily guarantee its utility in the applied setting.

Interpretation

An analysis of reading and spelling errors which highlights two subgroups of difficulty, i.e. children who are limited by inability to analyse word sounds into speech sounds, and children who have difficulty in retaining letter patterns as visual forms, should be useful in applied practice. Certainly, a comparison of a child's fluent word reading level with his spelling level and his use of phonic skills in reading and spelling will give the teacher an impression of the child's approach to deciphering the printed word. The test designers suggest, however, that the purpose of the test is not only to give global impressions but to provide guidelines for the remediation of the reading disability subtypes. Unfortunately, the generalities of the subtypes lead to prescriptions of such a general nature as to appear tritely obvious. It is suggested that the dysphonetic reader should be taught phonics while the dyseidic reader should build on his strength in phonics. If the child is mixed dysphonetic-dyseidic, his progress will be slower than if he has only one of the limitations. It is also asserted that we need to examine emotional factors more closely if a child is classed as having a non-specific reading problem, but it is self-evident that emotional aspects play a part for every child who is experiencing failure in achieving literacy.

There is clearly a discrepancy between the diagnostic instrument and the curriculum programmes designed to remedy reading and spelling difficulties. Whilst the test seeks to measure neuropsychological traits derived from a particular theoretical model, the remedial teacher will want to know exactly what phonetic rules and 'sight words' the child has mastered, and whether the child has learnt to compensate for any perceptual limitations by the use of context and meaning. As Kinsbourne (1982) has argued, we need to examine how the child is learning, so that he does not become labelled 'dyseidetic' because we have taught him to over-attend to phonic structure at the expense of attending to letter patterns as visual forms.

General evaluation

There are no agreed theories of reading, hence the theoretical underpinnings of reading failure depend largely on the particular views of the test designers. Whilst Boder's dichotomy appears to have intuitive credibility, alternative theoretical orientations emphasize other aspects, such as visual organization and memory (Orton, 1937; Bender, 1957), intersensory integration (see Birch and Belmont, 1964), temporal order processing (see Bakker, 1972) or verbal processing (see Vellutino, 1977). Whatever the labels used to describe cognitive or perceptual limitations in the acquisition of reading and spelling skills, reading is clearly not a unitary skill, but necessitates the acquisition and eventual integration of different skills. Vernon (1979), for example, identifies four possible phases in the development of the skill of reading, and stresses the importance of identifying the actual points of breakdown in learning to read. Although Boder's subtypes are a good start in attempting to obtain more homogeneous samples in reading research, sample selection depends on how the reading deficit itself is analysed. Therefore, further differentiation of sub-skills will become necessary both in research and in remediation, and should yield more refined criteria for the several possible weaknesses in reading.

Whereas Boder test results may be collected in a relatively objective manner, the choice of test items and the manner of scoring appears to be rather arbitrary. While the quantitative aspects of the test results must, therefore, be interpreted with much caution, the qualitative data are likely to be of help in supporting judgements made by the experienced and knowledgeable remedial teacher. By themselves, however, the test results will certainly not indicate what specific remedial action needs to be taken.

The nature of any constitutional weakness or reading problem may change with age and with teaching. The developing child also has a tendency to compensate for any limitations by the use of other strategies such as reliance on context and meaning. It would be unfortunate if the labels used in the Boder test were seen to imply stationary 'conditions' when, in many cases, appropriate practice and time are all that is needed.

References

Aaron, P. (1978). Dyslexia, an imbalance in cerebral information-processing strategies. *Perceptual and Motor Skills* **47**, 699–706.

Bakker, D. J. (1972). Temporal order perception and reading retardation. *In* "Specific Reading Disability: Advances in Theory and Method". (D. J. Bakker and P. Satz, Eds). Rotterdam: Rotterdam University Press.

Bender, L. A. (1957). Specific reading disability as a maturational lag. *Bulletin of the Orton Society* **7**, 9–18.

Birch, H. G. and Belmont, L. (1964). Auditory-visual integration in normal and retarded readers. *American Journal of Orthopsychiatry* **34**, 852–861.

Boder, E. (1968). Developmental dyslexia: A diagnostic screening procedure based on three characteristic patterns of reading and spelling. *In* "Claremont Reading Conference 32nd Yearbook". (M. Douglass, Ed.). Claremont, California: Claremont University Centre.

Boder, E. (1971). Developmental dyslexia: Prevailing diagnostic concepts and a new diagnostic approach. *In* "Progress in Learning Disabilities" (H. Myklebust, Ed.) Vol. 2. New York: Grune and Stratton.

Boder, E. (1973). Developmental dyslexia: A diagnostic approach based on three atypical reading-spelling patterns. *Developmental Medicine and Child Neurology* **15**, 663–687.

Forbes, C. (1968). "Graded and Classified Spelling Lists for Teachers". Cambridge, Massachusetts: Educators Publishing Service, Inc.

Ginn, R. (1979). "An Analysis of Various Psychometric Typologies of Primary Reading Disability". Unpublished doctoral dissertation, University of Southern California.

Harris, A. and Jacobson, M. (1972). "Basic Elementary Reading Vocabularies". New York: Macmillan.

Kinsbourne, M. (1982). The role of selective attention in reading disability. *In* "Reading Disorders, Varieties and Treatments" (R. N. Malatesha and P. G. Aaron, Eds). New York: Academic Press.

Orton, S. T. (1937). "Reading, Writing and Speech Problems in Children". London: Chapman and Hall.

Plunkett, M. (1961). "A Spelling Workbook (Grades 4, 5, 6)". Cambridge, Massachusetts: Educators Publishing Service, Inc.

Smith, F. (Ed.) (1973). "Psycholinguistics and Reading". New York: Holt, Rinehart and Winston.

Smith, M. (1970). Patterns of intellectual abilities in educationally handicapped children. *In* "Proceedings of the Fourth Annual Conference on the Educationally Handicapped". University of Redlands, California, 62–73.

Taylor, S. and Frackenpohl, H. (1960). A core vocabulary. *Research and Information Bulletin*, No. 51. Denver, Colorado: Educational Development Laboratories.

Vellutino, F. R. (1977). Alternative conceptualisation of dyslexia: evidence in support of a verbal-deficit hypothesis. *Harvard Educational Review* **47**, 334–351.

Vernon, M. D. (1979). Variability in reading retardation. *British Journal of Psychology* **70**, 7–16.

Whiting, S. and Jarrico, S. (1980). Spelling patterns of normal readers. *Journal of Learning Disabilities* **13**, 40–42.

Boehm Test of Basic Concepts

Reviewed by Andrew Sutton

Author: Ann Boehm
Publisher: The Psychological Corporation
Distributor: NFER-Nelson
Age range: Kindergarten, Grades 1 and 2 (USA)
1967
1968–71 (S); 1967–71 (M); 1969 (T:A); 1971 (T:B)
1971 Edition (M) reviewed
Group test

Test content

Boehm's test (to rhyme with 'games', not with 'homes' or 'therms') comprises of two parallel forms (A and B), each consisting of a pair of disposable booklets. Each pair of booklets contains fifty large, multiple-choice pictorial items in ascending order of difficulty, which the child marks in response to instructions read aloud by the teacher. For example, 'Now look at the shoe, the hat, and the sock. Mark an X on the *hat* . . . Mark an X right on the *hat*' (practice item, Manual, p. 2). The 'concepts' tested refer primarily to space (e.g. next to, behind), quantity (e.g. some, third), and time (e.g. after, always), example: 'Look at the animals walking in a line. Mark the *second* animal . . .' (test item, Manual, p. 3). The test is intended primarily for group administration.

There is a test Manual to cover both forms (from which instructions for administering the parallel forms are reprinted as two separate pamphlets), along with class record sheets for both A and B forms to record the results of up to 30 children. The test material is accompanied by a more recently published brochure stating the test's compliance with the USA *Education for All Handicapped Children Act* (1975) and relating the test to the *Boehm Resource Guide for Basic Concept Teaching*, a kit of curriculum materials.

Spanish translations of both forms are published in the USA for Hispanic pupils. There is no British adaptation, all the material (including the published brochure) being directed towards American users.

Purpose

The test 'is designed to measure children's mastery of concepts considered necessary for achievement in the first years of school' (Manual, p. 3) (i.e. the American Kindergarten Grade and Grades 1 and 2). According to the publisher's brochure: 'a surprising number of children simply do not understand some of the fundamental concepts essential to communication in the classroom . . . As a result they may achieve low scores and be categorized as lacking ability when, in fact, they may only lack experience with certain verbal concepts'.

The test concerns only 'concepts *as presented on the printed page*' (Manual, p. 4, footnote 3, Boehm's italics). Given this proviso, the purpose of the test is stated as two-fold, to identify:

'(a) individual *children* whose overall level of concept mastery is low . . . and
(b) individual *concepts* with which large numbers of children in a class may be unfamiliar' (Manual, p. 4).

The test is offered by its publishers as criterion referenced: 'It is the child's knowledge, or lack of it, that is the principle basis of the Boehm test's usefulness'. Norms, however, are provided, though an uncertainty about their use may be detected in the Manual: 'Since *BTBC* scores may be interpreted on an absolute or a relative basis, the normative information presented in this Manual is intended more as an informal guide than as the essential procedure for interpreting test results' (p .19). The parallel forms are intended for retesting to indicate the progress of a child or a class in concept learning.

Item preparation

Form A was developed in three stages. Pre-school and primary-grade curriculum materials in reading, arithmetic and science were reviewed for terms that occurred frequently, were rarely or barely defined and represented fairly abstract concepts or ideas. This stage is not described in any detail. The concepts selected were translated into pictorial, multiple-choice items and subjected to trials to eliminate problems of presentation (ambiguous wording, unclear artwork) and to eliminate items answered correctly by nearly all (98% or more) testees. Form A represents the best 50 items from this process, selected so that: (a) each measured a different concept; (b) had point-biserial correlations exceeding 0.30; (c) showed fairly even rises in per cent-passing values across age levels; and (d) together yielded per cent passing-values around 0.50 for kindergarteners. After further revision Form A formed the main basis for standardization.

Form B was designed to measure knowledge of the same concepts as Form A, using the self-same concept words, item by item. Compare, for example, 'Mark the bird on the *left*' (Form A, item 44) with 'Mark the tree on the *left*' (Form B, item 44). The author admits not achieving conceptual equivalence on certain items; compare 'Mark the bead that has string *through* it' (Form A, item 2) with 'Mark the dog that is going *through* the hoop' (Form B, item 2). Moreover, even items that appear thoroughly equivalent turned out not to be equivalent in terms of difficulty: for example, 'Mark the boy who is bending *forward* (Form A, item 39) was passed by 33% of kindergarten children at lower-socio-economic schools; 'Mark the chick that is bending *forward*' (Form B, item 39) was passed by 83% of such children.

The above data were drawn from a separate, smaller Equivalence Study which found an overall general compatibility between the two forms both in mean scores and through an equipotential procedure.

Administration

The test is for use by class teachers. The teacher requires a copy of the administration instructions and a demonstration copy of each booklet of the form being administered. Each child requires a copy of both booklets and a pencil or crayon.

Group administration is described. With younger pupils eight to twelve children are recommended per group. When 'large groups' are tested, it is advised that the children's work be monitored by a teacher's aide. There is no need for the children to be able to read or write to complete the test. Even their names can be written for them on the front of their booklets. Responses are made by crossing through the correct choice.

Each booklet is stated to take about 15 to 20 minutes to administer to kindergarteners, including time for general instructions and for sample questions. Older groups are somewhat quicker. Both booklets may be administered in a single session, though if booklet 1 is not holding the children's attention it is recommended to break off testing before starting the second booklet and return to it at a further session.

Each booklet begins with three sample questions which are not scored. There are three or four multiple-choice items per page, presented as bold, clear line drawings. Figures are consciously multi-racial and, though the artwork is American and more than a decade old, the pictures are not inappropriate for use with British children in the eighties. There is a non-verbal marker, a small picture of a familiar object, in the upper corner of each page, to which the teacher draws the child's attention to ensure that the place is being kept.

In the Manual the teachers' directions are clearly presented, with instructions to be read aloud presented in bold type. The key phrase in each item is read out twice and the actual verbal concept, to be read out with especial emphasis, is given in italics.

Given the author's caution about group size there seems no reason for the administration of this test to cause problems except in the case of the most atypical children who, in any case, would probably be best tested individually.

The test was prepared and published in American English, though this only occasionally jars to British ears in the teacher's instructions. It seems reasonable to deal with this by simple substitution, both when this involves words inessential to the concept being evaluated (e.g. 'trousers' instead of 'pants', Form B, item 35) and when it is the verbal concept itself that jars (most noticeably 'zero' used adjectivally, item 40, both forms).

Standardisation

Normative data are presented for Forms A and B, for each of nine groups (three socio-economic levels at three grades, kindergarten, 1 and 2) and for the beginning and the middle of the school year.

Form A, beginning-of-year norms

Data from over nine and a half thousand children in 16 cities across the USA, were collected in September and October, 1969.

Form A, mid-year norms

Data from over two and a half thousand children in five further USA cities were collected in November, 1968 and February, 1969.

Education officials in these cities had been asked to provide 'classroom groups from a fairly wide range of socio-economic background', selection being based on 'the socio-economic level of the *primary areas* from which the school drew their enrolments' (Manual, p. 19, again Boehm's italics). No criteria were offered the administrators in making this choice.

Form B

From the equivalence study separate regression equations were established for each of the 50 concepts, to calculate the likely difficulty of Form B items on the basis of Form A performance for all nine groups. These regression equations were then used to calculate Form B norms from the Form A standardization data.

Separate tables are given for Forms A and B for the percentage of children passing each item for beginning-of-year and mid-year testing, with separate figures for the three grades concerned and for low, middle or high socio-economic class (note, this refers to the class of the schools catchment area, not of individual pupils). Two further tables give percentile equivalents for total raw scores for beginning-of-year testing and mid-year testing, again subdivided for nine groups, though combining results for Forms A and B 'since total scores . . . were found to be equivalent' (Manual, p. 26).

No differential data are presented by sex and there is no account of chronological age or of ethnicity.

Scoring

The class record form is intended both as a scoring key and an interpretative aid to the teacher. By 'key' it is meant that each item is illustrated in miniature, correctly completed, beside the corresponding item number on the class record form: there is no direct key to booklet correspondence. Marking and scoring directly on to the class record form is stated to take about an hour for a class of 30 children, about 20 minutes more being required to transform columns into total scores per child and percentile ranks and rows into percentage passed per item.

Reliability

Split-half reliability coefficients and standard errors of measurement are reported for Forms A and B separately, for each of the nine—grade by class—groups: split-half reliability-coefficients ranged from 0.68–0.90 (Form A) and from 0.12–0.90 (Form B), standard errors of measurement from 1.4–3.0 (Form A) and from 0.9–3.4 (Form B). Alternative form reliability is presented in the form of correlations between total scores on Forms A and B, calculated from the equivalence study, coefficients for the nine groups ranging from 0.55–0.92.

Scoring reliability was checked on 200 class record sheets from the standardization of Form A. Almost half showed errors due to misplaced entries on the record sheet, though only five of these involved errors of more than two points per child: 'Since the errors . . . were found to affect total scores to such a limited extent, they might be considered minor' (Manual, p. 12). Out of more than 9500 cases in the beginning-of-the year standardization of Form A, only 2.5 per cent of total scores were incorrectly added up by their teachers, with only 0.2 per cent being more than two points out. Some errors were, however, substantial and Boehm recommends always cross-checking.

No data are reported on test-retest reliability, though Boehm draws the reader's attention to the general effect, apparent in the norms, that groups who do least well at the start of the school year (low socio-economic status, younger children) tend to make the largest gains over the half-year.

Validity

The test derives its validity empirically from the initial review (not described in detail) of curriculum materials. The Manual reports no independent validation studies or studies against other criteria. There have been no studies to validate the choice of 'basic concepts' against *British* curricular material. More fundamentally the Manual offers no basis for judging the generalizability of children's relative success at recognizing verbal concepts, as presented in this particular fashion, to wider classroom and developmental activities.

Interpretation

The Manual includes useful interpretative material that includes hints on remediation techniques, useful caveats on post-testing using the parallel forms and a supplementary list of very simple concepts, rejected from the standardization because they were too well known for further diagnostic work with children 'severely deprived of concept learning experiences' (Manual, p. 17). There is also a cautionary note on using the test for four-year olds.

No indication is made in the Manual of the existence of the *Boehm Resource Guide for Basic Concepts* which was presumably published later.

Test use

Experience suggests that the Boehm Test has been fairly widely used in remedial and special education in this country, in educational psychology and in speech therapy, though largely as an individual clinical instrument rather than as a group test to monitor class progress or for curricular purposes. It does not, however, appear to have been either a tool or the subject of formal research in Britain. Locke's (1978) judgement, in a review of readily available materials for assessing language development, made from a professional background in both educational psychology and speech therapy and from the present practice base of a teacher in special education, appears fairly to represent the niche that the *BTBC* has tended to fill in this country.

'It does not include items that were answered by 98% of all American kindergarten and first grade children . . . so it is a very limited use in most diagnostic work with children of that age and lower. But for children of seven and upwards it is a very useful guide, not only where language development is thought to be poor, but where other learning difficulties, particularly number difficulties, are suspected. It can also be used directly as a teaching programme'.

If this is a fair representation of British practice, then this diverges somewhat from the original intention of the test constructor.

General evaluation

In its present form the function of Boehm's test is rather unclear: this could put off or mislead some of those who might otherwise benefit from its use. It is advertised as a criterion-referenced test linked to teaching materials. As such it is a useful instrument. Its Manual, however, devotes considerable attention to normative data which, for all that the statistical analysis is clearly and honestly presented, is irrelevant to the test's qualitative and remediative functions.

Form B seems less than satisfactory: greater attention might have been usefully directed to whether an *alternative* form offers substantial advantages as a retest tool for a test of this kind.

The norms have an unsatisfactory base in that they are presented for socio-economic levels of *catchment area* not children. Their grade levels and beginning-of-year and mid-year norms are not translatable to Britain with its earlier school-starting age and flexible entry point to school. British teachers are advised not to use the norms.

More attention should have been given to establishing the criteria against which the test is referenced. More fundamentally, the term 'concept' merits greater attention in the Manual. While the distinction between children 'lacking ability' and lacking 'experience with certain verbal concepts' is an important consideration still unfortunately often ignored in assessment, as stated it can confirm implicit assumptions about human mental development also still all too frequent. The Manual would benefit from a clearer exposition of developmental theory.

Despite the above criticisms, Boehm's test provides easily administered materials and a workmanlike administrative Manual which can provide teachers with a salutory reminder both of the state of many children's 'readiness' and the demands of curricular material. It is easily adapted into British English and deserves wider consideration for ordinary classroom use as intended by its author rather than as a clinical tool. Its USA Hispanic adaptation suggests its possible value in addressing certain basic questions of bilingualism and double half-lingualism now being recognized in this country.

The flaws of this test perhaps reflect the time that it was prepared. It merits further development.

Locke, A. (1978). Measuring language development in children. *AEP Journal* 4, 28–32.

Classroom Observation Procedure

Reviewed by Caroline Gipps

Author: ILEA Schools Psychological Service
Publisher: ILEA
Age: final year infants
1979–80
Group test

Test content

The materials supplied include the following.

Children's workbook plus teacher demonstration cards

In the workbook the child has to write his or her name, write the words he or she knows, copy a sentence, draw a man and a woman, copy shapes and do simple tasks of visual discrimination, visual memory, identifying rhyming words, initial sounds and a short dictation task. These tasks are all done in small groups of four or five children. Then follow seven tasks which have to be done with the children individually, these are: reading alphabet names, giving the sound of various letters, identifying letters at the beginning of a word, phonic word-building, sound blending, an expressive language task in which the child has to tell a little story about a picture, short vocabulary test and finally (optional) the child may read a page from his or her reading book. The Teachers' Guide, which comes with the Procedure, explains in detail how each of the tasks is to be done.

Behavioural observation check-list

This contains 27 items under six headings: motor, visual, auditory, language, personality and environment. The items consist of two statements covering both extremes of the behaviour being rated, for example, under 'Language'— 'Spoken vocabulary and expressive language very restricted in content', to 'Can express ideas fluently using a wide vocabulary'. There is a rating scale of 0–4 ranging from 'Has extreme difficulty' via 'Average for group' through to 'Extremely competent'. There is no instruction given for this check-list beyond a simple one to total the marks for each section separately.

Data sheet

This is for additional data on the child and covers vision, hearing, speech problems and general physical condition, laterality, regularity of attendance in the infant school, number of previous schools attended, family size, date of school entry and experience of pre-school education. Information on how to code the data sheet is given in the marking guide-lines.

The content of the Procedure seems overall to be very comprehensive. It covers all the usual readiness tasks and some extra ones. Some of the tasks do seem a little hard, for example, the dictation exercise.

Activity cards

These are a set of colour-coded index cards containing ideas for classroom activities and tasks to extend the skills covered in the Observation Procedure, *viz* visual discrimination, motor skills, auditory skills, language and listening skills, reading, writing, motivation and personality. These activity cards look very useful for the classroom teacher and seem to provide a very comprehensive coverage.

Purpose

Classroom observation procedure

The Teachers' Guide says that the purpose of the Procedure is:

'(a) To provide the teacher with information about the group's general *levels of competence* in areas relevant to the learning process. This will provide a basis for planning and for a comparison with other groups of children of the same age.

'(b) To provide a *profile of the individual child* in order to plan his educational programme within the ordinary classroom setting.

'(c) *To identify children* who may need further assessment of their problems and subsequently extra help appropriate to their needs.'

Activity cards

'Once an individual child's profile has been completed it might suggest that further help is needed in one or more of the developing skills. No area of a child's development stands in isolation from another. It is because they are so inter-related that it is difficult at times to be specific about what help can be given. These cards represent a selection of ideas and suggestions for activities which can be done either with an individual child or group of children . . . for easy reference they have been divided into somewhat arbitrary areas. It will be the flexibility and enthusiasm of the teacher in developing and extending these activities which will bring about any positive result'.

Item preparation

The Teachers' Guide says only that 'This Observation Procedure has been developed by the ILEA Schools Psychological Service for use with top infant classes, with the collaboration of staff of selected schools and the Remedial Reading Service'. For the Activity Cards 'They have been put together by a group of teachers who have had a wide experience of teaching children with special needs'.

There is no information in the Teachers' Guide about piloting or item selection. However, an enquiry of the ILEA Schools Psychological Service indicates that items were piloted originally on a sample of 1000 children.

Administration

The Procedure is recommended for use in the first term of the final year in infant school but it is also suitable for older children with learning difficulties. Most of the work can be done in the ordinary classroom setting with small groups of four to five children working with a teacher and trained helper. However, five pages of the workbook require individual administration. None of the tasks should be regarded as tests but as a normal part of classroom activity. However, the teacher is reminded to observe the standardized conditions of administration; some of the tasks have a time limit, but there is no suggestion of speed required. The instructions to the teacher for administering the workbook are thorough.

Standardization

According to the Teachers' Guide 'The Procedure provides a profile of abilities. *It does not result in a standardized score for each child.* The implications and consequent interpretation of the results will involve staff discussions conference with the schools psychologist, the advisory teacher and some in-service training'. According to the ILEA SPS, the Procedure was not designed as a screening instrument but its value is seen to lie more in developing teachers' own skills.

Scoring

Marking sheet

The child's score on each part of the Procedure is marked on this sheet. The scoring of simple items is explained on this sheet and for items which are scored in a more complex way reference is made to the Marking Guide. This sheet has no separate instructions on how to fill out the columns and the reviewer found it confusing. The child ends up with a total score for each skill, *viz* reading, writing, motor, visual, auditory, language, language structure, expressive language, vocabulary, environment, personality and drawing.

Marking guide

This is a detailed guide to the tasks in the workbook which require a complex system of marking, including information on a diagnostic assessment of the child's reading aloud of a page from his or her reading book. The sections in the marking guide are called 'Appendices' and they are not related clearly enough to the pages in the children's workbook.

Individual learning profile

Class averages for each of the skills and the average of the top and bottom 25% are put into the Profile and the child's score is plotted over these. The result enables the teacher to see at a glance whether the child is average, above or below for the class.

Overall, the instructions for scoring are sufficiently adequate to make the task reasonably easy for the teacher.

Reliability

No information.

Validity

No information.

Interpretation

According to the Guide 'This initial observation can only provide a sketch of the child's functioning in some areas. Where evidence from it suggests the need for further investigation the child should be referred to the appropriate agency'. There is no further information given as to what sort of evidence might be required to suggest the need for further investigation.

General evaluation

Overall, this comprehensive observation procedure was rather difficult to follow. There are six different parts and it was not sufficiently clear which part should be done first, or which part went with which. What is needed is a simple covering page to provide pointers for the user. Otherwise, the Manual is adequate. The Procedure covers a good range of behavioural observations and activities and particularly useful should be the activity cards which are an obvious second stage to an observation process such as this. Within the ILEA the Procedure is introduced into a school with support and it may well be that if other LEAs are to buy this Procedure, they will have to produce a separate Introduction to the Procedure if they are not intending to provide the same level of advisory support.

By the summer of 1982 it is hoped that a video film of the Procedure will be available together with a booklet, and this will go into the National Film Catalogue. This video film is intended both as an introduction to the Procedure and as a useful form of in-service training for primary and infant teachers.

It is far more thorough than many of the other early identification procedures/screening instruments/observation procedures and though there is no information on reliability, validity or development, it is clear that the authors have depended on its apparent content validity and the extensive development work with teachers to validate their instrument. Overall, although there is no evidence from classroom teachers, it would appear that this is a useful classroom tool for the infant school teacher, particularly if introduced with adequate in-service training or advisory support.

Domain Phonic Test

Reviewed by Anne S. Hawkins

Authors: John McLeod and Joan Atkinson
Publisher: Oliver and Boyd
Distributor: Oliver and Boyd
Age: children with reading disabilities★
1972 (M, T)
No revisions apparent
1980 (M) printing reviewed
Individual test★★

★ The criterion for inclusion in this group may loosely be based on a reading age of less than 8:06 for those children who are retarded in relation to their chronological age.
★★ No restriction on sale or use is indicated in the Manual, but see remarks under Administration.

Test content

The Domain Phonic Test comprises two types of test:

Tests P1 to P4

These are made up of lists of words which are devised to assess a child's reading ability, his knowledge of letter names, letter sounds and blending ability.

Test P1 contains 48 three-letter words: consonant-vowel-consonant.
Test P2 contains 60 words, each commencing consonant-vowel blend.
Test P3 contains 69 words, each either consonant blend-vowel-consonant or consonant-vowel-consonant blend.
Test P4 contains 54 words, each containing vowel blend and consonant blend.

In these tests, the child is asked to read a word from a card. If he is unable to read the word, he is required to try to give the name of each letter, the sound of each letter and to attempt to blend the sounds to make up the word. If he still experiences difficulty, his immediate auditory sequencing memory for letter names and for phonemes will be checked by asking him to repeat the names and sounds which the tester gives. His blending ability will also be tested if necessary, after the tester says the sound.

Test P5

This is a phonemic discrimination test which assesses the child's auditory perception of differences within 50 pairs of words, each pair differing only in a single, close-related phoneme. In this test, the child is merely required to respond 'same' or 'different' according to his perception of the words. In addition to the diagnostic tests, material is also supplied for a remediation workshop and also guidelines for constructing remediation exercises and games.

Purpose

The tests are diagnostic, providing a means of pin-pointing 'any weaknesses which a child might have with single letter sounds, short and long vowels, and with consonant and vowel blends' which might therefore be contributing to the child's reading disability. It is suggested that it could be used as an early screening instrument for children who are already showing signs of having reading difficulties.

Item preparation

The Manual does not make it clear from whence the words for Tests P1 to P4 were selected. Clearly, their specific linguistic characteristics limit the range of possibilities. In addition, there is a suggestion on page 5 of the Manual that they may have been derived from Wepman's (1958) Auditory Discrimination Test. Worried by the possibility that the words in Wepman's test might be unfamiliar and thus the scores could be confounded by vocabulary knowledge, the present authors devised the supplementary test P5 made up of words 'all of which are in common usage' according to the Thorndike-Lorge (1944) count'. No details are given of pre-standardization trials but there are references to earlier work which used Wepman's test (McLeod, 1967) which may shed light on some of the test characteristics. In addition, there is quite a detailed rationale given for the design of the tests with supporting reference to research findings.

Administration

It is not entirely clear who the users would be but one must assume that these tests would not normally be for use in schools. Rather, they would be used by educational psychologists or speech therapists after the child has been referred for diagnosis and/or remediation.

These are power tests so the time required for the test is not specified. It will, in any case, depend on how retarded the child is for this dictates how much additional questioning is necessary. In the Manual, it is assumed that previous testing of ability and reading achievement will have permitted a rapport to have been established already between tester and child whereupon it is envisaged that the Domain tests will be completed within two sessions. Considerable care is taken to give practical details about how to encourage the child to produce his maximum performance.

Standardization

The Domain Phonic Tests are diagnostic instruments and have not been standardized.

Scoring

In the first four Domain tests, the errors of the child are recorded as substitution errors. Results for each phonic unit are collected together in tabular form to yield a profile of which phonic units are frequently difficult for the child. These test items are meant to be criterion referenced. No attempt is made to provide scores as such, nor any attempt to derive norms. It is the layout of the responses on the grids provided which gives an indication of what problems the child is having. Scoring Test P5 does involve a count of the number of errors. A check is included within the scoring of a possible invalidation of the test administration. Again, the scores of interest are not to be emphasized in numerical terms, but are merely to be taken as indicating whether or not the child's discrimination of phonemes within words is suspect.

Reliability

Studies not undertaken for the present test.

Validity

No studies described. Argument is based on content validity which is probably sufficient for the purpose of the test. There is some suggestion that part of the test may have been subjected to an evaluation of its power to discriminate between disabled readers and unselected controls (McLeod, 1967) but details are not supplied.

Interpretation

There is a great deal of guidance for interpreting the child's responses both in theoretical terms and also by example. Advice for relevant courses of action including further diagnostic testing and remediation is supplied. More material is supplied for relevant remediation work to follow on from the diagnostic testing.

General evaluation

These tests seem to provide an efficient way of diagnosing in considerable detail particular problems associated with phonic-based reading difficulty. The principles of content selection are clearly defined and supported by reference to some research findings in the area. The tests do not set out to assess semantic or syntactic skills.

The Manual is interesting to read and the authors state their intentions very clearly, making only the most realistic claims for their tests. The regular reprinting dates (1975, 1977, 1978, 1980) may well suggest its perceived value by practitioners. The accompanying workshop materials make it far more than merely a diagnostic test.

The content of the test may date with regard to vocabulary in common usage. Since there was anxiety expressed by the authors on this basis they saw fit to produce the supplementary Test P5 using only most common words from a

1944 frequency count—already far from current—this may be a problem. However, given the nature of the tasks for the children, I doubt whether vocabulary unfamiliarity really need invalidate the test since the critical factor is the child's ability to perceive and manipulate phonic structure. There is no real attempt to judge the child's reading ability based on this test, which merely provides supplementary information on this aspect. This being the case, vocabulary knowledge which would interfere with such an assessment, should not be a major problem. There is no really satisfactory way of ensuring equivalent familiarity across words except in the broadest terms and it would be wrong to over-emphasize difficulties associated with such dating since, in any case, the tests are only used to provide diagnostic evidence for a single individual and no comparison between children is intended. One further point about controls for word familiarity: with retarded readers it is unlikely that such controls would be particularly useful since such readers are unlikely to be typically knowledgeable on vocabulary, this probably being a secondary skill to reading and other language skills.

References

McLeod, J. (1967). Some psycholinguistic correlates of reading disability in young children. *Reading Research Quarterly* 2, 5–31.
Thorndike, E. L. and Lorge, I. (1944). "The Teachers Word Book of 30 000 Words". Bureau of Publications, Teacher's College, Columbia University.
Wepman, J. M. (1958). "Auditory Discrimination Test". 950 E. 59th Street, Chicago.

Early Learning: Assessment and Development

Reviewed by Anne S. Hawkins

Authors: Audrey Curtis and Mary Wignall
Publisher: Macmillan
Distributor: Macmillan
Age range: 5:03+
Individual test (but many observations take place in group setting)

Test content

A series of assessment devices, with appropriate activities to foster development, in the areas of:

movement skills—fine and gross motor, laterality;
perceptual skills;
communication—language and listening skills;
learning and memory;
emotional and social development.
The coverage of the tests is broad and should therefore provide a useful screening device. Most of the assessments are based on observations of behavioural responses. Many of the activities required of the child are those which either occur naturally in the course of the school day or may fairly easily be incorporated into regular teaching programmes.

Purpose

The intention of the authors is to provide a series of assessment devices for early identification of a child's areas of strength and weakness. Rather than merely providing early diagnosis, however, materials have been supplied for helping to alleviate the child's difficulties. Thus, the package is intended to be a 'learning package' with opportunity for regular feedback on the child's progress, rather than a diagnostic testing instrument.

Item preparation

The items or activities, have been selected on the basis of what 'most children of between 5 years 3 months and 5 years 6 months are able to carry out. Other activities have been included so that the teacher can identify the strengths of a child in any particular area' (Manual, p. 6).

No further information is given concerning the origin of these items nor is any mention made of any trials with the materials.

Administration

It is intended that all the activities 'should be seen as activities to be carried out during the normal school routine'. This may well encourage teachers to engage in casual (and therefore possibly unreliable) observations if their interests are focused on the one-off diagnosis of a particular child. They should be encouraged to adhere systematically to the suggestions in the Manual, although this might mean some radical impositions on their established teaching programmes, and to use the teaching and assessment materials for all their children. This should enhance the objectivity of the screening process.

Most of the activities require additional equipment, for example a PE bench, scissors, screw-top jar, etc. In general, these are the kind of things that most Primary schools already have available. The Manual contains a number of spirit duplicator masters for generating full sets of test sheets. The intention is that the time for using these test materials will be open-ended since they will be linked to an on-going teaching programme.

Standardization

None described.

Scoring

Copyright-free class record sheets are provided for recording all children's performances in the various activities. A system of superimposed ratings for subsequent testings is described whereby numbers of '1' entries and their colours gives a visual impression of the child's capabilities and progress over time. The judgements to be made are 'poor', 'average', 'good' and 'excellent'. Little guidance is given to establishing objective criteria for these scale-points and so the records kept will always be very context- and teacher-specific, making continuing assessment comparisons in later years problematical. If this visual impression of progress is to be at all useful each child should really be re-assessed (at least on all items within a particular category of development) in the same short period of time. It is difficult to see exactly how such a process would fit into the authors' intended *on-going* programme of individualized assessment and teaching. However, the recording of the results has an attractive simplicity which should serve to highlight extremes of ability within a class.

An additional record sheet is provided for recording the performance of each individual child. This takes the form of a pictogram-style chart again intended to convey a visual impression of a child's developmental profile. The transfer of information from the Whole Child sheet to the class record and vice versa is merely a duplication of the same information. The use of such charts and pictograms would need to be tried before any real opinion on their effectiveness could be passed. They appear to have a certain intuitive appeal and the instructions are reasonably clear.

Reliability

No studies described.

Validity

No studies described.

Interpretation

As indicated, the interpretation is based on the visual impressions of children's profiles from 'tally' charts and pictogram-style presentations. Interpretation is meant to be based on four broad categories of ability but no descriptions of these categories in relation to the specific items is given. Therefore, the judgements will tend to be very context-specific, i.e. what is 'poor' to one teacher, in one school or with one group of children may not be 'poor' to another teacher, or in another school or even with the same teacher and a different group of children.

No cautions are given concerning the strengths or weaknesses of comparisons based on these profiles. Nor is the reliability of the items for their diagnostic purpose tempered with 'may' or 'might'. For example, in the assessment of laterality on p. 14 of the Manual, the following sentence occurs: 'Right hand to left eye or left hand to right eye *indicates* cross-laterality'. It 'may' suggest a possibility of' but I doubt whether it really 'indicates'.

In general, the Manual gives too little guidance on criteria for assessing abilities and competences. Rather, it tends to focus too much on merely providing activities which may be used in these assessments.

General evaluation

The materials supplied should be viewed more as a package of teaching materials with record keeping facilities for obtaining some feedback on the effectiveness of the programme followed by each child. In helping to structure children's school experiences, this may well be very valuable. It is certainly more in keeping with the stated purpose of the authors than the supposition that the materials provide a rigorous diagnostic instrument. They may serve to alert a teacher to extremes of abilities in particular areas but then the prescribed action is for routine class activities rather than for more detailed diagnosis which such extremes may warrant. This being the case, it looks as if the authors feel that their materials can also serve to highlight less extreme strengths or weaknesses. In the absence of more information on the use of these materials, on their reliability and validity, it is impossible to determine whether such a claim is tenable. It remains unclear, also, to what extent class teachers require such a resource book of ideas for discriminating activities and structured schemes of learning, and hence how valuable a contribution this publication could make.

Early Mathematical Language

Reviewed by J. Tuson

Authors: Margaret Williams and Heather Somerwill
Publisher: Macmillan Education
Distributor: Macmillan Education
Age: 1st year infants
1982 (Handbook, booklets, materials)
Individual (or small group) assessment

Test content

The materials consist of six pupils' books containing pictures of a family of bears. The bears are shown engaged in activities which should be familiar to most young children. Each book deals with a different area of mathematics: position in space, number, length, weight and shape, volume and capacity and time. The books each contain 14 illustrations intended to provoke words which the authors consider necessary to the development of children's concepts and knowledge of the particular mathematics area. The illustrations are reproduced in the teachers' handbook together with the relevant vocabulary and questions recommended for prompting pupil response.

The concentration on aspects of geometry, e.g. position and size, makes the balance of content consistent with what is widely recognized as appropriate for young children. Within each mathematics area there is a fairly comprehensive coverage of the concepts crucial to development in that area.

Purpose

'. . . the Early Mathematical Language project has been developed in order to help the busy reception teacher assess the mathematical language a child has acquired in the first five years of its life' (Teachers' Handbook, P. 6). The authors stress the importance of not making assessments using these books in isolation but, in addition, other methods should be employed such as listening to children's conversation and asking children to draw pictures of a chosen subject. Assessment, in the form of discovering 'the breadth of each child's experience of life, and its relation to that of the others in the class' is seen as necessary 'before she (the teacher) can plan her classroom activities effectively'.

The authors offer a word of caution when discussing the limitations of the materials: 'This project will not provide a watertight tool for assessing children's acquisition of early mathematical language. Although all the materials have been tested with children, they are not intended as other than informal classroom supports. In drawing attention to their limitations, however, it must be stressed that their main purpose is to draw teachers' attention to the importance for children of acquiring the language that is basic to mathematics at an early age and, in addition, to provide assistance in monitoring the process' (Handbook, p. 9).

Item preparation

The Handbook gives no information on the development of the items. It is stated that all the materials have been tested with children but neither the origins of the items, nor the responses of children to them in the trials, is reported. There is little discussion on the areas of mathematics covered by the books and none on the particular illustrations.

Administration

The six pupils' books may be used to screen all children informally during their first year at school. 'Book 1: Position in Space' is intended to be used for assessment as soon as children are relaxed and happy in their new school environment. It is suggested that the other books be used when appropriate during the child's first year at school, either before introducing new work to see if the work 'is coming at the right time and to show up gaps in a child's knowledge, or to check a child's awareness of a concept after a selective programme of mathematical activities'.

The materials are organized with the intention that they may be used with a great deal of flexibility. In addition to the pupils' books, a set of spirit duplicator masters (three illustrations from each book) is also included in order that the materials may be used with groups of children. The authors do, however, suggest a routine which may serve as a model for test administration: 'The teacher should sit with the child in a quiet and familiar place, . . . and they should look at the book together. At first the child should be allowed to talk freely about each picture. If the child uses the required language in an intelligent way, then the teacher may assume that (s)he understands the word, and will note the fact on the record sheet . . .'. A pad of record sheets is provided with the materials and a comprehensive system of record keeping of all assessments is recommended. A few suggestions are also made concerning the follow-up to a child's failure to respond to a picture correctly.

Standardization

There is no mention of any standardization exercise in the Handbook nor is there any reference to what a teacher might reasonably expect from a class of five-year olds. The materials are not intended to be used formally for comparative purposes; they constitute an informal assessment procedure primarily concerned with diagnosis and mastery.

Scoring

No method of scoring is intended to be used. Children are judged to be able to use particular language appropriately or not and a record of their vocabulary should be kept. If a child does not use the required word but produces an acceptable alternative the authors recommend asking a suitable alternative question. If the child's response still does not make use of the particular vocabulary then it is recommended that a note be made and the child reassessed at a later stage or with different material (a number of the illustrations have been designed to duplicate key words).

Reliability

No test scores are allocated to children and so no traditional measure of reliability is reported, although perhaps comment might have been expected on the reliability of the basic observations.

Validity

Again there is no information given. The question of how the use of the particular vocabulary which is being assessed is related to mathematics performance is not fully addressed, nor do the authors discuss how a child's use of certain language is actually assessed by these particular illustrations. That language is an integral part of mathematics is discussed fairly widely elsewhere (e.g. Choat, 1978), but there is not a great deal in this material to convince a teacher of its own importance and relevance.

Interpretation

Although the tests are not formally scored the authors do give some guidance as to follow-up procedures when children fail to give the correct responses.

General evaluation

The materials do not constitute a test in the formal sense of the word; they are intended to be used as informal assessment procedures and the authors also include in the Handbook some suggestions for structured activities designed to stimulate the learning of mathematical language. If the authors were to give more information on how the items were developed and how children responded to illustrations then the importance of language in mathematics would be made more obvious. The Handbook is very readable and helpful and the record sheets are comprehensive. A great deal of flexibility may be employed when using the material which is important when dealing with young children. This flexibility is also important since in some illustrations the word to be elicited is not always the most obvious and the use of a family of bears means that the individuals are not particularly easy to distinguish.

One final point concerns the stereotypical gender differentiation in the illustrations. Although it is not always the case that the males are depicted as active and the females as passive, in many cases the family is shown with mother bear concerned with cooking, flowers and the children, father bear with the car, and the boy bear is shown to be playing with trains while his sister plays with dolls.

Reference

Choat, E. (1978). "Childrens' Acquisition of Mathematics". Windsor, Berks: NFER-Nelson.

First-Grade Screening Test

Reviewed by D. H. Lee

Authors: John E. Pate and Warren W. Webb
Publisher: American Guidance Service, Inc.
Distributors: NFER-Nelson; Educational Evaluation Enterprises;
   The Test Agency
Age: end of Kindergarten and early in first grade (USA)
1965 (S); 1966 (M, T)
1969 (M) (added references; no other revisions apparent)
Group test

Test content

The First-Grade Screening Test (FGST) consists of two small booklets—one marked 'Boys' and the other 'Girls'—each presenting twenty-seven paper and pencil tasks such as drawing a man, copying abstract shapes, tracing a path through dots, selecting pictures of objects named or defined by function. The pupil is asked to trace, copy or ring items. The pictorial standard of the items appears high and the format clear. The item content seems reasonably well balanced.

Purpose

The test is said to have been developed 'to satisfy a specific educational need: screening beginning or potential first-grade students to identify the few who will not, without benefit of special assistance, make sufficient progress during first grade to be ready for second grade the next year' (Manual, p. 5).

Concentrating as it does on picking out 'intellectual retardation, central nervous system dysfunctioning and emotional disturbance' (all claimed to be fundamental in impeding educational progress) the test can be said to be diagnostic and criterion referenced as a screening instrument. Although percentile norms are derived from the standardization exercise these are admitted to be of limited usefulness.

Item preparation

Items for inclusion in the test were, to quote the authors, 'inductively derived' and were selected 'to sample the child's accumulated fund of knowledge, development of his body image, perception of his own emotional maturation, accuracy of his perception of parental figures, perception of appropriate play, visuo-motor co-ordination, ability to follow directions and memory' (Manual, p. 46). All such items are frequently found in the psychometric literature and relate to familiar tasks in studies of handicapped pupils. The need to have this test of wide spectrum but limited length is further argued in justification of item choice.

Pilot studies on groups of 500 first-grade children (1962), 1500 first graders (1963) and 3500 kindergarten children (1965)—this last group 'drawn on a nationwide basis'—are reported to have determined the final form of the test using teacher reports, comments and grading of pupils—the latter as a criterion measure.

Administration

The test consists of a booklet with one item per page. There are separate booklets for boys and girls—the only differences being the gender of the key figures. It is intended for use by teachers and is untimed. It is recommended that sufficient time is allowed 'for most but not necessarily all' children to complete each page. The point is made that some children may not complete a test item however much time is allowed. Some 30–45 minutes is thought to be sufficient for most groups of testees. Apart from the test booklet a child requires only a pencil and eraser. The instructions are clearly set out and precise, and a useful touch is that phrases are underlined the exact number of times they should be stated aloud. As a guide to pupils and examiners each page carries a pattern of between one and four dots, offering a quick check that testees are working on the correct page.

Standardization

Following the sizeable pilot studies referred to above, 5534 first-grade children were drawn from a stratified sample of schools representing each geographic region of the USA. Sex balance was 51 per cent boys and the socio-economic, educational and urban-rural background of parents conformed to national norms. Percentiles were derived for each raw score point separately for an end of kindergarten group ($n = 3258$) and for the first-grade sample.

Reliability

No internal consistency measure was employed for this test of 27 items tapping several aspects of development. Two test-retest studies were carried out, one with a two-week and one an eight-week interval (sample of 347 and 407 respectively). Correlations of 0.84 and 0.82 indicate that the scores were moderately stable throughout the trial period. Inter-scorer reliability was also assessed as was intra-scorer consistency (at a four-month interval). Correlations of 0.98 in each case (samples of 189 and 129) are said to indicate a high degree of reliability.

Validity

External achievement standards were established using teacher ratings supplemented by scores from the California Achievement Tests, the SRA Achievement Tests and the Stanford Achievement Test (Forms J and W). A median score was derived for each child and became the 'general achievement score'. An overall product-moment correlation of 0.74 is taken by the authors to indicate 'that the FGST would be useful in the prediction of achievement scores'.

Using teachers' ratings of children's readiness for second grade work it was found that raw scores of 15 points and below (in the raw score range of 0-29 points) identified 76 per cent of the 'not ready' group while mis-identifying 9 per cent of the 'ready' group. Using teacher ratings again as criterion, it was demonstrated that each item discriminated significantly for placement in these categories. A further study found that a cutting-score of 19 points correctly identified 84 per cent of 144 first-grade children 'who would fail during the preliminary grade'. Finally, correlations of 0.55 and 0.67 were found between the FGST and a first-grade behavioural rating scale and a reading test.

Scoring

One point is awarded for satisfactory performance of each task except that the first item, Draw-A-Man, is given a score of three for successful completion of face, arms and legs. The maximum score for the twenty-seven items is therefore twenty-nine points.

Fairly comprehensive notes of guidance are offered in scoring those attempts which are straightforwardly pass or fail. Sample acceptable and unacceptable answers are provided and, with one or two minor exceptions, ambiguity or incompleteness is absent.

Interpretation

In relation to the purpose of this test—a first-grade screening device—the scoring system and interpretation of results seems adequate. The authors make the point that a locally determined 'cutting-score' is necessary to take account of, for example, availability of local support services. Some false positives or negatives will arise and suggested percentages of pupils requiring further investigation are given for each raw score cutting-point (e.g. 5 per cent for a cutting-point at 11 points).

In general, the advice appears cautious and sensible.

General evaluation

The FGST appears to be a modern, technically competent piece of work. The Manual has particularly clear and simple operating instructions. It should prove almost immediately accessible to any competent educationalist.

As an early school screening device it is obviously of restricted usefulness and is perhaps disappointing in its lack of profiling across skills and abilities. What is sacrificed here however, may be compensated for in its speed and ease of use. In the process it may well have avoided some of the rather suspect 'diagnostic' analyses of similar scales. It should be remembered, however, that this is a test developed and standardized for USA children.

The Frostig Developmental Test of Visual Perception

Reviewed by D. A. Sugden

Authors: Marianne Frostig and Phyllis Maslow, in collaboration with D. Welty Lefever and John R. B. Whittlesey

Publisher: Consulting Psychologists Press
Distributor: NFER-Nelson
Age range: 4–8 years
1961 (S); 1958 (pilot test)
1963 (S), 1964 and 1966 (M) (third edition); 1961 (T)
Group test

Test content

There are five independent areas of visual perception which comprise the test:
(1) Eye-Motor Co-ordination, involving the drawing of continuous straight, curved or angled lines between boundaries of various widths or from point-to-point without guidelines.
(2) Figure Ground, involving the ability to perceive certain geometric forms (the figures) against increasingly complex backgrounds (the ground).
(3) Form Constancy requiring the recognition of a figure which may vary in size, texture, shade or position without altering its basic form.
(4) Position in space, involving the ability to distinguish a particular form from other figures as it is presented in an identical, rotated or reversed position. Schematic drawings representing common objects are used.
(5) Spatial Relationships, involving the analysis of simple forms and patterns which consist of lines of various lengths and angles. The child is required to copy these lines using dots as guide points.

Purpose

The purpose of the test is to measure a variety of visual perceptual skills. The authors believe that some learning difficulties in children are accompanied by an impairment of ability to perform different visual perceptual tasks. The authors believed it necessary 'to map the normal development of visual perception as the first step toward establishing a 'perceptual quotient' for individual children. It was then possible to use the test to detect those children whose perceptual abilities were retarded in comparison with the norm' (1963 Standardization, p. 463). 'The Developmental Test of Visual Perception can be used either as a screening device for nursery school, kindergarten, and first-grade children, or as a clinical evaluative instrument for older children who suffer from learning difficulties' (1966 Administration and Scoring Manual, p. 6).

Item preparation

Test construction was preceded by observation of children referred to the Marianne Frostig School of Education because of learning difficulties. Many of the children had disturbances in visual perception particularly in the areas mentioned under Test Content above. Test construction, involving these five areas, took place on the basis 'that each of the five abilities developed independently of the others, and that there should be specific relationships between them and a child's ability to learn and adjust' (1963 Standardization, p. 464). These are not purported to be the only items involved in the total process of visual perception, but are seen as the important ones having particular relevance to school performance.

Preliminary construction of the test began in 1958 by first establishing which items could be used with nursery children, resulting in a pilot study in 1959. Children of different age were added, together with new items which eliminated ceiling effects, and these formed the second version of the test in 1960. These first two versions are described but not referenced in the 1963 standardization, which is based on tests in 1961 and referred to as the 'Third Edition'. The criteria used for the final selection of items in each subtest were good age progression and low degree of contamination with other abilities.

Administration

The test can be given individually or in a group. A group administration takes less than one hour and there are recommended maximums for the number of children who can be tested simultaneously at each school level. These range from 1–2 children at 3–4 years of age, to 20–40 for 8–9 year olds. All examiners should be experienced and familiar with the instructions and it is recommended that the test not be administered by a regular classroom teacher. An individual administration takes 30–45 minutes, and all 'disturbed or handicapped' children should be tested in this way. Various cautionary notes are given followed by the details of the administration of each individual test.

For the test each child is to be provided with a 35-page expendable booklet, coloured pencils, crayons and regular pencils. In addition there are 11 demonstration cards and transparent scoring tissues.

Standardization

The standardization procedure described in Frostig *et al.* (1964) involved 2116 schoolchildren between the ages of 3 and 9. The sample was derived mainly from white middle-class children in Southern California, which the authors readily admit is far from perfect. There were a few Mexican-American or Oriental children, and no Black-American children. The absence of a broad-based standardization sample is a deficiency, and comparisons of a given child's performance with this particular sample should be made with caution, especially with populations having different ethnic and social groupings.

Scoring

The authors claim a high degree of objectivity for the scoring if a careful adherence to the instructions is followed. There may be occasional situations where clinical judgement should be exercised. Instructions are given on how to score each individual item to obtain a raw score which is converted into a Perceptual Age defined in terms of the performance of the average child in the corresponding age group for each subtest. A Scaled Score is arrived at by dividing chronological age into perceptual age and multiplying by 10. Finally a Perceptual Quotient (PQ) is calculated and is a deviation score obtained from the sum of subtest scale scores after correcting for age variation. It is defined in terms of constant percentiles for each age group with a median of 100, upper and lower quartiles of 110 and 90 respectively, and other percentile ranks consistent with IQ values of the Wechsler Intelligence Scale for Children. The authors warn against the use of the PQ as a measure of a fixed ability, and it should not be used to suggest an expression of some common factor, as the test is based on the assumption that the five areas are different and relatively independent areas.

Reliability

Frostig *et al.* (1964) report test-retest reliability studies based on two or three week intervals, with reliability coefficients of 0.98, 0.80, 0.69 for the full range. Test-retest reliability correlations for each subtest ranged from 0.33–0.83 on 5–6 year olds ($n = 55$), and from 0.40–0.67 on 6–7 year olds ($n = 72$).

Split-half reliability coefficients based on the raw scores of four age groups between 5 and 9, ranged from 0.78 to 0.89 for total scores. There was some variability between the subtests. For example, subtest II gave a range from 0.91–0.93 while subtest IV ranged from 0.35–0.70.

Validity

For predictive validity, Frostig *et al.* (1964) report correlation coefficients of 0.44, 0.50 and 0.50 between the test and teacher ratings of classroom adjustment, motor co-ordination and intellectual functioning. However, Hammill and Weidesholt (1973) concluded that neither the total score nor the subtest scores related meaningfully to reading. The Frostig Test is assumed to measure five independent areas of visual perception and several factor analytic studies have attempted to validate this claim (Boyd and Randle, 1970; Chissom and Thomas, 1971; McKinney, 1971; Ward, 1970). These studies and others have usually isolated a single factor or, sometimes, two emerging from the total test battery suggesting that the use of the pooled figure may be valuable but that the independence of the subtests is questionable.

Interpretation

The raw score obtained on the test can be converted to a Perceptual Age, Scaled Score or a Perceptual Quotient. The Perceptual Age can be used in direct comparison with chronological age, e.g. 'He showed retardation of six months in his performance on Subtest I' (Revised Manual, 1966, p. 31). The Scaled Score is used to indicate a need for training in a particular area. A scale score of 8 or below on any subject is used as the criterion for this. If, using Perceptual Quotients, children fall into the lowest quartile the authors indicate that they are very likely to experience difficulties at school, and perceptual training is recommended.

General evaluation

The Frostig is a test that has been widely used, especially in the USA, to measure perceptual ability in young children and its relationship to learning difficulties. It is a test that is relatively easy to administer and score, although if a child devotes too much time to one item, the tester is not advised what to do.

Reliability for the total test is satisfactory both for test-retest and split-half, but is low for the individual subtests. It has satisfactory correlation with other measures of visual perception but low predictability for measures of academic achievement. The independence of the five factors has been questioned, and even though the authors acknowledge that the factors do not cover all of visual perception, it may be better to use the total test score rather than each subtest as a diagnostic instrument.

The test is useful in giving an overall evaluation of visual perception rather than specific details of visual perception relating to learning difficulties.

References

Boyd, L. and Randle, K. (1970). Factor analysis of the Frostig DTVP. *Journal of Learning Disabilities* **3**, 253–255.

Chissom, B. S. and Thomas, J. R. (1971). Comparisons of factor structures for the Frostig DTVP. *Perceptual and Motor Skills* **33**, 1015–1019.

Frostig, M., Maslow, P., Lefever, D. W. and Whittlesey, J. R. B. (1964). The Marianne Frostig Developmental Test of Visual Perception: 1963 standardization. *Perceptual and Motor Skills* **19**, 463–499 (Monograph Supplement 2–V19) (reprinted and distributed by Consulting Psychologists Press).

Hammill, D. and Weidesholt, J. L. (1973). Review of the Frostig Visual Perception Test and related training programme. *In* "The First Review of Special Education" (L. Mann and D. A. Sabatino, eds). Philadelphia: JAI Press, Grune and Stratton.

McKinney, J. D. (1971). A factor analytic study of the DTVP and the Metropolitan Readiness Test. *Perceptual and Motor Skills* **33**, 1331–1334.

Ward, J. (1970). The factor structure of the Frostig DTVP. *British Journal of Educational Psychology* **40**, 65–67.

Griffiths Mental Development Scales

Reviewed by R. Driver

Author: Ruth Griffiths
Publisher: Griffiths
Distributor: The Test Agency
Age ranges: 0:03–2:00 (Abilities of Babies)
          0:03–8:00 (Abilities of Young Children)
1947–53 (S); 1954 (Abilities of Babies); 1978 (Supplementary notes)
1960–61 (S); 1970 (Abilities of Young Children)
Individual tests (restricted use)

Introduction

The Griffiths Scale of Infant Development was first published in 1954. It was based on an extensive programme of observation of babies between the ages of three months and two years, at the Child Development Research Centre, London. The scale has been designed for use by psychologists, paediatricians and others concerned with the assessment of babies. It has five sub-scales and is of value in clinical diagnosis with both normal and handicapped children.

In 1970 an Extended Scale suitable for the assessment of children up to eight years of age (Griffiths, 1970) was published. Although the Extended Scale is designed to assess babies and young children from three months of age and incorporates many features of the Scale of Infant Development it has not completely replaced it in that the latter gives more detailed and reliable diagnostic information on babies. This review will therefore discuss each Scale separately.

The Griffiths Scale of Infant Development

Test content

The Scale is individually administered by a trained specialist. There are five sub-scales:

Scale A. The Locomotor Scale (includes items on body movement, balance, sitting, walking);

Scale B. The Personal-Social Scale (includes items on relation between baby, adults and the physical environment such as smiling, recognition of mother, feeding);

Scale C. Hearing and Speech (includes items on vocalization, pre-speech and evidence for active listening);

Scale D. Hand and Eye Development (includes items on the development of manipulative activities);

Scale E. Performance (includes items to assess the developing ability to reason in practical situations).

Each Scale is hierarchical and contains 52 graded items arranged in order of difficulty on the basis of the percentage of babies 'passing' them each month. Overall the Scale consists of 260 items, 3 items for each week for the first year of life and 2 items per week for the second year.

Purpose

The Scale was designed for use by clinical psychologists, paediatricians and others who require diagnostic information about the development of babies. The Scale, the first of its kind in this country, was produced as a result of an extensive programme of observations on several hundred babies ranging in age from 2 weeks to 24 months.

Administration

A standardized kit of equipment is required. The original publication (Griffiths, 1954) outlines the procedures for administering the test in detail. Supplementary notes have since been produced by a working party of the Association for Research in Infant and Child Development (1978). Administration time is between 20 and 40 minutes.

Standardization

This was undertaken with a sample of 571 children born between 1947 and 1951 and who were assessed by one examiner. The sample was not systematically constructed nor was it a random sample. In an attempt to obtain a sample of babies from a representative set of families the occupational status of the fathers was obtained and an attempt was made to match the distribution of grades of occupation of fathers of the sample cases with those in the population. However, in the absence of post-war British Census figures, the occupational composition of the USA population was used (a substitute which must be of dubious relevance).

Scoring

The separate subscales have been developed to be of comparable difficulty. This 'equality of difficulty' at each age level enables the profile of results on each subscale to be used for diagnostic purposes to indicate the existence of specific handicaps (the handbook discusses a number of cases). The baby's mental age and General Intelligence Quotient can be computed from the results on the separate scales; although a warning is given about problems associated with the interpretation of the General Intelligence Quotient in the first six months of life.

Reliability and validity

Sixty babies from the standardization sample were tested twice with an average interval of 30 weeks between tests. The results (reported in Griffiths, 1954) yield a test-retest correlation coefficient of 0.87.

Test use

Information on the Scale has been reported by Hindley (1965) who tested 80 children (43 boys and 37 girls), using the Griffiths Scale of Infant Development at 6 months and 18 months and the Stanford Binet (Form L) at 3 years and 5 years. In this study the parental characteristics (as indicated by the Registrar General's Classification of occupational status) of the children at the time of birth was representative of London Administrative County based on 1951 census data. The results indicated a positive correlation between scores on successive administration. Higher inter-correlations were obtained between adjacent ages (0.54–0.78) than between non-adjacent ages (0.32–0.40). The correlations between the infant scores and the later Stanford Binet IQs were small, and suggested that the scale has limited predictive validity for normal children.

Although there was no overall sex difference in the results, it was interesting to note that the social class differences in the scores appeared earlier for girls than for boys.

The Abilities of Young Children

Test content

There are six subscales, five are the same as for the earlier instrument, the sixth, Scale F is on Practical Reasoning. It includes items on simple arithmetic, use of money and comparison in size, weight, length, etc. of objects.

Purpose

The purpose of this Scale is similar to that for the Scale of Infant Development but extends its use up to eight years of age.

Standardization

The Scale was standardized on a sample of 2260 children aged from 3 months to 8 years. The testing took place in various locations in England, Wales and Scotland in the years 1960 and 1961. The parental characteristics as indicated by the Registrar General's Classification of occupational status was representative of the population (as determined in the 1951 Census).

Scoring

The separate subscales have been developed to be of 'equal difficulty' at each age thus enabling diagnostic information to be obtained from the subscale profiles. The number of items on each scale for the first two years have been reduced to 2 items per month in each subscale. There are 6 items per year on each subscale from year three to year eight.

Reliability and validity

Concurrent validity of the Scale has been assessed by testing 524 children aged 3 to 6 on the Griffiths Scale and on the Stanford Binet Test (Form L). Correlations of between 0.79 and 0.81 are reported at each of the ages. These correlations are quite high and suggest a substantial common factor between the two tests despite considerable differences in their subject matter. Correlations between the subscales and the total scale are reported and range from 0.64 for the Locomotor Scale to 0.78 for the Practical Reasoning Scale.

Interpretation

The Manual gives norms for each of the six subscales up to year eight and detailed information on the interpretation of the profiles for normal and handicapped children.

General evaluation

An important feature of the tests is the development of subscales of comparable difficulty, which enables the performance profile obtained to be used for diagnostic purposes. In some cases however, there appears to be reason to question the assignment of items to certain scales, and overlap exists between the scales which will reduce diagnostic usefulness of the tests.

The Griffiths Scales are no longer the only scales available for the assessment of babies. However, they are likely to continue to serve a useful purpose because of the breadth of behaviour assessed and the relatively short testing time required, compared with other similar tests.

The strength of the scales lies in the way they have been based on careful observation:

'One cannot stress too often the significance of careful and detailed observation of children if we are to understand them, perceive their thoughts, or interpret their behaviour. Still more important does this become for the investigator who is engaged in building a Scale of Tests. There is, in fact, scarcely any limit in this field of work, to what can be learned by the observation of children, at play, at home, on the street, in trains or buses, and in their own homes and gardens' (Griffiths, 1970, p. 7).

However, she herself acknowledges that 'there is a sense in which all test items may be regarded as social items' (ibid. p. 11).

Social behaviours change with time. The relevance of some items and their relative positions in the Scales may therefore need to be reviewed periodically. A revision of the scales is being undertaken but this will not be complete for a number of years.

References

Griffiths, R. (1954). "The Abilities of Babies." London: Association for Research in Infant and Child Development.

Griffiths, R. (1970). "The Abilities of Young Children". London: Child Development Research Centre.

Hindley, C. B. (1965). Stability and change in abilities up to five years. *Journal of Child Psychology and Psychiatry* **6**, 85–99.

The Harrison-Stroud Reading Readiness Profile

Brief Report

Authors: M. Lucile Harrison and James B. Stroud
Publisher: Houghton Mifflin Company
Distributor: NFER-Nelson
Age; 'first grade' (USA)
1950 (S); 1950 (M); 1949 (T)
1955 (S); 1956 (M, T)
No revisions apparent
Date of printing of review copies not stated
Group tests (Tests 1 to 5)
Individual test (Test 6)

There are six tests. *Test* 1, Using Symbols: the child pairs words and pictures (15 minutes). *Test* 2, Making Visual Discrimination: subtests a and b require the child to match a word with one chosen from four visually similar words (a,

14 minutes; b, 8 minutes). *Test* 3, Using the Context: one of three line drawings is to be selected as representing a word implied by a statement spoken by the tester (12 minutes). *Test* 4, Making Auditory Discriminations: the child identifies which of two line drawings on the right has a name, the first letter of which matches that of the name of one on the left (14 minutes). *Test* 5, Using Context and Auditory Cues: the child chooses one of three line drawings to match the initial consonant of its name to that of a person's name in a statement, read out by the tester, which gives a helpful context (13 minutes). *Test* 6, Giving the Names of the Letters: 42 upper and lower case letters (excluding those for which case makes little difference to form) are to be named (3 minutes).

The tests are untimed: approximate administration times are given above. Raw scores are converted to percentile ranks for each Test via a profile chart. The conversion is based upon 'over 1400 pupils' tested in 1955, taken from 28 different states (USA).

Infant Rating Scale

Reviewed by Anne S. Hawkins

Author: Geoff A. Lindsay
Publisher: Hodder and Stoughton
Distributor: Hodder & Stoughton
Age range: 5:00–5:06 (Level 1);
                7:00–7:06 (Level 2)
1981
Individual test

Test content

For each level, there are 25 items, each scored on a 5-point scale. The 25 items are grouped into 5 subscales derived from factor analysis of the IRS standardization data.

Subscales for Level 1

(1) Language—expressive and receptive	(7 items)
(2) Early learning—basic skills and attitude to learning	(8 items)
(3) Behaviour	(3 items)
(4) Social integration	(3 items)
(5) General development	(4 items)

Subscales for Level 2

(1) Language/Education—expressive and receptive
   language, basic skills   (11 items)
(2) Fine motor skills   (2 items)
(3) Behaviour   (6 items)
(4) Social integration   (3 items)
(5) General development   (3 items)

The IRS is not a test *per se*. Therefore, there are no specific test responses required. The teacher merely completes the proforma for the child being rated using scales of 1–5 where a low rating indicates a problem. It will be noted that the items are not spread evenly across the subscales, nor is there complete consistency between the names of the subscales across the two levels. There are a number of supplementary items to provide background information on the child, for example, items relating to hearing, vision and home circumstances.

Purpose

The IRS is intended to be used by class teachers in 'the analysis of their children's strengths and weaknesses'. It is 'to form part of the continuous monitoring process' during a child's early years of schooling so that the teacher will be assisted in planning that child's education. The IRS is presented as a screening instrument in response to the desire for early identification of children with special educational needs. Two main types of use are specified: comparison of a child's strengths and weaknesses, and comparison of a child with other children.

Item preparation

Items were originally selected on the basis of their perceived content validity. The number of items was reduced at pilot study stage by some unspecified means 'using experienced headteachers and teachers'. Items were selected on the basis that the percentages of children rated to be in the 'at risk' categories conformed to research expectations (cited in Rutter *et al.*, 1970; Davie *et al.*, 1972). The description of the pre-standardization work is a little vague and appears to have involved a fair degree of judgement in item selection. No clear details are given concerning the nature of the pilot study or studies. Two are referred to in the Manual; one related to refinement of items and scoring criteria, the other to the unsuitability of the IRS' use in certain types of school with a large proportion of recent immigrants.

Administration

The IRS is recommended for use by class teachers in infant and junior schools. No materials are required in addition to the record sheets supplied. The time required for completion will depend on how well the teacher knows the child or alternatively on how much time he is prepared to spend observing the child in order to ensure that his scaling of the child on the various items is reliable. The instructions are adequate, particularly since this is a simple and relatively quick scale to use. However, it is very unlikely that any scale of this kind can really achieve the stated intention that teachers will respond independently to each item.

Standardization

The standardization of Level 1 was carried out by the author on data collected from the total intake of 21 junior and infant schools ($n = 1342$) for the academic year 1975–76. When the children were 7 years old, they were retested on Level 2. The standardization sample had by this time been reduced to 916. The schools were selected 'to represent all types of area within the city (Sheffield) except those with a large proportion of recent immigrants from the sub-continent of India'. No reference is made to private schools. The sample was essentially 'opportunistic/judgemental'. The description suggests coverage but there is insufficient information to assess its representativeness. Tables of percentages of children being rated at each point on each item are presented for comparison purposes together with similar tables based on cumulative scores for the subscales and total scores.

The Manual makes no reference to separate subgroup distributions despite the fact that Lindsay (1980) states that there 'were highly significant sex differences in mean scores ($P < 0.001$) on 20 items, with girls always being rated better than boys' (a further two items were significant at the 0.01 level). Further reference to the treatment of subgroups by term of entry to the school will be found in the sections on Reliability and Validity below.

Scoring

The instructions should be relatively clear to most users of the test. The record form comprises the original scaling sheet and a separate profile/record sheet. A great deal of transferring of figures is required from the original scaling sheet and also from the Manual. This could be time consuming and might give rise to inaccuracies. A more direct recording chart should be devised to overcome these problems.

The instructions to teachers to mark each item 'as independently as possible', to select the category that 'is most appropriate', and to choose a category which 'reflects what the child actually does in your class now, rather than what you think he or she could do in a different situation or in the future' are essential guidelines but it cannot be assumed that teachers will readily be able to follow them. This is a problem inherent to this type of rating scale.

Questions relating to the aggregation of scores across items and subscales will be raised under Validity below.

Reliability

No inter-rater reliability estimation was made. This was justified on the basis that only the class teacher knew the child well enough to complete the schedule. A test-retest measure of Level 1 was carried out on 49 children (involving 17 teachers from 5 schools), with a two-week gap between rating. This is a very short test-retest interval, especially when alternative raters are not used for each child and, not surprisingly, high stability is reported. No details are supplied about how this small group of children were selected. No mention is made of any similar attempt to assess the reliability of Level 2. Lindsay (1980) describes how factor analyses were carried out for Level 1 items, but no information is supplied for this in the Manual and no indication is given of whether a similar exercise was carried out for Level 2.

The separate factor analyses were carried out on data collected from children after they had been in school for one to one-and-a-half terms, comprising three groups, presumably by the term of entry. The factor analyses appeared essentially the same for these three groups and the results were then amalgamated. No separate analyses for boys' and girls' results are reported in either the Manual or the Lindsay (1980) reference.

The factor analyses of item intercorrelations seem to have been undertaken expressly to determine the subscales, rather than to eliminate unsuitable items, and indeed those items which did not factorize conveniently have been pooled, regardless of their heterogeneity, into an extra subscale misleadingly labelled 'General Development'.

Validity

In addition to the judgements made of content validity and referred to vaguely in the description of item selection, predictive validity was examined by investigating the relationships between scores on the scale at 5 years with assessments at two later stages, namely at 7 and 9 years. There is some ambiguity as to what tests were administered when and to which children, particularly about the extent to which the assessment of predictive validity is being based on retesting using the same level of the IRS. Also, insufficient detail is supplied concerning the criterion tests used and the degree of overlap in, and sizes of, subsamples.

Tests in Education

Particular reference is made to a comparison between IRS Level 1 and Young's Group Reading Test with a sample of size 480, for which correlations are reported, being highest for the Language (0.51) and Early Learning (0.56) subscales and the Total score 0.51 with GRT ($n = 480$).

IRS Level 1 items are shown correlated with their 'equivalent' items on the IRS Level 2, but no attempt is made to define or clarify this equivalence. Since the numbers of items in the subscales for the two test levels differ, it is difficult to see what the author has used as his criterion of equivalence.

A measure of 'predictive efficiency' is derived in relation to 'hits' and 'misses' in classifying children to 'At risk' and 'Not at risk' categories, again using results on the Group Reading Test as the criterion against which to judge 'correct' and 'incorrect' prediction. The Manual only gives results for selected IRS Level 1 subscales (about 75 per cent 'hits') and Total Score (80 per cent).

Interpretation

A number of brief case studies are given to guide teachers in interpreting the scores. Indeed the principles of interpretation are basically simple provided the assumptions involved are understood and accepted. The implication is that the teacher should use this type of scaling procedure as a device to prompt or structure his evaluation of a child. It is not intended to be an end in itself and the Manual attempts to underline this purpose.

General evaluation

A number of points are still to be made concerning this rating scale. The Manual is highly selective in the information given concerning evaluation of its characteristics. No discussion is offered, for example, concerning the validity of scores comprised of aggregates of dissimilar subscales, particularly when there is an inherent weighting of the subscales introduced by the uneven distribution of numbers of items within these subscales. The 'rag-bag' items which did not factorize conveniently and therefore comprise a measure of 'General Development' have not been shown to form a valid subscale. Despite the author's own reported findings elsewhere (e.g. Lindsay, 1980) concerning the necessary modifications, these do not appear to have been made in this published version of the test. Nor are they discussed in the Manual.

It may be supposed that much of the statistical evaluation of the test characteristics will appear in the author's other writings, presumably his unpublished thesis (Lindsay, 1979). However, this would not readily be available to test users, and since journal articles will themselves only be summaries of research findings it must be concluded that the statistical information available for users of the rating scale is not adequate for a full understanding of its use and characteristics.

No general discussion has been made concerning the problems inherent in the use of such 5-point rating scales. Users should be warned of the assumptions made when comparisons or aggregates are made across schools and across teachers, for example. There was far too little demonstration in the Manual of the stability of the items across such contexts. Again, the question of the reluctance or otherwise of raters to use extreme categories is not addressed.

In conclusion, the Manual indicates that a great deal of test evaluation might have been carried out. The description of the procedures adopted, however, is often vague, ambiguous or over-selective. The usefulness of the scale remains extremely difficult to evaluate in the absence of the necessary evidence. It appears to have reasonably good coverage of developmental aspects. With the exception of the processing of the marks, it should be fairly easy to use. Provided the teacher uses it as a sort of check-list whereby he gains insight for planning a child's education then it may be useful. However, much will depend on the teacher's objective commitment to this purpose, and the committed teacher may not need such a check-list. As a means of keeping a profile record on the child, there may be grave problems encountered if interpretations have to cross contexts of school, teacher and school class. More warning of cross-context comparisons should be provided.

References

Lindsay, G. A. (1979). The early identification of learning difficulties and the monitoring of children's progress. Unpublished thesis, University of Birmingham.

Lindsay, G. A. (1980). The Infant Rating Scale. *British Journal of Educational Psychology* 50, 97–104.

Davie, R., Butler, N. and Goldstein, H. (1972). "From Birth to Seven". London: Longman.

Rutter, M., Tizard, J. and Whitmore, K. (1970). "Education Health and Behaviour". London: Longman.

Young, D. (1968). "Manual for the Young Group Reading Test". London: University of London Press.

The Infant Reading Tests

Reviewed by Ann Forrester

Authors: Alan Brimer and Bridie Raban
Publishers: Educational Evaluation Enterprises
Distributors: Educational Evaluation Enterprises
Age range: 4:07–7:00
1979 (M, T); S not stated
Age: infant schoolchildren
Group test

Test content

The tests consist of 6 subtests, 3 pre-reading tests suitable for all infants, and 3 reading tests, suitable only for children with 'some previous acquaintance with the printed word'.

Pre-reading Test 1

This consists of a series of styalized line drawings and shapes, enclosed in a row of boxes. To varying degrees, most but not all the drawings are representational, or bear some symbolic association to words. They are arranged in rows, to correspond to the words of sentences given in the Manual. In the first section of the subtest, the child is required to mark with a cross the box corresponding to a particular word from the related sentence. The same symbolic system is maintained throughout Pre-reading Test 1. In the second section, the child is required to mark with a cross, one of three boxes provided to the right of each row. The child must choose the box containing the symbolic drawing that will fit into the empty box in the row to the left, so that the 'symbol sentence' is meaningfully completed.

Pre-reading Test 2

This consists of line drawings, a key picture being placed on the left, and four test pictures to its right. The child is required to tick three of the four test pictures, having a sound in common with the key picture. The odd one out is left unmarked. A series of initial sounds are considered first, then final sounds, then vowel sounds, but for some unclear reason, the sections are not printed in the order in which they are to be administered.

Pre-reading Test 3

This presents sets of four symbols, ranging from abstract shapes, to letters, to real and nonsense words. The child is required to join with a line, the two identical elements among the set of four.

Reading Test 1

This presents sets of four printed words. The examiner dictates one word from each set, which the child is required to identify and mark on the test sheet.

Reading Test 2

Test 2 also presents sets of four printed words, but this time the examiner dictates a sentence, rapping with a pencil end to indicate where one word has been omitted from the sentence. The child is required to identify from the appropriate printed set, the word that is missing, and to mark it.

Reading Test 3

This consists of sets of short sentences. For each set, an initial sentence is printed on the left, and three possible follow-on sentences are printed on the right. For each set, the child must tick the box beside the chosen follow-on sentence.

Purpose

The tests are intended for diagnostic use, and claim to examine quite a range of skills. The pre-reading tests purport to examine 'linguistic competence, ability to use printed symbols, recognition of speech sounds, and discrimination of printed shapes varying in orientation'. The reading tests profess examination of word recognition skills, sentence completion and reading comprehension. The tests are considered relatively independent of any controlled reading vocabulary.

Item preparation

Trial items were given to an unspecified number of children in the age-range 4:07–7:00 in an unspecified number of infant schools. The total number of children employed is not stated, but a table given in the Manual shows that between 130 and 216 children took each of the Tests: these groups probably overlap. The content of the items was drawn from 'a specified universe', but this is not described. The form of the test tasks is claimed to be operationally defined, and developed from the author's investigations into early reading problems.

Administration

The tests are intended for use by teachers. Little equipment is needed: test forms and pencils for the children; the Manual and a blackboard and chalk for the examiner.

The Manual goes to some length in advising the examiner how to avoid arousing any anxiety in the children. The test can be given to groups of up to 8 children, but smaller groups, or even individual administration is recommended for children needing reassurance. The tests are untimed which, with the relatively small group size, enables the examiner to check that the children are proceeding correctly, and to give help turning pages, or repeating instructions as permitted. Examiners are warned against too much testing in one day:

no more than one subtest at a time is recommended, and testing time should not exceed 20 minutes.

The instructions for administration are specific and clearly laid out. It is permissible to alter the instructional words to a more familiar alternative: advice is given for such a contingency.

Standardization

Reference is made to a sampling design, which ensured relevant combinations of test data, from 4:06–7:00 year olds, but no other details are given. However, as the rationale of the tests and their scores are based on the Rasch model, the representativeness of the sample, and the abilities within that sample, might be claimed not to be a crucial matter.

On the other hand, approximate reading age norms are supplied, based on the raw scores from Reading Test 3. No information is given about how these were derived. It should be noted that once an attempt is made to supply any normative data, the representativeness of the sample becomes important. A calibration sample might well be only very roughly appropriate for normative purposes. With such a lack of rigour, the provisos concerning approximation and validity (see below) are indeed necessary. Unfortunately, in practical use, provisos tend to be forgotten. The provision of inaccurate norms cannot be recommended.

Scoring

Test items are scored either correct or incorrect: correct items gain one point. Criteria for correctness are given for Pre-reading Test 2, and a list of correct symbols is supplied for the first section of Pre-reading Test 1. (It is assumed that the examiner is able to work out symbol answers to the second half of pre-reading Test 1, but a printed list would have aided speed of marking.) In fact, a marking key, comparable to that provided for the reading tests, would have helped with Pre-reading Tests 1 and 2, though it is stated to be unnecessary. Each subtest is scored separately, and Pre-reading Test 2 is scored in three sections. Examiners are encouraged to look for orientation and sequencing errors, and generally to examine the child's pattern of response.

The summed raw scores are readily transformed to scale points for each subtest, by reference to a clear table in the Manual. A space is provided on the individual test sheets to record raw and scaled scores. A further table is also supplied whereby the raw scores for Reading Test 3 can be used as an approximate estimate of reading comprehension age.

A profile summary is provided at the end of Reading Test 3, in which the scale scores for the six subtests can be entered, and blocks can be shaded in to give a visual picture of the score pattern. The cut-off points for mastery etc., given in the conversion table, are not indicated on the blocks, though they easily could have been.

Reliability

Conventional and Rasch item analyses were conducted. The lowest reliability coefficient reported for the various subtests and sections, is 0.88, whilst most fall between 0.91 and 0.95. Reliability coefficients (KR-20), along with standard deviations and standard errors of measurement of raw scores, are provided in a table, but without a key to its interpretation.

Since the test formats involve multiple choice items, concern must be felt about the effect on scores of guessing. There is no instruction to the child to omit items if uncertain, a ploy which might have helped reduce guessing. In a test such as Reading Test 3, where a choice from three is required, some 30 per cent of items may show as 'poor' (i.e. poor fit) due to guessing. If the remaining 'good items' were rechecked, a further loss can be envisaged. In these circumstances, the suitability of the Rasch model itself must be queried, since this type of test would not satisfy the Rasch model assumptions. It would have been helpful to know what method was used to assess 'goodness of fit', and to know how the 'good items' were selected.

Validity

No validity studies are reported. Regarding the reading ages supplied, concurrent validity is disclaimed, the test task being described as different from that of most reading tests.

Interpretation

The conversion table for transforming raw scores to scale points, is banded to indicate levels of weakness versus mastery. Cut-off points at scale scores of 2 and 5, are related to probabilities of passing the test items of middlemost difficulty; children with high scale scores have more than a 50 per cent chance probability of passing, whereas children with low scale scores are unlikely to pass. The grounds for deciding these cut-off points appear to be arbitrary, and not the result of an educational investigation. If mastery level is not achieved, the need for further teaching is implied. However, the children's mastery, or lack of it, is defined by their relative scoring position, not apparently by any proven educational case to show that further teaching of the skills involved would be unproductive beyond the upper cut-off point: conversely, special need is not proven below a certain point. There is no educational information on minimum and maximum skill requirements which best facilitate reading progress. (If any comparisons were made with learning rates, or with teachers' views of satisfactory progress, they are not reported.)

The significance for a particular child of a discovery of weakness, is not clear. Relative weakness would be normal for a 5-year old, and further learning is obviously needed, but what is the teaching implication? Weakness is usually associated with inability to learn a skill given the usual learning environment but the weakness of the 5-year old can be expected to respond to usual measures, whereas similar weakness in a top infant, coming up to 7 years of age, might require extra attention, possibly with individualized emphasis. If it is implied that all children would benefit from more individualized teaching programmes, no supportive evidence is quoted to show that the degree of task analysis reflected in the Infant Reading Tests is necessary for everyone, nor that certain of the tests assess pre-requisite skills.

General evaluation

The tests are claimed to be operationally defined tasks, and to have been selected in the light of experience in investigating early reading problems. The descriptions of these operationally defined tasks, however, would benefit from greater task analysis.

The general description of purpose provided in the Manual introduction is acceptable, but the more detailed descriptions of what each subtest measures remain, in varying degrees, rather global definitions. This no doubt enhances the impression of unidimensional measurement upon which assumption the Rasch model rests. Where the component skills covered by the global definition, are essential to all items, the unidimensional measurement is preserved, but where the importance of the component skills is unequally represented in the test items, this assumption comes into question. Examination of test items suggest that this could be the case, for example, in Reading Test 1, where printed word is matched to spoken word. Though not specified, both visual discrimination and auditory sequencing skills are pertinent, but some of the words are visually confusing, whilst others require careful discrimination of phonic sequence. In this case there is a problem in assessing item difficulty levels which do not have a unitary source: the relative difficulty of visually and auditorily confusable items cannot be assessed, as the measure is no longer sample free.

As well as either exposing, or giving reassurance about such problems, more detailed task analysis would guide the test interpreter in the recommended analysis of response pattern (i.e. error analysis), which in turn would have implications for teaching.

The Rasch model itself is open to a degree of criticism. One particular shortcoming which might be pertinent in the case of this battery of tests, is the tendency for the standard error of measurement of the ability scores, to increase at the extremes of the range. It is the extremes of the scoring range, of course, which are of particular interest to the diagnostician. However, since the scale interval is relatively large (i.e. 7 point scale), error levels may not in fact, be distorting results unduly.

The references, sometimes indirect, to the Rasch model, and the explanation of how the cut-off points were established, seem to be aimed at impressing the Manual reader with authority. The details have little chance of being understood by infant teachers, and are insufficient to inform those in an advisory position, who may have a modicum of statistical knowledge. The justification offered for employing the mid-difficulty point in establishing the cut-off points, appears to be inaccurately stated, and must seem illogical even to the non-statistician. The Manual refers to test items arranged in order of difficulty (Reading Test 1), yet the justification refers to items written to be relatively homogeneous in difficulty. The mid-point would seem better justified on grounds of being a typical item, and of a level of difficulty likely to be passed by increasing proportions at every successive level of the ability range in question.

The Manual itself is well designed, with clear instructions, and content well organized into sections. Most of the test sheets too, are clearly presented, though Pre-Reading Test 3 is rather crowded and may overwhelm a young child, and Pre-Reading Test 2 might benefit from clearer drawings.

Though preventing the children from proceeding at their own pace, Pre-Reading Test 2 might be improved if the examiner named the various pictures. This would help overcome any drawing ambiguity, but more important, would ensure the children attached the intended label, and not some alternative, e.g. 'cake' when 'bun' was intended.

The tests are relatively recent, and reflect to a fair extent current thinking which attaches importance to assessing reading skills by using reading matter, i.e. letter shapes and sounds. The task set in Pre-Reading Test 1 seems the least appropriate on these grounds, based perhaps on a dubious theoretical analysis of the reading task. The second section, which introduces comprehension and syntactic structuring, could be rather demanding for a young child. The battery as a whole, however, represents quite a comprehensive cover of the various skills identified as involved in reading.

The Manual suggests that the tests can be used for determining 'what improvement a child has made after a period of teaching', but score increases can be compared and assessed only in terms of increasing probability of passing test items, i.e. in terms of increasing skill at the test task. This may allow a statement about the child's likelihood of success generally at tasks of this sort, but it does not reveal the child's actual success at chosen curriculum objectives;

nor does the test task necessarily constitute a pre-requisite skill for the attainment of those objectives, for indeed the skill might be best acquired through direct teaching of the chosen objective itself.

So, the meaning of the test scores and profile, in terms of mastery and achievement, must be queried, as must also the implications for differential teaching. The same objections apply to the cut-off points, which again are related to item content. As discussed in part above (Interpretation), cut-off points do not indicate what has been mastered in curriculum terms, nor whether mastery is essential, nor what point the child has reached in the range of reading performance to be acquired. In terms of the significance of mastery at that age, it is pertinent to ask whether the child's achievement represents an extreme case, or whether it is within expected variation for children of that age.

Perhaps it would have been more appropriate to provide conventional standardization norms for tests of the type and content found in the Infant Reading Tests, and to provide fuller guidance on how the scores can be interpreted, and on the limits of their usefulness.

Infant Screening Test

Reviewed by Anne S. Hawkins

Authors: Humberside Education Authority (P. Randall *et al.*)
Publisher: Macmillan Education
Distributor: Macmillan Education
Age range: 5–6+
1981
Group (small) and individual tests

Test content

The test materials comprise:
(1) Two developmental checklists, one for children at 5:00 and one for children 5:10–6:03.
(2) A series of initial screening tests which tap the following: visual motor expression/co-ordination, visual sequencing, auditory association, blending, word recognition, auditory reception sub-skills, sequencing and memory.
(3) A series of diagnostic tests to be used with those children who have been identified as possibly being at risk: visual reception (decoding), auditory reception (decoding), association skills, sequential skills, expression (encoding), reading difficulties.

There follows a section containing teaching programmes which are linked with the preceding diagnostic tests, with instructions for retesting, and a further section discussing ways of overcoming undesirable behaviour arising from social and emotional difficulties.

Purpose

'This test was constructed as an alternative to the usual test/diagnosis/classification system that merely placed children into categories for placement purposes by comparing their competence against a normative group' (Manual, p. 1). Instead the authors use 'a criterion-referenced approach in which levels of performance in specific abilities are postulated as necessary pre-requisites of formal learning at school'. Their model of the learning process, which guides their approach to assessment and remediation, is derived from Osgood's psycholinguistic model. The authors claim to have modified the model by reducing 'the number of postulated abilities of skill areas interacting to enable formal learning. Those omitted are the ones which have the smallest correlations with the severity of learning/communication difficulties'. They chose the model on the basis that it provided some coherent and dynamic system reflecting children's cognitive development, and would therefore be 'useful in the assessment of mental retardation, perceptual dysfunctions, speech disorders, severe reading disabilities and several other categories'. The authors imply, therefore, that their procedures which are based on this model, should provide a general purpose assessment programme for the learning/communication processes.

Item preparation

The selection of items was seemingly based on experiential judgement initially. The Manual refers to 'traditional test construction' being carried out but no details are given (Manual, p. 62). The statistical analyses reported relate to the scores which go to make up the subscales rather than to the individual items within the subscales.

The screening system was developed in Humberside and had been used there for the previous four years. Three pilot runs were made in the East Riding, Scunthorpe and Kingston-upon-Hull, divisions of Humberside Education Authority, on a total of over 1200 children. However, the analyses made seem to be aimed at specifying the characteristics of the test, rather than at making modifications to the test on the basis of these pilot findings. A 'technical report' in Appendix D only provides results from the third of the pilot studies which involved approximately 600 pupils from Kingston-upon-Hull.

Administration

The tests are intended to be used by teachers. The initial screening tests and checklists are provided for them as are the pupil profiles and test items for diagnostic assessments. Some additional modest types of equipment may be required but would usually be readily available in a primary school classroom. For example, the teacher needs to prepare a chart similar in layout to Test E on the initial screening test.

The test is ongoing and may require behavioural observations to be made over a considerable period of time. The 'paper and pencil' type tests are not lengthy. They are power tests and so no time limit is specified.

In general, the administration instructions are very detailed. For example, Appendix A gives clear descriptions of the practical procedures for the initial screening test with a discussion on how to ensure that the children really understand the tasks.

Standardization

The test is not supposed to be standardized to give norms. It aims to be a criterion-referenced diagnostic test. References are made to means and standard deviations, however, for the initial screening test and checklist totals. The actual identification of 'at risk' children is made according to cut-off points which are tabulated in the Manual (p. 56). It is not made clear here what is the relationship between these cut-off points and the column containing 'Mean' '±1.0 sd' and '±1.5 sd'. It later transpires (p. 63) that these are actually used as subtest norms, positive or negative cut-offs being indicated according to the directionality of each subscale.

The 'standardization sample' described is that for the last pilot study, based on Kingston-upon-Hull Primary Schools. 'Suitable schools were selected as having a wide ability range and diverse socio-economic catchment. A particularly cosmopolitan population was available' in this area. No more details are discernible with regard to the representativeness of the sample although the general impression is one of reasonable coverage.

Subgroup results are not reported, neither for sex, age, nor school types, etc. Indeed, there is a statement that analyses were carried out for the whole sample rather than for each age range 'in order to cut down on computation time' (p. 63). This sort of approach gives rise to much concern.

Scoring

The subscale scores are based on counting points according to specified marking schemes. Guidance is given concerning qualitative judgements but this is not always adequate to ensure stable criteria.

There seems to be a rather excessive amount of score transcribing if a clear visual impression is to be gained of the child's profile. The summary sheet is a simple tabulation of subscale scores. The more detailed profile sheet 'hides' the scores amongst the response layouts, and gives no immediate feedback without further reference to the Manual under the separate subscale diagnostic test headings.

Reliability

Results are reported for one of the pilot studies. It is not clear exactly what has been done to derive the reliability coefficients, however. For example, the Manual states that 'split-half coefficients exceed 0.88' (p. 64). It does not say how the halves have been 'split'. Similarly, 'Test-retest coefficients exceed 0.85' is meaningless without more information on who was tested and when.

Validity

In addition to the Infant Screening material, the children were also given the Carver Word Recognition Test (as the dependent variable which 'could justifiably be classed as an index of success at school') and their teachers completed the Bristol Social Adjustment Guide (Children in School). These two tests were used to establish concurrent validity. Multiple linear regression was used to determine how well the variables of the screening procedure related to the children's educational and social development. From an unexplained and badly laid out table (p. 64) one might infer that the best overall combination of screening variables correlates 0.83 with the Carver Test.

Discriminant analysis was used to check the validity of the screening procedure as an instrument for differentiating between those children who were 'at risk' from those not 'at risk': 85 per cent correct classification is reported. The 'at risk' group were further studied after being subdivided into those of particular problem types: 82 per cent correct classification is reported into 'normal' and three 'problem type' groups.

Interpretation

Score interpretation is very much restricted to cut-off points on the various subscales, as has already been described. In general, the advice for action is cautionary, based on what *may* be indicated rather than what is indicated. The process of assessment is designed to permit a gradual 'homing-in' on a particular child's problems while not subjecting other children to excessive irrelevant testing. There is also guidance given for developing the assessment findings into appropriate remediation programmes with further assessment guidelines for monitoring progress.

General evaluation

The Manual is difficult to assimilate, requiring constant referring backwards and forwards to details given elsewhere. The technical appendix is muddled, making global, and often meaningless, statements about the statistical techniques used. In the absence of a clear description of the pilot studies, it is impossible to evaluate either their value or the appropriateness of the selected statistics presented.

I feel that many teachers would find considerable problems in applying all of the diagnostic and remediation guidelines given in the Manual, simply because of the confusing presentation of all the information. Given that such guidelines should mainly only pertain to the minority of pupils, this criticism may be countered to a certain extent as the Manual does try to ensure a teacher reads the relevant material given particular findings in the initial screening test. This will, however, be no consolation to the teacher who has a child with lots of problems, or to the teacher who has lots of children with particular difficulties.

In general, the materials are difficult to evaluate because the Manual's style is not particularly easy, and background information is selectively omitted or presented elsewhere in a fashion which makes it less than accessible. Many key areas of information relating to the test's construction, evaluation and characteristics are regrettably glossed over while the authors nevertheless purport to provide them. This practice could be highly misleading to the reader.

Keele Pre-school Assessment Guide*

Reviewed by Charles F. Owen

Author: Stephen Tyler
Publisher: NFER-Nelson
Distributor: NFER-Nelson
Age: Nursery aged children
1980
Individual assessment

Test content

The Guide is divided into two sections. Section I is concerned with behaviour and consists of six 7-point scales. Only the end points are labelled (e.g. 'Tends to play alone—mixes well') and no guidance is given as to filling them in. Three

---

* 'Experimental Edition'.

unlabelled scales are also given, and users are encouraged to label them with 'any other feature of importance' (p. 29).

Section II is concerned with skills. It is subdivided into four areas, each with a number of items. The areas are: Cognition (with 6 items), Language (4), Socialization (2) and Physical Skills (3). Each item is a 5-point scale. All the points are labelled and some guidance is given as to the assessment of each point on the scale. For record keeping, the ratings on the 15 skill items are presented as a kind of pie-chart with concentric rings standing for the different levels of skill (1–5). Changes may be plotted on the diagram for repeated testing.

Purpose

This is not a test but a Guide, a guide for those working with pre-school children. It both suggests areas of importance and some scaling of them. It was developed as part of a DES Research Project on 'Play, Exploration and Learning' in pre-school children. As part of that study, 'we identified a need for some means of measuring . . . those aspects of behaviour which directly reflected the aspirations and values of the adults responsible for the children's care' (Foreword). 'The KPAG is not a test of intelligence or of general aptitude. The KPAG does not furnish a score or a set of scores . . . Rather, it represents a series of items which may furnish an outline of the child's development . . . The principal aim of the KPAG is to provide nursery staff with a flexible system capable of adaptation as the need arises' (p. 3). The benefits of the Guide, according to the Manual, are that it helps staff to ascertain the needs of individual children, to identify progress, and to evaluate their own practice.

Administration

The Guide has been designed for use by staff in nursery schools and similar places. It 'need not be completed in a single day' (p. 5). Section I requires behaviour ratings using information 'gained primarily through observation of the child in the nursery setting, together with discussion between all members of staff concerned with the child' (p. 6). The skills assessment of Section II should also be based on observation rather than testing: 'Where the assessor is unsure of the child's ability, even after periods of observation, . . . information may be obtained from participation in play. It should be emphasized, however, that the KPAG is not a test' (p. 6).

Standardization

The Guide has not been standardized and no guidance is given as to the level of behaviour and skill to be expected from children of different ages.

Reliability and validity

No data are provided.

Interpretation

About half a page is offered on interpretation. 'Just as the procedure requires a degree of flexibility on the part of the assessor, so too does the interpretation of the completed chart . . . Throughout, the need for flexibility of approach is paramount' (pp. 7–8).

General evaluation

The KPAG is a form of systematic record keeping for use by nursery staff. In this way it may be useful, from the staff's point of view, in that it draws to their attention aspects of the children's behaviour and development that might get overlooked. It helps in monitoring progress and (by implication) in evaluating their own progress. However, the total lack of guidance as to what level of behaviour or skill might be expected or appropriate for different ages of children may make the Guide difficult to use.

The Guide continually stresses that it is not a test, and should be used flexibly, in the way most appropriate to the user. It encourages adaptation of existing items and the addition of further ones to suit individual needs. In this determination to get away from the idea of 'testing' the Guide does unfortunately neglect even the simplest psychometric principles: no attempt has been made to see if the scales are used reliably by different members of staff (or even by the same member of staff) on the same child; the skill section is all in terms of 5-point scales of skills to be acquired in sequence, but there is no longitudinal data given on whether these are real sequences; and so on.

This is still an Experimental Edition, and perhaps some of these faults will be put right in the final version.

Language Imitation Test

Reviewed by Stephen Sharp

Authors: Paul Berry and Peter Mittler
Publisher: NFER-Nelson
Distributor: NFER-Nelson
Age: SSN children
Publication date not given; post-1976 indicated
Individual test

Test content

The Language Imitation Test (LIT) consists of six subtests. In the first five, the child's task is purely repetitive, i.e. he is required simply to duplicate an utterance on the part of the tester. Subtest 1, Sound Imitation, assesses the child's ability to reproduce single phonemes (such as the d in desk) on the grounds that problems here indicate failure in articulation which render the remainder of the test pointless. Subtest 2, Word Imitation, scores whole words instead of phonemes but is otherwise the same. Syntactic Control is the subject of Subtests 3 and 4. The former uses word combinations of four levels of difficulty ranging from subject-verb pairs to complete though simple declarative sentences. Subtest 4 continues to increase the complexity using interrogative, negative, passive and negative-passive forms of the same sentences. Subtest 5, Word Organization Control, uses 'organized word strings' of increasing length which, though not grammatical, contain some semantic sense, e.g. 'woman write letter pen'. The final component, Subtest 6, differs in that it requires Sentence Completion from the testee. In each case the incomplete sentence is read out and the child is required to supply any word or phrase semantically and syntactically appropriate for completing it.

Purpose

'The Language Imitation Test is designed to test language ability from a very basic to a relatively complex level. The main theoretical theme of the test is that when imitating sentences, words or sounds, a child brings his knowledge of language into operation. Mistakes in imitating language reflect breakdowns in this knowledge which may then be rectified by appropriate teaching programmes. Hence the ultimate objective of the assessment is to isolate those points where the child's knowledge of his language has broken down in order that appropriate teaching might be attempted' (Manual, p. 30).

The Manual stresses that the LIT is very much an experimental instrument, that its intended use is diagnostic and that it should be employed only in combination with other assessment techniques which provide a more complete picture of how the child copes with his 'language environment'.

Item preparation

The items were not arrived at by selecting the best of a large group of possibles. In fact the content of the actual items used is held to be of little importance. What matters is the hierarchical sequence of linguistic abilities tested and the principles of syntax, grammar and semantics embodied in the items. Thus, for example, Subtest 4 is directed at various syntactic transformations. The particular nouns and verbs used to build the sentences which exemplify those transformations are of little relevance.

However, the Manual does discuss the process whereby the principles tested were arrived at. A critical review of theoretical and empirical studies in this area is used to highlight the appeal and limitations of imitation as a tool of linguistic assessment. Then some feasibility studies are described in general terms, their aim being to assess the practicability of an imitation-based test and to investigate the best way to analyse errors as a function of increasing linguistic complexity. The result, a progression from phonemes to sentences, constitutes the subtests described above.

Administration

It is envisaged that the test will be administered by teachers without any special training. To this end a study was conducted on the ability of teachers to score accurately typical results from the tests (see comments below under Reliability). No materials are required other than the score sheet on which the results are recorded. The test is not timed; the children are just given as long as is necessary for them to respond. The instructions simply consist of the tester saying 'Say what I say, say . . .' or 'I want you to finish this off', as appropriate, followed by the stimulus utterance.

Standardization

The group consisted of all 108 severely educationally subnormal children in the former county of Cumberland. The Manual refers to this as 'the population study' rather than 'the standardization group' as it was not the intention to produce norms. This is partly because the test is diagnostic and still experimental and partly because age-related norms are less important when dealing with the subnormal due to the confounding effect of the degree of handicap. The population study was carried out by the authors in conjunction with an experienced educational psychologist. No date is given.

The distribution of the total test scores from the study are presented in histogram form and each subtest is individually analysed in tables giving the percentages of correct responses and the distribution over the various error categories (see Scoring below). The population study also yielded data on the relationship between the subscales and between the total test score and other variables (see Validity below).

Scoring

Two systems of scoring are used in parallel, one qualitative and one quantitative. The qualitative system concerns the categorization of errors. The result of each item is scored either as a correct response or as one of a number of error codes. For example in Subtest 5, the five possible errors concern the addition of words, the addition of word endings, changes of order, deletion of words and 'parroting' which means simply repeating the final item or items in the stimulus utterance. Other subtests have different error categories. In all cases the Manual provides detailed scoring instructions both by explaining the logic which defines each category and by providing examples of critical instances.

The quantitative scoring system arises out of the qualitative one by assigning a number of marks to each outcome. The correct outcome always carries the highest number of marks of course and the error categories carry various numbers according to the seriousness of the mistake. So for Subtest 5, the correct response carries three marks while the five error codes mentioned above carry respectively 2, 2, 1, 1 and 0 marks. For a given error categorization the number of marks follows directly and the resulting subtest and whole test results were used in the quantitative analyses in the Manual.

Reliability

A test-retest study was carried out on 25 severely ESN children. Commendably, instead of merely reporting a correlation coefficient, the Manual also gives tables of means and standard deviations for the two administrations. The first of these yielded a mean of 114 and a standard deviation of 48, changing to 119 and 50 on the retest. The correlation is high; rho (presumably Spearman's rank order correlation coefficient) was calculated at 0.98, though this may have been inflated by the use of a range of ages and perhaps age-related variation in degrees of handicap in the sample.

The Manual does not state who carried out this study, so one is left to assume that it was the authors. If so, the data throw little light on the possibly important problem of intermarker reliability. This was the subject of another study in which twelve teachers who had read the instructions once and studied a single worked example achieved 90 per cent accuracy in categorizing LIT responses. However, the teachers were working from written transcripts rather than more realistic (and difficult) sound recordings and their success rate does not provide convincing evidence of likely marker reliability in practice.

Validity

A group of 33 severely ESN children were assessed for age, LIT score, teacher ratings and vocabulary age on the English Picture Vocabulary Test (EPVT). The LIT yields correlations of 0.73 with EPVT score, 0.53 with teacher ratings and 0.26 with chronological age.

These results provide initial evidence of associative validity. The main evidence, however, comes from the population study where the 108 children were assessed on chronological age, EPVT score and the Weldall-Mittler-Hobsbaum Sentence Comprehension Test (SCT) as well as the LIT. The LIT had a correlation of 0.62 with the SCT, 0.59 with the EPVT and 0.19 with chronological age.

Evidence of construct validity comes from the intercorrelations between the subtests as calculated from the population study. These range from 0.37 between Subtests 1 and 4 to 0.92 between Subtests 3 and 5. 'Correlations between subtests provided further evidence of construct validity in so far as all subtests correlated highly with one another, but the highest correlations were found between subtests sampling similar skills . . . we may conclude that each subtest is sampling the same ability but at different levels of competence' (Manual, p. 22–23).

Further information on validity comes from a number of very briefly described studies which aim to relate performance on imitative tasks with that on language production tasks. An example of the latter is that children were given a series of pictures telling a story which the children were asked to relate in words. Insufficient detail is given to establish the degree of justification, but the Manual claims that language production tests correlate well with each other, with teacher ratings and with the LIT, but not with chronological age, thus providing more information of the associative validity of the LIT.

Interpretation

The Manual admits with laudable honesty that this aspect of the test is not well developed. The results of the test have not been incorporated into a proper scheme of remedial teaching. The LIT can not therefore, at least yet, be considered a prescriptive test. It does allow a detailed assessment of linguistic skills but it is up to the teacher to relate this to the rest of her knowledge of the child's language. 'In other words, the use that she makes of the LIT, is left to her own judgement' (Manual, p. 28). Hence the importance of using the test in conjunction with other techniques which can form a basis for its interpretation.

Test use

The Manual cites several published studies by Berry *et al.* using the test.

General assessment

Any overall assessment of the value of the LIT must take into account that as yet it is an experimental tool whose characteristics have only provisionally been investigated and whose applications are still very much up to the user. The paucity of the information relating to reliability and standardization is of least importance in a test of this kind but the lack of guidelines on implementing the results is more serious as the LIT is now an essentially diagnostic instrument with no basis for interpreting the diagnosis. As such it is hard to see that the test is more than a way of formalizing what the teacher already knows about the child. This process may itself have some value, but until further work is carried out to relate LIT results to remedial teaching programmes, much of the test potential will remain unfulfilled and its value will rest with the teacher's ability rather than its own merit.

Look: Visual Perception

Reviewed by A. P. Lonton

Authors: W. Brennan and J. Jackson
Publisher: Macmillan Education
Distributor: Macmillan Education
Age: Infant and young junior school children
1981 ('first published' and 'Revised edition')
Group test

Test content

The visual perception materials are predominantly teaching aids for young children, particularly those with developmental delay or specific difficulties. There are eight workbooks: 1, 2, 3, 4, 1A, 2A, 3A, 4A.

Book 1, and the parallel version 1A contain exercises in: hand-eye co-ordination, left/right orientation, visual discrimination, visual retention, visual rhythm and sequencing pictures in a story.

Books 2 and 2A aim to give practice in: Figure-ground discrimination, hand-eye co-ordination, visual discrimination, left/right orientation, visual retention, visual copying, visual closure, visual rhythm and sequencing pictures in a story.

Books 3 and 3A have exercises related to: hand-eye co-ordination, recognition of visual absurdities, left/right orientation, visual retention, visual discrimination, visual matching, visual copying, visual closure, visual rhythm, figure-ground discrimination, visual constancy and sequencing pictures in a story.

Books 4 and 4A have exercises in: hand-eye co-ordination, orientation in space, visual discrimination, figure-ground discrimination, visual retention, visual copying, left/right orientation, visual closure, visual rhythm, identifying relationships and sequencing pictures in a story.

Spirit duplicator masters are available for some of the exercises. Appendix 1 contains suggestions for supplementary materials which may be useful in generalizing the skills exercised in the workbooks. Individual record sheets enable teachers to chart the progress of pupils through the workbooks. Page 4 of the Handbook gives a sub-skill analysis which also provides the teacher with immediate information on which books and pages can form a programme to help the pupil who has problems with particular sub-skills.

Purpose

Though principally teaching materials, *Look* is within the ambit of this book of critical reviews of tests, because of the claim that different visual perceptual sub-skills can be assessed. The Handbook states that 'the material is developmental and the objective is to promote smooth and efficient maturation of perceptual skills' (p. 8). Emphasis is placed on the diagnostic-remedial value of the exercises (pp. 31–33). *Look* claims to provide 'a behavioural breakdown of visual perceptual skill into its significant sub-skills . . . and examination of the pupil's profile in the record shows up the pattern of strengths and weakness in his performance' (p. 33). This gives help to teachers in terms of devising remedial programmes for the areas of weakness.

Item preparation

No information is given in the Handbook on what pilot studies were conducted. Likewise, no reference is made to sampling procedures.

Administration

The materials are stated to be designed 'for classroom use within the rich curricula of infant and junior schools and the modified curricula of special schools . . . For those pupils with most severe delay or specific difficulty, remedial use of *Look* may extend into the early years of the secondary stage of education' (p. 8). The books are used in the sequence 1, 1A, 2, 2A, etc. Precise instructions are given for each page of each book in the Handbook. The teacher records the pupil's progress in an individual record sheet. Some pupils may need extra remedial help in the form of duplicated sheets of some of the exercises or other suggestions found in Appendix 1. The only additional equipment needed is a pen or pencil and a pair of scissors. The work is self-paced by the pupil.

Standardization

No details are given of standardization procedures, if, indeed, any attempt was made at trying out the materials before publishing the final version.

Scoring

In the record sheet the teacher enters the date the child reaches each page of the workbooks. On page 4 of the record sheet, the various exercises in the eight books are grouped under the sub-skills which are sampled. There are no precise instructions as to what is supposed to be done with this list, but presumably each exercise is crossed off when completed. Thus a record of progress with each sub-skill is built up.

Reliability and validity

No attempt is made to deal with the reliability or validity of the diagnostic profile.

Interpretation

No specific advice is given on score interpretation. However, it is implied that the sub-skill analysis should highlight weaknesses in one or more of these sub-skills of visual perception.

General evaluation

The material is correctly concerned with monitoring the progress of individual children (p. 41), but no evidence is given regarding its efficacy as a diagnostic or didactic tool. The nature of the sub-skills is expounded on pp. 20–28 of the Handbook, but no evidence is given to support this particular break-down of perceptual skills. No reference is made to relevant factor analyses. Since the mean 'Perceptual Age' at which the majority of children are able to do a particular item is not indicated, there is no guarantee that the materials are in the correct developmental sequence.

This material has some similarities to the Frostig (1966) teaching materials. Careful and authoritative reviews of the Frostig and related programmes have been carried out by Robinson (1972), Wiederhold and Hammill (1971) and Hammill, Goodman and Wiederhold (1974). The general conclusions reached are that Frostig type materials produce higher scores on Frostig type tests, but there is minimal evidence to support the assumption that there is generalization to other important aspects of learning. The effect of the programmes on intelligence, academic achievement and reading readiness was not clearly demonstrated. Particularly disappointing were the effects of such training on perceptual-motor performance itself. Some awareness is shown in the Handbook (p. 31) that previous work has lacked reliability and validity, but nothing is done to show that this material is any better. Until proper test construction exercises are undertaken, and appropriate evaluations of the efficacy of the teaching material, it remains difficult to say what value the materials have.

References

Frostig, M. (1966). "Developmental Test of Visual Perception". California: Consulting Psychologists Press.
Hammill, D. D., Goodman, L. and Wiederhold, J. L. (1974). Visual motor processes: can we train them? *Reading Teacher* 27, 469–478.
Robinson, H. M. (1972). Perceptual training—does it result in reading improvement? *In* "Some Persistent Questions on Beginning Reading". Newark, Del.: International Reading Association.
Wiederhold, J. L. and Hammill, D. D. (1971). Use of the Frostig-Horne visual perception programme in the urban school. *Psychology in the Schools* 8, 268–274.

Peabody Individual Achievement Test

Brief Report

Authors: Lloyd M. Dunn and Frederick C. Markwardt, Jr
Publisher: American Guidance Service Inc.
Distributor: NFER-Nelson
Age range: 5–18+
1962–69 (T)
1969 (S); 1970 (M, T)
Individual tests

This 'wide-range screening instrument' consists of five subtests, namely: Mathematics, Reading Recognition, Reading Comprehension, Spelling and General Information. Each subtest has 84 items plus 'demonstration and training exercises'. Items (e.g. multiple-choice diagrams, sentences to be read) and administrative instructions are presented on cards held in ring-binders which can be set up as 'easels'. Testees attempt only some of the 84 items in each subtest according to 'basal and ceiling procedures and rules'. Administration takes 30–40 minutes. Some items show the test's USA origins (e.g. cents, store, Fall, mail).

Norms based upon 2889 USA children from kindergarten to grade 12 (mostly aged 5 to 18) are presented for the subtests and the Total test in many forms: grade equivalents; age equivalents; percentile ranks for grade and terms; percentile ranks by age (to nearest three months); and normalized standard scores (mean 100, standard deviation 15) by conversion of the percentile ranks. Repeat-test reliabilities and correlations with the Peabody Picture Vocabulary Test are given for each subtest at several grade levels.

The Pupil Rating Scale Revised★

Reviewed by D. H. Lee

Author: Helmer R. Myklebust
Publisher: Grune & Stratton Inc.
Distributor: Academic Press
Age range: 5:05–14:00 (USA Kindergarten to 6th Grade)
1971 (T)
1971–1980 (S); 1981 (M, T) (revised version)
Individual test

Test content

The Pupil Rating Scale (PRS) is divided into five subscales: (1) Auditory Comprehension; (2) Spoken Language; (3) Orientation; (4) Motor Co-ordination; and (5) Personal-social behaviour. Each subscale is further divided, e.g. in the case of Auditory Comprehension (and Memory) the items are 'Comprehending word meanings', 'Following instruction', 'Comprehending class discussions' and 'Retaining instructions'. Of the five subscales, Personal-social behaviour is the most elaborated having eight items. Motor Co-ordination is least extensive with just three items: 'General co-ordination', 'Balance' and 'Manual dexterity'.

For each of these items there are five ordered statements descriptive of behaviour in a social setting. For example, under 'Following instructions', the extreme statements are 'Unable to follow instructions, always confused' and 'Unusually skillful in remembering and following instructions'. Each of these statements prompts the observer/teacher to consider its appropriateness as a description of the child/pupil in question and carries a weighting of between 1 and 5. A rating of 3 is described as 'average'; 1 and 2 are below average ratings, and 4 and 5 above average.

Purpose

The PRS was devised 'so that (children who have difficulties in learning which distinguish them from others in their class) can be more readily identified'. The 1981 revision reviewed here was primarily developed to 'present new data on standardization and on the extended age ranges to which The Pupil Rating Scale now can be administered'.

★ Sub-title: 'Screening for Learning Disabilities'

The rationale for the Scale, however, appears to be expressed in the following quotation from the Manual: 'The purpose of the Pupil Rating Scale is to identify children who have good mental ability, good hearing and vision, and adequate emotional adjustment, who do not have over-riding physical handicaps, but who still do not learn and achieve normally in school'.

Item preparation

The items were developed from Myklebust's previous work on various pathologies associated with learning disabilities, i.e. in neurological malfunctionings, cognitive deficits, sensory handicaps and disorders of language development. Myklebust states that 'Using a psycho-neurological-cognitive frame of reference . . . five areas of behaviour were chosen . . . These five areas . . . based on the observations of hundreds of learning disabled children, enable a critical, inclusive and definitive comparison of these children with normal children'. The items were also, states Myklebust, devised to meet the criterion of easy observation by 'experienced teachers'. A pilot study was undertaken and 500 3rd and 4th grade children were rated.

Administration

The PRS is intended for use by any qualified teacher who has known the target child for 'a reasonably long period'. The Scale is in pamphlet format. The five statements for each item are examined and the one reflecting the subject's ability is circled. The Manual suggests that ten minutes are required for each pupil.

Standardization

This Revised Scale has been re-standardized, i.e. norms have been devised for a much wider age range (from 'third and fourth-graders to kindergarten through sixth-graders') over the last ten years. Studies quoted by the author and done by his associates are dated 1972, 1977, 1979 and 1980. Sample sizes reported range from 500 (the pilot study) to 2176 for the 3rd and 4th grade pupils used for the original Scale. The Revised Scale was standardized on 1264 children, age 5–14 years inclusive. The sample was found in four large schools in a metropolitan area of the United States. Lower and middle-class and 'socially disadvantaged' children, including many black and Hispanic children, are represented in the sample. There appears to be no breakdown for sex. The 'opportunity' style of sampling reflects, no doubt, the diagnostic rather than normative nature of the test. Means and standard deviations are quoted for each item and for subscale totals.

Scoring

The Auditory Comprehension and Spoken Language subscales, with 4 items and 5 items respectively, each item rated on a 5-point scale, would yield a score of 12 and 15 points for the 'average' child. Scores from these subscales are totalled to give a Verbal Score. The Orientation (4 items), Motor Co-ordination (3 items) and Personal-social Behaviour (8 items) subscales would yield 'average' scores of 12, 9 and 24 respectively, giving an 'average' Non-verbal score of 45. An average score for the whole Scale, being the sum of these five subscale scores, would be 72 points.

The front sheet of the proforma incorporates, below the usual biographical data, adequate and clear space for presentation of summary scores.

Since the rating of each item is not based upon any specific elicited behaviour, qualitative and discretionary judgements are obviously required. Myklebust advises that the marker should have known the child for at least one month and should not rate more than 30 children, and that, to 'enhance reliability', meetings should be held to discuss the 'meaning and interpretation of each item'.

Reliability

As a 'screening test' relying on ratings of pupils on broad, generally agreed and qualitatively evaluated criteria, procedures for estimating the reliability and validity of the Scale have inevitably depended less on item analysis, repeat testing and inter-test correlations than on the general predictive performance on the Scale across clinical studies of, for example, pathological groups.

Evidence is quoted of two ratings, one year apart, of nonidentical but over-lapping groups comprising 1250 kindergarten to 6th-grade pupils on the first occasion and 994 on the second. It is the group, rather than individual scores, which are compared. The mean scores are compared across occasions and on this basis high stability is claimed. Inter-marker reliability was assessed using 49 teachers across all items in the five behavioural categories. The mean scores were, with few exceptions, very similar and the teachers are reported to have discriminated 'satisfactorily' between impaired and non-impaired groups. No information is given on the extent to which the teachers could have been influencing each others' judgements.

Validity

A study of 2176 children compared the PRS with the Learning Quotient battery of 'psycho-educational tests' developed by Myklebust in 1968. The PRS is reported to have separated the same children into the same diagnostic categories in a highly consistent way. In other studies the PRS was found to have high validity in accounting for the percentage variance in each of the five behavioural areas when differentiating between normal and learning-disabled children, to be valid across all 24 items in separating impaired and normal children and to be high in concurrent validity when predicting, e.g. reading readiness in kindergarten children. In still other studies the PRS was found to correlate 'highly' (0.42–0.53) with educational achievement but at a lower level with intelligence (i.e. verbal, perceptual, spatial and non-verbal abilities). This is expressed as an advantage by the author since the PRS is not intended to measure 'cognitive ability'.

Interpretation

The Scale was designed purely as a screening procedure and it is claimed that some 15 per cent of pupils were identified by the Scale as being 'at or near the failure level in their respective schools'. Myklebust emphasizes that, once detected, each child would be further studied so that his or her specific disturbance or disability can be determined'. Data are given to justify the selection of certain cut-off points for inclusion in the 'at risk' group.

General evaluation

No great claims are ostensibly made for this test. It is modestly described by the author as being a screening device, useful for teachers and other 'contact' professionals in providing a ten-minute assessment of where a pupil stands, relative to his peers, in certain large areas of day-to-day activity which have developmental significance. Myklebust stresses that a much fuller diagnostic investigation would be needed before serious clinical conclusions could be drawn and remediation and/or management planned and implemented.

The choice of these five 'behavioural characteristics' as subscales conforms largely to accepted practice in the case of four of them. Language and gross/fine motor development are classically important areas in developmental psychology and it would be remarkable if any serious screening device ignored them. The separation into expressive or receptive aspects of language is also time-honoured. Myklebust's use of 'Orientation' as a major component of his Scale is, however, more surprising. Some items might have high 'g' loadings (e.g. judging relationships and time) and others have more obvious body-image implications. This seems to make it a mish-mash and the eccentricities apparent in the factor-analytic findings reported for this 'characteristic' are not too surprising. Rating scales of this kind, using numerical weightings to encapsulate what are essentially behavioural/verbal entities is notoriously prone to randomness and inaccuracies. The extension of these items to incorporate an age-range down to 5 years seems unconvincing, especially when faced with items such as 'Usually disregards feelings of others' (this under 'Tactfulness').

Despite these reservations Myklebust's Scale seems to fulfil a useful role in the rapid screening of 'at risk' pupils in the upper ages of the range recommended by the Manual. Myklebust is a skilled and experienced researcher and special educationalist and this shows in the technical side of the production and revision of this Scale. The Scale is 'user-ready', the Manual and operational procedures adequate and the research support thorough. The impression remains, however, that the Scale would have been well left unextended although the revision itself is valuable. British users should bear in mind the provenance of the test and exercise caution in applying the tables of norms.

Reading Readiness Inventory

Reviewed by Caroline Gipps

Authors: J. Downing and D. Thackray
Publisher: Hodder & Stoughton
Distributor: Hodder & Stoughton
Age: Infant school
1976 (T); 1971, 1975★
Individual test

Test content

This is a check-list rather than a test. There are four parts covering physiological, environmental, emotional motivation and personality factors, and intellectual factors. Under each heading is a list of questions, for example:

Is speech normal?
Has the child contact with books at home?
Has he a dislike for books?
How quick is the child at learning new things?
The response to the majority of these questions is a simple yes/no.

Under emotional, motivation and personality factors there are only four questions. These ask about any *severe* emotional or personality problems, whether there is a marked dislike of books, what the child's special interests are which may be used in motivation for reading, and whether a child knows that

---

★ The inventory is not sold accompanied by a Manual. For this the user has to purchase separately the UKRA Monograph "Reading Readiness" by Downing and Thackray (2nd ed, 1975, London: Hodder & Stoughton).

pleasurable things can be found in books. These four items can hardly be considered to cover the areas suggested by the heading.

Intellectual development is more widely covered but the cognitive development section requires very subjective judgements to be made and a fairly sophisticated knowledge of the child's understanding.

Purpose

There is no information about purpose on the inventory, but according to the publisher's blurb which comes with the sample, it is:

'1. A four-page check-list designed to focus attention on the most significant reading readiness indicators and to provide a convenient, structured basis for classroom observation.

'2. Will help teachers to make their pre-reading programmes more effective.

'3. May also be used as a record sheet for completion over a period of time'.

According to Downing and Thackray's book the purpose is:

'To provide a starting point for teachers who wish to develop their own reading readiness chart we propose tentatively the following inventory of factors to be considered in judging a child's preparedness for the tasks involved in the beginning stage of learning to read' (p. 95).

And

'We have . . . proposed (1975) a *Reading Readiness Inventory* . . . which teachers can use to organize their knowledge of each child's development in the learning to read process . . . this inventory is . . . a summary of our findings from our review of research on this topic. It lists the factors we have found to be important in fitting the child for reading' (p. 97).

Note

The Inventory should not be confused with the Thackray Reading Readiness Profiles published also by Hodder and Stoughton, dated 1974. This is a group test for use by reception class teachers, the test was standardized and tables are given for converting raw scores to norm-related grades.

Item preparation

No information.

Administration

No information.

Standardization

No information.

Scoring

No information.

Reliability.

No information.

Validity

No information.

Interpretation

No information.

General Evaluation

Downing and Thackray's book explains in detail the authors' view of reading readiness. Sections include all those headings covered in the Inventory (and more) but no attempt is made to connect these sections with the Inventory. The book reproduces the Inventory in the last chapter but does not discuss it in detail. In effect *there is no manual.* The user is given no guidance as to how the (in many cases highly subjective) items might be completed. For example, 'In his own language or dialect, how fluent is the child?' or indeed, what to do once these judgements have been made. In order to make much use of the Inventory, the teacher must read and absorb the book and make his/her own connections with the items in the Inventory.

Why have the authors produced this Inventory after the Thackray Reading Profiles? It seems to be for two reasons—first, that the usual reading readiness tests barely touch on cognitive development, and secondly, because they feel that teachers' judgements based on the 'directed observation of pupils' behaviour' are more reliable than reading readiness tests. They cite some (rather dated) research indicating that teachers' judgements of reading readiness correlate more highly than reading readiness test scores with later reading success.

> 'Teachers and parents also should view commercial claims for readiness materials or readiness tests with a degree of caution. With regard to published tests, none have proved superior to the professional judgement of the teacher. Indeed, teachers' assessments have been found to be slightly better. Readiness programmes which have been published have also been found in research to be no more than *as good as* informal procedures invented by individual teachers for their own classrooms'.

In conclusion, this is not a test and was not intended as such, hence the lack of information on item development, standardization, validity and reliability. However, as a check-list it should be accompanied by a good teachers' guide and the Downing and Thackray book is not suitable as it stands. Until such a guide is produced (if indeed the publisher and authors are still interested in doing such a thing) the value of the Inventory can only be described as extremely limited.

Reynell-Zinkin Developmental Scales★

Reviewed by R. Driver

Author: Joan Reynell
Publisher: NFER-Nelson
Distributor: NFER-Nelson
Age: Visually handicapped children aged up to 6 years
1974–78 (S); 1979 (M, Record Sheet)
Individual test (restricted use)★★

Purpose

The developmental scales are designed for use by professionals for the assessment of young visually handicapped children, aged 0–5 years. The purpose of the scales is to explore with each child the areas of learning and development of particular importance for visually handicapped children. It is intended that this assessment will lead to the planning of a programme of help which can be carried out by parents.

Test content

The instrument includes six scales of mental development:
social adaptation;
sensori-motor understanding;
exploration of environment (orientation);
response to sound and verbal comprehension;
expressive language (structure);
expressive language (vocabulary and content).
Each scale contains between 12 and 36 checkpoints. For example, items include such observations as 'Drinks holding cup himself', 'Active grasp of an

---

★ '. . . for Young Visually Handicapped Children': Part I Mental Development.
★★ 'The scales are intended to be used only by people with relevant qualifications who have responsibility for the assessment and developmental guidance of handicapped children. This includes doctors, psychologists, and certain special groups such as teachers of blind children' (Manual, p. 12). Only a brief review is offered for this test in view of its specialist usage.

object put into his hand', 'Exploration of surfaces', 'Reaching for source of sound in correct direction', 'Telling the use of objects'. In each case guidance is given about the performance required for success on the item (Manual, pp. 34–37).

The user is required to assemble a kit of objects for parts of the assessment. Specifications for this test material are given in the Manual.

Development of the Scales

The scales were developed in the period 1970–75 at the Wolfson Centre, Institute of Child Health, London. Children with multiple handicaps including visual handicaps were referred to the Centre for assessment. The scales were developed in response to a need for assessment instruments for such children in a clinical setting. Both 'motor' and 'mental' assessment instruments were developed however, only the 'mental' assessment scales have been published to-date.

Data

Scores on each of the scales for sighted, partially sighted and blind children up to age 5:03 are given. The data was based on a study in which 203 recordings were made from 109 children. The sample was selected to eliminate children with severe associated handicaps.

Other supportive materials

The Manual is clearly presented and includes copies of papers relating to the development of the scales and descriptions of types of visual handicap in addition to the detailed instructions for administration, age score tables and a list of test material. An individual record sheet lists the checkpoints on each of six scales for coding, and gives a table for summary scores and background information.

Sentence Comprehensive Test

Reviewed by C. D. Elliott

Authors: Kevin Weldall, Peter Mittler and Angela Hobsbaum
Publisher: NFER-Nelson
Distributor: NFER-Nelson
Age range: 3:00–5:06
1979 (Experimental Edition)
Individual test

Test content

The test consists of six practice items followed by 60 scored items, which are divided into 15 subtests of four items each. These subtests correspond to different grammatical structures or sentence types. Each of the four items in each subtest is identical in sentence structure, which allows 'a reliable assessment of each structure to be made' (Manual, p. 8). The list of subtests—sentence types—is as follows:

Subtest	Sentence type	Example
I	Simple intransitive	The horse is eating
II	Simple transitive	The boy is reading the paper
III	Intransitive with adjective	The old man is reading
IV	Transitive with adjective	The fat lady is pushing the pram
V	Plural	The girls are skipping
VI	Past tense	The boy has slipped
VII	Future tense	The dog is going to jump
VIII	Passive	The boy is being pushed by the girl
IX	Simple negative	The boy is not crying
X	Transitive negative	The boy is not riding the bicycle
XI	Comparative	Can you see two big pencils—which is the bigger pencil?
XII	Superlative	Here are some fat ladies—which is the fattest lady?
XIII	Simple prepositions	The mouse is in the box
XIV	Harder prepositions	The horse is in front of the tree
XV	Embedded phrase	The dog with long legs is jumping

For each of the items, the child is shown a page from a picture book on which are four black and white drawings. The child's task is to demonstrate that he has understood a spoken sentence by identifying, through pointing, which of the four simultaneously presented pictures corresponds to the sentence spoken by the tester.

'Thus, following the target sentence "The boy is reading the paper" the child has to point to the picture illustrating this sentence from the four pictures illustrating alternative grammatical interpretations:

The boy is reading the paper (target sentence);
The *girl* is reading the paper (subject varied);
The boy is *tearing* the paper (verb varied);
The boy is reading the *book* (object varied)' (Manual, p. 8).

Incorrect responses are coded. 'This coding allows the tester to see at a glance whether the child is making consistent types of error or not which may prove useful in devising suitable remediation strategies if remediation proves necessary' (Manual, p. 35).

All items have exactly the same format and method of administration. The test is individually administered. The authors state that 'With very young children it may prove preferable to spread the testing over two or even three sessions . . . the test normally only takes about 20 minutes to administer' (Manual, p. 9).

Purpose

The main aim of the sentence comprehension test is 'to attempt to assess objectively the child's ability to understand various language forms in the relative absence of contextual or other cues to meaning' (Manual, p. 5). The authors emphasize that the SCT is not a standardized, normative test. 'The value of the test lies in the extent to which it permits the user to come to a better understanding of the ways in which the child deals with sentences of varying complexity. It should help to pinpoint sentence constructions which are a cause of particular difficulty and thereby lead to more systematic and specific approaches to remediation' (Manual, p. 8). Nevertheless, although the authors disclaim its use as a normative test, means and standard deviations of scores for various groups of children are presented in the Manual, which also contains some tentative mastery norms for each of the 15 subtests, although the authors urge the user to show considerable caution in interpreting and using these norms.

The authors clearly see one of the major functions of the SCT will be as a simple screening instrument which might be used by infant school teachers. 'If the test is used as a quick screening device in nursery and infant classes, the teacher will, over a period of time, be able to identify children whose performance on SCT is markedly different from that of the majority' (Manual, p. 8).

The authors, however, also envisage the test being used by other professional workers such as speech therapists and psychologists. 'Those who work with children with delays or disorders of language development will no doubt be using a wide variety of other measures of language and intellectual development; for them, we hope the test will provide more detailed diagnostic pointers which can provide one of the foundations of an intervention programme' (Manual, p. 8).

Item preparation

The sentence comprehension test is the outcome of a number of studies. The test was originally devised by Angela Hobsbaum and Peter Mittler and preliminary work on it began in 1966. This work is presented in some detail in the test manual.

'In developing a test of *sentence* comprehension, it was necessary to attempt to reduce the influence of other verbal factors influencing comprehension. The most obvious of these was the vocabulary employed in the sentence. In order to test a child's comprehension of the simple active affirmative declarative sentence form, one would be more likely to be successful with "The mouse is eating the cheese", than with "The rodent is consuming the gorgonzola". In order to minimize the likelihood of difficult vocabulary interfering with comprehension of structure, the Burroughs (1957) Vocabulary of Young Children list was used, so as to employ primarily only those words which fell among the 500 most frequently used words' (Manual, p. 10). Efforts were made in the selection of alternative sentences, to use words which were all similar to the originals, but which were also sufficiently semantically distinct and pictorially unambiguous.

Development work on the SCT took place in London, Manchester and Birmingham, as a result of which various changes were made both to sentences and to the pictures presented to the children, until the final published experimental version of the SCT was ready.

Administration

The instructions for test administration are clearly stated in the Manual, although the print is a bit small and rather densely packed. It would, therefore, be easy for a tester who is unfamiliar with the test, or who is under some time pressure, to miss some important features of test administration. This reviewer, therefore, recommends any potential test users to familiarize themselves thoroughly with the instructions ahead of testing. Apart from this small criticism on a point of presentation, the instructions themselves are generally satisfactory.

The child does not require any materials. The tester requires a record form for each child (disposable) and a re-useable picture booklet for the presentation of each item. The record form itself is a single sheet and contains error codes for incorrect responses so that these can be quickly and easily recorded. The test is not speeded—the tester proceeds at the optimum pace for the child.

Standardization

Trials of the experimental version of the sentence comprehension test were carried out on two groups of children, drawn from the Birmingham and West Midlands area. The representativeness of the sample is thus open to question, as the authors admit.

Data were gathered on two samples of children: (a) 50 'near five-year olds' who had just started at infant schools, and (b) 160 children aged between 3 and

5 years, 119 of whom attended nursery schools and 41 attended playgroups. The date of collection of these data is not given, but since the date of publication of the SCT is 1979, we can assume the data collection to have taken place in 1976 to 1978.

Basic data are provided in the Manual (p. 25) for three groups of children whose mean ages were 3:06, 4:06 and 5:00 respectively. Means and standard deviations are given for their scores on the English Picture Vocabulary Test, together with the total score on the Sentence Comprehension Test and the mean number of subtests passed. The percentage of children who passed each subtest are also reported for each of these three age groups. In addition, extrapolations are presented (p. 27) which give some tentative norms. A table gives the chronological ages by which 50 per cent and 75 per cent of children passed each subtest. It is stressed in the Manual that 'such information is still only an approximate estimate based on relatively small samples. There is a need to collect further test data to add to the existing two samples in order to provide more accurate estimates. We hope to be able to provide such information in a subsequent edition' (Manual, p. 24).

Scoring

Scoring instructions are given clearly in the Manual and the position of the picture which correctly illustrates the sentence given to the child is clearly indicated on the record form, together with error codes for the alternative pictures. The record form enables two scores to be obtained from the administration of the test. *First*, it is possible to obtain a total score for the child on the whole test, i.e. the total number of items out of 60 which the child gets correct. *Secondly*, it is possible to estimate how many subtests have been passed. Each subtest consists of four items. If three or four items are passed in a subtest then that subtest is said to have been passed. The subtests are not arranged in ascending order of difficulty, so no discontinuation rules are recommended by the test authors: each child should be given all items in the test.

Reliability

The children in sample (a) (as described under Standardization) were tested on the revised SCT and were subsequently retested on the SCT three weeks later. The test-retest reliability coefficient was 0.78 for total score and 0.76 for the number of subtests passed. They also conducted a split-half reliability estimate and this, corrected for length of test, was 0.88.

For the sample of 160 three–five year olds (referred to as sample (b) above) were tested on the SCT and approximately half were retested 7–10 days later.

The test-retest coefficients for total scores and subtests passed, were 0.87 and 0.83 respectively. The corrected split-half reliability was 0.90. It should be noted that for this sample the reliability coefficients which are reported appear to refer to the whole sample which covers a relatively wide age range. Since age is positively correlated to both total score and to the number of subtests passed on the SCT, *this will have resulted in an inflation of the reliability estimates*. These reliabilities, which were higher than those for sample (a), should therefore be treated with caution. No standard errors of measurement for either total score or number of subtests passed are given in the Manual. This is, of course, consistent with the authors' statement that they do not expect the test to be used normatively.

One further point should be made. For sample (a) the pass rate over the two occasions of testing increased by more than 10 per cent for 6 out of the 15 subtests. For sample (b), three out of the 15 subtests showed an increase of more than 10 per cent in pass rate. Accordingly, the authors recommend that 'When used as a screening device, it may well be prudent to retest children on the subtests they fail a week or two after the initial testing, so as not to *under-estimate* their receptive skills' (Manual, p. 19).

Validity

The 50 five-year old children in sample (a) were given, as well as the SCT, The English Picture Vocabulary Test, the Reynell Development Language Scales, Raven's Progressive Matrices, and three subtests from the Illinois Test of Psycholinguistic Abilities. The correlation of the SCT total score and number of subtests passed with the EPVT, the three ITPA tests and the Reynell Receptive Scale were all substantial (in the range of 0.59 to 0.71 and 0.50 to 0.63 respectively). Much lower, barely significant correlations of around 0.3 were found between the SCT variables and the Reynell Expressive Scale, and between the SCT variables and Raven's Progressive Matrices. The authors claim that 'Perhaps the most persuasive proof of the specific validity of the SCT as a measure of receptive language lies in the large discrepancy between the correlations with expressive language (0.27) and with receptive language (0.61)' (Manual, p. 19).

Similarly, for the three–five-year old children in sample (b), correlations with the vocabulary age on the English Picture Vocabulary Test and the total score and number of subtests passed on the SCT were also high, being 0.74 and 0.71 respectively.

Although all the subtest intercorrelations are shown for this sample, no factor analyses of this correlation matrix are reported. A word of caution here, however, as in the case of the reliability coefficients for sample (b), it is likely that the subtest intercorrelations will have been inflated to an indeterminate extent by using all the children in this sample because of their wide age range.

Interpretation

Guidance and cautionary advice are given to users of the test at various points in the Manual on the use and interpretation of scores. Users are urged to be cautious in their interpretation of the scores of individuals in terms of the sample data provided, because of the small sample sizes reported in the Manual.

The authors clearly consider that the use of the SCT as a profile test is its most appropriate application, giving the test user some indication of the range of language mastered by a child. Furthermore, the error coding which is given on the record form may, the authors hope, prove useful in helping test users to devise suitable remediation strategies. However, the Manual contains no suggestions for remedial procedures.

Test use

The reviewer knows of no major studies where the use of this test has been reported. The Manual, however, is well referenced with previous studies on the use of the earliest test materials.

General evaluation

The Sentence Comprehension Test represents an original approach to the assessment of language comprehension in young children. For current use it has two major limitations. These are *first*, the relatively narrow age range covered by the test, and *secondly*, the rather small number of children who were tested and whose results were used as the basis for the analyses reported in the test manual. Nevertheless, for teachers, speech therapists, psychologists and other workers who work a good deal with children in the three–five year old age range or who work with handicapped children whose level of language functioning is in this range, the test will provide a useful addition to their assessment armoury. If the test is used, as its authors hope it will be used, for the assessment of a child's ability to understand a range of sentence constructions, rather than as a normative instrument, the test will provide users with useful insights into children's language comprehension.

However, if test users wish to have some normative evaluation, it is likely that they will turn to other tests which have a more substantial data base, such as the Reynell Scales or the British Ability Scales' Verbal Comprehension Scale. To make this test maximally useful, therefore, it is important for the authors to collect further representative data on larger samples of children so that good normative information, as well as diagnostic information, may be obtained from the test by potential users.

In future editions, it would be helpful for the instructions for administration and scoring to be more helpfully and clearly laid out in the Manual.

The Visual Pattern Recognition Test and Diagnostic Schedule

Reviewed by Stephen Sharp

Author: Diane Montgomery
Publisher: NFER-Nelson
Distributor: NFER-Nelson
Age range: 4:07–5:06
1979 (M, T)
Individual test

Test content

There are four subtests consisting of 8, 5, 5 and 10 items. In subtest *A* the child is shown a sequence of between 3 and 6 coloured dots of diameter 16 mm, its task being to place coloured counters below the given sequence so as to duplicate it, in terms of both number and colour. In subtest *B* the principle is the same except that instead of consisting of coloured dots, the target sequences are made up of black dots, short (16 mm) vertical lines and long (25 mm) vertical lines. Again, the child is required to duplicate each sequence from similar response materials provided.

The other subtests involve letters, so after subtest *B*, the child is given a break then a letter recognition practice test. This consists of five items each of which has a target letter followed by a row of five letters one of which is the same as the target letter. The child's task is to identify the target from within the row. Subtest *C* has the same format but instead of a single letter, the target and distractors consist of meaningless sequences of two to five letters. In subtest *D*, words are used and range from easy targets (do) to difficult (aeroplane), but again the task is to pick out the target from a list of three or four alternatives.

The subtests are intended to cover all stages of word recognition, starting from simple dots, and progressing to arrangements of dots and short and long lines. These were chosen because 16 of the 26 letters of the alphabet can be made out of these symbols including the problem letters, b, d, p and q. Then the recognition of letter sequences is assessed and finally proper words are used.

Purpose

'The scores of the VPR are of value in determining whether or not certain types of help are needed in order to bring a child to reading readiness'.

'The most important function of the test is as a diagnostic tool. It focuses the teacher's attention on specific, highly relevant pre-reading behaviours and cues her to their absence. A check list of these should be made during and after test administration. This information may be used in devising a suitable schedule of training in pattern recognition where this is found necessary'. (Manual, p. 4).

Item preparation

The Manual gives little information. Mention is made of two pilot studies involving 34 and 30 children as a result of which 'some alterations were found to be necessary, e.g. the shortening of some of the subtests and minor adjustments in order. A letter recognition test was shown to have no power to discriminate between the majority of children tested' (Manual, p. 5) and so was relegated to the practice test described above. Apart from this no details are given of how the final version was arrived at.

Administration

The instructions in the Manual are intended to enable any primary school teacher to administer the test. The second pilot study indicated that 'the materials were suitable for easy use by teachers' (Manual, p. 6). The materials consist of coloured counters for subtest one and black counters, long and short black sticks for subtest 2. The other parts of the test are of the paper and pencil variety.

There is no time limit on the test and every effort is made to elicit correct responses from the children, even if several prompts are necessary. The Manual provides verbatim instructions and prompts to be used by the tester and describes as closely as possible how to deal with a range of probable difficulties which may be encountered with children of this age and how far to persevere before deciding that the child has failed.

Standardization

The standardization group consisted of 120 children from a school in the south-east of England. All were tested by the author. Information about the socio-economic profile of the sample is given but no details about how or why those children were selected. Maybe this does not matter as the data derived from the group were not used to construct age-related norms. 'Perceptual readiness quotients are not given as these would be no more informative than the raw scores. The raw scores are found to be equivalent to standardized scores as a correlation of 0.99 $(n = 87)$ was found during standardization—thus no conversion of scores is necessary' (Manual, p. 4).

Thus the standardization data were not used to standardize the test as this is normally understood. In fact the Manual does not make it clear exactly what the data were used for. A second group of size 38, this time tested by their teachers, is described and their performance related to that of the main sample but, apart from a table in the appendix, it is not mentioned again in the Manual.

In general, the information on standardization is unclear, scanty and poorly exploited. The diagnostic nature of the test presumably explains the lack of emphasis on this aspect and also goes some way to mitigate the effects.

Scoring

Detailed instructions are given concerning the detection and classification of errors. Items are scored dichotomously and any error causes that item to be deemed incorrect. The significance of different types of errors is treated at some length in the Manual—see the comments under Interpretation below.

A sample score sheet is given in the Manual along with suggestions for recording useful supplementary information during administration. The four raw subtest scores are each divided by the number of items in the subtest and these means are summed and divided by four to arrive at a test mean. Comprehensive tables are provided for these divisions in case they should be beyond the user's powers. In fact, two pages of the Manual are given over to a confusingly laid out table which lists the result of dividing by four. Using this procedure with subtests of different lengths means that some items carry more weight than others. Why this was done, rather than simply dividing the total score by the total number of items, is not explained.

Reliability

Five groups, three of size 10 and two of size 25, were used to calculate reliability coefficients by the method of 'equivalent forms'. No details are given of what these forms were or how they relate to the final version. They seem to come from the pretesting stage, an impression reinforced by the reference to these five groups as the 'pilot studies', although the combined size of the five groups (80) does not match the sum of the two pilot groups (64). Things are complicated even further by a four-week gap between testings and by the mixing of data gathered by the author and by teachers 'who had no training but who were given the instructions for administration and scoring and were asked to read them carefully'. For what they are worth, coefficients ranged from 0.75–0.85 with a mean of 0.81. No details are provided about the ages of the children in these groups so it is impossible to assess how close these figures are to fixed-age estimates.

Validity

Correlation coefficients are given between test score and teachers' assessments of reading performance for groups of size 15 ($r = 0.64$), 19 ($r = 0.73$) and 42 ($r = 0.73$). The Manual reports that for the last group, the effect of holding age constant is to increase the coefficient from 0.73 to 0.85, i.e. that the fixed-age coefficient is higher than the variable-age one, a truly astonishing result. Less surprisingly, it is stated that when the teacher is an experienced teacher of reading, the coefficient can be as high as 0.90. Finally correlations are given between test score and Registrar-General social class for 45 boys ($r = 0.22$) and 42 girls ($r = 0.12$).

Unfortunately, the value of all this information is lessened by its haphazard presentation. Many groups are mentioned and the size is given each time but it is not possible to work out how the groups are related to each other, what their characteristics were or how they were selected. It is difficult therefore to assess how much information the results contain about the meaning and usefulness of the test.

Interpretation

It was stated that no age-related norms are provided but the Manual does give two tables which contain verbal summaries of children in each of six age-score groups. These groups are arrived at by splitting scores into three bands (15–40 per cent, 45–70 per cent and 75–100 per cent) and ages into two (4:07–5:00 and 5:01–5:06). For each group, comments are given on the approximate level of perceptual readiness reached by the child along with some indication of likely future teaching needs. It is odd that age is taken into account only to the extent of division into two categories, since the Manual contains a graph showing marked increases in test score over all the target age range.

Another table gives raw scores and means of children in each of five Reading Categories on the Rainbow Reading Scheme. These data are not employed elsewhere, however, and it would have been better to have analysed them properly and included them in the section on validity.

The Manual section labelled 'diagnostic' provides descriptions of 30 behaviour types, relating both to the test responses and the child's ancillary behaviour, which allow the teacher to build up a highly detailed remediation profile. Unfortunately, no discussion is given of how the profiles might be applied once they have been compiled. Instead, five case studies are presented (including the perceptual readiness quotients disdained by the rest of the Manual) which describe the test performance and subsequent development of typical children. Finally, details are given of a range of follow-up learning programmes which the teacher can prepare so as to aid the development of children at various levels of ability. The materials involved in these programmes are illustrated and specific instructions relating to administration are given, almost as specific as the test instructions themselves. However, the programmes are not related in any precise way to the test results and ultimately amount to a series of general suggestions for developing pre-reading skills rather than an implementation of a particular set of test data.

General evaluation

The Manual gives the impression that the test author knows considerably more about young children and the way they learn to read than about the statistics of educational testing. Those sections relating to children—administration, descriptions of behaviour types, follow-up programmes—are thoughtfully written and incorporate a good deal of interest in and experience of the subject matter. Those sections on technical support—standardization and the assessment of reliability and validity—lack the clarity of layout and the organization of the data necessary to provide an adequate appreciation of the strengths and weaknesses of the test.

The Manual also shows signs of having been put together in a hurry, e.g. page 9 states that 'on the next page a completed score sheet is shown' whereas the sheet is in fact blank. This and similar errors indicate that little emphasis has been given to precision in the Manual.

The test may provide an interesting supplementary aid to confirm reading problems of which the teacher is already aware, but the small number of the items, and the imprecision with which the results are supported by the Manual, restrict the value of the test to circumstances where it is being used diagnostically and where the teacher has good overall knowledge of the abilities of the child.

Walsall Infant Screening Procedure

Reviewed by C. J. Phillips

Stage 1, including Classroom Observation Guide (revised February, 1980). *Authors:* P. G. White, S. Richards, and E. C. Raybould
Stage 2, Basic Skills Checklist in Number (revised September, 1981). *Authors:* P. G. White and E. C. Raybould
Stage 2, Basic Skills Checklist in Reading (revised September, 1980). *Authors:* J. E. Solity and E. C. Raybould
Publisher: Psychological Services, Walsall Education Department
Age : infant school children in mid-group and final year Individual procedure

Introduction

The Walsall Infant Screening Procedure (WISP) is an example of a local education authority's setting up systematic screening for the early identification of children with learning difficulties, in its infant schools. Other examples are Birmingham (Tansley, 1976) and Croydon (Bryan and Wolfendale, 1973). One of the authors of the WISP is co-editor of a symposium on the topic of early identification (Wedell and Raybould, 1976). The subject has been reviewed by Marshall (1976) and by Leach (1981).

Identification procedures, in the initial stage(s), attempt to apply a set of common and explicit criteria to all of an age group, not only to cases that immediately claim teachers' attention. They are systematic, 'in order to guard . . . against . . . certain children . . . being overlooked'. Determination of 'the earliest feasible stage in their school career' for screening pupils must allow for the variety of social experience of school beginners and for their differences in accommodating to the social environment of school. The WISP judges 'a good practical time to begin . . . the process is during the middle year of infant schooling'. Infant schools vary in admission age and class structure (e.g. 'vertical' grouping); 'the middle year' is interpreted to mean children of age about 5:06–6:06 years, who have been attending school for at least two terms.

Screening instruments of the kind under review rely entirely upon information which teachers possess and upon their professional judgements. Hence, the rationale is 'to provide (them) with a framework for observing children's responses to the normal process of teaching, in the normal class situation, in the "here-and-now"'. To this extent, the children identified as 'at risk' are 'those . . . currently causing concern'. If it is successful, interventions can be made much sooner than would often otherwise be the case. Therefore, longer term prediction is also in mind. The complexity of the undertaking can briefly be noted here. It would be unethical to persuade teachers, even if it were possible, to make no use of the insights gained from submitting their observations to the framework. On the other hand, one must seek evidence of the validity of the framework from its effectiveness in predicting significant outcomes, including the nature and prevalence of learning and behavioural problems in, say, junior school years. The dilemma is not an insuperable obstacle to objective investigation and it is hoped that initiatives like Walsall's will lead to reports of long-term studies in the field.

Origins

Seventy-two teachers from 30 infant schools took part in a pilot study in 1976–77 'to develop and evaluate an initial screening instrument with children in the middle infant year group'. The Infant Screening Procedure, Stage 1, is a revised form from that study. Specimens of the Classroom Observation Scale (COS), Class Record, and Year Group List, form an appendix to the manual, Section V (pp. 16–25) of which is a Guide to the use of the COS. The authors cite 'The Bullock Report' (DES, 1975), which included a recommendation that local authorities should initiate this kind of thing in relation to literacy.

Screening stages

The sequence in outline is as follows:

Stage 1. Use of the Classroom Observation Scale (COS) to identify an 'at risk' group 'for within-school help and/or further investigation of teaching needs'.

Stage 2. Use of Basic Skills Checklists in Reading and in Number, with identified 'at risk' pupils.

Stage 3. Follow-up by (a) attention to children's needs, and (b) individual investigations.

It is the formal instruments for Stages 1 and 2 that are reviewed here.

Stage 1: Classroom Observation Scale

Content

The COS consists of 23 items to be rated on five-point scales. All the scales are arranged to give the highest value to the most positive attribute. Each scale is well described operationally, so as to concentrate the teacher's attention on a characteristic that she will immediately recognize (e.g. *Self help:* 1. Needs constant help with personal needs; Extremely reliant on teacher; 2. Considerable help needed from teacher; 3. Satisfactory; 4. Fairly independent; needs only occasional help; 5. Completely independent . . . in caring for own personal needs). The items are grouped under six headings—the number of items is shown on the right—as follows:

(1) Listening Skills (Receptive Language)	(4)
(2) Speaking Skills (Expressive Language)	(4)
(3) Physical Skills	(3)
To include self-help competence	
(4) Early Learning Skills	(5)
Refers to reading, number concepts, writing, drawing, and fine manipulation	
(5) Attitude to Learning	(2)
(6) General Social Behaviour	(5)
Includes peer relationships, teacher co-operation, and appropriateness of behaviour.	

'Attitude to Learning' has only two items: interest/eagerness, and concentration/perseverance. In view of the overall aim, if it is not too narrowly restricted to assessment of present attainments, one might think that there are too few items, giving insufficient weight to attitudes; teachers have more information in this area, to which others have given greater importance (e.g. Stott, 1978).

Scoring

Composite scores, with a range from 23–115, are weighted sums of item ratings, using the steps 1–5. Composite scores are to be used to draw up a rank order for a school's whole age group, expressing the 'overall level of concern felt about a child's educational and social standing'. Section III (pp. 8–13), 'Finalising the "at risk" group', contains many sound recommendations for determination of a 'realistic cut-off point' and for the consideration of factors in addition to the rank ordering that should influence the school's actions on behalf of selected individuals. These factors are physical problems, speech/articulation difficulties, hearing, vision, poor attendance, and language other than English spoken at home. Taking full account of these factors, after rank-ordering by the COS, would meet some of the critical points to follow.

Interpretation

Aside from the statistical problem of conflating the 23 ratings, which is probably not very important, there is the major issue of what the composite score means. There can scarcely be any doubt about the status of the small number receiving very low or very high scores, say, those below 40 and above 100. But for the majority, summing COS scores postulates that the items operate cumulatively. This seems unlikely. Factor analysis of an instrument devised by Herbert (Wilson and Herbert, 1978, pp. 49–59; Philips *et al.*, 1972, pp. 74–75) for 6–7 year olds, showed distinct factors: (1) social competence associated with reading and auditory-vocal functioning, (2) problem behaviour, and (3) emotional and social development. The second and third factors had almost no connection with basic educational skills.

It is stressed that the COS is not a normative instrument, not a 'test'; but all of its items, and the composite score, are quantitative, with frequencies typical of interval scales. Although each school rightly holds the responsibility for interpretation and action, the scale is conceived as a measuring instrument for a large population, defined regionally and over time. What framework of judgement should the teacher be encouraged to employ? One expects some schools to have as few as, say, five per cent 'at risk' cases. In others, serving families of great social disadvantage, it might be of the order of 30 per cent, even before taking account of the educational problems of children from ethnic minority families. Social justice demands the use, although not the exclusive use, of a normative frame of reference.

Finally, would the COS alert schools to children with specific learning difficulties, so that their progress comes under closer scrutiny, and the junior schools are not left to go through the protracted process of discovering those with special needs? One looks forward to answers to such questions.

Theoretical evaluation

A great value in such procedures, as the present example, is not the instruments themselves, but the effect that use has on teachers' thinking. Therefore, the conceptual framework of their devising is important. Currently this is a critical issue for psychologists, more than it is for teachers. The WISP illustrates the problem. It is fashionable to denigrate normative tests of attainment in basic educational skills; with young children, it is said, they are not reliable, they are not predictive of future progress, etc. Why should one need high reliability and long-term prediction, in order to draw attention to significant degrees of backwardness in six-year olds? It is indeed worthwhile to reiterate that many factors 'play a crucial part in determining an individual child's relative success or failure in school, notably his social background and development, sensory and physical adequacy, and very importantly, the extent to which his particular needs are catered for'. Why does the imparting of this message oblige psychologists to jettison the distinctively psychological concept of cognitive development?

Stage 2: Basic Skills Checklist in Number

The purpose of checklists in reading and number—the second R has largely dropped out of sight—is 'to provide more detailed information on the attainments of children of top-infant age who have already been nominated . . . as being in need of special help' at Stage 1.

The Number Checklist is a 'substantial revision' of a pilot production carried out with stratified samples of children to represent the range of number attainments, as judged by their teachers, at average age 7:06 years (Kinsella, 1980). Further developments included an examination of the literature on basic number skills and consultation with teachers. Revision included 'more items sampling . . . practical use of number for problem solving' and 'fewer items devoted to formally laid-out, written calculations'. The purpose of the instrument is 'to sample key numerical steps only' in basic number concepts and the four operations.

Content

The areas of attainment are partly implied in the advice to users that failure on an item may indicate 'the need for . . . checking . . . in other areas not included . . . (e.g. pre-number skills, conservation, language of size and shape, seriation, etc)', and that one 'may wish to assess the extent to which . . . competence on basic operations is "underpinned" by understanding of the concept involved'.

The Checklist consists of 42 items, falling into five sections—the number of items is shown on the right—as follows:

(1) Equivalence/Correspondence   (6)
    Matching and comparing sets: making
    sets of more, the same, and less.

(2) Cardinal Number   (12)
    Counting, recognition, naming, writing
    from dictation, visual and oral sequencing,
    place value of two digits.

(3) Four Operations: concrete problems   (12)
    Four rules, including multiplication and
    division by 2, 3, 4 and 5, with and without
    aids.

(4) Knowledge of Signs   (5)
    Recognition, naming, writing from dictation,
    and writing into number sequences.

(5) Four operations: written formal   (7)
    Conventional sums and insertion of
    missing elements in equivalence statements.

Questions on the relative value of numbers (Item 2.9) are possibly ambiguous. The answer to 'What number is more than 7, 3 . . . 15, 23?' could be, say, '100' in all cases; and 'What number is less than 2, 10 . . . 17, 29?' might be, say, '1' repeatedly.

Materials

The checklist is in fact the manual of instructions and the test itself. The latter is very well arranged, so that when child and teacher face each other, the displays are presented to both; on the latter's page are shown the materials needed, the task, instructions to child, and the criterion for passing; and on the child's page, the visual stimulus material. The child does not mark the Checklist; for those items requiring a written response, there is an Answer Sheet. It and the Teacher's Record are not reproduced in the Checklist. The only other material required is a set of 24 blocks or counters.

Administration

The testee responds to most items as follows: (1) by constructing sets of counters, or adding to or removing from sets; or (2) by pointing to selected displays; or (3) orally, stating numbers, naming symbols, saying 'same', 'different', or interpreting. The intention is that all items should be given, unless the teacher knows that the child will fail, except that two items are used only if the preceding item is passed, and two items, when the preceding item is failed. The test requires the child's full attention and co-operation. It is given individually 'in as quiet and distraction-free a setting as possible'. It is not timed. No estimate of time needed is stated, but one would expect it to require at least 30 minutes, preferably in a single session.

Scoring

Each item consists of a number of examples of the same type, usually three or four. The criterion for passing an item is success on all examples that 'require reproduction of information', and not more than one error where 'practical demonstration of mastery is required' (Kinsella, 1980). Passes are not added to form total or sectional scores. Within sections, items are probably in order of difficulty.

General evaluation

The items 'have been selected to provide a sample of commonly agreed basic skills in Number'. A consensus is hard to come by, because much depends upon the curriculum of the particular school, at this educational stage. Therefore, the present endeavour should be well received seeing that so little has appeared which has general usefulness. One investigator of infant school children's thinking found no satisfactory instrument in being and 'a test of mathematical understanding was specially constructed, focusing on the conceptualization of simple numerical and geometrical relationships' (Lunzer *et al.*, 1976; Lunzer and Dolan, 1977). For these very reasons, it is difficult to view the Walsall instrument without normative reference. Within a normative context, one sees that there are many items that only a minority of children could pass, especially in Sections 4 and 5. One is uncertain of use of the information with 6–7 year olds who give concern, for those tasks which the majority of the class would fail.

The authors are at pains to declare this is *not* a norm-referenced test. Notwithstanding the claim to immunity from psychometric constraints by the criterion-reference school, one would like to see, in due course, a report on item facility from a large and representative sample of children.

Stage 2: Basic Skills Checklist in Reading

Behind this system for investigating children 'who are experiencing difficulty in learning to read' by sampling 'skills and knowledge in different areas of reading' there lies, of course, a particular set of ideas as to how reading is acquired by six-year olds. It is controversial ground with regard to both the psychological processes and their sequence, and the universality of the story. It is unlikely that an examination of 'all the available literature on reading', the first stage in devising this instrument, would have led to consensus about the component skills which are 'thought to be important in learning to read'. At the second stage, the views of teachers were sought on the importance of the components itemized, for instruction in the infant school. At the third, 100 top-infant pupils from five schools were tested, and a final selection of items was made to take account of difficulty, depth, and significance for future instruction. Before making some critical points on the outcome of these labours, it needs to be stressed, I think, what a very ambitious undertaking it is, and how much greater the resources would need to be.

Content

There are five areas of assessment, within four of these there is a sequence of items to be followed at each point at which the child is not successful in the task. The areas and items within them are:

1 Knowledge of own name in written form
   (1) Writes own name.
   (2) Recognizes own Christian name/surname out of a set of five names.
2 Sight vocabulary
   (1) Recall: reads 20 words correctly.
   (2) Recognition: recognizes orally presented words, not successfully read at 2.1, by pointing.
   (3) Selection of one of five printed words to match a picture; no error in 10 examples.
   (4) Word matching, by pointing to one of four words which matches a stimulus word; no error in four examples.
3 Phonic skills
   (1) Correct reading of 16 phonically regular words of one syllable.
   (2) Initial or final consonant replacement, to read ten three-letter words of CVC form.
   (3) Recall of letter sounds of 26 letters of the alphabet.
   (4) Recognition of letters by pointing in response to oral presentation of items failed at 3.3.

(5) Discrimination by selecting a printed word, (i) visual search for 'odd man out', (ii) auditory discrimination of initial or final consonants in words.

4 Comprehension
  (1) Contextural cues in a story: child provides five missing words, in printed story read aloud to him.
  (2) Contextural cues in sentences: child provides a word to complete five sentences, presented visually and orally.

5 Language of instruction
  From his reading book, child is required to identify examples of punctuation, beginnings and endings of words and lines, etc. No criterion for passing is given, unlike all other items. This task is not administered if the subject passes the first items of all other sections.

Materials

Other than the manual, the only materials required are the child's own reading book and individual record sheets. The instructions for administration are clear and the organization of the materials is very good.

Comments

Of central interest is the sequence of items in Sections 2 and 3. It is stated that their order 'should not necessarily be taken as an intended or recommended teaching sequence'. However, it may be supposed that the sequence is analogous to raising the power of magnification in order to take a closer look at components. If that analogy includes the notion that success on an item denotes high probability of success on later items in the chain, which need no investigation, one would hope for empirical demonstration in the future that this is indeed the case. For example, are children who can read all the 16 phonically regular one-syllable words (item 3.1), usually able to recall the sound values of *all* 26 letters of the alphabet, including 'q' and 'x' (item 3.3)? Is the test of recognition of phonically regular words (3.1) of comparable difficulty to the test of sight vocabulary (2.1)? One estimates the latter to represent a reading-age of between 6:00 and 6:06 years; but the former test is fairly difficult, including graphemes that are known to less than 50 per cent of infant school pupils according to Williams (1971). The section on phonic skills may be thought of as an analysis of word-building skills for words that are unfamiliar or not readily recognized from context. One misses from the analysis the important component of syllabification: the ability to recognize the syllables in compound regular words.

Items in areas 4 and 5 are unlike the rest and are particularly useful, in that they do not form part of widely used attainment and diagnostic instruments by Daniels and Diack, Schonell, Southgate, etc. But item 4.2 may need modification. The task is 'to say appropriate words' to complete sentences. Although instructions to the child include: 'there is a word missing . . . tell me the word that is missing', many young children would complete the sentence 'The boy ran to school—.' in meaningful ways that employ *more than one* word (e.g. 'because he was late'). By the criterion, 'any word that is grammatically correct', such a response is a failure, but completion by an adverb is more difficult than providing the nouns to end the other four examples.

Picture/Word Correspondence (item 2.3) is like Southgate's Group Reading Tests 1 (q.v.). Such tests are difficult to devise; among other things, they call for close examination of the response frequencies to the 'wrong' words; that seems to be needed particularly for the examples 'father', 'hand', and 'mother' (Southgate, 1958).

Testing that eschews a normative frame of reference, but which rests upon developmental trends, presents problems. At this stage of education, even within the age span of only 12 months, age contributes significantly to the variance of measured literacy. It may be found that more than twice as many in the youngest quartile are unable to pass the sight vocabulary test (2.1) as in the oldest quartile. Depending upon the criteria adopted for the first steps in the detection sequence, either an excessive number of younger pupils will come under scrutiny, or a disproportionate number of older ones will be overlooked.

Conclusion

Walsall's Infant Screening Procedure and the materials prepared for it by the Authority's educational psychological service, are the most ambitiously conceived and thoroughly worked out of any scheme known to this reviewer. It is to be hoped that revisions will appear in the future, based upon experience of their use.

References

Bryan, T. and Wolfendale, S. (1973). "Guidelines for Teachers No. 1". Director of Education, London Borough of Croydon.

Department of Education and Science (1975). "A Language for Life" (The Bullock Report). London: HMSO.

Kinsella, C. (1980). The development and testing of a criterion referenced checklist in number for use as part of an infant screening procedure. Unpublished dissertation, University of Birmingham.

Leach, D. J. (1981). Early screening for school learning difficulties: Efficacy, problems and alternatives. *Occasional Papers* 5, 46–59; Division of educational and child psychology, The British Psychological Society.

Lunzer, E. A., Dolan, T. and Wilkinson, J. E. (1976). The effectiveness of measures of operativity, language and short-term memory in the prediction of reading and mathematical understanding. *British Journal of Educational Psychology* **46**, 295–305.

Lunzer, E. A. and Dolan, T. (1977). "Making Sense, Vol. Two: Appendices". Nottingham University School of Education.

Marshall, C. P. (1976). Screening procedures for the early identification of children in need of help. *Association of Educational Psychologists Journal* **4**, 2–13.

Phillips, C. J., Wilson, H. and Herbert, G. W. (1972). *Child Development Study (Birmingham 1968–71), Part 1*. Centre for Child Study, University of Birmingham, and CORE 2 (3), 1978.

Southgate, V. (1958). The construction and applicability of a group reading test for children of low reading ability. Unpublished Master's Thesis, University of Birmingham.

Stott, D. H. (1978). "Helping Children with Learning Difficulties". London: Ward Lock.

Tansley, A. E. (1976). Special educational treatment in infant schools: 6 1/2 year old screening. *In* "The Early Identification of Educationally 'At Risk' Children". K. Wedell and E. C. Raybould, Eds). University of Birmingham: Educational Review Occasional Publication No. 6.

Wedell, K. and Raybould, E. C. (Eds) (1976). "The Early Identification of Educationally 'At Risk' Children". University of Birmingham: Educational Review Occasional Publications No. 6.

Williams, P. (1971). "Swansea Test of Phonic Skills Manual". Schools Council/Oxford: Blackwell.

Wilson, H. and Herbert, G. W. (1978). "Parents and Children in the Inner City". London: Routledge and Kegan Paul.

Woodcock Reading Mastery Tests

Brief Report

Author: Richard W. Woodcock
Publisher: American Guidance Service, Inc.
Distributor: NFER-Nelson; Educational Evaluation Enterprises
Age range: 4–18 (USA Kindergarten to grade 12)
1971–72 (S); 1973 (M, T)
Individual tests

The five tests are prepared in two Forms, A and B. The tests are:

Letter Identification: a set of 45 items sampling letters of the English alphabet in a variety of type styles.

Word Identification: a set of 150 words to be read aloud.

Word Attack: 50 pronounceable nonsense words to be read, testing phonic and structural analysis skills

Word Comprehension: 70 analogy items, e.g. bird (is to) fly (as) fish (is to) _____ .

Passage Comprehension: 85 items using a cloze procedure with oral response.

The items are presented as cards in a ring binder which can be set up as an 'easel'. Administration can be limited to 30 to 40 minutes by use of a 'basal and ceiling levels' procedure for selecting the most appropriate groups of items on each test for a particular child.

USA norms provide a variety of conversions for the raw scores on the five tests and for Total Reading scores, including both norm-referenced and criterion-referenced scales.

Word Order Comprehension Test

Reviewed by N. C. Graham

Author: Gillian Fenn
Publisher: NFER-Nelson
Distributor: NFER-Nelson
Age range: 4:00–5:06 ('children with language delay or disorder')
1979 (M, T)
Individual test

Test content

There are nine subtests containing items which test respectively the following linguistic forms:

(1) proposition *on;*
(2) proposition *under;*
(3) subject–object *nouns (1);*
(4) subject–object *nouns (2);*
(5) subject–object *pronouns;*
(6) indirect object *nouns;*
(7) indirect object *pronouns;*
(8) indirect object with prepositional phrase *nouns;*
(9) indirect object with prepositional phrase *pronouns.*

Each subtest has 10 items which consist of a stimulus sentence which can be spoken, read or signed and a response display of two pictures. One of these expresses the content of the sentence exactly while the other is a plausible but incorrect alternative. The principle on which the alternative is constructed is not discussed. The subject must perceive the sentence in whichever modality is being used and point to the picture which expresses its content.

Purpose

The test is intended to assist psychologists, speech therapists and teachers, especially teachers of the deaf or mentally handicapped in the assessment of children presenting problems of language delay or disorder. In particular the test claims to assess the ability of children to comprehend 'words in sentences' (i.e. in grammatical sentences) as distinguished from understanding them as separate lexical items.

The test is intended to be used diagnostically and for remedial purposes. In particular it should prove helpful in distinguishing those deaf children who appear to be reading fairly competently but who are not, in fact, understanding much of what they are reading.

Item preparation

No information is given as to how the items were prepared or why these particular linguistic forms and vocabulary were chosen rather than others. The principles of language sampling used is not specified. A pilot study is reported but no details are given of whether or how the results were used in item selection or development.

Administration

Recommended users are psychologists, speech therapists and teachers of the deaf and mentally handicapped children. The materials come in a stout box and consist of the following in addition to the test manual:

(1) Sets of pairs of pictures for each subtest. Some sets are used for more than one subtest.
(2) Corresponding sets of sentence cards to be spoken and/or 'signed' by the Tester or read by the subject.
(3) One set of answer cards for scoring.
(4) Separate, individual scoring sheets for each subtest with space for six subsequent retests and provision for noting the mode of presentation.
(5) Individual record summary sheets for each subject tested.

The test is individually administered and is untimed. Emphasis is placed on the necessity of gaining rapport and holding the attention of subjects with different handicaps. The details of 'signing' to be used in conjunction with lip reading for deaf pupils are left to the testers own skill and expertise. The test is somewhat complicated to administer but not more so than many other individually administered published tests.

Standardization

Since the test is designed to be used diagnostically and is criterion referenced rather than normative very little in the way of standardization has been performed. However, information is given about a Pilot Study which established the approximate range of suitability of the test in terms of the performance groups (unspecified) of normal children from 'lower socio-economic home backgrounds' in the age range 4:00–5:05 years.

The tables show: (1) the number who were given each subtest; (2) the number 'correct' (i.e. scoring maximum points); and (3) the percentage (2) is of (1). These results are taken rather uncritically to indicate that the test is unsuitable for children whose level of language development is equivalent to that of normal children over the age of 4:09 years. A further pilot study is reported briefly in which over 100 deaf or mentally handicapped children were tested on this test and on the Reynell Developmental Language Scales or the Peabody Picture Vocabulary Test. No correlation with either of these tests was obtained. The carrying out and reporting of both of these studies leaves a lot to be desired in scientific rigour.

Scoring

The instructions for scoring are clear and the key convenient to use. It is suggested that scoring be carried out only when administration is completed. Record forms and summary sheets are adequate and convenient to use.

Reliability

No studies of this kind are reported.

Validity

No studies of this kind are reported.

Interpretation

The test is presented as a criterion referenced test (though this term is not used). Anything less than 100 per cent success (with a leeway of one item wrong) is judged as diagnostically significant to be further explored by retesting and checking for systematic misunderstanding of sentence or vocabulary and/or for remedial action (unspecified). Caution is advised about the frequency of retesting not so much because of practice effects (which are claimed to be nonexistent for the test) but because of the possibility of the loss of interest and motivation on the part of the subject which would invalidate the results.

General evaluation

In the opinion of the present reviewer the textual and pictorial materials of the test are produced to a very high standard but its psychometric and diagnostic properties are largely unexplored. The minimal psychometric data supplied in the manual is quite inadequate for drawing conclusions about the test's usefulness. The items do not appear to have been developed according to any psychological or linguistic theoretical criteria and even lack anything more than superficial educational validity. The remedial action which it is advocated should arise from indications provided by failure on one or more of the subtests is totally unspecified. Though potentially an interesting test it has been published in an underdeveloped state.

Language

List of reviews

Bowman Test of Reading Competence	117
The Burt Word Reading Test	121
Diagnostic Spelling Test*	127
29rrell Analysis of Reading Difficulty	128
Edinburgh Reading Tests	133
Edwards' Reading Test	142
English Progress Test A	147
English Progress Test A2	149
English Progress Test B2	152
English Progress Test B3	154
English Progress Test C2	156
English Progress Test C3	159
English Progress Test D2	161
English Progress Test D3	165
English Progress Tests: E, F2, F3, G	168
English Progress Test E2	173
Gap Reading Comprehension Test	175
Gapadol Reading Comprehension Test	179
Gates McKillop Reading Diagnostic Tests	181
Graded Word Spelling Test	185
The Holborn Reading Scale	190
Hunter-Grundin Literacy Profile	195
Learning Through Listening	210
London Reading Test	215
Macmillan Diagnostic Reading Pack	219
Moray House Junior English Test 5	222
Moray House English Test 41	225
Moray House English Test (Advanced) 2	227
Neale Analysis of Reading Ability	230
Neale Analysis of Reading Ability: Adapted for use with blind children	235

---

* Brief report only.

The Primary Reading Test 241
Reading Comprehension Test DE 243
Reading Level Tests (Experimental Version) 246
Reading Test AD 252
Reading Test BD 255
Reading Tests EH1, EH2, EH3 259
The Reading Vocabulary Tests 263
Salford Sentence Reading Test 267
Schonell Reading Tests 271
Senior English Tests★ 278
Southgate Group Reading Tests: Test 1 279
Southgate Group Reading Tests: Test 2 282
SPAR Spelling and Reading Tests 286
The Standard Reading Tests 291
Tests of Proficiency in English: Listening, Speaking,
    Reading, Writing 302
Thackray Reading Readiness Profiles 304
Transitional Assessment: English★ 309
Wide-Span Reading Test 310
Word Recognition Test 314
Young's Group Reading Test 318
Young's Group Reading Test 323

See also:

Basic Skills Assessment Program 435
Boder Test of Reading-spelling Patterns 11
Bristol Achievement Tests: English 437
Domain Phonic Test 30
The Infant Reading Tests 59
Language Imitation Test 72
Richmond Tests of Basic Skills 449
Reading Readiness Inventory 85
Sentence Comprehension Test 89
Vocabulary and verbal tests under 'General Abilities' 460
Word Order Comprehension Test 111

Bowman Test of Reading Competence

Reviewed by Christine Mabey

Author: Anthony J. Bowers and Margaret Mann
Publisher: Science Research Associates
Distributor: Science Research Associates
Age range: 7:10–10:09
1980 (M, T); S not stated
Group test

Test content

This test consists of four passages involving the cloze procedure. Each passage, of continuous prose, has had a number of separate words deleted and replaced by a marker line. The testee is required to write in the missing words. The four passages, preceded by a short practice passage, are of increasing length and difficulty.

Purpose

The claimed purpose of the test is in 'identifying, measuring and improving comprehension, and in assessing language competence. By determining how well a child can supply words which have been deleted from a passage, we can gain a measure of the degree of difficulty which he has with the concepts and language it presents' (Manual, p. 1). In addition, it is claimed that the test 'provides a means of separately assessing semantic and syntactic abilities as they relate to reading comprehension' (Manual, p. 1).

Item preparation

The four passages included in the test are said to have been 'ranked in ascending order of difficulty using the Fry Readability Formula (Fry, 1968), their assessed levels ranging from 6 years 0 months to 12 years 0 months. While some cloze passages contain deletions at repeatedly regular intervals, deletions in the Bowman Test have been made specifically to represent as many areas of syntactic and semantic significance as possible, and to take into account both forward-acting and backward-acting cues. Since Rankin (1970) has indicated that the contextual cues within a cloze test may in fact be far removed from a particular cloze unit, certain deletions have been made in order that their successful completion will indicate a full comprehension of the whole passage' (Manual, p. 3).

It is not clear how many different passages or items were piloted although the authors refer to: 'pilot surveys and initial analysis to identify non-discriminating items' (Manual, p. 3).

Administration

Nowhere in the Manual do the authors specify the age groups or school year groups or level of reading ability for which the test is recommended, although of course the provision of age standardized norms implies something of these characteristics. However, *en passant*, they state: 'clearly, the child must have a basic knowledge of the English language in order to read it' (Manual, p. 1). From looking at the standardized sample and statistics derived from that, it would seem that the target age group is 7:10–10:09 years.

Children require a test booklet and a pencil for the test. The usual instructions about seating the children to avoid copying is included. The test is untimed but the authors state: 'in practice, 20 minutes will usually be sufficient time for most children to complete it or to achieve their best attainable score' (Manual, p. 1). No further guidance is given as to whether all children should be allowed to work until all have completed as much as they are able or whether the test should be stopped when 'most' (however, in practice, that is defined) have completed. Such lack of precision can make an important difference to children's scores. The effect of a timed test on younger and/or less able children will be to 'depress' their scores whereas, particularly if there are 'ceiling' problems, e.g. with older, more able children, an untimed test will provide the best possible achievement for the less able and possibly under-estimate the real difference between their ability and that of others. Each method is acceptable but if the test is administered under different conditions (as is possible given the ambiguity in the Manual's instructions) then interpretation of the results from the different administrations is difficult.

The instructions for administering the test are brief and possibly, given the lack of attention paid by some test users, it would have been preferable for more precise instructions with specific wording to have been included.

Standardization

The sample on which the test was standardized contained 2393 children whose ages ranged from 7:07–11:04. They were drawn from eight local education authorities (no information is provided as to how these were selected) some attending primary and some middle schools. Although how these schools were selected is not known 'the twenty-five schools from which the sample population was drawn were chosen to provide a representative cross-section of results from inner-city, suburban, rural and semi-rural communities' (Manual, p. 3). The date of standardization is not given. From the date of publication and references cited it is assumed that it was prior to 1979.

Standardized scores and reading comprehension ages were constructed from the raw scores of 2331 children in the age range 7:10–10:09. These 'were derived' from the smoothed regression of raw scores on age at the fiftieth percentile' (Manual, p. 4).

Scoring

The overall raw score for a child is given by the total number of correct responses. The common problem of discretionary judgements in marking tests using cloze procedure, is eliminated by specific answers being provided for each item (by means of templates). Further, there is a specific instruction: 'Do not accept similes which are not given on the scoring key' (Manual, p. 1). However, this procedure is equally open to question. Although the reviewer only had one template for part of one passage, an immediate criticism springs to mind. For example, looking at one sentence in 'The Thing': 'It moved very fast, yet it didn't appear to _____ legs' (Test Booklet, p. 4) only one response—'have'—is given as acceptable in the scoring key. Why 'possess', for example, should not be credited is unclear.

There is a problem also about the treatment of misspellings. The instruction is: 'Give credit for incorrectly spelled words which are obviously correct answers' (Manual, p. 1). However, the bizarre nature of many junior aged children's spellings is such that different markers could score the same response differently, i.e. as incorrect or as a misspelt correct response. Tables are provided to convert the raw score into either a reading comprehension age (range from 7:08–11:01 years) or into a reading 'quotient' (presumably standard scores). For the latter chronological age is grouped into 3-month age bands. Instructions for both are clear. However, to be able to provide reading comprehension ages up to 11:01 when the oldest child included in the standardization sample was stated to be 10:09 is questionable.

Subscores are also provided as each item is categorized as either 'semantic' or 'syntactic'. Subscores are the total number of correct responses in each category. T-score equivalents for these subscores are given at each of 6 age levels (each covering a 6 month age band) in a conversion table similar to that for converting overall raw score to reading quotient.

Also provided is a class record sheet on which can be recorded, for each child, his chronological age, raw score, reading age, reading quotient, subtest scores and whether the difference in subtest scores is significant, and if so at which level. The provision of such a summary sheet is obviously a useful adjunct for a class teacher.

Reliability

Test-restest reliability was 0.95 for a second administration of the test after a two-week interval ($n = 166$). Overall internal consistency of the test was computed using the KR-21 Formula, yielding an estimate of reliability derived from a single administration to 2331 children of 0.94.

The Manual points out the limitations to the obtained scores as reflecting an individual's 'true' ability. Standard errors of measurement are given for each of the 3-month age bands. Typically these are 3.4 or 3.5.

Separate data relating to 'the subscores were derived from an analysis of the results of 720 children, 120 in each of six age bands. Reliability coefficients, calculated by the split-half method with Spearman-Brown correction ranged from 0.89 to 0.94 for semantic scores . . . and from 0.87 to 0.94 for syntactic scores' (Manual, p. 4).

Validity

Content validity is claimed somewhat tautologically on the grounds that: 'Insofar as comprehension of a passage is indicated by the child's ability correctly to cloze on that passage by filling in the deleted words, the Bowman Test possesses content validity' (Manual, p. 4).

Two measures of concurrent validity are presented. The first is based on the test scores of 174 children who were given the Spar Reading Test, a test of verbal comprehension, shortly after they had completed the Bowman Test. The correlation was $r = 0.86$. Secondly, teachers of 1528 children in the sample population were asked to rate each child's reading ability on a nine-point scale, taking into account speed and fluency decoding ability, skill in using contextual cues and comprehension of written material. Product-moment correlation coefficients for six age groups ranged from 0.73 to 0.82 with a median r of 0.78' (Manual, p. 4).

Interpretation

Apart from pointing out the confidence which may be placed on a test score reflecting an individual's true 'ability', little other guidance is given about interpreting results. Scores below a specified number for each of the passages are said to 'indicate that the child is probably unable to read the passage with any understanding' (Manual, p. 2).

As far as subscores are concerned, the Manual suggests that when there is a T-score disparity (i.e. semantic competence exceeds syntactic or vice versa) which is statistically significant as given in the Manual, 'then specific remedial action may be indicated from the weaker area' (Manual, p. 2). Further, if the

Class Record Sheet is completed and a number of discrepancies in T-scores occur it is suggested that 'this will then provide a convenient method of reviewing the teaching groups performance as a whole' (Manual, p. 2).

General evaluation

Cloze procedure is a useful technique in providing information about, not only levels of reading ability, but also in indicating areas of reading difficulty. However, when used in a norm-referenced test more information about aspects of the test construction are required than is provided in the Manual for this test. In particular, information which would allow one to use the test with confidence is lacking on certain points: notably item preparation and the standardization sample. The reliabilities presented are acceptable but the validities are limited. The lack of precision about the timing of the test could produce different scores for the same children (or children of the 'same ability') tested under different conditions. Further, even with the limited information available to the reviewer, the suggested marking, both in respect of acceptable responses and spelling errors, seems questionable. The subscores would seem to have a limited purpose. In all, one would wish for greater detail about the test construction, some clarification and amendment of the administration and marking, and further details of its actual use before recommending it with confidence.

References

Fry, E. (1968). Readability formula that saves time. *Journal of Educational Measurement* 3, 189–196.
Rankin, E. F. (1970). The cloze procedure—its validity and utility. *In* "Measurement and Evaluation of Reading" (R. Farr, ed.). New York: Harcourt, Brace and World.

The Burt Word Reading Test

Reviewed by Jenny Hewison

Author: Cyril Burt; adapted by P. E. Vernon and others
Publisher: Hodder & Stoughton for the Scottish Council for Research in Education
Distributor: Hodder & Stoughton
Age range: 6:04–12:00
1921: 1938 (S, M) (revised); 1952 (S)
1974 (S) (restandardization); 1976 (M, T) (revision)
1976 (M, T) printings reviewed
Individual test

Test content

The test consists of 110 individual words, printed 5 to a line, which the child must read aloud from a card. The words are listed in roughly increasing order of difficulty. Responses are recorded, on a separate sheet, by the person administering the test.

Purpose

No specific purpose for the test is claimed, but a general, non-diagnostic assessment of reading development is the intended purpose, judging by the tone and content of the Manual. The test is said not to be appropriate for the diagnosis of specific disabilities in backward readers: 'the teacher must realise that other and more specific tests are required to identify the problem faced by this type of child' (Manual, p. 2).

Item preparation

The original selection of words for inclusion in the test took place more than 60 years ago; and the grounds for inclusion or exclusion have since become lost in the mists of time, at least so far as the average test user is concerned. The ordering of the 110 words has, however, been examined quite recently, and is discussed under Standardization below.

Administration

The instructions given in the Manual for administering the test are clear and generally adequate. No materials are required other than the printed list of words, from which the child reads aloud. Responses are recorded by the teacher, either on another copy of the word list, or on a separate sheet. The manner of recording responses is not discussed; credit is only given for items pronounced correctly, so no information other than a tick or a cross need be recorded. Some teachers may, however, prefer to record children's incorrect responses, on the grounds that, 'the main types of error a backward reader makes will help in a preliminary diagnosis of his disability' (Manual, p. 2).

Children are encouraged to read through the list at their own speed. No time limit is imposed, and no indication is provided in the Manual of the length of time likely to be required. Other test reviewers have suggested that only 'a few minutes' are likely to be needed (Vincent and Cresswell, 1976).

Standardization

'The 1974 revision of the Burt Test has not only yielded up-to-date norms, but a revised word order that takes into account changes that have occurred in the relative difficulty of the words' (Manual, p. 2).

Burt's original standardization of the test was published in 1921, and a major restandardization by P. E. Vernon appeared in 1938. The 1974 standardization, like Vernon's was carried out in Scotland, but differed from its predecessor in that it was based on a national sample: over 2000 children took part, spread evenly over the seven years of the primary school. A sophisticated cluster sampling technique was used. A random sample of classes was first drawn from each year group, then either the older or younger half of each class was selected for testing. A brief account of the standardization exercise is given in the Manual, but further details are provided in a technical report, available from The Scottish Council for Research in Education (Thorpe, 1979). According to the report (p. 1), the sampling procedure used for the standardization 'ensured a nearly equal probability of selection for each child in the target population'. Special schools, grant-aided and independent schools were excluded from the study, and their pupils were therefore not represented in the calculation of age norms.

Two kinds of norms were calculated, reading ages and 'class norms'. The reading age appropriate to each raw score value was determined by plotting median reading score against age, and using regression analysis to fit a straight line through the plotted points. Adjustments were made to obtain a better fit towards the lower end of the scale; and the very youngest children of all, those below 6:04 years were excluded altogether from the reading age standardization, because their reading progress was insufficiently regular. The Manual therefore advises that no attempt should be made to use the Reading Age Norms for children in their first year of school, even if their raw test score falls within the range of the table 'since the reading ages that would be obtained by so doing might be misleading' (Manual, p. 7).

Class norms 'relate the performance of a child to that of Scottish pupils in the same stage of their primary course' (Manual, p. 9). They are given in the form of percentiles, e.g. 10 per cent of final year juniors obtain scores of 62 or less. Unlike the reading age norms, the class norms may be used for children in their first year of school, but they are only strictly applicable at the end of the school year.

In the standardization exercise, it was found that the order of difficulty of some of the words had changed since the previous rearrangement in 1938. A new word order was therefore adopted for the 1974 revision of the test; and a list of the 23 words found to have shifted in position by eight places or more is included in the test Manual.

In addition to the 1974 restandardization figures produced by the Scottish Council for Research in Education, published norms are also available from a similar exercise which was carried out in Cheshire at about the same time, and in which about 6000 children took part (Shearer and Apps, 1975). Both the reading age norms and the revised word order obtained in the Cheshire study differ slightly from those obtained in Scotland.

Scoring

A child's score on the Burt test is simply the number of words read aloud correctly; that score is then looked up in a conversion table, and a reading age or percentile point read off directly. (For some unexplained reason, the authors of the Manual thought fit to include each conversion table twice, once in the text and once in an appendix. In a document only 17 pages long, and containing no other tables, this is so unnecessary as to be confusing.)

Some guidance is given in the Manual about the scoring problems caused by pronunciation and dialect differences; and teachers are given the reasonable general advice that 'pedantic accuracy should not be expected' (Manual, p. 5).

Reliability

Reliability coefficients of 0.98 by the split-half method, and 0.97 by the KR-20 method are claimed in the Manual; but no information is given about the sample or subsample of children on which these figures are based. The Manual warns teachers that 'even a test of such high reliability has an error of measurement', but adds that in 19 cases out of 20, 'a reading age obtained using this test is . . . likely to lie within six months of the pupil's "true" reading age' (Manual, p. 12).

Validity

The only reference made in the test Manual to the concept of validity is a defensive statement in the introductory chapter, in which criticisms of the test are being discussed; 'The test has a high degree of reliability, and produces scores which correlate well with other measures of reading ability—i.e. it has a satisfactory validity' (Manual, p. 2). 'A compelling face validity' is claimed in the conclusion to the technical report (p. 22), but the question is not further discussed there either.

In the Burt test, children are awarded points if they correctly pronounce words aloud. There are obvious problems, discussed in more detail below, in calling this activity 'reading'. To take just one example, children may be able to pronounce correctly words with which they are entirely unfamiliar, and which they do not understand; or indeed they may be unable to pronounce correctly words with which they are familiar and do understand, but which they have never before been called upon to read out loud (highly skilled adult readers encounter both types of word frequently).

Teachers will inevitably hold different views about what reading *is*, and hence about what a reading test should measure; but the validity question is at the heart of most criticisms of the Burt test, and to omit all discussion of it from the test Manual is really quite inexcusable.

Interpretation

The concept of reading developing underlying the Burt test is so simplistic that virtually no advice on score interpretation is required. A score of 41 means a reading age of 7:05 years, and that is that. Users are reminded that it is only the 'average' child who has a reading age equivalent to his or her chronological age. 'Discrepancies between the two, if large, require further investigation' (Manual, p. 5), is the only advice for action which is given.

On the test sheet itself, a space is provided for teachers to fill in a child's 'Mental Age—if known'. Calculating mental ages and juxtaposing them with reading ages and chronological ages is an old-fashioned practice which can be dangerously misleading. It is a pity that the 1974 designers of the test did not take the opportunity of discouraging this kind of simplistic thinking by omitting any mention of 'mental age' from the revised version of the test card.

In the Manual, which is designed for use by teachers, a word of caution is given regarding the essential unreliability of all tests. The technical report, however, goes much further on this point, and states that the Burt test's inherent error of measurement 'implies that it is not possible to make precise statements of individual reading ages, a point which must be recognized by those using the test' (Thorne, 1979, p. 11). Since this is exactly the purpose for which most teachers do use the Burt test a more strongly worded warning about over-interpretation should certainly be included in the test Manual, and not just in the technical report.

Test use

Some useful references are:
Evans, R. (1976). The prediction of educational handicap—a longitudinal study. *Educational Research* **19**, 57–68.
Peace, W. M. (1974). Reading surveys: is inadequate sample follow-up creating a false picture of standards? *Journal of the Association of Educational Psychologists* **3**, 9–12.
Pumfrey, P. D. and Naylor, J. G. (1978). The alleviation of psycholinguistic deficits and some effects on the reading attainments of poor readers. *Journal of Research in Reading* **1**, 87–107.

Rennie, E. F. N. (1980). The West Riding screening six years on. *Educational Research*, **23**, 47–50.

Sawyer, C. E. and Brown, B. J. (1976). Laterality and intelligence in relation to reading ability. *Educational Review* **29**, 81–86.

Tobin, D. and Pumfrey, P. D. (1976). Some long-term effects of the remedial teaching of reading. *Educational Review* **29**, 1–12.

Vincent, P. (1973). An investigation of the effect of summer holidays on children's reading attainment. *Journal of the Association of Educational Psychologists* **3**, 8–12.

General evaluation

When first published, the Burt test was said to be appropriate for children aged between 5 and 16 years. Subsequent standardizations have dropped the upper limit to 14 and then to 12; and the 1974 exercise has also raised the lower limit for assessing reading ages from 5 years to 6:04. Even so, the recommended age range for the test is still very wide, spanning six full years of primary schooling. This fact alone recommends the test to many teachers, who wish to follow children's reading progress for prolonged periods, without the difficulties involved in changing tests along the way.

A technically competent standardization exercise was carried out for the Burt test only a few years ago, so relatively up-to-date norms are available. The Manual is easy to read, the test is quick and simple to administer, and raw scores may be converted directly into the convenient and familiar form of reading ages. Added to which, many teachers like what they know, and the Burt test has certainly been around for a very-long time.

The above list of positive features accounts for the continuing popularity of the Burt test in schools. All is not as satisfactory, however, as at first appears. The concept of reading upon which the test is based is, as previous reviewers have argued, 'basically archaic' (Vincent and Cresswell, 1976). This is an argument about validity: does the Burt test measure reading ability, across the age range for which the test is intended, as that concept is generally understood? The answer quite clearly is that it does not. The test measures a child's ability to pronounce correctly a list of words isolated from context. The argument that this *is* what is meant by reading ability is obviously unsustainable; so defenders of the test must argue instead that the ability measured by the test, develops so closely in step with reading ability that the former may safely be used as an index of the latter. The high correlation of the Burt test with other reading tests is the evidence adduced in support of this argument.

The crucial questions therefore become: in establishing the validity of a reading test, is it sufficient simply to demonstrate relationships with other reading tests; and further, if another test *is* acceptable as a yardstick, does a high correlation between the two sets of scores necessarily mean that one of those tests may satisfactorily be used as a proxy for the other?

To take the first point, most tests currently available do not do justice to the complex network of skills which constitutes reading ability, and therefore cannot be said to 'measure' that ability in any meaningful sense. High intercorrelations with inadequate yardsticks do not establish a test's validity. (It should also be pointed out that many tests published in the last thirty years have been validated using the Burt as a yardstick. High correlations are often built into the relationships amongst tests, and consequently cannot be adduced as independent evidence for the validity of any one of them).

On the second point, even if a satisfactory yardstick of reading ability were available, the fact that Burt scores correlated highly with it would not be sufficient grounds for using the Burt test as a substitute measure of that ability. As children grow from 6 to 12 years of age, many aspects of their mental and physical development correlate one with another. Even if no substantive relationship exists between two attributes, if both are highly correlated with age, then they will also be correlated with each other. Further, if a substantive relationship does exist, as between height and weight for example, the fact that the two measures are correlated over a large span of childhood does not mean that weight can be used as an adequate proxy for height as far as any individual child is concerned. Most teachers use reading tests to provide them with information about individual children: in these circumstances, proxy measures are to be avoided whenever possible, and measuring instruments chosen instead which at least begin to do justice to the complex skills they purport to assess.

References

Shearer, E. and Apps, R. (1975). A restandardization of the Burt-Vernon and Schonell Word Reading Tests. *Educational Research* 18, 67–73.
Thorpe, W. G. (1979). "Technical Report on the 1974 Standardization of the Burt Word Reading Test". Research Services Unit: Report No. 6. Edinburgh: The Scottish Council for Research in Education.
Vincent, D. and Cresswell, M. (1976). "Reading Tests in the Classroom". Slough: NFER.

Diagnostic Spelling Test

Brief Report

Authors: Denis Vincent and Jenny Claydon
Publisher: NFER-Nelson
Distributor: NFER-Nelson
Age range: 7:08–11:08
1979–80 (T)
1981 (S); 1982 (M); 1981 (T)
Group test

Forms A and B of the test booklet both contain 7 separately administered subtests. In addition, a dictation task is described in the Manual. *Test 1*—Homophones: a choice is to be made of one spelling out of the two offered in order to correctly complete a sentence (e.g. there, their). *Test 2*—Common Words: a sentence completion task; a line drawing is given to cue the missing word. *Test 3*—Proof-reading: identify and make corrections to incorrect spellings in a printed handwritten passage. *Test 4*—Letter Strings: a line drawing representing a word is accompanied by four words containing a common letter string, which can be used to complete the spelling of the indicated word. *Test 5*—Nonsense Words: which nonsense word in each group of four such words looks as though it could be—in terms of letter structure—an English word? *Test 6*—Dictionary Use: eight seconds are allowed for testees to find and circle, in a 'dictionary' of 94 words, each of ten words announced by the tester. *Test 7*—Self Concept: ten 3-point rating scales ('like me, not like me, not sure') about spelling (e.g. 'I am rather careless over my spelling').

Norms based on over 4000 children are given in the form of standardized scores (mean 100, standard deviation 15) for each month of age for total raw scores. Correlations between preliminary forms of the DST and numbers of free writing errors were found to be in the range 0.51–0.83.

Durrell Analysis of Reading Difficulty

Reviewed by Sandra Johnson

Author: Donald D. Durrell
Publisher: Harcourt Brace Jovanovich, Inc.
Distributor: NFER-Nelson
Age range: 8–13 (and non-readers)
1937, revised 1955 ('New Edition')
Individual Test

Test content

The Durrell Analysis of Reading Difficulty comprises of a battery of diagnostic tests: including tests of oral reading, silent reading, listening comprehension, spelling, handwriting, and phonic skills. The oral reading and the silent reading tests consist of equivalent sets of eight paragraphs of graded difficulty, and there is in addition a third equivalent set of supplementary paragraphs. The listening comprehension test contains seven paragraphs. Every paragraph in each kind of test has a group of direct recall comprehension questions associated with it.

Word recognition and analysis are evaluated by means of a set of word cards and a cardboard tachistoscope (quick flash device) and there are also tests of letter identification (naming and matching) and of letter sound recognition. In addition, spelling lists are included, as are instructions for conducting a handwriting test.

Individual record booklets contain detailed checklists of difficulties for most of these tests, tables of norms usually also being included. The booklet contains provision for notes to be made of the child's school and medical records and of relevant psychological factors.

Purpose

The test battery is principally diagnostic in function: 'The primary purpose of the analysis is to discover weaknesses and faulty habits in reading which may be corrected in a remedial program' (Manual, p. 3). Having completed the battery of tests, information from the various checklists of difficulties is transferred to a 'check list of instructional needs' in the individual record booklet, and on the basis of this information a remedial plan is outlined.

Item preparation

No information is given on the way in which the paragraphs contained in the oral reading, silent reading and listening comprehension tests were created or selected, or on what procedures were carried out to establish the equivalence of their graded levels of difficulty. Neither is any information provided about the compilation of the word list used in the word recognition test, nor about the construction of the spelling lists.

Administration

Test users are advised to use a group screening test to select poor readers for this individual diagnostic testing (which can take between 30 and 90 minutes per child). Very detailed advisory notes are offered to test administrators: these cover conditions of testing, verbal interaction with the child, test administration order, timing and record-keeping. Further, more specific, directions are given for each kind of test.

It is assumed that the oral reading test will be used first, and for this it is necessary for the administrator to establish a 'basal paragraph' (read without errors) and an 'upper level' (seven or more errors or more than 2 minutes time needed to complete reading) for the child. There are instructions for recording the child's miscues and eye-voice span. When each paragraph has been read, the administrator assesses the child's level of comprehension of the test by eliciting direct recall with a series of specific questions.

The paragraphs used for the silent reading test are suggested from those used for the oral reading test. Eye movements are noted during the reading. When the child has finished reading a paragraph the administrator elicits free recall of the story content, and then questions the child to prompt direct recall of items not already volunteered. There is an optional probe of the child's imagery.

The listening comprehension test requires the administrator to read a paragraph to the child (a paragraph suitable for the child's age or grade) before asking specific questions to elicit direct recall of story content.

A series of word cards and a tachistoscope are supplied for the word recognition and word analysis test (instructions are given to the test user on how to operate the tachistoscope). The child is asked to pronounce each flashed word. Whenever a word is mispronounced, it is revealed for the child to study before attempting a revised pronunciation (the 'analysis' test). The procedure is continued until seven successive mispronunciations are made on the flash test, words thereafter being given longer exposures. Seven successive mispronunciations on the 'analysis' test signal the end of this particular assessment.

The letter naming test is intended to be given only to non-readers or very poor readers, and this is followed for these children by a letter identification test and a letter matching test *only* if they failed the first test. The tachistoscope is again used for the letter matching test, and also for the test of visual memory of words. This latter is also intended only for very poor readers, and the child is required to identify within a list of letters or words that which is flashed (for about 0.5 sec) by the tachistoscope.

Another optional test intended only for non-readers or very poor readers is that of hearing sounds in words. Here the child is required to circle all words in a list which begin, end, or begin *and* end, as the case maybe, with a particular letter sound (the sound is verbalized by the tester in an appropriate example word). Children failing this test on hearing sounds in words can be given a test on learning to hear sounds in words, in which some tuition is given before testing begins.

Intermediate-grade children are given a test of visual memory of words, in which they are required to write from memory words flashed by the tachistoscope.

In the test of phonic spelling of words the child is asked to write 'just as they sound' 15 words verbalized by the tester. The *spelling test*, on the other hand, contains 40 items. The tester pronounces each word, reads an illustrative sentence containing the word, and then repeats the word before requesting the child to write it.

In the handwriting test the younger children (8-year olds) are asked simply to write two or three words, older children being asked to copy for a timed period (1 minute) a paragraph read earlier.

When the child has completed a particular test, the administrator records the child's score, if appropriate, and completes the relevant check-list of difficulties.

Standardization

Norm tables are given for most of the tests in the Analysis battery, but little information is given on how these were derived other than that they were based on 'no fewer than a thousand children for each test' (Manual, p. 32). This apparent lack of rigour in standardization procedures, or at least in the formal recording of those procedures, is considered acceptable by the author in whose opinion 'the check-lists of errors are more important than the norms' (p. 32).

Scoring

In both the oral reading and the silent reading tests, the time taken by the pupil to read each paragraph is noted and matched to a set of norms for that paragraph. The outcome of this is to allocate the child to a grade level (age group) and a position in that grade (high, medium, low). Where these classifications differ across paragraphs the test user is advised to take the median. In addition, the number of questions answered correctly is noted— two or more questions unanswered being taken as indicative of poor comprehension for that paragraph. For the silent reading test only, norms are also given for volunteered recall. The word recognition and word analysis test is scored by allowing one mark for each word correctly pronounced. A child is given a score for 'flash' and for 'analysis' pronunciations—the latter presumably subsuming the former, and these are matched to a table of norms to classify the child into a high, medium or low position in an appropriate grade. Simple error counts are made in the letter naming and matching tests. For the remaining tests (other than the handwriting test) the final score is the number of correct responses, and in each case this can be compared with a series of grade norms.

Reliability

No information is contained in the Manual about the reliability of any of the tests included in the battery.

Validity

No comment is offered in the Manual on the validity of the various tests, although the author does state that 'the items on the check-lists are those of highest frequency and significance in remedial work'.

Interpretation

The foreword of the Manual states that 'the Durrell Analysis is designed for use by experienced teachers', because 'educational analysis requires teaching experience in the subject studied' and 'the inexperienced person has difficulty in interpreting the faulty habits observed and in providing a priority schedule for remedial instruction'. Thus, although the author offers some notes of guidance with regard to such aspects as increasing a child's reading motivation and improving word recognition skills and general reading comprehension, the burden of planning an effective remedial programme on the basis of a child's performance on the Analysis rests with the test user.

Information about difficulties the child experienced in the various tests is interpreted and transferred to a check-list of 'instructional needs'; this then determines the remedial plans. The author suggests ways in which the check-list information can be supplemented by the results of informal assessments conducted in the normal classroom situation (for example, assessments of reading interest and effort, word skills, speed of reading).

For non-readers or very young readers, the check-list of instructional needs includes sections on listening comprehension and speech, visual perception of word elements, auditory perception of word elements, phonic abilities, learning rate and reading interest and effort. The check-list for older children consists of sections relating to listening comprehension and speech, word analysis abilities and spelling, oral reading abilities, silent reading and recall, speeded reading abilities, study abilities and reading interest and effort.

An experienced reading teacher would have no difficulty in devising an appropriate remedial program for a child given the extensive diagnostic information provided through use of the Analysis.

General evaluation

The Durrell Analysis has undoubted value as a diagnostic tool in evaluating areas of weakness in reading (and, to some extent, in speech). The items contained in the various check-lists of difficulties have a timeless quality which will ensure their continuing relevance.

The tables of norms, on the other hand, have little to offer the modern-day user. The adequacy of the standardization procedure and sample on which they were based must be in doubt given the sparcity of information offered in the test manual on this point. The norms are also American-based (and, therefore, inevitably of limited value to British test users) and out-dated.

Edinburgh Reading Tests

Reviewed by Jenny Hewison

Authors: Godfrey Thomson Unit, University of Edinburgh (Stages
1, 2 and 4); Moray House College of Education,
Edinburgh, (Stage 3)
Publisher: Hodder & Stoughton
Distributor: Hodder & Stoughton
Age range: 7:00– 9:00 (Stage 1)
            8:06–10:06 (Stage 2)
           10:00–12:06 (Stage 3)
           12:00–16:00 (Stage 4)
Stage 1: 1975 (S); 1977 (M, T)
         1981 (M, T) printings reviewed
Stage 2: 1971 (S); 1972 (M, T)
         1980 (M, T) (second edition)
Stage 3: 1972 (S); 1973 (M, T)
         1981 (M, T) (second edition)
Stage 4: 1975 (S); 1977 (M, T)
         1980 (M, T) printings reviewed
Group tests

Test content

Each of the tests in the series is made up of several distinct subtests. In *Stage 1*
(two forms a and b), these are Vocabulary (20 items), Syntax (30), Sequences
(20) and Comprehension (21). In *Stage 2*, the subtests are Vocabulary,
Comprehension of Sequences, Retention of Significant Details, Use of Context, Reading Rate and Comprehension of Essential Ideas, each containing 20
items. *Stage 3* contains Reading For Facts (35 items), Comprehension of
Sequences (41), Retention of Main Ideas (20), Comprehension of Points of
View (36) and Vocabulary (35). *Stage 4* contains Skimming (30 items),
Vocabulary (35), Reading for Facts (30), Points of View (35) and Comprehension (25). Throughout the series, responses are indicated by underlining or
ringing the chosen answer from a list of alternatives; by ordering a list of letters
to correspond to the suggested order of words in a sentence, or sentences in a
paragraph; and occasionally, by writing onto a dotted line an answer obtainable
from the text or from a supplied list of alternatives.

Each subtest in each stage contains two or three different types of item.
Vocabulary is assessed using the following techniques: the selection of the right
word to go with a picture (Stage 1) or to complete a sentence (Stages 1, 2 and

3); the choice of a single word to 'condense and summarize the meaning of an extended phrase' (Stage 2, Manual, p. 30); the selection of a word or phrase to fit into a precis of a given passage (Stage 3); the selection of a common phrase to fit into a sentence (Stage 3); and the selection of synonyms (Stages 3 and 4).

'Concepts of sequence are essential to reading at any level' (Stage 1, Manual, p. 27). These concepts are tested by asking children to select the first word from a scrambled sentence (Stage 1); to put in order a scrambled question and answer sequence (Stages 1 and 2); and to put in order four or five sentences making up a simple paragraph (Stages 2 and 3).

The other subtests do not reflect developing themes in this systematic way; consequently only a piecemeal description of their contents can be given. In the *Syntax* subtest (Stage 1), children must cross out those words in simple sentences which 'do not belong'; select words to fill the gaps in a story from a list of syntactically distracting alternatives; and answer questions about sentences, which depend for their correct response on an understanding of 'the complexity of written English idiom' (Manual, p. 26). A variety of techniques are used to test the development and refinement of comprehension skills. The *Comprehension* subtest in Stage 1 requires children to extract information from a picture; to make simple inferences; and to use an element of imagination in drawing conclusions about how people feel from the remarks they make. The *Retention of Significant Details* subtest (Stage 2) assesses children's ability to extract simple information from print, and to retain it—briefly—in memory for subsequent use: a more subtle and highly developed version of this skill is tested in the subtest *Retention of Main Ideas* (Stage 3). The *Use of Context* subtest (Stage 2) assesses children's ability to 'make sense of a new word by completing the sense of the context in which it appears' (Manual, p. 32).

Children's ability to understand in detail the information contained in a passage and to distinguish what a passage does say from what it does not say, are skills which are tested in *Comprehension of Essential Ideas* (Stage 2), and *Reading for Facts* (Stages 3 and 4); while the *Comprehension* subtest in Stage 4 examines the ability to grasp general principles, to paraphrase, and to draw inferences from what has been read. The two subtests referring to *Points of View* (Stages 3 and 4) assess pupils' ability to make inferences from a variety of clues, and to connect different ideas together into a coherent whole. Finally, two subtests are designed to assess children's ability to read and make appropriate responses under pressure of time (*Reading Rate*, Stage 2; and *Skimming*, Stage 4).

Purpose

The tests were designed for use by teachers, 'to assist in the teaching of reading. Such tests can provide information that will help the teacher, whether she is organizing group activities or attending to the special needs of an individual child. In the light of the test results she can adapt her methods and choose her teaching material to remedy a weakness or satisfy a strength'. By using a wide range of item types, the tests assess a large sample of the tasks likely to face a child of a particular age. 'It is to be hoped that (the tests) will help the teacher to appreciate more clearly both the general attainment and the particular strengths and weaknesses of each child'. In addition, the tests were designed to 'enable the teacher to evaluate the success of her own teaching methods with respect to the whole, or to special areas of reading' (all quotes from Stage 1, Manual, p. 3).

Item preparation

No information is given in the Manuals about the preparation of items. A description of the 'rationale' of the various subtests is provided: for example, the Use of Context subtest in Stage 2 is given the following rationale: 'This subtest sets out to measure the essential skill by which our vocabulary is built up: the ability to make sense of a word by completing the sense of the context in which it appears'.

The different item types are then described in more detail, e.g. items D1 to D8: 'These items confront children with unfamiliar words in otherwise straightforward sentences'. Items D9 to D16 show 'the variation in meaning which different contexts and different adjuncts can together give to such common words as "cut" and "put"'. In this way, the authors' intentions are made explicit: what is lacking is any mention of the process by which these intentions were realized, and a set of tests was designed and constructed (all quotes from Stage 2, Manual, p. 32).

Administration

The instructions for administration given in the Manuals are clear and comprehensive. The tests were explicitly designed for use by teachers, and to require 'no special psychological expertise in administration or in the interpretation of results' (all Manuals, p. 3).

In the Stage 1 test, the teacher reads out to the class what they must do, section by section: in Stages 2 to 4, pupils work from written instructions, but each subtest is separately timed by the teacher. In all cases, only writing implements and test booklets are required by pupils taking the tests. Practice items are incorporated into the beginning of every section of the Stage 1 test, and are worked through by the teacher and the class together. The sections of Stage 1 are not precisely timed, and teachers are advised to stop children working on a section 'after three minutes, or when about three-quarters of the children seem to have done all that they can' (Manual, p. 5). It is also stated that 'no page should take more than three minutes to complete' (p. 4), and the element of ambiguity in these instructions is not resolved.

It is recommended that testing for Stage 1 should occupy two sessions, in order to reduce fatigue, and that administration should, if possible, be completed in the course of one day. It is estimated that each of the two sessions is likely to last about 25 minutes. Stage 1 is available in two parallel forms (a and b), which are printed in different coloured ink, and designed to be used simultaneously as a means of preventing copying or other cooperative working. (The other recommended use of the parallel forms is in the monitoring of reading progress over time, when practice effects may result if the same form were used on different occasions).

Stages 2 and 3 each consist of a practice section, containing examples of all the item types to come; and two separately administered parts to the test proper. The practice sections which take 30–35 minutes, are worked through with the class by the teacher, item by item. Part I of the test proper occupies about 40 minutes, and Part II about 35 minutes, in both Stages 2 and 3. Stage 4 contains no practice section, and is therefore taken in only two sessions, each of 30 minutes working time. No more than 24 hours, it is recommended, should elapse between the administration of Parts I and II of the tests, or between the practice and Part I sessions of Stages 2 and 3. A watch with a seconds hand, or a stopwatch, is needed for the timing of the independent subtests making up the separate parts of Stages 2 to 4.

As will be apparent, the administration of the Edinburgh tests is a complex and lengthy business, requiring detailed organization and timing. The instructions contained in the Manuals for Stages 2 and 3 are, however, admirably clear and well laid out, so the careful user is unlikely to encounter many problems. The instructions in the Stage 1 Manual are somewhat cramped by comparison, with the result that it is very easy to lose one's place in the script. The Manual for Stage 4 is quite satisfactory in this respect, because few instructions are needed.

Standardization

Each Manual in the series contains a Statistical Appendix, describing the test standardization. The form of the exercise was essentially the same for all four Stages of the test: samples of pupils from state schools in Scotland, and in England and Wales, were obtained by dividing the country or countries into areas, choosing a representative education authority from each area, then drawing from each chosen authority a random sample of schools which took population differences between areas into account. A single class was then selected from each school, in an attempt to give an average class enrolment of 30 within each authority. The classes were also selected to give an equal balance between the sexes, and to give as even a distribution as possible over the age range in question, but specifically 'remedial' classes were excluded. The aim was to test, at each stage 3000 in Scotland, and 3000 in England and Wales. Unfortunately, it was not possible to adhere strongly to this plan, as a number of authorities refused to participate; and several more placed constraints on the lists of schools from which the sample was to be drawn, or requested that changes should be made to the sample after it had been selected. A number of schools also failed to co-operate, and had to be substituted by others; and absenteeism amongst pupils was a problem in the upper age ranges.

At each stage, some of the pupils tested were found to be outside the specified age range, and so were excluded from the standardization sample. The final numbers of children on which the standardization tables are based are shown below.

	Scotland	England and Wales
Stage 1	2500	3013
Stage 2	2700	2593
Stage 3	2865	2793
Stage 4	2282	2216

Raw scores may be converted into standardized scores (referred to as deviation quotients) based on a normal distribution with a mean of 100 and a standard deviation of 15, or into reading ages; both sets of conversion tables were constructed using linear regression techniques to model the relationship between raw score and age.

For the Stage 1 test, separate conversion tables were produced for boys and girls: a third set of standardized scores was also calculated, based on the total sample, but no reading age table was produced for the sexes combined. The statistical appendix provides additional information on the differences between the sexes; between the samples from Scotland, and from England and Wales; and between the two parallel forms of the test (each of the parallel forms was administered to half the sample, but no other information is given about this part of the standardization exercise).

For the Stage 2 test, separate conversion tables were produced, not for the two sexes, but for the samples from Scotland, and from England and Wales: no combined tables are given. Limited information on the sex differences observed in the standardization sample is given in the statistical appendix.

Stage 3 follows the same principle as Stage 2: separate conversion tables are given for the samples from Scotland, and from England and Wales, with limited information on sex differences being provided in a statistical appendix. The Stage 4 Manual also follows this pattern, but the statistical appendix is lengthened to include a complicated procedure for the calculation of standardized scores based on the total sample. No equivalent procedure is described for reading ages.

Norms are also provided for the various subtests that make up the four tests in the series. Unlike the main standardization tables, these norms make no allowance for age: 'all children with a particular subtest raw score are awarded the same standardized score, whatever their age and sex' (Stage 1, Manual, p. 20; a similar statement appears in the other Manuals). This simplified procedure can be used, because the subtest norms are only intended for use in comparisons between different aspects of the performance of any one child, and not for comparisons between children.

The subtest standardized scores range over the odd numbers between 1 and 15: in an unsuccessful attempt to reduce the user's confusion, the Manuals state that these figures are just a simplified version of the quotient scale; and provide tables by way of illustration. (The Stage 3 Manual is an exception here; subtest standardized scores on this test take values between 1 and 40; and the relationship to quotients is not discussed).

Some information on age differences in subtest scores is given in the statistical appendix to each test Manual, together with information on sex differences, differences between the samples from Scotland, and from England and Wales, and for Stage 1, differences between the two parallel forms of the test.

The standardization data presented in the Stage 2 test Manual were collected in 1971, the Stage 3 data were collected in 1972, and the Stage 1 and 4 data in 1975.

Scoring

Clear instructions are given in the Manuals for the scoring of the tests, and well laid out scoring keys are provided. Sensible guidelines are given for the few occasions when an element of discretionary marking is permitted.

A profile sheet is provided at the end of each test booklet. Page totals are transferred to this sheet, totalled for each subtest, and for the test as a whole. The total raw score obtained may then be directly converted, using the appropriate table (see Standardization above), into a reading age, or combined with the child's age and converted, again using the correct table, into a standardized score (a 'deviation quotient'). Clear instructions are given for the use of these tables.

If desired, subtest standardized scores may also be obtained by reference to the appropriate table. These scores may then be plotted on a profile chart, and their pattern inspected.

Reliability

Reliabilities (KR-20) were calculated for the various tests and subtests. For

Stages 1 and 4, whole standardization samples were used. For Stage 2 ($n = 198$) and Stage 3 ($n = 368+$ for each of England and Wales, and Scotland) were used. Reliability coefficients ranged from 0.95 to 0.97 for whole tests, and from 0.73 to 0.95 for subtests. It is interesting to note that subtest E was excluded from the calculation at Stage 2, because KR-20 reliabilities were considered inappropriate for a highly speeded test.

No other reliability data are reported. Most notably absent in this context is any discussion of the relationship between the parallel forms of the Stage 1 test, or any reference to test-retest reliabilities.

Validity

'The test's content validity is assured as far as possible by its constructors' working in association with the steering committee of teachers and reading experts' (Stage 1, Manual, p. 31. A similar sentence appears in all the other Manuals). The question of validity is not further discussed in the test manuals. A statistical annexe to the tests is planned; and will include correlations between the stages of the Edinburgh and other tests, factor analysis and item analysis data and estimates of the tests' predictive validity.

Interpretation

Clear and sensible advice is given on the interpretation of the overall test score. In particular, the numerical properties of 'deviation quotients' are well explained; and simple tables record the percentages of children in the standardization sample who scored at or below specified quotient levels. A section entitled 'Cautions' appears in every Manual, immediately after 'Total scores: calculation and interpretation of quotients'. This section includes discussion of the reliability of test scores, and the use of group tests in making decisions about special education and warns, in addition, that 'changes in reading standards may gradually render the standardization inaccurate' (Stage 1, Manual, p. 13; other Manuals also).

The interpretation of the overall test score is only the beginning, however. Lengthy sections follow in all the Manuals on the interpretation of subtest scores and the patterns they present. Once the subtest profile has been drawn up (as described in 'Scoring' above), the next step is to make a judgement about which, if any, of a pupil's results are 'sufficiently exceptional to demand special attention'. A special set of procedures is described, to enable teachers to make these judgements systematically and without bias (in addition to judgements about individual children, further procedures permit assessments to be made about the pattern of performance of whole classes). In all the Manuals, several pages are then devoted to going through the subtests one by one, discussing the rationale of the items, and offering interpretations of unusually high and low subtest scores. These sections tend to be highly repetitive, and the advice given in them is often bland, or self-evident, or both. On the other hand, the general advice given about investigating low scores (find out what the child found difficult) is both sensitive and sound; and so is the advice about not concentrating remedial resources on pupils with interesting patterns of deficits, at the expense of those whose overall level of performance is poor.

The test authors recognize that the Edinburgh's usefulness as a diagnostic instrument is likely to be more limited than originally intended, because, as they themselves point out, the subtests 'agree closely with each other about almost every pupil; that is, the subtests are highly correlated' (Stage 1, Manual, p. 24). The correlation coefficients given in the statistical appendix to each Manual provide the evidence for this assertion.

In the light of this evidence, it seems reasonable to suggest that the amount of space devoted in the Manuals to the interpretation of subtest scores is excessive, and that a pruning exercise should be carried out before the tests go into another edition.

General evaluation

This overview is organized around three main topics: the nature of the skills measured by the Edinburgh tests; the usefulness of the tests as 'diagnostic teaching aids' (publisher's advertising material); and the adequacy of the test standardization procedures.

The Edinburgh tests provide much richer and more comprehensive information about children's reading performance than most other commercially available group tests. Obtaining the information does, however, require a substantial investment of teacher time and effort: administering one stage of the Edinburgh tests can take up to two hours. Teachers faced with a choice between different tests should bear in mind that quality and convenience can seldom be maximized at the same time: this necessarily means that any one test will not serve all purposes equally well, since quality will be more important for some purposes, and convenience for others.

The range of skills tapped by the Edinburgh is commendably wide. That said, it remains the case that the tests' content validity is based on no sounder evidence than plausibility: more searching investigations are required. Most items and subtests do have a powerful claim to face validity, but there are occasional exceptions. Subtest E in Stage 2 asks children to choose one word from three possibilities to complete a sentence, and to do this repeatedly and at speed. The correct response is a word which the child has read within the previous two or three lines. This requires a degree of repetition so great for some items, e.g. Item 1, that good readers might reject the 'right' answer as inappropriate, and choose instead a word which continues the narrative, rather than just repeats something which has already been said.

Lastly on this subject, the content of the tests raises questions about the continuity between the skill domains of 'reading', 'English' and 'verbal reasoning'. The series is entitled 'The Edinburgh Reading Tests', but the range of skills assessed is much wider than that conventionally subsumed under the term 'reading'. Since no consensus exists about the skills which characterize good readers of secondary school age, the test authors have had to make their own selection, and they have chosen to venture in some cases quite far afield. Users need to give thought to whether the boundaries of 'reading' adopted by the test devisers correspond to the boundaries they would choose to adopt themselves. Certainly, most of the special types of reading assessed in Stages 3 and 4 are not explicitly taught in schools, as 'reading' or as anything else, and the test authors anticipate that the Edinburgh test itself might encourage teachers to change their practices in this respect (the effect of any widespread change on the test standardization would then presumably need to be investigated).

Moving on to consider the usefulness of the tests as 'diagnostic teaching aids': on the evidence available, the publisher's claims in this respect seem to be exaggerated. The subtests of the Edinburgh tests, as chosen and as constructed, agree with each other about almost every pupil. This being the case, the amount of space devoted in the Manuals to the analysis of subtest scores is out of all proportion to the usefulness of the exercise, and needs to be reduced if unrealistic expectations are to be avoided. In any future rewriting of the subtest sections of the Manual, the authors would also do well to clarify some parts of the text: users are given no clear explanation about how the bandwidths for isolating 'exceptional' scores were decided upon, nor why they are sometimes asymmetrically placed about the central score on the subtest profile; terms like 'median' are not explained for several pages after understanding of their meaning has first been assumed.

Finally, the question must be asked: how satisfactory are the test standardization procedures used for the Edinburgh? The answer must then be given: not as satisfactory as they might have been in a number of important respects. First of all, it was a mistake to exclude remedial classes from the standardization sample (this decision is mentioned in the Manuals, but its important implications are not discussed). The under-representation of weak readers in the standardization sample will necessarily lead to an artificially high estimate of 'average' performance. A child whose performance was indeed 'average' with respect to the whole age group would appear below average when judged according to this inflated standard. (Schools without remedial classes would have had their 'remedial' children included in the sample, so the final mixture of pupils obtained is altogether uncertain). The problem of the missing weaker readers is likely to be exacerbated in the Stage 4 test, because of the high number of children who were unable to be tested owing to absenteeism from school.

The second important problem relates to the changing standardization samples used for the different stages of the test. Stage 1 has separate standardizations for the two sexes; Stages 2–4 for two different geographical regions. It is therefore impossible to follow a child's reading development from Stage 1 to Stage 2, and use the same yardstick on the two occasions.

The sex differences revealed in Stage 1, and the changing pattern of regional differences revealed in Stages 2–4 are interesting in themselves, and should have been discussed in greater detail: any explicit comment on the latter is in fact scrupulously avoided. Also deserving comment are the discontinuity in the subtest mean score increases with age found in the Stage 1 test (Manual, p. 30), the arbitrary weights used in the regression analysis of the Stage 2 data (Manual, p. 36), and the difference in difficulty level between the parallel forms of Stage 1 (Manual, p. 30). A few words of additional explanation are also required in connection with the reading age standardizations: for example, the idea that a score of 55 on the Stage 1 test represents a reading age of 7:08 for a boy but only 7:01 for a girl is likely to be confusing, because teachers are not accustomed to thinking of reading ages in these relative terms. Finally, the distinction between 'mental age type' and 'deviation' quotients is unlikely to be as familiar to teachers as the test constructors assume.

The Edinburgh then is impressive in its breadth, disappointing as a diagnostic instrument, and sometimes irritating in its technical presentation. The flaws should not, however, be allowed to obscure the virtues: as a comprehensive assessment of reading performance, the Edinburgh has few serious rivals.

Edwards' Reading Test

Reviewed by Tessa Roberts

Author: Peter Edwards*
Publisher: Heinemann
Distributor: Heinemann
Age range: 6–13
1976 (Australia)
1980 (revised, UK edition); S not stated
1981 (M) printing reviewed
Individual tests

---

* UK edition prepared by Ruth Nichols, Adviser for Special Education, Berks.

Test content

The test materials consist of a Reading Selections Booklet, a Pupil's Record Booklet and a Manual. This is really a small battery of tests consisting of the following:

(1) *Edwards' Quick Word Screen Test.* A series of eight graded word lists ranging from what is termed a 'six-year level' to Level 13. Each list contains ten words which the child is required to read unhesitatingly as sight vocabulary.

(2) *Oral Reading Test.* A series of eight passages of continuous prose ranging from Level 6 to Level 13 with an optional practice piece at the beginning. Each passage is accompanied by a list of questions and the child is required first to read the passage aloud and then to answer the questions verbally when the passage has been removed.

(3) *Silent Reading Test.* Another series of eight passages of continuous prose ranging from Level 6 to Level 13, together with a series of lists of related questions. The child is required to read the passage silently. It is then removed and the questions asked and answered verbally.

(4) *Listening Comprehension Test.* Passages from either the Oral or the Silent Reading Test selections which have not previously been attempted can be used and these are supplemented by additional passages at Level 12 and 13. The teacher reads the passage aloud and the child is required to give verbal answers to the associated questions.

(5) *Edwards' and Summers' Word List.* 'This list comprises the 100 most frequent words in English prose materials. They are listed in rank order'. The list may be used to provide a reading test in which case the child is required to read unhesitatingly down the list or to provide a spelling test in which case he is required to write the words as they are dictated to him.

Purpose

'The Edwards' Reading Test enables the teacher to evaluate reading skills in different situations in oral and silent reading. It will help the teacher to establish a pupil's reading level and to select materials appropriate for the pupil's reading programme' (Manual, p. 3). *The Edwards' Quick Word Screen Test* is 'to establish the level at which the reader can respond to single words on sight. This test may help to establish the reading level to use for the initial test of Oral Reading' (Manual, p. 4). *The Oral Reading Test* is 'to establish an instructional reading level and to offer the opportunity for the tester to diagnose the type of error made by the reader' (Manual, p. 5). *The Silent Reading Test* is 'to establish the pupil's silent reading level, testing recall and speed, so that this can be compared with his oral reading ability' (Manual, p. 7). *The Listening Comprehension Test* is 'to contrast the pupil's ability to recall information presented orally with his ability to recall material he has to read himself' (Manual, p. 8). *The Edwards' and Summers' Word List* 'can form a test of a pupil's basic sight vocabulary and will give guidance in planning a sight reading programme for him'; '. . . as a spelling test, it will help the pupil and his teacher to identify commonly used words for which the child needs more writing practice' (Manual, p. 8).

Item preparation

There is little indication of the way in which items were prepared. The Quick Word Screen Test is said to consist of words from each year level (6 to 13) but there is no information about the criteria used to relate them to a particular age group. The passages for all reading or listening tests are said to have been 'checked for reading level with several readability techniques' but the techniques are not actually specified. There are three references which might enable the potential user to investigate this but two appear to be inaccurately dated and two are sufficiently obscure to make it unlikely that a teacher would be able to locate them. The Edwards' and Summers' Word List is presumably based on a study of English prose materials but no reference to this work is given.

No information is offered about pilot studies or trials of the materials.

Administration

The test is for children ranging from those reading at the level of an average 6-year old to those at the level of a 13-year old. The separate tests in the battery are designed to be used in conjunction with each other in that one test can help to establish a suitable starting point for another. Children progress from one level of a test to the next until they exceed the maximum number of errors specified as permissible. All work is oral with the exception of the spelling version of the Edwards' and Summers' Word List. The Oral and Silent Reading Tests are timed but there is no time limit specified. For each of the tests the Reading Selections Booklet and Pupil's Record Booklet are required. In addition, a stop watch is required for the Oral and Silent Reading Tests and the use of a tape recorder with the Oral Reading Test is recommended for the tester who wishes to analyse at leisure the errors in a child's oral reading. Clear step-by-step instructions are given for the administration of each test and a simple and comprehensible system of notation is proposed for recording particular errors or reading habits in the Quick Word and Oral Tests.

Standardization

No information is given about standardization procedures but as the test manual has clearly been written for teachers who may wish to use the test diagnostically this may be a deliberate omission.

Scoring

Scoring varies from test to test but involves simple counting of errors in reading and correct answers to questions. There are clear guidelines on what is to be considered as an error and as an acceptable answer and since most of the questions involve only literal comprehension of the passage there is little scope for the scorer to make subjective judgements about responses. After each test, the teacher judges the performance as either satisfactory or unsatisfactory according to criteria set out in the Pupil's Record Booklet. These are in terms of number of correct responses made without hesitation for the Quick Word Test; comprehension, accuracy and speed for the Oral Test; comprehension and speed for the Silent Test. For the Listening Comprehension Test, it is simply stated that 70 per cent recall is required. When a child has fulfilled the criteria at a particular level of a test, the date is entered in the appropriate place on the first summary page of the Pupil's Record Booklet. Achievement on the Edwards' and Summers' Word List is recorded in multiples of ten words, the date being entered below the appropriate number in terms of either a reading or a spelling performance. A profile of developing skills is thus built up.

Reliability

There is no indication that reliability studies have been carried out.

Validity

There is no indication that validity studies have been carried out but the test draws a certain validity from the fact that it is based on commonly accepted items of reading behaviour.

Interpretation

The test can be used to establish a profile of a child's reading abilities and to chart the progress of these over a number of years by means of the summary sheet provided. It is claimed that this information can itself be used to establish an individual reading programme by offering guidance on the level of reading material which would be suitable for the child to read on his own (Independent Reading) or with an adult (Instructional Reading). This section of the Manual is not very clearly written but the suggestion appears to be that a comprehension score of over 70 per cent is necessary in either situation while an accuracy score of 90 per cent is necessary for Instructional Reading and 95 per cent for Independent Reading. One difficulty of interpretation lies in relating the test levels achieved in these respects with reading material generally available. A means of relating the test levels to the comparative book lists of Moon and Body is offered in the Manual but beyond this the usefulness of the test for this purpose would depend on how well established the level of difficulty of other reading materials could be considered to be. For children found to have an uneven profile of reading development teachers are referred to specific sections of Edwards' own book (Edwards, 1978) for helpful, practical suggestions.

General evaluation

The test offers a means of investigating a child's skill in performing a variety of reading tasks although this is by no means comprehensive: the questions asked are largely concerned with literal comprehension, for example. In the absence of any information about field trials or pilot studies its usefulness depends on the degree to which it is possible to accept the validity of the tasks and the confidence which can be placed in the criteria used for judging competence. Unfortunately this is largely a matter of faith. No evidence beyond a list of references is provided to support the allocation of materials to age levels and the tasks themselves are subject to possible sources of contamination. The requirement that word lists should be read without hesitation, for example, is likely to disadvantage certain types of personality; the testing of comprehension through recall might place more emphasis on memory than comprehension, particularly when specific words from the text are required; no account is taken of any prior knowledge that the child might possess. The criteria for judging competence are also unsupported by evidence. Certain reading speeds and accuracy and comprehension levels are suggested as satisfactory but again only general references are given. Nothing in the test is inherently improbable but without any external points of reference it is difficult to see great advantage over criterion-referenced tests which a teacher might make up to suit particular requirements.

For the most part, the Manual is clearly written, the tests easy to administer and likely to provide useful insights into a child's reading performance. The Pupil's Record Booklet is similarly clear although much of the information from the Manual is duplicated and there may be problems of recording data when a child needs more than one attempt to achieve the criterion score and where the use of a passage for the Listening Test may obscure the charting of a profile of development.

A recently published test which can be related to classroom practices could be a helpful instrument for the teacher but without more information about its rationale and construction, it is difficult for him to use it with confidence.

References

Edwards, P. (1978). "Reading Problems: Identification and Treatment". London: Heinemann.

Body, W. "Books for Reluctant Readers: Graded Lists of Selected Books for Older Readers". Reading: Centre for the Teaching of Reading, University of Reading.

Moon, C. "Individualised Reading: Comparative Lists of Selected Books for Young Readers". Reading: Centre for the Teaching of Reading, University of Reading.

English Progress Test A

Reviewed by N. C. Graham

Author: A. F. Watts
Publisher: NFER-Nelson
Distributor: NFER-Nelson
Age range: 8:00–9:00
1953 (M); 1963 (T); S not stated
No revisions apparent
1977 (M); 1979 (T) printings reviewed
Group test

Test content

Four kinds of item are used to test progress in English:
(1) Sentence completion, requiring the addition of one word.
(2) Category membership, which is also framed as a sentence completion task, e.g. A ROBIN is a kind of——(BIRD).
(3) Questions on comprehension of a printed passage in which only a single word is required.
(4) Question answering—requiring plausible 'made up' answers which should be sentences.
There are 10 items of each kind.

Purpose

The test purports to give teachers 'an idea of the progress a pupil has so far made in mastering the English language'. Standard scores are provided so presumably the test is to be used normatively.

Item preparation

No information is given as to why these particular items rather than many others are used. They appear to be backed by some (unstated) common-sense notion.

Administration

Since only teachers are mentioned it is presumed that no other users are intended. The materials consist of a booklet incorporating both the test items and space for the written responses. The test is not a speeded test: pupils are to be given adequate time to complete each page. Clear instructions are given in the booklet for answering questions but it is advised that the tester should read these aloud at the commencement of each page which should be timed separately.

Standardization

No information as to the procedures used is given except that standardization was carried out on 3199 children in the age range 8:00–9:00. The resulting data were used to derive standardized scores with a mean of 100 and a standard deviation of 15. Bands of scores carry a designated alpha-numeric grade from A1 to E2 each representing 10 per cent of the standardization sample. No information is provided about the sampling frame or sampling procedures. A table of allowances for age by months within the age range 8:00–9:00 is supplied. No differentiation by sex is mentioned.

Scoring

There is an element of tester judgement in the scoring and this is most marked in the case of the sentence answers. A key giving correct answers plus acceptable alternatives is provided. Partial credits for less than wholly acceptable answers are allowed in some cases; examples are given. Answers have to be not only acceptable but 'polite'! It is not entirely clear as to how the scores for each part of the test are to be entered on the front of the answer book.

Reliability

Reliability was measured by KR-20 from a sample (unspecified) drawn from the standardization sample. This was found to be 0.96 with a standard error of measurement of 3.0. Reference is made to the interpretation of this as indicating that 'true' tests scores of 19 out of 20 children will be within + or −6 points of their obtained standardized scores. No further details are given.

Validity

The manual provides no information which has a bearing on the validity of the test though it appears to be assumed that face validity can be judged by inspection of the test items.

Interpretation

The tables of standardized scores and age allowances allow a particular score to be evaluated against the standardization sample. The range of scores is divided into 'deciles' with each successive 10 per cent carrying a grade from A1 at the top to E2 at the bottom.

General evaluation

The age of this test taken in conjunction with the vagueness of the standardization information given makes it unlikely that it will be of any use in the 1980s. Theoretical notions of what constitutes language competence have progressed so far as to undermine even what face validity the test might be thought to possess.

English Progress Test A2

Reviewed by Don Labon

Author: B. Barnard
Publisher: NFER-Nelson
Distributor: NFER-Nelson
Age range: 7:03–8:11
1965 (S(; 1966 (M); 1962 (T)
No revisions apparent
1979 (M); 1980 (T) printings reviewed
Group test

Test content

This 42 item test samples vocabulary and reading comprehension, together with applications of sound-symbol associations and of grammatical and spelling rules. In most cases, item response involves either copying or constructing a written word. Altogether the test taps a reasonably representative range of literacy processes.

Purpose

Whilst not spelt out as such in the Manual, the test's evident purpose is to provide single norm-referenced measures of general English Language proficiency, with emphasis on literacy.

Item preparation

The Manual provides no indication.

Administration

This appears to be straightforward, insofar as administration of a group test to 7-year olds can be. Instructions for the teacher are adequate and the format of the answer booklet is clear. Some preliminary teaching of the meanings of the words 'rhyme', 'plural' and 'opposite' is involved. The test is untimed, and could take rather more than an hour.

Standardization

The test was administered, in the mid-sixties, during the autumn term, to all the children between 7:03 and 8:11 in two borough education authorities. Raw scores, at monthly intervals, were converted to standardized scores with mean 100 and standard deviation 15. Whilst sample size is more than adequate, approaching 5000, there is no indication in the Manual of steps taken to check whether the standardization samples were representative of the age group population in the country as a whole. The apparent lack of an urban/rural mix in itself opens the sample's representativeness to question. Additionally, the standardization has made no allowance for seasonal effects.

Girls scored significantly higher than boys (a difference in mean of 3.6 standardized score points), but norms for both sexes are combined into a single table.

Scoring

The test form also serves as an answer sheet and is therefore not re-usable. Scoring by hand is fairly rapid, though partly subjective, as some misspellings of some responses are acceptable and the Manual's guidance is only partial. Conversion from raw to standardized scores, through use of a table, is straightforward.

Reliability

From analysis of the responses of 368 of the standardization sample, using KR-20, internal consistency emerged as very high, with a coefficient of 0.97, indicating a standard error of measurement of some 2.5 points.

Validity

Inspection of the items indicates a reasonable content validity, but no concurrent or predictive validity studies are reported in the Manual.

Interpretation

For within-school or within-authority comparisons, the standardized scores can be used with some confidence. The Manual's reporting of the test's standardization, however, does not justify anything more than a very broad interpretation of the scores in terms of national norms. Because there is only one composite conversion table, literal interpretation of standardized scores could lead to a slight under-estimation of boys and over-estimation of girls relative to their own means. The test will differentiate hardly at all amongst children with reading and/or writing difficulties. For example, almost an eighth of the standardization sample obtained 2 or less correct answers among the test's 42 items.

Although the test is designed to provide a norm-referenced global measure, it has a few uses for criterion-referenced diagnostic purposes. For example, certain weaknesses in generating irregular plural forms of nouns or past tense forms of verbs could be identified through the test and then remedied.

General evaluation

Lack of information concerning constructional stages and a lack of validation necessitate the test's being reviewed with some reservations. It is, nevertheless, internally consistent and fairly easy to use, and should prove serviceable for broad within-school or within-authority comparisons.

English Progress Test B2

Reviewed by John Gray

Author: NFER Guidance and Assessment Service in conjunction with the
  English Group of the Surrey Educational Research Association
Publisher: NFER-Nelson
Distributor: NFER-Nelson
Age range: 8:09–9:09
1969 (M); 1959 (T); S not stated
No revisions apparent
1979 (M); 1980 (T) printings reviewed
Group test

Test content

There are nine blocks of questions in this test. Each block is devoted to testing a particular skill. 'The questions asked test the ability to provide rhymes and opposites; to change nouns into the plural and verbs into the past tense; to spell and punctuate; to write sentences and to read a passage and answer questions on it' (NFER Catalogue, 1980, p. 30).

Purpose

English Progress Test B2 was constructed in conjunction with the English Group of the Surrey Educational Research Association, to provide a means of estimating the attainment in English of children in the second year of the primary school. An attempt has been made in devising the items to abolish the 'tick the right answer' type of question, and to concentrate upon questions where the child is required to write a word or sentence as his answer'. It is essentially a normative test.

Item preparation

No information is provided on this topic in the Manual. It is not clear whether the items within each block are ordered in terms of difficulty although they probably are.

Administration

The test is a 'group' one intended for teachers to administer to their entire classes. 'There is no precise time limit for the test, since it is desirable that each child should have as long as proves necessary to complete it. In practice, it has been found that most children finish within 40 minutes'. The instructions to the children taking the test are to 'work carefully but not to waste time'. No advice is offered to the teacher about how to respond to requests for clarification or assistance *once* the test is underway, to decide when to collect in the scripts of children who have not finished or to decide which children it might not be appropriate to administer the test to in the first place.

Standardization

The test was 'administered for the purposes of standardization to a representative sample of children in the age range 8:09–9:09'. The scores of 5458 children were collected and standardized to a normal score distribution by comparing each child 'with a representative sample of children of exactly the same age'. Extrapolations were employed to provide standardized scores for children outside the age-range of the sample (i.e. aged 8:06, 8:07, 8:08, and 9:10, 9:11, 10:00). For younger children in the sample (those under 9) a raw score of 1 represents a standardized score of 80. No subsequent work appears to have been conducted to establish whether the standardization is still appropriate some twenty years after its initial construction.

Scoring

The Manual states that 'a list of correct answers is given in the key. Except where otherwise stated, answers differing from those listed must be regarded as wrong. Each numbered question gains one mark'. Some examples of how 'discretion' should be exercised in marking the 'Sentence Construction' items are offered.

Reliability

A KR-20 coefficient of 0.97 is reported with a standard error of measurement of 2.64. This coefficient was 'calculated from the answer pattern drawn up from a random sample of 246 scripts taken from the standardization sample'.

Validity

Face validity is assumed from the nature of the items tested. Other types of validity are not discussed.

Interpretation

No advice is given in the Manual on the interpretation of standardized scores (although the NFER Catalogue (1980) refers to this topic). The problems of using the test for both younger and older children in the recommended age-range are touched on but only in technical language.

General evaluation

This test needs to be seen in the context of the era (the days of a universal eleven-plus) in which it was produced. It seems, essentially, to have been designed to produce overall standardized scores, which might then subsequently be rank-ordered. Those wishing to use it actually to measure 'progress' would need to consider very carefully whether it covered a sufficiently wide span of abilities and attainments to suit their purposes, since it might not provide suitable scores at two points in time. It is not suited to diagnostic purposes.

Users would need to decide whether the test items themselves matched their view of what 'English' might be for this age-group. Since well over half the items relate to grammar, punctuation and spelling it might, more appropriately, be termed a test of 'English usage' and would probably need to be supplemented by other tests. Scores on many of the blocks are likely to be influenced by whether children have covered this specific item as part of their curriculum although the Manual does not point this out.

The test will do little to provide useful information about 'below average' children. Its dated appearance and directive tone may, indeed, discourage the less able, few of whom will have had the experience by this age of working in silence on their own for 40 minutes without any interaction with the teacher. It seems unfortunate that for this group, in particular, the first instruction to the pupil is to 'Fill in the following particulars' (a feature of several NFER tests) rather than a request to 'Please write your name here' and the ordering of the items is such that children may become stuck whilst tackling the first page of questions. There are no practice items before the test begins.

The review copy of the test was a 44th impression which indicates that it has been widely used. Schools not already using the test might want to compare it closely with others to see which is most suited to their purposes.

English Progress Test B3

Reviewed by John Gray

Author: Not stated
Publisher: NFER-Nelson
Distributor: NFER-Nelson
Age range: 8:07–9:09
1970 (T); 1972 (S); M undated

No revisions apparent
1979 (T) printing reviewed
Group test

Test content

Forty multiple choice items are used in various ways to cover aspects of English usage such as: the use of synonyms; use of class names such as 'fruit' and 'cutlery'; sentence construction; and comprehension based on a short prose passage.

Purpose

The 1982 NFER-Nelson Catalogue states that the purpose of the English Progress Series is 'to measure the progress which . . . pupils have so far made in mastering certain aspects of language' (p. 30). With respect to this test it describes the purpose as 'to assess a child's ability to use words correctly'. No statement about purpose is made in the Manual. The Catalogue and the standardization table in the Manual indicates that the test is suitable for the age-range 8:07–9:07; the front page of the Manual, in contrast, indicates the age-range 'approximately 8:00–9:06 years'. (Those wishing to use an NFER test on children in this area and age group may also wish to consider English Progress Test B2 reviewed above).

Item preparation

No information is provided on this topic.

Administration

The Manual briefly describes typical procedures for the administration of an NFER group test. The test is untimed but is said to require about 45 minutes to complete.

Standardization

The most minimal of details are provided in the Manual about the 1972 standardization of the test. These indicate that there were 3789 children in Eastern England from urban/rural areas in the standardization sample. There may, one infers, be some 'test ceiling' problems with older, more able children. The Manual reviewed did not indicate that the test had only been 'provisionally standardized', a fact which emerged in subsequent correspondence.

Scoring

A marking key indicating the correct answers is provided and the directions for marking the test are clear.

Reliability

No information is provided on this topic in the Manual.

Validity

No information is provided on this topic in the Manual. However, since the test items seem fairly straightforward they probably test what they were intended to test.

Interpretation

No guidance is provided on this topic in the Manual.

General evaluation

It seems odd that a test which was copyrighted in 1970, has reached its 8th impression and was prominently displayed in the 1982 NFER-Nelson Catalogue should have such a limited Manual. It consists of three typed double-sided photocopied sheets which merely provide standard instructions for administering the test, some brief guidance on marking it, a list of the correct answers and a raw score conversion table. It is also unfortunate that information about the 'provisional' nature of the standardization, which emerged in subsequent correspondence, is not explicitly mentioned either in the Manual or in the 1982 catalogue. None of these factors need necessarily deter experienced users of NFER tests but inexperienced users would need to consider very carefully whether the test met their aims and purposes in the teaching of English, and hence, in its assessment.

English Progress Test C2

Reviewed by Charles F. Owen

Author: Valerie Land
Publisher: NFER-Nelson
Distributor: NFER-Nelson

Age range: 9:09–10:09
1971 (M); 1961 (T); S not stated
No revisions apparent
1980 (M, T) printings reviewed
Group test

Test content

This test contains some multiple-choice questions, some where the child supplies an answer and some open-ended questions. The multiple-choice items concern comprehension of a short passage, synonyms, missing words from a paragraph, and transformation of sentences to the past tense. Questions where the child has to supply a correct answer include punctuating a sentence and supplying missing words in sentences. Two open-ended sections have no single correct answer: these involve elaborating given sentences and sentence completion. 'An attempt has been made in devising the items to abolish the "tick the right answer" type of question' (Manual, p. 2).

Purpose

The test is designed for use by teachers to 'provide a means of estimating the attainment in English of children in the third year of primary school' (p. 2). This estimate of attainment is in terms of a standard score, and so is relative to other children; it does not give information on an individual child's strengths and weaknesses.

Item preparation

No information is given about the origins of this test.

Administration

This is a group test. The children fill in their answers on a test form. The tester reads out some short instructions, which are not reproduced on the test forms. There are no practice items. There is no time limit on the test, and consequently no breaks between sections. The Manual suggests that most children finish within 40 minutes.

Standardization

Very little detail is given about standardization. The standardization sample consisted of 5499 chosen to be a 'representative sample of children in the age range 8:09–10:09' (p. 2), but no information is given as to how they were selected, of what they were 'representative', their geographical distribution (presumably British), how many schools were involved, year of standardization, and so on.

Scoring

The Manual contains a list of correct answers, which gain one mark each. For the sentence completion test 'specimen' answers are given, but the only guidance to marking is that 'the response may be of any length, provided it is sensible and grammatical' (p. 3). The other open-ended test, the elaboration of sentences, may get 0, 1 or 2 marks, which 'markers are invited to use their discretion in allocating' (p. 6): the only guidance is that this is a test of 'a child's ability to write creative English' (p. 6) and not a test of spelling or grammar.

Reliability

A random sample of 222 from the standardization sample gave a reliability (KR-20) of 0.97, which is high for a test with such a limited age range. No information is given as to the reliability of scoring the open-ended questions, which could easily have been obtained.

Validity

The test has a high content validity, but there are no data on its relationship to other measures.

Interpretation

A table is provided to convert raw scores to standard scores (mean 100, standard deviation 15) for each month of age, from 9:06–11:00. The table exceeds the range of ages in the standardization sample, so the top and bottom three months were 'extrapolated', and their validity is dubious.

General evaluation

The high content validity of this test may make it attractive to teachers. On the other hand, the fact that it provides no diagnostic guidance but only a standard score makes it of limited use. The scope for individual variations in scoring the open ended questions makes even this standard score a little suspect.

English Progress Test C3

Reviewed by A. Stibbs

Author: Not stated
Publisher: NFER-Nelson
Distributor: NFER-Nelson
Age range: 9:09–10:08
1976 (M); 1970 (T); S not stated
1977 (m); 1980 (T) printings reviewed
Group test

Test content

For each testee there is a five-page A4 booklet in which they are to write the answers to fifty items. Answering requires underlining words in lists to indicate which ones would best fill spaces, selecting phrases from lists to fill gaps, arranging jumbled phrases to make meaningful paragraphs, answering questions about information in both a poem and a prose passage, choosing synonyms for words in the poem and the prose passage, indicating where unpunctuated sentences end, and using conjunctions to join given sentences. The language of the items is that of genteel primers, and bears little relation to that of children of the age for which the test is intended. There is no time limit.

Purpose

According to the Manual, the test 'has been constructed to provide a means of estimating the attainment in English of 9–10 year olds'. The Manual says nothing about the content validity of the test. Perhaps the designers implicitly define 'English' as selecting or ordering given words and phrases, answering 'literal comprehension' questions, using conjunctions and recognizing sentence ends (a much more narrow definition than most junior school teachers would accept). More likely, they know but will not tell something which teachers do not know about the correlation between, on the one hand, performances at tests of these narrow skills and, on the other hand, 'attainment in English' in the wider sense in which teachers might define it.

Item preparation

The Manual discloses nothing about either the rationale or the method by which items were designed, chosen or apportioned.

Administration

Children are to be seated at different desks, given pencils and face-up booklets, deprived of all other materials, and allowed as much time as they need (which the Manual says will be less than 45 minutes for most of them). The tester instructs them to fill in the details on the front page (name, date of birth, etc.), then to begin the test with a given verbal formula. There is no indication of how many children at a time can be tested; that presumably depends on the vigilance of the invigilator(s).

Standardization

This was performed on a 'representative sample' (no details of selection given) of 5747 third year juniors. Using Lawley's method (see Introduction) separate conversion tables were constructed for boys and girls because the girls had a significantly higher mean raw score. Extrapolation of two months at each end of the age range has been used.

Scoring

The Manual has a marking key. With one exception there is comprehensive and implicit advice on dealing with such anticipated problems as those of negative scores for some items (rights minus wrongs), changed answers, and misspellings. The exception is the following direction: 'In certain items there may be other correct answers, and those given in the marking-key are intended as a guide to the types of answers which may be accepted'. No further guidance as to what criteria might be used in recognizing 'other correct' answers is given.

Reliability

The internal reliability was estimated by calculating KR-20 for 408 scripts drawn (on unstated criteria) from the standardization sample. The result obtained was 0.96, with a standard error of measurement of 2.9.

Validity

The Manual gives no hint that there has been any consideration of the test's content validity, predictive validity, associative validity, or concurrent validity.

Interpretation

The only aid to interpretation is that it should be used only in the summer term, since it was then that standardization data were obtained.

General evaluation

This is a very well designed test from the points of view of presentation, administration, marking and scoring. However, the Manual provides no information about the design of the test items nor about the content validity or the concurrent validity. On the surface, it is a test of familiarity with a miscellany of conventions to do with formal written language and to do with comprehension questions. Yet the publishers call it an 'English Progress Test'. There is a danger that teachers will take the competences which it tests as representatives, rather than symptoms, of progress in English, so that they will provide a model—even limits—for the materials, practices and objectives of teachers of English to upper juniors.

Because of its format and its title, a test like this tempts teachers to abuse it (for instance by using it more than once with the same group). The designers should have taken more account of this, both in the prominence of their warnings against such abuse, and by presenting scores in ways which were obviously unhelpful in assessing 'progress' on the results of this test alone.

English Progress Test D2

Reviewed by Jenny Hewison

Author: J. Henchman
Publisher: NFER-Nelson
Distributor: NFER-Nelson
Age range: 10:07–11:08
1969 (T); 1971 (M)
Group test

Test content

This test is designed to assess the traditional subject matter of 'English language' lessons, namely a knowledge of grammar, punctuation and vocabulary.

The test consists of 75 items, spread unevenly across 11 sections. For the most part, the items in any one section all tap the same skill, e.g. the ability to transform sentences from the active to the passive voice, or vice versa; or the ability to find one word which means the same as a series of words underlined in a sentence; or the ability to link two short sentences by means of an appropriate conjunction. One section asks for punctuation marks to be inserted into simple sentences; another for nouns to be replaced by pronouns. In other sections, different types of question are used to assess simple paragraph comprehension. The response required of the child varies slightly from section to section, but usually consists of writing the required word or phrase onto a dotted line. Sometimes the child must choose from a list of options, printed at the head of the section, but on other occasions, a more open-ended format is adopted, and the child must write in words of his or her own choosing.

Purpose

'English Progress Test D2 was constructed to provide a means of estimating the attainment in English of children in the fourth year of the primary school' (Manual, p. 2).

The test Manual contains a standardization table, which permits a child's score to be judged relative to the performance of other children of the same age.

From the stated aim, and the presence of the standardization table, it must be inferred that in the author's view, 'attainment in English' can be adequately represented by the sample of skills tapped by the test; and further, that attainment may be adequately summarized in the form of a single standardized score.

Item preparation

The origins of the test and its component items are not described in any way: more specifically, no information is provided on the selection of skills to be covered in the test, or on the choice of items to represent those skills.

Administration

The instructions given in the Manual for administering the test are clear as far as they go, but exhibit the major shortcoming that the specified introduction gives the children no idea of the nature of the tasks which will confront them. Only by opening the booklet and reading each section's instructions can children learn what they have to do; and questions are only allowed before the test has begun and the booklets opened. One worked example is provided at the beginning of certain sections, but a sample of practice items for the children to work through under guidance before the beginning of the test proper would also have been helpful. Teachers who are confronted by queries arising in the course of the test are given no advice as to how to deal with them—in the absence of fully adequate initial instructions, this is an important omission.

To take the test, each child requires only a test booklet and a pen or pencil. The test is not timed, 'since it is desirable that each child should have as long as proves necessary to complete it' (Manual, p. 3). Most children are said to finish within 45 minutes.

Standardization

A table is provided in the Manual for the conversion of raw scores into standardized scores, taking age into account. To construct the standardization table, the test was administered to 'a representative sample of fourth year children in the age range 10:07–11:08'. All children of the right age in two areas were included, plus a 'representative sample from a third', 4096 raw scores being collected altogether. Conventional procedures were then used to construct from the raw scores and children's ages a set of standardized scores, with a mean of 100 and a standard deviation of 15.

The conversion table in the Manual spans the age-range 10:06–12:00, i.e. a wider range than that of the sample studied. The additional values were obtained by extrapolation downwards or upwards as required.

Data for the standardization exercise were collected in 1963–4. No information is given about the areas, schools or children used in that study: so it is impossible to know in what terms the sample was 'representative', as claimed by the author.

A sex difference was found in the standardization sample, girls scoring on average about 4 points higher than boys. Users of the test are advised to take this finding into account, but are not told how best they might do so. The increase in score with age was found not to be significantly different between the two sexes, 'Hence a mean value was used in constructing the conversion table for the test'. Once again, no attempt is made to discuss, for the user's benefit, what implications these findings and decisions might have for the interpretation of individual test score.

Scores

A four-page marking key is provided, with quite clear instructions for its use. Listed in the key are the correct answers to all the closed-ended items, with alternative spellings as permitted. One of the test sections contains only open-ended items. Teachers are given a few words of advice about marking these, but otherwise told to use their own discretion. The key gives no specimen answers for this section, so differences of opinion may arise between markers about the scoring of these items.

The number of correct answers is totalled for each page. and then for the test as a whole. This mark, and the child's age, are then looked up in the conversion table according to simple instructions provided in the Manual, and a standardized score is obtained. Boxes are provided on the front of each test booklet for the recording of page subtotals, raw score total, age and standardized score.

Reliability

To calculate a reliability coefficient for the test, a random sample of 241 scripts was taken from the standardization sample. KR-20 was applied to the observed pattern of scores, and a value of 0.97 was obtained. No further details of this exercise are reported.

There is no discussion of inter-marker agreement, even though some discretionary marking is included in the scoring of test responses.

The standard error of the test was found to be 2.71. The Manual states that slight modification to this figure are required when comparing children of different ages, but gives only a brief and confusing explanation of why this should be so.

Validity

The test is intended as 'a means of estimating the attainment in English of children in the fourth year of the primary school' (Manual, p. 2). Since no reference is made to validity in the test Manual, potential users must of necessity examine the test closely and judge for themselves if the range of skills represented corresponds to their own view of the essential components of 'attainment in English'. Teachers whose views are in broad agreement with those of the test author must still take it on trust that the skills in questions are adequately assessed by the items selected: teachers who believe that this test leaves essential skills unexamined will undoubtedly prefer to look elsewhere for a means of estimating their pupils' attainment.

Interpretation

A very brief explanation of standardized scoring procedures is given in the Manual. Users are further told that 'Standardized scores of 75, 90, 100, 110 and 125 are obtained by children who do better than the bottom 5, 25, 50, 75 and 95 per cent respectively of children of their own age in the standardization sample' (Manual, p. 2). No other advice or guidance is given on the interpretation of test scores.

General evaluation

This test reflects a very traditional view of the range of skills which it is necessary and sufficient to assess under the heading of 'attainment in English'. Although the copyright date of the test is 1969, the standardization data were collected in 1963–64. Almost two decades have passed since then, and ideas about the English curriculum have changed and diversified. Many teachers will not consider English Progress Test D2 to be a suitable instrument for assessing English as the subject is currently taught in their schools. Others may consider that the skills tested are 'necessary but not sufficient', and may wish to use the test as only one part of a wider assessment exercise. All users of the test ought, however, to bear in mind that 20-year old norms must be treated with caution, especially since curriculum change has undoubtedly been widespread in the intervening years.

If the test author's view of education in English is accepted, a number of problems still remain. The standardization and reliability data reported in the Manual are inadequate, while the question of validity—even in the author's own terms—is not discussed at all. The test was designed to assess attainment in English, not in reading, but the two skills cannot properly be separated in a test of this kind; a fact which must have implications for score interpretation, though this possibility is not discussed. Finally, the vocabulary of some of the items has become dated: few girls tie a ribbon in their hair these days, and going 'to the pictures' is not the common expression it once was. Users of the test should be prepared to use their own judgement on these and other points, even though no words of caution are included in the test Manual.

English Progress Test D3

Reviewed by Roger Murphy

Author: Not stated
Publisher: NFER-Nelson
Distributor: NFER-Nelson
Age range: 10:03–11:08
1972, 1975 (S); 1970 (M, T)
No revisions apparent
1979 (M) printing reviewed
Group test

Test content

The test has 50 items which are claimed to test the ability to use words in a contextually correct manner, elementary punctuation and comprehension. The test has eight sections, which employ somewhat different methods for testing these skills. Various types of response are required, including short answers to comprehension questions, filling in missing words in passages and sentences, breaking up a passage into sentences, arranging jumbled sentences into a paragraph and putting capital letters and punctuation into unpunctuated sentences. The two comprehension sections differ only in that one relates to a poem and the other to a prose passage. It is difficult to say definitely what each item in the test is testing, but there appears to be more emphasis on word usage than the other two skills, and punctuation appears to be tested less frequently than anything else.

Purposes

The test is intended as a test of English attainment, allowing teachers to compare the results of individual children with national norms. It could be used for diagnostic purposes although this is not mentioned in the Manual.

Item preparation

No information is given about how either the individual items or the test as a whole were constructed.

Administration

The Manual implies that the test is suitable for children across the whole ability range, although the conversion table indicates that the test may not provide any discrimination amongst children with IQs outside the range of 76–132. The test is relatively simple to administer: each child is provided with a test booklet in which detailed instructions are given at the start of each section. All responses are written into the booklets. There is no fixed limit for the test, and although the Manual states that 'most children finish within 45 minutes' (Manual, p. 2), experience of using the test has revealed that several children in a group of middle-range ability may be expected to take considerably longer than that. In some sections of the test, where the items are unlike anything children of this age are likely to have encountered elsewhere, quite a bit of time may be spent working out what is required.

Standardization

Standardization of the test was carried out in 1972 and 1975 using the scores of 7813 boys and girls. 'Representative samples of children in the age range 10:03–11:08' were used, although no details are given about how they were chosen or what they were supposed to be representative of. Lawley's method (see Introduction) was used for constructing the conversion table. No separate norms are given for separate groups and no indication is given even about the relative number of boys and girls in the standardization samples. Finally, the conversion table itself is not all that clearly labelled, suggesting for example, that it can be used for raw scores from 0–24 whereas it actually covers the full range of scores from 0–50.

Scoring

A list of correct answers is given in the Manual. It indicates that there may be other correct answers, but does not seem to allow for this in questions 13–19, where one of two quite reasonable possibilities is excluded by the specific marking instructions. Scoring the test is quite time consuming: many responses will require close examination. The Manual recommends that ticks should be placed in the margin and totalled at the bottom of each page.

Reliability

The only reported reliability estimate is a KR-21 of 0.96. This was derived from the same sample on which the standardization of the test was carried out, but no information is given about whether all of the data were used together, or whether the children were divided into the different samples or into the different age groups that were represented. There is no discussion of the possible effect on the reliability of practice, which because of the unfamiliar nature of some of the items could be a significant factor.

Validity

There is no information in the Manual about any validity studies of any kind being carried out on the test.

Interpretation

The Manual explains how the conversion table may be used to convert a raw score of a child of a given age into a standard score. It also explains how a standard score may be interpreted in terms of the child's standing in relation to 'the relevant age group'. However, the population of children that the standardization sample is supposed to represent remains undefined. It is doubtful whether this type of interpretation really does the test justice and it may well be that teachers would gain more from looking at the sections of the test children do well on and those they do less well on and use this information for diagnostic purposes.

General evaluation

The test is an interesting one in that it contains a range of different types of items. This is, however, both an advantage and a disadvantage in that children can find such a variety of tasks stimulating and interesting, but in a number of cases they will fail, not because they do not have the skills required for the item, but because they misunderstand the instructions.

The rationale behind the construction of the test remains a mystery as do most of the procedures used to standardize it and estimate its reliability. Furthermore, its validity appears as yet to be untested.

English Progress Tests E, F2, F3 and G

Reviewed by Roger Murphy

Author: J. Henchman and E. Hendry (Test F2), S. M. Unwin (Test G); not stated (Tests E and F3)
Publisher: NFER-Nelson
Distributor: NFER-Nelson

Test E
Age range: 12:00–13:00
1956 (T); S not stated
No revisions apparent
1972 (M); 1971 (T) printings reviewed

Test F2
Age range: 12:03–13:08
1963 (T)
Some revision implied
1971–72 (S); 1977 (M)
1977 (M); 1979 (T) printings reviewed

Test F3
Age range: 12:09–13:08
1969 (S); 1963 (T); M undated (duplicated)

No revisions apparent
1980 (T) printing reviewed

Test G
Age range: 13:04–14:02
1962 (T)
No revisions apparent
1975 (S); 1976 (M)
1977 (M); 1980 (T) printings reviewed
Group tests

Test content

These four tests are all similar in style to other NFER English Progress Tests (e.g. A2 and D3). They contain a range of different item types which test the children's vocabulary, spelling, punctuation, reading comprehension, expression and grammatical usage. The items mostly require a short or one word answer which can be written into the test booklet.

Purpose

The complete set of tests is designed to provide a continuous assessment of the progress made by children in the use of English from 8–14 years of age. For example, it is claimed about Test E that it 'in no way seeks to indicate what *should* be taught, but sets out an array of tasks which are common to many schemes of work and which are part of more liberally conceived programmes' (Manual, p. 2).

Item preparation

In no case is any information given about how either the individual items or the tests as a whole were constructed.

Administration

Apart from the difficulty of deciding which test to use, all of the other administrative details appear to be fairly straightforward. In each case the children write their answer in the test booklet and so these are not reusable. No precise time limits are given for the tests, but in each case a rough estimate is given for the maximum amount of time it is expected that most children will need to finish the test. For Tests E and G this is 40 minutes and for Tests F2 and F3 it is 45 minutes.

Standardization

Test E

The Manual states that the test 'has at present been only provisionally standardized, and the norms should be used with caution' (Manual, p. 2). No further details are given about the 'provisional standardization' and as the test was first published some 26 years ago and has now gone to its 11th impression this seems to be a somewhat unfortunate state of affairs.

Test F2

Standardization was carried out in 1971 on 4759 children (12:03–13:02 years) from a Midland non-industrial urban/rural LEA, and in 1972 on 1295 children (12:06–13:09 years) from a North East England urban LEA. The Manual states that 'it was felt that the data in the two samples could not be satisfactorily combined to produce a national standard with confidence' (Manual, p. 2). Thus two separate local standardizations of the test exist for two unspecified LEAs and users of the test are invited to select 'the conversion table which appears to be most appropriate for the schools locality' (Manual, p. 2). Once again this seems somewhat unsatisfactory for a test that has been on the market for such a long time. The conversion table was constructed using Lawley's method (see Introduction).

Test F3

No details of any standardization of this test are given in the Manual. A provisional conversion table (December, 1969) is included, however, and above this it is stated that it is based on 1563 boys and girls. No information is given about when the 1969 provisional conversion table is expected to be replaced.

Test G

Standardization was carried out on 3061 boys and girls (13:04–14:02 years) in a Midlands urban LEA in the summer term of 1975. Again Lawley's method was used for constructing the conversion table. The Manual states that the standardization sample was not representative of national standards and 'the tables should be used with care, bearing in mind that the sample was a Midlands urban area' (Manual, p. 2). It is difficult to imagine how much use such a table and such information about it are to a teacher in another area who wants to use the test.

Scoring

Full scoring instructions are given in each of the Manuals. Each test booklet has to be marked item by item. In some cases the person doing the marking has to exercise judgement about whether to accept answers as being correct. Tables are provided for transforming raw scores into standardized scores for each of the tests. These are easy to use but are of dubious value (see comments under Standardization).

Reliability

Test E

A value of 0.95 is quoted, which is based on an application of KR-20 to 185 of the standardization sample scripts. No information is given about how this sample was chosen and no other reliability estimates are provided. The Manual states that the internal consistency estimate 'is high for a test of this type' (Manual, p. 2). It also points out that it leads to a standard error of measurement for the test of 3.4.

Test F2

The Manual quotes a KR-21 of 0.95, based on 1295 scripts from the urban standardization sample and a standard error of measurement of 3.4.

Test F3

No reliability estimates are provided.

Test G

A KR-21 of 0.92 and a standard error of measurement of 4.3 are quoted. No information is given about the sample from which these estimates were derived other than that it included 3061 scripts. The Manual points out that one child in twenty can be expected to be given a standard score that is in error, either above or below the hypothetical true score, by more than 8.6 points.

General comment

In general, information about the reliability of these tests is somewhat disappointing. Nothing is available for one of the tests and in the other three cases only internal consistency methods are used. Virtually no information is given about the samples that were used, so it is difficult to evaluate the worth of the measures that are provided.

Validity

There is no information in the Manuals about any validity studies of any kind being carried out on any of these tests.

Interpretation

As with the NFER English Progress Test D3, the Manuals imply that the main interpretation of test performance will be through a conversion of raw scores into standardized scores, which can then be used as a guide to where each child stands in relation to the population that the test was standardized on. Quite apart from the fact that the standardization samples, in every case, are likely to be unrepresentative of the national cohort, this exercise seems of dubious value to most class teachers.

No attempt is made to suggest any diagnostic use of the test results, although this might easily be developed in relation to the performance of individual children or groups of children on the various parts of the tests.

General evaluation

It may be that this is a very useful series of tests for English teachers and others interested in the English attainments of 12- and 13-year olds, but it is disappointing to find that such a widely used set of tests appear to have been poorly standardized and validated. The complete absence of any information about how the tests were first constructed and why they were constructed is a mystery. As can be seen from the target age-groups specified at the start of this review, these tend to overlap somewhat. None of the Manuals for the four tests gives any guidance about how a teacher with a group of 12- or 13-year olds should choose which test to use. Presumably each test is slightly harder than the one preceding it but this is not explicit in the Manuals.

Presumably a test that goes to an 11th impression (Test E) and is still in use after some 26 years is meeting with some kind of consumer approval. It is unfortunate that the test constructors have not been able to quantify or evaluate the results of such extensive use in order to assure other potential users of the test's credentials.

A final worry about the poor standardization and validation of the tests is that common types of test bias such as sex bias and cultural bias may have been built into the tests and remained undetected.

English Progress Test E2

Reviewed by E. P. Duggan

Author: not stated
Publisher: NFER-Nelson
Distributor: NFER-Nelson
Age range: 11:00–12:09
1963 (T)
1971–72 (S)
1977 (M); 1979 (T) printings reviewed
Group test

Test content

Eight basic test-tasks are used: transformations of nouns to pronouns and infinitives to other verb forms; sentence writing; vocabulary (synonyms); word completion (spelling); punctuation; comprehension; language experience (proverbs, homonyms); organization of ideas (sentence-sequencing) giving 70 items altogether. Response requirements vary from one word to full sentences.

Purpose

The Manual (p. 2) states that the test is intended as a measure of foundation skills and not intended as a guide to English teaching. Additionally, it is said, scores will indicate which children are in need of remedial help in basic literacy. The test is intended to be diagnostic of the range and standard of English attainment in order to assist teachers in planning the nature and level of their approach to the teaching of English. These claims are perhaps a little extravagant: while those aspects of English outlined in the Manual are tested, the test is normative in intent. For the particular group tested standards might be established for the kind of tasks set by the test, but there must be some doubt that these do in fact act 'as means of determining pupils' readiness for more or less sophisticated work in a wide variety of curricula' (Manual, p. 2). However, the manual does say, 'It is not claimed that isolated practice at exercises such as those employed in the test itself will lead to greater real mastery of literacy skills' (p. 2). Agreed.

Some statements are a little naive, e.g. 'it is likely that the underlying ability factor is largely that of verbal ability' (p. 3). Not really surprising in an English Progress Test! What is surprising is that the word 'data' is used as a singular noun (Manual, p. 3).

Item preparation

No details are given, only that the present form of the test arose from item analyses of trial versions given to groups of about 370 pupils. No indication of numbers of items or trial versions employed prior to standardization, and no item sampling frame is referred to.

Administration

Test E2 is clearly intended for class teachers of English. The instructions are laconic and simple except for one sentence: 'All sources of information, pens, rulers and rubbers should be removed before work starts' (p. 4). The test is untimed, it is considered that most children will complete the test within 45 minutes. The format of the instructions and procedure follow the same pattern as for Verbal Tests BC and CD but are far more condensed.

Standardization

This was done in three stages in November 1971, October 1972 and June 1972, each in a different area—Midlands urban, Eastern rural and South-Eastern urban/rural. A sample of 8709 children (4416 boys, 4293 girls) in the age range 11:00–12:09 were tested, and the Manual curiously refers to all the children as being in junior schools. Standardized score conversion tables employ Lawley's method (see Introduction). Roughly equal numbers of boys and girls of the same average age were used in each of the three areas noted above. Girls' mean scores were statistically significantly higher than the boys' (0.1 per cent level), but separate norms are not provided. Although standardization data were based on the age-range 11:00–12:03, the test claims to cover the range 11:00–12:09 years. It must be presumed that extrapolation was performed for the extra 6 months, although not stated in the Manual.

Scoring

Instructions are simple and clear, but no guidance is given on checking total right and wrong answers or double marking, etc. The scoring key is well-laid out, with explanations, alternatives or permitted variations noted where appropriate. The key for items 46–52 is a little confusing, particularly for lay administrators, although some attempt has been made to clarify why alternative sequences to the one considered fully correct are permitted. It might have been better if this item had been constructed unequivocally. Boxes for recording score totals, age and standardized score are given on the front page of the test.

Reliability

This was computed using KR-20 from 'the answer pattern on 257 randomly selected test scripts from the standardization sample' (Manual, p. 3) with a value of 0.96. The standard error of measurement at 12:00 years is 2.91; at 11:00 it is 2.96 and at 12:09 is 2.94. The use of these values to form a confidence interval is explained.

Validity

None reported.

Interpretation

The pupils' performance, inferred from the standardized score, can be described in terms of relative standing within a single age group. Instructions on the use of the conversion tables (Manual, pp. 10-11) to determine each pupil's standardized score from his raw score are given.

General evaluation

The information given by this test about a pupil's performance in English is limited. In fact, it is difficult to understand what it conveys that any reasonable teacher of English could not ascertain in the normal course of lessons. The amount of subsidiary explanation in the marking key suggests that the test itself is not comprehensive or precise in relation to its intended outcome.

This reviewer spent a great deal of time analysing the various aspects of the test, which suggests that busy class teachers may not find it particularly apposite to their needs for diagnosis. The Manual is adequate; no undue or global claims are made for it.

Gap Reading Comprehension Test

Reviewed by Margaret Thurston

Author: J. McLeod; 'this edition' (M: 1970) prepared by Derek Unwin
Publisher: Heinemann
Distributor: Heinemann
Age range: 8–12 (Australian grades II to VII)
1965 (Australia)
1970 (M, T) (Great Britain); S not stated
1981 (M); 1980 (T) printings reviewed.
Group test

Test content

There are two alternative forms of this test: Form B and Form R. Each of the tests consists of a series of short passages of increasing difficulty (Form B has 7 passages; Form R has 8 passages).

The test adopts a modified cloze procedure in the presentation of the test passages. There are 44 gaps in the text of each test for the pupil to complete with his own response. These gaps are not at uniform intervals, each of the deleted words is replaced by a dotted line and the pupil writes his response on these lines.

Form B and Form R are alternative rather than parallel tests; they are meant to augment rather than duplicate each other. They are intended for children aged 8:00–12:00 years. A pupil may be given one or both of these forms to arrive at a reading age or reading quotient.

Purpose

The GAP test is a test of reading comprehension for children aged 8:00–12:00 years. The author claims that it is a more valid test of reading comprehension than completing questions based on a written passage because the 'only stimulus to which the child must respond is the reading passage itself; there are no extraneous questions to constitute an intervening variable' (Manual, p. 5). The pupils responses to the gaps in the text are then measured against the criterion of the responses of 'first class readers'.

Item preparation

The idea for the use of modified cloze to assess children's reading comprehension arose from an experiment to estimate the readability of children's books, using Taylor's (1953) cloze redundancy technique. 'This research centred round the "cloze" procedures in which words from a test are struck out at random and the readability of the test is defined by the ease with which a reader can supply the missing words. That is the readability varies as the redundancy of the text' (Manual, p. 8).

The GAP test was originally devised by Dr John McLeod, 1965. The passages were selected from a variety of sources ranging from early school readers to Winston Churchill's "History of the English Speaking Peoples", using the method outlined above. Approximately one word in ten was deleted and the selected items given to undergraduate students to complete. The material was then revised to include only those items on which such 'first class readers' were fully agreed. From this material two alternative tests were compiled; Form J and Form M. These two prototype tests were then given to children in the Gap State Primary School, Brisbane, Australia. The results of these trials were then compared with the results obtained on the Watts Reading Comprehension Test and the Schonell Silent Reading Test B. Correlations between the tests ranged from 0.72–0.82. The tests were then re-administered three months later to determine test-retest correlations and the effect of practice. As a result of these trials it was decided to use the same practice examples for both forms of the test so that the two tests could be administered simultaneously to adjacent children to eliminate the possibility of copying. The forms were then printed on different coloured paper: Form R in red and Form B in blue. These were then given to a second sample of University students to confirm the answers of 'skilled readers'.

Administration

This test is designed to be administered to a group of children at the same time. Each pupil will need an answer booklet and a pen or pencil. The red and blue forms are given out alternatively so that children next to each other are completing different forms. The Manual gives clear directions for the administration of the test. The pupils work through two practice examples with the teacher to ensure they understand what they have to do; the script is helpfully printed on the back cover of the Manual. Alternative answers are discussed and the 'best' answer obtained. The pupils are instructed how to alter an answer if they wish to do so. The pupil is then allowed 15 minutes to complete the test.

Standardization

The Manual does not contain a lot of detail about standardization. The tests were originally standardized in Queensland, Australia, on a stratified random sample of 2009 schoolchildren of Grades II to VII inclusive. Further trials were carried out on over 1000 children in schools in Aberdeen, Glamorgan, London and Suffolk to recalculate the 'scoring tables' (i.e. test score to reading age conversion tables) for use in Britain.

Scoring

A marking key is provided in the Manual. This gives one acceptable word for each gap. These words are based on the responses of 'expert readers' in Australia. A word is only marked correct if it occurs in the marking key. Incorrect spelling is not penalized but the word must be semantically correct. One mark is scored for each correct answer. Either one or both tests may be given to a pupil and the score converted to a Reading Age by using the three separate tables provided for Forms R, B or R + B. A pupil's Reading Quotient may be calculated using the Reading Age and employing the literal quotient or ratio method.

Reliability

Again, the details are meagre. Reliability was assessed by calculating the equivalence of Forms B and R within school classes. A correlation of 0.83 was obtained. The standard error of measurement for Forms B and R together (88 items) was estimated at 2.76 points.

Validity

The Australian evidence of concurrent validity using the Watts Reading Comprehension Test and the Schonell Silent Reading Test B for comparison are reported in the Manual. In Great Britain the results from GAP test were compared with results on the Schonell B test. An overall correlation coefficient of 0.73 was obtained; these data were obtained, it seems, from the standardization sample and may have been used to assist in recalculating the reading ages.

The author refers the reader to the work of Fries (1963) and Bormuth (1967) for the theoretical basis for accepting the GAP test as a test of reading comprehension.

Interpretation

Tables are provided in the Manual to convert the raw score obtained from Form B, R or B + R together to a reading age, then a reading quotient. No further advice on interpretation is provided.

General evaluation

The test is simple and quick to administer and as such will appeal to the class teacher, although it is not really designed to pick out the really good reader in the older age group. Most children seem to enjoy doing the test as it presents them with a realistic situation and is short. However, some teachers may not be keen to penalize children who respond with a plausible word which does not appear in the marking key. Particularly as this marking key is based on the responses of 'first class' readers in Australia over 12 years ago. There would seem to be a need for up-to-date trials of these tests in Great Britain to establish the responses in 1983 of the 'first class' reader.

References

Bormuth, J. R. (1967). Design of readability research. *Proceedings of 11th Annual Convention of the International Reading Association* **11**, p. 485.

Fries, C. C. (1963). "Linguistics and Reading". New York: Holt, Reinhart and Winston.

Taylor, W. L. (1953). Cloze Procedure: a tool for measuring readability. *Journalism Quarterly* **30**, 415–433.

Gapadol Reading Comprehension Test

Reviewed by Margaret Thurston

Authors: J. McLeod and J. Anderson
Publisher: Heinemann
Distributor: Heinemann
Age range: 7:03–16:11
1972 (Australia)
1973 (M, T); (Great Britain); S not stated
1979 (M); 1980 (T) printings reviewed
Group test

Test content

This test has two alternative forms Y and G. Each of the forms consists of 8 passages of writing, in which words have been omitted; two of the shorter pages are for practice only. The passages were taken from various sources including encyclopaedias, fiction and non-fiction publications. A modified cloze procedure is used. The gaps in the text are not at regular intervals; the gaps are indicated by broken lines; the number of dashes indicating the number of letters in the missing word. An answer box at the side of the text is provided for each missing word. Form Y has 83 gaps; Form G has 81 gaps. The pupil has to provide words to fit the gaps and write them on the answer box provided on the right hand page of the answer booklet.

Purpose

The Gapadol is a test of Reading Comprehension. It was designed to follow on from the GAP Test and is for use with adolescent children 'to identify their retarded and superior reading ability (Manual, p. 2). It can be used with children aged 7:03–16:11 years. As with the GAP Test the suitability of a pupil's responses is judged against that of 'first class readers'.

Item preparation

The Manual is very brief and refers the reader to the GAP Test Manual and to McLeod and Anderson (1970) for an explanation of cloze technique and item construction.

Administration

Each pupil needs an answer booklet and a pencil or pen. The two forms G and Y can be given simultaneously to alternate pupils to eliminate the possibility of copying. The tests may be used for successive assessments with the same pupil to help eliminate practice effect. Alternatively, the two forms of the test can be given on successive days to the same pupil, and the average score used to arrive at a reading age, the author claims this achieves a more sensitive and reliable measure of reading comprehension.

Details for administration are provided in the Manual. The pupils work through two examples together with the teacher and then complete the rest of the booklet by themselves. Each child is allowed 30 minutes to complete each test.

Standardization

No details of sample size, dates of trials, etc. are given in the Manual. The statistical information provided is presumably based on the original Australian population. The reader is again referred to the GAP Manual as 'similar techniques were used in the construction of the present-tests' (Manual, p. 2).

Scoring

A marking key is provided for both Forms G and Y. Only the words given in the marking key are to be scored as correct: a different word even if appropriate is not allowed. A pupil is not penalized for incorrect spelling, but the correct word must be intended. A pupil's score can be calculated on just one test or the average score of both tests can be used.

Reliability

The evidence of reliability studies is scant and those figures presented must presumably be based on the original Australian trials. Internal consistency coefficients and standard errors of measurement of individual scores are given for five different year groups from 7:03–16:03 years. They range from 0.84–0.93, median reliability coefficient 0.91, with the median standard error of measurement 3.47.

Validity

No information about any validity studies is provided in the Manual.

Interpretation

Two tables of norms are provided which are presumably based on Australian trials. Table 1 lists the norm for each age group and the 90th and 10th percentiles are said to indicate 'superior reading ability' and 'reading retardation' respectively. Table 2 converts raw scores to reading ages.

The tables are designed to assist teachers detect children who require special attention, however no further advice on interpretation or subsequent action is provided.

General evaluation

As with the GAP test the simplicity and ease of administration of the test will appeal to the teacher and pupil. Teachers who have used the test have been satisfied that it does indicate the above average and below average reader adequately with older junior and 1st and 2nd year secondary pupils. Teachers feel that it would assist the presentation of the test and help to eliminate the pupils confusion, if the words could be inserted in the text or alternatively the gaps and answer boxes numbered, as sometimes pupils have missed out whole pages. Also teachers may have reservations about not being able to allow a plausible answer if not contained in the marking key.

The original test, which has not been revised, was first constructed and published in 1972. The published tables of norms are now quite old and based on the original Australian trials. There seems to be a need to carry out more up-to-date trials based on a British population, if score interpretation is to be meaningful today.

Reference

Mcleod, J. and Anderson, J. (1970). An approach to the assessment of reading ability through information transmissions. *Journal of Reading Behaviour* 2, 116–143.

Gates McKillop Reading Diagnostic Tests

Reviewed by Margaret Thurston

Authors: Arthur I. Gates, Anne S. McKillop and Elizabeth Cliff Horowitz
Publisher: Teachers College Press

Distributor: The Test Agency
Age range: 6:06–12+ (US grades 1–6)
1962 (1st edition)
1979–80 (S); 1981 (M, T) (2nd edition)
Individual tests

Test content

This version is the second edition of a battery of tests first published in the US in 1962. It is made up of a battery of 15 subtests designed to assess a child's reading and writing skills. It is not intended that all children should be given all the tests or that the tests should be given in any particular order. The subtests include:

(1) Oral Reading—7 passages to assess the pupil's use of context, meaning and word form cues.
(2) Reading Sentences—4 sentences of phonetically regular words.
(3) Words: Flash—40 isolated words.
(4) Words: Untimed—80 words.

A section headed 'Knowledge of Word Parts; Attack' includes the following subtests:

(5) Syllabication—17 pronounceable two and three syllable nonsense words.
(6) Recognition and Blending—12 items of common word parts.
(7) Reading Words—phonetically regular, single syllable nonsense words.
(8) Letter Sounds.
(9) Naming Capital Letters.
(10) Naming Lower Case Letters.

Recognising the Visual Form of Sounds:

(11) Vowels.

Auditory Tests:

(12) Auditory Blending—15 words.
(13) Auditory Discrimination—14 pairs.

Written Expression:

(14) Spelling—40 words.
(15) Informal Writing Sample

There are two booklets to be used when giving the tests: 'Test Materials' and the 'Pupil Record Booklet'. The 'Test Materials' booklet if reusable and contains all the material to be read by the pupil. 'The Pupil Record Booklet' is needed for each pupil and is used by the teacher to record responses and errors, and by the pupil for spelling and informal writing. The teachers' Manual is needed for test administration, scoring and interpretation and is aimed to assist the teacher to decide which of the tests are appropriate for each individual child.

Purpose

This battery of tests is designed to provide a detailed profile of a child's reading and writing skills together with an assessment of a child's strengths and weaknesses in reading and related areas. They are primarily for use with children aged 6:06–12:00 years but they can be used with older children who are experiencing difficulty in learning to read.

Item preparation

A brief rationale for each of the test items and the skills they are designed to test is included in the Manual. There is no further information or theoretical basis for the selection and content of these particular subtests.

Administration

The battery of tests is designed to be given individually to pupils aged 6:06–12:00. They can also be used with older children experiencing reading difficulty.

The teacher needs the two booklets 'Test Materials' and 'Pupils' Record Booklet'. Full instructions for administration and recording responses and errors are included in the Manual. The reader is warned that any marked deviation from the directions given in the Manual will invalidate 'grade scores'. The pupils responses to the test items should be recorded accurately and fully. The Manual also advises that the tests should only be given when the pupil is in 'good physical and emotional condition for testing'. They recommend that testing should be carried out in a quiet secluded place.

Not all children need to do all the tests. It is the teachers responsibility to be able to assess which tests are necessary to give the required diagnostic information. The teacher makes a careful record of the pupil's responses and errors in the 'Pupil Record Booklet'.

Standardization

Details are brief. The tests for the second edition were given to 600 children in grades 1 to 6 in the Spring and Fall of 1979 and the Spring of 1980 in the USA.

These children attended 10 different schools. Sixty-five per cent of the schools were private; 35 per cent were public. The majority of the schools were in urban areas. Fifty-one per cent of the sample were male and the sample included Caucasian, Negro and Oriental English speaking pupils.

Scoring

A detailed guide for scoring and recording errors in the Oral Reading Test and Reading Sentences Test is included in the Manual. Grade score tables are provided for the following tests: Oral Reading, Words: Flash, Words: Untimed, Spelling. These tables convert raw scores into 'grade score norms'. These can in turn be rated as High, Medium or Low in relation to the child's actual age and grade. The subtest item scores are recorded on the first page of the pupil's record booklet.

Validity

The information is brief and mainly refers to the 'Oral Reading Test'. Correlation coefficients were obtained from children's scores on the Gates-McKillop and Horowitz Oral Reading Test and on the Gates-McGinitie (*et al.*) silent reading test. Comparisons were made at various grade levels. Correlations ranged from 0.68–0.96. Higher correlations were obtained with the younger children than with the older children.

Reliability

The test-retest correlation for 27 children on the Oral Reading Test was 0.94 (time interval not stated). Fifty test protocols for the Oral Reading Test were scored independently by two testers to obtain inter-judge reliability. Comparisons of the error classifications showed 94 per cent agreement for the first four paragraphs of 458 words and 91 per cent agreement for the final 3 paragraphs of 746 words. No information concerning other subtest reliabilities and intercorrelations is provided.

Interpretation

The Manual gives detailed guidelines for interpreting errors and test scores on each of the subtests. In the sections devoted to interpretation, grade norms, based on the original sample and trials, are provided for comparison and to help the teacher decide if a pupil's score is low, normal or superior for his age group. This allows the teacher to judge what particular skills in an individual are undeveloped, normal or superior and on the basis of this a programme of work can be planned.

The authors stress that these tests and scores are not meant to provide a comparison of one child with another but a means at arriving at a more comprehensive understanding of each individual and often further observation and investigation will be necessary to provide a complete picture.

General evaluation

This battery of tests does provide a detailed profile of a child's reading skills. However, as Pumfrey commented (1976), they do not include a test of reading comprehension; they rather concentrate on the mechanical, decoding aspects of the reading process. In the second edition of the tests the authors suggest a further test of silent reading should be given to the pupil. They recommend the Gates-MacGinitie Reading Test which measures a pupil's vocabulary and comprehension.

The evidence reported of standardization, validity and reliability studies is meagre and was carried out in the USA; as such it is difficult to relate the grade scores to the needs of children in British schools. However, this does not seem to be of great importance in this instance as the tests are primarily meant to be a diagnostic tool rather than comparative. It is the pupil's errors, and method of tackling the reading situations that is important, together with the teacher's interpretation and future planning.

The battery of tests takes at least one hour to administer for each child, therefore its usefulness seems to be mainly for the specialist teacher or the class teacher who requires more detailed and systematic information about particular children. It would certainly be very time-consuming to administer to a whole class and it is difficult to see how, for the majority of children, it would yield any additional information to that already collected by an experienced teacher in her day to day record keeping and observations.

The Manual is rather difficult to follow and needs to be read very carefully. However, it does contain useful guidelines and information on error analysis and interpretation of pupil responses.

References

Pumfrey, P. (1976). "Reading Tests and Assessment Techniques". Sevenoaks: Hodder & Stoughton.

Graded Word Spelling Test

Reviewed by C. J. Phillips

Author: Philip E. Vernon
Publisher: Hodder & Stoughton

Distributor: Hodder & Stoughton
Age range: 5:00 to Sixth Form pupils and college/university entrants
1976 (S); 1977 (M) (no test form)
1981 (M) printing reviewed
Group test

Introduction

This is a test of spelling vocabulary. In the last half-century few British spelling tests of other types have appeared (Lambert, 1951; Fleming, 1936; Peters, 1975). Choice of spelling vocabulary tests has been largely limited to instruments devised and standardized forty years ago or more; the only exceptions are Test 11 of the Standard Reading Tests (Daniels and Diack, 1958), for which no standardization data are reported, and the SPAR tests of Dennis Young (q.v.). Vernon's test 'is unashamedly old-fashioned, being similar to the Burt and Schonell tests' (Manual, p. 3). It is a normative scale for the assessment of ability to write English words correctly, when they are orally presented. Compared with the interest in reading and arithmetic, the second of the three Rs has been a very neglected field for decades. Although spelling is only part of written expression, some teachers acknowledge its importance; they will wish to assess objectively pupils' spelling skills from time to time. In the investigation of specific problems of literacy learning, educational psychologists require a reliable modern instrument for assessment of spelling ability, which is often an important diagnostic sign. Cognitive psychologists are giving greater attention to the subject than hitherto (Frith, 1980).

Content

Vernon's test has improvements over its progenitors. There are many homophones and near homophones in the language; numerous examples occur in Schonell's Graded Word Spelling Tests A and B (1932; 1950); for example, 'son', 'four', and 'pair'. Vernon's test has uniquely few such words. In his Spelling (Graded Vocabulary) Test, Burt (1921) wrote that the dictated words should be enunciated clearly and moderately slowly 'but are not to be enshrined in an illustrative context' (1921, p. 316). Experience showed that the stimulus word needs to be 'embedded in an explanatory sentence' (Schonell, 1950, p. 69). Vernon provides the sentence to accompany each word.

The test is based on 'the reasonable assumption that children or students who perform well or badly on a fairly short list of arbitrarily selected words would be likely to perform similarly on any other words at the same levels of difficulty'. Hence it is like other long established graded word tests of reading and spelling. Those by Burt and Schonell had ten words per year; this test has 'approximately six words for each age group from 6:0–18:0 years and over', so extending the range of attainment to 'the level of well-educated adults' (p. 4), but reducing the sample of words for each attainment year. Experience of use will show if that sample is sufficient.

In criticism of the graded word spelling test by Schonell, it was recommended that 'future authors . . . would do well to select their words not from adult vocabulary counts, but from words actually used by children of different ages in free writing' (Moseley, 1974). Of the first twenty words in Vernon's test, 19 occur in the high frequency list of the spoken vocabulary of infant school pupils (Burroughs, 1956) and/or in the list by Hildreth (1948).

Item preparation

Words were chosen 'to sample a wide variety of spelling difficulties'; words which 'appear in widely used standardized tests were avoided'. The 'main basis for choice . . . was the Macmillan Spelling Series . . . supplemented by more difficult words chosen at random from a dictionary'. Selected words were 'then divided into thirty-six tests of thirty words each . . . Three parallel tests were designed at each (age) level'. From testing of pupils in Birmingham and in Calgary, Alberta, 'eighty words were chosen which covered the whole age range as evenly as possible' (p. 5).

Standardization

Cross-sectional standardization of the finished test was carried out in 1975 in Canada and on '3313 pupils in . . . schools in the county of Northamptonshire', England, 'which was considered to be likely to be reasonably representative of the country as a whole'. Schools of average level for their area, and average classes in each school were tested. The author draws attention to uncertainty about the representativeness of the English samples at secondary school level 'where different types of schools . . . and different classes within schools tend to vary widely in levels of achievement' (p. 12); he invites results from future users. 'The classes tested for standardization purposes were spread over a wide age range, so that numbers per age group were only moderately large, and sometimes doubtfully representative' (p. 15).

Administration

The test is suited to group and to individual testing. For the former, the tester must judge from the median age and the scholastic standard of the group, the set of words to be used. Guidance is given in a table (p. 6). Except for children under eight years, requiring fewer words, 40/48 words are dictated in about 30 minutes. It is not a speed test, but a maximum of about 15 seconds is allowed for the writing of each word, following its presentation in the form: '(The next word is) *cat*. The *cat* has five kittens. (Write the word) *cat*'. Initial instructions to the testees include the request to write with separate letters, not joined, but 'words written in cursive script are accepted . . . provided they are sufficiently legible to be scored'. The norms apply only to written words, not to oral responses such as one might require for some disabled children. It will often be the case with groups that supplementary testing of easier or harder words is needed for a minority of low or high scoring subjects. A useful alternative is provided in two tables (p. 11) for extrapolation of adjusted scores from raw scores.

Individual testing proceeds by the traditional method of establishing a basal level and testing up to a 'ceiling', which is defined as ten errors, not necessarily consecutive. With many seven-year olds the criterion of ten errors is probably too stressful. No materials are needed other than the Manual. Group testing, especially of younger children, is facilitated by the preparation of widely ruled and numbered answer sheets.

Scoring

Each correctly spelled word counts '1'; no partial credits are given. Credit is not given for correct spellings which are not the word dictated, or not the correct part of speech. The total score is to include the number of easier words omitted. Generally the test is not suitable for group administration to pupils before the last term of infant schooling. Many children at that age are still prone to graphical errors (incorrect orientation of letters). Perhaps one should not penalize such mistakes when there is no doubt of the writer's intention—not possible, of course, on confusions such as 'b' and 'd'—but the author gives no guidance on this point. Mixtures of upper- and lower-case letters should be accepted.

Norms

Norms for the interpretation of raw scores are expressed as Spelling Age. The tested words are in established order of difficulty. 'The percentage of correct responses to each word were tabulated at each available age level, and approximate . . . spelling ages were interpolated, i.e. the age at which 50 per cent . . . might be expected to pass the word' (p. 5).

Maximum score on the test is 80; the highest spelling-age is 15:10, at the score of 60. The user should be aware of the considerable range of spelling skills in average mixed classes, at least in English junior schools. The spread is usually much wider than that of comparable tests of reading. This is a feature of the present test, as it was of the Schonell tests. Distributions of spelling ages tend to be positively skewed. For these reasons, it is 'desirable to include words ranging from, say, three years below to three years above the average age of the class to cover the full range of ability likely to be present' (p. 4). Although there is no empirical evidence, it is likely that teachers are less aware of the spread of spelling abilities in classes than they are of other basic school subjects. Deviation Quotients are also provided (i.e. standard scores with mean 100 and standard deviation 15), at intervals of five points from 70 to 130, for two-monthly age levels from 5:06 to 17:06+ for English subjects. There are separate norms for Canadian pupils between 6:00 and 8:05, above which age there were found not to be significant differences between the two countries.

Reliability

Internal consistency is reported as about 0.94, based on corrected split-half coefficients from samples at Grade 4 and Grade 7. This measure of reliability may be an underestimate; it is based upon 'scores of class groups . . . more homogenous than a representative year group' (p. 15). The standard error of measurement of a Spelling Quotient is 3.7 points.

In a longitudinal study of pupils in a number of Coventry schools, this reviewer found (report in preparation) a correlation of 0.87 between the results of group testing in first-year juniors (mean age 8:2) and individual testing 12 months earlier; the subjects were 153 indigenous children.

Test use

Yule *et al.* (1981) include the Vernon spelling test in a report on the relationship of the WISC-R to educational attainments for 87 school leavers in the Isle of Wight. From the same principal author (Yule *et al.*, 1982) came data on the relationship of the Vernon test with other tests of ability and school attainments in a sample of 160 London school children aged 6–12 years; their results show a significant positive correlation between age and spelling quotient.

General evaluation

The Graded Word Spelling Test appears 40 years after the author's Graded Word Reading Test. Psychologists and others will be grateful for his continued interest in devising basic tools for educational assessment, with characteristic thoroughness and flair.

References

Burroughs, G. E. R. (1956). "A Study of the Vocabulary of Young Children". (University of Birmingham, Institute of Education, Monograph No. 1) Edinburgh: Oliver and Boyd.

Burt, C. (1921). "Mental and Scholastic Tests" (2nd ed, 1947). London: Staples Press.

Daniels, J. C. and Diack, H. (1958). "The Standard Reading Tests". London: Chatto and Windus.

Fleming, C. M. (1936). "Kelvin Measurement of Spelling Ability". Glasgow: Gibson.

Frith, U. (Ed.) (1980). "Cognitive Processes in Spelling". London: Academic Press.

Hildreth, G. (1948). A comparison of the Dale, Dolch and Rinsland word lists. *Journal of Educational Psychology* 39, 40–46.

Lambert, C. M. (1951). "Seven Plus Assessment: Spelling". (The Northumberland Series). London: University of London Press.

Moseley, D. (1974). Some cognitive and perceptual correlates of spelling ability. *In* "Spelling: Task and Learner" (B. Wade and K. Wedell, Eds). Birmingham: University of Birmingham. (Education Review Occasional Publications Number Five).

Peters, M. L. (1979). "Diagnostic and Remedial Spelling Manual". (Revised edn). London: Macmillan Educational.

Schonell, F. J. (1932). "Essentials in Teaching and Testing Spelling". London: Macmillan.

Schonell, F. J. and F. E. (1950). "Diagnostic and Attainment Testing". Edinburgh: Oliver and Boyd.

Young, D. (1976). "SPAR Spelling and Reading Tests". London: Hodder and Stoughton.

Yule, W., Gold, R. D. and Busch, C. (1981). WISC-R correlates of academic attainment at 16:06 years. *British Journal of Educational Psychology* 51, 237–240.

Yule, W., Lansdown, R. and Urbanowicz, M-A. (1982). Predicting educational attainment from WISC-R in a primary school sample. *British Journal of Clinical Psychology* 21, 43–46.

The Holborn Reading Scale

Reviewed by Ann Forrester

Author: A. F. Watts
Publisher: Harrap
Distributors: Harrap; The Test Agency
Age range: 6:06–11:00 years
1948; reissued and copyrighted in 1980
1980 (M, T); 1982, reprinted; S not stated
Individual test

Test content

The scale consists of 33 sentences which are claimed to be 'arranged in order of difficulty, both as regards their mechanical elements, and as regards their comprehensibility' (Manual, p. 1). In addition, a set of related questions are supplied for the examiner to read out. For example, the child is asked to read: 'The dog got wet and Tom had to rub him dry'. The examiner may then ask: 'It says that Tom rubbed the dog because it was . . . *what?*'. The child is asked the related questions with the sentences still in view. The first 16 questions are to be answered orally, with one or two word responses; the later ones, which include mainly multiple-choice questions, can be answered in writing if preferred.

Purpose

The test is intended as a normative measure of the child's progress in mechanical word recognition, and of ability to comprehend the sentences read.

Item preparation

No information is given about the basis on which the sentences were constructed, chosen, and subsequently modified. The sentences were tried out with children between the ages of 5:06 and 11:00 years, but the numbers of children used and the nature of the trial group are not specified. The order of items was altered during these trials, and further verbal modifications made during a 'preliminary standardization', but again, no details are given about what this involved, or the rationale adopted. It is implied that the resultant items increase in difficulty (mechanical and comprehension) at a uniform rate. No information is given about how the comprehension questions were formulated or tested, e.g. for ambiguity or for psycho-linguistic level.

Administration

The test is untimed. Materials needed are the sheet of sentences, the test Manual, and, if written answers to the comprehension questions are sought, pencil and paper for the child; a blackboard is then suggested for the examiner's use. No reference is made to categories of potential users.

A number of queries could arise due to the instructions being insufficiently full and clear. The ceiling for prompting is fairly obviously the ceiling for testing, though not stated. Prompting is not explained: should the examiner merely supply the word or help with word-building? The point at which the comprehension questions should be given is not indicated either; presumably they are interspersed between the child's sentence reading. When seeking written answers to the multiple-choice comprehension questions, the examiner is instructed to show the possible choices on a blackboard. The test, so far described in terms of individual administration, seems now to refer to a group situation. Perhaps the comprehension questions can be given separately, after all the sentences have been read aloud, if preferred. No instructions are given regarding starting points, or regarding discontinuing the comprehension questions, though later questions are considered unsuitable for children under 7 years of age.

Standardization

The standardization is notable for its lack of reported detail. The time of the testing is not mentioned, and the target population is not specified; the latter can only be deduced in reverse from the information provided about the sample population.

The standardization sample was drawn from 30 schools of different types, and this is claimed to ensure a representative sample. No details about sample selection are given. The sample covered children between the ages of 5:06–10:06, grouped by 6 month age spans. Numbers in each group varied from 181 to 393. These details, however, are quoted in reference to the scores for mechanical reading. It is not clear whether standardization studies were also carried out for the comprehension scores, but it would seem that comprehension scores were merely appraised in relation to the mechanical reading scores, and not assessed in their own right.

The average number of sentences acceptably read by each age group was determined and plotted. The result was approximately linear, and considered justification for a set of age norms in which there was a regular increase with age, in the number of sentences a child was expected to read, i.e. one further sentence every 3 months. There is no report of this being justified statistically, and the explanation of the discrepancies between observed and expected scores, is statistically naive.

The norms are presented in terms of age scores, but no indication is given of the range of scores found in any one age group, nor of their distribution. No guidance is given on whether the age norms are to be applied to comprehension, as well as to mechanical reading, though the Manual itself, in discussion, refers to actual numbers of sentences comprehended.

Scoring

The fourth word the child is unable to name without help, sets the reading age score. Age norms are provided in 3-month intervals, opposite each sentence. The examiner reads off the child's reading age from the sentence in which this fourth unread word occurs. Instructions are given for the dubious practice of converting the reading age to a reading quotient.

Scoring for comprehension is less clear. No correct answers are supplied, and no attempt to correct for guessing is applied to the multiple-choice questions. The questions are either answered correctly or incorrectly, but no further transformation of the raw result is explained. No kind of record form is supplied to aid the examiner in scoring or making notes.

Reliability

No reference is made to any reliability studies; the subject of reliability is not discussed at all.

Validity

No validity studies are reported either, though the test does have a measure of 'face validity', i.e. on the surface it would appear to be assessing a child's ability to read with a measure of understanding.

Interpretation

The system in which raw scores are converted to reading ages makes it difficult to determine the significance of below or above average performances at any given age. The spread of scores is affected by various factors, not least by the non-equivalence of the skills to be learnt at different stages, e.g. the simple sound-blending skills of the infant reader, compared to the word attack skills of an upper junior. Wide variations at one age level may be normal or insignificant, but of considerable significance at another. The conversion of reading ages into reading quotients by a straight proportional calculation, disregards this issue too. Similar significance cannot be attributed to reading quotient regardless of age, any more than to chronological age-reading age discrepancies, and it would be erroneous to seek educational interpretations of fluctuations in the quotient.

The Manual invites the examiner to compare scores for mechanical reading and comprehension. Lower scores for comprehension are reported to be usual, which makes nonsense of the age norms as a measure of comprehension. Even comparing numbers of sentences read and comprehended, no interpretation of discrepancies can be made unless the distribution of scores in the population are known to have similar statistical characteristics (means and distributions): in this case they do not, the means being different for a start. No educational significance can be attached to minor differences in test scores. The Manual acknowledges this, but can give no guidance on the reliability of larger apparent differences, or about their degree of abnormality.

The educational interpretations offered throughout the Manual, should be viewed with due scepticism and caution. They are largely applied unnecessarily to score patterns which are explicable purely in statistical terms, and although some inferences have plausibility in their own right, they cannot be justified from the test data.

General evaluation

The reading test is easy to administer, but the Manual is not sufficiently explicit in its instructions. The multiple-choice comprehension questions add some complications. The child must remember all the possible choices, or be able to read enough of their written presentation, to give them due consideration. (Guidance is not given on how much the child may be helped by spaced reiterations, etc.) Indicating choice by writing (a), (b), (c) or (d) introduces the possibility of perceputal errors being attributed to lack of comprehension. It would be preferable too, if the instructions in the Manual were not interspersed with discussion passages.

The discussions reflect the out-dated thinking underlying the reading scale. The scoring system and the related concepts of age scores, true quotients (in contrast to deviation quotients), and the retardation measures derived from them, have since been found wanting. The sweeping explanations of test results are of a very general nature, giving little detailed suggestion of where, how and why they have affected the individual child's attainment; presumed obvious, they are not questioned, but have a facile ring today.

The actual sentences seem somewhat stilted in places, reminiscent perhaps of the style encountered in 'ancient' school readers. It is very likely that children's reading and general language experience has changed sufficiently over the intervening years, since 1948, to alter the familiarity and difficulty level presented by the sentences and their vocabulary. The accuracy of the norms, when referred to the children and the educational system of today, must be queried, both as a normative measure, and as a reflection on changing standards (the language today probably develops differently; the standards are not necessarily worse or better).

Being a sentence reading test, scope is given for the application of a range of reading skills, phonic, sight vocabulary, syntactic and semantic. Such use of context is not possible in the various word reading tests, and to this extent, the Holborn permits a fuller assessment of a child's likely performance in a natural reading situation, and so gains in face validity. There appears, however, to have been no attempt to grade the sentences in terms of this range of skills, nor have issues such as word frequency, vocabulary and concept development, been considered in any detail. Adjustments were made on a more overall pragmatic basis.

In conclusion, it can be said that the test has the benefit of a degree of contextual reading, but is is doubtful how much reliance can be placed on the norms, since these are outdated, and the test items are difficult to evaluate, the whole scale lacking rigour in its item analysis and standardization, and being devoid of reliability and validity studies.

Hunter-Grundin Literacy Profile

Reviewed by Caroline Gipps

Authors: Elizabeth Hunter Grundin and Hans U. Grundin
Publisher: The Test Agency
Distributor: The Test Agency
Age ranges: 6:06–8:00   (Level 1)
            7:10–9:03   (Level 2)
            9:00–10:00 (Level 3)
Published about 1981
Group test (most scales)
Individual test (spoken language scales)

Introduction

Following some general comments, I will deal with each of the constituent parts of the Literacy Profile in turn.

Test content

Each of the three levels contains group tests of reading for meaning, spelling, free writing, an individual spoken language test and some attitude to reading measures. The reading for meaning scale is the main item of the battery and may be used in isolation from the others.

Purpose

'The purpose of the profile is to enable schools and teachers *to monitor individual pupil's progress* and to further this process in several important language and literacy skill areas through *diagnostic teaching*'. The profiles provide an effective, yet simple and easily administered 'system of monitoring' of the kind called for in the Bullock Report's first principal recommendation: 'a system of monitoring should be introduced which will employ new instruments to assess a wider range of attainments than has been attempted in the past . . . On the basis of the test results it is possible to assess how much progress each child has made in basic reading, writing and spoken language skills, and to determine what should be the priorities as regards further work in these areas, and what level of material and tasks will suit each individual child best' (Level 1 Manual, pp. 1–2).

Item preparation

Nowhere is there any information given on item preparation nor information on early trials, piloting, etc.

Administration

The tests are designed for use in normal classrooms by teachers with whole classes of children. Materials required are all provided in the test packages, all that is needed in addition is a pencil for each child. Some of the tests are timed, others not. Generally, administration is quite straightforward and good details are given in the Manuals for administration, including precise wording for examples and so on.

Standardization

In general the information on standardization is very limited and patchy. We are told that for Level 1 the data used for the development of norms for calculating standard scores were based on the results of over 2800 children in 70 participating schools in 23 LEAs in England, Scotland and Wales. For Level 1 we are told that the schools represented city, small town and rural areas covering a wide socio-economic range. However, there is no information given on the number of, for example, boys as opposed to girls, the date of standardization, the length of time over which the tests were given; nor is there a breakdown of the SES of the sample (Level 1, Manual, p. 5). For Level 2 we are told that the norms were based on the test results of over 2400 children from 50 schools in 21 LEAs in England, Scotland and Wales and again no information is given on a detailed breakdown of the sample (Level 2, Manual, p. 5). For Level 3 standard scores and norms were based on the test results of over 2400 children from 50 schools in 21 LEAs—again no information is given on the ages of the children, sex or distribution of SES (Level 3, Manual, p. 4).

We will now deal with each of the sub-tests in each level in turn.

(1) Attitude to Reading Scale

Level 1

Content

This attitude scale boils down to one item 'How do you like reading books?' embedded in a list of five questions, none of the others relating to reading. For example, the first one is 'How do you like going to bed?' There is one practice item—'How do you like eating ice-cream?—and the child has to indicate degree of like or dislike by marking one of five faces showing various states of like or dislike.

Purpose

'The purpose of the attitude scale is to assess the children's attitude to reading as an activity compared to a selection of other activities' (Level 1, Manual, p. 6).

Scoring

The child's attitude to reading is expressed simply as A, B, C, D or E depending upon which funny face he marked, A being 'like very much', E being 'dislike very much'.

Standardization

'There are, naturally, no norms for children's attitude to reading, or to any other activity for that matter. The purpose of this assessment is mainly to identify those children whose attitude to reading is negative'. (Manual, p. 8).

Reliability and validity

No information. One can only comment on this so-called subtest that it is so gross, and uninformative as to be less than useless. To make a technical criticism, one must also say that one item can hardly be called an attitude scale, nor can it have much reliability.

Level 2

Exactly as Level 1.

Level 3

The scale does not exist at this level.

Interpretation

The authors say that where the children's attitude to reading is shown to be negative, story books of all kinds and all levels of difficulty should be available; indeed, they suggest that books out of favour with educationists such as Enid Blyton, comics, etc. should also be available to children because children enjoy them.

(2) Reading for Meaning Scale

Level 1

Content and purpose

It is a cloze procedure test, based on a story about Grump, the dragon. There are 45 places where the text is broken and the child has to indicate which of four alternative words is the appropriate one to fill the gap. The authors have obviously tried to embed the test in the text but have ended up with what looks like a daunting and rather confusing double page. Although the words themselves are not difficult the task, and its presentation, do seem so for top infants; indeed, as the Manual itself says '. . . successful results on a cloze reading test indicate that the pupils are using valuable reading strategies involving context cues, prediction or psycho-linguistic "guessing and checking" skills, . . .' (Manual, p. 12).

Reliability and validity

There is no information at all on the number of children involved in the reliability and validity exercises. Is one supposed to assume that it is 2800 children?

Reliability

The KR-20 value is given as 0.98.

Validity

We are told that the reading for meaning scale has 'obviously high construct validity', i.e. the task the children are asked to perform is very similar to the task involved in the real life situation of reading meaningful text. I would disagree with this; the page looks very difficult, off-putting to an adult and bears no resemblance to what one would do normally in a reading task. We are also told that the task is, for example, much more realistic than that of reading isolated words (with which one must agree) or reading isolated sentences (which is arguable). Another measure of validity is provided by the correlations reported between the reading for meaning scale and six well known reading tests. These are given as Neale (0.87), Holborn (0.84), Southgate Group Test 2 (0.82), Schonell GWRT (0.81), Young's Group Test (0.80) and Burt WRT (0.74). These figures, however, must be considered meaningless in the absence of any information on age of the children concerned, size and breakdown of the sample. We are told, however, that 'these data show that reading for meaning Level 1 measures, to a great extent, the same aspects of reading ability as other tests using meaningful texts (Neale) or sentences (Holborn, Southgate and Young), but that it also assesses word recognition, as witnessed by the high correlation with Schonell, the most commonly used word reading test at this level' (Manual, p. 10). We are told that the standard error of measurement for an individual child is 2.5 standard score units—again, with no information as to how this figure was obtained. 'In summary, it can be concluded that reading for meaning Level 1 provides a highly reliable and valid measure of reading ability in a way which is unusually "economic" in view of the relatively short testing time and the use of group testing procedure' (Manual, p. 10).

Scoring

This is perfectly straightforward and good, clear instructions are given also for converting test scores to age-related standard scores and reading ages.

Interpretation

Guidance is given for reading diagnosis. The Manual identifies three reasons for possible low scores:

(1) A low rate of reading, i.e. a slow reader.
(2) Failure to use sufficiently wide context.
(3) Failure to read with even a minimum of understanding.

The Manual points out that children with roughly the same total score can show evidence of different kinds of weakness in their reading. Their future reading tasks should then be chosen with a view to helping them overcome that particular weakness. According to the authors, giving pupils practice in cloze technique is a useful way of improving reading skills.

Evaluation

If among other things, the layout of the test were improved it could be a useful tool. However, the information on reliability and validity is so scanty as to make the whole test questionable. The diagnostic information supplied to teachers is limited and could only have limited value.

Level 2

Content

As Level 1 but involving a longer passage called Baba Yaga the Witch, with 55 spaces where the child has to choose the correct word from four alternatives. Instructions for administration and marking are the same as for Level 1.

Reliability and validity

Exactly the same comments apply as for Level 1. The KR-20 coefficient is given as 0.97. We are told that the scale has high construct validity because it is like a real life task. For validity, correlation coefficients between scores on this test and six well-known reading tests suitable for 8-year olds have been calculated: these are given as Holborn (0.86), Schonell GWRT (0.79), Young's Group Test (0.82), Burt's WRT (0.75) and NFER Reading Test AD (0.78). 'These data show that reading for meaning Level 2 measures, to a great extent, the same aspects of reading ability as other tests using meaningful text (NFER, Holborn, Southgate and Young), but that it also assesses word recognition, as witnessed by the high correlation with Schonell, the most commonly used word reading test at this level'. The authors conclude that this scale provides a highly reliable and valid measure of reading ability in a way which is unusually economic in view of the short testing time and the use of group testing procedures.

Interpretation

The authors tell us that this is regarded by many teachers as the most important test of the battery and that it represents a significant improvement on tests like Schonell and Burt. However, the diagnostic help provided by the authors is extremely limited. 'Children who are performing below the average on this scale need as much help, encouragement and instruction as the teacher can provide, including the assistance of any teacher aides and parent helpers'.

There are then suggestions that children help each other, that they have books read to them, that cassettes of stories are available and that all the notes about improving attitude to reading are relevant to improving reading ability. Then the authors say that for backward readers there should be an emphasis on reading meaningful prose that is likely to appeal to the child, words should not be taught in isolation, the child should be encouraged to use all the cues available to find the meaning of an unknown word, they should try to learn to guess unknown words, should be given plenty of prose, reading material should not be limited to basic reading schemes which are usually very dull. This is the sum total of the diagnostic information for teaching reading.

Level 3

Test content and purpose

This is a similar task as that for the earlier levels but again it is an even longer passage, about Rusty the Robot, and contains 60 places where the child has to choose the correct word from four alternatives.

Reliability and validity

The Kuder Richardson reliability coefficient is given as 0.97. For validity, correlation coefficients were obtained with five well-known reading tests suitable for 10-year olds: these are given as Holborn (0.83), NFER AD (0.81), Schonell GWRT (0.79), Young's Group Test (0.76) and Burt GWRT (0.76). The same comments about reliability and validity apply as for Levels 1 and 2.

Interpretation

The information given is again exactly the same as for levels 1 and 2, but with slightly different examples which relate to this story rather than the other stories.

(3) The Spelling Scale

Level 1

Content

The spelling test is done by dictation. The test sheet contains a short story with 20 gaps; the teacher reads aloud the story including the missing words and the child's task is to write the missing word into the gap.

Purpose

'The spelling scale assesses children's ability to spell common English words in a situation where the words are defined, not only by the way they sound when dictated, but also by the context of the story in which they appear. This eliminates, as far as possible, the risk of misunderstanding about the words to be written, a risk which can be considerable if words are dictated out of context' (Manual, p. 13).

Reliability and validity

Kuder-Richardson reliability coefficient is given as 0.93 'which is a very high value for a test of 20 items'. Again no information is given on sample size, etc. We are told that the construct validity of this test as a measure of spelling ability is 'obvious' since it engages children in the writing of common English words in a meaningful context. We are told that no comparison can be made with other tests because there are none designed for this age range in this country, but the authors conclude that the spelling test gives a highly reliable and valid measure of a child's ability to spell words that are within his vocabulary.

Interpretation

The Manual gives examples of types of error that indicate: (a) the child has a spelling problem but not a reading problem; (b) the child has a spelling problem along with a reading and language problem. The Manual emphasises that for remediation attention should be focused on reading development and not on spelling development *per se*.

Evaluation

As spelling tests go, and there are very mixed views about whether spelling tests are useful, this may well be quite a useful task. It is certainly much better to have the test words embedded in context than just tested individually in isolation.

Level 2

Content and purpose

The same as for Level 1 but a different story is used which is slightly more difficult and the child has to spell 22 instead of 20 words.

Reliability and validity

KR-20 is given as 0.90 which, we are told, is a high value for a test of 22 items. Construct validity is again obvious. As in Level 1 there were no British spelling tests with which a comparison could be made, so instead the authors correlated scores on the spelling test with the number of words correctly spelt in the free writing test. For Level 2 this correlation is 0.84 as it was for Level 1, i.e. children's ability to spell words prescribed in the spelling test correlates highly with their ability to spell the words they themselves choose to use in their free writing. Again, there is no information on the numbers involved in these reliability and validity calculations. Instructions, scoring and conversion to standard scores are exactly the same as for Level 1.

Interpretation

There are some slightly more direct suggestions here, starting with the degree to which spelling should be considered a problem, particularly at this age range. The sort of suggestions are that lessons in phonics which were perhaps too abstract for younger children may now assist spelling as much as reading. If a child is struggling with reading and writing then it is wise to defer emphasis on spelling improvement until adequate skills in reading and writing are evident. It is important to teach the alphabet. Ability to consult a dictionary is a most important skill, children should be encouraged to correct their own first drafts and to correct those of other children.

Level 3

Content

Uses the same technique as the previous levels, but with a different story with more difficult words and there are 25 of them.

Reliability and validity

KR-20 is 0.92 which again we are told is a very high value for a test of 25 items. The same comments apply about construct validity and about not being able to make comparisons with other spelling tests. Comparison of spelling scores with spelling performance on the free writing test showed a correlation of 0.81 at this level. Instructions, scoring, conversion to standardized spelling age and spelling diagnosis are as for Levels 1 and 2.

(4) Free Writing Scale

Level 1

Content

Ten minutes is allowed for the child to write a piece on 'On the Way to School'. There is no preparation given beyond the instruction that the teacher wants the children to write about the 'things they see and the things that happen on the way to school', since preparation of the sort normally carried out before children write stories at this age would make standardization impossible.

Purpose

'The Free Writing task makes it possible to assess various aspects of children's writing in relation to examples of writing typical of children at different ability levels'.

'There exists no objective test that can give a standard score for free writing, comparable to standard scores for reading and spelling. Free writing must always be assessed on the basis of *expert judgement*, and the best available expert is the individual teacher. The judgement can, of course, be based on children's writing in informal situations, where they can choose the topic freely and spend as much time as they like on their writing but in order to assess how the writing of any particular group of children compares to that of a large, representative sample of children it is necessary to obtain samples of writing in a more formal, standardized situation' (Manual, p. 17).

Scoring

Guidelines are given to the teacher for making a rating on four aspects; legibility, fluency, accuracy and originality. These are rated in grades A to E. Examples are given of pieces of writing which have been judged at levels A to E. (NB These are all from first year junior children whereas early on in the Manual attention has been concentrated on using the profiles at the end of the infant school). These, however, are overall grades for each piece of writing, not for the four separate aspects, and the teacher is not given any indication of how she might set about combining the four different grades to one overall one. Indeed, it seems most unlikely that many teachers will bother with the scoring technique as it would be time-consuming to master.

Reliability and validity

The Manual points out that the reliability of teacher judgements in this sort of assessment will depend on the way in which the teacher does the scoring. The

Manual suggests that by working together teachers will come to share standards of judgement. We are told that the validity of the free writing test is entirely of the construct validity type, that is if the aim is to assess children's ability to write whatever they may wish to communicate, then any task that initiates written communication must be a valid task. The authors concede that whether a totally free task is more valid than a restricted task depends mainly upon which aspects of writing ability you wish to assess, and how much emphasis should be put on originality and creativity. No guidance is given to the teachers as to what emphasis should be put on originality and creativity given the restrictive task set. They point out that many children find a totally free task much more difficult than a slightly restricted one as it does not give them any help to get started.

Evaluation

This is nothing more than an old-fashioned, unprepared, timed essay but with a detailed marking or scoring system. It seems unlikely that teachers will want to spend the time necessary to master the scoring system and to co-operate with other teachers in order to produce a reliable measure.

Level 2

Content and purpose

This is exactly the same task as in Level 1, including the ten minute rule. Strangely enough, the scoring instructions, i.e. the instructions for teacher ratings are exactly the same as for Level 1. One would have thought that different standards would have been set for the grades A to E for 8–9 year olds than for 7–8 year olds.

Reliability and validity

As for Level 1.

Interpretation

This scale, we are told, involves a brief essay on the same topic each year so that the pupils' work can be compared and progress monitored. If progress from one year to the next is not evident, then the teacher should review the curriculum in this field of classroom work and allocate more time to it. This is the main diagnostic point for this section. Other points made are that more enthusiasm can be generated for free writing by the introduction of regular class magazines, newspapers, etc. and also the extraordinary suggestion that children should always be encouraged to write a second and even third draft of any piece of free writing after the teacher has given help and advice. This seems to be a sure way of discouraging young children from going freely into free writing.

Level 3

Content and purpose

Yet again, this is exactly the same task as for Levels 1 and 2. The children have to write an essay about the things they see and what happens on the way to school. The slight difference is that at this age level they are asked to consider as well the things that *might* happen on the way to school. Ten minutes are allowed and exactly the same instructions are given for teacher ratings on exactly the same four aspects. Again the same grades are given for the same levels of writing although the children are now three years older than when they did Level 1.

There is, however, a very slight difference in the grading for fluency in that a different number of words is used for the different criteria for Level 3 than was used for Levels 1 and 2: e.g. Grade A at Level 3 is a story of 150 words or more, whereas at levels 1 and 2 it is a story of 100 words or more.

Reliability and validity

As for Levels 1 and 2.

Interpretation

As for Level 2. NB In the Appendix examples are given of graded pieces of free writing on the essay task, these are all for end of second year junior pupils, and again the overall grades are given rather than those for the four aspects.

(5) Spoken Language Scales

Level 1

Content

There is a large picture of an adventure playground, the child's task is to look at the picture and tell the teacher what is going on in it. The test is not timed but the Manual tells us that it should only take about three minutes for each pupil (this test, of course, has to be given individually).

Purpose

'The spoken language scales included in the literacy profiles help to focus the teacher's attention on a number of important aspects of language development, and provide a simple and practical means of keeping records of the progress of individual children' (Manual, p. 21).

Administration

It is suggested that the child's response be recorded on a tape recorder so that marking can be carried out later and relaxed during administration of the task, but this is the only piece of equipment needed apart from the picture which is supplied with the test. The script suggests verbal instructions from the teacher to the child: 'Start by saying: "I want you to look at this picture and tell me what is going on in the picture", or *words to that effect*'. It seems most strange that at this point they should provide instructions which are, as it were, optional. They do, however, say that the wording the teacher decides to use should be the same for every pupil; it would seem simpler to have told the teachers to stick to the wording in the Manual.

Scoring

The teacher is given guidelines for rating the piece of speech on confidence, enunciation, vocabulary, accuracy and imagination, within each of these five aspects giving a grade from A to E. Examples are provided of pupils' responses to the spoken language test, there are ten examples from pupils 'about to leave the infant school or just beginning junior school'. They are given as examples ranging from very poor to very good and are ordered according to the vocabulary aspect, however, they are not assigned any grade and thus the examples seem of limited value, but 'the examples given here are particularly useful for teachers of classes with a limited range of variation. For example, in a class with highly "verbal" children the teacher may not appreciate that even those children who are below average for the class are above average for their age group. Our examples should help the teacher to assess her own pupils in the proper "perspective"' (Manual, p. 22). There is no suggestion as to what to do with the child who scores at various levels in the various aspects of spoken language.

Reliability and validity

No information is given.

Level 2

Content

Exactly as for Level 1, including the scoring instructions.

Interpretation

We are told that too little time is allocated in schools for the development of skills in spoken language, and yet this is the skill we use most commonly throughout life. Self-confidence is highly dependent on the ability to communicate easily and children should be given as much opportunity as possible to practice spoken language skills. 'Many areas within the curriculum can benefit from a problem-solving approach based on small group discussion'. We are then told that the topic cannot be discussed fully in the Manual but we are referred to three books which should be of assistance to those who would like to have more information and ideas.

Level 3

Content

Exactly the same task as for Levels 1 and 2. The only slight difference in the scoring is that slightly different criteria are used for the vocabulary grade, e.g. Grade B at Level 3 is when the pupil uses some 75–90 different words, while at Level 2 it was 60–90 different words. Otherwise there is absolutely no difference between the scales. Again, there is no information on reliability or validity.

General evaluation

Diagnostic teaching

Rather confusingly, in the Manuals for Levels 2 and 3, though not for Level 1, there are three pages devoted to diagnostic teaching. In fact the script is exactly the same for both Levels 2 and 3. We are told by the authors that use of the profiles is intended to make it easier for teachers and heads to 'monitor individual pupil progress throughout the primary school years, from chronological ages of about 6:06–12 years. This is a far wider age band than is actually mentioned in the information about the individual scales and seems to be a rather grandiose statement. The Manual goes on, 'In the case of reading, comprehension and spelling, this monitoring is an accurate measure, since these tasks are standardized, and a large population of similar children have enabled us to give you precise information about how well your individual pupils are progressing'. Really, one must question this sort of comment. The Manual tells us also that the profiles can help teachers and heads compare the progress of their pupils as a group with the progress of similar children throughout Britain.

Attitude to reading scale

Perhaps it has some general interest.

Reading for meaning

Looks a difficult task for children of the lowest age but could be a useful test; it is the only one which provides any information on reliability or validity and does provide standardized scores.

Spelling

This is an adequate test, if indeed one wants to use a spelling test. It also provides age-related scores.

The reading for meaning and the spelling tests are the only ones which have a certain amount of (albeit very limited) diagnostic information, and the only ones to change from Level to Level.

Free writing task

This is of highly questionable value, the emphasis being on the scoring system which class teachers are unlikely to want to use with their own children given the time involved.

Spoken language scales

The least well prepared and presented apparently. There is no information on reliability or validity, no practice example suggested for the child who may be completely put off by the use of a tape recorder, no diagnostic suggestion and no examples of pieces of work in different grading categories.

All in all one wonders why the authors bothered to publish anything other than the reading for meaning and spelling tasks. Presumably it is because they are committed to a notion of literacy which involves attitudes, speaking and writing as well as reading and spelling, but they have rather spoiled the value of the reading and spelling tasks by including these poorly developed scales in other skills.

Finally, though information is given on reliability and standardization for some of the scales information on the samples involved is nowhere near detailed enough, nor is the information on test development.

Learning Through Listening *

Reviewed by A. Stibbs

Authors: Andrew Wilkinson, Leslie Stratta and Peter Dudley
Publisher: Macmillan Education (for Schools Council)
Distributor: Macmillan Education
Age ranges: 10–11 years (Test Battery A)
                      13–14 years (B)
                      17–18 years (C)
1976 (M, **T); S not stated
1980 (M) printing reviewed
Group tests

Test content

There are three batteries of tests, each battery intended for a single year-group. Each battery is presented as an audio tape of spoken material (both spool and cassette forms are available). Nearly all the 'testees' instructions are on the tape. Pupils' multiple-choice answer sheets for all the batteries are made from a set of spirit duplicator masters which are bound separately from the Manual.

Battery A has tests to measure five different 'elements of listening comprehension' (Manual, p. 1) (for the status of these 'features' see the section on Validity below). These elements are the abilities to understand content, contextual constraints, phonology, register and relationships between speakers. Evidence of these understandings comes from correct choices of comprehension-type answers, missing pieces of conversations, meanings conveyed by emphases, phrases in odd registers and statements about the relationships between speakers, respectively. Battery B follows the same pattern, and so does Battery C except that it omits the 'phonology' tests (an omission which is unexplained in the Manual, but justified in QL ("The Quality of Listening", p. 45) by the authors' feeling that all the 'phonological skills' tested in A and B would have been mastered by 17+.

Each battery has about 70 items and, with a 'changeover break' in the

---

* Schools Council Oracy Project Listening Comprehension Tests.
** 'Manual' refers to the Teachers' Manual for "Learning Through Listening". Information has also been taken from the book "The Quality of Listening" by the same authors, sponsor and publisher. This will be referred to as 'QL'.

middle, each takes about an hour and a half to administer. The recordings simulate material from pupils' home and school life. As might be expected from the authors of the urbane, wordly and sometimes facetious QL, the recorded material is up-to-date and humorous.

Purposes

In the Preface to the Manual, the authors claim that the tests can be used diagnostically to 'measure problems and levels of understanding, perhaps in relation to other language abilities', to 'add another dimension to existing examinations in English', and as 'developmental materials'. They also add, without disapproval, that they have been used as a test of understanding for 'English as a second language' and/or 'English as a foreign language' speakers. These proposals for use of the test are ingenious, but seem to lack conviction, perhaps for the reasons implied in General Evaluation below.

Item preparation

There is no information about item preparation in the Manual, but there are hints in QL. For some items, spontaneous conversations were recorded, transcribed, scripted, tidied, and re-enacted for recording (p. 34). For other material the authors were driven (one suspects with little reluctance) to creative scripting. For Test 5 in Battery A (as 'register test') material was 'substantially transcribed' from actual BBC news bulletins (p. 51). A recording of part of a real university lecture was used for a content test in C (p. 90). Chapter 6 of QL describes how the pilot tests were evolved through discussion then modified in the light of trials and teachers' conversations. The impression is given that preparation was, eventually, scrupulous and systematic.

Administration

Booklets are made up from the spirit masters. Testees are equipped and disposed as for an examination. All the instructions for answering the questions are on the tape, so this aspect of test procedure is standardized. The Manual gives clear instructions to users on how to ensure that the tape is audible to all candidates. Each battery requires the use of two separate booklets and both sides of one cassette or spool, with a changeover period in-between.

Standardization

Following trials in small samples with each of the batteries, Test Battery B was standardized on 1152 3rd year secondary-school pupils. A conversion to standard scores with a mean of 100 and standard deviation of 15 is provided.

No details of how these pupils were selected are given in either the Manual or QL. No attempt is made to provide norms for test batteries A and C. The authors are a little coy about the reasons for this (in QL) but, since B was designed first, one can infer that the explanation is that the time and money of the Schools Council Project ran out. For reasons suggested in General Evaluation, below, the omission is not serious.

Scoring

The Manual shows how marking keys can be made to fit over the testees' duplicated answer sheets. As the answers are multiple choice, there are few interpretation problems; the marker is instructed to ignore answers which hedge bets. Battery C, in accordance with the greatest sophistication of its intended takers, has items which explicitly invite testees to provide more than one right answer. The instructions ensure that this causes no problems for testees or markers, though it does make negative scores possible.

For Battery A, raw scores are used. For Battery B, raw scores are converted to standardized scores, mean of 100 and a standard deviation of 15, using a table provided in the TM. For Battery C raw scores for the five tests are converted to a score ranging from -100 to $+100$ but not standardized.

Reliability

For each battery an opportunity sample (between 130 and 180 children) was selected from which reliability and validity coefficients were calculated. The reliability of the total score within each battery was estimated by the split-half method and figures were obtained for A, B and C of 0.78, 0.83, and 0.84 respectively. No test-retest reliability coefficients were established.

Correlations between tests in the same battery were in the ranges 0.28–0.49, 0.01–0.44 and 0.04–0.49, for A, B and C respectively. Test-total score correlations were in the ranges 0.52–0.66, 0.51–0.67, 0.70–0.81. To the lay reader of the Manual, the inter-test correlations may seem low. The Manual (and QL, for that matter) gives no guidance as to whether these low figures should be treated as a matter of congratulations to the test-designers (because they show the degree to which the different tests *discriminate* between putative separate listening factors) or whether they should be treated as a matter for commiseration (because they show the different degrees to which some of the tests succeed in measuring a putative *general* listening factor). An emphasis in the Manual suggests the latter: 'the test battery is designed to produce a score which represents performance on the *complete battery*' (p. 4). On the other hand, the clarity with which listening is analysed (in QL) and the fact that the authors bothered to establish inter-test correlations suggest that the differences are important. The mention of 'diagnosis' in the preface to the Manual is ambiguous: it could refer to diagnosis in which listening was an element (along with other language modes) or to diagnosis of particular strengths and weaknesses in particular elements within listening.

Validity

Since, as the Manual's preface claims, the tests are unique, there could be no comparison of their results with other tests of listening comprehension in order to establish their concurrent validity. Similarly, it is fair to assume that teachers would be insufficiently practiced in thinking about listening comprehension to provide opinions of the tests which would establish their content validity. So the authors seem to have decided that their own informed consensus would provide a face validity which was a sufficient basis. However, the authors did give other tests to the small samples of children referred to under Reliability. For 4th-year junior children, Battery A had correlations of 0.45 and 0.41 with Richardsons' Simplex Intelligence Test and Schonell's Silent Reading Test B. For the 3rd-year secondary children, Battery B had correlations of 0.60 with Heim's AH4 Group Test of General Intelligence, and correlations of 0.75, 0.73, 0.35 and 0.28 were found for the four parts of Bate's Secondary Reading Test, namely, vocabulary, comprehension, speed and speed again. Among the sixth-form and FE students, Battery C gave correlations of 0.54 with AH4 and 0.72 with the NFER Senior English Test. QL also reports a comparison of scores on the test with scores on a personality test: no significant correlation was found.

The authors do not discuss (in either the Manual or QL) possible interpretations of these correlations, although the difference between the correlations of test scores with the different parts of Bate's reading test provoke speculation about whether performance on, specifically, 'language' tests would be a better predictor of performance on these listening tests than would performance on either an intelligence or a reading test, and also whether some sort of 'speed of listening comprehension' might have made a useful contribution to the batteries.

General evaluation

Listening, as the authors implicitly admit, is a social interaction in which visuals, kinesic, and proxemic cues usually play a part. The authors admit that these sorts of cues can play no part in their tests (QL, p. 29), but they minimize the importance of this as when they try to make a virtue of the necessity of not having vision in an analysis of a TV advert. Since the tests were published, video-taping has become easy and commonplace: if the tests were revised now, video-taping should be exploited to make them more life-like—just as audio-taping was exploited to make these tests more life-like than they would have been if they had used, say, dictation.

Another quibble is that the tests ignore accents (though QL raises the problems they cause, pp. 42–43). An 'element of listening comprehension', a test for which it would have been within the wit and gusto of the authors to devise, is the ability to understand a variety of regional accents without being thrown by unfamiliarity with them, prejudice for or against them, or stereotyped assumptions about the meaning they convey.

On the surface, a more serious question about the test concerns the treatment of listening as a collection of separable factors or skills. Some mention has already been made of this under Reliability above. In reality, listening is a whole task involving intuition, social experience, and general contextual knowledge, never separable elements, far less multiple choices. In QL the authors admit the drawbacks of a separate skills approach (p. 65) symptomatically in the context of discussing the *teaching* of listening, a discussion with assumptions which might seem to undermine the relevance of the tests. The context of that admission is symptomatic for the same reason that the criticism is serious only on the surface: the tests seem to have a covert teacher-training function which is more important than the overt pupil-testing function. Where an analytical approach to *testing* may have misleading results, analysis may be helpful in *thinking* about listening because the categories are rungs in a ladder which can be kicked away once it has been climbed. The balance of content in QL (less than half of which is directly about the tests) together with many remarks within it (exemplified below) suggests that the design of the tests was a front behind which the authors could use their Schools Council commision to think out, write up, and disseminate a valuable model of listening comprehension. "The Quality of Listening" is as good a textbook on listening—indeed on language as communication—as I know; it is terse, elegant, witty and down-to-earth. This 'report' of the Project, rather than the tests which were its more obviously practical outcome, is what should reach teachers, so that their consciousness about listening is raised to the point where they can make informed, comprehensive and discriminating judgements about, and exercises for, their pupils' listening, using everyday classroom material. As the authors say, 'the great value of the tests (lies) in their "backwash" effects in the classroom—the developing of an awareness of the features and functions of the spoken language'.

The tests are probably as good as could be conceived in this unexplored field where standardized testing is at best premature and more likely fundamentally inappropriate. The test items are illuminating examples of general points in an excellent textbook on language as communication especially in the oral and aural modes. They are possibly the price which had to be paid for that book.

But the effective, if not official, importance of the tests in the Project's outcome is well conveyed by the qualification to measuring and emphasis on understanding in the last sentence of QL—a book which teachers would do better to buy than the tests:

'(Listening) can be analysed; it can, if necessary, be measured; and it certainly needs to be more fully understood'.

London Reading Test

Reviewed by Neville Bennett

Authors: Working Party of Teachers and ILEA Research and Statistics
    Group
Publisher: NFER-Nelson
Distributor: NFER-Nelson
Age range: 10:07–12:01 (4th year junior); 10:11–12:04 (1st year secondary)
1978–1980 (M, T); S not stated
Group test

Text content

Parallel forms of the test are provided each containing three passages of increasing level of difficulty. Levels of difficulty are based on the assessment of commonly used textbooks in ILEA (Innder London Education Authority) secondary schools, using the Flesch Readability Formula (see, e.g. Gilliland and Merritt, 1972). Comprehension of the first and second passages is tested by the cloze technique. Words are deleted from the passage at regular intervals and children must supply the missing words. 'If the child fills about 90 per cent of the gaps correctly he can read the passage unaided; if less than 75 per cent of the gaps are filled correctly the material is too difficult' (Manual, p. 5).

The third passage is designed to stretch the more able children and here comprehension is tested by a series of questions covering the whole range of comprehension skills following Barrett's Taxonomy of Reading Comprehension (see, e.g. Clymer, 1968). Since the passages are of a known level of difficulty predictions can be made about the child's ability to cope with the material to be encountered in secondary school.

Purpose

The test was constructed at the request of members of the ILEA Central Consultative Committee of Headmasters and Headmistresses who were concerned with the problem of communicating information about children's reading attainments on transfer from primary to secondary schools. The main purpose was thus to produce a 'survey/screener' test which could be administered in familiar surroundings. The scores are designed to provide information on children's reading attainment and patterns of ability and to indicate those children who may need remedial teaching in secondary school. Parallel forms are provided in order to allow alternation of the forms used year by year.

Item preparation

Several passages were analysed from the most commonly used first-year secondary-school texts in English, History, Geography and Science using the Flesch formula. This gives a Reading Ease Score range of 100 (very easy) to 0 (very difficult). The range in these texts was from 49 to 96 (Neale Reading Age equivalents of 11.8 years down to 7.7 years). The three passages in each form of the test were therefore written to cover this range. The first passage is the easiest and the third the most difficult. Thus the child who can only just cope with the first passage is likely to experience difficulty with most of the secondary school texts.

A rationale for the use of cloze procedure and the Flesch formula is provided in Appendix 2 and 4 of the Manual. The Barrett Taxonomy is described in Appendix 3 but no reason given for its adoption.

A group of six teachers wrote the test in conjunction with the ILEA Research and Statistics group but no information is provided on the choice of passages or pre-standardization trials. However, it is recorded that the passages were written with ILEA's multi-racial population in mind and test items were constructed which did not handicap children from any one cultural background.

Administration

A practice test is first administered to familiarize the children with cloze procedures. The main test is untimed but one hour is recommended. It should be undertaken under normal classroom conditions without previous notice. Instructions to teachers are clear and unambiguous.

Standardization

Each form of the test was standardized twice with independent samples in the last term of junior school and the first term of secondary school. This was carried out to make allowance for any possible fall-off of attainment over the summer break. For each standardization both national and ILEA samples were used.

The National Foundation for Educational Research provided the national sample. For this ten LEAs were chosen and twelve schools in each LEA were selected from the DES list. Each sample of primary and secondary children numbered 5000 but only Form A was standardized on the full sample. Form B was tested on 1000 children and standardized by calibrating it against Form A. The ILEA primary school sample was obtained by a stratified random technique. Fifty schools were used to provide two samples of approximately 1000 children. The secondary school sample was constructed by matching samples according to the percentage of children in the three Verbal Reasoning (VR) groups accepted by secondary schools. Schools were selected to provide two samples whose VR group percentage compositions were the same as that of the year group. Twenty schools provided two samples of approximately 1000 children.

Norms are provided separately for fourth year junior and first-year secondary children. Separate sex norms are not provided. Analysis of raw scores indicated the superiority of girls but, with the exception of one analysis, these were not statistically significant. The date of standardization is unstated.

Scoring

With cloze techniques there can be many acceptable answers. Acceptable alternatives 'guided by statistical and other considerations' are therefore provided in the marking keys. If the child's response is not included in these keys then it is deemed incorrect. However, an incorrectly spelt but recognisable word is marked correct. A general rule is that if in doubt mark incorrect. Scoring procedures are clear and extensive and include a section on how to calculate the reading quotient, and the relationship between standardized scores and percentile levels.

Reliability

The only reliability measure provided is for internal consistency (KR-21) which was found to be 0.95 for the ILEA sample and 0.93 for the national sample. No sample size is provided nor is there a separate reliability measure for junior and secondary children. The reliabilities of cloze procedures and the Flesch formula are not evaluated.

Validity

Only concurrent validity is discussed. Several of the schools involved in standardization had tested their pupils with other tests during the Summer term. Those scores were correlated with those derived from the London Reading Test. The samples were small (44 to 293) and probably unrepresentative and show a median correlation of 0.80 with such tests as Daniels and Diack Test 12, Neale, Gap and Schonell. These findings were interpreted as being 'high enough to indicate a measure of concurrent validity but low enough to reassure us that the test may be measuring something more than the traditional tests do' (Manual, p. 60). What that 'something more' might be is not considered.

Interpretation

The guide to interpretation is limited to the use of the test for screening purposes. It is suggested that 35 be regarded as the critical raw score, i.e. 'all children scoring less than 35 points should be individually assessed by a remedial teacher on entry to the secondary school' (Manual, p. 56). It is further suggested that for all children the raw and standard score be passed on to the secondary school together with any other useful comments.

A warning is given that the test's powers of discrimination are concentrated at the bottom end of the distribution. As a result there is inadequate discrimination between children scoring well above average. It is claimed that such scores are valid but that care should be taken if scores are being compared between groups containing a large percentage of children whose performances are above average.

General evaluation

The development of the test represents an attempt to provide valid information on a significant educational problem—the difficulties some children experience reading and comprehending secondary-school texts. A screening device based on the difficulty levels encountered in such books, using the Flesch formula as a comparative tool, is thus, at face value, a valuable addition. It may prove to be so but as yet there is insufficient data on aspects of validity. Content validity is assumed instead of being ascertained. A factor analysis might, for example, have been able to establish the match between item content and the underpinning model, i.e. Barrett's Taxonomy. This might also have shed some light on what the London Test measures which is different from other tests. Also since the major claim is that the test predicts how well children cope in secondary schools a measure of predictive validity could have been expected. Given the high concurrent validity the question of differential predictive validity of the London Test in relation to other tests must be raised.

The test does offer a raw criterion score to identify children at risk although this too may change with experience. It is perhaps regrettable that the only implication to emanate from score interpretation is that at-risk children should be tested yet again in secondary school.

The use of the test as a screening device holds distinctly more promise than that as a survey instrument. Although standardization would appear adequate the lack of discrimination in the upper half of the distribution is a major drawback.

References

Gilliland, J. and Merritt, J. (1972). "Readability". London: University of London Press.

Clymer, T. (1968). What is reading? Some current concepts. Reprinted in Merritt, J. and Melnik, A. (Eds) (1973). "Reading: Today and Tomorrow". London: University of London Press.

Macmillan Diagnostic Reading Pack

Reviewed by Anne S. Hawkins

Author: Ted Ames
Publisher: Macmillan Education
Distributor: Macmillan Education
Age range: 5:00–9:00 ('reading ages')
1980 (M, T)
Group test

Test content

There are 28 tests or check-lists within the package. They include a wide range of reading skills as follows: knowledge of key words, letter matching, matching upper/lower case letters, visual memory (recognition and reproduction), transcription of sounds, sound value of letters, auditory discrimination, auditory memory, blending 2/3-letter words, phonic readiness, final consonant blends and consonant digraphs and initial consonant blends, consonant and vowel sounds, consonant blends and digraphs, spelling regular 2/3-letter words, reading strategies, long vowel and vowel digraphs, vowel digraphs, application of structural analysis, identification of root words, suffixes –s, and –ed and –ing, spelling words with short vowel and consonant blends and digraphs, syllabication, spelling regular single-syllable words.

These items are distributed as appropriate to developmental stages across reading ages 5–6 years, 6–7 years, 7–8 years and 8–9 years.

Purpose

The test is intended to be integrated within a teaching programme and to form part of an on-going diagnostic process. The teacher is encouraged to go beyond the formal one-to-one diagnostic testing procedures to a less formalized diagnostic/intervention approach based on group activities. The teacher would not be able to adequately test all children regularly on a one-to-one basis. Group testing will enable the teacher to interact more effectively with all of the pupils, and bring about more remediation even though the teacher does not at first have the results of all the tests for a given child. The group sequential test process permits the teacher to provide some individually relevant work to correct weaknesses as they are uncovered.

The materials have been devised for use in an on-going programme by the teacher. The remarks at the foot of p. 10 of the Manual recommending their use by an external agency as diagnostician in a one-to-one situation rather than the teacher are therefore rather surprising and a little ambiguous. It is possible that 'third alternative' should read 'first alternative' on the penultimate line. Otherwise, the sentiment expressed here seems to contradict the purpose stated throughout the Manual. I am not convinced that external diagnosticians would want to use these materials as they stand for they do not appear to be designed in a way which would easily fit into one or even a series of one-off diagnostic sessions, and rarely is there sufficient interaction between external agency and classroom teacher for a child to be 'treated' by both with this integrated form of diagnostic/intervention programme. The same might be less true if the 'external agency' was a specialist remedial teacher operating extensively within the school. However, the suggestion in the Manual is that these materials were first and foremost designed for the purpose of training and encouraging the *class* teacher to structure the teaching more appropriately, based on guided observations and testing preferably in a *class* situation.

Item preparation

No details are given in the Manual concerning the selection of the individual test or observation items, other than those which are implied by the nature of the linguistic tasks. There is a brief reference to one small study concerning the hierarchical nature of the test process whereby a short-cut may be taken by the teacher on the grounds that 'if a pupil can spell phonically regular words, the same pupil will *probably* be able to blend similar words'. This notion is developed in the test programmes outlined for teachers in the forms of flow-charts for each of the reading-age stages whereby the testing logic is presented as a series of diagnostic decisions with action indications. The selection of test materials by the teacher for a particular pupil will be guided by prior diagnostic decisions and that pupil may or may not encounter all parts of the testing package.

Administration

As has been stated, the tests are not time restricted. They are to form part of an on-going programme of diagnosis and intervention by the class teacher. A major feature of the materials is the attempt to train the teacher to become a reading diagnostician. The Manual therefore must teach the teacher! The development of reading skills being of the complexity that it undoubtedly is, then the Manual has a difficult task of conveying rather technical and specialist ideas to relatively lay persons. The instructions are detailed but it will take most teachers some time to internalize them for use in individual let alone group situations. This may put some teachers off the 'do-it-yourself' approach. I suspect that many teachers would find administering the tests easier if they had been able to study the materials in a work-shop, in-service or initial-training setting initially.

Prior to using these tests, the teacher must establish approximate reading-ages for the pupils. A range of suitable group reading tests are recommended.

Standardization

These tests are diagnostic profile/intervention programmes. They are not standardized.

Scoring

For most of the tests, the score is merely a matter of counting either the numbers correct, or the numbers of errors. A 0–10 conversion scale is provided for each test so treated and a Profile Graph is then completed by the teacher, so that she can fairly readily see the low-spots in a pupil's abilities. The instructions are adequate and the response sheets are clearly laid out. There is guidance given for cases where the teacher must make judgements concerning necessary action.

Reliability

No reliability studies are reported.

Validity

No validity studies are reported. Copious references are supplied to research in the areas covered by the test which may serve to establish content validity.

Interpretation

There is much attention paid to the interpretation of the results in the Manual, and relevant references are supplied with each test area. It will be remembered that one of the purposes of this test package is to educate the teacher in diagnostic and remediation techniques. Extensive guidance is featured in the Manual with suitable cautions, for example, that which categorically states that the test does not provide a spelling programme. This is backed up with a reference to an alternative source of such a programme should the results on this Macmillan test indicate that a pupil's difficulties may lie in that area.

Similarly, practical hints on the sequencing in the tests are given to prevent a child being wrongly diagnosed as having difficulties on what are in fact skills of a secondary nature to more fundamental aspects.

It is, of course, always possible that a teacher will overlook such cautions, and this is a shortcoming which must be inherent in any attempt to provide a do-it-yourself programme of this kind.

General evaluation

This package gives the impression of being an ambitious programme which will only be adopted by the more dedicated teachers. I feel that the concept is admirable but that initial or in-service training would be necessary for most teachers to use it to its full potential. The demands it makes on the user are considerable.

The materials seem to be well-presented and the Manual is very detailed with a great many avenues of further exploration highlighted for the teacher.

It would have been interesting to hear of the use of this package in the classroom. There is only a superficial and impressionistic description of teachers' reports on their experiences in using the programme. It is impossible to evaluate the programme adequately in the absence of research findings concerning its use.

Moray House Junior English Test 5

Reviewed by E. P. Duggan

Author: The Godfrey Thomson Unit, University of Edinburgh
Publisher: University of London Press
Distributor: Hodder & Stoughton
Age range: 8:06–10:06
1967 (S); 1970 (M, T)

No revisions apparent
Review copies dated only 1970 (M, T)
Group test (restricted)★

Test content

There are seven practice items and 90 test items. These are of the multiple-choice type requiring the children to fill in blanks, underline words or sentences or insert punctuation marks. The items deal with comprehension of prose passages, sequences of words and phrases; opposites, adjectives, adverbs, conditional clauses, tenses, plurals, rhyming words and punctuation. The test is well graded in difficulty and the balance and variety of content is adequate.

Purpose

JET5 has no stated purpose, but is presumably diagnostic. The test appears to be for classroom use only (cf. MH ET41 which, according to its Manual (p. 8), '. . . has been in private use amongst Education Authorities since 1966').

Item preparation

There is no report of the origin of the items, item sampling frame nor of any early trials.

Administration

The only materials required are sharpened pencils (plus a reserve held by the supervisor) and the test booklets. The test is timed and requires a minimum total time of 70 minutes, made up of 15–20 minutes for the practice test, a 10–15 minute interval and 45 minutes for the test proper. For the practice test a blackboard is required on which the supervisor illustrates the response requirements of the test, e.g. word in brackets, underlining *one* word or phrase, fill in gaps, etc. The examples are left on the board during the test proper. The instructions are adequate, simple and clear.

Standardization

The test is designed for a target population of children aged 8:06–10:06. The

---

★ Available to schools with the permission of the local Chief Education Officer.

Manual states: 'It is similar in construction and administration to the two previous tests in the series, JE3 and JE4' (p. 9). The test was standardized in 1967, presumably by Moray House, on scores obtained by one complete year group of 12 247 children in one large county authority. No details of the standardization sampling other than the above are given. Lawley's method (see Introduction) was used to produce the conversion table. Separate norms for boys and girls are not given, but a sex difference is reported of 7.8 points of raw score favouring girls, equivalent to about 4.6 standardized points.

Reliability

The Manual gives no details of the reliability of the test.

Scoring

The instructions for scoring stress the need for independent checks on the marking of each script, to follow the marking key without deviation and where indicated in the key, to ensure that spelling is correct. One mark is awarded for each correct response. If the method of answering is wrong and the content of the answer is correct, credit is given. The scoring key is spaced to facilitate page marking. The record of the child and summary sheet for marks, accurate age and EQ are placed on the front sheet of the test booklet. Instructions for transforming raw scores to standardized scores ('English Quotients') are given.

Validity

Correlations with MH Verbal Reasoning Test 5 and MH Arithmetic Test 5 were 0.89 and 0.83 respectively for a random sample of 201 children from the standardization group.

Interpretation

Guidance on the use of the raw score conversion tables is clearly outlined, covering all possible scores for the test at intervals of one month in the age-range defined for the test, and are easy to use, giving the EQ as indicated above. Users are cautioned against undue extrapolation below the minimum and above the maximum ages defined, but gives guidance for doing this for ages up to 3 months below or above the defined test age limits.

General evaluation

The test appears to have face validity and is generally well-graded. Users should have no difficulty in following the guidelines laid down in the Manual. The content of the test is reasonably up-to-date. The absence of reliability data should not be due to its age (1967 standardization), but perhaps a satisfactory value is implied by the authors' experience with earlier tests in the series (MH JET3 and MH JET4).

Moray House English Test 41

Reviewed by E. P. Duggan

Author: The Godfrey Thomson Unit, University of Edinburgh
Publisher: University of London
Distributor: Hodder & Stoughton
Age range: 10:06–11:06
1966–68 (S); 1968 (M, T)
No revisions apparent
1979 (M) printing reviewed
Group test (restricted)*

Test content

There are 115 test items. These are of the multiple-choice type requiring the children to fill in blanks, underline words, phrases or sentences, and so on. There is a good variety of content. The items deal with comprehension of prose passages, sentence completion, spelling, word order, adjectives, tenses, plurals, word definitions, rhyming words and punctuation. The balance of content is adequate. The test is well graded in difficulty.

Purpose

ET41 has been used since 1966 to determine selection for grammar schools and to control promotion to other post-primary courses for the age-group stated.

Item preparation

No report is given of the origin of the items, item sampling frame, nor of any early trials.

---

* Available to schools with the permission of the local Chief Education Officer

Administration

The only materials required are sharpened pencils (plus a reserve held by the supervisor), and the test booklets. The time required is 40 minutes. The instructions are adequate, simple and clear.

Standardization

Designed for a target population of children 10–12 years old, the standardization was based on the raw scores of 4381 boys and 4267 girls from three English Education Authorities—one county and two boroughs (the same sample was used to standardize Arithmetic Test MHA41). The norms were prepared using Lawley's method (see Introduction). A sex difference of 5 points in favour of girls was found in the standardization group, equivalent to about 2 points of standardized score. The Manual (p. 9) reports that the size of this difference varied considerably from one area to another.

Reliability

A KR-20 coefficient of internal consistency was calculated using a random sample of 201 scripts drawn from one area. After controlling for the effect of age, the value was found to be 0.97.

Scoring

Instructions for marking in both this test and the Moray House Junior English Test 5 (q.v.) are identical. They stress the need for independent checks on the marking of each script, to follow the marking key without deviation and where indicated in the key, to ensure that spelling is correct. One mark is awarded for each correct response. If the method of answering is wrong and the content of the answer is correct, credit is given. The scoring key is spaced to match up with responses in the test booklet. Alternative correct responses are noted although these are rarely allowed.

Instructions for transforming raw scores to English Quotients (EQs) are given. The record of the child and a summary sheet for page marks, accurate age and EQ are placed on the front sheet of the test booklet.

Validity

Intercorrelations between ET41, 'a verbal reasoning test' on the same day and MH Arithmetic Test 41, 14 days later with 2065 children, were found to be 0.91 and 0.86 respectively. No interpretation of these data is given.

Interpretation

Use of the raw score conversion tables is clearly outlined, covering all possible scores for the test at intervals of 1 month in the age-range defined for the test, and are easy to use, giving the EQ as indicated above. Users are cautioned against undue extrapolation below the minimum and above the maximum ages defined, but gives guidance for doing this for ages up to 3 months below or above the defined test age limits.

General evaluation

The test appears to have face validity, is generally well graded and suitable for the purposes indicated in the Manual. The items of the test are mostly technically competent. Given the Manual, users should have no difficulty in following the guidelines laid down. The content of the test is reasonably up-to-date, i.e. modern use of the test should maintain the internal consistency indicated.

Moray House English Test (Adv.) 2

Reviewed by E. P. Duggan

Author: The Godfrey Thomson Unit for Educational Research
Publisher: University of London Press
Distributor: Hodder & Stoughton
Age range: 12:06–13:11
1953–56 (S); 1961 (M, T)
No revisions apparent
1967 (T) printing reviewed
Group test

Test content

The test items cover the following: comprehension of prose or poetry passages, rhymes, appropriate words, synonyms, oppposites (antonyms), blanks in words and sentences, word meanings, punctuation and syntax. The responses required are underlining words, phrases or sentences, filling in blanks, code answers, sentence completion by underlining. There are 120 items in the test which are graded in difficulty.

Purpose

The Manual says that 'A child is assessed by a consideration of his standing in a representative group of children exactly as old as himself' (p. 9). The English Quotient (EQ) derived from the test claims to measure this. The Manual also states: 'Many education authorities in England have used it as part of their admission examination to technical and commercial schools or to classify children for late transfer from modern to grammar schools' (p. 9). Thus, the users are teachers in schools administering the test on behalf of the education authority. Implicitly the test could be used within schools for diagnostic or screening purposes.

Item preparation

No report is given on this.

Administration

Apart from the test booklets, a sharpened pencil and a reserve supply of these, no further materials are required. The test is timed to last exactly 40 minutes. The administration instructions are clear, concise and unequivocal, and follow precisely the pattern of most Moray House Tests seen by the reviewer. The script in the Manual is satisfactory.

Standardization

This was carried out by the Godfrey Thomson Unit at Moray House in 1954 and 1956 in 3 education authorities on a total of 2597 children over the age range 12:06–13:11. The sample contained approximately equal numbers of boys and girls. The norms so obtained in an attainment test such as this 'must always be of a somewhat tentative nature. Performance will depend on the school syllabus and on the time devoted to the subject' (Manual, p. 9). The scores were classified according to each month of age and from these data Moray House prepared the conversion tables to provide standardized scores for the range 12:00–14:00, thus entailing some extrapolation. No details are given on the exact numbers of boys and girls, the mean raw scores for each, nor of sex differences in scores.

Scoring

Instructions for marking are clear and adequate and the scoring key is well spaced to facilitate marking. Each page of the test carries columns for recording marks for correct and incorrect responses. On the front cover is a summary sheet for entering details of the child, page scores and the standardized score ('English Quotient').

Reliability

No item analyses are reported. The reliability coefficient was calculated using KR-20 from a random sample of 200 scripts from the complete year group of 1042 children in one area. After partialling out age effects, the value was found to be 0.97.

Validity

The content validity of the test appears to be satisfactory. For a year group of 906 children, correlations of the test with MH Arithmetic (Adv.) 2 was 0.76 and with MH Verbal Reasoning Test (Adv.) 11, a test for a 13+ age-group, was 0.87. Two years prior to the standardization, two MH Verbal Reasoning tests and two MH English tests had been administered to the same children, yielding correlations of the order of 0.89 with the verbal reasoning tests and 0.94 with the English tests. These show satisfactorily high-predictive validity.

Interpretation

The Manual considers that if the test is used for allocation purposes it is desirable to administer the test as near to the date of transfer as the administrative conditions permit. Instructions are given clearly for the use of the conversion table with an example to illustrate and check this. The maximum raw score allowed for in the tables is 109 (out of 120) because of the difficulty of the test. Extrapolations to upper ages of 14:00–14:06 and to lower ages of 12:00–11:06 are described, but are not recommended outside these limits.

General evaluation

This is a good test commensurate with its stated purposes. One group of items is suspect—the items 6–10 on p. 1—where matching word rhymes are used. For example, 'Gas' is given six possible choices, one of which is to be underlined; 'Mass' is given as the correct response, but if, for example, the test is given in Nottinghamshire or Lincolnshire the response could well be given correctly as 'jazz' since the local dialects pronounce 'gas' as 'gazz'. This merely underlines the need to state in which areas of the country the test has been used for standardization. Otherwise, items appear appropriate for their purpose.

Teacher users should have no difficulty in following the Manual instructions for administration, marking and interpretation in this test.

This test was constructed in 1953, standardized in 1954–56 and its copyright date is 1961. It is largely a test of English usage. If English is still being taught within the framework of syntax and of classical and quasi-classical literature, the test remains appropriate. If, however, under recent curriculum changes, wherein English tends to be part of an integrated syllabus, and where selection for the secondary sector has changed dramatically, then this test may no longer be apposite.

Neale Analysis of Reading Ability

Reviewed by P. D. Pumfrey

Author: M. D. Neale
Publisher: Macmillan Education
Distributors: Macmillan Education; NFER-Nelson
Age range: 6:00–11:11 (extrapolation to 13:00)
1958 (M, T); S in mid-fifties
1966 (M, T) (2nd edition) reviewed here
Individual test

Test content

The Neale Analysis of Reading Ability comes in three parallel forms A, B and C. Each form consists of six passages of prose. Each passage is a complete narrative and is illustrated by a picture designed to provide a context increasing the appeal and utility of the material. In addition the passages are graded according to length, vocabulary level and sentence structure. Details of the procedures are only briefly described in the Manual. Further information can be obtained by consulting the PhD thesis on which the test is based.

The test booklet, containing all three forms of the instrument plus three supplementary optional tests in a spirally bound format, is reusable. Separate consumable sheets for recording a child's test reponses are available for each of the three forms of the test. These record sheets allow the child's reading rate, reading accuracy and comprehension of the passages to be recorded. Six types of error in oral reading are recorded during administration of the test. The record form also contains copies of the supplementary diagnostic tests of the names and sounds of letters, auditory discrimination through simple spelling and the blending and recognition of syllables.

The child is asked to read aloud each passage. Criteria for starting and discontinuing testing are based on the number of errors made in a passage. Passage 1 is followed by four questions designed to test the pupil's comprehension of the material. The other passages each have eight questions.

Purpose

The test is intended to 'provide a sympathetic and stimulating situation in which his (the child's) difficulties, weaknesses, types of error, persistence and attitudes could be assessed' (Manual, p. 3). It provides normative information concerning the individual child's reading rate, reading accuracy and reading comprehension. This information, together with the pattern of errrors made by the pupil and responses to the (optional) supplementary tests, provides a basis for '. . . making more subtle assessments of weaknesses and strengths upon which a wise reading programme for the individual can be planned' (Manual, p. 35). How this desirable end might be achieved is only hinted at in the mere 400 words devoted to 'Use and Interpretation' in the short Manual.

Item preparation

Initially fifty passages were devised. Of these, twelve were selected, two for each age level from 6–11 years, and used in a pilot study involving a random sample of 192 children. The results were analysed in terms of 'word difficulty, sentence-structure complexity as reflected in answers to comprehension questions, children's preference for theme and optimum length of test for each age' (Manual, p. 11). From these results a model of age-appropriate passages was devised thereby enabling new passages to be written as alternatives at each level.

A random sample of 500 pupils representing a 'good cross-section of the population' was selected from four schools. Analysis of the results of 439 pupils confirmed the appropriateness of the grading of the tests and the methods of scoring. Close correspondence between pupils' scores on parallel forms of the test was also established.

The brevity of the Manual means that only a cursory outline of these procedures is presented.

Administration

The child will require the reusable booklet containing the three forms A, B and C of the test. The examiner must have the Manual to the test, a record form appropriate to the form of the test that the pupil is about to take and a stopwatch and pencil.

The test material is well organized and the instructions for its administration are clear. However, considerable practice in recording the six error categories is required if results are to be reliable and valid. The instruction to the child to 'remember the story as you read it' can be criticized as inadequate to establish an appropriate set towards comprehension in an oral reading test. A practice passage would have been a useful addition in this respect. There is insufficient space to record, easily, children's responses to the comprehension questions.

The author claims that administration takes between 10 and 15 minutes. In the reviewer's experience, and that of other teachers known to him who use the test, this is an under-estimate of the time likely to be needed especially if one is testing children with reading difficulties.

The three supplementary diagnostic tests are recommended, but not prescribed, for all children who obtain low scores on the first reading passage of any form of the test.

Standardization

Standardization was carried out on a sample of 2000 children selected from 13 schools. The 'size, area, social background, age and sex' of the sample was controlled (Manual, p. 11). No details are given in the Manual of the distribution of these characteristics. The numbers of children taking the three forms of the test were unevenly spread as follows: Form A, 1221; Form B, 522; and Form C, 489. The sample size tested in each year group is relatively small. This has implications for the accuracy of the norms.

It appears that no children in the standardization sample older than that of top junior age (i.e. 11+) were tested. The reading ages for rate and comprehension are based on extrapolation above age 11:10 years; whilst for reading accuracy this is so above 11:11 years. The Manual does not include an account of how the age norms were derived or the extrapolations carried out.

Scoring

In respect of reading accuracy, rate and comprehension the child's raw scores can be converted to three reading ages. The provision of percentiles and/or deviation quotients for each age group would have been helpful.

Neale recognizes the limited diagnostic utility of the three indices provided by the test and stresses the need for their interpretation in relation to a child's particular background, personality and pattern of reading errors. The importance of clinical assessment is stressed but little guidance given as to how this might be achieved.

The three supplementary tests have brief instructions concerning their administration. These tests are not scored to allow inter or intra-individual comparisons. They are to be used to make explicit 'particular difficulties of an individual child with basic processes in reading' (Manual, p. 8).

Reliability

The parallel form reliability of accuracy scores is high, 0.96 being the lowest of the reliability coefficients presented for samples from the four year-groups. The parallel form reliability of the comprehension coefficients from the same groups are somewhat lower but still adequate, the lowest reported coefficient being 0.92. As there are more items in the accuracy test than in the comprehension, this could account for some of the difference. No information is given concerning the reliability of the rate of reading score.

The means, standard deviations and intercorrelations between the three tests are not presented. Coupled with the absence of information concerning the reliability of the rate scores, this makes the statistical interpretation of a profile impossible.

Validity

Using samples of 200 9-year olds and 200 11-year olds, the validity of the test was assessed by correlating a pooled score for rate, accuracy and comprehension with a pooled score from another battery comprised of three tests aiming to measure the same three aspects of reading. High coefficients of 0.95 are reported for each age level. The failure to present separate validations in respect of each of the three aspects of reading is a weakness. The high intercorrelation of the three aspects of reading is suggested by the comments on the factor analyses. Insufficient detail of procedures or results is presented to allow an informed consideration of such matters by the test user.

Interpretation

Reading ages for rate, accuracy and comprehension can be obtained. These are of value insofar as the sample on which the standardization data were obtained was representative of a particular population. The Manual is not as clear as it might be in this respect.

The validity of simultaneously testing reading rate, accuracy and comprehension is suspect. The three aspects are interdependent in oral reading. In this instrument they vary together with no adequate control. For example, accuracy can be sacrificed to rate of reading or vice versa. Comprehension can be affected by the rate/accuracy relationship of a child's reading.

The interpretation of a child's pattern of errors is left largely to the judgement of the tester. The same applies to the three supplementary tests that may, or may not, be used.

Test use

This instrument has been used widely in many studies in which *individual* testing of reading is deemed important. The following are examples.

References

Bookbinder, G. E. (1970). Variations in reading test norms. *Educational Research* **12**, 99–105.

Cartwright, D. and Jones, B. (1967). Further evidence relevant to the assessment of i.t.a. *Educational Research* **10**, 65–71.

Hornsby, B. and Miles, T. R. (1980). The effects of a dyslexia-centred teaching programme. *British Journal of Educational Psychology* **50**, 236–242.

Lunzer, E. A., Dolan, T. and Wilkinson, J. E. (1976). The effectiveness of measures of operativity, language and short-term memory in the prediction of reading and mathematical understanding. *British Journal of Educational Psychology* **46**, 295–305.

Netley, C., Rachman, S. and Turner, R. K. (1965). The effect of practice on performance in a reading attainment test. *British Journal of Educational Psychology* **35**, 1–8.

Pumfrey, P. D. and Lee, J. (1982). Cultural group, reading attainments and dialect interference. *Journal of Research in Reading* **3**, 133–145.

Riding, R. J. and Pugh, J. C. (1977). Iconic memory and reading performance in nine-year-old children. *British Journal of Educational Psychology* **47**, 132–137.

Rutter, M. and Bartak, L. (1973). Special educational treatment of autistic children: a comparative study—II. Follow-up findings and implications for services. *Journal of Child Psychology and Psychiatry* **14**, 241–270.

Ryle, A. and Macdonald, J. (1977). Responses to reading as perceived by boys with and without specific reading retardation and behavioural disorders: a repertory grid study. *Journal of Child Psychology and Psychiatry* **18**, 323–334.

Sturge, C. (1982). Reading retardation and antisocial behaviour. *Journal of Child Psychology and Psychiatry* **23**, 21–31.

Thompson, M. (1978). A psycholinguistic analysis of reading errors made by dyslexics and normal readers. *Journal of Research in Reading* **1**, 7–20.

White, M., Batini, P., Satz, P. and Friel, J. (1979). Predictive validity of a screening battery for children 'at risk' for reading failure. *British Journal of Educational Psychology* **49**, 132–137.

Yule, W. (1973). Differential prognosis of reading backwardness and specific reading retardation. *British Journal of Educational Psychology* **43**, 244–248.

General evaluation

This test has proved popular with many reading specialists, educational psychologists and research workers involved with individual children, particularly children with reading difficulties.

The Neale Analysis of Reading Ability has many weaknesses. Several of these are specified in preceding sections of this review. They relate to its construction, standardization and the interpretation of the data the test provides. Such weaknesses mean that the test cannot fully meet the professional requirements of users that Neale rightly identified and aspired to meet.

Neale sought to provide a bridge between the assessment of inter and intra-individual differences based on conventional test theory and a more clinically oriented approach based on a child's patterns of errors. At the time when it was first produced, it was in the latter field that it showed most promise. It is probably on this, coupled with the authority and orientation of the institution in which it was developed, that the test's popularity has been based. The fact that there was no other equivalent British constructed alternative available in one handy package also contributed to its popularity with many professionals, despite its limitations.

The Manual, whilst easy to understand, is so brief that technical aspects of construction, validation and interpretation are only dealt with superficially.

Neale Analysis of Reading Ability
Adapted for use with blind children

Reviewed by P. D. Pumfrey

Author: Adapted by J. Lorimer
Publisher: NFER-Nelson
Distributor: NFER-Nelson
Age range: 7:06–13:05
Source test: 1957–58; 1966 (2nd edition)
Adapted: 1977 (M, T)
Individual test★

Introduction

A review of the 1966 edition of the Neale Analysis of Reading Ability (NARA) is presented elsewhere in this book (p. 227). The technical and professional strengths and weaknesses of the instrument are there described in relation to the purposes that the test was designed to fulfil. It is *not* proposed to repeat those comments here.

The adaptation by· J. Lorimer of the NARA for use with blind children is built on the original test constructed by Neale. The review of the 1966 edition

---

★ For use by experienced teachers of the blind.

test provides an essential context within which to set that which follows. There is no substantial difference between the first and second editions of NARA.

In the review of the braille edition, additional points consequent on the modification of the original test for use with blind children will be presented.

Test content

The original version of NARA contains a series of graded narratives which the child reads aloud. Each passage of text is accompanied by a picture. In the braille edition, it is claimed that the function of the picture is performed by an introductory sentence read aloud by the tester prior to the child reading each narrative.

There are three parallel forms of the test, A, B and C, each comprised of six graded narratives. The test booklet is reusable: the forms for recording a pupil's responses are consumable.

A practice test has been added. It is to be used at the tester's discretion in circumstances where familiarization with materials and procedures is likely to be helpful to the child. Three supplementary tests are contained on the pupil's record form which is the same as for the original NARA. In Lorimer's manual, no reference is made to the use of these additional tests.

Purpose

The author's aims in adapting the NARA for use with blind children were to provide a braille test providing both 'reliable quantitative measures of accuracy, comprehension and rate in reading' (Manual, p. 1) to provide 'diagnostic information which reveals specific difficulties and indicates the type of remediation needed' and to develop an instrument for 'evaluating the results of experiments with new teaching techniques and materials' (Manual, pp. 1–2).

Item preparation

After surveying the available British reading tests, it was decided to adapt the original NARA for use with blind children by producing a braille version. On the assumption that the child's understanding of the narrative was not unduly dependent on visual experience, it was concluded that the pictures in the original test could be replaced by a verbal instruction and that an optional practice test should be devised.

Braille code difficulties were assessed for each of the three forms A, B and C. An examination of the constructions that would be required in the braille edition indicated that the distribution of 'easier and harder signs was approximately the same in each series of narratives' (Manual, p. 4). The problems of simultaneously assessing a child's reading accuracy, comprehension and rate were recognized. Despite this, it was concluded that the NARA 'appeared to the best available test for use with blind children' (Manual, p. 4).

Administration

The test booklet used by the child will contain the three forms A, B and C in braille. The appropriate four page record sheet, a stop watch and pencil are required by the tester.

It is held 'that blind children read braille at about one third of the pace of sighted children using print' (Manual, p. 12). Hence an increased limit of 12 seconds for the recognition of a word was adopted. This will tend to increase markedly the time taken to administer the test. It is strongly recommended that testers be experienced teachers of the blind who have taught braille and are aware of the problems faced by children in learning the medium. Additionally, users should be familiar with the Manual and materials of the original NARA and knowledgeable in the field of mental measurement.

The recording of six types of oral reading errors is required. To achieve facility requires considerable practice. Criteria are specified for discontinuing testing when a given number of errors is reached in a particular passage.

Standardization

This posed many formidable difficulties. Some children read both braille and large print by sight. Some children have attended ordinary schools and started to learn to read there prior to being transferred to a special school for the blind; others have been blind from a very early age. Not all blind children can learn to read braille. A considerable proportion of blind children have additional mental and/or physical handicaps likely to adversely affect their progress in reading more severely than does their blindness. The total population of blind pupils is relatively small.

These issues are discussed in the Manual and the problem of identifying an appropriate standardization sample is squarely faced. 'In selecting the sample . . . an attempt has been made to eliminate or reduce to negligible proportions the adverse effects of anomalies arising from differences in reading mode and from the late entry to a blind school' (Manual, p. 8). The two selection criteria adopted were, first, to include only children who read by touch. Secondly, those pupils entering a blind school after the age of seven years were accepted provided that they were touch readers and had been learning braille for at least two years. Whilst this sampling specification has important weaknesses insofar as the interpretation of children's scores is concerned, it has the major advantage of being explicit on this key point.

A preliminary trial involving 150 pupils in six schools was carried out, *not* with the final braille form of the NARA but using the vocabularies from the narratives arranged as word-recognition tests. To have used the braille form of NARA with these 150 pupils would have prevented the children's inclusion in the standardization sample. As the group formed a significant proportion of the total population, this would not have been desirable. The results from this preliminary trial indicated the suitability of the words in that accuracy scores increased steadily between 7:06 and 13:00 years.

The standardization sample included all children between the ages of 7:06 and 13:06 years in special schools for the blind in Britain who met the selection criteria. In total there were 299 pupils representing 55 per cent of the entire population of pupils attending such schools. The remaining 45 per cent were either unable to score on the test or failed to meet the selection criteria. Children who were untestable were excluded. Had they been given scores of zero and included in the standardization data, the norms for children who could begin to cope with the task 'would have been too distorted to be realistic' (Manual, p. 10).

Scoring

The pupil's responses are scored for accuracy and comprehension. As the administration of each passage is timed, the child's rate of reading can also be calculated. Age norms for accuracy, comprehension and rate of reading are given. The accuracy scale of raw scores runs from 1–100. The age equivalents for scores above 83 and below 14 are obtained by extrapolation. The comprehension scale of raw scores is from 0–44. Age equivalents for scores above 31 and below 6 are obtained by extrapolation. Rate of reading per minute scale has scores ranging from 5–103. Age equivalents for scores above 40 and below 11 are obtained by extrapolation. Because reading braille by touch reduces reading speed compared with reading print, it is recommended that the child's rate of reading for each separate passage be calculated also. Percentile rankings for accuracy, comprehension and rate are also provided for each of the six year-groups on which the test was standardized.

Reliability

Parallel form reliability coefficients for each of the six age-levels are presented for the three possible paired comparisons of forms A, B and C. Accuracy coefficients ranged from 0.990 and 0.997; comprehension coefficients ranged from 0.959 to 0.996 and rate coefficients from 0.953 to 0.998.

No other details of test reliability are presented.

Validity

As no similar standardized measures of braille reading ability were available at the time, it is stated in the Manual that this aspect of concurrent validity could not be explored. In view of earlier mention of the Lorimer Braille Recognition Test (1962) and the Tooze Braille Speed Test (1962) this statement seems somewhat cavalier, despite the limited scope of the other instruments.

It is claimed that, for the blind, this test is as valid as the original version was for the sighted. This assertion is based on 'the striking similarity of the patterns of results obtained by braille readers in the present study and by print readers in Neale's research sample' (Manual, p. 11). (Presumably the same reservations concerning validity mentioned in the review of the original test also apply).

An analysis of item difficulty is reported by Lorimer as having revealed clear discrimination between good and poor readers and between age levels for all three measures in all forms of the braille edition of NARA.

Interpretation

Concurring with Neale, Lorimer considers that the results of the standardized assessment of accuracy, comprehension and rate are of limited value unless simultaneously considered in relation to a child's chronological age, personal characteristics and history of learning to read. The need for the tester to appreciate the nature and degree of additional handicaps is stressed, as is the importance of knowing whether a child is on medication.

The assessment of intra-individual strengths and weaknesses and the diagnosis of causes of difficulty in reading require the tester to observe the child's attitudes, reactions and reading habits. The pattern of reading errors must also be described and utilized in the diagnostic process. Little indication is given in the Manual as to how the standardized data, the pattern of errors and the clinical observations enable Lorimer's purpose to be attained.

Lorimer considers that the test gives reliable and valid indices of reading accuracy, comprehension and rate and that a passage-related pattern of errors can be identified. If this is so, the instrument will enable a child's progress in braille reading to be assessed. This is valuable. It also allows the assessment of the efficacy of teaching techniques and materials. Less readily apparent is the utility of the pattern of errors in devising the 'type of remediation' needed. Despite this caveat, the adaptation is an advance on what was previously available.

Test use

Although the braille version of NARA is relatively new, it has been widely used with visually handicapped pupils in this country (Lorimer, personal communication). Currently the test is being used by workers at the Research Centre for the Education of the Visually Handicapped (University of Birmingham) in a ten-year longitudinal study of the cognitive development and school attainments of blind and partially-sighted children. The research started in 1973 when the children were aged five years. To-date the braille version of NARA has been used three times with each of the 120 pupils involved (Lorimer, personal communication; Tobin, personal communication).

General evaluation

Whilst the original and second editions of the NARA have some weaknesses (as have all other individual diagnostic tests), Lorimer is well aware of these defects and specifies some salient reservations in his manual. The simultaneous assessment of accuracy, comprehension and rate is one. Problems of interpreting both normative profiles and error patterns are others.

Despite these issues, the braille adaptation of NARA represents a thoughtful and meticulous attempt to provide an instrument for the individual diagnostic assessment of braille users' reading, though evidence for reliability and validity is somewhat limited and the characteristics of the standardization sample present some problems concerning normative interpretation within the context of braille readers. Further evidence for the test's validity and utility will probably accrue relatively slowly by virtue ot the size of the population for whom the test is designed and the restricted number of potentially competent users.

The adaptation will enable important inter-individual comparisons of braille readers' reading attainments and progress over time to be made using the test. The efficacy of methods of teaching braille can be more objectively assessed than previously. Links between the data provided by the individual diagnosis of reading difficulties and the specification of reading or reading related activities likely to enhance the child's reading attainments have still to be adequately forged both for the blind and the sighted. Without instruments such as Lorimer's adaptation of the NARA, the opportunity for facilitating these links would be reduced.

References

Lorimer, J. (1978). The limitations of braille as a medium for communication and the possibility of improved reading standards. *British Psychological Society Division of Educational and Child Psychology Occasional Papers* 2, 60–67.
Tobin, M. J. (1978). An introduction to the psychological and educational assessment of blind and partially-sighted children. *British Psychological Society Division of Educational and Child Psychology Occasional Papers* 2, 9–16.

The Primary Reading Test

Reviewed by Helen Quigley

Author: Norman France
Publisher: NFER-Nelson
Distributor: NFER-Nelson
Age range: 6:08–10:07
1978 (S); 1979 (M); 1978 (T)
1980 (M) printing reviewed
Group test

Test content

The test is an untimed, multiple-choice, group reading test. Level 1 is designed for children aged 6:04–8:03 at 31st December, while Level 2 is designed for children aged 8:04–10:03 at 31st December. Each level of the test begins with several multiple-choice picture items where the child has to circle the name of the article in the adjacent box, while the remaining items are simple sentence completion tasks where the child has to select the word that 'fits' the sentence, from a choice of five. Each test has 48 items but Level 1, being designed for younger children, has a greater proportion of picture items.

Purpose

In the words of the author 'the two levels of the test provide an overall assessment of the ability to apply reading skills for the understanding of words and simple sentences in the early stages of learning to read' (Manual, p. 2). The tests are normative tests. The author also suggests that Level 1 can be used as a word recognition test for screening infants of below average ability. In this case, the teacher reads out the test items to the children.

Item preparation

Twelve thousand children distributed in schools throughout the UK in the four year-groups from the second-year infants to the third-year juniors were involved in piloting the test. Four approximately parallel tests, each containing 56 items, arranged in an estimated order of difficulty, were distributed equally within each school class. An item analysis was carried out for a sample of English and Scottish children on each of the 224 items of the four forms and for each of the four year-groups involved. The 48 items, which constitute each of the final tests, 'were chosen to provide an even gradation of difficulty, to maximize discrimination between high and low reading ability and to minimize differences of achievement between boys and girls' (Manual, p. 7).

Administration

The tests are designed to be used by teachers in a normal classroom situation. The instructions are clear and there are no unusual features in the administration. The test is untimed, but 'It is expected that most children will have reached their ceiling of attainment in one normal 30-minute lesson period' (Manual, p. 2). Each child requires a non-reusable test booklet and a pencil or pen.

Standardization

The two tests were administered to a total of about 8000 children distributed throughout the UK in accordance with the proportions shown in "Statistics of Education" (1976). For the main standardization, 1500 children in each year group from second-year infants to third-year junior were involved. A further 1500 infants in their second year were involved in standardizing Level 1 as a word recognition test while further groups of 150 children in the two last years of the junior school and the two first years of the secondary school, were involved in a further validity study. Although tables are provided for converting raw scores to reading ages and standard age scores (mean 100, standard deviation 15), the method of construction of these norms, is not clearly described.

Scoring

The scoring instructions are clear. A scoring key is given and one point is awarded for each correct answer. The child's raw score is then interpreted as either a standard age score, a stanine score or a percentile score, using the norms provided. Separate norms are provided for Scotland.

Reliability

First- and second-year juniors took both forms of the test. The author has used the correlation between Level 1 and Level 2 as a measure of the test-restest reliability of the test, which proved to be 0.85 and 0.86 for the two year-groups respectively. For the other year-groups, test-retest reliabilities were estimated, using KR-20.

Validity

The content validity of the test was assessed by asking teachers to assess their children independently on a nine-point scale of reading skill and comprehension. Agreements between teachers' assessments and scores on the primary reading test were as high as 0.89 for second-year juniors. A sub-sample of children in third- and fourth-year juniors and first- and second-year secondary schools were also tested on the Reading Comprehension Test of the Richmond tests of basic skills. A correlation of 0.82 was obtained between scores on the two tests.

Interpretation

Little guidance is given on the interpretation of the scores.

General evaluation

This test amply meets its author's claim that it provides 'an overall assessment of the ability to apply reading skills for the understanding of words and simple sentences in the early stages of learning to read'. The material is not very exciting but the test is well constructed and produced in a workmanlike fashion. It can be recommended to teachers seeking a basic word recognition or sentence completion test.

Reading Comprehension Test DE

Reviewed by P. D. Pumfrey

Author: E. L. Barnard
Publisher: NFER-Nelson
Distributor: NFER-Nelson
Age range: 10:02–12:01
1967 (S); 1971 (M) (provisional); 1970 (S)
1976 (M) (revised)
1981 (M); 1980 (T) printings reviewed
Group test

Test content

The test consists of eight varied passages; seven prose extracts and one verse extract. Each passage is followed by between four and eight questions totalling fifty in all. Most of these are multiple choice but some require a short written answer, usually a quotation, taken from the previous passage.

Purpose

The test aims to assess four related aspects of reading comprehension: Global Understanding (an appreciation of the meaning of the passage as a whole); Detail (ability to extract the facts given in the passage); Inference (going beyond the facts presented); and Understanding of the use of individual words and phrases.

Item preparation

The Manual reports that '. . . considerable numbers of passages and questions were tried out . . . to establish items which were of a satisfactory level of difficulty throughout the age range, and which were also discriminating satisfactorily between children in this age group' (Manual, p. 2). An analysis of item type by passage is presented in a 4 × 8 matrix. Items are mainly multiple choice but some require a constructed response.

Administration

The test is designed for use with pupils aged between 10:00–12:10 years of age. The test booklet can only be used once. Administration is untimed but it is suggested that a double period be allowed. 'Most children will have finished within 50 minutes'. Thus those who finish early must be set 'quiet work to do' (Manual, p. 4).

Standardization

The test was standardized on 13 070 children (6659 boys; 6411 girls) aged between 10:02–12:01 years from four different local authority areas plus a further 879 older pupils (417 boys; 462 girls) from an urban area in the North West. The entire population of pupils, other than absentees, of the appropriate age group in each local authority area was tested. Whether these were samples of pupils representative of the national population is not established, although one assumes that the large sample was a planned one. The original standardization was carried out in 1967, though this is not made clear in the 1981 reprint of the Manual. The claim that each child 'is assessed by comparing him with a representative sample of children of exactly the same age' is important (Manual, p. 3), but without further details one has legitimate reservations concerning it. Additionally, even if one is entitled to make such a comparison, the dates when the normative data were collected are important to the interpretation of scores currently obtained by pupils.

Scoring

The scoring instructions in relation to a small minority of the multiple-choice items and most of the constructed response items are left to the marker's judgement in respect of variations from the listed acceptable answers. This is an unquantified source of error variance.

From the raw scores, standardized scores with a mean of 100 and a standard deviation of 15 for each monthly chronological age group between 10:00–12:10 years are readily obtained. One set of tables for both boys and girls is provided, although the younger girls in the standardization sample obtained a significantly higher mean score than the boys.

No comparison of children's relative performance on the four aspects of comprehension that the test is designed to measure is possible, other than by a comparison of raw scores. The relationships between pupils' scores on these four facets of reading comprehension are not given. Any interpretation of a profile of these abilities using the present Manual would be based on clinical intuition.

Reliability

One study concerning the instrument's reliability is cited. This involved a random sample of 317 scripts from *one* of the areas in the standardization sample. An internal consistency coefficient of 0.96 (KR-20) is reported.

Validity

No evidence is presented concerning any aspect of validity.

Interpretation

The nature of the standardized scores based on overall performance on the test is briefly yet lucidly explained in the section on standardization in the Manual. There is no section on interpretation as such and no cautionary notes are sounded concerning the problems posed by the age of the test and sex differences in attainment on it in certain groups. The four aspects of comprehension that the test aims to measure are not empirically substantiated; hence their interpretation is likely to be less valuable and certainly more suspect than the authors of the test suggest (Manual, p. 2).

General evaluation

A test that aims to compare children's ability to understand complex passages rather than single sentences has much to commend it in principle. A second aim of identifying different aspects of reading comprehension is also of theoretical and practical importance. This test provides one means of assessing the former but has weaknesses due to the age of the material, the lack of information on the representativeness of the standardization sample, the test's reliabilities and validities. In respect of the second aim, the test constructor's aspiration remains that. The situation has not changed since an earlier review (Pumfrey, 1977).

The format of the test is interesting and worthy of development. Its utility in providing valid information for either institutional or personal decision making in its present form is suspect.

Reference

Pumfrey, P. D. (1977). "Reading Tests and Assessment Techniques". Sevenoaks: Hodder & Stoughton.

Reading Level Tests (Experimental Version)

Reviewed by Jenny Hewison

Author: Not stated
Publisher: NFER-Nelson
Distributor: NFER-Nelson
Age range: 7:00–8:11 (Part 1); 9:00–10:11 (Part 2)
1970, 1974 (T); 1961 (M)
1977 (M); 1980 (T) printings reviewed
Group test

Test content

The test consists of eight short passages, constructed to meet specified 'readability' criteria. The measure of readability used derives from the work of Fry (1968, 1969), while the concept itself is defined as 'a measure of how difficult a passage is, taking into account the age level of the group in question' (Manual, p. 3).

Pupils' comprehension of the test passages is measured using a cloze procedure: marker lines replace words which have been deleted from the text, and the child's task is to write in the words that are missing. The rationale underlying the test is that, 'A pupil's capacity to understand the prose is measured by the accuracy with which he can supply the missing words' (Manual, p. 2).

The passages are arranged in order of difficulty, and printed in two separate booklets of four passages each. These two parts of the test are intended to be appropriate to first- and second-year juniors, and third- and fourth-year juniors respectively; and the content of the passages is intended to reflect the reading interests of this age group (7–10 year olds).

Purpose

'The tests were designed to assess how efficiently pupils can comprehend prose material of known readability. Pupils are assessed primarily in terms of how well they cope with reading matter—not in relation to other pupils' (Manual, p. 2). Only an experimental version of this test is available at present. It is not intended for use as an alternative to established tests, but rather as a source of supplementary information to guide teachers in the selection of reading materials for their pupils.

Item preparation

The Manual states that, in 1974, sixteen cloze passages were written to conform to selected readability levels, drawn from Fry's Chart, and specified in terms of the two Fry dimensions of prose difficulty, syllable length (calculated as the average number of syllables per 100 words) and sentence length (the average number of sentences per 100 words). The vocabulary for the passages was drawn largely from "Key Words to Literacy" (McNally and Murray, 1968) and "Words Your Children Use" (Edwards and Gibbons, 1968) to ensure that it would be familiar to most children.

Words were randomly deleted from the passages on a one-in-ten basis, and the resulting material tried out on a sample of about 740 children from a number of different junior schools (no criteria for the selection of schools or children are specified, and no information is given about them). 'Words which failed to discriminate between pupils who performed exceptionally well or badly on the test in general were replaced in the main text' (Manual, p. 4); while words found to be either very easy or very difficult were retained as omissions in order not to alter the task difficulty, but were not included in the scoring key for the revised form of the test, as they contributed nothing to its efficiency as a measuring instrument.

Correlation coefficients were calculated between the two Fry dimensions of syllable and sentence length, and the mean cloze scores obtained for each passage. Values of 0.7 and 0.8 were obtained, and interpreted as indicating that 'the difficulty of the passages tended to follow the readability of the passages moderately well' (Manual, p. 4).

From the original 16 passages, 8 were selected according to unspecified criteria to form the present version of the test. (The test user is not informed about the preliminary work which presumably took place on this test between 1961, the copyright date of the Manual, and 1974 when the test passages were written).

Administration

Since the tests are 'appropriate only for pupils who have reached a moderate level of word recognition skill', it is recommended that in cases of uncertainty, teachers should first screen their pupils by administering a standardized test covering initial and intermediate reading skills. It is recommended that pupils below the following raw score points, which represent the level of attainment of the average 7-year old on the tests named, should not attempt the Reading Level Tests: Reading Test A (NFER), 11 points; Gates McGinitie Primary A (Vocabulary) (NFER), 34; Carver's Word Recognition Test (Hodder & Stoughton), 30; Young's Group Reading Test (Hodder & Stoughton), 19. Pupils who possess the required basic reading skills may be given the two parts of the Reading Level Test either in conjunction or independently.

Before using the test, teachers are advised to familiarize themselves with the notions of cloze procedure, readability and independent, instructional and frustrational reading levels. A brief introduction to these ideas is given in the Manual. Detailed introductions for the administration of the test are also given. Practice examples are provided on the front of the test booklets, and are worked through by the pupils in response to precise but over-lengthy instructions read aloud to them from the Manual. Using the examples, the teacher indicates that alternative words and incorrect spellings may sometimes be acceptable. The test itself is untimed, and the only materials required are a test booklet for each child, and pens or pencils for writing in the missing words. No estimate is given of the amount of time likely to be required for administering the test.

Standardization

The Reading Level Test differs from most established measures of reading attainment in that it is not designed to assess a child's performance in relation to that of other children, but rather in relation to texts of varying degrees of difficulty. A number of equivalences must be demonstrated or otherwise established for this method of assessment to be convincing. Passage difficulty, as measured by raw cloze score, must bear a direct relationship to passage readability, as measured by the Fry dimensions of syllable and sentence length. In turn, 'readability' as measured must be expressible in terms of age norms, and children's performance must be classifiable in terms of 'Comprehension Levels'—independent, instructional or frustrational—at each readability age level.

The two tables of page 8 of the Manual permit a child's raw score on any one passage, or on certain combinations of passages, to be translated into a qualitative assessment of how well that child can comprehend material of the age level represented by that passage, or passages. So, for example, any child obtaining a raw score of 4 on passage B, which is known to be of readability level 6–7 years, may be said to be reading that material at the instructional level of comprehension. The correspondence between raw score and comprehension level—the central theme of this test—should, however, be treated with caution, since values of the former 'were chosen provisionally and may be altered as a result of further research' (this statement appears on p. 3 of the Manual, not on p. 8 with the tables to which it refers).

Since no proper standardization data are reported, it is impossible to judge how sound is the empirical basis for the test's complex theoretical rationale. The only link in the argument which is even briefly discussed in numerical terms is that between raw cloze score and the readability dimensions of syllable and sentence length; and even this discussion is unconvincing. The adequacy of Fry's own standardization procedure is highly relevant, but is not discussed and conscientious users would need to make their own further enquiries amongst the reference material cited.

It may be said that only a rough and ready correspondence is required between performance indices and categories of prose complexity, if the sole aim of the exercise is to guide teachers in the rough and ready process of selecting reading materials. It must also be remembered that the test is still only being published in an 'experimental' form. None the less, by any criteria, the reported standardization data are inadequate, and should be improved upon in any future revision of the Manual.

Scoring

In any use of cloze procedure, the problem arises of how to score an answer which is not the original deleted word, but which is 'equally appropriate to the author's purpose' (Manual, p. 6). Markers of the Reading Level Test are advised to use their discretion in giving credit to alternatives, and a number of guidelines are provided. Difficulties are most likely to arise with the enjoinder that, 'Care should be taken not to allow words which are semantically appropriate but stylistically incongruous or inferior' (Manual, p. 6), since variations in judgement are inevitable. It is asserted that few children will be incorrectly assessed as a result of discretionary marking but this claim requires substantiation. Misspelt, but otherwise acceptable answers are allowed, and quite detailed guidelines are given on this particular point. A marking key listing a few acceptable alternatives, and also some disallowed words is provided.

After the raw scores from the various passages have been entered into a box on the front of the test booklet, users are left in some doubt as to what they are supposed to do next. A second box on the test cover invites entries under the headings, 'Independent', 'Instructional' and 'Frustrational', but it is not clear how four raw scores are to be converted into three such entries, especially if an inconsistent gradient of errors is observed across the four test passages. The Manual is silent on this question.

Reliability

The only reported item of relevant information is that, 'The overall reliability of the test by the internal consistency method (KR-20) was found to be 0.96' (Manual, p. 4). It must be presumed, as it is not stated that this figure refers to data from the eight passages which constitute the final full test, that it was abstracted from the larger study of the original 740 children. No further information is given about this sample, not even its age distribution.

At a more general level, some discussion of the reliability of cloze procedures or readability estimates would have been valuable.

Validity

It is not possible to assess the validity of the Reading Level Test in its own terms, namely as a measure of how well pupils 'cope with reading matter', since no validity information is provided on the cloze and readability technique upon which the test is based. The authors point out that the test is still at an experimental stage, and argue that the validation of test and techniques cannot properly be accomplished until both have been extensively 'tried and tested' in British schools.

Interpretation

Insufficient advice is given on the interpretation of test scores. As mentioned above in the context of 'scoring', after administering the test to a pupil a teacher is faced with raw cloze scores from 4 or 8 passages. The test is designed to provide information of guidance to teachers in the selection of reading materials for their pupils, and to this end two tables are provided in the Manual

(p. 8) relating cloze score to readability. However, the instructions which accompany these tables are too brief, and leave many questions unanswered. It is unclear, for example, how information from the various passages is to be integrated if an inconsistent pattern is observed; and unclear, too, whether it is desirable to make any allowance for the age of the child when interpreting test results, and using them as a guide in the selection of materials.

General evaluation

A complaint, often made, about traditional tests is that the reading ages or standardized scores that they yield are in themselves unhelpful as guides to what a teacher should do next. The teacher's task is to select material appropriate to the child's current level of performance; hence any assessment procedure offering a short cut to this goal ought, in principle, to be welcomed and widely adopted. According to the copyright date in the Manual, work on the Reading Level Test began more than 20 years ago, yet the test is still said to be in an 'experimental' form, no adequate standardization, reliability or validity information is available, and the contents and layout of the Manual still leave much to be desired.

It must therefore be asked why the Reading Level Test has not met with a more enthusiastic response. One reason might be that it appeals neither to advocates of formal testing, who would be disappointed by the lack of appropriate standardization and other data, nor to advocates of cloze and readability techniques as methods of informal assessment, since they would be disappointed by the strongly test-like appearance of the answer booklets, and the formality of the administration procedures.

The test Manual invites teachers to try out the test in their schools and report on their experiences. Unfortunately, an informal validation of this kind cannot substitute for proper test construction procedures and until the latter are carried out and reported, the Reading Level Test is unlikely to gain further in popularity.

References

Edwards, R. P. A. and Gibbon, V. (compilers) (1973). "Words Your Children Use: A Survey of Words Used by Children in Infants' Schools with the Resultant Graded Vocabulary" (1st edn). Burke.

Fry, E. B. (1968). A readability formula that saves time. *Journal of Reading* **11**, 513–16.

Fry, E. B. (1969). The readability graph validated at primary levels. *The Reading Teacher* **6**, 534–538.

McNally, J. and Murray, W. (1968). "Key Words to Literacy and the Teaching of Reading" (Revised edn). Schoolmaster Publishing Co.

Reading Test AD

Reviewed by Sandra Johnson

Author: A. F. Watts
Publisher: NFER-Nelson
Distributor: NFER-Nelson
Age range: 8:00–10:07
1955 (T)
Revised 1965
1977 (S) (restandardized); 1978 (M); 1970 (T)
1980 (M, T) printings reviewed
Group test

Test content

Thirty-five multiple-choice sentence completion items constitute this speeded test, which is intended for use with 2nd- and 3rd-year juniors, i.e. 8–10 year olds.

Purpose

Nowhere in the Manual is the purpose of the test explicitly stated. The test can loosely be termed a test of reading comprehension, and the outcome of its use is to allocate to each child a standard score and/or a reading age.

Item preparation

The Manual contains no information about the way the test was constructed, although there is a brief reference to the fact that item order reflects graded difficulty (p. 3).

Administration

It is clearly assumed in the Manual that this test will usually be administered as a group test. The administration instructions are very detailed, and these include directions on timing and supervision in addition to giving a well-defined administration script. Great emphasis is placed on the need to adhere strictly to the specified 15-minute testing time, and, given the absence of a parallel form, on the need for vigilance in preventing copying. Two example items are worked with the group by the supervisor before the test session begins. The children then proceed to work independently through the test, completing each sentence by underlining in pencil on the test sheet itself the one word from a selection of five which they consider to be the missing last word of the sentence.

Standardization

The test was restandardized by testing, in March and April 1977, samples of 4582 2nd-year juniors and 4781 3rd-year juniors who were chosen 'according to a stratified random technique designed to make it representative of the population in England and Wales' (Manual, p. 2). No further details are given of the sampling technique itself, but from other descriptive information about the resulting sample (numbers of LEAs, schools and pupils) it can be inferred that it was a complex sampling scheme, probably with whole teaching groups selected within each chosen school at the final sampling stage. Lawley's method (see Introduction) was used to produce two tables (one per school year-group) for the conversion of raw scores to standard scores (mean 100, standard deviation 15).

Statistically significant differences were recorded between the performances of boys and girls at all ages—the discrepancy being in favour of girls and decreasing slightly with increasing age. However, conversion tables are not given for boys and girls separately.

Scoring

A marking key is contained in the Manual, correct word-choices being allowed one mark, all other choices attracting no marks. If a gap of five consecutive wrong choices occurs then no marks are credited to pupils for any correct choices beyond that point. This latter rule is justified in the Manual on two counts: the graded difficulty of the test items, and the results of an answer-pattern analysis of pupils' test scripts (no details given). A rather unconvincing attempt is made to further justify this criterion on statistical grounds.

Reliability

The internal consistency of the test was calculated for each year-group on the basis of the responses of a random subsample (approximately 10 per cent) of the total standardization sample, and a KR-20 value of 0.92 is given in each case. Standard errors of measurement of 4.22 and 4.34 in standard score units are quoted for 2nd years and 3rd years respectively.

Validity

No comment is contained in the test manual on the validity of this test.

Interpretation

It is possible through use of the test, to assign reading ages to individual children and/or to rank children in terms of their standard scores. However, no guidance is given to the non-technical user on how to further interpret, and therefore perhaps to act on, this information. While the attention of the test user is drawn to the size and the meaning of the standard error of measurement, and to the implications with regard to the reliability of an individual pupil's standard score, no elaboration is offered of the properties of the standardized distribution itself; that is, the test user is given no guidance on the way in which children can be assigned percentile rankings on the basis of their standard scores. A non-technical user may, therefore, be uncertain about how to judge particular standard scores, and therefore be unsure about a suitable cut-off criterion for identifying children for further testing or remedial help.

Test use

Reading Test AD was formerly known as Sentence Reading Test 1, and was used, along with a number of other tests, in both of the Kent Inquiries. In the first inquiry, conducted in 1954 (Morris, 1959), the test was used to assess the reading standards of all 7–11 year olds in the 60 schools in the Kent sample. In the second inquiry (Morris, 1966), the reading standards of children were assessed each March as they moved through the 2nd, 3rd and 4th years of junior school between 1955 and 1957 (the test results, not surprisingly, showed evidence of a marked ceiling effect for many of the better readers even as 2nd-year juniors).

It was also used to monitor changes in the reading standards of 8-year olds in Aberdeen between 1962 and 1972 (Nisbet *et al.*, 1974). The whole population of 8-year olds in Aberdeen was tested in each of these two years; the conclusion was that standards at age 8 were relatively unchanged over that time-period.

The test is currently in use, probably for screening purposes, in a number of primary *and* secondary schools. It was noted, for example, in the Bullock Report (DES, 1975) that 15 per cent and 5 per cent, respectively, of their national random samples of primary and secondary schools used this particular test.

General evaluation

Reading Test AD would seem to have potential as a quick, easy to administer screening test, particularly given its very recent restandardization. Administration would, though, be simpler had a parallel form been available.

The value of the test results to class teachers could have been greatly increased had the Manual contained some comment on what the test is actually designed to measure (together with information about its validity in this respect), and had it spelt out the practical significance of a pupil's position on the standard score distribution.

References

DES (1975). "A Language for Life" (The Bullock Report). London: HMSO.
Morris, J. M. (1959). "Reading in the Primary School". London: Newnes Educational (for NFER).
Morris, J. M. (1966). "Standards and Progress in Reading". Windsor, Berks.: NFER.
Nisbet, J., Welsh, J. and Watt, J. (1974). Reading standards in Aberdeen: 1962–1972. *Educational Research* **16**, 172–175.

Reading Test BD

Reviewed by John Gray

Author: not stated
Publisher: NFER-Nelson
Distributor: NFER-Nelson
Age range: 7:06–10:04
1969 (S); 1971 (M); 1970 (T)
No revisions apparent
1980 (M, T) printings reviewed
Group test

Test content

The test consists of 44 questions graded in difficulty. For each question pupils are asked to select the one alternative from the five one-word choices offered which most appropriately completes the gap in the sentence.

Purpose

'Reading Test BD is a reading test of the sentence completion type. It is intended for use throughout the primary school (i.e. ages 7–11) although its usefulness is limited with the poorer readers amongst the 7 year olds and the better readers amongst the 10–11 year olds.

'It covers approximately the same age range as the NFER Reading Test AD by A. E. Watts, which is also a sentence completion test, but the two are not parallel tests. Although they may be treated as alternatives, fulfilling similar functions, the questions in the two tests are not exactly parallel in difficulty nor were the standardizations performed at the same time' (Manual, p. 3).

Elsewhere the manual remarks: 'In deciding which of the two reading tests to administer it is worth bearing in mind that Reading Test AD is easier than Reading Test BD and therefore more appropriate for the younger or lower ability group' (p. 4).

The Watts test (AD) has been more widely used as a way of assessing standards.

Item preparation

No information is provided in the Manual on this topic.

Administration

Detailed directions about how the test should be administered are contained in the Manual. Four practice items for use with the whole group are provided on the front page; children are required to underline the most suitable alternative in each case. The time allowed for the test is 20 minutes plus 5–10 minutes for practice. Advice about the suitability of the test for non-readers is provided in the section on 'guessing'.

Standardization

Previously known as Primary Reading Test 2, the test was standardized, in 1969, on samples from four different geographical areas with somewhat different age-groups, which were then combined. Two separate, raw score to standardized score, conversion tables are provided 'because there is a significant difference between the rate of increase in scores of the 1st-year children and that of the 2nd- and 3rd-year children' (Manual, p. 3). One conversion table covers 1st-year children in the age-range 7:00–8:08, based on a sample of 5332 children. It should be noted that since the youngest children actually tested were 7:06 the scores provided 'have been extrapolated downwards to 7:00'. The second conversion table covers 2nd- and 3rd-year children in the age-range 8:00–10:04 and is based on a sample of 9978 children. 'Less data existed for the 4th-year children (10–11 years) than the other ages. It has been decided that a satisfactory "final" conversion table for this age group cannot be produced from the present data but a duplicated provisional table covering the age-range 10:00–11:04 can be supplied if required' (p. 3). Girls averaged 2.6 points of standardized score higher than the average for boys.

The NFER Catalogue (1980) indicates that the test was restandardized during 1978; no new norms were available, however, with the specimen copy reviewed here.

Scoring

Instructions for marking the test are provided. The total is obtained by counting the correct answers directly from the script. The test is designed to produce a single total score. No subtest scores are available.

There is a section in the Manual (p. 6) on the influence of 'guessing', no correction being seen as necessary in the light of field trials; this conclusion is qualified only with respect to non-readers and weak readers where a strategy for identifying 'guessing' is suggested.

Reliability

Figures for test-retest and 'internal consistency' correlations are reported as measures of reliability. The test-retest correlations were based on a 'selected group' of 337 children who were tested on two occasions about three and a half weeks apart. The reported correlation is 0.92. The correlations for each year-group separately (based on samples of just over 100 in each case) are also of this level. Virtually identical correlations were obtained for scores which were 'corrected' to take account of 'guessing'.

Internal consistency was measured using the KR-20 coefficient. The coefficients are presented separately for 2nd, 3rd and 4th years and are based on between 211 and 241 pupils in each case. Reliabilities of 0.94 (with a standard error of measurement of 2.5) are reported for 2nd- and 3rd-year pupils and of 0.95 (standard error, 2.2) for 4th years.

Validity

Face validity is assumed. The Manual reports an investigation designed to compare 'any discrepancies between the standards set' by Reading Test BD as opposed to Reading Test AD which was administered one month later to a sample of 462 children in one London Borough. The AD test produced a score approximately one point higher than the BD test, but the Manual argues that this difference can be almost entirely accounted for by 'maturational effects'. Validity was also investigated by comparing scores with teachers' estimates although no details are given of this analysis.

Interpretation

Some elementary guidance on the conversion of raw scores to standardized scores is offered.

General evaluation

Tests of this kind (although not, it should be noted, this particular test) have featured prominently in debates about standards of reading and whether these have changed over time. Concern in the early seventies that they might have fallen (Start and Wells, 1972) led to the establishment of the Bullock Committee which, in turn, conducted a wide-ranging review of the teaching of language and literacy (Bullock, 1975). Bullock was emphatic in its evaluation of the tests which had been used in Start and Wells' research. 'We do not regard these tests as adequate measures of reading ability. What they measure is a narrow aspect of silent reading comprehension' (p. 16) they declared. They were particularly concerned about the effects that the 'datedness' of several of the items might have had on the apparent trend of standards over time and stressed that, at best, sentence completion tests of this type can only measure units of language up to a sentence long rather than the ability to extract themes or follow arguments. Readers considering use of this test might find it helpful to refer to the second chapter of the Bullock Report for a fuller discussion of these issues.

The NFER Catalogue hints at some of these limitations but also argues that its reading tests 'provide a reliable picture of pupils' ability to cope with fairly steeply graded reading tasks. The sentence-completion tests approach reading as a process requiring both structural and vocabulary knowledge as well as general experience of written forms. None of the tests are intended as a substitute for individual diagnosis of backward readers' (NFER Catalogue, 1980, pp. 25–26).

With respect to Reading Test BD itself my impression is that the 'datedness' argument is less applicable—the vocabulary employed is still contemporary if, on occasion, somewhat literary in flavour. Whether the 'narrowness' of the reading skills tested is important will depend on the uses to which it is intended to put the results. The test does provide a simple means of obtaining a summary reading score which *probably* correlates quite highly with the skills tested by other lengthier tests and procedures. The "Primary Survey" (DES, 1978), conducted by members of HM Inspectorate, employed a reading test of a similar kind without comment and subsequently analysed it against a number of other variables from which it derived conclusions for educational policy.

References

DES (1975). "A Language for Life" (The Bullock Report). London: HMSO.
DES (1978). "Primary Education in England". London: HMSO.
Start, K. B. and Wells, B. K. (1972). "The Trend of Reading Standards". Slough: NFER.

Reading Tests EH1, EH2, EH3

Reviewed by Helen Quigley

Author: S. M. Bate
Publisher: NFER-Nelson
Distributor: NFER-Nelson
Age ranges: 11:02–15:09 (EH1)
　　　　　11:02–15:09 (EH2)
　　　　　11:03–15:07 (EH3)
1971–74 (S); 1975 (M); 1970 (T)
1976 (M); 1980 (T) printings reviewed
Group tests

Test content

EH1, 2 and 3, are three separate reading tests which can be administered together or independently. EH1 is a vocabulary test, containing 60 items of the sentence completion, multiple-choice type. EH2 is a comprehension test with 7 prose passages each followed by 5 questions. The majority of the questions are multiple choice. EH3 is a speed of reading test which consists of 2 long prose extracts with periodic brackets, in which the child underlines one word to 'continue the sense'.

Purpose

The stated purpose of the tests is 'to assess performance in different aspects of reading in the first 4 years of secondary schooling'. The authors cite 4 such aspects of reading:

(1) Global understanding (understanding of what the passage as a whole has been about).
(2) Detail (extracting the facts given in a passage).
(3) Inference (going beyond the facts given).
(4) Understanding of individual words and phases.

No source is given for this view of the reading process, nor is an assessment made of the extent to which the tests measure these various aspects.

Item preparation

The authors state that 'in compiling the tests, considerable numbers of questions and passages were tried out in all year groups and statistical analysis performed to establish items which were of a satisfactory level of difficulty throughout the groups and which were also discriminating satisfactorily within each group' (Manual, EH1 and 2, p. 2). No further details are given. In particular, the authors omit to state how the items devised are related to the stated purpose of the tests.

Administration

For all three tests, an individual, non-reusable, pupils' booklet is provided. The child marks this book in pencil. Detailed instructions are given. The method of administration is very straightforward and the instructions are minutely precise. EH1 and 2 are untimed, while EH3 is very strictly timed (the administrator needs an accurately calibrated stopwatch).

In EH1, the child is required to underline the words in brackets which he thinks makes best sense. In EH2, the child is asked either to underline the correct answer or to write a few words in response to a specific question. In EH3, the child is asked to read the continuous passages and, whenever he or she reaches a group of words in brackets, to underline the word that makes the best sense and then read on. In all three tests, the instructions are straightforward, clear and simple. EH1 and 2 are untimed but in EH3, the supervisor is asked to stop pupils after a certain period of time and to make sure all of them stop and turn over to the next page.

Standardization

Tests EH1 and EH2

These standardizations were carried out by the NFER 'between 1971 and 1974'. A total of 21 390 children (EH1) and 17 117 children (EH2), were tested in 6 different areas in England. The authors do not state why these areas were chosen nor what is the balance of numbers of children between these areas. The children were tested in year-groups (e.g. 11+, 12+). There appear to be wide variations in the size of the year-groups, e.g. for test EH1, 13 278 children were tested in the 11+ year-group but only 1591 in the 13+ year-group. Furthermore, not all year-groups were tested in all 6 areas, for example, in the 12+ and 13+ year-groups, children were only tested in 'a predominantly rural county in eastern England'. The authors do not say why the standardization followed this pattern. They have, however, stated that 'where only one area has been used to provide age group norms, national norms have been projected, based on the performance of pupils in this area on other tests'.

There were approximately equal numbers of boys and girls in all samples. In no case was there a significant difference in ages between the sexes. The mean scores for each age group of each sex were calculated. The authors state that 'the differences between the performance of boys and girls are significant except in the case of EH1 for the age ranges 12 plus and 13 plus'. They give a combined conversion table for each age group. Surprisingly, in EH1, in every age group, the mean score of the girls was less than that of the boys. This is not a common finding. Separate conversion tables are provided for each year group. This leads to a puzzling feature of the test—the ages within the year-groups show some overlap. For example, children of ages 12:00–12:07 feature in both the 11 plus and 12 plus age groups and there is similar overlap in all the other age groups. This leads to the situation where a child with a specific raw score receives two different standardized scores, depending upon the year-group conversion used. For example, a child of 14:04 scoring 37 raw score would receive a standardized score of 100 when referred to the 14 plus year-group but 107 referred to the 13 plus year-group. Similarly, a child of 14:04 with a raw score of 50 would achieve a standardized score of 115 when considered a member of the 14 plus age group but one of 123 when referred to the 13 plus age group. There may be a good reason for this discrepancy— perhaps school year-group is the key—but it is not mentioned in the Manual. The instructions simply state that 'to use the conversion tables, find the column corresponding to the child's exact age and the row corresponding to his raw score, the cell where the row and column intersect contains the child's standardized score'.

Test EH3

Only a provisional standardization of EH3 appears to have been carried out. This was done in 1973 in 'a rural county in North West England' and involved 4352 children, covering the age range 11:03–15:07. The sample consisted of 1239 children aged 11–12, 1273 children aged 12–13 and 1840 children aged 13–15. No further details are given of the standardization sample. This casts doubt upon the representativeness of the sample. However, the authors do state that the standardization is only provisional.

Scoring

Tests EH1 and 2

These are scored in a straightforward fashion with each correct answer counting for one point. Conversion tables for converting raw scores to standardized scores (based on a mean of 100 and standard deviation of 15) are provided.

Test EH3

As this test is a speed test, the 'score' is the amount the child has read in the fixed time. This is assessed by counting the number of brackets in which the child has underlined one answer. This gives an 'attempt' score for the child. The instructions say that this 'attempt' score is then to be converted to a rate score using the table provided. This table gives the cumulative percentage of the sample of 163 children who reached each point (the ages of the children concerned are not given in this table). A set of conversion tables are provided to turn these raw scores into standardized scores. Instructions for the use of these conversion tables are not provided, nor is there an explanation of the method by which they were constructed. The tables are available for three age ranges.

The brackets in which the children have to underline words are irregularly spaced throughout the text.

Reliability

No reliability data are provided for Test EH3. KR-20 reliability coefficients are calculated for each year group in tests EH1 and EH2. The numbers involved in each group range from 219–430 and the KR-20 reliabilities range from 0.94 down to 0.81. The standard errors of measurement have been calculated from these and range from 3.76–6.48.

Validity

There are no studies quoted giving the correlation between scores on these tests and other reading tests. As far as content validity is concerned, it has already been noted that the test is designed to assess 4 facets of reading prowess but the relationship between these aspects of reading prowess and the content of the test has not been explained and it is hard for the lay observer to see it.

Test use

This test has been used by the ILEA in its literacy survey. The ILEA, apparently, had problems with the standardization (ILEA Literacy Survey: 1976 Follow-Up; ILEA 412, 1977).

General evaluation

The contents of these tests are not very interesting and the material may not appeal to the children at whom it is aimed. There are inadequacies in the standardization and the relationship of the material to the stated aims of the test is unclear.

The Reading Vocabulary Tests

Reviewed by Ann Forrester

Authors: Alan Brimer and Herbert Gross
Publisher: Educational Evaluation Enterprises
Distributor: Educational Evaluation Enterprises
Age range: 6:09–11:11
1979 (M, T); S not stated
Group tests

Test content

The two parallel forms of the test each contain 36 sentences, each of which has a single word missing. Five numbered words are printed below each sentence, one of these being the missing word. The child has to select the appropriate word and record its number in a space provided to the right of the sentence, though other clear methods of indicating choice are accepted.

Purpose

The tests are described as measuring 'understanding of individual words in the context of sentences', and were 'developed as measures of reading comprehension for Primary Schools'.

Item preparation

Items, from which the two parallel scales were to be formulated, were given preliminary trials, but no information is given about how these trials were conducted, or about the source of the items themselves.

Administration

A test sheet is needed for each child, along with a pencil or ballpoint pen. The examiner needs a copy of the Manual, a stop-watch for preference, and a blackboard and chalk for demonstration. The children are allowed 30 minutes to work at the test; the time needed to give the instructions would be quite brief.

The instructions for the children and directions for the examiner are very clear and explicit, and well laid out on the front page of the Manual. In the case of young children, it is permissible to adapt the instructions to ensure that the children know what to do, but the examiner is warned to avoid helping with the actual test questions.

Standardization

Standardization data are tabulated but have very little accompanying explanation. Both forms of the test were standardized, using the same sample, but no dates are given, nor information about sampling design, nor of number of schools involved. Only primary schools were used, though the test is also recommended for use with first-year secondary pupils. Boys and girls of primary ages were more or less equally represented: other variables affecting the constitution of the sample are not mentioned.

Statistical data are given by sex and by upper and lower age groups. The upper age limit is 11:11—presumably the limit of the standardization group—but the lower junior limit is not specified. There were 500 children in the total sample.

The raw score distribution was normalized and age-score regressions calculated, to provide deviation-type standardized scores (mean 100, standard deviation 15). Tables provide an adjustment at six-month intervals for Forms A and B separately. In addition, raw scores may be converted to 'scale scores' which, 'based upon a system of "sample-free" measures, provide a scale of 20 points covering the 7–12 age-range in which all the intervals are of equal size'. This, the only explanation of the 'scale scores', continues: 'It is possible through these scores to make direct comparisons of levels of reading for children of different ages' (Manual, p. 2). Presumably this is a reference to a use of Rasch scaling methods (as also, for example, in The Infant Reading Tests). This may not be apparent to all readers, from the description given in the Manual.

Scoring

Instructions for scoring are clear and straightforward. The child's answers are aligned with a key printed in the Manual for ease and speed of marking. Raw scores are then readily transformed into standardized scores or scale scores by reference to the tables provided. No correction for guessing is suggested. Raw and transformed scores can be entered at the head of the child's test sheet.

Reliability

Conventional and Rasch item analysis was carried out, using data from the standardization sample, and certain items were discarded as a result. Reliability coefficients (KR-20) and standard errors of measurement were calculated for each form, using the raw data from the final standardization. Internal reliability coefficients are 0.80 and above for the 2–3 year upper and lower age groups. Estimates based on the whole group inevitably raised the coefficient (around 0.9), since the age range was wider.

Reliability was also measured by comparing the parallel forms. In this case the coefficients were slightly lower. There is no report of test-retest measures.

It should be noted, that when the total sample was grouped by both age-span and sex, the subgroups were small in numbers (e.g. 96 girls below 9 years), thus reducing confidence in the estimates pertaining to such groups.

Validity

No validity studies are reported. Considered on 'face validity', the task bears some resemblance to the stated test purpose, but presents as a more specific semantic, syntactic and decoding task than the rather vague 'understanding' skill described, (i.e. words in context, etc.).

Interpretation

The little guidance given refers to the scale scores; the standardized scores, being declared of familiar form, are not discussed. Direct comparison of reading levels for children of different ages is invited, using the scale scores. The wisdom of this guidance, and indeed of producing the scale scores at all, can be queried. The meaning of 'equal intervals' should be questioned. The actual skills involved in the harder sentences are not necessarily mirrored in the easy ones, so that an improvement of, say, 2 points, at one end of the scale does not have the same meaning or significance as a 2-point improvement at the other end. The Manual does not strictly invite comparison of score changes, but there is a real risk that the scale would be used in this way, and no warning is given against it. The need for comparison of children of different ages is unclear. Grouping the advanced youngster with the slow older child has distinct disadvantages (different learning rates, different teaching techniques required, social effects), and the setting of similar work for children of different ages, scoring the same points, would not take account of age interest, nor of suitable styles of presentation. The needs of children of different ages will vary, as do the skills through which they attain. Inter-child comparisons, if for educational purposes, are more meaningfully made by reference to the standardized scores. Moreover, age equivalents of raw scores can be readily deduced from the table of standardized scores, should they be needed for matching materials graded with regard to comprehension level.

A table of percentile equivalents for the standardized scores would, perhaps, have been more useful than the scale score points.

General evaluation

The tests provide a relatively quick and easy measure, in a well-tried form, and undoubtedly involve the children in reading with a degree of comprehension (the full description, 'understanding of individual words in the context of a sentence', seems more pedantic than meaningful).

The form of response, required from the child, perhaps owes more to the objective of quick, easy and accurate marking than to accurate assessment of the child. The selection of a number equivalent for the chosen word, and its transfer to the correct space on the right of the page, is very open to error. Children with directional difficulties are likely to read off the number to the right instead of the one to the left of the chosen word, and young children particularly, are likely to make mistakes in aligning their response with the item, with resultant omissions and confusions. It would have been preferable if the children were asked to ring or underline their chosen word, though this would reduce the ease of marking, or at least require the supply of a marking template at extra cost.

An instruction to remind the children about turning over, or an instruction to the tester to check this point, might be helpful. In many other respects the Manual is well designed, though exceedingly brief; it provides insufficient technical data, and inadequate guidance on interpretation.

From a technical viewpoint, a larger standardization sample might have been desirable, particularly in view of the amount of 'processing' carried out, i.e. the sub-groupings considered, and the age-span of the adjusted scores. Also standard errors of measurement for the standardized scores and comment on how they should be applied would have been useful, and possibly more useful than the same information which *is* supplied with regard to the raw scores.

The tests do have the advantage of being quite recently developed, so the normative data can be taken as currently relevant if we can trust their representativeness. The claim that the scores provide 'sample-free' measures is presumably based upon use of the Rasch model in the development of the test, but that claim depends heavily on its assumptions being adequately met. There is no discussion on this point.

Salford Sentence Reading Test

Reviewed by A. Stibbs

Author: G. E. Bookbinder
Publisher: Hodder & Stoughton
Distributor: Hodder & Stoughton
Age range: 6:10–11:09
1974–75 (S); 1976 (M)
No revisions apparent
1981 (M, T) printings reviewed
Individual test

Test content

There are three cards (Forms A, B and C) each with 13 different sentences of increasing difficulty and decreasing print size, and each with the instructions for administration printed on the back. Testees are to read the sentences on one card aloud and in order, whilst the tester records and counts errors. A figure representing a reading age is printed at the end of each sentence.

Purpose

The Manual says the test is of 'the basic mechanics of reading . . . to give an accurate and speedy assessment of reading attainment up to a reading age of 10:6+'. The assessment is normative, though the emphasis on median scores in the Manual might suggest that the author envisages its use especially for distinguishing above-average readers from below-average readers. Although the tester is instructed to record as well as count errors, there is no suggestion that the record of errors could be analysed for diagnostic purposes. The test seems to be designed on an assumption that 'the basic mechanics of reading' are signalled by word recognition, and that word recognition is indicated by a recoding of word-signs into word-sounds. It is noteworthy that the Manual describes the test, despite its title, as a test of word recognition rather than as a test of sentence reading. One would not quibble with this, especially when the sentences are peculiar combinations of graded words (very like those on the more familiar Holborn Scale) which it is hard to imagine being uttered or written. For example:

> 'Arthur's unusual and attractively shaped moustache certainly improved his appearance' (A: 12). 'This restaurant has an enviable reputation for serving delicious dishes' (C: 13).

Incidentally, the use of names, especially of place names or persons' names with spelling patterns unusual for English, seems to introduce an unnecessarily chancy element into word recognition by juniors and top infants.

Item preparation

'The test was constructed largely on a trial-and-error basis' (Manual). Increasing length and unfamiliarity of word was assumed to relate to difficulty. Pilot tests were carried out on unspecified 'samples of children', then revised items were tried on 'further samples of 50–100' children until norms were 'fairly well equated' and inter-test correlations, between the three forms of the test and between them and the Schonell Graded Word Reading Test, of 0.95+ were obtained. The norm with which scores for each test was compared was the revised norm for the Schonell Graded Word Reading Test. So the method by which the test was devised suggests that it is really only a way of measuring Schonell GWRT scores without using the Schonell Test.

Administration

The teacher is to give the junior or top infant pupil a card on which is printed one of the three forms of the test, and invite the pupil to read from the beginning (or from a later point from which the testee can still read two successive sentences without error). The teacher is then to record and count errors in the reading and stop at the end of the sentence in which the sixth error is made. An error is defined as an incorrectly 'read' (i.e. pronounced?) word not spontaneously corrected by the testee, or a pause of 6–7 seconds. The teacher is to correct errors straight after they are made except when it is judged that there is no disadvantage in waiting until the sentence is completed.

A form of words for introducing the test is recommended in the Manual and in the instructions on the back of the test card. There is a warning against using the same form of the test twice in a 12-month period. The procedure is straightforward and the instructions are clear, but it might help teachers if the Manual gave a rough estimate of the time it might take to give the test to 30 children.

Standardization

The Schonell GWRT was used as the norm in the initial standardization which was performed on 250 randomly selected children from five Salford schools which—on the evidence of the Schonell GWRT—'represented national standards'. (The current norms for the Schonell GWRT are based on trials with Salford children too). Forms C and B of the test, respectively, were then given to 20 000 juniors and top infants in successive months of June and median Reading Ages (RAs) were obtained which were, for each age group, within a month of the previous or next year's RA plus or minus 12 months.

Scoring

The teacher counts errors and at the end of the sentence in which the sixth error is made, the teacher stops the test and calculates the testee's RA using a simple formula. The Manual defends the formulating of results as Reading Ages rather than as standardized scores because they are more handy for the teacher. The Manual also gives a table for converting the RAs into percentile rankings, a table constructed by the analysis of scores of children in 3 age-groups in a representative sample of about a quarter of the 'entire population' (which presumably means of the 2500 used for the comparison of the medians 12 months apart).

Reliability

Trials with 250 Salford schoolchildren produced ranges of reading ages with medians equal or 'very close' to the median chronological ages, and correlations between scores on each form, for each year-group, between 0.95 and 0.99. There was also a test of groups of about 50 children at a year's interval on two forms of the Salford Test and on the NFER BD Test. Figures are given which suggest that the Salford Test had a better test-retest reliability than the NFER.

Validity

Scores on forms of the test were also correlated with those on eight other English tests (though the samples vary from as few as 28 to only as many as 82 and single—different—year-groups were used for the separate correlations). Not surprisingly, in view of the way the test was devised and standardized, the best correlation was found to be with the Schonell Graded Word Reading Test.

Interpretation

The Manual has a simplistic approach to the concepts of 'reading attainment', 'the basic mechanics of reading', 'word recognition' and 'reading age'. It advocates no caution in interpreting the scores or, in using them, to make judgements about children's reading aptitudes, attitudes or materials. The formulation of scores as reading ages to the nearest month gives them a semblance of precision which is misleading. There is no warning to be specially cautious in interpreting the scores of children with accents unfamiliar to the teachers, especially the scores of children for whom English may not be a first language.

General evaluation

This test has obvious physical advantages over the better-known Holborn reading test and over the popular Schonell and Burt word recognition tests to which it is also comparable. It has three forms. It is printed on stiff card. It has instructions on the back where—except in the case of illegal photocopying of the front—they cannot become divorced from the test and be replaced by inaccurate folk-memories of the scoring system. The cut-off point of the scores offers no temptation to use the test inappropriately with secondary pupils.

From the rather terse reporting of the Manual, it seems that the reliability of the test has been established but rather unsystematically and only on Salford children in June. The important criticisms of the test concern its validity. Its validity is 'borrowed' from that of the much earlier Schonell Graded Word Reasoning Test, with all the dubious assumptions behind that test about the relationship between pronunciation and word recognition and about the contribution of word recognition to 'reading'. The danger in these assumptions is that they may lead teachers to teach atomistically as well as test atomistically, without regard for the meanings of texts and the attitudes of readers.

However, the presentation of the graded words in this Salford Test as quasi-sentences may have some pedagogical, if not methodical, usefulness, because it suggests that reading has more to do with construing combinations of words than with barking out single words, even though the sentences in the test are neither predictable nor contextualized like sentences in 'real reading'.

For junior-school teachers who need a screen or a reassurance for their complex, intuitive judgements about children's reading attainments, this test would provide a convenient and easily-administered prop. Its unfamiliarity (compared to the Schonell, Burt and Holborn tests) is an argument in its favour because none of its parallel forms are likely to be as well-known (literally—by heart—in the case of some) to the testees. However, it is misnamed, since the sounding out of words in artificial combinations is hardly 'sentence reading' or even, arguably, 'reading'.

Schonell Reading Tests

Reviewed by A. Stibbs

Author: Fred J. Schonell
Publisher: Oliver & Boyd
Distributor: Oliver & Boyd
Tests
R1 Graded Word Reading Test (GWRT)
R2 Simple Prose Reading Test (SPRT)
R3 Silent Reading Test A (SRTA)
R4 Silent Reading Test B (SRTB)
Age ranges*: 5–15 years (R1)
      6–9 years (R2)
      7–11 years (R3)
      9–13 years (R4)
1942–1945† (T); 1955 (M)
1971 (S: R1); S dates incomplete
1978 (M†); 1970–80* (T) printings reviewed
Individual tests: R1, R2; Group tests: ‡ R3, R4

Test content

The four tests are separate, but have a single Manual with separate sections for the different tests with none of the text referring to all four at once.

The Graded Word Reading Test (R1: GWRT) is presented as an array of 100 words, five to a line, the lines themselves being paired. The words increase in strangeness as pairs of lines show a decrease in print size. Individual children are to read the words aloud, in the order in which they are printed, to the tester.

The Simple Prose Reading Test (R2: SPRT) consists of four paragraphs of continuous prose ('My Dog'), the first in very large print and the other three in large print. It is to be read aloud to the tester and there are questions for the tester to ask the testee about the passage when the passage has been taken away from the testee.

---

* Taken from Appendix 5 of Schonell and Goodacre (1974). Neither publication dates nor target populations are explicit or completely inferrable from the Manual and tests supplied.

† The 'Manual' referred to below is the "Handbook of Instructions", 12th impression, copyrighted and first published in 1955.

‡ Schonell and Goodacre (1974) classified the set of all four tests as 'individual tests', but it is clear from wording in the Manual ('Give to each pupil . . . and instruct them') that R3 and R4 are intended as group tests.

Both Silent Reading Tests (R3: SRTA and R4: SRTB) consist of a series of very-short, unrelated 'comprehension' passages (most less than 50 words in length) each with follow-up questions. In SRTA each of the 18 passages has questions on literal comprehension requiring various methods of answering— writing one-word answers, selecting the correct word from a list, filling in a missing word, choosing a response and following apt instructions about underlining, and so on. SRTB (the harder one) is less eclectic: two (or occasionally three) gaps near the end of each of the passages (rather longer than in SRTA on average) have to be filled with words from lists provided. Both SRTs contrive to keep the evidence of reading attainment uncontaminated by writing attainment.

Many teachers will know much of the GWRT by heart almost as well as their pupils; as a result of over-using it they may never again be able to pronounce 'canary' and 'angel' correctly! Similarly, the narrator's dog, cat, and Fred's mice, which occur in the opening sentences of SPRT, SRTA, and SRTB, respectively, will be old friends. The choice of words in GWRT is referred to below. It is clear that in the other three tests there has been an attempt to use material of interest to young children (e.g. dogs, cats, mice). However, the dated gentility of the SPRT ('He is able to catch a brightly coloured ball in his mouth') may be specially confusing to pupils who are reading *aloud* in the *first* person, i.e. simulating their own story telling. SRTA uses a miscellany of information, bits of story, and two verses. One of these, No. 12, so displaces the rhyming word (which is the answer to the question on it) that it may appear nonsensical to the reader. The SRTB passages are mostly bits of narrative (some quasi-fictional and some quasi-historical), but information about migrating birds, icebergs, hop plants and cotton goods creeps in towards the end. Hans and Yaina appear in SRTA and Caesar in SRTB.

Purpose

The Manual says nothing about the purpose of the test. However, since it was clearly thought necessary to devise all four tests, and since they are presented as a package, one can infer that they are supposed to fulfil different functions and that together these are supposed to add up to a model of reading attainment. There is a hint of differentiation within some of the individual test instructions too. SPRT provides norms for three separate attainments—reading correctly, reading quickly, and answering questions about what has been read (the last after the text has been taken away so that as well as being a test of comprehension it is a memory test—rather than a reference-skills test). The Manual suggests that SRTA can be used to measure speed of reading as well as comprehension, and an aside in the notes on administering GWRT says that '. . . word analysis and synthesis . . . (is) . . . one of the things revealed by the test' (p. 4). Schonell and Goodacre (1974) describes the GWRT as 'a measuring instrument' of a pupil's 'power of word recognition' with the aim 'to discover the total number of these words that the testee can read' (Appendix 4). The notions of reading, comprehension, analysis and synthesis which appear to lie behind the GWRT are discussed below.

Schonell designed separate diagnostic tests of reading, but a record of the errors made in a GWRT could possibly be used by experts to diagnose particular weaknesses in aural discrimination or pronunciation. A note in the Manual 'On the Use of Silent Reading Test B with Older Pupils Backward in Reading' suggests that (but not how) comparing numbers of errors made in the test with time taken to complete the test could be used to choose remedial exercises (presumably because they would help a teacher to distinguish backward from merely careless readers). In Schonell and Goodacre (1974) it is suggested that a note of 'mispronunciations and errors' (on the GWRT) could be used in 'planning a suitable remedial diagnostic programme for the pupil' (Appendix 4).

Item preparation

There is no information on item preparation in the Manual, but for the GWRT Schonell and Goodacre (1974) tell how the 100 words of the GWRT were 'selected from 300 words administered individually to approximately 60 children in each of ten age-groups. The words were then arranged in continuous order of difficulty'. Because usage changes it is reasonable to assume that some words in Schonell's 'hundred' will have become less familiar (e.g. 'canary') and others more familiar (e.g. 'university' which occurs a 'year' after 'canary' in the GWRT). Familiarity, as well as 'analysis and synthesis', plays a part in word recognition and in pronunciation, so the order of difficulty will have changed since the test was devised. Experience bears this out. It would be very easy to revise the order simply by counting the number of children in a large random sample of testees who mispronounced each word. The normative function which the original version of the GWRT has come to fulfil presumably acts as a disincentive to publishing such a revision.

Administration

All the tests are extremely straightforward to administer. They are quick, and easy to understand (even for children who have not done them before) and they have thorough and sensitive 'tester scripts'.

It is a pity that the ubiquitous GWRT is printed on paper which soon—given its over-use—becomes tatty. Teachers tend to photocopy the front, which carries the graded words, but not the back, which carries the instructions. So the word-lists are passed on with the reverence which characterizes the preservation of sacred texts whilst the instructions are subject to the vagaries which characterize oral traditions. In my first two years of teaching I was required to measure 'Schonells' with an instructionless sheet and told three different folk-versions of the scoring system, all wrong.

Standardization

The Manual does not mention standardization, nor does it refer to any technical literature. The 1971 revised norms printed on the back of the current print of the GWRT refer to Appendix 4 of Schonell and Goodacre (1974). There, a little (only) is said about how Bookbinder obtained the revised norms, but nothing about how the original norms were obtained. In the revision, norms up to 7:06 years were obtained from a sample of 300 Salford children and the reader is referred to an article by Bookbinder. The norms for older children were obtained from blanket tests on 10 000 Salford children, taking Salford's 67th percentile as the National Norm (mean) because of the Salford children's performance on nationally standardized IQ tests.

Pumfrey (1977) cites a recent revision of the word order and a restandardization which differs from what he calls 'the publisher's 1972 revision' but less so from Schonell's original norms.

Scoring

The scoring of all the tests is extremely easy: that is part of their appeal. The GWRT is correctly scored by counting the number of words pronounced correctly (and abandoning hope of further words correctly pronounced only when ten successive mistakes have been made). The SPRT provides tables from which Reading Ages (RAs) for word recognition, comprehension and speed can be read off by using totals of pronunciation errors, number of questions answered correctly, and time taken to read the piece aloud. For both SR tests it is sufficient to read the RA from the total of correct answers. In the Manual, the Instructions for Administering the GWRT show how to convert an RA into a Reading Quotient (as a ratio of ages, not as a deviation score).

Reliability

The Manual mentions no reliability studies, but for GWRT Schonell and Goodacre (1974, Appendix 4) report—with no further details—that 'the reliability coefficient on retests of groups of children was 0.96'.

Validity

It is hardly an exaggeration to say that the Schonell Reading Tests, especially the GWRT, are 'self-validating'. They have been familiar instruments throughout almost the whole careers of even the longest-serving primary and secondary English teachers. They are by far the most popular reading tests. The Bullock Survey (DES, 1975) found that R1, R3 and R4 were the three most popular reading tests in terms of the numbers of secondary schools in which they were used (Table 84), and in primary schools those same three tests were the first, fourth, and fifth most used, respectively (the Burt and Holborn word-recognition tests—rivals of Schonell's GWRT—taking second and third places) (Table 39). This dominance has been reduced more recently (Gipps and Wood, 1981) but it is fair to say that R1 is so widely used that reading attainment is virtually defined as scoring on the GWRT. It is so handy, quick and easy to score that it is used in both primary and secondary schools for such purposes as streaming, screening for remedial reading withdrawal, monitoring progress at reading, providing a shorthand description of reading ability at 11+ transfer, and providing a check on subjective holistic assessments of reading ability.

For this reason, to say that the GWRT had content validity would be almost tautologous. The Manual finds no need to discuss the validity of any of the tests. Furthermore, the norms for the GWRT are so long established that they are sometimes used as the norms against which to standardize other tests (the Salford Sentence Reading Tests, for instance). So it becomes meaningless to discuss the concurrent validity of the GWRT with respect to such tests. The Manual does not discuss it.

In view of its widespread use, it is important to ask what GWRT so handily and popularly measures. The Manual mentions 'comprehension' and 'speed' in relation to R2, R3, and R4. So R1—if it is not otiose—presumably measures some other, perhaps lower-order, reading factor such as size of vocabulary (see 'Purpose' above). It is noteworthy that the Manual mentions recording 'the number of words correctly read' (p. 4). It implies that evidence of such 'correct reading' is 'the testee's pronunciation' (p. 4). It says 'word analysis and synthesis' is 'one of the things revealed by the test' (p. 4). 'Guessing should *not* be discouraged' and testees should be allowed 'to see if there are any further words they recognise' (p. 5). From this it seems that 'correct reading' entails 'recognition' but that recognition is conditional upon correct pronunciation and is a process in which (phonic?) analysis and synthesis play a part, as does guessing. Chapter 1 of Schonell and Goodacre (1974) provides a rationale for linking word recognition with sound recognition and sound reconstruction. This could possibly explain the apparent contradictions in the Manual's implications. The chapter also asserts the importance of meaning, but meaning only in the sense of the reference inhering in isolated words. (At a coarse level, this concept of meaning is adequate for content words, and it is noteworthy that the GWRT unlike its rivals—the Burt and Holborn word-recognition tests—consists entirely of unambiguous content words).

So for the GWRT to measure 'reading', it seems we need to make a number of assumptions:

(1) reading is recognizing words;
(2) words correctly pronounced have been (or are) recognized;
(3) incorrectly pronounced words have not been (or are not) recognized;
(4) analysis and synthesis leads to recognition/correct pronunciation; and,
(5) guessing is a desirable part of reading (and since the GWRT provides no semantic context this must mean guessing from phonetic evidence—knowing the complex rules of English spelling and seeing if phonic reconstruction yields a sound which the testee recognizes).

It is easy to think of counter evidence to these propositions from experience. Words we have never seen before are understood if they are met in supportive contexts; we can correctly pronounce many words we do not recognize and do not understand; we recognize and understand many words we cannot pronounce. However, it could be argued that these are special cases, such as the GWRT is careful to avoid, just as it avoids using function words or ambiguous content words with meanings specially dependent on context. But the GWRT does not avoid such cases. For example:

(1) it does contain words which even advanced readers may not recognize ('homonym', 'metamorphosis');
(2) it contains eminently pronounceable words which the 'readers' may not have seen before and may not know the meanings of ('classification', 'procrastinate'), and—following the success of the pop group which has put a month on the nation's 'Schonell R.A.'—'adamant');
(3) it contains words which children may recognize even though they cannot pronounce them ('miscellany', 'colonel').

The GWRT also contains words which defy phonic reconstruction ('ceiling', 'gnome', 'orchestra'). The degree to which these will provide difficulties may depend upon the method by which the testee has been taught to read. The Manual seems to assume that readers will use a 'phonic' reading process ('analysis and synthesis'). In the period since the Test was designed, however, methods of teaching initial literacy other than those based on phonics have gained some currency: the Manual takes no account of this. There have also been well-argued claims that phonic recoding can play no part in competent, silent, speedy reading so its emphasis in initial literacy could be harmful in the long run (see Smith, 1978). So the widespread use of a test with the assumptions which seem to lie behind this one might propagate a model of reading which does not help the pupils of the teachers who use it. It is a pity that the norms of the GWRT overlap those of SRTA and SRTB because the silent reading tests, whatever their faults, do not suggest that reading entails reading *aloud*.

Interpretation

All the scores for the tests are convertible into Reading Ages, which are popular with teachers because they seem to give an instant indication of whether children are above or below average, catching up or slipping back, or whatever, and whether or not a group is, on the whole, up to a national norm.

The tables for SPRT in the Manual do make it clear that testees can have different RAs according to whether one considers their pronunciation, speed or comprehension. It is a pity that this potentially subversive discrimination is not given more prominence, so that it could suggest to users of the tests that children might have different RAs according to the mood they are in, their attitude to the tester, their interest in the content of the test, and so on.

The tables are misleading because they provide seeming equivalences between the numbers of items correct and RAs given to the nearest month. This can tempt teachers to test children on the GWRT every month in the hope that they will get one more word right each time and thus demonstrate steady and constantly monitored 'progress'. With such a handy test this misuse is quite practicable, and the Manual does not warn against it.

General evaluation

The Schonell Reading Tests have been so popular for so long because they are simple and speedy, and they painlessly yield easily-interpretable results. They are easy to do and easy to administer. The GWRT especially has a seductive simplicity with its magic 100 words and its simple scoring system. But by contemporary standards the tests are deficient. They are dated in vocabulary and do not have parallel forms, despite their familiarity even to the testees. The Manual tells the user nothing about the purpose, target population, item design, validity, or reliability of the tests, nor the range of confidence with which the results should be interpreted. The popularity of the tests has led to their norms being used to validate other tests. The disputable model of reading inferrable from the Manual and the implicit claims of the test have influenced teachers of reading to the extent that the GWRT, at least, has become self validating. The use of the tests has become a pseudo-scientific excuse for teachers to avoid making professional pragmatic judgements about the range, degree, and balance of children's reading abilities. So the tests, which were once, no doubt, a blessing, have become a curse.

References

DES (1975). "A Language for Life" (The Bullock Report). London: HMSO.

Gipps, C. V. and Wood, R. (1981). The testing of reading in LEAs: The Bullock Report seven years on. *Educational Studies* 7, 133–143.

Pumfrey, P. D. (1977). "Reading: Tests and Assessment Techniques". Sevenoaks: Hodder & Stoughton.

Schonell, F. J. and Goodacre, E. (1974). "The Psychology and Teaching of Reading" (5th edn). Edinburgh: Oliver & Boyd.

Smith, F. (1978). "Reading". Cambridge: Cambridge University Press.

Senior English Test

Brief Report

Author: NFER 'with the help of teachers in the field of technical education'
Publisher: NFER-Nelson
Distributor: NFER-Nelson
Age range: 16:00–18:00
1964 (T)
1975 (S); 1976 (M)
1976 (M); 1982 (T) printings reviewed
Group test (restricted)*

This is to be used 'primarily as a test of the basic knowledge of English for general entry groups in Technical Colleges, or their equivalent' (Manual, p. 2). The 56 items test comprehension, vocabulary, grammar skills and the ability to construct sentences and to summarize. Both completion items (including a crossword) and free-response items are employed. Marking is said to be 'completely objective'. Testees are allowed one hour.

Monthly-corrected age norms (mean 100, standard deviation 15) are given for boys based on over 1300 technical college students. KR-20 for 374 students was 0.92. No validity studies are reported.

---

* 'It is not available to schools except where a Technical College prefers to conduct its selection and allocation procedure within the school framework and makes copies available to a school' (Manual, p. 2).

Southgate Group Reading Tests: Test 1

Reviewed by Neville Bennett

Author: Vera Southgate
Publisher: Hodder & Stoughton
Distributor: Hodder & Stoughton
Age range: 5:08–8:01
1957 (S); 1959 (M, T)
No revisions apparent
1978 (M); 1980 (T) printings reviewed
Group test

Test content

Three parallel forms—Forms A, B and C—are provided each containing the same four practice items. Each form consists of 30 items. Two types of item are presented: (1) a box containing a picture and a selection of five words wnere the child has to locate the word representing the picture; and, (2) a box of the same size as above but containing a selection of five words only. Here the child has to locate the correct word from a verbal instruction; for example, 'Now point to box number four. The one with no picture. Listen carefully while I tell you which word to look for. This time I want you to look for the word "the". Find the word "the" and draw a ring round it' (Manual, p. 10).

Purpose

'It is expected that this new group test will provide teachers with a simple, speedy and reliable method of making a preliminary assessment of the level of reading ability of those pupils who are still in the initial stages of learning to read' (Manual, p. 5). The author envisages the test as a preliminary survey of reading ability, which, when necessary, can be followed by individual reading tests.

Item preparation

A full account of the construction of the test appears in a thesis housed at the University of Birmingham. Development took five years during which time 16 tests were constructed comprising 676 items and tried out on children aged 6–7 years and with older children of low reading ability. Item analyses were carried out using the technique of upper, middle and lower thirds. Items with low validity values were discarded together with items which did not fall within the required levels of difficulty. New items were devised as necessary until the present levels of validity and reliability were achieved. There is no definition of 'low validity value' or any indication of the level of difficulty utilized.

Administration

The test instructions are given orally with the children responding in the test booklet. The test is untimed. The whole group of children work each item together, the tester waiting until all are finished before proceeding to the next item. To children who cannot answer the question the tester should say 'If it is too hard just leave it'. The total time envisaged, from commencing the practice items, is approximately 15–20 minutes. It is suggested that no more than 20 children be tested at one time and should be spaced out to avoid copying. The tester is warned against offering any assistance. The instructions to teachers are clear and concise and a script is provided for each item.

Standardization

The standardization was carried out by the author but was limited to the City of Worcester. The entire population of children in the City aged from 5:08–8:01 on June 30th, 1957, were tested, giving a total of 2329. Each child completed two of the three parallel forms providing scores on 4658 scripts. Form A was completed by 1161 children, Form B by 2329 and Form C by 1168.

It is claimed that there is no reason to suppose that the reading ability of the children in Worcester differs markedly from those elsewhere in the country; but this claim is unsubstantiated. Similarly unsupported is the claim that 'it may well be that norms established in this way will prove more reliable than those which would have been achieved by using a sample of children from a wider area' (Manual, p. 18).

Norms are based on reading ages in preference to standardized scores on the rationale that these are more understandable and meaningful for teachers. The method of achieving these norms was based on median raw scores. Percentile norms are not available. Norms for each sex are not provided even though data are reported to indicate that by the age of seven girls are some five or six months ahead of boys in reading ability on this test. More recent—although still dated—norms for seven-year olds are available from the data of the National Child Development Study (see Test Use).

Scoring

The correct answers for each item in the three forms of the test are provided and answers other than those are not allowed. Incorrect marking mode is allowed, however, e.g. a square drawn round a word instead of a ring. The correct number of items is recorded on the front of the test booklet. The table of norms is then entered to gain a reading age. It is assumed that teachers know how to do this since no explanation is given.

Reliability

Information on reliability is limited to the relationship between parallel forms since the author argues, contentiously, 'that agreement between parallel forms may be said to be the most stringent measurement of the reliability of a test'. The reader is directed to a table on p. 24 (actually on p. 21) of the Manual to show that the greatest difference in mean raw scores is insignificant at the 1 per cent level ($t = 1.6$). In addition, two of the parallel forms were administered to 96 children in one infant school. The product-moment correlation between the two sets of raw scores was 0.95.

Validity

Information concerning validity is limited to concurrent validity. Three studies are reported. The first compared teachers' estimates with test scores in two small samples ($n = 40$ and 35) of six-year olds. The correlations gained were 0.95 and 0.88. The second study related the scores of 76 six-year olds on the Southgate Test with those from five 'well known individual reading tests'. The correlations ranged from 0.87–0.94. Finally, 949 children aged 5 years 6 months to 14 years 11 months completed both the Southgate Test and the Schonell Graded Word Reading Test and a correlation of 0.89 was found between the two sets of scores.

Interpretation

No interpretation is provided. This is presumably based on the assumption that teachers will know what action to take on the basis of a reading age.

Test use

In 1965 the test was used by the National Child Development Study on a representative national sample of over 14 000 seven-year olds (Davie *et al.*, 1972). A marked ceiling effect was found, making the test suitable more as a screening device rather than a monitoring instrument.

General evaluation

At the time of the development of the test in the mid 1950s there was what the author describes as a 'vital gap' in the testing field whereby no group-administered test was available to teachers to make an accurate assessment of the levels of attainment of children under the age of seven. This is no longer true, but if evaluated on the basis of the original aim then the levels of concurrent validity achieved with individually administered tests would indicate that the aim has been achieved. Set against this, however, must be doubts concerning limitations in item content, in standardization and reliability.

The purpose of the test is to assess 'reading ability' but reading as a process is not considered. This is simply a test of word recognition. Also, despite the author's claims that children in the City of Worcester could be treated as representative of the country as a whole there is no evidence to support this. The standardization took place a quarter of a century ago and it would thus be wise to treat the norms with caution. A restandardization is overdue and if undertaken the opportunity should be taken to present more comprehensive information on aspects of test reliability.

The test is designed for use by teachers of young children or older children with reading difficulties but it is difficult to envisage what information the test provides which could not be easily gained during the normal process of children reading to their teachers.

Reference

Davie, R., Butler, N. R. and Goldstein, H. (1972). "From Birth to Seven". London: Longmans.

Southgate Group Reading Tests: Test 2

Reviewed by Neville Bennett

Author: Vera Southgate
Publisher: Hodder & Stoughton
Distributor: Hodder & Stoughton
Age range: 7:00–8:11
1960 (S); 1962 (M, T)
No revisions apparent
1976 (M); 1980 (T) printings reviewed
Group test

Test content

Two parallel forms—Forms A and B—are provided each containing the same five practice items. Each form consists of 42 items, all of the sentence completion type. There is a choice of five words for the last word in each sentence and the child has to choose the most appropriate, e.g. 'A sheep's babies are called *lame calves look lambs lamps*'.

Purpose

The test has been designed for use in conjunction with Test 1 to form 'a two-fold assessment of reading ability during the period of learning in which the skill of reading is being acquired, that is, from the early beginnings of reading until the level of reading ability of an average child of 9 or 9.6 years' (Manual, p. 7). Test 2 is thus planned as a consecutive test to Test 1 and is concerned with the range of reading skill which extends from the ability to read the final books in most infant reading schemes to that level of reading ability at which the child is considered literate, i.e. a reading age of about nine years. Tests 1 and 2 used in conjunction 'will enable the busy teacher to make rapid assessments of reading ability from the early beginnings of reading until such time as the basic skill of reading has been taught' (Manual, p. 7).

Item preparation

In the course of the construction of the test ten separate tests comprising 584 items were devised and administered to children in the age range 6:00–10:11. At each stage item analyses were carried out using the techniques of upper, middle and lower thirds. Items with low validity values were discarded as were those which did not fall within the required levels of difficulty. As with Test 1 definition of 'low validity value' is not provided nor an indication of the level of difficulty required.

Administration

Instructions for administration are extensive and include a script for each of the practice items and a separate script for the test proper. Children complete the 42 items by ringing the appropriate sentence ending. Fifteen minutes is allowed for the test during which time the teacher should walk around the room checking that the children are working. Some guidance is allowed particularly when a child cannot find the right word or cannot read the sentence. In such circumstances the teacher can tell the child to try another item. On no account can help in reading the word or sentence be provided.

The two parallel forms of the test have been prepared with the possibility of simultaneous administration to allow for the testing of large groups without the possibility of copying. In such circumstances children sitting next to each other are presented with different forms of the test.

Standardization

The standardization was carried out by the author but was limited to the City of Worcester. The entire population of children in the City aged 7:00–10:11 on May 31st, 1960 were tested, a total of 3751 children; 1739 completed Form A and 1771 Form B (the scores of 241 children aged 10:09–10:11 were excluded because of ceiling effects).

Norms are in the form of reading ages rather than standardized scores. This is in part based on the aim of the test to provide teachers 'with a simple rank order of attainment' and partly due to the distribution of raw scores. Age-related percentile norms are not available although histograms are presented to show the raw score distributions for children aged 7:00–7:02, 7:09–7:11 and 8:09–8:11. These show some disturbing trends. In the youngest age group the modal score is zero comprising 18 per cent of the sample whereas in the oldest group the modal score is 40 with 40 per cent of the sample scoring 39 or over. The distribution for the middle age range is distinctly bi-modal with modes at 0 and 39.

The test is designed to cover the age range seven years to nine years. The histograms clearly show that marked floor effects are likely at the lower age level and equally marked ceiling effects at the upper. Establishing separate norms for boys and girls was considered but rejected. Differences between raw scores on Form A were not significant although they were on Form B for the age 8:11. It was thus decided that 'no useful purpose would be served by the creation of separate norms'. As with Test 1 the norms are based on median raw scores.

Scoring

The correct responses are provided in marking keys and answers other than those listed are not allowed. An incorrect marking mode is allowed, e.g. drawing a rectangle, or underlining a word instead of ringing it. Each correct answer receives one mark but after five consecutive wrong answers or omissions no further marks may be credited. The total score is thus the number of correct items obtained before a block of five consecutive wrong answers. The raw scores are converted to reading ages by reference to the table of norms although no explicit guidance is presented on how this is achieved.

Reliability

Reliability is covered in two lines, and reports only the correlation between Form A and B. This was 0.96 in a sample of 253 children aged 7:06–8:05 from six primary schools in one local education authority.

Validity

Information concerning validity is limited to one study of concurrent validity. The 253 children referred to above were administered Form A and B together with Sentence Completion Test 1 (NFER) and Schonell's Graded Word Reading Test. The NFER test is a group test and the correlations with Form A and B were 0.85 and 0.88. Correlations of the two forms with the Schonell test were 0.82 and 0.83.

Interpretation

No interpretation is provided.

General evaluation

Although designed as an assessment of reading ability the process of reading is not considered. Content validity is assumed, but doubts must be expressed about the suitability of sentence-completion items to fulfil the aim of the test. A wrong answer could be due to inability to read the sentence or lack of the necessary knowledge to choose the correct alternative. As such a number of the items appear more akin to those in a verbal reasoning test.

The standardization is limited to the population of one city over twenty years ago and thus the norms must be treated with caution. The distribution of raw scores from this testing programme provides serious indications of floor effects among the younger children and marked ceiling effects among the older children.

Lack of adequate discrimination, an out-dated standardization, and doubts about validity together with insufficient evidence of reliability seriously limit the value of this test as a survey instrument. Nor is it easy to perceive its usefulness as a diagnostic instrument given the item content, lack of interpretative detail and the unknown relationship between item content and the content of contemporary reading schemes.

SPAR Spelling and Reading Tests

Reviewed by C. J. Phillips

Author: D. Young
Publisher: Hodder & Stoughton
Distributor: Hodder & Stoughton
Age ranges: 7:01–11:03; 11:00–14:09 (1st-year juniors and backward readers
   and spellers to school-leaving age)
1976 (M, T); S not stated
1980 (M); 1980, 1981 (T) printings reviewed
Group test

Purpose

The SPAR tests are presented as 'a means of following the progress towards
literacy of children of a wide range of ability in the first year of junior schools
and of less able pupils to the age of 15:11 . . . Although it is envisaged that
teachers will use both the spelling and reading tests . . . in order to compare and
contrast results, the two (tests) can . . . be used independently' (Manual, p. 1).

Test content

Spelling

For the testing of spelling ability Young provides two banks each of 150 words,
in order of difficulty, from which can be drawn, by an ingenious procedure, ten
equivalent tests of 30 words without overlap, and many more sets with partial
overlap. By this means one has parallel tests, so avoiding the effects of coaching
and practice, 'and the reliability of the scores can be increased by averaging the
results of two (or more) tests' (p. 1).

No information is given on the selection of words. Of the 300 words, 270 are
reported to appear in the 500 words of highest frequency (List 1) in young
children's oral vocabulary (Burroughs, 1957); a further 22 are in Burroughs'
List 2. As to the establishment of order of difficulty for spelling, 'the facility
level of each item was determined from at least two analyses of over 300 papers
from junior and from backward secondary pupils. Samples were equated by
reference to items common to several samples'. Some information, but not
enough, is given about the equivalence of parallel forms of the spelling test: for
145 subjects, the mean difference between two forms of the test was 0.07 points
of raw score.

About 10 per cent of the words appear in Schonell's Graded Word Spelling Tests A or B (1950). The order of difficulty for these words is very similar, but there are a few differences which may reflect vocabulary changes over the intervening 40 years. A few words are common to the SPAR test and Vernon's Graded Word Spelling Test (q.v.), which was also standardized on English children in the 1970s; their positions in the sequence are fairly close.

Reading

The test is in two parts. The first, having 15 items, requires selection of a word from four or five nouns to match a picture. The second part consists of 20 unfinished sentences, to be completed by one of six words. The short sentences are either general knowledge statements (e.g. We put stamps on *letters*) or synonyms (e.g. Loyal means *faithful*). The format is the same as the author's Group Reading Test (q.v.), but the content is different. In the Manual for that test (Young, 1968) there is more information on construction than the test under review; it includes the statement, items were designed to minimize 'demands on vocabulary, general knowledge and intelligence (for) the picture items and the easier sentence items'. That policy seems to apply to the SPAR reading tests also, from inspection of the picture vocabulary. There are two parallel forms, A and B.

Standardization

The reading and spelling tests were standardized in the 1970s, on pupils from junior schools 'known to be representative of the national pattern of achievement in NFER and Moray House tests' (Manual, p. 17). There were 1864 subjects in the standardization sample for the spelling test and about twice that number for the reading tests.

Administration

Directions for administration of the tests are good and very clear. The two parts of the reading test are preceded by three practice items. The parts are timed, but it is not a speeded test since the prescribed times are maximal 'for the benefit of very poor readers'. Total administration of the reading test takes about 20 minutes; about ten minutes should suffice for the 30-item spelling test. 'Each item is presented in a uniform fashion, i.e. by giving the number of the item, the word to be spelled, the phrase or sentence embodying the word and, finally, the word again'. The tester provides the phrases or sentences; unless he is very experienced, they should be prepared in advance of testing.

Scoring

'Such difficulties as there are in marking a spelling test usually arise from misreading of poor handwriting'; credit should be given when doubts can be resolved. The author rightly proposes to give credit also 'for knowledge of the correct sequence of letters and to ignore reversals and inversions of the letters themselves' such as may be written by young children and those with 'perceptual difficulties' (pp. 7–8).

In the testing of reading by multiple-choice items, some children are prepared to respond to items they cannot read, but since there is no way of obliging all testees to conform to this practice, one needs to control, as far as is possible, for 'guessing'. The SPAR reading test, unlike, for example, the Southgate tests (q.v.) which it resembles, has an error ceiling, allowing no credit for correct response after ten errors have been made. No evidence is given, but the number of errors strikes one as rather high in a test of 45 items.

The marking templates, Forms A and B, of the Group Reading Test (op. cit.) may be used with the SPAR Reading tests which are not provided with marking keys. It should be noted that the SPAR tests are not equivalent forms of Young's earlier reading test: the norms are different.

Norms

Raw scores are convertible to attainment ages and to quotients, i.e. standard scores with mean 100 and standard deviation 15. Probably no justification for the use of 'reading age' and 'spelling age' is necessary, but one would expect the user to be offered guidance on the interpretation of 'quotients'.

Correct spelling of 3 to 25 words, out of a maximum of 30, represents spelling ages ranging from 6:00 to 10:07 years. Thus the number of words, less than five on average, to represent a year of spelling gain is rather few. Equivalent spelling ages below a raw score of 7 are extrapolations, the standardization population ranging from 7:01 to 11:03. The same inference can be made for reading scores below 16. The range of reading ages is 5:09–10:08 years for corresponding raw scores of 6 and 42 in the 45-item tests. For reading and spelling, attainment ages are expressed in decimal fractions of years, not in months. A reason for this seems to be the inclusion of equivalent scores from the Graded Word Reading tests of Burt, Schonell and Vernon and the Schonell Graded Word Spelling Tests in the conversion table (p. 28). The sources of these extra data are not declared, but the implication is that samples were tested by those instruments as well as the SPAR tests.

Tables 1 and 3, for spelling and reading respectively, convert raw scores to quotients for monthly intervals between 7:00 and 8:11, i.e. the range of ages for first-year juniors at the beginning and the ending of the school year, when age is reckoned in completed months. For pupils approaching nine years, a ceiling effect begins to operate: unless one's purpose is only to discriminate among average and below-average readers and spellers, the tests become less and less appropriate for normal groups above the first year of junior school.

Two further tables, 2 and 4, give quotients for ages 8:00–15:11, i.e. from second-year juniors to school-leaving age. These tables overlap by a year those already mentioned, yielding different quotients. This feature must surely be confusing to many users, since it is not explained that the number of years in school, as well as pupils' age, forms a basis for the standardization. If there is some value in having a measure of attainment status for older slow-learning children, its expression in terms of standard scores lays claim to metric precision that is unwarranted; expectancy tables or percentile ranks in broad bands of age and rank would be sufficiently informative, less liable to misuse, and statistically more responsible. 'At the secondary level the norms depend on calibration from . . . nationally standardized tests' of attainment published by NFER and Moray House. No further information is given. A valuable feature of the norms for older subjects is the fact of their being based on reading and spelling results from the same samples, amounting to nearly a thousand subjects.

'In both reading and spelling, girls show a superiority of 3 points of raw score at 8 years. In reading this decreased to less than 1 point at 11 years, but for spelling the difference was maintained thoughout the junior range' (p. 17). Possibly the convergence of reading skills in boys and girls at 11 years is due to the ceiling of the test. Like most tests of educational attainment, the sexes are not treated separately in the norms, it being argued that 'common tables for boys and girls are of greater practical value to the practising teacher than separate tables of norms'.

Reliability

Data from testing of groups in junior schools provide information on reliability of spelling scores by equivalent forms, given on the same occasion or within 14 days: mean correlation coefficients of 0.93 from four spelling tests given to 125 children aged 8:03, and a coefficient of 0.95 from two forms to 125 children at 8:09. The parallel forms, A and B, of the reading test correlated 0.95 at age 8:09 and 0.93 at 11:00. These results are as high as one can hope for.

Validity

Interesting and suggestive results are reported from correlating raw scores for a number of groups, all exceeding a hundred subjects (pp. 29–31). At 8 years, the reading test correlated 0.90 with NFER Reading AD; at about the same age, the spelling test correlated 0.93 with Schonell Graded Word Spelling. At 11 years, the NFER English Test 20 correlated 0.78 with SPAR reading and 0.68 with SPAR spelling. Two essays were assessed for spelling; the results correlated 0.68 with the spelling test.

Tables (A to E) report other correlation coefficients, including those with the author's Oral Verbal Intelligence Test. He notes that with increasing age correlations of spelling with reading, mathematics, and intelligence tests progressively weaken; and he warns against making the 'assumption that difficulties with reading and spelling are due simply to lack of intelligence' (p. 17).

General evaluation

This is an unusual test publication, bringing together normative measures of reading and of spelling. Pupils' skills in those two aspects of literacy are highly correlated, but 'there is a minority with . . . specific weakness in spelling that affects the ease and confidence of written expression'. The author aims to 'provide a complementary approach to the testing of literacy at a simple level . . . alerting the teacher to the need for remedial measures' in spelling (p. 1). Such an approach is needed to help remedy a widely neglected educational problem. But the goal is not fully attained in the SPAR Tests because insufficient guidance is provided in the interpretation of scores. For pupils of a given age range, one can determine, at various levels of probability, when a pupil's spelling falls significantly below expectation for his reading skill. Are such intra-individual comparisons to be expressed in terms of attainment ages, or quotients? If the latter, two features of the comparison need explanation. First, the unreliability of a difference between scores on two tests is large; at the 5 per cent convention, the difference has to be about 12 points on the SPAR quotients. Secondly, the margin of difference may not be treated as a constant; it has to be about twice as great in the highest quartile of reading as in the lowest. Or, if regression, with standard scores, is not to be the model, some other model for relating levels of attainment in spelling to reading skills, in a normative context, ought to be expounded and elaborated for practical use.

It appears from the range of attainment levels that the additional purpose of assessing progress among slow learners in secondary education might be realized, as well as the detection of specific problems in written expression. It is stressed that the tests are not diagnostic; but the need for more than one testing of reading and spelling is not sufficiently stressed.

The SPAR tests are appropriate to the routine testing of the basic skills of first-year juniors. For use with its other target population, older children with delay in reading and/or spelling, independent studies are needed.

No reports of use have been noted in the research and technical literature.

The SPAR Tests have been reprinted a number of times and they are rightly popular among school teachers. It is an inexpensive production. It deserves a manual with better layout, having somewhat fuller technical information, and containing more explanation and guidance to users.

References

Burroughs, G. E. R. (1957). "A Study of the Vocabulary of Young Children" (University of Birmingham, Institute of Education, Monograph No. 1). Edinburgh: Oliver & Boyd.

Schonell, F. J. and F. E. (1950). "Diagnostic and Attainment Testing". Edinburgh: Oliver & Boyd.

Vernon, P. E. (1977). "Graded Word Spelling Test". London: Hodder & Stoughton.

Young, D. (1968). "Manual for the Group Reading Test". London: University of London Press.

The Standard Reading Tests

Reviewed by Barry Stierer

Authors: J. C. Daniels and Hunter Diack

Publisher: Hart-Davis Educational (formerly published by Chatto & Windus)

Distributor: Hart-Davis Educational

Age range: Children 'still in the primary stage of reading (i.e. with reading ages up to nine years)'.

1958; S not stated

No revisions apparent

1979 printing reviewed

Individual tests (Tests 1–10)

Group tests (Tests 11 and 12)

Test content

In keeping with the authors' view that 'in recent years it has come to be generally acknowledged that in reading a number of different skills are involved' (p. 7), the Standard Reading Tests consist of 12 separate tests, 'each with a specific function to perform' (p. 13). The 12 tests are presented together in a single hardback volume which includes a few background notes to the tests as well as brief instructions for each test.

The flagship among the dozen tests is *Test 1*, the Standard Test of Reading Skill, for it is this test which is 'designed to be given to every child who, it is evident, has not fully mastered all the skills involved in reading' (p. 7). It is also this test for which norms, reading ages, reading quotients and 'Reading Standards' have been calculated and provided. The test consists of 36 sentences in question form, each sentence presented on a separate page of the book (and also available separately as a set of cards). The test is fundamentally a word-recognition test, in that the 36 sentences are made up only of words selected for their gradually increasing phonic complexity. The first 26 sentences are merely short questions which children are invited to answer 'yes' or 'no', while questions 27–36 present, in addition, four alternative answers which are to be read out by the testee. Here again, the four alternative answers are in essence vehicles for the presentation of words in increasing phonic complexity, rather than comprehension questions *per se*.

Test 2, Copying Abstract Figures, consists of four abstract line drawings which children are asked to copy.

Test 3, Copying a Sentence, consists of a single sentence ('The dog sits in his box'), with an accompanying picture.

Test 4, Visual Discrimination and Orientation Test, consists of four pages, each presenting several 'matching' exercises. A figure is shown in the left-hand column; four figures are presented to the right of it, only one of which matches the single figure. Children are asked to match the single figure with its likeness to the right. These figures range from representational drawings of familiar objects to abstract line drawings, to hand-drawn letters, to printed groups of letters.

Test 5, Letter Recognition Test, consists of a single page with five lines of five letters each, thus including every letter in the alphabet except 'x'. Several variations in approach to the use of these letters are suggested in the Manual.

Test 6, Aural Discrimination Test, consists of a single page with twelve small representational line drawings, intended for the assessment of children's discrimination of initial sounds.

Test 7, Diagnostic Word-Recognition Tests, 'consists of a battery of eight word-recognition tests—each with its special function' (p. 137). Each of the eight tests uses an identical format, i.e. several lines of semantically unrelated words to be read aloud by the testee. Each test reflects a different phonic concept, as outlined below.

Test 8, Oral Word-Recognition Test, consists of two pages, each presenting several lines of four semantically unrelated words which are read out by the tester and identified by the testee.

Test 9, Picture Word-Recognition Test, is linked to the previous test. It consists of four pages, each presenting four lines of four semantically unrelated words preceded by a line drawing representing one of the four words. Children are invited to identify the word which corresponds to the 'meaning' of each picture.

Test 10, Silent Prose-Reading and Comprehension Test, consists of a single page presenting a short prose passage of approximately 150 words. Two pages follow this story, one with four drawings and one with 10 questions related to the story. One of the questions asks the testee to select the picture which 'best fits the story you have just read' (p. 199).

Test 11, Graded Spelling Test, consists of four lists of 100 words each. The 40 words are graded according to phonic complexity. A table of norms is presented for the calculation of 'spelling ages'.

Test 12, Graded Test of Reading Experience, consists of 50 sentences. For each sentence one of the words has been substituted with four alternative words in brackets, and children are asked to select the word from among the multiple choice which renders the sentence meaningful. A table of norms is also presented for the calculation of 'reading experience ages'.

Purpose

Test 1—Standard Test of Reading Skill

This test enables all children to be assigned a 'Reading Standard'. There are seven such standards, reflecting the authors' theory of qualitative stages in the growth of reading skills. Each of the seven Reading Standards is described in moderate detail, although these notes are expressly not intended to replace the teacher's 'detailed, qualitative, diagnostic interpretation' which is 'an art which the teacher gains by judiciously blending teaching experience and the scientific understanding of the nature of the skills involved in fluent reading' (p. 19). Included in these notes describing the characteristics of each Reading Standard are suggestions as to which among the further eleven tests children at each Standard should be given.

Test 2—Copying Abstract Figures

This test is 'designed to discover something about the child's perceptual development and of his hand-eye co-ordination' (p. 13). It is intended that the test should be given to '(1) all children who record Grade 0 on the Standard Test of Reading Skill; (2) those children who, it is suspected, have difficulty in left-right orientation and who as a result of this frequently confuse certain individual letters and misread certain words where left-right orientation is specially involved; and (3) those children whose eye-hand co-ordination and hand motor-control seem to be impaired' (p. 99).

Test 3—Copying a Sentence

'This test is basically a more difficult version of Test 2. It will tell the teacher something of the child's experience in seeing and copying letters' (p. 13). It is suggested that the test should be given to '(1) children who record Standard 0 in the Standard Test of Reading Skill; (2) children who are border-line 'successes' and 'failures' in Test 2; (3) pupils who in the Standard Test of Reading Skill appear to be guessing at many words by concentrating attention on only part of the words; and (4) pupils who only just succeed in getting into Standard I on the Standard Test of Reading Skill' (p. 107).

Test 4—Visual Discrimination and Orientation Test

'This test is designed to determine more exactly what the child sees when he looks at pictures, diagrams and letters and to pick out those children who have not yet reached the stage of perceiving with left-right orientation, an important principle of identity' (p. 14). It is suggested that the test should be given to '(1) children who score Standard 0 on the Standard Test of Reading Skill; (2) children for whom the results of Tests 2 and 3 suggest some deficiency in left-right orientation; (3) children who make errors in the Standard Test of Reading Skills which suggest that the child either confuses mirror-image letters or the left-right order of letters of words' (p. 113).

Test 5—Letter Recognition Test

'The letters of the alphabet are here printed in a special order, with detailed test items to discover the degree of skill in letter-recognition' (p. 14). It is suggested that the test should be given to '(1) those children who, in the Standard Test of Reading Skill, score Standard 0 or Standard I and who seem to have no firm grasp of the letters and their sounds; (2) those children who give wrong sound-values to particular letters in the Standard Test. This sometimes happens with children who score relatively highly on the Standard Test as a whole' (p. 125).

Test 6—Aural Discrimination Test

'This test has been designed to help the teacher discover how acute is the aural discrimination of a child when he listens to words' (p. 14). It is suggested that the test should be given to '(1) children who score Standard 0 on the Standard Test of Reading Skill; (2) those children who appear to score better on the Standard Test than would be expected from their performance on Test 5 (Method 'c'); and (3) children who make particular mistakes in initial sounds of words in the Standard Test' (p. 131).

Test 7—Diagnostic Word-Recognition Test

A test intended to discover more about children's ability to apply phonic rules in decoding individual words.

Test 7A (phonically simple two- and three-letter words) should be given to '(1) children scoring Reading Standard 0, I, and II; (2) those children who tend to make errors in recognising, or in associating the right sound-values with certain particular letters; and (3) children who appear to have difficulty in synthesizing some words from their component parts' (p. 139).

Test 7B (consonantal blends at beginnings of phonically simple words) should be given to '(1) children of Reading Standard I and II; and (2) children having difficulty in reading phonically simple words, whatever their Reading Standard (p. 141).

Test 7C (consonantal blends at ends of phonically simple words) should be given to '(1) children of Reading Standard I and II; and (2) children having difficulty in reading phonically simple words whatever their Reading Standard' (p. 147).

Test 7D (polysyllabic phonically simple words) should be given to '(1) children of Reading Standards I, II and III; and (2) children having difficulty in reading polysyllabic words, whatever their Reading Standard (p. 151).

Test 7E (graded phonically complex words) should be given to 'children scoring a Reading Standard of II, III, IV and V, especially those children who show uncertainty in the recognition of various digraphs (p. 155).

Test 7F (common words with irregular spelling) should be given to 'children of Reading Standards II, III, IV and V, especially those who show a tendency to phoneticize common irregularly-spelt words' (p. 161).

Test 7G ('reversible' words) should be given to 'all children who in any other test read one or more words reversed' (p. 165).

Test 7H (nonsense syllables) is 'not one of the tests that should be used frequently. Some teachers may feel, with some justification, that they should never use it at all. There are two types of child with whom this test may be found useful: (1) the very rare, glib reader who pays practically no attention to what he is reading; and (2) the child who has mastered the basic skills of reading but who is not sure enough of this principle to permit him to utter "nonsense"' (p. 169).

Test 8—Oral Word-Recognition Test

'This test is designed to discover something about the child's ear-eye co-ordination. The child has to recognise in print words spoken by the teacher' (p. 14). It is suggested that the test should be given to '(1) children who have shown in the Standard Test of Reading Skill that they often make wild guesses at words by looking at one or two letters in the words (usually the first or the last letters) and saying any word that begins or ends with these letters; (2) children who, though reading tolerably well, appear to have difficulty in picking out the individual sounds in spoken words; (3) children who confuse certain pairs of letters, e.g. *b* and *d*; and (4) all children who are given Test 9 (this test is suitable only for children who score Standard I, II, III or IV in the Standard Test)' (p. 173).

Test 9—Picture Word-Recognition Test

'This tests the ability of the child to choose from amongst other words the names of pictured objects' (p. 14). It is suggested that the test be given to '(1) children who show a disposition to guess words from the context; (2) children whose word-recognition ability is relatively high but who appear to be "word-calling"—reading aloud without comprehension; and (3) all children who are given Test 8' (p. 181).

Test 10—Silent Prose Reading and Comprehension Test

'This is a test of comprehension of a passage of prose' (p. 14). 'The test is about Reading Standard V level. It should be given to those children who reach Reading Standard V or VI on the Standard Test, yet whose independent silent reading appears to be below this level. Test 1 demanded an understanding of what was read aloud. This text gives an indication of the extent to which a pupil is getting the meaning out of his silent reading' (p. 193).

Test 11—Graded Spelling Test

It is suggested that the tests be given to '(1) any child or group of children in the school for whom a spelling test is felt to be necessary; (2) those children who, though reading well in the oral and picture word-recognition tests (Tests 8 and 9), are reading rather less well in the word-recognition tests (Test 7); (3) children who read better in the nonsense syllables test than would be expected from their performance on the other word-recognition tests; (4) those children who make mistakes in reading due to incorrect phonic rendering of irregular words; and (5) children in Reading Standard III who are making any type of reversal error (List A only)' (p. 201).

Test 12—Graded Test of Reading Experience

'This is a test, for children who score very highly in the Standard Test of Reading Skill, of the extent to which reading skills have been used in practice. It is as much a vocabulary test as a reading test' (p. 14). 'Children scoring

Standard IV, V and VI on the Standard Test of Reading Skill, and especially those children whose performance in the Standard Test leads the examiner to suspect a mechanical approach to reading at the expense of comprehension' (p. 207).

Item preparation

Very little information is provided about the principles upon which this battery of tests was constructed. It is therefore possible only to infer, from various brief discussions in the book about the nature of the reading process, the method by which the authors prepared and ranked items in the different tests.

Underlying the entire battery is the authors' view that the process of reading is comprised of a number of discrete visual and auditory skills which enable the reader to translate 'the letters of words, in a given order, into sounds that have meaning' (p. 7). The authors' emphatic support for the phonic approach, not only as a method for the teaching of reading but also as the key to an understanding of the reading process itself, needs to be fully taken into account in any consideration of the test's applicability to classroom settings. A young reader is seen to move through a series of distinct developmental stages, or 'Reading Standards', each one characterized by the ability to recognise words of increasing phonic complexity. Hence a modern child's ability to recognise words such as 'professionals' or 'astro-challenger'—both words of considerable phonic complexity—would be considered by the authors to be examples of 'reading experience' rather than of 'reading skill', since it would not necessarily result from an ability to translate letters into sounds. Such a view of the reading process reinforces the notion of reading as a passive, mechanistic motor-sensory activity rather than an active engagement with the language of a text, and reduces the act of reading to the processing of individual words rather than of running text. This runs counter to many recent advances in knowledge about reading (cf. e.g. Smith, 1971, 1978) and needs to be seriously considered by the classroom teacher before adopting the test.

The items presented in the main test (Test 1, the Standard Test of Reading Skill) were prepared according to *a priori* criteria devised by the authors and therefore did not, apparently, require standardization. The authors claim to have overcome the weaknesses of other more conventional word recognition tests which list words according to statistically-established relative difficulty. Such approaches are, by implication, unreliable and quickly become outdated. The authors have instead presented words which become increasingly more complex phonically, which they claim reflects the words' innate difficulty rather than their perhaps temporary accessibility. Thus, the authors claim, the sentence 'Do bells ring?' is inherently more difficult to read than 'Has a camel a hump on its back?' which is presented earlier in the test. That children who are able to read the first of these two sentences are nearer to becoming readers than those who cannot is neither defended by the authors using empirical evidence nor borne out by recent studies. All that can be said with certainty is that children who are taught to read using an approach based on training in phonic skills are more likely to perform well on the test than other children in the early stages.

Although the information provided about the preparation of the items in Test 1 is seriously insufficient, Tests 2–12 are even less thoroughly explicated. No evidence from empirical studies is presented to support the implicit view that more can be discovered about a child's (poor) performance on a word-recognition test by administering further tests of visual and auditory skills. Furthermore, although children assiduously trained to improve their performance on these tests of sub-skills might achieve higher scores on the more general Standard Test of Reading Skill, there is no evidence that such training would increase their effectiveness as readers generally.

The language and subject matter of many of the items throughout the battery will offend many teachers. Much of the language is stilted, archaic and reminiscent more of the 1920s than even of the 1950s when the test items were written (e.g. 'whilst getting off the bus', 'Has a cup a lid?'). Although in some cases this linguistic awkwardness was an inevitable result of the authors' determination to use only phonically simple words at the beginning of the test, such language will no doubt cause confusion for many modern children, perhaps especially those for whom English is not their mother tongue. The culture and gender bias is also worrying. Many items require familiarity with middle-class customs in order to answer them sucessfully (e.g. 'When we go out to a friend's house for tea, we often find that the table is already laid with cups and (visitors, sand, sausages, saucers)') and there are numerous references which are now more historical than contemporary (e.g. 'A steam engine usually runs on (rails, reels, stoves, signals') and 'A place where talking films are shown is called . . .'). Of the 50 items in the Graded Test of Reading Experience, nine items refer to boys and men, and only one deals with girls or women; and even that one will not tap the 'reading experience' of all readers, male or female ('The most important female participant in a wedding is the (groomsman, bridegroom, mother, bride)').

Despite the authors' insistence on the importance of *a priori* criteria in selecting and grading words for the test, and despite their eschewal of statistical procedures, they do indicate that some attempt was made to try out the instrument on a sample of children and, moreover, to study the extent to which their *a priori* criteria correlate with more conventional measures:

'In spite of the fact that the questions were placed in a particular order on *a priori* grounds . . . experiment has shown that the *a priori* order of difficulty coincides very closely with the statistical order of difficulty throughout the entire test' (pp. 15–16).

Details of this experimentation are not available for inspection, which is especially unfortunate in view of the age of the test (1958) and in view of its fundamental limitations already discussed. It is also ironic that after the authors' rather pious attempts, not only to appraise the relative phonic complexity of words independent of their empirical difficulty, but also to discredit conventional methods of statistical analysis, they proceeded to establish—and felt impelled to report—that their procedure correlated with conventional statistical measures. The problem was successfully identified, but the attempted solution broke no new ground.

Administration

Tests 1–10 are individual tests; Tests 11 and 12 are individual or group tests. Instructions are clearly presented; all tests are untimed.

Standardization

As already mentioned, no information on standardization is given either within the Manual or elsewhere. Standardization procedures would presumably have been inconsistent with the principles underlying Test 1, since emphasis was placed on the difficulty of the words comprising the test rather than on the ability of a given population of children to recognize them. Hence the notion of reading ability as an attribute distributed among children appears to have been abandoned, or at least subordinated to the inherent difficulty of words.

Although norms are presented with Tests 11 and 12, no information is provided about their derivation.

Scoring

Except for Tests 1, 11 and 12, no instructions for scoring are provided. 'The reason is that the others are tests of skills which *must* be completely mastered if normal progress is to be made. Therefore . . . pupils are expected to give 80–100 per cent correct answers' (p. 12).

For Test 1, marks are awarded for the correct rendering of each sentence—three marks for each sentence 1–26, and one mark for each of the five parts in sentences 27–36. 128 marks are therefore possible overall, and reading ages and Reading Standards are then calculated using the tables provided.

For Test 11, the Graded Spelling Test, one mark is given for each word correctly spelt (maximum 40). Total marks are then converted into 'spelling ages'.

For Test 12, the Graded Test of Reading Experience, one mark is given for each correct answer from the multiple choice, maximum 50, and 'reading experience ages' are then calculated. No marking key is provided with this test, the correct answers presumably being self-evident.

Reliability and validity

No information whatsoever is provided. It must be concluded therefore that the ultimate reference for the tests' validity must be the authors' limited and outdated model of the reading process.

Interpretation

As already mentioned, the authors offer very little *direct* guidance as to how the results of the various tests should be interpreted and acted upon, asserting that the 'detailed, qualitative, diagnostic interpretation' of the results 'is an art which the teacher gains by judiciously blending teaching experience and the scientific understanding of the nature of the skills involved in fluent reading' (p. 19). The content of the tests and the way in which they are presented, however, allow little real flexibility of interpretation. No scope is given to interpret a poor result on the main test (No. 1) in terms other than those suggested by the skills assessed in the subtests. Even so, the few suggestions actually ventured by the authors either exemplify the narrow circularity of their testing-teaching model, e.g. (p. 126):

'Test 5 gives valuable evidence about the child's readiness to proceed on a systematic course like the Phonic Word Method course of the *Royal Road Readers*' (Daniels and Diack, 1954);

or are entirely open-ended, e.g. (p. 143):

'If it is discovered that any blend is giving trouble, it should be dealt with through specially devised activities' (unspecified).

Test use

The Bullock Committee reported (DES, 1975) that the tests were in use in 17.7 per cent of primary schools in early 1973, and that three of the 93 local education authorities responding to their survey reported that the test was used as part of an LEA testing programme. Nearly ten years later, the Evaluation of Testing in Schools Project at the University of London Institute of Education found that the test was used in 7 LEA testing schemes and that 18 of the 80 primary schools surveyed reported that the test was used in some capacity in the school (Gipps *et al.*, 1983).

At the time of writing (early 1983) the test was in its fourteenth impression (1979), which indicates a steady popularity for some 25 years. However, this may be attributable to its ease of administration and of scoring/conversion to reading ages rather than to widespread support for the tests' underlying principles.

General evaluation

As previously mentioned, the diagnostic function of the tests is either narrowly circular or entirely open-ended. Children scoring poorly on the tests are seen to be deficient in certain phonic skills; a programme of training in the phonic skills is therefore recommended to boost these children's scores. The link between this cycle and real reading is not demonstrated. Having thus limited the teacher's scope for interpretation, the authors then refrain from specific advice as to how these various phonic deficiencies may be remedied.

It is difficult to imagine any purpose which could be effectively served by the use of this battery of tests other than to appraise children's dexterity in certain rudimentary phonic skills. Too little information is provided, about the principles underlying the test's construction, for practitioners to make informed decisions about its applicability. Whether the seven Reading Standards delineated by the authors relate with any validity to the characteristics of real readers—particularly those real readers who have been encouraged to view the process of reading as an active engagement with the language of a text rather than as the passive decoding of individual words—remains doubtful, and certainly is not discussed in the Manual. Since these Reading Standards are central to the use of the battery as a whole this uncertainty renders the entire system suspect. Teachers familiar with recent psycholinguistic and sociolinguistic work in the area of reading, which has reinforced the importance of the reader's sense-making strategies and of the social and textual determinants on reading will be alarmed at the authors' suggestions that children who 'appear to be guessing at many words by concentrating attention on only part of the words' (p. 107) require remedial help and further testing.

References

DES (1975). "A Language for Life". (The Bullock Report). London: HMSO.

Gipps, C. V., Steadman, S. D., Blackstone, T. and Stierer, B. M. (1983). "Testing Children: Standardized Tests in LEAs and Schools". London: Heinemann Educational Books.

Smith, F. (1971). "Understanding Reading". New York: Holt, Rinehart and Winston.

Smith, F. (1978). "Reading". Cambridge: Cambridge University Press.

Tests of Proficiency in English: Listening, Speaking, Reading, Writing

Reviewed by Ian Plewis

Author: Not stated
Publisher: NFER-Nelson
Distributor: NFER-Nelson
Age range: 7:00–11:11 ('Immigrant children of junior-school age')
1973 (M, T)
Group test: Listening, Reading, Writing
Individual test: Speaking

Test content

There are four skill areas—listening, speaking, reading and writing. For each skill area, there are four levels of difficulty—level one, level two, level three part one and level three part two. Each listening and reading test uses multiple-choice items and picture items are used for levels one and two. The reading tests are tests of reading comprehension in English and they parallel the listening tests. The writing test at level one parallels the speaking test at level one and both use 25 picture items. The other tests are a mixture of picture and verbal items.

Purpose

'The function of the test is threefold . . . to help teachers with *placement* to decide whether new pupils should be placed in special language classes or given any extra tuition, and whether pupils in special classes are ready to return to normal classes. Secondly, they should give teachers specific linguistic information for each child tested, which can be used as a *diagnostic* guide for future teaching. Thirdly, they should be helpful to teachers monitoring the *progress* of their immigrant children' (General Guide, p. 3). 'The scores indicate not where a pupil stands in relation to others, but what he can do in terms of the skills tested', i.e. the tests are criterion referenced. 'There is no question of "passing" or "failing" any of the tests' (p. 6).

Item preparation

Successive trials of a pool of items were carried out on four groups of Asian and three groups of West Indian children, the groups being defined by length of time in English schools. There were about 200 children in each group. A 'discrimination index' was calculated for each item and used either to reject or to modify items.

Administration

The tests are suitable for all junior-school immigrant children providing they have spent a few weeks in the country. 'With older, more able children it should be possible to administer all three tests of any one skill area in the same morning'. If more than one skill area is to be tested, the following order should be used—listening, speaking, reading and writing. The speaking tests are individually administered but the others are administered to groups of pupils who just need pencils. A tape recorder is needed for listening tests at levels two and three and a tape recorder and microphone needed for the speaking tests.

Standardization

Norms are not provided since it is not intended that the tests be used for comparative purposes.

Scoring

The scoring for the listening and reading tests is unambiguous. The items in the writing and speaking tests are open-ended and so scoring requires more judgement by the teacher, but detailed instructions are given for all four skill areas. For writing and speaking at level three, the total score is made up of two components—intelligibility and average length.

Reliability

Internal (KR-20) estimates are presented for the listening and reading tests except, inexplicably, for listening, level one. They vary from 0.63–0.85 with a median of 0.80. Standard errors of measurement are also given for these tests. No information is given on the composition and sizes of the samples on which these figures are based. Inter-rater reliabilities were calculated for the speaking and writing tests. 'A relatively representative set of 50 scripts were chosen for each test—these were then scored by two different markers'. The resulting correlation coefficients varied between 0.85 and 0.98 with a median of 0.95.

Validity

No information is given.

Interpretation

A good deal of qualitative material is provided to help with interpretation. Scores are given for each test 'above which a child can be said to have succeeded at the level being tested' and 'below which a child cannot be said to have reached the level being tested'. However, the user is given no guidance about the interpretation of scores between these limits, which are widely spaced.

General evaluation

The tests are comprehensive, the Manuals are adequate and the pictures are clear, if rather old-fashioned. However, it would be reasonable to expect teachers to be given more guidance about interpreting scores in the light of the stated purpose of the tests. It is particularly difficult to see how teachers could assess progress from the information given. Also, the tests were piloted only on Asian and West Indian children and so may not be suitable for other immigrant groups. Furthermore, there are no longer 'immigrant' children as in the early 1970s and it is not clear that these tests have much value in their present form. The technical information provided is not really adequate with nothing on validity.

Thackray Reading Readiness Profiles

Reviewed by Christine Mabey

Authors: Derek and Lucy Thackray
Publisher: Hodder & Stoughton
Distributor: Hodder & Stoughton
Age range: 4:08–5:08
1973 (S, Profiles 1–3); 1974 (M, T)
No revisions apparent
1981 (M); 1980 (T) printings reviewed
Group test

Test content

The test consists of 4 subtests, or Profiles:

(1) vocabulary and concept development;
(2) auditory discrimination;

(3) visual discrimination;
(4) general ability.

For each of the first three Profiles the administrator works through each item orally with the group to ensure that each child understands what is required.

The first profile (vocabulary and concept development) requires the child to select the correct picture, from four, to match the spoken word. There are 23 items preceded by 2 practice items. The second profile (auditory discrimination) requires the child to match two pictures with the same initial letter(s). In this there are 3 practice and 17 test items. The third profile (visual discrimination) involves the child in selecting the same word (from a choice of four) as is written on the left of the paper. This contains 3 practice and 27 test items. Unlike the previous two Profiles the administrator only verbally administers the first 5 items, after that children are told to complete the remaining items on their own. The final profile (general ability) is an adaptation of Harris' (1963) revision of the Goodenough Draw-A-Man test. In this the child is asked to draw a picture of 'Mummy'.

Purpose

The purpose of the Profiles is clearly set out in the Manual. They aim to 'measure directly or indirectly the most important skills and abilities contributing to readiness for reading' (Manual, p. 3) and, further, to be diagnostic with information which 'can be used to provide a stimulating programme of pre-reading activities which includes those specific skills and abilities which are so important for learning to read easily and profitably' (Manual, p. 2).

Item preparation

The authors report briefly their own work over the preceding decade and test users are referred to earlier work both in the field of reading readiness generally and in the development of these Profiles (Thackray, 1965; Thackray, 1971; Downing and Thackray, 1971). They report that:

'a number of Profiles have been devised, tried out in schools and evaluated in research reports. One outcome of this on-going research has been to establish the most important reading readiness abilities which can be measured satisfactorily, namely Vocabulary, Auditory Discrimination, Visual Discrimination and General Ability. In more recent years work has been concentrated in these four important areas of readiness and experimental Profiles in each area have been devised, tested and improved. Item analysis has been continuously carried out to determine item difficulty and item discrimination of all measures. A careful study of each item, together with its difficulty index and its discrimination index, revealed those items which best served the purpose for which the Profiles were intended. In the final version, only those items which were within the facility range of 25% to 75% and had a very high discrimination index were used for standardization purposes. The average discrimination index of the items retained is 0.59, which is considered exceptionally good' (Manual, p. 28).

Certainly, the work both as background to and in developing the Profiles has been more intensive and thorough than is generally the case.

Administration

The test is intended for reception class children soon after they start school for the first time; 5 to 6 weeks after is suggested. The target age-group is derived from the standardized sample (which reflects the different age at which children first start school throughout the UK): age range 4:08–5:08 years.

It is recommended that the children's class teacher administer the Profiles: 'as rapport will already have been established with the children, her voice will be familiar to them, and she is the one who will make the immediate and direct use of the results of the Profiles' (Manual, p. 5). Groups of 8–10 children are recommended to be tested at one time, though it is suggested that more could be tested with the help of an assistant. The authors suggest that if any child does not respond to the group situation he may be given the Profiles individually provided the same wording is followed exactly. Instructions are given for seating the children so that copying is difficult. The children need a test booklet and pencil.

Although paced by the teacher and, therefore, untimed, it is estimated that the first three Profiles will take 20 minutes to administer and the fourth 10 minutes. It is suggested that each is given on separate occasions, although two might be administered on the same day. Detailed instructions are given in the Manual about the administration with precise wordings. Further, users are cautioned: 'The precise wording of the instructions has been worked out with great care and must be followed exactly, word for word, if valid results are to be obtained' (Manual, p. 5). Given the variations adopted by test administrators, such precise instructions and wording are to be welcomed.

Standardization

Standardization of the first three Profiles took place in October, 1973, based on a sample of 5500 children 'drawn from 350 schools in England, Scotland, Wales and Ireland . . . who had started school in September, 1973, and had been in school approximately six weeks at the time of the standardization. The children ranged in age from 4 years 8 months to 5 years 8 months and the average age was 5 years 0 months' (Manual, p. 28). Although the sample design is not clear the sample size is much larger than is often used for standardizing tests.

Since the target group for the purposes of the test is all new school entrants, no age conversions are provided despite the large age range. Scores for each Profile are grouped into 5 ratings: A to E: 'B, C and D are each approximately 1.0 standard deviation in width. A and E are the extremes beyond 1.5 standard deviations above and below the mean respectively. Level A includes the top 7% of the standardization group, level B the next 24%, level C the middle 38%, level D the next 24% and level E the lowest 7%' (Manual, p. 17). It should be noted that this standardization does not apply to Profile 4 for which no information is available.

Scoring

Clear instructions are provided for scoring the first 3 Profiles. A child's score on each is the number of correct items. This raw score is then converted into a rating for each of the Profiles using a simple table. The fourth Profile is the least satisfactory in this respect. The child's drawing is rated, as for the other three Profiles, from A to E. However, scores are not given for particular parts of the body (as in the original version) but a verbal description of the attributes of each rating is provided accompanied by four pictorial examples of each rating.

Reliability

Coefficients of internal consistency are provided based on a random sample of 196 children drawn from the standardization sample. 'All computations were done using raw scores and the reliability coefficients were obtained by the split-halves technique using the Spearman-Brown formula corrected for length' (Manual, p. 29). The reliability coefficients for the three Profiles were 0.80, 0.81 and 0.90 respectively.

Validity

High content validity is claimed for the Profiles since their basis is the research studies into areas of importance for developing reading. For example, the authors point out 'research has clearly shown that for learning to read successfully the ability to make auditory discrimination among consonantal sounds at the beginning of words is a vital specific skill. Profile 2 measures this skill directly' (Manual, p. 30).

Evidence of predictive validity is given both from work on earlier experimental versions by the authors and also from a sample of 525 children tested in February, 1975. At that point (average age 6:06 years) the children were tested for Accuracy and Comprehension on the Neale Analysis of Reading Ability and their score correlated with their earlier scores on the Profiles (mean age 5:00

years). The correlation coefficients obtained by using the product moment method are tabulated. They range from 0.41 for Visual Discrimination with Neale Comprehension to 0.50 for Auditory Discrimination with Neale Accuracy. A table of the correlation coefficients obtained on the most recent experimental versions with reading achievement scores on a variety of tests is also provided. The mean ages of the children for that comparison were 5:04 years and 6:06 years. The correlation coefficients were highest for Visual Discrimination, between 0.48 and 0.58, and lowest for Vocabulary, between 0.45 and 0.49.

Interpretation

In order to interpret the raw scores the teacher is referred to a conversion table of raw scores into ratings (A to E). The expected percentages falling into each rating is given. The authors then suggest that once a child's Profile has been established 'the teacher can use this information to devise a more effective pre-reading programme, bearing in mind each child's strengths and weaknesses in the important reading readiness skills which have been measured' (Manual, p. 24). A number of practical suggestions are made covering the three areas.

Again Profile 4 is the weakest in this respect. To rate the drawing may well be difficult. Further, the general discussion of additional information which can be derived from the children's drawings (despite the caution) is somewhat questionable.

Test use

McMichael has reported two studies using the Profiles in different ways. The first was concerned with estimating whether anti-social behaviour preceded reading disability or the reverse. The Thackray Profiles and Rutter Scale (B) were used as screening devices and the Southgate Reading Test, the Columbia Mental Maturity Scale and Rutter Scale (B) as criterion measures. A multiple regression analysis showed that once the contribution of the Profiles to the variance in reading test scores had been taken into account anti-social behaviour as such had little to add (McMichael, 1979). In the other study the Profiles were used to screen children for selection to a programme devised to boost reading (McMichael, 1980).

General evaluation

This is a well piloted and standardized test with precise objectives and limited target group. The reliabilities and validities presented are acceptable. The child's test booklet is attractive and the Manual is clear and precisely worded in order to minimize user variability. The use of Profile 4 (the drawing of 'Mummy') is less than satisfactory, however, in most respects. As a measure of 'general ability' it is questionable; data on its construction, reliability, etc., are lacking; the scoring lacks precision and the interpretation is questionable. However, this is not an essential part of the test and could easily be disregarded.

References

Downing, J. A. and Thackray, D. V. (1971). "Reading Readiness". London: Hodder & Stoughton.

Harris, D. B. (1963). "Children's Drawings as Measures of Intellectual Maturity. A Revision and Extension of the Goodenough Draw-A-Man Test". New York: Harcourt, Brace and World.

Thackray, D. V. (1965). A study of the relationship between some specific evidence of reading readiness and reading progress in the infant school. *British Journal of Educational Psychology* 35, 252–4.

Thackray, D. V. (1971). "Readiness to Read with i.t.a. and t.o." London: Geoffrey Chapman.

McMichael, P. (1979). The hen or the egg? Which comes first—anti-social emotional disorders or reading disability? *British Journal of Educational Psychology* 49, 222–238.

McMichael, P. (1980). School intervention with disadvantaged children. *Educational Studies* 6, 65–77.

Transitional Assessment: English

Brief Report

Author: A collaborative project of NFER and London Borough of Hillingdon
Publisher: NFER-Nelson
Distributor: NFER-Nelson
Age range: 'last term in junior school'
1978 (M, T)*
Group assessments

This 'bank of modular assessment exercises' was designed to provide information to be passed on to a child's receiving secondary school. The eight modules

---

* Full details of the project are contained in Sumner, R. and Bradley, K. "Assessment for Transition: A Study of New Procedures". Windsor, Berks: NFER-Nelson. The Administrative Manual, supplied with the specimen set, is primarily concerned with the assessment procedures.

call for four essays (autobiographical, descriptive, explanatory, story writing) and exercises in sentence writing, punctuation, closure ('cloze' technique) and comprehension.

Criteria are provided for marking the essays and the sentence writing modules along with keys and guides for those modules giving rise to more defined responses. Assessment of raw scores is reported in terms of a profile of 'Stages' achieved.

Wide-span Reading Test

Reviewed by Christine Mabey

Author: Alan Brimer (incorporating material written by Herbert Gross)
Publisher: NFER-Nelson
Distributors: NFER-Nelson; Educational Evaluation Enterprises
Age range: 7:00–14:11
1972 (M, T); S not stated
'Revised Edition'★
Group test

Test content

Two parallel versions of the test are provided: Form A and Form B. These can be used either for retesting within the same year or for simultaneous administration to minimize copying. Each version consists of 80 items which become progressively more difficult. Each item consists of an incomplete sentence which is completed by selecting one word from another sentence, printed to the left of the incomplete test item. The test, although continuous, is divided into eight levels, four for secondary-aged and four for primary-aged children. Some of the items seem particularly culture bound and it is difficult to accept that they have recently been ordered in order of item difficulty. On Form A, for example, item 10 reads: 'The salt of the earth are the hewers of wood, and the drawers of water'. With the word 'drawers' to be selected to go with 'chest of . . .'. For the youngest age level (first-year juniors) the average child is expected to achieve 14 correct items.

★ The Manual used for review is copyright 1972 but labelled 'Revised Edition' although no date for revision is given. The Manual was reprinted 1973, 1974, 1976, 1978, 1979, 1980.

Purpose

Two objectives are stated for the test. The principal purpose is: 'to measure the level of reading comprehension . . . within the range defined by the beginning of competent silent reading and the full development of reading comprehension effectiveness'. Further claims are made for the tests: 'As measures of reading comprehension, they assess the child's skills in decoding printed symbols into meaningful sounds of language, in fitting meanings to groups of sounds, and in construing the structural relationship of meanings in their total semantic and syntactical context' (Manual, p. 7).

A secondary purpose for the test is diagnostic: 'to indicate the areas of reading skill within which low-scoring children may have difficulty'. However, the author warns that 'Since the skills in reading can only be as good as the aural language competence of each individual permits, no claim is made that specific reading disability is being distinguished from general language disability; rather, the diagnostic indicators point to the profitable lines of further investigation of the child's weaknesses' (Manual, p. 7).

Item preparation

No details are provided in the Manual on this.

Administration

As the test covers such a wide range (7:00–14:11 years) children in different year-groups are recommended to begin at different points in the test. Although the test is aimed at eight year-groups, there are six separate starting points since both first- and second-year juniors start at the beginning while fourth-year juniors and first-year secondary children start at the same point.

Each child needs a (reusable) test booklet, an answer sheet and pencil or pen. The administrator needs supplies and a stop-watch. The usual instructions about seating in order to minimize copying are given. 'Timing must be accurate', stresses the author, 'the time-limit is thirty minutes, at whatever level the test is being used, and it is preferable to use an accurate stop-watch. If a stop-watch is not available then a watch with a seconds hand should be used and the time at which the test is begun and what the time will be thirty minutes later noted on a spare sheet of paper' (Manual, p. 8). If the test is also to be used for diagnostic purposes (for children of third-year juniors and older) the children then attempt the items which preceded their starting level and 'testing continues immediately after the first thirty minutes . . . Allow as much time as is necessary for each child to reach the point at which he first began. Allow no more than thirty minutes' (Manual, p. 9).

Standardization

Few details are provided about the sample on which the test was standardized. The author merely states that the tests 'were standardized on a sample of children drawn to represent the national distribution of schools of various types. Schools also represented a wide geographical spread throughout England and Wales' (Manual, p. 12). The sample sizes for each year group or 'level' (and conversion to standardized scores is within each separate level) were approximately 950. Children were tested on two occasions, half with Form A on the first occasion while the other half were first given Form B.

The method of obtaining standardized scores was 'by combining data in various ways and smoothing the resulting distributions before normalizing them. Age adjustments were computed by determining the regression coefficients of raw score upon age within subgroups and by using the mean of relevant coefficients to derive the adjusted values' (Manual, p. 12).

Scoring

Considerable details are given in the booklet for scoring both the attainment level and diagnostic indicators and marking keys are provided. As far as the attainment level is concerned each item has only one correct response and a child's raw score is the total number of correct responses. Standardized scores are provided for each level, i.e. each year group, in a conversion table with raw score plotted against level. A second table has then to be consulted for age adjustments within level. This seems needlessly complicated and the provision of a single conversion table incorporating raw score and age allowance would be easier and quicker to use. In addition a percentile chart is included for interpreting the standardized scores.

Scoring on a 'nominal' scale is also provided, 'This "scale" is derived by identifying the point in the test which represents the highest level of the child's effective functioning' (Manual, p. 11). This is determined by finding the latest point in the test at which the child has three correct answers out of four consecutive items. The middle of the three responses is the nominal scale point.

Scoring of the diagnostic indicators is more complicated and valid diagnostic indicators—in the areas of decoding, linguistic and vocabulary—are only derived if there are 10 or more identifiable responses within the category. Considerable detail is provided on criteria to identify responses contributing to a diagnostic category and interpretation of indicators. It is important to note that the author only claims to provide diagnostic *indicators* and not to provide a diagnostic test.

Reliability

Evidence of reliability is provided from the inter-correlations of the two forms. These are provided for each of the eight year-groups. They range from 0.95 for second-year juniors to 0.89 for third- and fourth-year secondary children. Estimates of the standard error of measurement derived from these are also provided and range from 3.5 for the second-year juniors to nearly 5.0 for two, older secondary age-groups.

Validity

No information is provided in the Manual about the validity of the test as a reading comprehension measure.

Interpretation

As noted above, conversion tables are provided along with a percentile chart.

Details are provided for interpreting the diagnostic indicators, explaining the sorts of problems, or the area of problems which the child may have if he scores highly in a given category. However, the author is aware of the limitations with these. 'The absence of positive diagnostic indication does not necessarily imply that no difficulty exists in that direction and whenever a child's reading comprehension is so low as to give concern to the teacher a range of specific diagnostic tests should be given and the help of an educational psychologist or counsellor sought' (Manual, p. 11).

Test use

Three studies of interest have been traced which have used this test, two of them involving deaf children. The first of these by Conrad (1977) specifies that he used the test untimed which, according to the Manual, is not permissible. Further, it was administered individually rather than as a group test. This study was concerned with the reading levels of school leavers (age range 15:00–16:05 years) from schools for the deaf or partially hearing. Kyle (1980) also used the test with deaf children, but for a younger age-group (7–9 years), comparing their reading ability with that of a normal control group. The third study, by Whittaker (1977), involved a wide age range—from 11–17 years, i.e. beyond the provision of standardized scores. The sample studied were consecutive entrants to an assessment centre over a six-month period in 1975. One attraction of the test was the wide age-range covered but the author also cites as a reason that 'it uses linguistic ability to a greater extent than a multiple choice test'.

General evaluation

The lack of detail about test and item preparation, the standardization and validities are matters of concern. The sample size for standardization is small and the standard errors of measurement relatively high. If it were to be used for assessing *individuals'* levels of reading comprehension the range which one would have to place around an obtained score as an estimate of 'true' score would be so wide as to be of little practical value. The diagnostic indicators seem particularly weak. In particular, they are only indicators. Further, the time to be spent on the testing—up to a full hour of continuous testing—is longer than usually recommended, particularly as it would be low-achieving or 'problem' children who would be involved in the full testing.

From a user view the conversion from raw to standardized scores seems needlessly cumbersome. It seems possible that the desire to produce a test covering a very wide age-range has meant sacrifices in the construction and standardization of the test.

References

Conrad, R. (1977). The reading ability of deaf school-leavers. *British Journal of Educational Psychology* **47**, 138–148.

Kyle, J. (1980). The reading development of deaf children. *Journal of Research in Reading* **3**, 86–97.

Whittaker, E. M. (1977). Aspects of intellectual and educational functioning of boys admitted to the regional assessment centre. *Association of Educational Psychologists Journal* **4**, 24–30.

Word Recognition Test

Reviewed by John Gray

Author: Clifford Carver
Publisher: Hodder & Stoughton
Distributor: Hodder & Stoughton
Age range: 4:06–8:06
1970 (M, T); S not stated
No revisions apparent
1980 (M); 1981 (T) printings reviewed
Group test

Test content

The test comprises 50 items designed to assess the following aspects of 'word recognition': (1) initial letter errors; (2) distortion or twisting of letters; (3) mid-vowel errors: (4) serial distortion of letters; (5) reversal of words; (6) errors in common word endings; (7) initial multiple construct errors; (8) combined vowel errors; (9) regular (phonic) and irregular (sight) words. The teacher provides a stimulus word orally from a sentence given in the Manual and the child underlines the word in the test he believes the teacher has spoken, five or six choices being offered for each occasion.

Purpose

'The Word Recognition Test . . . is designed to give the teacher two assessments of a child's word recognition ability: (a) the child's overall level of ability in word recognition which is provided by the child's total correct score on the test; and (b) an analysis of the child's errors and difficulties in word recognition, achieved by a close study of the type of correct and incorrect responses made by the child'.

'The test assesses word recognition (not "conceptual" reading in the sense of comprehension) from the earliest stages of letter knowledge to a level normally achieved at about 8 years 6 months. The test is constructed differently from the normal word-list type of test, and though a child may know a word in its normal context, he may find difficulty in deciding the answer when the same word is presented within a structured group of alternatives. It is these difficulties that the . . . test illuminates' (Manual, p. 1).

Item preparation

The 50 items incorporated in the test were derived initially from an 'extensive battery of 300 test items which were used to investigate aural (sound) and visual factors in word recognition' (Manual, p. 9). The 'original try-out battery' from which the 50 items were finally selected, however, seems to have consisted of around 100 items administered to only 148 children. The final items in the test itself were chosen to 'reflect a level of ability around the age of 6 to 6.5 years, this being the crucial area of the early stages of word recognition . . . Easier and more difficult items (22) were added to extend the range of the test, to ensure greater reliability, and to give the children at the very early stages an introduction to the test' (Manual, p. 11). In addition, the discrimination of each item was calculated before selection, items ranging from 0.60–0.94, just over half (26) falling in the range 0.70–0.79, with the next largest group (15) falling in the range 0.60–0.69. Details for individual items, however, are not supplied.

Whilst the selection of items to be incorporated in the test seems satisfactory there must be some doubts about the nature of the sample upon which these analyses were based: the Manual indicates that infant children, lower juniors and a remedial class were involved but it does not indicate the proportions or representativeness of each group in this sample.

Administration

Detailed instructions for the administration of the test are provided, up to 30 minutes being required. The test can be given to large groups of the older children, to individuals or smaller groups of younger ones. An alternative activity is provided for children experiencing difficulty on the first page of the text. A detailed script is provided for the teacher.

Standardization

There must also be some doubts about the manner in which the test scores were standardized. The Manual refers, intermittently, to the 'final sample of 1005 children' but provides no systematic details whatsoever of who these children were or how they were chosen. It seems likely that the majority of the children in this so-called 'final sample' were aged between 7:00–8:06 years. Carver argues that the 'distribution of median scores of the children aged 7 yr 0 m to 8 yr 7 m (7:00–8:07) . . . showed a reasonably steady progression' (Manual, p. 20) and uses this finding to justify a straight-line extrapolation to produce 'Word Recognition Ages'. He reports: 'The median score of the 1005 children in the final sample was 43, the mean age being 7 yr 9 m (7:09). A line was drawn from the established theoretical upper limit through the median score and extended downwards . . . (from the graph) it can be seen that a score of 12 . . . yields an age level of 4 years. This was remarkably close to the median score of 11 obtained by the children in the age group 4 yr 0 m to 4 yr 4 m (4:00–4:04) in the original sample' (Manual, p. 21).

Given the absence of any systematic details about the nature of the sample upon which these extrapolations were based, along with some minimal details about the progression of scores, however, it would seem wise to treat the resulting Word Recognition Ages with the greatest caution, using them merely as broad indicators of the levels children have achieved.

Scoring

The instructions in relation to marking the test are straightforward.

Reliability

High figures are quoted for reliability, based on the sample of 148 children to whom the test battery was originally administered. Using KR-20, $r = 0.98$; using split-half (odd/even) reliability, $r = 0.95$. It will be noted, however, that these values will have been inflated due to the sample spanning a three-year age range.

Validity

High correlations with other tests of reading are reported. With the Schonell Graded Word Reading Test the correlation was 0.90 based on 79 junior children; for a group of 168 'retarded readers taking remedial education' the correlation with the Burt (Rearranged) Word Reading Test of reading was 0.82. It is difficult to know what to make of these figures, given the small size of the samples, the wide age range and the restricted ranges of children tested.

Interpretation

A section of the Manual is devoted to possible uses of the test, with particular reference to its diagnostic potential. This section, in tandem with the schematic discussion of 'levels' of word recognition, is likely to prove useful to those undertaking remedial action on the basis of the test's results. The back page of the test provides additional space for the teacher/tester to make detailed notes on the child's 'pattern of errors' and, as such, may serve as a baseline against which to assess progress in specific areas.

Test use

Marshall reports that this test has been employed as part of 'a diagnostic battery given by remedial teachers or psychologists' in a screening programme devised by Moseley. Moseley (1975) reports upon a project which began in 1974 in the London Borough of Barnet when '3373 top-infant children were given the test and 12% of most backward and retarded were seen individually for further assessment'. A new method of scoring the test was devised at the same time which yielded a more adequate profile of different types of errors. Pumfrey and Naylor (1978) employed the test, along with others, on a sample of 60 children as part of an investigation into psycholinguistic deficits in retarded readers and Pumfrey refers to its extensive use 'for screening purposes in the Manchester area' where Carver was originally an experienced remedial teacher.

General evaluation

This test might contribute to a battery of test information on children aged 7+ employed for screening purposes; it could also subsequently assist in diagnosing aspects of children's specific difficulties in relation to word recognition and form a basis for remedial action. I am doubtful, however, whether the information available in the Manual about its characteristics and standardization is sufficient to justify giving it a prominent role in the identification of children in need of remedial education; to be on the safe side one could only employ it as a very preliminary screening device. Carver claims that the test could be used with 'children of 4–5 years who have some knowledge of word recognition' and there might be certain instances (e.g. a research project) where such use might be contemplated. However, it is difficult to know how such children might respond since most of the piloting appears to have been conducted on older children.

Overall, it seems unfortunate that the efforts which went into constructing this test in the early sixties have not been matched by equivalent efforts to discover more about its characteristics and behaviour in practice with larger, more representative samples of children.

References

Marshall, C. P. (1976). *Journal of the Association of Educational Psychologists* 4, 2–12.
Moseley, D. (1975). "Special Provision for Reading". Slough: NFER.
Pumfrey, P. (1977). "Reading: Tests and Assessment Techniques". Sevenoaks: Hodder & Stoughton.
Pumfrey, P. and Naylor, J. (1978). The alleviation of psycholinguistic deficits and some effects on the reading attainments of poor readers. *Journal of Research in Reading* 1, 87–107.

Young's Group Reading Test

Review (1) by Caroline Gipps

Author: D. Young
Publisher: Hodder & Stoughton
Distributor: Hodder & Stoughton

Age ranges: 6:05–7:10 (2nd-year infants)
             7:00–8:10 (1st-year juniors)
             8:00–12:10 (older below-average pupils)
1968–69 (M, T)
1974–79 (S) (re-standardized); 1980 (M, 2nd edition)
1980 (M); 1980–81 (T) printings reviewed
Group test

Test content

There are two alternate forms, A and B. Each form of the test consists of one sheet of paper printed on both sides which functions as a combination of test sheet and answer paper. The first side consists of 15 pictures illustrating words of increasing difficulty. By the side of each picture is a list of three, four or five words from which the child has to select, by putting a ring around it, the correct one. The second side of the test sheet contains 30 sentence completion items ranging from 'Cows give—' to 'Remember means—'. In all cases the missing word is at the end of the sentence and there are six alternatives given. In both forms A and B, 12 of the last 17 items are vocabulary ones of the 'Remember means—' type. Both parts of the test are preceded by three practice examples.

Purpose

'The test is suitable for children in the final year (especially the last term) of the infant stage, and in the first year (especially the first term) of the junior stage, and with older, below-average pupils. The test was designed for easy application and quick marking. The alternate forms facilitate use in normal classroom conditions—that is, by one teacher to a full class—as children sitting next to each other can be given different forms. The one line sentence items help to confine the length to a single sheet, and this both simplifies administration (particularly to less able infants) and permits the provision and use of marking templates for ease of scoring' (Manual, p. 3).

Item preparation

'The picture items and the easier sentence items were constructed to minimize the demands on vocabulary, general knowledge and intelligence. Since marking by template was planned, the sentence items were limited to one line, and typically, the more difficult item thus takes the simple form of finding a synonym . . . The distractors (the wrong answers) for the easiest items were selected with the aid of the lists in "Words Your Children Use" (Edwards and

Gibbon, 1964). The item analysis used separate samples for the sexes and employed a method of converting the percentage of passes to probits so that discriminating power and facility levels could be more easily calculated . . . Though some items with strong sex bias were eliminated, care was taken to avoid selecting items in a way that would eliminate any general sex difference' (Manual, p. 19).

This is all the information given in the Manual on item preparation. Thus there is no information on the item sampling frame and the sentence about not selecting items to eliminate general sex differences is vague in the extreme. The questionable practice of the use of synonyms for the more difficult items seems to be related solely to the need to keep the items to one line.

Administration

The test assumes normal classroom conditions of a full class and one teacher, the only materials required are the test sheets and pencils. They suggest that both forms are used, children sitting next to each other using different forms, to reduce the amount of copying. Four minutes are allowed for the picture items and nine minutes for the sentence items. The section in the Manual on administration is comprehensive and thorough.

Standardization

The sample for the new (1980) norms was drawn from 'three widely separated areas' and testing was carried out between 1974 and 1979. The sample size was 21 711 infants, 5560 first-year juniors and 1867 pupils aged 8:07–12:10. There is no information on the number of boys and girls tested, the sample design, what proportion was from metropolitan or county areas, etc., beyond the description 'part urban and part rural'. The score distributions from each of the three areas were independently calibrated by means of 'nationally standardized tests' (Salford Sentence Reading Test, the Burt, Schonell and Vernon Graded Word Reading Tests) and in the calibrated form the data were combined to produce tables of reading quotients. These are given separately for three different age bands, 6:05–7:10, 7:00–8:10 and 8:10–12:00, i.e. corresponding to infants, juniors and the older below-average junior children. There is also a table of equivalent scores for Young's and the Salford Sentence Reading Test, Burt, Schonell and Vernon.

The Manual discusses the problem of testing children on reading as young as 6:05. Scores of children at such a young age vary with the age of admission, degree of overlap between the reading scheme and the test vocabularies, teaching methods and the timing of phonic training. 'For many reasons, therefore, the lower reading ages are best regarded as a convenient extension of a scale intended for use with children older than 6:05, and certainly not as a guide to our expectations for younger children'. In any case the age norms below 7:00 were derived from equivalences with the Burt score using a sample of only 315 children. There is no information on the number of children who were in either the last term of infants or the first term of juniors, the so-called target population, and indeed this may well be quite a small number.

The problems mentioned above and the fact that this restandardization was carried out over five years, suggest that the standardization procedure is not as thorough as it should be. Indeed, as the author points out in the Preface to the Manual, the original standardization itself was obviously not satisfactory as the new norms differ from the old ones except in the eight- to ten-year age range which is not the range for which the test is really intended.

Scoring

The scoring is straightforward, no subjective judgements being required. Templates are available, instructions for conversion of raw scores to reading quotients and reading ages are given and are clear.

Reliability

The parallel forms were administered on the same occasion to 100 7 year-olds. The resulting reliability coefficient was 0.95 and the standard error of measurement was 2.38. 129 children (average age 7:01) were retested on the same form after a week, and the standard error of measurement was 2.49. Also 475 children (average age 7:02) were given the parallel form 2–7 days after being given the initial form. Standard error of measurement was 2.27. For a sample of 886 children who were given the test twice (no information on the average age of the children or the gap between test and retest), the standard error of measurement was 2.18.

We are told that the 'reading age scale is uniformly reliable up to a Reading Age of 8:05 with six points of a score corresponding to 0.6 of a year. Above this the reliability progressively decreases' (Manual, p. 30).

Validity

Predictive validity

One hundred and thirty children aged 7:06 were given Young's test and the Vernon Graded Word test. Three years five months later they were given the NFER English test 16 and the correlations between 'quotients' were: Vernon and NFER English, 0.76; Young's test and NFER English, 0.77. This latter correlation is claimed as showing satisfactory predictive validity for the Young's test over this period of time.

Concurrent validity

This was assessed by correlating the results of the test with the results of other tests taken at the same time and with class teachers' judgements of reading ability. Eighty children aged 7:06–8:06 were given NFER Reading Test AD, Young's Group Reading Test, the Neale Analysis of Reading Ability and the Vernon Graded Word Reading Test. Teachers' ratings of these children were obtained in the form of orders of merit and these 'were quantified by scaling against the Young scores'. The correlation between the Young's reading test score and the Neale accuracy score was 0.88. For the Young's reading test score and the Neale comprehension score the correlation was 0.74. The Manual claims that the correlation between the teacher's assessment and the score on the Young's test—value 0.93—also supports the validity of the test.

Interpretation

The section of 'Examining the Results' (Manual, p. 17) is thorough and should be useful to the class teacher, 'If the test has been properly administered and carefully marked, the results will, in general, confirm the opinions of teachers who know the children; but there may be some surprises and the following remarks are intended to help in resolving the doubts that may arise'. It includes caveats such as that very high or very low scores should be treated with caution, and that discrepancies between teachers' assessment and test score could be due to the unreliability of testing. This section does suggest courses of action to follow, these are not diagnostic but do go further than the follow-up suggested by many reading tests.

Test use

Bailey and Rogers (1979) used the Young's Group Reading Test to validate an infant reading check-list which they developed in Essex. Young's Group Reading Test was administered to children leaving infant school in the years 1976, 1977 and 1978. Mean scores rose from 105.34 to 108.35 during this period. The difference in mean scores and standard deviations was significant at the 0.01 per cent level. The authors of the infant reading check-list take this rise in Young's reading test scores as support for the value of their check-list and the screening process in which it was involved.

Marshall (1976) carried out a survey in 1973 of Schools Psychological Services in England, Scotland and Wales asking about procedures for the early identification of children with educational or behavioural difficulties. Sixty-two per cent of the 138 LEAs that replied were using some form of identification procedure. This survey found that Young's group test of reading (and also intelligence) was the most popular with 17 LEAs using the group reading test.

More recently, Gipps and Wood (1981) found that the Young's Group Reading Test was the most popular reading test in use by LEAs for group testing of children for monitoring, screening or record-keeping purposes. Some 33 LEAs used the Young's group reading test in 1979 compared with 9 LEAs using the next most popular test.

General evaluation

This test is, above all, quick and easy to administer. It is also cheap, hence its popularity in LEAs. There is no doubt that it is useful as a rough guide to overall standards given a class, school or LEA (with a caveat about the standardization). It is also useful to look at an individual child's progress over the very short span from the last term of infants to the first term of juniors. However, it provides little feedback for the teacher and certainly none that is diagnostic. One must question the extensive use of synonyms in a reading test but the greatest criticism is the inadequate information on the standardization.

References

Bailey, T. and Rogers, C. (1979). Screening, diagnosis and prescription: an infant reading check. *Association of Educational Psychologists Journal* 5, 1.

Edwards, R. P. A. and Gibbon, V. (1964). "Words Your Children Use". London: Burke.

Gipps, C. and Wood, R. (1981). The testing of reading in LEAs: the Bullock Report seven years on. *Educational Studies* 7, 133–143.

Marshall, C. P. (1976). Screening procedures for the early identification of children in need of help. *Assocation of Educational Psychologists Journal* 4, 2.

Young's Group Reading Test

Review (2) by Christine Mabey

Author: D. Young
Publisher: Hodder & Stoughton
Distributor: Hodder & Stoughton
Age ranges: 6:05–7:10 (2nd-year infants)
　　　　　　 7:00–8:10 (1st-year juniors)
　　　　　　 8:00–12:10 (older below average pupils)

1968–69 (M, T)
1974–79 (S) (re-standardized); 1980 (M, 2nd edition)
1980 (M); 1980–81 (T) printings reviewed
Group test

Test content

Two parallel versions of the test are provided, Form A and Form B, primarily for simultaneous use to minimize copying. Each version is in two sections with preliminary practice items for each. The first section consists of 15 picture items for each of which the correct word (from a choice of 3–5) needs to be chosen. The second section has 30 items involving sentence completion from a choice of 6 words. The test is almost entirely a vocabulary test with even the latest items involving the choice of a synonym for the test item. For example: 'Ability means ——————— (skill)' (Form B, Item 45). The test is printed on both sides of a sheet and the pictures on the first side are clearly drawn and seem to appeal to 7–8 year-old children.

Purpose

No aims are specified in the Manual except the age-groups for which it is suitable: 'the test is suitable for children in the final year (especially the last term) of the infant stage and in the first year (especially the first term) of the junior stage, and with older, below-average pupils'. Further, it is claimed that the test 'was designed for easy application and quick marking' (Manual, p. 3).

Item preparation

The author reports that:

> 'the picture items and the easier sentence items were constructed to minimize the demands on vocabulary, general knowledge and intelligence . . . The distractors (the wrong answers) for the easiest items were selected with the aid of the lists in "Words Your Children Use" (Edwards and Gibbon, 1964).

> 'The item analysis used separate samples for the sexes and employed a method of converting the percentages of passes to probits, so that discriminating power and facility levels could be more easily calculated (Das, 1964). Though some items with strong sex bias were eliminated, care was taken to avoid selecting items in a way that would eliminate any general sex difference.

> 'All score levels of the test were equally represented in the 3600 papers used in the final analysis' (Manual, pp. 19–20).

Unusually—in the reviewer's experience—the author reports on an investigation into whether the instructions had been understood. This was done by 'considering the papers of the worst scores of a sample of 1162 infants of average age 7:01. It could be surmized that 7 of the 11 children who failed to score had not understood the instructions. One child who was subsequently ascertained as "unsuitable for education in school", had ringed the pictures. The other six children had ringed more than one word per item. It was subsequently confirmed that all these children were non-readers and, moreover, were of low intelligence' (Manual, p. 20). The author further reports 10 children who had apparently understood the nature of the task but had failed to hear or remember the instruction to work across the page. The author concludes that this should more correctly be interpreted as an error of supervision.

Administration

The test is designed to be given in normal classroom conditions, i.e. a full class and one teacher present who administers the test. It is recommended that desks are rearranged to avoid copying and that children with some hearing loss sit near the front where the teacher's lips can be clearly seen. Children need a pencil and a copy of the test. It is advised that alternate Forms (A and B) be given to children sitting next to each other to minimize copying.

A maximum time allowance of 4 minutes for the picture items and 9 minutes for the sentence items is stated. It is stressed that this is a maximum time allowance for the benefit of very poor readers and that it is advisable to arrange a quiet occupation for those children who need much less than the full 9 minutes.

Full and precise instructions are given in the Manual for the introduction of the test and the explanations of the tasks required. Further, specific wording is provided for the actual test administration. In addition, the administrator is advised to walk around while the children are working through the test to ensure that they are following the instructions correctly.

Standardization

The standardization for the revised edition (used for this review) differed from that of the original version. For the revised edition norms are based on surveys, between 1974 and 1979, in three 'widely separated areas', part urban and rural. How far these areas were, or were thought to be representative of the country as a whole is not discussed. It is stated, further, that 'the score distributions from each area, calibrated by means of nationally standardized lists, were found to be consistent with each other' (Manual, p. 22). The numbers involved in these samples were 21 711 infants, 5560 first-year juniors and 1867 older pupils aged 8:07–12:10.

These samples were used to construct tables with a mean of 100, standard deviation of 15 and provide reading quotients in three separate conversion tables for infants, aged 6:05–7:10, first-year juniors, aged 7:00–8:10, and below-average second-year juniors and older pupils aged 8:00–12:00.

No separate norms are given for boys and girls although it is reported that girls showed a 'superiority of 5, 3, 2 and 2 points of quotient at 7, 8, 9 and 10 years' (Manual, p. 22). The reason for this is that separate norms would conceal the differences in reading ability at these levels.

Scoring

Instructions for marking are explicit. Only one answer for each item is acceptable and templates are provided for ease of marking. In order to lessen credit being given to guesses when by chance the correct answer is provided, scoring is discontinued after the tenth mistake has been made. This point was decided on after examining the effect of using two different methods; cut-off after a fixed number of mistakes ('cumulative' cut-off) and cut-off after a fixed number of mistakes occur consecutively ('block' cut-off). The author reports that 'for a sample of 183 pairs of scripts the improvement in reliability was found for increasing the number of mistakes from nine to twelve or from four to six. For a sample of 354 pairs the ten-mistake cumulative method showed a small (but not statistically significant) increase in reliability compared with the five-mistake consecutive method' (Manual, p. 21).

Reliability

Reliability is reported for various measures. First, the two forms were administered on the same occasion to 100 7 year-old children. The inter-form correlation was 0.95 with a standard error of measurement of 2.38. A different measure of reliability—of stability—was obtained by administering the same form to 129 children (average age 7:01) a week after they had first been tested with it. There was a practice effect, estimated at 2.52 points of raw score, and a standard error of measurement of 2.49. A measure of the reliability of equivalence and stability was obtained by giving 475 children (average age 7:2) the parallel form two to seven days after the initial testing. As in the previous instance the coefficient is not quoted but the standard error of measurement—of 2.27—is provided. In all, some 886 children were tested and retested: the mean difference was 2.27 with standard error of measurement of 2.18. All these different measures provide reasonable reliabilities.

The author makes clear, however, that reliability is not uniform across all ages for which standard scores are provided. 'The reading age scale is uniformly reliable up to Reading Age 8:05, with 6 points of score corresponding to 0.6 of a year. Above this the reliability progressively decreases.

For a given age the quotients differ little in their reliability. At 7:00 (Table 1) six points of raw score correspond to 8 or 10 points of quotient. At 9:00 (Table 3) this is reduced to 7 or 8. In short, the quotients for the older children are more reliable' (Manual, p. 30).

Validity

The author does not claim high content validity for his test but he makes an interesting comment on the criticisms of such tests:

> 'Test results are sometimes thought to have low validity when the criteria used are based on comparison with books and reading for pleasure and information. However, the inadequacy of a subjective approach is demonstrated by investigations showing that, despite their quite different content, graded word reading tests and Moray House English tests correlate highly. Terms such as "word recognition" and "comprehension", when applied to tests certainly mislead if they are taken to imply correspondence between tests and distinct abilities' (Manual, p. 24).

Information is provided on the predictive validity of the test using data from an earlier version. One hundred and thirty children aged 7:6 were tested on the earlier version and the Vernon Graded Word Reading Test. 'Three years and five months later they were given NFER English Test 16 and the correlations between quotients were: Vernon/NFER English, 0.758: Young prototype/NFER English, 0.77. These correlations may be claimed to show satisfactory/predictive validity for both tests over this period' (Manual, p. 4).

Concurrent validity was assessed from a sample of 80 children, mean age 8 years (area not known), who were tested with the following tests: NFER Reading Test AD, Young Group Reading Test (Forms A1 and B1), the Neale Analysis of Reading Ability (Form A) and the Vernon Graded Word Reading Test. Further, the teachers' opinions of the children were obtained in the form of orders of merit. Correlation coefficients of 0.93 with the teachers' orders of merit, 0.88 with Neale Accuracy Age, 0.88 with Vernon Graded Word Reading Test, 0.88 with NFER Reading Test AD and 0.74 with Neale Comprehensive Age were obtained.

Interpretation

A long section is provided on interpreting the results, under the title 'examining the results'. In the reviewer's experience this is one of the most detailed interpretations provided in a reading test manual. First, it is suggested that the raw scores should be examined to see how they compare with the teacher's own order of merit. The author counsels: 'if there are discrepancies keep an open mind, for it is when the test result differs from the teacher's opinion that it may be most productive'. The obvious point (which is often ignored) of checking for marking error is advised. If marking is correct, the author refers again to the degree of unreliability in testing and refers the user to the detailed statistics on this. Further, the differences between individual children in dealing with test material is emphasized: 'some children impress more when they are reading familiar material to their teachers, while others, having more independence of attack, do unexpectedly well with tests' (Manual, p. 17). Caution is also recommended for interpreting very high or very low scores and the author points out that children scoring within a few points of 45 (the ceiling) should not be assumed to be similar in achievement.

Guidance is given on converting raw scores into both reading ages and reading quotients. The conversion tables for these are accompanied by a percentile table showing the distribution for a normal population. The advantages of using reading quotients (or, more precisely, standardized scores) are spelt out with precise instructions for establishing a child's chronological age.

Advice is given for interpreting the results of two testings at different periods in time when gains are thought to have been made. The effects of both practice and error measurement are pointed out and the user is again referred to the detailed sections on validity, reliability and practice effects.

Finally, there is a section on the action to be taken following examination of the results. Various tests and types of tests are suggested either to confirm the obtained score or provide indicators of the areas of weakness. These are followed by practical suggestions and the enlisting of various specialist services.

Test use

This is a popular, much used test as is evidenced by its frequent citation in research reports. Marshall (1976) reported that in a survey of 160 School Psychological Services in England and Wales, in 1973, 17 local authorities were using the test for screening purposes. In fact, it has been for screening purposes that the test has most often been quoted. Crowther (1971) reported the test use with first-year junior-school children in Surrey. There it was used as a preliminary tool to identify ESN, gifted and children whose reading quotient was less than their IQ. Bailey (1979) reported its use in Southend by the Schools Psychological Service (SPS) for screening children in top infants and top junior classes. In addition the SPS devised on Infant Reading Check (IRC) with items on visual-motor tasks, auditory tasks and acquired knowledge. All children who scored less than 90 on the Young test were given an IRC. Interestingly enough Bailey also used the improved mean scores for the age group from the Young test over three years (1976–8) to suggest that the screening procedure with its accompanying feed-back and discussion in the schools had had a positive effect. Marshall and Wolfendale (1977, pp. 228–237) also used the test with a teacher check-list (based on observation) to screen children experiencing difficulties. The work they reported was in Croydon and the Young test was only used in the first term of second-year juniors as the Neale test was used in the top infants and first-year juniors. Perhaps the most interesting use of it as a screening instrument is contained in Booth's report (1980) of routine screening in Grampian of Primary 2 children. He points out that the standardization for 6:06 year olds covers children with very different amounts of education because of different authorities entry policies: from one to two years. In Grampian, however, there is a standard, single entry date so that all children have the same amount of schooling. He, as were the other reports listed, was using the 1968 version of the test. This he restandardized on 1531 Grampian children to give a mean of 100 and standard deviation of 15. In comparing the resulting scores with the 1968 Young standardization he found a marked difference at the lower age points, e.g. at 6:06, but roughly the same mean scores at 7:06. This is an important qualification to remember if the test is being used for example with top infants who have either had more or less schooling than the average. An example of the test being used as a measure of attainment is given in Lindsay's report (1980) of an Infant Rating Scale (IRS) used in Sheffield LEA. There the IRS was administered to the children on intake to identify learning difficulties. The Young test was then given to the children when they reached top infants to assess the predictive value of the IRS. Gray (1979) has reported a slightly different, but probably equally common, use of the test in his report on teacher effectiveness in infant school. In that study children in two consecutive years were tested at the beginning and end of the top infants year. The use in that context was to measure relative reading gain of children taught by different teachers.

General evaluation

This is a popular test and, if used for the correct age groups, provides useful screening or attainment measures. It is rightly popular with teachers for its quickness of administration and marking, clarity of manual, with practical instructions for follow-up, and attractiveness to children. Information in the Manual is detailed about its construction, reliability and validity which are all acceptable. More precise detail about the representativeness of the standardization sample would have been useful. However, the practical section on interpreting and using the results is particularly welcome.

The only significant reservation which should be made concerns the test's use or rather misuse. It is designed for the transition period from infants to juniors and when used for that age band is perfectly acceptable. However, even with first-year juniors its value may be limited as examination of the conversion tables demonstrates. For example, older children (8:08–8:10) in this year are expected to score 38–39 out of a total possible 45 items in order to achieve a standard score of 100. Similarly, a child of that age scoring at the 'ceiling' is credited with a standard score of only 113–115. Caution in interpreting scores at the ceiling have been pointed out by the author. Potential users would be advised to consider carefully the age group they wish to test and the purpose of their study.

References

Bailey, T. and Rogers, C. (1979). Screening, diagnosis and prescription: An infant reading check. *Association of Educational Psychologists Journal* 5, 47–51.

Booth, G. (1980). Effects of length of schooling upon early reading attainment. *Educational Research* 23, 57–59.

Crowther, C. R. (1971). Educational screening: A pilot report. *Remedial Education* 6, 37–9.

Edwards, R. P. A. and Gibbon, V. (1964). "Words Your Children Use". London: Burke.

Gray, J. (1979). Reading progress in English Infant Schools: Some problems emerging for a study of teacher effectiveness. *British Educational Research Journal* 5, 141–157.

Lindsay, G. A. (1980). The Infant Rating Scale. *British Journal of Educational Psychology* 50, 97–104.

Marshall, C. P. (1976). Screening procedures for the early identification of children in need of help. *Association of Educational Psychologists Journal* 4, 2–12.

Marshall, C. P. and Wolfendale, S. (1977). "Screening and Early Identification of Children with Problems in Reading: Research and Classroom Practice". London: Ward Lock Educational.

Mathematics

List of reviews

APU Arithmetic Test 332
Basic Mathematics Test A 336
Basic Mathematics Test B 341
Basic Mathematics Test C 344
Basic Mathematics Test DE 348
Basic Mathematics Test FG 351
Basic Number Screening Test 354
Essential Mathematics 356
Graded Arithmetic-Mathematics Test 359
Group Mathematics Test 362
The Leicester Number Test 369
Mathematics Attainment Test A 373
Mathematics Attainment Test B 377
Mathematics Attainment Test C1 380
Mathematics Attainment Test C3 382
Mathematics Attainment Test DE1 385
Mathematics Attainment Test DE2 387
Mathematics Attainment Test EF 390
Mathematics Topic Tests 394
Moray House Mathematics Tests 396
The Nottingham Number Test 401
Number Test DE 404
Profile of Mathematical Skills 406
Secondary Mathematics Item Bank 410
Senior Mathematics Test* 416
The Staffordshire Test of Computation 416
Transitional Assessment: Mathematics 419
Yardsticks: Criterion-Referenced Tests in Mathematics 422
'Y' Mathematics Series 424
'Y' Mathematics Series 430

* Brief report only.

See also:

Basic Number Diagnostic Test　　　　　　　　　　　　　8
Basic Skills Assessment Program　　　　　　　　　　435
Bristol Achievement Tests: Mathematics　　　　　　442
Bristol Achievement Tests: Study Skills　　　　　　445
CSMS Science Reasoning Tasks　　　　　　　　　　670
Early Mathematical Language　　　　　　　　　　　37
Richmond Tests of Basic Skills　　　　　　　　　449
SRA Reading and Arithmetic Indexes　　　　　　455

APU Arithmetic Test

Reviewed by B. L. M. Chapman

Authors: S. J. Closs and M. J. Hutchings
Publisher: Hodder & Stoughton
Distributor: Hodder & Stoughton
Age range: 11:08–18:11
1976 (M, T); S not stated
1977 M, T) printings reviewed
Group test

Test content

This is a single timed test in arithmetic, covering the age-range 11–18 years, which the Manual stresses is an achievement test and not an aptitude test. The 50 questions begin by testing a straightforward evaluation of arithmetic expressions mixed with evaluations of simple problems specified in sentential form. Subsequent questions then deal with knowledge of proportion, percentage, estimation of area and simple probability. In the main, questions can be solved mentally by sequential processing of partial results, but a few may be most quickly solved by resort to simple algebra which may lead the testee to using 'rough-working' procedures.

For the most part the test makes little demand upon a knowledge of units of measure although some of the questions on mensuration refer to metric measures of length. All of these could be answered correctly without a specific knowledge of those units. To this extent the test is reasonably free of local cultures within the western scientific community. It may be, however, that the patterns of correlation with mathematics results in the General Certificate and Scottish Certificate of Education, which are discussed later, are due to this freedom from particular curricular fashion.

Purpose

The test was designed as one of general arithmetic attainment, not tied to particular curricula, but clearly by its use of arithmetic symbolism it is specific to the familiar form of western educational culture. It is designed to test arithmetic concepts through calculation yet not to impose difficulty of calculation nor to test perseverance in calculation. Quite explicitly it does not seek to test algebra, geometry, trigonometry, matrices or calculus. The acronym APU might suggest that it is a product of the Assessment of Performance Unit set up by Department of Education and Science in Britain to study educational attainment on a national basis. This is not the case, however, and as the Manual makes clear the acronym refers to Applied Psychology Unit at the University of Edinburgh whose test predates the setting up of the Assessment of Performance Unit.

Item preparation

No details of any kind are given about item selection although the Manual is very specific about standardization procedures.

Administration

The instructions on administration in the Manual are exemplary in their attention to detail and general advice to the examiner. The test is administered as a group test with one expendable test form for each pupil and the time allowed for the completion is 25 minutes.

Standardization

Standardization was carried out using pupils drawn from a random sample of secondary schools throughout the UK. In drawing this sample considerable care was exercised to maintain a balance between schools of different size and to obtain a sample of schools which were geographically representative of the UK. The final sample consisted of 14 schools which, despite the care exercised, may be regarded as rather a small number to properly represent the attributes among which a balance was sought.

Sampling of pupils within these schools was carried out by age-group and a very comprehensive table of distribution statistics for the sample is published.

In the 11–17 years age group the sample sizes vary from 294–1591 but in the 18 years age group the sample is down to 130 pupils. The Manual includes a caveat for the interpretation of percentile scores for the 16–18 years age group because these children are by definition those who are staying on to take leaving certificates and are thus a self selected group. Although the meticulous reporting of the standardization procedure inspires confidence it is unfortunate that there is no comment on the distribution of ages by sex or of any difference in the means for the sex groups. Date of standardization is not reported.

Scoring

Layout of the test form is extremely clear for the pupil with a bold answer column on the right of each page and good regular alignment of questions with answers. Marking is equally straightforward with one double page of the test Manual devoted to answer keys matching each of the pages on the test form. In the few cases where alternative answers are acceptable these are also clearly marked. It is difficult to envisage any improvements to this procedure short of machine-readable code.

Total scores of correct answers are converted to percentile ranks for each age year-group using tables of norms derived from the standardization procedure.

Reliability

Two indices of reliability are given, one being a measure of internal consistency based on a part-whole (item-test) correlation similar in assumptions to those of KR-20, and the other from test-retest correlation. The first was carried out only for the 15–16 years age group while the second was reportedly only done with a sample of 13 year-old pupils. The reliability indices are respectively 0.91 and 0.96. There is some confusion in the text, however, because elsewhere a table of standard errors of measurement is given for each of the age ranges 11–18 years and this claims to be based upon test-retest results for which no details are given. The test-retest which is described for the 13 year-old pupils involved tests given only one week apart which for this kind of test would seem to be rather too short an interval.

The Manual is at pains to point out the meaning and inference to be drawn from the standard error of measurement though it falls into the very common error of failing to state whether this is for the raw score or the derived score. Because, in this case a percentile scale is used, it is reasonably safe to assume that the standard error of measurement refers to the raw score.

Validity

As the Manual correctly indicates, in a test of this kind, the content is so closely related to what one seeks to measure that validity can be assessed in terms of the extent to which the test content samples the curriculum. Nevertheless, a series of figures for concurrent validity are quoted. Perhaps the most relevant comparison in terms of similarity of test aims is the Vernon Graded Arithmetic-Mathematics Test which yields a correlation with the APU Arithmetic of 0.88. Also of great interest is a table of correlations with various papers on the Scottish Certificate of Education and the General Certificate of Education. The highest figure in this table is the correlation between APU Arithmetic and the arithmetic paper of the SCE which is 0.75. In terms of predictive validity this is not very useful in that neither paper adds substantially to a prediction the other made upon a knowledge of age alone. Among the other subjects, however, the relative magnitudes of the correlations follow a familiar pattern with all of the sciences being correlated with APU Arithmetic but the coefficients becoming progressively smaller as the subjects become more applied in the vocational sense.

What is most striking about this table is the comparison, subject by subject, between the SCE and the GCE. For each of the three subjects maths, physics and chemistry at 'O' level the correlation coefficient with APU Arithmetic is about half for the GCE what it is for the SCE. This suggests very strongly that there is an attribute of the Scottish curriculum which, irrespective of subject speciality, forms a common element not shared by curricula in the rest of the UK. It is impossible to guess what this may be but there is no doubt that on the figures presented the APU is a much better predictor of success on these three subject areas in SCE than it is in GCE.

Interpretation

A table provides percentile equivalents of raw scores for each year group 11–18.

General evaluation

In terms of the well-defined aims of the test there is no doubt that this is, both administratively and in terms of standardization, one of the most satisfactory tests available. Its avoidance of particular fashionable procedures in education and adherence to basic competence makes it attractive as a test likely to withstand the erosion of time. In some respects, however, this same centrality of approach which avoids curricular differences makes it less satisfactory as an index of mathematical attainment, particularly in the context of testing pupils against national expectations.

Despite the protestations of the Manual this implies that when given in the context of a body of pupils who have been subject to similar treatment the test has much to commend it as an index of aptitude for arithmetic learning. It does little to test transfer of training or lateral thinking with arithmetic concepts but essentially tests the ability to reproduce that which is common to all arithmetic processes.

Without doubt the quality of the administrative Manual as an instrument for educating the test user is very high and having consideration for the context of use of many educational tests this is a very desirable asset.

Basic Mathematics Test A

Reviewed by Jim Ridgway

Author: not stated
Publisher: NFER-Nelson
Distributor: NFER-Nelson
Age range: 6:09–8:02
1975 (S); 1971 (M); 1971 (T)
No revision apparent
1980 (M, T) printings reviewed
Group test

Test content

There are 40 items which cover the use of a number of mathematical operations across a wide range of topic areas. The operations represented (written here in order of the number of questions devoted to each) are: equating, counting, adding, ordering, subtracting, and with just two questions to each, classifying, multiplying and dividing. These operations are applied to a variety of topics (quantities, ideas or domains), namely: size, shape, volume, fractional parts, the interpretation of bar charts and pictograms, place value, area, money, length, weight and time (reading a clock). Scores can be derived for each operation and for each topic.

Instructions for each item are administered orally. In the test booklet, items consist of clear line drawings separated by solid lines. Pupils respond by writing in answers, shading areas, circling and crossing out response alternatives, and drawing lines.

Purpose

The Manual says:

> 'This test was constructed to provide a measure of how well a child has grasped and developed the ideas he has met in the early part of his junior school.
>
> 'In addition to the comparisons between children, this test aims to give some diagnostic information about a child's individual strengths and weaknesses . . . It is believed that this information will be valuable to the junior school teacher in directing the child's subsequent mathematical learning.
>
> 'It is hoped . . . that the test results can be interpreted as reasonably "pure" measures of mathematical attainment' (Manual, p. 3).

Standardized scores are available from a large sample of children. As well as the diagnostic functions outlined above, the test can be used to

(1) roughly relate the mathematical attainment of the individual and the class to peers elsewhere in the country;
(2) rank order children within a class;
(3) provide the teacher with feedback about the strengths and weaknesses of lessons on different aspects of mathematics; and,
(4) identify children in need of special education.

Item preparation

No data are available on how the items were developed, nor is there any information about piloting studies which may have been conducted. Clues about the construct validity of each item can be obtained by examining the diagnostic scoring scheme for each item.

Administration

The test is administered orally to overcome the problems which poor readers face when presented with written mathematics problems. The test, then, requires pupils to understand spoken English, and to possess elementary writing skills. Children need a response booklet, a pencil and a rubber. 'The proper administration of an oral test requires particular skill and it is recommended that this test should be given by an experienced teacher' (Manual, p. 4). Questions are read aloud by the test administrator, one item at a time. The administrator has to judge when all the children have finished each question, before proceeding to the next item. The time taken to administer the test will, obviously, vary depending on the speed of the slowest child in each group. The Manual recommends that the test be administered in two parts, separated by (say) the mid-morning break. The test should not be given to a group of more than 45 children. The script for administering the test provided in the Manual for the administrator is perfectly clear.

Standardization

'The test was standardized on 6073 children (3178 boys, 2895 girls) from two areas, one being an urban area in Midlands and the other being a London Borough. The tests were administered during 1975 . . .' (Manual, p. 3). The mean age of the children in the sample was 7:06. Children's scores were grouped together in age bands one month wide to provide normative data for the calculation of standardized scores. Standardized scores are available for the age range 6:09–8:02. A conversion table in the Manual shows the standardized score of an individual child given the child's age and raw test score. Values for children aged 6:09–8:06 are provided: entries for children in the range 8:03–8:06 have been extrapolated from the data, not observed, and so should be treated with some caution. Within each age band of one month, the standardized scores are arranged so that they have a mean of approximately 100 and a standard deviation of 15. The Manual provides a guide to the interpretation of these standard scores in terms of the percentage of children who attained less than a given standardized score.

'The data was (*sic*) considered sufficient to give a fair approximation to the "national standard" ' (Manual, p. 3). We have no way of evaluating this rather strong assertion. Certainly the sample size is adequate, but its representativeness of the population as a whole is debatable. However, the test will be used most commonly to monitor class performance, and the performance of individual pupils, in order to provide feedback to the class teacher about the competence of the class and the needs of individual pupils. Comparisons with notional 'national standards' may give rise to local gloom or euphoria, depending on the outcome of the comparisons but are far less use to the teacher than an analysis of the strengths and weaknesses of children in the different topics covered.

'The difference in terms of raw scores between boys and girls was found to be not significant. Nor was the difference in the increase of score with age significant . . .' (Manual, p. 3).

Scoring

The test booklet contains a well laid-out score summary sheet. Instructions for marking are laid out clearly. The scorer's discretion for the acceptance of 'wrong' answers is specified unambiguously. Quite reasonably, the reversal of numbers, mirrored numbers and misspelled words are permitted. The scoring procedure offers some checks against scorer errors.

An overall raw score is calculated for each script, which can be converted to a standard score. The score summary sheet provides a box labelled 'score band'—a useful reminder to the user of the errors inherent in measurement, and the dangers of over-interpreting small differences between pupils.

The scoring scheme also offers a profile of the mathematical attainment of each child. Each question in the test is identified as assessing skills relevant to at least one operation and to at least one topic. A simple check-list, completed while scoring the test, allows the child's scores on each operation and each topic to be determined.

Reliability

The only reported reliability test is that of internal consistency (KR-20) which was found to be 0.91. The sample consisted of 261 individuals chosen randomly from one of the areas taking part in the standardization. A value of 0.91 corresponds to a standard error of measurement of 4.54. Caution should be exercised since it seems no adjustment for age changes over the 2-year age range was used. The Manual explains how this value is to be interpreted and used when comparing individuals, in a straightforward manner.

Validity

None are reported. Inspection of the test items, however, taken together with the profile scoring scheme, provides strong clues about the content validity of the test items. Since the test is a measure of mathematical attainment, rather than of some mystical latent trait of mathematical ability, parallel items are easy to construct. Indeed, many primary school teachers will already possess relevant item banks in the form of work cards!

Interpretation

Raw test scores and standard scores can provide a rough idea about overall class performance compared to classes in an urban area in the Midlands and in a London Borough. They can also be used to rank children within a class in order of their mathematical attainment. At least as useful is the prospect of identifying areas of relative weakness, both of the individual and of the whole class, to enable remedial action to be taken. The classification of test items into scores on different topics and on the use of different operators provides a strong indication of the nature of the difficulty experienced.

General evaluation

The test provides a relatively easy way of providing the class teacher with feedback about teaching performance and about the needs of individual pupils. The Manual is clearly written, and provides a straightforward guide to test use. A good feature is the use of a score band for each individual, rather than a score. The test booklet is clear and easy to use. The test items are, by and large, unambiguous although two minor amendments could usefully be made:

(1) Questions 3 and 4 show a triangle which should be bisected exactly, and is not;
(2) Questions 15 and 18 use a bar chart with pictures of bags of crisps. The Manual assertion that 'One picture stands for 5 bags of crisps' (Manual, p. 9) may leave some pupils confused about which 'picture' was being referred to.

Using the test diagnostically may prove to have benefits beyond the immediate test scores obtained. An obvious benefit is to allow the teacher to pinpoint topics which have not been dealt with adequately in the lessons (or which might not have been covered at all). A less obvious benefit may come simply from the teacher's analysis of the items into operator and topics, and the translation of the analysis into classroom mathematical activities. A notion which should be central to mathematical learning is the applicability of mathematical operations across a wide range of topics both inside and outside the classroom. If this test causes teachers to increase the number of topics which are used to illustrate the different mathematical operators, and thus help pupils generalize the rules they learn, it will have served a very useful function.

Another good feature of the test is the transparency of the rules for item construction. Teachers should be able to generate parallel items, easier items, and more difficult items all with similar construct validity, for teaching and re-assessment purposes. This process of de-mystifying tests is useful in itself. Since the test is an attainment test, it should be clear just what is being attained. A focus on 'attainment', rather than 'ability', casts the teacher in a role of a transmitter of knowledge, rather than one of observer of human intellectual development.

This test is similar in format to Mathematics Attainment Test A, which is also reviewed in this volume. Basic Mathematics Test A should be used in preference to that test because of:

its potential use as a diagnostic test;
the attention devoted to analysing items;
the wider spread of operations across topics.

Basic Mathematics Test B

Reviewed by J. R. Hartley

Author: not stated .
Publisher: NFER-Nelson
Distributor: NFER-Nelson
Age range: 8:07–9:07
1973 (S); 1976 (M); 1971 (T)
No revisions apparent
1977 (M); 1980 (T) printings reviewed
Group test

Test content

Basic Mathematics Test B is administered as an oral test and consists of 40 items; several are multiple choice but the majority require a constructed response using numbers, number sentences, diagrams and shapes. The tasks are varied and the test requires the child to classify, order, count, equate in terms of number, size and shape, and deal with arithmetic operations and relations, fractions, areas and volumes, time, weight, and the interpretation of pictograms. Units follow the metric system and, where needed, are printed for the pupil in the seven-page test booklet.

Purpose

The test is the second of a series designed to encompass the 7–15 age-range. It aims to 'measure children's understanding of the fundamental relationships and processes which form the basis of all mathematical work'. The Manual states that the authors have attempted 'to eliminate, as far as possible, the effect of different teaching methods' so the scores would provide a fairer basis for comparison, but there are no explicit details on how this was achieved. The test administrator gives instructions, and also the questions, orally; as well as a total score, children's answers are used to give diagnostic information and a profile of individual strengths and weaknesses. Thus a secondary aim of the test is to provide the teacher with some guidance for 'directing the child's subsequent learning' (Manual, p. 2). The NFER invites comment on the usefulness of this feature.

Item preparation

The test is similar in type and content to the Maths Attainment Test B and the experience gained was used, presumably, in the construction of the test being reviewed. An experiment was constructed to detect any advantages for an oral administration (readers are referred to the Manual for Maths Attainment Test B for further details), and the results suggested that 'the oral presentation significantly increases the scores for all readers, but this effect is greatest for the poor reader' (Manual, p. 2).

Each item has also been analysed to indicate the skills and conceptual understanding it requires from the child (e.g. ordering, equating, knowledge of place value, or fractions). This is shown on a grid so that across the span of questions the teacher can obtain an elementary profile for the child. In many of the columns of the grid the number of data points is small (e.g. only one item requires knowledge of approximation, only one of place value, only two of fractions) and consequently is of limited value. On the other hand, ordering, equating and knowledge of addition are each needed in approximately ten items, and so these data should be more informative. No report on the value of such diagnoses is given or referenced in the Manual.

The test booklet is carefully composed and clearly presented (though a slight omission on the picture labelling of Question 4 was noticed) with figuring and print-size suitable for junior school children.

Administration

The instructions for administrators are comprehensive but to the point; they give advice and explanation as well as direction, and underline difficulties which the teacher/administrator might experience, and draw attention to details which might go unnoticed. The test is given orally, which requires particular skills, so the administrator is cautioned to know the test thoroughly and to follow the given instructions carefully. For example, there is advice on judging when children have finished each question, and on dealing with queries through the repetition of instructions or questions.

Each child needs only a pencil and rubber. The test is not speeded: 'each child, even the slowest should be given time to answer each question' though 'if after a reasonable length of time there are some children still writing, the teacher should allow a moment or two more, then go on to the next question' (Manual, p. 3). Consequently, the 40-item test takes longer to administer than the concentration span of pupils, and it is suggested a break (perhaps the mid-morning school break) is taken after Question 25. No data are given on completion time but the test is likely to occupy much of the period before and after this break.

Standardization

The standardization studies were administered in 1973 and used 6878 children (3563 boys, 3315 girls) taken from one urban area in the Midlands and one in West Yorkshire. The Manual notes that this sample cannot be judged as representative of a properly drawn national sample and cautionary comments are made about the interpretation of the raw score to standardized score and age norm table, for which Lawley's method was used (see Introduction). The standardization sample had an age range 6:07–9:07. In this table this age span was extrapolated to 8:04–8:06 and to 9:08–9:10 years, so again caution is urged when comparing data in these ranges. A small table and paragraph illustrates the meaning of standardized scores. Their distribution is arranged to have a mean of approximately 100 and a standard deviation of 15, and an example illustrating use of the table is given. There were no significant differences between the sexes either in terms of raw score distributions or score increase with age.

No data are available on the supplementary performance analysis classification grid referred to earlier. (NB. If the investigator places the main emphasis on the diagnostic information supplied by this grid, then the lack of a truly representative sample for the standardization table assumes much less significance).

Scoring

The scoring scheme and instructions for marking are clearly set out. A full marking key is provided which includes notes/examples on problems which could occur when evaluating junior school children's scripts, e.g. number reversal, numbers written backwards. A child is not penalized for underlining instead of ringing an answer, nor for writing his answer in words, nor for putting it in the wrong place: 'if his intention is clear and correct then his answer is given a mark'. Each question which is completely correct is given one mark and no half marks are allowed.

A feature of the test is the classificatory grid which is attached as a cut-out page (with the record summary table) to each test booklet. Details on how to mark off the relevant skills/ideas components under each question is detailed and illustrated. A full key to these classifications is also provided.

Reliability

The reported reliability, based on KR-20, is 0.91. This internal consistency statistic was calculated from a random sample of 362 scripts drawn from the standardization study. The age range of this reliability sample matched that of the larger group (8:07–9:07). The standard error of measurement at the mean age of 9:01 years is 4.51 (i.e. the conventional error band for a child's obtained standardized score is about 9 points). A suitable cautionary note on interpretation is included in the Manual and a reference on test reliability and errors of measurement is also given.

Validity

No comments or references to validity studies are given, though similarities of the test to the Mathematics Attainment Test B are noted.

Interpretation

Guidance on interpreting scores, and the skills/ideas classificatory grid, is adequate and makes clear links to the content and type of questions forming the test. The Manual invites comments on the effectiveness of the grid as a diagnostic tool and as a teaching aid, so presumably further discussion will appear in later editions.

General evaluation

The test was constructed and refined during the mid-1970s as part of a series of basic mathematics tests spanning the junior and secondary school age ranges. The Test B is an oral test and so is not sensitive to the reading skills of pupils; its booklet is well presented, and the Manual contains sound and detailed direction on administration and marking. The test itself includes a useful range of content and types of items.

A feature which will interest teachers is the diagnostic information given in addition to the raw and standardized scores. The idea is that through the analysis of performance on the items, profiles under the skills/ideas components can help the teacher in giving guidance to pupils and permit more informed comparisons to be made between groups of children. Such data should be useful but under many of the skills/ideas headings (and there are 21 in all) the data points are small in number and might not be sufficiently specialized to meet the needs of the teacher. Only further studies and comments from practitioners will permit a proper evaluation.

Basic Mathematics Test C

Reviewed by B. L. M. Chapman

Author: not stated
Publisher: NFER-Nelson

Distributor: NFER-Nelson
Age range: 9:08–10:09
1971–72 (S); 1970 (M); 1970 (T)
No revisions apparent
1980 (M, T) printings reviewed
Group test

Test content

The 50 items demand a wide range of mathematical skills, knowledge of terminology, spatial judgement and inference of meaning from information presented in sentences and diagrams. The test 'aims to measure children's understanding of the fundamental relationships and processes which form the basis of all mathematical work. The questions are designed to eliminate as far as possible the effects of different teaching methods . . .' (Manual, p. 1). Although this claim may be true within the context of current curricular norms in Britain it is evident that a number of items reflect a particular curricular stress which would not be stable with regard to time or location within English speaking cultures. Thus seven of the items make assumptions about the terminology and accepted practice of set theory, three about the interpretation of histograms and four about metric units of measure. Although in most cases the instructions with each question are clear, in one question they have been abbreviated to an extent which allows them to be construed as making an impossible demand on the testee.

Layout is extremely clear with the exception of the cover page where an excess of zeal in boxing instructions has led to an unfortunate and confused grouping. In this respect a notable omission is any reference to the age range of the test on the cover of either the test or Manual despite the fact that each of the tests in the series to which this belongs has its own Manual. The testee responds directly on the test form which makes for simplicity and clarity both for the testee and marker.

Purpose

The Manual makes no mention of the purpose of the test but claims that because of its freedom of effects due to teaching methods, already referred to, it forms a 'fairer basis of comparison than those yielded by our Mathematics Attainment Tests'. This implies that it is regarded as an attainment test and clearly it is geared to the recent requirements of British primary schools.

Item preparation

The origins of the items is unstated and no reference is made to any item selection or screening procedures.

Administration

The test is administered as an untimed group test requiring a Manual for the teacher and one test form for each pupil. It is anticipated that most children will have finished the test in 50 minutes but some children may take more than an hour. The Manual advises the issuing of two sharpened pencils and a ruler to each child. Instructions on the sequence of administration are clear and detailed while being sufficiently concise to be read while administering the test.

Standardization

We are told only that the test was standardized on all third-year children in primary schools in two selected areas (unnamed) during the school year 1971–72. The scores of 4371 boys and 4175 girls were collected and used to construct the score conversion tables using Lawley's method (see Introduction). The age range on which the standardization was carried out extended from 9:08–10:09. The standardized scores for children aged 9:07 and 10:10 were obtained by extrapolation.

Scoring

The scoring key is as clear as the instructions for administration but no form of mask is provided for responses which are scattered over the area of the seven pages. The tester first has to record right and wrong answers in the right hand margin of each page of the test form and then to derive totals for each page. Page totals of both right and wrong answers are to be recorded on the front cover of the test form, added up (along the row) and finally converted to a standardized score. This is an unduly laborious process which is likely to take an inexperienced tester at least ten minutes for each pupil and can scarcely be done in less than five minutes. There is also a 'diagnostic grid' which classifies items by topic within the curriculum, but no reference is made to this in the Manual.

Reliability

A KR-20 reliability coefficient of 0.95 is reported giving a standard error of 3.30 at the mean age of 10:02. This was derived from a subsample of 397 children although no details are reported of the age range of this sample. The section on standardization is commendably explicit about the implications of this standard error for scores awarded to children, pointing out that in only one case in twenty is a child's obtained standard score likely to exceed or fall short of his true score by more than seven points. Since this is a point frequently overlooked by test users it could be given even more force by referring to the numbers and extent of likely errors when testing a class of 40 pupils.

Validity

No evidence of content validity is offered and in the light of the claims made for the test it is left to the user to assess the suitability of the test for his or her own purposes. While the validity of the test as a measure of attainment in current primary school practice is very plausible this is not the nature of the claim made in the Manual. Instead it is asserted that the test 'aims to measure children's understanding of the fundamental relationships and processes which form the basis of all mathematical work' (Manual, p. 1). This is clearly a claim relating to cognitive processes arising from and pertaining to mathematics but removed from curriculum content and as such is very questionable indeed.

Interpretation

The provision of standardization tables printed to the nearest decimal integer on a scale whose mean is 100 and standard deviation 15 can only be expected to lead to such scores being ascribed to individual pupils. This tendency is even further exacerbated by the provision of separate norms for boys and girls even though they only differ by a single standardized unit. Notwithstanding the cautionary note about standard error already referred to, the presentation of material to which the tester must actually refer to gives an overriding impression of accurate measurement. The situation would be somewhat alleviated by standardization into centile groups or better still by a set of conversion graphs on which the band of standard error was clearly shown. Preferably the scale of such graphs should be chosen so as to defy the derivation of standards scores of unwarranted accuracy.

General evaluation

As a test of general mathematical attainment for primary school use this instrument can be expected to provide a reasonable measure for monitoring curriculum coverage among classes and groups of pupils. Used in this context, however, the cumbersome marking procedure is likely to make the test unattractive to the teacher or head whose main concern is with school-based assessment. Its use as a screening instrument for making decisions on placement or measuring ability would be highly questionable because of its dependence on curriculum.

Insofar as the diagnostic grid classifies items by curricular topics its use may help to identify omissions in teaching for a whole class of children or for individuals who may have been absent. The classification is, however, contentious in a number of respects and since it pays no regard to cognitive or operational criteria its use in diagnosing particular conceptual problems is dangerous. No reference is made to the presence or use of this grid in the Manual.

Basic Mathematics Test DE

Reviewed by Charles Desforges

Author: not stated
Publisher: NFER-Nelson
Distributor: NFER-Nelson
Age range: 10:05–11:07
1971–73 (S); 1970 (M); 1967 (T)
No revisions apparent
1979 (M); 1980 (T) printings reviewed
Group test

Test content

The test comprises 55 items the design of each of which reflects a 'deliberate attempt to get away from a topic oriented system of, e.g. fractions . . . and concentrates on ideas basic to the handling of mathematics . . .' (Manual, p. 5). For each item mathematical material is presented in the form of a table, equation or diagram. Each has an associated question or instruction which the testee must read and respond to. It is not necessary to show any working although this is permitted. The testee must select and write out appropriate information, draw a diagram or complete tables, grids or equations.

The items, testing the understanding of sets, relations, representation and the four basic mathematical operations, are distributed throughout the test. The precise procedures tested are sets (sorting, set membership, subsets, non-membership, complement, the union and intersection of two sets and of three sets), relations (ordering, equality, equations, equivalence, equivalent fractions, whole part relations, place value, number patterns, permutations, combinations and probability), representation (single and multiple comparisons from interpretations of tabulated data and histograms, interpretation of representation of an algebraic identity and of a Venn diagram) and operations (reflection, addition, subtraction, multiplication and division).

Purpose

The aim is to 'measure children's understanding of the fundamental relationships and processes which form the basis of all mathematical work' (Manual, p. 2). It is a norm-referenced test which additionally 'aims to give some diagnostic information about a child's individual strengths and weaknesses'. (Manual, p. 2). Moreover, the questions are 'designed to eliminate as far as possible the effects of different teaching methods, so that the scores from these tests will give a fair basis for comparison of children following different schemes'.

This claim is questionable since some of the contents of the test seem peculiar to the contents of particular junior school mathematics schemes and text books. Thus while the items may be fair across teaching methods it is likely that the test would be selectively invalid with respect to the contents of different curriculums.

Item preparation

The classification used to isolate the mathematical skills and behaviours involved in answering each question was developed by Bishop (1968). No further information on item preparation is available.

Administration

The test is designed to be administered by teachers. The testees are to 'work in conditions under which they can do their best' (Manual, p. 3). Each testee should have a response booklet, two pencils and a ruler. A reserve of sharpened pencils is advised. The test is untimed but 'most children will have finished in 50 minutes.' Some gainful activity to occupy the early finishers should be planned and provided for. Instructions to the administrator are clear and include a script of instructions to be read out to testees. The script is sufficient and concise.

Standardization

The test was standardized on a sample of 3740 boys and 3722 girls tested during the period 1971–1973. The age range of the sample extended from 10.5–11.07

(mean age 11.01). No further information is presented on the sample or its design.

Standardized scores, prepared by use of Lawley's method (see Introduction), are presented at monthly intervals of chronological age for the age range 10:00–11:11. Standardized scores for children aged 10:00–10:04 and 11:08–11:11 were obtained by extrapolation. No subgroup norms are provided. Instructions are given to locate each testee in a 'score band'. The addition and subtraction of six points of standardized score provide the true score within 95 per cent confidence limits.

Scoring

Scoring instructions are concise and unambiguous. No discretionary marks are permitted. A scoring grid, printed on the end sheet of the response booklet, is completed to provide a breakdown of the child's strengths and weaknesses in respect of the mathematical domains tested (sets, relations, representation, operations). A summary table, printed on the back page of the response booklet, shows the testee's age, raw score, standardized score and score band.

Reliability

A random sample of 304 scripts was used to calculate the internal consistency reliability (KR-20) coefficient of 0.96, with a standard error of measurement of 3.2.

Validity

No comment is made on the validity of the test.

Interpretation

No advice is given on how to use the test scores for the claimed diagnostic purposes. It may be said that its use for identifying gross gaps in content coverage or comprehension seems self evident. The notion of 'score band' is introduced to the test user and the significance of a particular standard score in respect of the 'true' score is commented on. No comments are offered about the utility of the scores other than that they permit comparisons with other testees to be made.

General evaluation

The test is very well produced. The arrangement of pages and page layout are exemplary. The Manual is clear and straightforward. The utility of the test is, however, open to question. Whilst the content of the items seems to be a very broad sample of the contemporary primary school mathematics curriculum it may be asked whether it samples any particular school's curriculums and to the degree that it did not it would be selectively unfair. The test was standardized over eight years ago and it is likely that teachers' (and hence pupils') experience with the sorts of contents tested will have been enhanced.

The pedagogic utility is also questionable. What follows from comparing one child with another or with a reference group is not at all clear in pedagogic terms. The use of the test in identifying weaknesses has no clear advantage over more direct methods such as monitoring the child's work book.

Almost all the test items require considerable reading ability. This suggests that they do not demand an understanding of mathematical concepts only. Weaker readers are likely to be seriously disadvantaged whatever their level of mathematical competence.

Reference

Bishop, A. J. (1968). Four unifying ideas behind primary mathematics. *Primary Mathematics* **6**, 21–30.

Basic Mathematics Test FG

Reviewed by John K. Backhouse

Author: not stated
Publisher: NFER-Nelson
Distributor: NFER-Nelson
Age range: 12:00–14:06
1969 (S); 1971 (M); 1969 (T)
Undated additions to Manual apparent
1980 (T) printing reviewed
Group test

Test content

The test contains 55 constructed-response items, which include use of arithmetic operators, number series, simple tabular and graphical representations, fractions, decimals and percentages. There is little geometry, apart from mensuration, and normal school algebra is not represented.

Purpose

The test 'aims to measure children's understanding of the fundamental relationships and processes which form the basis of all mathematical work. The questions are designed to eliminate as far as possible the effects of different teaching methods, so that the scores from these tests will give a fairer basis for comparison than those yielded by our Mathematics Attainment Tests. A child's total score on this test gives an indication of his level of mathematics *attainment*. Knowledge of this score makes it possible to compare a child with others in his class or year group who completed the same test at the same time' (Manual, p. 1). Comparisons with pupils in other schools, by means of standardized scores, may be made using the *provisional* conversion tables provided.

Item preparation

No details of how the items were prepared are given in the Manual. It would have been of particular interest to know exactly what 'fundamental relationships and processes' are included in the test, and what weight is given to each.

Administration

Clear instructions are given to the teacher as to what to tell the children. There is no time limit for the test and the teacher is told to see that each child settles down to a book or something quiet on finishing the test. Most pupils finish within 50 minutes (Ferri, 1971, p. 79).

Standardization

Three tables for finding standardized scores are provided from the following samples:

(1) 1579 children 'being educated in one of 83 different secondary schools: streamed or non-streamed, Grammar, Secondary Modern or Comprehensive' (Manual, p. 1).
(2) 3536 children in an urban industrial area; and,
(3) an unspecified number of children.

The age ranges for the three tables are respectively 12:09–13:08, 12:01–13:04 and 13:00–15:00. Warnings are given that the first sample is small and that the nature of the second should be taken into account in consulting that table. It appears that the second and third tables have been added since the preparation of the Manual in 1971. The standardization was carried out in 1969. A table is provided which converts standardized scores to percentiles.

Scoring

A scoring key is provided in the Manual and it is well laid out for easy marking. A check is provided for by recording the numbers of correct and incorrect answers on each page. For two items the child has to draw lines, which may lead to doubt as to whether the response is correct but otherwise the marker should normally be left in no doubt.

Reliability

No item analyses are given in the Manual. Values of KR-21 of 0.95 and 0.94 (standard errors of measurement 3.2 and 3.9) are given for the first and second samples respectively.

Validity

Validity is not discussed in the Manual.

Interpretation

An example is given of a score with 95 per cent confidence limits calculated from the standard error of measurement. No other guidance on the interpretation of scores is given.

General evaluation

The test booklet is clearly printed and from the point of view of the pupil it is an advantage to be able to write the answer in the booklet. Constructed responses may well be preferred by the teacher on educational grounds and, if the number of tests to be marked is small, the teacher may obtain further information from wrong answers which can lead to remedial work. The writer has reservations about the content of the test if, as the norms indicate, it may be used at any time in the third year of secondary education. It has been pointed out that no attempt was made to discuss the validity of the test, nor is the method by which the items were selected indicated. The test is intended to measure understanding of fundamental relationships and processes and the prospective user is advised to inspect the content of the test closely to see whether it covers the relationships and processes appropriate to the pupils to be tested.

The present Manual (dated August, 1971) is still in duplicated form, but there is a suggestion that it may be printed. It is strongly urged that the printed version should set right the deficiencies noted above.

Reference

Ferri, E. (1971). "Streaming: Two Years Later". Slough: NFER.

Basic Number Screening Test

Reviewed by P. S. Clift

Authors: W. E. C. Gillham and K. A. Hesse
Publisher: Hodder & Stoughton
Distributor: Hodder & Stoughton
Age range: 7:06–11:06; older retarded children
1976 (S)
No revisions apparent
1979 (M); 1980 (T: Form A); 1979 (T: Form B) printings reviewed
Group test

Test content

There are two equivalent forms of the test, A and B. Each consists of 30 items of a range of difficulty suitable for normal 7–12 year-olds and retarded older children. Fifteen of the items test number concepts, e.g. place, value, series, grouping, conservation; and 15 number skills: '. . . the processes involved in basic computation rather than the ability to do complicated "sums"' (Manual, p. 4). The items included were '. . . determined by our understanding of the development of children's number concepts, an appreciation of the changing nature of mathematics in schools, but above all by practical experience and detailed discussion with class teachers' (Manual, p. 3).

The tests make no demands on pupils' reading ability: testees' papers contain only numbers, diagrams, and pictures. All instructions are given orally from a script given in the Manual.

Purpose

The aims are 'to give a quick assessment of a child's understanding of the basic principles underlying the number system (number concepts) and the processes involved in computation (number skills) . . . to help identify the child whose number attainments are low for his age or who is failing to make continued progress' (Manual, p. 3).

Item preparation

The items included 'are a minute fraction of those used during item try-outs in schools, and feedback from children and teachers has been a major factor in determining whether an item was acceptable, or not' (Manual, p. 3).

Administration

The children each need a test form, and something to write with. Two separate versions of the test instructions (group, individual) are given in the Manual and should be read out by the tester, 'as naturally as possible' but 'should not be significantly altered or added to'. The test is untimed, leaving the responsibility for pacing with the administrator.

Standardization

The test was standardized in 1976, in February and March, on a total of 3042 children in the age range 7:06–11:06, 'in the city area of Nottingham' (Manual, p. 4). No breakdown of this sample by age is given, nor is the proportionate social composition of the schools involved indicated. Given also that Nottingham city may have particular policies regarding primary school mathematics, the extent to which test standardization based on this sample is applicable to the population of 7–12 year-olds in England and Wales as a whole is thus uncertain, although the authors claim that a similar procedure used with their Leicester and Nottingham Number Tests has yielded norms 'which have been found satisfactory' (Manual, p. 4). A table for converting raw scores to Number Ages (i.e. age equivalents) is given in the Manual. Percentile norms are not available.

Reliability

The reliability of the test was estimated by correlating children's scores on the two separate forms (A, B) administered one week apart. The product-moment correlation was 0.93. This cannot properly be evaluated without knowing how many children were involved, and moreover this value will be inflated by the wide age-range of the children used (see Introduction).

Validity

The authors propose a content validity: 'the test directly samples the attainment it is measuring' (Manual, p. 4). This is unarguable, but 30 items are very few on which to judge the mathematical skills and concepts of pupils aged between 7 and 12 years. Evidence is also given of concurrent validity in the form of a correlation of 0.82 between teachers' prior ratings of their pupils' attainments and their subsequent scores on the test. These teachers were all in one school, however, and as with the reliability, the value will be inflated by the wide age-range used. The evidence would be more convincing had *all* the teachers involved in test standardization taken part in this form of validation.

Interpretation

No direct advice is given in the Manual on the interpretation of either the raw scores or the 'Number Ages' to which they may be converted.

General evaluation

This calls itself a 'screening' test. As a screen it is pretty coarse, thus of value only if what you want is a quick, rough and ready indication of how individuals or groups (class, year group) stand *vis-à-vis* their peers. It is far too coarse to offer *diagnostic* information, nor do its authors claim that intention. Further, because the standardization was carried out within a limited and possibly atypical area (Nottingham City), its use to measure *standards* (i.e. in comparison with the 'national population') is dubious. Within any given group of suitable age, however, comparisons made on the basis of what it measures are valid, thus used periodically it can offer useful indications of *progress*, both of individuals and of groups. That it makes no demands on literacy is a very useful characteristic at the lower end of its range of applicability and with older, retarded children.

Essential Mathematics

Reviewed by Charles Desforges

Author: L. M. Bental
Publisher: NFER-Nelson
Distributor: NFER-Nelson
Age range: Top infants, juniors and backward 11–14 year-olds
1973 (experimental version)
1973, 1974 revisions
1976 (M, T) versions reviewed
Individual test

Test content

The test contains 22 small exercises each forming the context for a brief, structured interview in which the testee's comprehension of a particular mathematical concept or skill is explored. Mathematical concepts covered include ordering, counting, money (including change up to £1), simple sums and equations (including four rules with quantities up to 10 and addition and subtraction of tens and units), more/less, bigger/smaller, comparison of fractions, names of shapes, simple mental arithmetic including use of multiplication, length, telling time and days of the week.

All the items 'could reasonably be assumed to be part of the knowledge of the vast majority of eleven year-old children admitted to an ordinary (i.e. not a special) secondary school . . . The number of items per topic is related to the amount of exposure the pupil is likely to have had to that topic before the age of eleven' (Manual, p. 1). The problems are presented orally by the tester and frequently involve the use of concrete objects or diagrams. The testee is not required to read anything. He is required to say his answer or sort or point or, occasionally to record a response. As well as information and instruction about the test *per se*, extensive teaching notes advising on remedial activities are included in the Manual.

Purpose

'Failure in mathematics is often due to unrecognised gaps in knowledge or understanding . . . The items were selected because they cover knowledge that must be acquired by the child to make progress in learning mathematics. They are . . . a precondition for following a secondary mathematics course . . . This test, and the accompanying notes, aims to identify these deficiencies, to guide the teacher in a technique of close observation of the pupil and to suggest some remedial teaching methods' (Manual, p. 1).

Administration

Since the purpose of the test is to inform remedial teachers it is best administered by the teacher. A pencil, ruler, some bricks or blocks, marbles or pebbles and some buttons are required. The test should be conducted in a quiet, private place. The importance of a calm, supportive atmosphere is stressed. The test is not timed but it appears that the average 12 year-old takes 30 minutes. It is advised that younger or disturbed children should receive the test in two or three parts. The tester follows the detailed schedule but is advised to modify or extend it as appropriate. The tester is required to make detailed records of the child's answers and behaviours on test.

Standardization

'Because the information provided by the test is specific to the individual child, norms would be inappropriate' (Manual, p. 2). Since the purpose is to identify remediation needs and design teaching, the omission of norms seems entirely appropriate.

Scoring

The test does not provide a score but a record of behaviours and verbal responses. The instructions for marking the record are necessarily general rather than specific. The importance of detail and flexibility are stressed.

Reliability

'It must be pointed out that no detailed statistical analysis of children's answers has been undertaken. Any generalizations or opinions reflect the experience and ideas of the author' (Manual, p. 4). Since the teacher is encouraged to modify the test and since allowance is made for a variety of answers which are interpreted rather than scored, it is argued that statistical analyses are inappropriate.

Validity

'It was considered necessary to establish that the items did indeed constitute "Essential Mathematics" for a pupil about to begin a secondary maths course, and that most average children in this age range were able to complete the test successfully . . . A study has been made of the performance on the test of children chosen by their own school as being of average mathematical attainment'. The size of this sample is not specified but it is recognised that the definition of 'average' would vary from school to school and that the sample was 'not chosen to be representative of any particular group' (Manual, p. 2).

Of the 22 items, the study showed that six were answered correctly by almost 100 per cent of testees, six were answered correctly by 75 per cent or more, two by 70 per cent or more and a further three by 50 per cent or more. One item did not distinguish between average and slow learners but was retained because it was considered to be a 'particularly important topic'. The topic is a comparison of fractions and it seems no effort was made to alter the item. This seems to betray a certain amount of confusion as to whether the nature of 'essential mathematics' was to be empirically or rationally established. Four items are not mentioned in respect of this validity study.

No report is available on whether the decisions made on the basis of the test are valid; that is, whether the test actually picks out particular children with particular difficulties.

Interpretation

There are extensive and detailed notes on interpretation. It is acknowledged that 'It is difficult to provide hard and fast rules for interpreting a test of this kind in which the teacher may modify the test . . .'; and 'It must be pointed out that . . . any generalizations or opinions reflect the experience and ideas of the author' (Manual, p. 4).

Following these cautions general advice is given on the approach to children with learning problems. This is interwoven with detailed, specific comments on the interpretations of responses to particular items. Much of the interpretative comment is unexceptional and not very helpful. For example, with reference to an item demanding the identification of odd numbers, 'Failure here is usually due to a lack of learning experience or to difficulty in understanding the word "odd"' (Manual, p. 5). Some comments are more contentious, as in 'If a child cannot name three out of four shapes, I would suspect perceptual impairment' (Manual, p. 7).

General evaluation

The interpretation section is followed by several pages of ideas and tips on how to help children with specific problems. These ideas seem part of the common stock of professional knowledge. For example, 'Many (children) cannot work out change from 50p or £1. I use real or plastic money and contrive shopping situations' (Manual, p. 9).

At best the test is unexceptional. Apart from encouraging, in a general sense, the detailed observation of children as a prelude to interpreting and ameliorating their difficulties it seems to have little to offer.

Graded Arithmetic-Mathematics Test

Reviewed by John K. Backhouse

Authors: P. E. Vernon and K. M. Miller
Publisher: Hodder & Stoughton
Distributors: Hodder & Stoughton; The Test Agency

Age ranges: 5:03–11:08 (Junior); 11:06–18+ (Senior)
1949; 1971 (decimalization, interim edition)
1976 (metric edition) (other revisions indicated)
1979 (M); 1980 (T: Junior); 1979 (T: Senior) printings reviewed
Group test

Test content

The junior test contains 70 items, almost all of which are completion type. Items include examples of the four rules, simple money sums, fractions, linear algebra with one unknown, place value, volume and simple geometric relations. There are later starting points for 8+ and 9+, 10+, and 11+ classes (or pupils in individual testing). The senior test contains 65 completion type items, the first 33 of which also appear in the junior test. The additional items include examples of algebraic manipulation, trigonometric functions, bases and logarithms.

Purpose

The authors do not define the purpose of the test directly but state that it has been used especially in the following contexts: '1. Assessing the attainment of individual retarded or problem primary school children by educational psychologists. 2. Grading the mathematical competence of school leavers on entry to technical courses' (Manual, p. 3).

Item preparation

The method of content sampling was to model a large number of items on different textbooks. These items were then tried out but 'the great majority of them had to be dropped, not merely because of the wide discrepancies in age at which they could be answered in different schools, but also because they often showed such irregular progress, or even no progress at all, in pass rates with increasing age. . . . If the present edition, then, appears old-fashioned to mathematics teachers, and as representing little advance on the 1949 edition, this is the reason' (Manual, p. 3).

'In the preliminary trials, much larger numbers of items were given to classes in Canadian and English schools, totalling some 3000 pupils. Those items which covered the desired range of ability most evenly, and showed consistent rises with age level in both countries, were selected in order to make up the two final tests' (Manual, p. 12).

Administration

Pupils write their answers on the test blank. Most will have no difficulty in filling in the details required on the front. The administrator is told to read aloud the printed instructions on the front of the test, slowly, drawing attention to the three pages of questions and, if using the junior form, pointing out to the class where they should start. There are no practice questions. Thirty minutes are allowed and it is apparent that speed of working may be expected to affect a pupil's score. The test may also be administered orally. The heading on p. 6 of the Manual would have been more appropriately given as 'Oral Administration' rather than 'Oral Version'. There are also instructions for individual testing and advice is given to precede the test with one of reading.

Standardization

The English norms are based on 2280 infant and junior pupils, and 2029 secondary pupils all from Northamptonshire, together with 916 Scottish infant and junior pupils. It is not stated further how these pupils were spread across the age ranges for which norms are available. Norms are given for intervals of 3 months for 5:03–11:08 (junior test) and 11:06–16:02 (senior test) and also for two further age ranges, 16:03–16:11 and 17:00–18+. The standardized scores, termed 'deviation quotients', implicitly have a mean of 100 and standard deviation of 15. They are given in the tables at 5-point intervals from 70 to 130 (Canadian norms are also provided).

Scoring

There are clear instructions for scoring. Since virtually all the items are of the completion type, the scoring key has three columns headed 'Correct response', 'Acceptable alternatives', and 'Not acceptable'. In some cases mathematically incorrect alternatives are 'Acceptable', e.g. a volume expressed in cm or cm^2, or an erroneous decimal point. In others mathematically correct but incompletely processed alternatives are 'Not acceptable', e.g. 28/14, 25/100, $2+2+2+1$. Scoring by two markers is recommended since many answers may be doubtfully right or wrong.

Reliability

'The consistency or reliability of scores was calculated by taking several classes at various ages from 8 to 16, and finding the correlations of scores on odd-numbered items with even-numbered. After correction, the coefficients were all 0.90 or over, and the average was 0.92' (Manual, p. 16).

Validity

Validity is not discussed in the Manual.

Interpretation

It is suggested that the standardized scores are expressed to the nearest multiple of five, and suitable tables are provided. The standard error of measurement (termed the standard error of a deviation quotient) is given as 4.2 on both tests. Ninety-five (incorrectly referred to as *five*) per cent confidence limits are mentioned and given 'the reason why it was suggested that quotients should be expressed to the nearest five points' (Manual, p. 16). However, on these grounds the two standardized scores 5 points either side of that obtained from the tables come within the confidence limits. It would have been better to make this explicit to the user.

General evaluation

The title of the test does not make evaluation easy, nor does the lack of a clear description of its purpose. The reviewer's impression is that the questions are very hackneyed, no doubt representing the textbook questions on which the authors modelled the items. The prospective user will need to peruse the content of the tests carefully in the absence of any attempt to establish content validity. There are, for instance, very few questions on geometry. A class teacher could learn something from errors made by pupils but the user who wants large numbers of scripts marked would be well advised to consider alternative multiple-choice tests.

Group Mathematics Test

Reviewed by Jim Ridgway

Author: D. Young
Publisher: Hodder & Stoughton
Distributor: Hodder & Stoughton
Age range: 6:06–7:11; and various backward pupils up to 12:10
1969 (S); 1970 (M); 1970 (T)
1977–78 (S)
1989 (M), 2nd edition; 1980 (T) printing reviewed
Group test

Test content

Both forms of the test consist of two practice items followed by 58 test items. Attempts have been made to make the two forms exactly parallel: the operations used, and the topic are the same in questions with the same number on each form. Fifteen of the items are straightforward addition problems, presented in ascending order of difficulty; 15 of the items are straightforward subtraction problems, again presented in ascending order of difficulty. The remaining items are spread thinly across a range of mathematical operations (including: multiplying, counting, ordering, using fractions, series, addition and subtraction, dividing, telling the time, judging size, matching, sharing and place value). These operations are applied to a variety of domains (including: areas and shapes, and to everyday objects like animals and food).

More than half of the items assess addition and subtraction skills directly. When multiplication and division items are added to these, we find that more than two thirds of the test is devoted to the direct application of these rules. The choice of other operators and domains is patchy in the extreme; no rationale is provided for the choice of operators or domains of the 8 items which do not assess number skills.

The computation items are all presented in horizontal form. While this form is appropriate for calculations which involve single digits, it seems inappropriate for the more difficult items like '114 + 178 =   '. Here the memory load imposed on pupils who can add three digit numbers if presented vertically may result in them getting these items wrong. Children are required to write down either the answer itself, or a letter corresponding to one of the response alternatives. Half of the test is administered orally, in order to overcome the problems that poorer readers would experience when presented with written material. Nevertheless, the wording of some of the questions requires some above-minimum language skill to unravel the mathematical question which is being set.

This edition of the test is different from the first edition in that it provides new test norms, slightly revised instructions, and the results of investigations conducted using the first edition. The first two items are now practice items; otherwise the test remains unchanged. The revised Manual provides separate norms for infants, first-year juniors and older pupils. 'The original tables . . . produced distortions in . . . the quotients of the younger children within a year-group . . .' (Manual, p. 2).

Purpose

The test is one of five tests developed by the author to assess the mathematical ability of children in primary schools. It focuses on upper infants and lower juniors, but can also be used to assess older, less able, children. The series of tests 'afford a means of following the progress of children without risking the distortions that can arise from using tests standardized without a common basis' (Manual, p. 3). The test can be used for: the identification of children in need of special education; following the progress of an individual child over time; assessing the overall mathematical ability of a class; providing feedback to the teacher on class performance and the teacher's own assessment skills.

'Though diagnostic clues can be only incidental in a test primarily designed for general assessment, in a few cases something may be gained' by comparing 'a child's subtest scores (oral with computation or addition with subtraction)', such comparisons 'are best made in the light of the school or class averages' (incomplete sentence, Manual, p. 20). Its use as a diagnostic test is severely limited.

Item preparation

Little or no information is provided about how the items were prepared. We learn nothing about the author's intentions, nor about his rules for constructing items from the Manual. One quarter of the test items are addition problems in the form of conventional equations (e.g. '$1 + 1 = $'). One quarter of the test items are subtraction problems in the same form. The remaining half of the test items are administered orally, and are largely devoted to addition, subtraction, multiplication and division. Indirect justification for such a narrowly based test can be found '. . . the same large general factor appears in diverse sets of items and indeed in sets of items which could easily be supposed to be testing quite different aspects of mathematics' (Manual, p. 22). Data presented to support this assertion omit important information.

Administration

The test is administered in two halves, preferably before and after break. Each half contains an oral section and a computational section. In the oral section, the administrator reads each question aloud and allows 7 seconds for the children to write their answers. The computational section is timed for 8 minutes. The total testing time should be less than 50 minutes.

Less able children can take the test as four subtests; more able children can take the whole test in one sitting. By giving adjacent rows of pupils different forms of the test, the risk of copying can be minimized. The test can be given by one teacher to a full class. Children need a pencil each. The administrator needs a watch with a second hand.

The administrator's script provided in the Manual is satisfactory. The task of ensuring that children understand the items is emphasized. The language used in some of the orally administered questions could be simplified. This is intentional, however, to 'recognise and reinforce, in the test situation, the place of language in mathematics' (Manual, p. 20).

Standardization

Standardizations have been conducted by the author. 'The second standardization is based on a total of 3175 scores from children aged 6:07 to 13:01. The numbers were: infants, 1064; first-year juniors, 613; second-year juniors, 650; older backward children, 848. The standardizations for the three youngest groups depend on samples drawn from schools of known characteristics and the procedure can therefore be regarded as one of indirect calibration' (Manual, p. 21).

The author conducted a study in which a group of children took the test under review (the GMT) and tests from his 'Y' series, at different ages:

'The comparability of the standards of the GMT and the "Y" series was checked by analysing the records at three "first" schools, i.e. schools admitting infants and lower juniors (these schools were not in the standardization samples). The group of 101 children who had taken all three of the tests GMT, Y1 and Y2 had successive median scores of 32.11, 26.88 and 24.86. At ages 7:02, 8:02 and 9:02 these scores correspond to quotients of 101, 100 and 100. The differences are not statistically significant. The five tests therefore afford a means of following the progress of children without risking the distortions that can arise from using tests standardized without a common basis' (Manual, p. 3).

Tables of mathematics quotients, which are standardized scores with a mean of 100 and a standard deviation of 15, are provided. The quotients are provided for different test scores, in one-month age bands. Separate tables are provided for infants (6:05–7:10), juniors (7:00–8:10) and older pupils (8:00–12:10). A table relating test scores to Mathematics Ages is provided as 'an alternative scale for very backward children whose quotients may be difficult to interpret in practical terms' (Manual, p. 19).

No precise information is provided about the date of standardization ('data collected in 1977 and 1978'), nor any about how the samples of children used in the standardization were chosen. Thus, test users who hope for an exact comparison with a notional 'national standard' will be disappointed. However, the main uses of the test, namely the identification of children who are performing badly, tracking performance of individuals over time, and rank ordering pupils, are relatively unaffected by criticisms of the representativeness of the standardization sample.

The two test forms appear to be of equal difficulty. 'The item analyses enabled the items to be distributed between the two forms so that inequalities in facility level were balanced. A comparison at 10-point intervals between matched samples (587 scripts) showed neither form to be consistently easier' (Manual, p. 21). 'The differences between the median scores of the sexes are slight and equal weight was given to both sexes in producing common norms (Manual, p. 21).

One would like to be assured that the author has looked both for significant differences in mean score between the sexes, and for significant differences between the two regression coefficients of age on score for the two sexes, rather than merely comparing median scores. However, for most of the uses to which the test is put, small differences will probably be unimportant.

Scoring

The scoring scheme is straightforward, and is adequately described in the Manual. The scorer's discretion is clearly specified; for example, reversal of figures is allowed, but transposition of digits is not. Right and wrong answers can be marked as such on the answer sheet, and columns totalled easily. Summaries of the four 'subtests' are written on the front of the answer sheet and added to give the child's total score. This is then converted to a standard score by using the child's age and test score to index the appropriate Table in the Manual. The answer sheet could be improved by providing a space for the child's age to be written, and space for the standard score, alongside the raw score, at the top of the sheet.

Reliability

Little evidence is provided directly about the reliability of the test; however, its reliability can be inferred indirectly. It would be most surprising if a test with such a small variety of items had any reliability coefficient below 0.8. Some idea about internal consistency can be gained from a study of 83 children (ages, and the nature of the sample unspecified). The correlation between the oral and computation section was $r = 0.84$. Using the Spearman-Brown correction for test length to assess the reliability of the whole test gives a value of $r = 0.91$. The section on validity below provides data which suggest strongly that the reliability of the test is high.

The standard errors of measurement for samples of children who were tested on both forms of the test, with a one-week interval between tests are presented. The overall estimate of the standard error of measurement is 2.7 points (raw score). Using the raw score standard deviation from another study reported in the Manual, the test-retest correlation between parallel forms on different occasions can be estimated as 0.94.

Validity

'Two investigations show satisfactory concurrent and predictive validity for the GMT. The correlation between the GMT and the *Leicester Number Test* . . . for 145 children was 0.85 (average age 6:11, GMT SD 10.8, LNT SD 11.3). The GMT scores of 153 children at 7:2 were correlated with their "*Y*" *Mathematics Series* Y1 scores at 8:2 and their Y2 scores at 9:2. The correlations were: GMT/Y1, 0.87; GMT/Y2, 0.86' (Manual, pp. 21–22). It is difficult to understand the author's claim that these data show satisfactory predictive validity for the GMT, since no external criterion of mathematical ability is involved. No data are provided on the range of the children's ages. A wide age-range could inflate the estimate of the correlation coefficients if raw scores were employed.

'. . . the following correlations, calculated from the scores of 83 children, show a considerable overlap between the oral and computational sections despite their apparent individuality. Moreover, there is a similar overlap between the whole test and an oral verbal intelligence test having no mathematical content': (a) oral section with computation section, 0.84; (b) oral section with Non-Readers Intelligence Test (NRIT), 0.79; (c) computation section with NRIT, 0.80; (d) Total with NRIT, 0.83 (Manual, p. 22).

Again, there are difficulties in interpreting these data, because the distributions of the children's ages and of the scores on all the tests are not given. A wide age-range can lead to an over-estimation of correlation coefficients.

Further data are presented in which the GMT has been correlated with: NFER Picture Test A ($r = 0.68$; $n = 145$); Moray House Picture Test 2 ($r = 0.80$; $n = 161$); Non-Readers Intelligence Test ($r = 0.73$; $n = 145$; $r = 0.78$; $n = 161$); Southgate Group Reading Test 1 (forms A and B) ($r = 0.73$; $n = 145$); Young's own Group Reading Test (forms A and B) ($r = 0.73$; $n = 161$). These data appear to show that the GMT relates quite strongly to tests of general (ill-defined?) ability and reading; but we cannot be sure just how strong the relationship is for the reasons given above.

Interpretation

The interpretation of scores is quite direct. Normative comparisons are made with data provided in the Manual, or between pupils. Sensibly, given the purposes of the test, and the size of the standardization sample, standardized scores outside the range 70–130 are simply recorded as < 70 or > 130. Other qualifiers on the use of the tables of norms are also provided. Two examples will suffice to illustrate the Manual's style.

'Teachers of children above first-year junior level should note that for these older children the content of the test is too limited for unqualified acceptance of the highest quotients. The Y2 in the *"Y" Mathematics Series* is probably more appropriate when the quotients exceed 85' (Manual, p. 19).

'Table 4 has a limited use mainly as an alternative scale for very backward children whose quotients may be difficult to interpret in practical terms. Above a mathematics age of 8.5 years the content of the test is too limited to provide a satisfactory scale. Below 6.5 the age scale is arbitrary . . .' (Manual, p. 19).

General evaluation

The test purports to measure the mathematical ability of infants and first-year juniors and is one of a series of tests designed to assess children aged 6:06–11:10. It can also be used for older, less able children. The range of items chosen is very narrow, focusing almost exclusively on the operations of addition, subtraction, multiplication and division. The format of some of the items presents difficulties to the children which are irrelevant to the mathematical operations to be performed.

In my view, there is a considerable danger in presenting teachers with the view that mathematical attainment in the first few years at primary school is best assessed by examining performance on these four operations alone. A number of tasks face the teacher of mathematics. Helping pupils to master skills is an obvious task. Less obvious is the job of alerting pupils to the beauty of mathematics; to the joys of discovery; to the excitement of finding regularities in the world around them. One of the problems in mathematical education is that primary school teachers of mathematics often have had little mathematical training themselves, and indeed may not have experienced the beauty, joy and excitement of mathematics as pupils. Teaching these aspects of mathematics requires both considerable skill and a good deal of confidence. It certainly involves a good deal more than the practice of arithmetic. Presenting teachers with a notional 'national standard' of mathematical ability, which relates only to basic number skills, is a remarkably negative thing to do, since it implicitly denies the relevance of other useful mathematical activities.

The implication in the Manual that the skills of using the basic mathematical operators relate strongly to verbal ability and general intelligence also has strong, negative, pedagogical implications. Since attainment relates so strongly to general intelligence, and intelligence is relatively stable over time (?) what impact can the teacher have upon the education process? What remedial action should the teacher take for a class or an individual who 'under performs'? Sit back and watch nature take its course, or try harder at drill and sums? Neither of these alternatives is likely to bring children closer to the joys of mathematics.

The Manual is deficient in a number of respects. Most important, inadequate data are presented to permit the user to assess reliability and validity. No data are provided about the nature of the standardization sample. Less important, the style is turgid, and the contents need to be re-arranged to make them more readily accessible to the user.

The test has some use for discovering children who are performing below par on the basic mathematical operators. The fact that it is one of a series of tests allows the progress of an individual child to be followed over time. However, the philosophy implicit in the choice of items concerning the nature of mathematics in primary schools is sufficiently pernicious to outweigh the test's usefulness for other purposes.

The Leicester Number Test

Reviewed by K. Lovell

Authors: W. E. C. Gillham and K. A. Hesse
Publisher: Hodder & Stoughton
Distributor: Hodder & Stoughton
Age range: 7:01–9:00
1968 (S) (1st-year juniors); 1970 (M, T)
1972 (S) (2nd-year juniors)
1973 (M) (2nd edition)
1978 (M, T) printings reviewed
Group test

Test content

The 54 items of the test cover: counting; number equivalence (conservation); number relativeness (larger, smaller, etc.); number sequence (seriation); grouping; simple fractions; addition, subtraction, multiplication, division.

Purpose

'The test is designed to assess a child's understanding of basic concepts of the number system, as well as his grasp of the "four rules" of conventional calculation' (Manual, p. 1). It was constructed particularly to discriminate among the less able 25 per cent of the age groups and, for this reason, a relatively large number of easy items were included.

Item preparation

The Manual indicates (p. 2) that there were two preliminary draft forms of the test. But apart from the general statement given under Purpose, below, no details are given as to how the initial items were determined, the criteria and procedures used to select from these, or details of the populations used. But it is claimed that the test will 'differentiate among children whom most arithmetic tests leave as an undifferentiated non-scoring or minimally-scoring mass'. It is also stated that care was taken to achieve a 'balanced heterogeneity amongst the items so that a reasonably comprehensive estimate of a child's numerate ability is obtained'.

Administration

The authors state that the test requires a teacher experienced in test administration. Although this is an untimed test, the Manual suggests that 42–56 minutes may be required for the overall administration depending upon the size and composition of the group being tested. Clear directions are given as to the classroom arrangements to be made and the actual words to be used. Each question is read out by the teacher as the pupil follows in the test booklet. Pupils are instructed to put down their pens when they have finished each question so that the teacher can judge when to read the next one.

Standardization

This took place in two stages. The scores of pupils aged 7:01–8:01 years were standardized on 557 non-immigrant children in the City of Leicester in October, 1968. There were 284 boys and 273 girls. While the sample size is not large the authors claim that it was a stratified sample of approximately one seventh of the total age group. Since it is maintained that the sample is representative of the City of Leicester, the authors claim that the standardized scores will be representative of other large urban areas but not necessarily of the country as a whole. But it must be noted that there were very few pupils aged 7:01 and 8:01 years in the sample. The frequency histogram (Manual, p. 4) shows the raw score distribution to be negatively skewed as would be expected since it was the intention to discriminate among the bottom 25 per cent of the distribution. Raw scores are converted to standardized scores [although referred to as 'Quotients' (mean 100, standard deviation 15)] and to percentile levels in the table provided (Manual, p. 15).

The scores of pupils aged 8:00–9:00 years were obtained from a representative sample of second-year junior school children in the City of Nottingham in September 1972 (469 non-immigrant pupils: 236 girls, 233 boys). Once again the raw score distribution is negatively skewed as intended, and raw scores are converted to standardized scores and percentile levels in the score conversion table. Few details are, in fact, given of the standardization procedures for this age group in the Manual, and readers are advised by the authors that the full details of these procedures are contained in the Manual of the Nottingham Number Test.

Scoring

The instructions for marking are clear. The marks for each question or each part of a question are indicated, together with acceptable answers for each question and each part of a question. Instructions are also given for marking reversals and inversion of figures.

Reliability

In respect of the age group 7:01–8:01 years, 512 of the 557 non-immigrant pupils retook the test one week after the first administration. The test-retest correlation coefficient was 0.92 yielding a standard error of measurement of 4.2. As for the age group 8:00–9:00 years, 422 of the 469 non-immigrant pupils retook the test one week after the first administration. The test-retest correlation coefficient was 0.91 giving a standard error of measurement of 5.0.

Validity

The authors take the view that they are directly testing what they sought to measure and so 'validity is not a serious problem'. Further, 'good validity can be assumed providing the coefficient of reliability is high' (Manual, pp. 6 and 17). In other words, content validity is assumed.

But some other information is provided. For the younger age group, scores on the first administration of the test for 499 pupils gave a product-moment correlation coefficient of 0.64 with scores on the NFER Mechanical Arithmetic Test 2A, the tests being taken within one week of one another. Scores for 513 pupils of the same age group correlated 0.585 with scores on the NFER Picture Test 1 with a one week interval between tests. It is difficult to see how these modestly-sized correlation coefficients, which might be said to reflect concurrent validity, add much to the users' knowledge. All one can say is that the Leicester Number Test has some 41 per cent of common variance with the NFER Mechanical Arithmetic Test 2A, and some 34 per cent of common variance with NFER Picture Test 1.

Three months before the test was given, teachers of the older age group were asked to rate pupils on a 7-point scale according to their judgement of the children's understanding in number and proficiency in written arithmetic. The teachers had known the pupils a whole school year and pupils were rated in two classes of 28 and 29 children respectively. The Spearman rank order correlation coefficients between ratings and test scores were 0.71 and 0.79 respectively. These figures may be taken as estimates of concurrent validity.

Interpretation

The authors intended this test to scale pupils. Interpretation is straightforward in that for each raw score a standardized score and a percentile level is given, for each age group separately. Thus, used as the authors intended, interpretation is easily made. But the following point should be noted. A number of test items involve counting in one form or other. Counting is a skill universally and spontaneously acquired by normal children, and seems necessary for understanding the natural number system. Early and self-invented arithmetic involves counting procedures applied to real objects. Various procedures for accomplishing the same purpose are then taught in school but children often fail to grasp the rationale for these written methods, with the result that pupils make many errors. Users thus might wish to observe if there is a basic weakness in counting skills (as there is in many very backward children at these ages) or whether such skills are present but errors reside more in the written methods. In other words, for detailed interpretation, information is needed on how the raw score is made up.

General evaluation

This test is easy to administer, mark and interpret, if used as the authors intended. No reading is required. The standardization for the younger age group was carried out on a small number of pupils although the authors defend this on the grounds that stratified samples were used. In respect of the older age group, users must consult another Manual for details of the standardization. The reliability for each of the two age groups is acceptable using the test-retest procedure. Little can be said about validity; the authors consider that this is not a serious issue for the reason stated.

For the reviewer there are two useful points about the test. It discriminates better than many other tests between the less good performers. Second, it has questions involving counting in different guises. However, responses to the latter questions need to be supplemented by individual interviews using the kinds of tasks employed by Gelman and Gallistel (1978).

Reference

Gelman, R. and Gallistel, C. R. (1978). "The Child's Understanding of Number". Cambridge, Mass.: Harvard University Press.

Mathematics Attainment Test A

Reviewed by Jim Ridgway

Author: not stated
Publisher: NFER-Nelson
Distributor: NFER-Nelson
Age range: 7:00–8:06
1969–71 (S); 1978 (M); 1970 (T)
No revisions apparent
1979 (M); 1980 (T) printings reviewed
Group test

Test content

Forty-two items cover the use of a number of mathematical operations across a wide range of topic areas. Operations covered include equating, adding, subtracting, multiplying, dividing, counting, ordering, classifying and equating. These operations are applied to the topics (quantities, ideas or domains) of fractional parts, area, money, bar charts, size, volume, weight, place value, shape length and telling the time. The spread of operations across topics could be wider. For example, three questions on fractional parts all use shaded areas; all three questions on division take the same form.

Instructions for each item are administered orally. In the pupils' booklet, items consist of clear line drawings separated by solid lines. Pupils respond by writing in answers, circling and crossing out response alternatives, shading areas and drawing lines.

Purpose

'This test was constructed in 1968 to provide a measure of mathematics attainment of first-year junior school children. The aim is to test the child's grasp of a wide range of mathematical ideas . . .' (Manual, p. 2). Standardized scores are available from a large sample of children. The test can be used to:

(1) roughly relate the mathematical attainment of the individual and the class to peers elsewhere in the country;
(2) rank order children within a class; and,
(3) identify children with special educational needs.

Item preparation

No data are presented about how the items were developed, nor is there any information about any pilot studies which may have been conducted.

Administration

The test is administered orally to overcome the problems which poor readers face when presented with written mathematics problems. The test requires the pupils to understand spoken English and to possess elementary writing skills. 'The proper administration of an oral test requires particular skill and it is recommended that this test should be given by an experienced teacher' (Manual, p. 3). Each child needs a response booklet and a pencil. The test takes from about 30–60 minutes to administer, depending on the speed of the children. It is recommended that the test should not be given to a group of more than 45 children. Questions are read aloud by the test administrator, one item at a time. The administrator has to judge when all the children have finished each question, before proceeding to the next.

The script for administering the test is perfectly clear. One improvement might be made. Pupils are asked to write their date of birth on the front of the response booklet. This seems a difficult thing for a child aged 7:00 to do; it would probably be better if these data were taken from the class register by the teacher.

Standardization

'The test was standardized on all the first-year children in primary schools in five selected areas during the school years 1969–70 and 1970–71. The scores of 6764 children were collected (3515 boys and 3249 girls)' (Manual, p. 2). No information is provided about the nature of these 'selected areas', and so the normative data can be used only as a rough guide to the relative performance of any individual or group under consideration. For some purposes, of course, like rank ordering pupils and the identification of pupils with special mathematical needs, normative data which are representative of the population as a whole, are of relatively little importance.

The mean age of the children in the sample was 7:10. Children's scores were grouped together in age bands one-month wide to provide normative data for the calculation of standardized scores. Standardized scores are available for the age range 7:00–8:06. A conversion table in the Manual shows the standardized score of an individual child, given the child's age and raw test score. Within each age band of one month, the standardized scores are arranged so that they have a mean of approximately 100 and a standard deviation of 15. The Manual provides a guide to the interpretation of these standard scores in terms of the percentage of children who attained less than a given standardized score.

'With the children in the standardization sample the superiority of boys over girls amounted to 1.3 points of standardized score with a standard error of 0.4 points. The difference between the sexes is significant at the 1 per cent level, therefore it is recommended that in all assessments with this test the two sexes be considered independently of each other, unless it has been shown that the sex difference is not present in the sample tested' (Manual, p. 2). Separate sex norms, however, are not presented.

Scoring

The instructions for scoring are clear for the most part. However, although the marker is instructed to allow misspelled items to be counted as correct, no guidance is given on numbers which are written in mirror form, or with the digits reversed (e.g. 61 to 16).

Two items require children to draw hands on a clock face provided, to represent 'quarter to one', and '25 past nine'. In the sample answers, regions of acceptability for the position of the hands are provided. However, in both cases, the centre of the regions point directly at the relevant number on the clock face. Thus for '25 past nine', the answer is accepted if the minute hand is in the region 23 to 27, and the hour hand in the region 43 to 47. So an answer where the hour hand points at 48, and the minute hand at 25 is 'wrong', but if the hour hand points at 43 and the minute hand at 27, it is 'right'.

The scoring sheet provides some check against errors in scoring. A raw score is calculated for each child and can be compared to the normative data provided in the Manual.

Reliability

The only reported measure of reliability is that of internal consistency (KR-20) which was found to be 0.94. The sample consisted of 259 scripts obtained from one of the representative standardization samples. A value of 0.94 corresponds to a standard error of measurement of 4.54. The Manual explains how this value is to be interpreted and used when comparing individuals, in a straightforward manner.

Validity

No studies are reported. Inspection of the test items provides clues about the content validity of the test items. Since the test is a measure of mathematical attainment, items have been chosen which reflect topics commonly dealt with in first-year junior mathematics. Their design seems to follow no systematic pattern; some operations seem over-represented, and tied to specific topics (three questions on fractions all use shaded areas); others seem to be under-represented.

Interpretation

A raw score and standardized score is available for each child, which purport to reflect mathematical attainment. These scores certainly allow the user to relate the child to his classroom peers, and both the child and a class to a large (unspecified) sample of school children from the same age range. However, since the test has no diagnostic function, the scores can only be used as a source of either congratulations or exhortations to try harder to learn (and teach). No prescriptions for improving performance can be made, unless the teacher analyses the test for himself in terms of the difficulty of the items for his class, and in terms of the possible content validity of the most difficult items.

General evaluation

The test consists of a collection of items which represent, in a rather unsystematic way, mathematical topics dealt with by first-year junior pupils. It would benefit considerably from a detailed study of the content validity of the items.

The test can be used only for normative studies, that is to say, for comparing individuals with their peers (either in class, or nationally). Test scores, then, serve only to provide feedback on some fairly vaguely defined 'attainment of mathematics'.

Teachers of mathematics must have theories (either explicitly stated or implicit in their teaching) about the processes involved in mathematics learning, and have clear conceptions about the operations which are accessible to children and the topic areas which will maintain their interest. Since mathematics lessons involve a good deal of problem posing and problem solving, teachers also have notions about the signs and symptoms of mathematical attainment. A test which purports to measure mathematical attainment without attempting any operational definitions is of limited use. How should teachers respond if their classes are found to perform well below the norms set out in the Manual? They can 'try harder', or they might try to rationalize the results on the following grounds: that the normative data are atypical; that these children are less able; that the class had an 'off-day'; and so on. Nothing in the Manual or the test items provides the basis for teachers to re-appraise their own teaching.

The test would be considerably more use if the Manual analysed the nature of the mathematical operations dealt with. This analysis could cover the operations commonly taught, together with content areas (measuring rooms, cutting cakes, weighing things) which are relevant to the interests of children of this age. A clear discussion of how items are to be constructed to assess the child's mathematical attainment would be most valuable. This sort of analysis lends itself naturally to the development of the test as a diagnostic instrument. If pupils have difficulty with a certain class of problem, there are strong reasons to suppose that they have either had inadequate exposure to problems of this sort, or that they have been inadequately taught.

Discussion of the nature of the mathematical operations assessed will provide strong clues about remedial (or indeed new) teaching which will improve the overall performance of the individual child. Discussion of the rules for constructing items should allow the teacher to develop worksheets, graded in difficulty level to facilitate learning, and to provide the basis for subsequent testing to evaluate the effects of the remedial lessons.

It would help greatly if the clear format of the test items and the lucid exposition in the current Manual were transferred to any new test developed along these lines. These principles (but not the rules for item construction) have been embodied in *Basic Mathematics Test A*, also reviewed in this volume. That test should be used in preference to *Mathematics Attainment Test A*.

Mathematics Attainment Test B

Reviewed by David Jesson

Author: not stated
Publisher: NFER-Nelson
Distributor: NFER-Nelson
Age range: 8:00–10:08
1965 (S); 1970 (T)
1977 (S); 1978 (M) (restandardized)
1980 (M); 1979 (T) printings reviewed
Group test

Test content

There are 42 questions in this orally administered test covering a range of mathematics appropriate to second-year junior children. The questions cover six major themes: number recognition and counting (3 items), interpreting operations on number (16), applying numbers to simple measures (6), fractions

(8), spatial appreciation (6) and three further questions on patterns in number. The items to be tested are presented in two parts, the Manual contains the questions themselves (to be read aloud by the administrator) whilst the test booklet has the visual, verbal or numerical material that is to be used in answering each. All except three items require a constructed response. In 1978 the test was republished in similar form but with a conversion table extending its use to third-year junior school children.

Purpose

The questions in this test were constructed by a panel of Worcestershire teachers in order to test the mathematical experience and understanding of second-year junior school children. An orally administered version was published to reduce the problems in assessing the mathematical ability of weaker readers. A small-scale research study had shown that whilst all children showed significant increases of score when using this type of test as opposed to an identical test read by the children themselves, the greatest gains were made by those scoring in the lowest 25 per cent of NFER Reading Test AD. The test is intended therefore to reduce incidental problems of reading in assessing children's mathematical experience and understanding. It is essentially a normative test.

Item preparation

No information is given on this in the Manual nor on the framework of objectives assumed.

Administration

The test is intended to be administered by experienced teachers. It is designed for class use and detailed instructions for oral administration are given in the Manual. There is no precise time limit specified for the test as a whole, for 'each child should be given time to answer each question'. On average 45 minutes is reported as the approximate time required for full completion. There are no practice items, the test proceeds by the administrator reading aloud one question at a time to which the children write their answer in the test booklet. Advice is given on how to respond to children's requests for clarification or assistance—and this forms part of the introductory instructions.

Standardization

The test was originally standardized in June, 1965. The restandardization was carried out by the NFER in April, 1977, using stratified random sampling. The sample covered two year-groups: 2nd-year juniors (8:00–9:08, $n = 3747$) and 3rd-year juniors (9:00–10:08, $n = 4176$). For the conversion tables extrapolations were employed to provide standardized scores for children outside the age-range of the sample (i.e. aged 9:09, 9:10 and 10:00 for the second-year table). These extrapolated scores are likely to contain a higher degree of error hence greater caution is required when interpreting such results. Results for girls and boys are combined since no statistically significant differences were found between them.

Scoring

The Manual states that 'answers that can be accepted as right are given in the marking key. No alternative answers can be accepted'. Some examples of how discretion should be exercised in marking drawn or estimated answers are offered.

Reliability

KR-20 was calculated separately for 2nd- and 3rd-year junior children. For 2nd-year children, based on a sample of 348, this was 0.93 with a standard error of measurement of 4.05, while for 3rd-year children it was 0.92 with a standard error of measurement of 4.14 (based on a sample of 280 children). The implications of the standard error for assessing the range within which the 'true' score is likely to lie are detailed within the Manual.

Validity

Content validity is assumed, other types of validity are not discussed.

Interpretation

The Manual presents a description in qualitative terms of the nature of standardized scores. Separate conversion tables are presented for second-year and third-year children. The lack of precision in a particular score is discussed in relation to the standard error of measurement, but it would be helpful if this information were to be included on the conversion table itself.

General evaluation

This test was originally designed for second-year junior pupils and it is this use which will be mainly discussed in this report. The major features of this test that make it a useful instrument for second-year junior school children are: its oral administration, its relative appropriateness of content, and its appropriate centring on the age range for which it is stated to be applicable. It does not offer a yardstick for the measurement of purely computational ability and indeed does not give any diagnostic information. The test does not reflect all that is appropriate in children's mathematics at this level; work on shape, visualization and problem solving is omitted. These considerations should be taken into account when deciding whether the test content reflects sufficiently the curriculum balance in the users' classroom.

The test appears to be appropriate for average and below-average children, but is probably too easy to discriminate adequately between the most able children. Its main use will be to provide internal information on children's standards on a year-to-year basis as well as means of reporting in a rank-ordered manner to parents.

The extension of the standardization of this test to third-year junior children is reported. If the test is rather easy for the more able second-year junior children, it is likely that its value in the third year would be restricted to children of average ability and below. Its oral administration could still be of value at this stage.

Mathematics Attainment Test C1

Reviewed by P. Coxhead

Authors: Teachers of Surrey Educational Research Association; and NFER
Publisher: NFER-Nelson
Distributor: NFER-Nelson
Age ranges: 9:07–10:07 (3rd-year junior)
                10:07–11:07 (4th-year junior)
1970 (M); 1969 (T)
1977 (S) (restandardized)
1980 (T) printing reviewed
Group test

Test content

The test consists of 50 items, some in completion format, some in multiple-choice format. Most items are verbally posed. The test is not divided into sections but appears to cover a wide range of topics. 'The test includes questions on graphs, simple geometry, base, series and number patterns, fractions, arithmetical processes and equations' (Manual, p. 2).

Purpose

The test 'was designed to measure the child's knowledge and understanding of mathematics rather than his mechanical skill. Computation has therefore been kept to a minimum' (Manual, p. 2). Other parts of the Manual make clear that the purpose is to produce age-standardized scores, rather than to be diagnostic or criterion referenced.

Item preparation

No information is given in the Manual on item preparation other than that the test was 'constructed by a group of primary mathematics teachers acting as members of the Surrey Educational Research Association'.

Administration

The test is untimed; it is suggested that 'most children will have finished in 50 minutes but some may take rather more than an hour' (Manual, p. 3). Pupils respond directly onto the test booklet in pencil. Clear instructions are provided in the Manual, including a 'script' for administrators.

Standardization

The standardization reported in the Manual is dated March–April, 1977. A stratified random sample of the year groups corresponding to 3rd-year junior (9+ to 10+) and 4th-year junior (10+ to 11+) was used, totalling 3689 in the former age range and 3831 in the latter. The method of age standardization is that by Lawley (see Introduction). No sex differences were found, and a single set of norms is given.

Scoring

A marking key is provided, indicating alternative acceptable answers where appropriate. Clear tables are provided for conversion of raw scores to age-standardized scores (mean 100, standard deviation 15). Space is provided in the front of the answer booklet to record the raw and standardized scores.

Reliability

The internal consistency reliability is reported (KR-20) as being 0.95 for both 3rd- and 4th-year juniors ($n = 372$ in both cases), giving a standard error of measurement of between 3.2 and 3.5 standard score points.

Validity

No information on validity is provided in the Manual beyond the brief statements on test construction noted above which might be thought to relate to content validity.

Interpretation

No suggestions are made as to how the age-standardized scores should be interpreted.

General evaluation

The test itself apparently originated in 1969, which could mean that the content is somewhat dated although inspection does not suggest this. Restandardization was carried out in 1977. The test and Manual assume that the user simply wants age-standardized scores, knows how to interpret them, and is not concerned with issues such as validity, coverage, or curriculum relevance. If this is indeed the user's position then the test can be recommended but the lack of detail in the Manual is a poor reflection on the NFER which ought surely to set the standards in this area.

Mathematics Attainment Test C3

Reviewed by K. Lovell

Authors: A group of Middlesex teachers on behalf of Middlesex Education
 Authority
Publisher: NFER-Nelson
Distributor: NFER-Nelson
Age range: 9:08–10:08
1965 (S); 1970 (M); 1970 (T)
Revised: 'decimalized and metricated'
1978 (M, T) printings reviewed
Group test

Test content

There are 50 questions which cover the following ground: operations on number (14 questions); problems involving number (14); fractions (5);

interpretation of graphs (8); test of number base (3); symmetry (1); selection of reasonable answer (1); measurement of length (1); solution of simple algebraic equations (1); use of analogy (1); and, use of induction (1).

Purpose

On p. 2 of the Manual it is stated that, 'In this test an attempt has been made to test understanding rather than skill in computation. For this purpose adequate time must be allowed for pupils to think about the questions—the test is not devised to assess speed of calculation'.

Item preparation

The purpose of the test no doubt determined the general nature of the questions initially selected for consideration. But no details are given about the actual items tried out, how the final test questions were selected, or the population used.

Administration

The administration of the test is straightforward, the Manual giving the actual words to be used both before and after the test booklet is given out. Instructions are also printed on the front cover of the test booklet. Since sufficient time is given for all pupils to complete the test, the examiner must, when the group form is used, see that the faster workers get on with other activities after their booklets have been closed and set aside.

Standardization

'The test was standardized on all third-year junior school children in nine of the Greater London Boroughs in the Summer Term, 1965' (Manual, p. 1). The table given for converting raw scores to standardized scores was constructed from the scores of 20 175 pupils (10 293 boys, 9882 girls). Lawley's method (see Introduction) was used in making the table. But the Manual does not say if the authors consider that the table can be safely used outside of the nine Greater London Boroughs which are not identified.

The age range of the children tested was from 9:08–10:08 years with a mean age of 10:02 years: the standardized scores for pupils aged 9:03–9:07 years were obtained by extrapolation. But the Manual carefully points out that 'This test was standardized before the decimalization and metrication alterations were made. Although care has been taken to match the replacement questions to the old ones, the standardization should be regarded with caution' (Manual, p. 2).

Scoring

Clear instructions are given for scoring. Answers that can be accepted as correct are given in the marking key. Each correct answer scores one mark—no half-marks are given.

Reliability

The scripts of 274 pupils, a one-tenth sample of all children in one London borough, was used for calculating reliability. The only reported test was one of internal consistency (KR-20) which gave the value of 0.97. This yields a value of 2.55 for the standard error of measurement of the test at the mean age of 10.02 years.

Validity

In respect of content validity no relevant comments are given in the Manual other than the very general point made under Purpose above. To establish concurrent validity, scores on the Moray House Junior Arithmetic Test taken in the Spring Term of 1965 were available for 6013 pupils in the standardization sample. The product-moment correlation between the two sets of raw scores was 0.89.

Interpretation

The authors intended that it should be an instrument which *scales* pupils in respect of their understanding as given by their performance. For this purpose the interpretation of raw scores is straightforward in that the standardized scores are given in the conversion table for each raw score for each month of age. But interpretation in the sense of obtaining a measure of a pupil's depth of understanding of the mathematical ideas and processes tested is a more complex matter requiring a group test to be supplemented by individual interviews.

General evaluation

This test was devised in the early 1960s. Although it might have been regarded by some teachers as innovative at that time, it would certainly not have been so thought even ten years later. It is not possible to say how the authors arrived at the particular items finally selected, or how the number of items in each item type was determined.

Nevertheless, it could be a useful test if used just as the authors intended, namely to *scale* pupils in respect of their performance. Its reliability is acceptable; the administration and scoring straightforward. The figure for concurrent validity (0.89) suggests that it taps much the same skills as the Moray House Junior Arithmetic Test. Although only a limited amount of reading is required, some poor readers may understand more than their poor performance suggests. To assess understanding the reviewer reiterates that such a test needs supplementing with individual interviews.

Mathematics Attainment Test DE1

Reviewed by Charles Desforges

Author: not stated
Publisher: NFER-Nelson
Distributor: NFER-Nelson
Age range: 10:01–11:05
1966–67 (S); 1970 (M); 1970 (T)
Revised: decimalized and metricated
1979 (M); 1980 (T) printings reviewed
Group test

Test content

The test comprises 45 items mainly in the form of verbally presented problems. The problems demand the application of one or more mathematical skills relating to speed, time, volume, area, angles, money, number bases, four rules, missing numbers, codes, fractions, percentages, measuring and histograms and graphical interpretation. The testee has to write out the correct answer to the problem.

Purpose

It is a norm-referenced test. It is evidently a revised version of an earlier test, the revisions taking the form of decimalization and metrication.

Item preparation

No information is available on item preparation.

Administration

The test is designed to be administered by teachers. Each testee should have a response booklet and two pencils. A reserve of sharpened pencils is advised. The test is untimed but, 'most children will have finished in 50 minutes' (Manual, p. 40). Gainful activity to occupy the early finishers should be planned and provided for. Instructions to the administrator are clear and include a script of instructions to be read out to testees. The script is concise and clear.

Standardization

The test has not been standardized in its present form. The original, premetrication form was administered to top year-groups in primary schools in 'selected areas' in 1966–67. Scores were collected from 5123 boys and 4905 girls as a basis on which to construct tables of standardized scores. The age range of this sample was 10:01–11:05. The standardized scores were calculated using Lawley's method (see Introduction).

Standardized scores are given for children of chronological ages from 10:00–12:00. Extrapolation was used to obtain scores from 10:01 down to 10:00 and upwards from 11:05 to 12:00. The extrapolation of seven months upwards is noteworthy.

It is claimed that the decimalized version of the test is a little harder than the original form although no evidence is given for this nor for the degree to which it is harder. It is surmised, however, that with increasing familiarity with decimal and metric units, the tendency of the test to underestimate testees will decline.

No subgroup standardized scores are provided although it is recommended that should the test be used for allocating children, the two sexes should be considered independently (see Introduction).

Scoring

Scoring instructions are concise and unambiguous. No discretionary marks are permitted.

Reliability

Reliability was assessed using KR-20 as an index of internal consistency. A random sample of 250 scripts from the original standardization sample provided the data for this calculation. It is thus no more pertinent to the revised version of the test than the original exercise. The KR-20 value was 0.96 giving a standard error of measurement of 2.84. The point that an obtained score may be taken to fall within certain limits of the true score at a 95 per cent level of probability is made.

Sampling errors of estimation of the age allowance are recognized and suggested modifications to the standard error related to age are quoted as 2.88 at age 10:00 and 2.92 at age 12:00. It is implied that these have little impact in the determination of attainment standardized score for practical purposes: 'in only one case out of 20 is the obtained score likely to exceed or fall short of the true score by more than 6 points' (Manual, p. 3).

Validity

No comment is made on the validity of the test. Content validity would have to be estimated by the test user by comparing the test items with a particular mathematics curriculum.

Interpretation

No advice is given on the significance, utility or limitations of the test scores.

General evaluation

Since the test was standardized 16 years ago in a premetrication form its serious use (for example in making allocation decisions) should be questioned.

In respect of validity, many if not most of the items have a familiar appearance and close correspondence with primary mathematics curriculums. However, what is missing from the test may be crucial. There are no items on, for example, sets, Venn diagrams, permutations, probability, spatial relations or reflection. The content is thus very much pre 'modern maths' and to that degree its use would be discriminatory against children working such a curriculum.

Mathematics Attainment Test DE2

Reviewed by J. R. Hartley

Author: not stated
Publisher: NFER-Nelson
Distributor: NFER-Nelson

Age range: 10:01–11:09
1968–69 (S); 1970 (M, T);
No revisions apparent
1979 (M); 1980 (T) printings reviewed
Group test

Test content

There are 46 items spanning a diverse range of mathematical tasks which are aimed at 'testing understanding rather than computation'. Approximately one-third of the items are versions of multiple-choice questions, the remainder requiring a constructed response or a selection and ordering of data or statements. The test includes questions on mathematical/arithmetical operations, equations, transformations and number sentences, small problems, ordering of statements to specify a procedure, areas and perimeters and shape comparisons. Questions involving 'old' units have been updated to decimalization and the metric system. Where such amendments were made they 'were examined carefully' to ensure the content was kept the same or similar, and the difficulty 'about the same'. However, as children are taught and understand more about decimal and metric measurements . . . the replacement questions 'may underestimate a child's ability for a little while'. The test itself is clearly printed in a seven-page booklet.

Purpose

The test was developed during 1966 and 1967, in order to provide a test somewhat broader in content than traditional arithmetic tests of the time. The questions were accordingly designed to assess mathematical understanding, rather than skill in computation.

Item preparation

Few details are given, beyond the test development (1966–67). The modified version of the test (with decimalization and metric units) was standardized in 1969. However, the criterion regulating which item types were developed and which questions retained on trials, or the size and sampling of the development groups, is not stated.

Administration

Instructions for administrators are clearly set down in the Manual. The test is untimed and self paced by the pupil; however, 'most children will have finished in fifty minutes though some may take rather more than an hour'. Each pupil will need a Question Booklet into which answers are written, a pencil, ruler and some other work to do quietly when he has finished the test. The administrator is also reminded to check that unit conventions, e.g. cm^2, are understood.

Standardization

After collecting test data on the original version of the test in 1968/9, the modified version (updated on decimalization/metric system of units) was administered to 3541 pupils (1838 boys, 1703 girls) later in 1969. 'No significant differences were found' and the standardization was constructed using the pooled data from both administrations. The total sample of children numbered 10 012 with approximately equal numbers of boys and girls. However, no details are given on how the sample was drawn and if it covered urban/rural, and types of school, for example, in a representative manner. In this sample, raw score differences between the sexes were slight, their mean ages the same (11:00 years) and differences in the increase in score per month between boys and girls were not significant. Accordingly, mean values were used to construct one common conversion table (using Lawley's method) for boy and girl pupils between raw and standardized scores for each month of increasing age from 10:00–11:11 years (the scores for ages 10:00, 11:10 and 11:11 were found by extrapolation). The meaning and use of the conversion tables are adequately explained in the Manual.

Scoring

The scoring scheme is simple. Each question has a maximum mark of 1, for which the answer has to be completely correct. No half marks are given. The Manual clearly sets out when alternative phrasing, incorrect units or incorrect copying of words should not be penalized.

Reliability

The only reported reliability is that of internal consistency. On the basis of a random sample of 241 pupils from one of the standardization groups, KR-20 was found to be 0.95. A value of 3.44 was given for the standard error of measurement of the test at mean age 11:00.

Validity

No comments on the validity of the test or its constructs are given.

Interpretation

The purpose of each item is clear from its content, and the authors provide the raw score to standardized score conversion table. The standardized scores are normally distributed with a mean 100 and standard deviation 15. Brief examples show these scores can be used to interpret an individual's performance in relation to his own age group. Further examples of their use in making comparisons between pupils of differing ages would be welcome.

General evaluation

The test was designed and norms constructed during the late 1960s. Since then there have been significant developments in the mathematics curricula and in teaching methods. Although the aim of the test is to assess attainment through understanding rather than computation, the task range and type is varied and no data or discussion of their validity is given. Thus, if the test is to be used seriously in attainment, it would benefit from a refurbishing of tasks, a reappraisal of performance norms and some studies of its validity. Until these are done its uses should be more modest—perhaps in making local comparisons between groups or as a group comparability measure. Even here interested teachers are advised to reassure themselves that the types of questions are relevant to their purposes, and relate to the children's maths experience and the curriculum.

Mathematics Attainment Test EF

Reviewed by John K. Backhouse

Author: not stated
Publisher: NFER-Nelson
Distributor: NFER-Nelson
Age range: 11:00–13:01
1972, 1974 (S); 1975 (M); 1972 (T)
Some revisions apparent (see review)
1975 (M); 1979 (T) printings reviewed
Group test

Test content

The specification 'was drawn up to reflect the present "common core" topics in secondary schools for the age range 11–13' (Manual, p. 8). On pages 9 and 10 of the Manual, the 60 items are classified according to six behaviour types (adapted from Wood and Skurnik, 1969) and five broad content categories. The behaviour types are:

(1) Knowledge: recall of definitions, notations and concepts.
(2) Technique and skill: computation, manipulation of symbols.
(3) Comprehension (Translation): to translate symbolic forms.
(4) Comprehension (Interpretation): to understand problems.
(5) Comprehension (Extrapolation): to follow and extend reasoning.
(6) Application: of appropriate concepts to unfamiliar mathematical situations.

The content categories are: (1) Number (Concepts) (14 items); (2) Number (Operations) (17 items); (3) Space (11 items); (4) Tabular/Graphical Representation (9 items); and, (5) Geometry (9 items). These categories are further subdivided into 39 specific categories, 10 of which are not represented in the test.

Purpose

'Mathematics Attainment Test EF is designed to assess understanding of mathematical concepts rather than computational skills, and in content and behaviour sampling it is similar to the other tests in the mathematics attainment series' (Manual, p. 2). It is intended to provide standardized attainment scores for pupils in two age groups: 11:00–12:07 and 12:00–13:06.

Item preparation

No further information on item preparation is given in the Manual.

Administration

Instructions for administration are clearly laid out in the Manual (pp. 4–5) and instructions to be given by the teacher to the pupil are printed in bold type. The test layout has been changed and reference to this is made in the Manual; there is some confusion over page numbering in this respect but it should not confuse the teacher. Most pupils are expected to finish in 50 minutes; if standardized scores are to be found, this time should not be exceeded.

Standardization

'The scores of 8969 pupils (4939 boys and 4030 girls) in the 11 + age-group and 2609 pupils (1403 boys and 1206 girls) in the 12 + age-group were used to provide data for the conversion tables' (Manual, p. 2). Lawley's procedure was used. The standardized scores obtained are normally distributed, with a mean of 100 and a standard deviation of 15. 'The standardization data were collected during 1972 and 1974. The age range of the pupils tested was 11:01 to 12:05 (mean age 11:10) for the 11+ age group and 12:00 to 13:01 (mean age 12:06) for the 12+ age group. The standardized scores for 11:00, 12:06 and 12:07 for the 11+ age group and 13:02 to 13:06 inclusive for the 12+ age group have been obtained by extrapolation' (Manual, p. 2).

Scoring

Pupils mark their answers on a separate answer sheet. Clear directions for scoring are given. As the items are multiple choice, it is possible to use a stencil and the instructions for its use incorporate a check.

Reliability

'The scripts of 362 pupils in the 11+ age-group and 357 pupils in the 12+ age-group formed the random samples used to calculate the reliability coefficients of the test. For the 11+ age-group the KR-20 reliability coefficient was found to be 0.90, giving a standard error for the test of 4.64 at mean age 11:10. For the 12+ age-group the KR-20 reliability coefficient was 0.92 giving a standard error of 4.34 at mean age 12:06' (Manual, p. 3). The paragraph continues with a sentence which appears to blur the distinction between internal consistency and test-retest measures of reliability.

Validity

Validity is not specifically discussed but the item specifications given in the table on pages 9 and 10 are an attempt to establish content validity.

Interpretation

In addition to the conversion tables to provide standardized scores, the Manual gives guidance on p. 3 on the interpretation of these scores. Standard error of measurement is referred to as 'standard error' and values are given for the mean age of each group. The Manual provides an example for a pupil with a standardized score of 105 who may be expected to have a 'true' score in the interval 96–114, using twice the standard error of measurement. It is also explained that comparison of pupils at different ages is also affected by sampling errors of estimation of the age allowance. Some examples of 'modified standard errors' are given but no indication is given to the user about how to make such comparisons.

Test use

The test was used in 1973 by Newbold (1977) for first-year pupils at Banbury School. A factor analysis is reported and the test was found to load highly (0.88) on the first rotated factor, which was described as 'traditional scholastic'. There was a negligible loading on the second factor which was described as 'creative'.

General evaluation

This test, with a separate answer sheet and marking stencil, will appeal to those with many scripts to mark. Of much greater import, however, is the content of the test. The test constructor has, as may be seen under 'Test content', made a move towards establishing content validity by the two-way specification of items. The user must, of course, still examine the test to see whether the content of the pupils' courses will be adequately sampled by the test. While the standardizing sample for the 11+ age-group is large, no indication was given of the types of courses followed by the pupils. This means that the user cannot be sure whether his or her sample is drawn from the same population as the standardizing sample.

For a test which is designed to assess understanding of mathematical concepts rather than computational skills, it is disappointing to find that 63 per cent of the items appear to be testing Knowledge or Techniques and Skill, when Bloom (1972, p. 204) suggests that Comprehension is the lowest category to test understanding. The classification grid should, according to the test constructor, be interpreted with some reservation. This accords well with the writer's belief that the behaviour type depends on the pupil's experience. Nevertheless, the classification grid is a feature of the Manual to be welcomed: it makes explicit the test constructor's intention and the user may make use of the information it contains to assist him or her to decide whether the test is suitable for the purpose it is wanted to serve.

References

Bloom, B. S. (ed.) (1972). "Taxonomy of Educational Objectives. Book 1 Cognitive Domain". London: Longman.

Newbold, D. (1977). "Ability Grouping: The Banbury Enquiry". Windsor, Berks: NFER.

Wood, R. and Skurnik, L. S. (1969). "Item Banking". Windsor, Berks: NFER.

Mathematics Topic Tests★

Reviewed by P. Coxhead

Author: Frances C. Morrison (Manual)
Publisher: Guidance Center, Faculty of Education, University of
   Toronto
Distributor: The Test Agency
Age range: 11–16; Canadian Grades 5–9 (Test 1); 4–6 (Test 2); 5–8 (Test
   3); 5–7 (Test 4); 6–9 (Test 5)
1974
No revisions apparent but Form B said to be in preparation
1974 Form A only reviewed
Group tests

Test content

Five tests were available for review, covering Number and Numeration,
Addition and Subtraction with Whole Numbers, Multiplication and Division
with Whole Numbers, Operations with Fractions and Multiplication and
Division with Fractions. Each test contains from 24–40 items which group into
sets concerned with subtopics within the main topic of each test. Completion-
type items are used in Test 2, multiple choice in the rest. Form A of each test,
as reviewed, uses some Imperial units; a Form B is said to be being produced
using only metric units.

Purpose

The tests are designed to offer diagnostic information on specific topics for
both individuals and groups and thus 'to provide feedback to both teachers and
pupils at various levels'. There is no attempt to provide norms of any kind.

Item preparation

The tests were developed in the Research Center of the Ottawa Board of
Education. Tables of specifications were drawn up for each topic on the basis
of which the items were composed. Several versions were prepared and tried
out, the major trials involving some 10 000 students at the appropriate grade

---

★ 'Elementary Series for Grades 4–9'.

levels. A separate report is available giving full details of the development of the series (Research Report 73-06, available from the Ottawa Board of Education, 330 Gilmour Street, Ottawa, Ontario, Canada).

Administration

Tests 1, 3–5, are multiple choice and are designed to be answered using the separate answer sheets provided. Test 2 is to be answered in the question booklet. Each test is designed to require from 20–40 minutes to complete but as the tests are not speeded, time should be allowed for most pupils to finish. Clear directions for administration are given in the Manual.

Standardization

The tests are intended solely for diagnostic purposes so that standardization is not appropriate.

Scoring

When the separate answer sheets are used, scoring can be simplified by using the stencil-type keys which are provided. A key is also provided for hand scoring the completion type items in Test 2. Individual Record Forms and Class Record Sheets are available, the former providing for up to three repeated administrations.

Reliability

No reliability data are given. Such information may be considered unnecessary for a *purely* diagnostic test; the Manual does suggest in some places that the total scores on the tests may be useful, in which case reliability estimates should have been provided.

Validity

The validity of a test designed primarily to diagnose specific weaknesses in a pupil's understanding of a mathematical topic can be demonstrated by showing: (1) that the topic has been completely specified in terms of a series of specific subtopics or objectives, and (2) that each objective is tightly related to an item or set of items. More evidence as to point (1) could have been provided, although full tables of specifications are reported. Point (2) is well covered and should make highly specific diagnosis possible. For example, Test 4, Operations with Fractions, is first divided into 7 subtopics (e.g. Addition of Fractions with Like Denominators), each of which is then divided into 3–7 objectives (e.g. changing sum to mixed number in lowest terms) with one item for each.

Interpretation

Very full and clear guidance is given as to how the results can be interpreted, either for individuals or for classes, although a little more caution over the reliability of single items would be preferable. Whether many teachers have the time to regularly complete a detailed Class Record Sheet for say 32 items by 35 pupils is another matter!

General evaluation

The series of tests have the 'feel' of being carefully prepared for their major purpose: the diagnosis of specific strengths and weaknesses in a pupil's understanding of a range of mathematical topics. When available, Form B using only metric units will be more appropriate in the UK, but with suitable amendments to a few items even Form A of the tests can be thoroughly recommended. Since the user can select the precise test to be used by topic, the Canadian origin should pose no problem.

Moray House Mathematics Tests

Reviewed by E. P. Duggan

Author: The Godfrey Thomson Unit, University of Edinburgh
Publisher: Hodder & Stoughton
Distributor: Hodder & Stoughton
Age ranges: 8:06–10:06, JMT2
         10:00–12:00, MT7
         10:00–12:00, MT10

JMT2
1970 (M, T); S not stated
1980 (T) printing reviewed

MT7
1971 (S); 1972 (M, T)
1979 (M) printing reviewed

| **MT10** |
| 1974–76 (S); 1976 (M, T) |
| Group tests (restricted)★ |

Test content

These three versions of Moray House Mathematics Tests all follow very similar types of items, so can be dealt with together mainly. The total number of items, however, in each, does vary a little—60 in JMT2, 65 in MT7 and 70 in MT10. The items cover the four rules of addition, subtraction, multiplication and division presented in different kinds of problems: area measure, graphs and mapping, fractions, unknowns in simple equations, number series and simple problems. The type of item covers number sequences, multiple patterns, graphical interpretation, manipulation of signs, numerical manipulation. Response requirements for all are simple—filling in blanks, underlining or entering responses in brackets.

There is some ambiguity in some questions: e.g. in item No. 11 (p. 3) of JMT2, what is needed should be made more explicit; item No. 12 (p. 3) should explicitly state that there must be no overlap in the shapes to be counted. The balance of content varies between the three tests. It does not seem to this reviewer that this test is very searching on the use of basic rules and concepts. MT7 and MT10, as befits tests for older pupils, are more thoughtfully graded, and cover well the basic skills, including numerical manipulation, sign inversion in arithmetical processes and so on.

Purpose

JMT2 is, as its title implies, the second in a series. It is a diagnostic type of test. MT7 and MT10 have both been used by LEAs in the secondary selection process, as well as for controlling promotion to other post-primary courses.

Item preparation

No information is provided on this.

Administration

Recommended users for all tests are teachers in primary junior and middle schools. JMT2 is for general diagnostic use within the school or class. The

---

★ Available to schools with the permission of the local Chief Education Officer.

other tests in addition are authorised for official use and administered by teachers. Guidance in the three Manuals for preparation and supervision of the test are worded identically, while the instruction for administration of MT7 and MT10 are identical, those for JMT2 are modified slightly to cater for the younger pupils, including use of a blackboard for examples. JMT2 takes exactly 40 minutes, the other two tests 45 minutes each exactly. In each case the test rules are read by the supervisor. Children need only a pencil and test booklet, the supervisor holding a reserve supply of pencils. The script for administration of the test in all three Manuals is satisfactory.

Standardization

JMT2

This was standardized with its companion Verbal Reasoning Test Junior 7 and English Test Junior 6. The Manual (p. 8) states: 'The total effective sample consisted of 1618 children between the ages of 8:10 and 10:06 who worked all three tests'. What exactly 'effective' meant in this context is not explained. The sample was drawn from 12 areas situated in all parts of England and 'balanced for type' (again this is not explained). Within each area, five or six primary schools were drawn at random, and within each school a class was randomly selected within the age-group. Nevertheless, this attempt at rigorous sampling of children is an improvement on those for the Verbal Reasoning and English Moray House tests. The Manual states that the sample should have been a satisfactory representative sample of the total population, but voices the suspicion that the least bright children may have been under-represented and warns that caution should be exercised in interpreting 'Mathematics Quotients' (MQs) below 90. Likewise, brighter children are likely to obtain higher MQs than those taking JMT1 or tests in the Junior Arithmetic series as these latter tests were standardized in semi-competitive conditions. Presumably this means they were given for selection or promotion purposes. A further very interesting point in comparison with other MH tests is that a mean raw score difference of 0.58 points was found favouring *the boys* in the standardization sample; boys also improved faster than girls. Hence separate conversion tables for boys and girls are provided for the test. This standardization procedure has been dealt with at some length since it points to a more serious attempt at rigorous sampling; but goes further than some Moray House procedures in producing separate tables when the sex mean difference is as low as 0.50 points, whereas other tests having a mean difference as large as 7.6 points of raw score found good reason for keeping the tables combined for the sexes (but see Introduction).

MT7 and MT10

The wording for the standardization procedures in both Manuals is almost identical, and indeed seems to be a common format for all Moray House tests. This may or may not be good for teacher users, suggesting a uniformity of method, which may give a false sense of confidence in the figures so obtained even if the representativeness differs from test to test. Both tests used a standardization sample of the 'semi-competitive' type referred to above, i.e. an opportunity sample presented by the needs of LEAs for tests used in selection and promotion procedures. Thus for the standardization of MT7, 11 376 boys and girls in the four LEAs were used to determine the MQ norms. For MT10, 2022 children in two LEAs were used. Neither stated the number of boys and girls except to state they were 'in approximately equal proportions' (p. 8). In both tests, boys were shown to have 'slight superiority'. For MT7 (1086 boys, 956 girls) this was 2.3 points of raw score (about 2 MQ points), while for MT10 (525 boys, 508 girls) the difference was 2.9 points of raw score (about 2 MQ points).

Reliability

KR-20 coefficients were found to be 0.96 for JMT2, 0.96 for MT7 and 0.95 for MT10. All were based on random samples of 201 scripts drawn from the standardization samples.

Validity

JMT2 scores were correlated with the companion tests of Verbal Reasoning 7 and English Test 6 and the correlations were 0.85 and 0.80 respectively. MT7 scores were correlated with MHT86 (Verbal reasoning) and MH English Test 41, giving coefficients of 0.89 and 0.81 respectively. The Manual for MT10 reports that: 'Correlations between MT10 and other tests were not available' and quotes intercorrelations for two preceding tests in the series with MH English and Verbal Reasoning Tests. It is not clear what conclusion is to be drawn from these statements. No studies of validity with respect to *mathematics* are reported for any of these three tests.

Scoring

Again, the scoring instructions for all three tests are highly similar. They are clear, concise and satisfactory. The scoring keys are equally clear and satisfactory. Scoring is simple for all three, one mark being awarded for each item answered correctly. Each test has a summary sheet on front cover of the the test booklet with spaces for the MQ and test age of the child.

Interpretation

For all three tests the Manuals give guidance on the definition of 'Mathematics Quotients'. However, the conversion tables for JMT2 differ from all other MH tests reviewed in certain respects: (1) separate tables are provided for boys and girls, and (2) MQ scores are given for each point of raw score to which correction factors may be applied for each month of age within the age-range.

The other two tests have combined conversion tables for boys and girls from which the MQ can be read directly for any child, given the child's accurate age and raw score. Users are given examples of the procedure. MT7 and MT10 indicate that in interpreting MQs those of value 75, 90, 100, 110 and 125 denote the upper limits of the lowest 5, 25, 50, 75 and 95 per cent respectively of the standardization group. JMT2 does not give this information. MT7 and MT10 Manuals suggest that, since attainment test norms are necessarily tentative, performance in the test depends on the school syllabus and the time given to the subject in school, and that the conversion tables are based on the assumption that the sample is a satisfactory representation of the whole population. The size and scope of the samples used suggest this assumption is speculative rather than factual. JMT2 does not deal with the interpretation of the norms.

All three tests give guidance on extrapolation of MQ scores beyond the age limits for which the test was designed, warning against further extrapolation beyond those specified and against placing confidence in any such extrapolated MQ values.

General evaluation

The three tests were all produced in the 1970s. They cover broadly basic concepts in number, manipulation of the four rules varied in the contexts of money, mensuration, time and numbers themselves, simple graphical interpretation, fractions and series. MT7 and MT10 carry the testing into more complex problems appropriate to the older age-ranges. The balance of content is, on the whole, adequate. JMT2 is diagnostic, the other two are used for competitive selection processes. The Manuals, again on the whole, are adequate and should be clearly intelligible to the intended users. No information is given on item preparation, sampling frames or item analysis. Standardization of the tests is adequate for their intended purposes of diagnosis and selection, but care should be exercised in applying the tests for purposes outside those stated. Hence it seems desirable that more information should be made available to the user in relation to the sex composition of the sample, and, perhaps more importantly, the location and nature of the areas from which the samples were obtained, for example the ethnic and socio-economic mix. The reliability of all three tests seem satisfactory, but from the intended users' point of view, more and clearer interpretations of the intention and meaning of the correlations with tests in other cognitive areas needs to be given, otherwise a false inference about validity of the tests might ensue.

The Nottingham Number Test

Reviewed by Neville Bennett

Authors: W. E. C. Gillham and K. A. Hesse
Publisher: Hodder & Stoughton
Distributor: Hodder & Stoughton
Age range: 9:01–11:00
1972 (S); 1973 (M, T)
No revisions apparent
1979 (M); 1980 (T) printings reviewed
Group test

Test content

The eight-page answer booklet contains 88 items which aim to measure children's developing grasp of the base-ten number system. The test is divided into 'number concepts' and 'number skills', a dichotomy which the authors recognise as accurate in degree only. Number skills cover the calculation skills of the 'four rules' including fractions and decimals. Number concepts cover place value and series together with subgroupings of items related to the concept of series—proportion, grouping and what the authors call 'number relativeness', e.g. larger and smaller.

This test is a direct development of the Leicester Number Test and in common with that test the major guide in determining test content was the Schools Council report 'Mathematics in Primary Schools' published in 1965.

Purpose

The general aim is to assess what is considered essential in any primary mathematics programme. More specifically, 'The test is designed to:

(a) indicate areas of weakness in individual children;
(b) provide a basis for grouping for teaching;
(c) detect gross educational failure as part of a comprehensive attainment assessment programme;
(d) make possible, in conjunction with the Leicester Number Test, a continuous appraisal of attainment in number through the junior school;
(e) give some guidance as to the content and emphasis of an essential part of primary school mathematics' (Manual, p. 1).

Item preparation

There is little to indicate how the items were chosen. The authors claim to have been guided 'by the need to have adequate and balanced representation of the concepts and skills we are seeking to test as well as adequate representation of different levels of difficulty' (Manual, p. 2). However, there appears to have been prestandardization trials since it is claimed that some items were eliminated or modified where the verbal instructions appeared to constitute a difficulty.

Administration

The test is administered orally by the teacher with each child responding in the answer booklet. The test is untimed but on average is expected to take about 50–55 minutes. The Manual instructions for administration are clear and concise, including, for example, when to pause and how long for. It is suggested that an invigilator be present as well as the teacher.

Despite the clear and unambiguous Manual instructions, the oral and untimed nature of the test does place responsibility on the teacher for judgements regarding pacing and momentum. The guiding principle stated in the Manual is to avoid causing unnecessary anxiety by hurrying and to allow enough time for those children who are clearly capable of writing an answer.

Standardization

The test was standardized in the last week of September, 1972, and readministered one week later to obtain an estimate of reliability. The population was limited to the City of Nottingham. The City was stratified into four areas and schools selected proportionately. The sample is claimed to be representative of the population of third- and fourth-year juniors in Nottingham although all immigrant children were excluded from the norms. This left a standardization sample of 509 third years (264 boys, 245 girls) and 516 fourth years (253 boys,

263 girls). The readministration one week later sampled 472 third-year and 483 fourth-year non-immigrant children.

Raw score distributions for both years and for the subscales and full scale are given in frequency histogram form as are the means and standard deviations of raw scores. From these it is apparent that children find the number concepts subtest considerably easier than the number skills.

The scores are arranged to have a mean of 100 and a standard deviation of 15 in the score conversion table and percentile levels are also provided. However, the standardized scores do not incorporate an age allowance within each age-year. The rationale for this is that whatever their chronological age they are treated as equivalent for teaching purposes. A warning is given about comparing such scores with those on other tests which incorporate such an allowance. Norms for the two sexes are not provided.

Scoring

Instructions for marking and a marking key are provided. These clearly show which items are to be scored for number concept and number skill. The number of marks are to be awarded strictly as indicated. Where acceptable variations are allowed, e.g. lines placed through a number instead of underneath, these are indicated. The marks achieved on each page of the test are transferred on to the front page of the answer booklet prior to ascertaining the number quotient and percentile rank.

Reliability

The only reported reliability estimate is that of stability (test-retest). This reliability coefficient together with a derived standard error of measurement is reported for each subscale, and the total scale for both age groups. The subscale coefficients vary between 0.91 and 0.94, and the total scale values are 0.94 for third years and 0.96 for fourth years. No details are provided concerning the internal consistency of the test.

Validity

The construct validity of the two scales of number concepts and number skills is not demonstrated. Indeed the authors admit that these labels are essentially descriptive and highly correlated. Validity of the total scale is based solely on content, i.e. 'since the test actually samples what is taught, satisfactory validity essentially follows from satisfactory reliability' (Manual, p. 6). As a check on this assumption class teachers in one school ranked their pupils on a 7-point scale according to their judgements of the children's understanding of number and proficiency in written arithmetic 12 weeks before test administration. Spearman's rho between test scores and rankings ranged from 0.67 to 0.85 for third years and from 0.54 to 0.87 for fourth years. It is stated that these are satisfactory.

Interpretation

'Quotient' (actually a standardized score) and 'Percentile' are not explained, neither is there any guide as to how class teachers can make effective use of the information provided. A breakdown of the item components of number concepts and skills might have been useful for diagnostic purposes.

General evaluation

The test is designed both as a norm referenced and as a diagnostic measure. It seems unlikely that teachers would wish to use it in the former capacity particularly since any comparisons made would be with children in the City of Nottingham a decade ago. This same limitation applies to its use as a research instrument.

The usefulness of a diagnostic test will depend crucially on the match between taught and item content, and here there are grounds for concern. The authors limit the range of the test to 'what is considered essential' in primary mathematics based on a dated source. Many mathematics schemes have been developed since 1965 and are in extensive use. As such the match of item content to contemporary mathematics curriculum is unknown. A further factor in the value of tests of this kind is that a number of those schemes incorporate diagnostic measures as an integral part of the package.

Nevertheless the Manual is adequate in most respects. Details of administration and marking are clear and concise but aids to interpretation are almost totally lacking.

Number Test DE

Reviewed by Jack Wrigley

Author: E. L. Barnard
Publisher: NFER-Nelson
Distributor: NFER-Nelson
Age range: 10:08–12:03
1965 (S); 1970 (T)
No revisions apparent
1978 (M); 1979 (T) printings reviewed
Group test

Test content

Fifty items test the pupils' understanding of the four number processes (addition, subtraction, multiplication and division). The items contain relatively unfamiliar notation, especially novel, but easily understood, symbols in an attempt to measure understanding rather than simply acquired knowledge.

Purpose

It is claimed that a pupil who 'understood' the four number processes would be able to use them logically as a basis from which to generalize and draw inferences and hence be able to solve relatively unfamiliar problems. Experimental results, quoted later in this review, lend support to this claim.

Item preparation

No details given in an otherwise excellent and informative Manual.

Administration

Careful instructions are given in the Manual designed to ensure that each pupil is able to work in conditions under which they can do their best, consistent with some standardization of procedure. The test is untimed; in practice most children will have finished in 50 minutes, though some may take more than an hour.

Standardization

The test was standardized (in 1965) on large samples of 3rd- and 4th-year junior school children ($n = 855$ and 2329 respectively) and on 3398 1st-year secondary school pupils in one county authority. Details of the distribution are given in the Manual and a conversion table, based upon a pooling of the data from different year groups, is supplied to provide standardized scores in the usual form. As this test is one of understanding it is reasonable to suggest that the norms will not date readily and that they are still reasonably accurate.

Scoring

Good instructions are given. In most cases the correct answer is obvious to the marker and one mark is given for each correct response. In one question to which a variety of responses can be considered correct the Manual gives explicit guidance on the issue.

Reliability

The scripts of 500 children aged 11:03–12:03 in four schools representative of the first year at secondary school were used to calculate a KR-20 reliability coefficient of 0.96. The standard error at mean age 11:06 is 2.84; at 10:06 and 12:06 a standard error of 1.94 should be used. These statistics are of course highly satisfactory for a test which has certain novel features.

Validity

The Manual gives a table of correlation coefficients measuring the relationship of the test with other reputable intelligence, problem and mechanical arithmetic, and verbal tests. These correlations ranged from 0.55–0.86. The test correlates better with general school ability than with tests of mechanical and problem arithmetic. Correlations with teachers' ratings, NFER non-verbal Test DH and the Schonell Word Reading Test were lower, of the order of 0.5–0.6. The statistical results suggest an interesting new type of test tapping an important ability related, within the mathematical field, to general ability.

Interpretation

It is easy to interpret the scores using the table of standardized scores and there seems little doubt that the test is a reliable measure of general rather than verbal ability within a mathematical context.

General evaluation

The test is well constructed and a valiant attempt has been made to produce a test of understanding of the four number processes in such a way as to be not too dependent on the mathematical notation used by an individual teacher. Obviously the test is context bound and does measure mathematical ability and understanding within the school situation. But it is relatively independent of controversies with regard to 'modern' and 'traditional' mathematics. It makes sense to use such a test if one wishes to measure understanding rather than knowledge.

Profile of Mathematical Skills*

Reviewed by P. Coxhead

Author: Norman France
Publisher: NFER-Nelson

* Levels 1 and 2.

Distributor: NFER-Nelson
Age ranges: 8:04–11:09 (Level 1)
11:04–14:09 (Level 2)
1978 (S); 1979 (M, T)
Group test

Test content

The Profile consists of a series of subtests. For Level 1 there are 7 subtests: Addition, Subtraction, Multiplication, Division, Operations, Measurement and Money and Extensions. For Level 2, two further subtests are added: Fractions, Decimal Fractions and Percentages and Diagrams. The items are arranged in increasing order of difficulty in sets of four across the page, each set relating to a different topic within the subtest. Completion format is used throughout rather than multiple choice.

Purpose

The Manual (Teachers' Guide) suggests a twofold purpose for the Profile. First, for an individual pupil, 'the best assessment derives from the long acquaintance that an experienced teacher has with the individual child. It is when these two prerequisites—long experience and acquaintance—are lacking that the value of an authoritative estimate of mathematical ability and skill provided . . . will be fully demonstrated' (p. 8). Secondly, an analysis of results for a class can be used to discover weaknesses which may need 'remedial treatment for the class or groups within the class'. Since each subtest is itself divided into topics with four items per topic, it is claimed that such weaknesses can be located with some precision.

Item preparation

The items in each subtest were chosen from a larger pool of 256 items administered in a number of schools in Doncaster, Wolverhampton and Leeds in 1977. The origin of this pool of items is not stated, nor is the rationale behind the initial division into subtests. About 2000 pupils ranging from 3rd-year junior to 2nd-year secondary were used at this stage. The internal consistency reliabilities of these initial subtests ranged from 0.91 to 0.97 (KR-20). The results were used to revise the Profile to 'provide an even graduation of difficulty, maximize discrimination of ability and skills and minimize differences of achievement between boys and girls' (p. 12). Details of how this was achieved are sparse (but reference is made to a paper by the author of the Profile) and in particular the validity of the division of the items into subtests is not demonstrated.

Administration

Level 1 is designed for second- to fourth-year junior pupils, although the tables provided in the Manual enable standard scores to be calculated for a somewhat wider age range of 8:00–13:00 years. Level 2 is designed for first- to third-year secondary pupils, with the Manual again providing standardization for a somewhat wider age range of 10:00–15:00 years. The Extensions subtest is, for each Level, designed to measure 'more advanced development, particularly for the average and better than average pupil', whereas the other subtests are intended to be 'most effective at and below the average level of ability' for diagnostic purposes.

The Profile is to be used untimed, with one or more mathematics lessons allowed per subtest. The subtests can be taken in any order and presumably some could be omitted since norms are provided separately, although this would not yield the complete Profile. Pupils answer directly on the test booklets in pen or pencil and, it is suggested, may also be provided with a sheet of plain paper for working. The directions in the Manual and on the test booklets are clear.

Standardization

Standardization was carried out in June, 1978, using 8000 pupils (1300–1400 for each of six age-groups) 'distributed throughout the regions of the United Kingdom in accordance with the proportions shown in Statistics of Education 1976'. No other information is given as to how the sample was obtained although it is claimed that it was 'fully representative of the United Kingdom school population'. This claim cannot be assessed in the absence of more detailed sampling information.

Age-related norms for each subtest are provided in the form of Standard Age Scores (mean 100, standard deviation 15), Percentiles, Stanines and Mathematical Ages. Norms are provided separately by sex (see Introduction).

Scoring

Correct answers are provided for scoring all subtests at each Level. For most items, only one answer is regarded as correct but, where appropriate, alternatives are indicated. Very clear tables are provided for the conversion of raw scores on each subtest into age-standardized scores and using these the complete profile can be recorded on the front of the individual answer book or on the special charts available which have space for up to 5 repeated uses of the Profile.

Reliability

For the central year group for each Level of the Profile, split-half internal consistency reliabilities were calculated for each subtest using a random 1 in 6 subsample ($n = 219$ for Level 1, $n = 170$ for Level 2). These ranged from 0.82–0.96. For the remaining year groups, internal consistency reliabilities were estimated for each subtest using KR-21 ($n = 1300$ approximately). These estimates ranged from 0.68–0.96. The great majority of quoted internal consistency reliabilities are considerably above 0.80. Since the major use of this instrument is via a profile of subtest scores, the reliability of *differences* between the subtest scores is of importance. In the absence of the correlations between the subtest scores, these reliabilities cannot be checked but the suggestion in the Manual that differences of 15–20 points of Standard Age Score should be regarded as worthy of further investigation seems reasonable. This means that if profiles are plotted as suggested (as shown, for example, on the cover of the Manual) differences of up to a third of the full scale of 60 points of Standard Age Score may not be meaningful; yet these differences *look* dramatic when so plotted.

Validity

Three arguments concerning validity are presented in the Manual. First, there is content validity. The Profile consists of sets of four items per topic, with topics being grouped into subtests. However, as no information is provided as to how the topics were chosen (by the author?) or as to whether this choice would be judged appropriate by, for example, teachers, doubts must remain over the content validity. Secondly, it is argued in the Manual that where there is scope for argument concerning validity, 'there can be few better guides than a factorial (*sic*) analysis'. It is not at all clear from the Manual exactly how the factor analytic results presented are intended to be used in supporting validity, since for one thing they suggest that there are perhaps only four dimensions underlying the Profile rather than seven or nine subtests. No clear evidence is presented to show that the items are most meaningfully (and hence validly) grouped into the particular set of subtests employed, rather than any other set. Thirdly, a measure of concurrent validity was obtained by correlating the *total* score on all subtests with teachers' estimates of mathematical ability. This produced values falling from around 0.65 for junior school pupils to 0.29 for third-year secondary pupils.

Interpretation

Very clear tables are provided for the conversion of raw scores on all subtests into various age-standardized forms—Standard Age Scores, Percentiles,

Stanines, and Mathematical Ages. Caution concerning the uncertainty to be attached to an individual score is prominent in the Manual, although as noted above, perhaps under-stressed in relation to differences between subtest scores.

General evaluation

A major weakness of the Profile, as presented in the Manual, lies in the failure to provide evidence that the topics covered in the subtests are relevant and appropriate in breadth and depth to the curriculum in UK schools over the age range concerned. Users will need to make their own assessment of the Profile by inspecting the list of topics provided in the Manual and the items themselves.

It is also difficult to evaluate the soundness of the standardization in the absence of further details concerning the sampling procedures employed in the main part of the development of the Profile. The internal consistency reliabilities are adequate when subtests are considered individually. For many users, the strength of the Profile will be that it offers just that—a profile—as opposed to a single total score. However, profiles inevitably invite the user to pay attention to *differences* and the standard error of subtest differences implied in the Manual is uncomfortably high. To be fair, this is probably a weakness of most practicable profiling techniques.

Within these limitations, the Profile is clearly and attractively presented and could be valuable to users who have sufficient testing and scoring time available.

Secondary Mathematics Item Bank

Reviewed by David Jesson

Author: Compiled by M. Puroshothaman for Guidance and Assessment
    Service, NFER-Nelson
Publisher: NFER-Nelson
Distributor: NFER-Nelson
Age range: 12–15
1976
Group test

Test content

The Item Bank contains 186 questions covering 10 distinct topic areas drawn from the subject matter of secondary-school mathematics. The particular selection of content was made after a survey of teachers' views of the relative importance of some 48 topics and the most appropriate age group for which they should be introduced. The content categories are given as: (1) properties of number of operations; (2) properties of fractions and decimals; (3) algebraic manipulations; (4) general structures; (5) graphical representation; (6) symmetry; (7) algebraic method in geometry; (8) properties of figures; (9) everyday mathematics; (10) constructions. The objectives are given as: Knowledge, Technique/Skill, Comprehension (Translation), Comprehension (Interpretation), Application, Comprehension (Extrapolation), Concrete Operation and Formal Operation. A classification of the test content by behavioural objectives is also given (Manual, p. 38).

Purpose

This is an experimental version of a proposed new form of test instrument. 'The purpose of the bank is to provide (mathematics) teachers with a wide range of items so that they can choose appropriate materials (for a test) in accordance with the pupils' experience and their own teaching intentions'. A subsidiary aim that emerged as the testing programme proceeded to produce a bank of items that 'enables a pupil's score on a particular set of items to be put on the same scale as other pupils' responses to different sets (or tests)'. In effect this means that the underlying purpose of the test constructors was to provide a common scale (perhaps called 'Mathematical ability') along which pupils who had followed different courses could be assessed and hence compared (Manual, p. 5).

The stated purpose and its possible achievement has been a matter of dispute and no convincing evidence has as yet been produced to indicate that such a single scale (or unidimensional trait) can be discovered to exist.

Item preparation

Considerable information is presented on this. Practising teachers contributed a pool of 429 items according to a two-dimensional blueprint relating content categories to objectives for 2nd- to 4th-year secondary school children. On testing these, conventional item analysis revealed severe problems with the *stability* of the facility and discrimination indices across different age groups. This made impossible the assembly of reliable tests from the item pool. At this stage new trials were held designed so that pupils attempted only items that 'matched approximately their attainment in mathematics'. Common items were included to link tests together and make measurement along a common scale a possibility. A 'model' was used to assess how well the assumption that relatively more able children should be consistently more successful in responding to any item. Items which did not 'fit' this model (known as the 'Rasch model') were either rejected or retained with cautions as to their use. The resulting test contains 186 items of which 23 are marked either as not fitting the model or as being appropriate only to pupils of above-average ability, but were retained because of the importance of their content.

Administration

This is an Item Bank from which teachers select questions to form a test, no directions are given to guide the administration of any test which is formed.

Standardization

In the conventional sense standardization was not carried out. The Item Bank is designed on a different basis from a norm-referenced test—teachers select the number of items they wish to include and the maximum score of a candidate is thus determined simply by the length of the test.

Instead of using a model based on an underlying normal distribution of ability, in the construction of the Item Bank it is assumed that the probability of a pupil obtaining a correct answer to any question depends on the difference between his ability and the difficulty of the item. For an item equal in difficulty to a pupil's ability it is assumed that the pupil has an even chance of getting that item either right or wrong. The procedure by which the scale of difficulty is established and quantified is called the 'calibration' of the scale. This was carried out using 5 tests of 60 questions each drawn from a total of around 220 and including common items in each successive pair of tests. These tests were given to the following groups:

> Draft 2B, bottom half of ability range in Year 2 ($n = 474$ pupils); Draft 2A, top half of ability range in Year 2 ($n = 490$); Draft 3, full ability range in Year 3 ($n = 474$); Draft 4B, bottom half of ability range in Year 4 ($n = 430$); Draft 4A, top half of ability range in Year 4 ($n = 523$).

No information is given on the meaning or interpretation of top/bottom half, nor of what ability measure was used.

Each draft gave rise to a different calibrated scale and in order to put all the items on a common scale 'draft 2 was chosen as the one to which the difficulty values in the other drafts could be most profitably linked'. Recalibration was then carried out but no details of this are presented.

The resulting scale of 'mathematical' difficulty and ability runs from 35 for the least difficult items to 75 for the most difficult. The assumption of the Rasch model is that a person's ability can be measured by the difficulty of the items he gets correct. Conversion tables have been constructed to convert a raw score, on tests of length from 15 to 40 items, into an ability measure (each with an associated standard error of measurement).

Scoring

Once the test has been assembled scoring is achieved by totalling the number of correct responses.

Reliability

Conventional measures of test-retest reliability or internal consistency are not reported. The Rasch model makes the *assumption* that only two factors come into play when a pupil encounters a test item—the pupil's ability and the item's difficulty. In theory nothing else influences the outcome of a pupil's attempts to answer the question. However, the Manual indicates that further investigations were to be conducted to explore this in collaboration with users of the Item Bank.

Each ability measure in the conversion tables has an associated standard error which has been estimated from the Rasch model. This 'error' is always smaller at mid-range, and for longer tests. If a test is 'appropriately' set in terms of the ability of the group who take it the standard errors of the ability measure are around 2.0 for shorter tests and around 1.5 for longer. This is not unexpected, in general longer tests are more reliable than shorter and most tests are more reliable at the mid-point of their range. The standard errors rise sharply towards the extremes of each scale.

Validity

The responsibility for assembling an appropriate test is placed on the user.

Interpretation

Tables are provided for the conversion of raw scores to ability measures. No guidance is given in interpreting these.

General evaluation

An item bank with questions of clearly defined measurement characteristics, the operation of which gives unambiguous information about student performance and attainment, has obvious attractions. Conventional item analysis, which uses two measures to determine an item's characteristics, facility and discrimination, has been fairly convincingly shown to lead to possible inclusion of items that discriminate for the wrong reason—since they may reflect more than one source of variation in ability in the population and hence to be not characteristic of the actual ability under test. It has also been suggested that determining whether the discrimination of an item is appropriate to the ability under test or not is an extremely difficult if not impossible task (see Bryce, 1983). How this problem can be resolved has been a matter of considerable controversy, much of it centring on the use of a latent trait model of which the Rasch model used by the NFER in the construction of this item bank is one example.

To use the Rasch model a test designer assumes that underlying the performance of a student on a test is a single trait of ability on the items sampled by the test. Clearly this *is* an assumption, and testing its validity may result in the rejection of items because they do not 'fit' the model. In the period since the publication of this item bank and consequent to the suggestion that the Rasch model was an appropriate tool for the national monitoring of mathematics by the Assessment of Performance Unit, considerable concern has been expressed over this issue (Wright, 1977; Wood, 1978; Pollitt, 1979; Goldstein, 1979).

Practically this concern has been over the nature of the items 'rejected' by the model and in particular whether tests constructed in this way validly reflect the categories both of subject content and intellectual functioning that underlie the acquisition of knowledge by the individual. It is also not clear to what extent different teaching emphasis may influence the perceived difficulty of an item. At a more fundamental level the assumption that there exists a single underlying trait, in this case mathematical ability, has also been questioned. (An assumption that attainment tests measure 'something' surely underlies all attempts at their construction, but the precise definition of what that is is not made explicit in norm-referenced tests). Considerations prompted by a review of the controversy should be taken into account in any evaluation of the Secondary Mathematics Item Bank.

The sample of 186 items (reduced to 163 if rejected items are excluded) can hardly be said to cover extensively the whole range of mathematical objectives taught in the 2nd to 4th years of all secondary schools. The assumption that by using a selection of such items one can assess all pupils' mathematical ability on a common scale must at least be regarded as open to question. A preliminary survey of the feasibility of developing an item bank (Sumner, 1975) contributed nearly 600 items in the 10 subject categories used here. It is not clear how the particular selection of items in the bank were chosen. Evidence presented by Bryce (op. cit.) suggests that items may be rejected by the model because the topic is taught in different ways and that the questions do not discriminate 'as they should' because systematic differences in teaching methods alter the perceived difficulties of items for different groups of pupils.

Secondly, although one of the assumptions of the Rasch model is that items which 'fit' pose the same order of difficulty to all students it would seem appropriate to test this assumption rather rigorously. The calibration of the model was carried out using relatively small numbers of pupils classified only crudely by 'top half' and 'bottom half' of ability range. Thus it cannot be said that evidence presented about the operation of the item bank is anything more than indicative. To be an effective tool of measurement an item bank must be rigorous in its specification, comprehensive in its coverage and be shown to have operating characteristics which match the assumptions of the test designers.

Under these circumstances it is not surprising to find that there are no references to uses of the item bank reported. If the role of teaching method and other possible sources of variation in the discrimination of items can be disentangled from the 'ability' of pupils undertaking the test, an item bank would represent a very significant advance indeed in our capacity to assess and monitor pupils' performance. To be practically useful an evaluation must make comparison with other sources of test information on pupils in the age range.

One advantage of an item bank is in the freedom it gives teachers to construct tests which contain material directly related to that which has been taught. Even if the suggestion that the test represents ability on a single uniform scale of mathematics is not fully justified, it would appear that such a test could present diagnostic information that is generally unavailable from standardized tests. The availability of appropriate coverage could be improved by a substantially increased supply of questions. But any teacher faced with the choice of a norm-referenced test or a test based on this item bank would have to consider whether the detailed information on pupil performance available from a suitable selection of items outweighed in value the more general norm-referenced information provided by other tests. In the reviewer's opinion the present item bank offers some useful scope for experimental use, while it is to be hoped that the technical questions raised elsewhere will not deflect test developers from tackling the difficulties inherent in creating appropriate and objective measuring instruments.

References

Bryce, T. G. K. (1983). Rasch fitting. *British Journal of Educational Research* 7, 137–153.

Goldstein, H. (1979). Consequences of using the Rasch model for educational assessment. *British Educational Research Journal* 5, 211–220.

Pollitt, A. B. (1979). Item banking. *In* "Issues in Educational Assessment". SED Occasional Papers, London: HMSO.

Sumner, K. (1975). "Tests of Attainment in Mathematics in School: Monitoring Feasibility Study". Windsor, Berks: NFER.

Wood, R. (1978). Fitting the Rasch model—a heady tale. *British Journal of Mathematical and Statistical Psychology* **31**, 27–32.

Wright, B. D. (1977). Misunderstanding the Rasch model. *Journal of Educational Measurement* **14**, 219–225.

Senior Mathematics Test

Brief Report

Author: NFER 'with the help of teachers in the field of technical education'
Publisher: NFER-Nelson
Distributor: NFER-Nelson
Age range: 16:00–17:11
1963 (T)
1975 (S); 1976 (M)
1976 (M); 1979 (T) printings reviewed
Group test

The test 'was designed to assess the mathematical attainment level of general entry groups in Colleges of Further Education. It is intended for use in allocation to the various courses available, particularly in the more technical subjects' (Manual, p. 2). The 50 completion-type items include the basic computational skills, including some verbally stated arithmetic problems, and basic algebra and geometry. Time allowed is 45 minutes.

Standard scores (mean 100, standard deviation 15) are available with monthly age corrections for boys and are based upon a sample of 1340 engineering student entrants. A KR-20 of 0.95 is reported for a sample of 352 students. No validity studies are reported.

The Staffordshire Test of Computation

Reviewed by R. A. Davies

Authors: M. E. Hebron, W. Pattinson
Publisher: Harrap
Distributors: Harrap; The Test Agency

Age range: 7–14+ years
'1974 revision'; S not stated★
Group test

Test content

The test consists of two sheets. *Sheet 1* has 46 mechanical items involving the four rules applied to number and decimal money. The most difficult items are:

	Number	Money
Addition	3 digit numbers involving carrying	3 pence values totalling more than one pound
Subtraction	a three digit number from a three digit number	a two digit pence value from one pound
Multiplication	a three digit number times a single digit number	12 times a single digit pound and pence
Division	a three digit number divided by a single digit number	single digit pound and pence divided by 11

Sheet 2 has 46 items, two-thirds of them requiring the understanding of verbal instructions or descriptions. They involve the application of the four rules to number, money, metric measures of length, area and volume, and to time. There are items covering percentages and simple interest. Within 46 items the coverage is fairly limited.

Eyeball assessment by the reviewer suggests that the most difficult item requires the calculation of the weekly earnings of a machine operator given the number of parts produced per minute, the pay per 100 parts, the hours per day and days per week worked. Another item asks for the earnings of 3 men in 6 weeks if 2 men earned 56 pounds in 4 weeks. In both the items the basic information and the answers seemed unrealistic and to militate against pupils being encouraged to look at their answers critically and to question whether they seem reasonable. In a period of inflation items like these involving money need frequent revision.

One item seemed unclear. A given sum of money invested was worth a greater sum of money after 10 years. The testee was asked to calculate the annual rate of interest. The answer was based on simple interest. An able testee

★ First publication date not stated. Nature of revision not stated. Standardization took place in late February; year not stated.

might well assume that compound interest was required and perhaps leave the item unattempted.

Purpose

The authors claim that the test 'measures accuracy in computation, sampling comprehensively the skills acquired during the ages 7–15 years . . . It is useful in detecting specific weaknesses in the case of individual pupils and for establishing a pupil's status within his age group' (Manual, p. 1).

Because of its restricted length the extent to which the test can sample these skills or detect specific weaknesses is fairly severely limited. By implication the test is intended for pupils aged 7–15 years.

Item preparation

There is no information about this in the Manual.

Administration

The test is untimed. All testees are to be encouraged to attempt both sheets 'unless it is obvious that the second sheet is too difficult'. This sounds unsatisfactory. A testee could be incorrectly discouraged from attempting Sheet 2. It would be better to administer Sheet 1, mark the results and then decide who should not attempt Sheet 2.

Sheet 1 is to be answered on the test form; Sheet 2 on paper normally used by the testees.

Standardization

Means and standard deviations of test scores are given for 4079 children from 'two mixed urban/rural areas' in eight age-groupings 7+–14+. The year of standardization is not given but it is stated that the time chosen for the operation was late February, 'i.e. the middle of the school year'.

Scoring

The Manual contains straightforward instructions. Most items carry one mark; a few of the more difficult items carry two marks.

Reliability

Split-half reliabilities are quoted as 'ranging from 0.96 in the primary years to 0.97 at the age of 14 years'. No more details are given.

Validity

'A further approach tested validity by comparing the total score on the Staffordshire Test with those for Concepts and Skills on the Nottingham Number Test. At 9-and-a-half years the correlations were 0.86 for Concepts and 0.78 for Skills; at 10-and-a-half years they were 0.82 and 0.85 respectively'. Again, no details of the samples or dates are given.

Interpretation

One table gives means and standard deviations for each year of age from 7–14. There are no data for months within years. There is no means of determining an arithmetic age below 7+ or above 14+.

Another table is headed 'Conversion Table: Standard Scores according to age on September 1st': 'age' refers to whole years only. Under 'Purpose of Test' in the text it states 'The Standard Scores are geared to the same unit as the usual group test of intelligence, and can be used as an indication of whether a pupil is working at his true capacity'. Not everyone in the field of education would subscribe to the views underlying that statement.

General evaluation

The usefulness of the test will be affected by the limitations mentioned above in the section on Interpretation. The scope of Sheet 1 would enable it to be used only as a very crude diagnostic instrument. The total score on the test compounds mechanical and problem applications of computational skill which are more helpfully kept separate. In general, the Manual gives only limited information.

Transitional Assessment: Mathematics

Reviewed by Jack Wrigley

Author: not stated
Publisher: NFER-Nelson
Distributor: NFER-Nelson
Age range: Transition from primary to secondary school
1978; 1979 printings reviewed
Group test

Test content

The ten modules cover various areas of the general primary school mathematics curriculum but cannot be taken to be exhaustive. The areas chosen for the modules are: (1) Numbers, (2) Addition, (3) Subtraction, (4) Multiplication, (5) Division, (6) Properties of the four operations, (7) Shape, (8) Ratio, percentage, proportion, (9) Money, (10) Problems. Each module of 12 items is presented in a separate booklet varying in size from 2 to 6 pages.

Purpose

To assist transition from primary to secondary school by providing structured information obtained objectively on recognised and specified areas of the mathematics curriculum.

Item preparation

Full details are given in Sumner and Bradley (1977). Clearly a great effort has been made by the research team in consultation with others in various working parties to analyse the appropriate content and then to produce suitable items. Trials were carried out, in 1975, in the London Borough of Hillingdon involving three secondary schools and eight feeder junior schools ($n = 650$). A thorough item analysis was carried out and facility and discrimination indices are quoted for all items. The General Guide provided and the reference quoted make clear that the preparatory work was impressive.

Administration

There are no time limits for any of the modules and the atmosphere during testing should be the same as when the children are working on mathematics worksheets.

Standardization

The Administrative Manual says that 'No attempt was made to standardize the marks' (p. 6); but the General Guide gives a cumulative frequency curve (p. 12) from which percentile equivalents of total scores may be read off; and it also gives (pp. 16–20) score and stage distributions for each module. No doubt the authors would wish to de-emphasize the normative uses of the tests; they point out that the samples used during development of the modules are not claimed to be fully representative.

Scoring

Each of the 12 items within the 10 modules is given a score of 1 for a correct answer. The marking key makes procedure both simple and completely objective. Within each module it is suggested that the scores be presented as a profile (or vector) corresponding to three stages. Stage 1 (Basic) corresponds to the first four questions, Stage 2 (Intermediate) the next four, and Stage 3 (Advanced) to the final four items. Thus a pupil is allocated a score such as, for example, (4, 3, 2) or (4, 3, 1). More information is thus provided than when the total score itself is used. It is, however, immediately obvious that the part scores will be more unreliable than the total score and that there will be anomalies of the kind (2, 3, 4) were some pupils score more highly on the apparently more difficult sections. Both the Guide and the Manual report approximate data for the relative frequency of such anomalies. However, in the context of transition from school to school it may be that encouragement to the users to consider the scores in a way different from the conventional makes sense.

Reliability

The General Guide reports reliability coefficients ranging from 0.62–0.78 based upon the 1975 trials. For tests of only 12 items such values are to be expected. Again, the Administrative Manual de-emphasizes use of normative and other statistical characteristics. Indeed, it is somewhat vague about the results achieved with the earlier samples and cautious in claiming only that 'the 1977 results are fairly stable in relation to earlier results'.

Validity

None quoted.

Score interpretation

As can be seen from the method of scoring discussed above the score interpretation is somewhat novel. Maximum information is squeezed out of a limited test. Since this means some loss of reliability and since the validity of the test consists almost entirely of face validity it is necessary to proceed with caution in interpreting scores. The Guide claims that 'By looking at the child's stage allocation on different modules, information on his or her strengths and weaknesses can be obtained' (p. 8). This reviewer hopes that results derived from this kind of test would indeed be used continuously and that the information provided would be supplemented by more obvious results derived from the actual secondary school context.

General evaluation

These tests (together with similar ones in English) are a bold attempt to provide objective information of a kind which used to be summarized in various selection tests at 11 +. By testing basic, and therefore limited content, the tests can be used in varying school environments either at the end of the primary phase or the beginning of the secondary phase. Useful, but only if supplemented sensibly.

References

Sumner, R. and Bradley, K. (1977). "Assessment for Transition: A Study of New Procedures". Windsor, Berks: NFER.

Yardsticks: Criterion-referenced Tests in Mathematics

Reviewed by Jack Wrigley

Authors: adapted from USA tests by C. Milward and I. Fraser, with the assistance of A. Austin and P. Bruckland
Publisher: NFER-Nelson (by arrangement with Houghton Mifflin Company)
Distributor: NFER-Nelson
Age range: first six years of schooling
1975; 'reprinted with corrections' 1977, 1978, 1979, 1980
Group tests

Test content

The tests identify the stages of growth in mathematics for the first six years of schooling. The stages are enumerated in terms of behavioural objectives and for each objective there is a group of test questions. There are six different books each corresponding roughly to one year's work in mathematics. Taken as a whole, the tests cover all the main mathematical activity within the British Primary School.

Purpose

The tests are criterion referenced in mathematics and measure performance in relation to the skills mastered. They attempt to serve a role in the sequence: teach, test, evaluate, follow-up, and to measure mastery, i.e. total success in the ability to answer all questions correctly for each mathematics objective.

Item preparation

The British editions of the test are based on a scheme first published in 1973 in the USA. Programmes of teaching mathematics during the first six years of schooling were analysed and behavioural objectives written for the six levels. Question writers were drawn from schools, colleges and universities. Each item was checked for consistency and validity. In the UK the entire series was evaluated by a panel of British educationalists (names not stated) and practising teachers were involved from the outset. No details are given of actual trials or prestandardization.

Administration

The tests can be used by primary school teachers who are provided with the pupil booklet, a behavioural objectives index, a class record and a list of objectives at all levels. This information is included in six management guides corresponding to the six levels for the pupils' books. The management guides are excellent though there is a common element to all six guides.

Standardization

No details are given on standardization. The main effort appears to have been placed in item writing, behavioural objectives, etc. Mastery is assumed if pupils make only one error at any particular level but there is no apparent experimental evidence available.

Scoring

Simple recording of items answered correctly, one mark for each correct answer.

Reliability and validity

No details given. It is stated that 'each item was checked for consistency and validity in measuring its particular objective' and 'test questions were examined and reconstructed or rewritten where necessary to conform with UK courses and practises'. The user thus has to judge the face validity and content validity for himself relying on the thoroughness of the process described.

Interpretation

The scores are interpreted simply in terms of mastery at the various levels and can be used either for selecting objectives to use in a revision test or for identifying points of difficulty. It is generally necessary for pupils to understand throughly the work of the preceding objective before they can master the next one.

General evaluation

American tests revised for the British market should be used with caution. Great care appears to have been taken to make the content thoroughly British and little worry remains on this count. The tests have good breadth and are technically competent if it is admitted that criteria-referenced tests do not need elaborate empirical studies of reliability and validity. The tests appear up-to-date, easy to administer, and would help teachers analyse the weaknesses of their pupils. They should, however, be used with some caution since a too slavish adherence to the guidelines with regard to failure at any particular level could lead to a somewhat peculiar style of learning and teaching. More evidence is required with regard to the publisher's statement that one failure per test is acceptable. Used with care the tests could help a teacher or an LEA pinpoint individual weaknesses and difficulties. Used with lack of discretion a pupil might be stuck for an unduly long time at a particular level of learning.

'Y' Mathematics Series

Review (1) by B. L. M. Chapman

Author: D. Young
Publisher: Hodder & Stoughton
Distributor: Hodder & Stoughton
Age ranges: 7:05– 8:10 (Y1: Forms A and B)
                8:05– 9:10 (Y2: Forms A and B)
                9:05–10:10 (Y3)
               10:05–11:10 (Y4)
                8:05–14:10 (Y2X, poor readers and slow learners).
1979 (M, T); S not stated
Group tests

Test content

This series comprises a set of four tests covering the years of junior education from age 7:05–11:10. Each of the adjacent pairs of tests overlap by six months allowing for the possibility of testing some pupils on either of two tests. In addition Y2 has been specially standardized for poor readers to span the age range 8:05–14:10.

Tests Y1 and Y2 are divided into three distinct sections, the first of which is orally administered and involves testing concepts and skills commonly taught in the British primary curriculum such as number, spatial judgement, time, class inclusion and linear measure. This section studiously avoids technical terminology found in some mathematics schemes but in one item in each test it uses English incorrectly and in two other items uses a very obscure form of words. Such lapses are, however, far from typical. The second section involves computation in a variety of forms, and the third section sets computational problems in the form of short sentences. Both of these latter two sections are read by the pupil. Written responses are required in all three sections. Both tests Y1 and Y2 are available in two parallel forms, A and B.

Tests Y3 and Y4 have only one form each and neither has any oral section. Each is divided into a computation section of 20 items and a problem section of 30 items. The problems draw on a wide selection of source information involving diagrams, graphs and situational statements but all entail a calculation and a numerical outcome.

In the main the layout and presentation of items is clear to the point of being exemplary but in tests Y3 and Y4 some unfortunate indenting of item numbers mars the effect in the problem section making some items difficult to find. This is done to ensure that all responses are written by the pupil in the right hand margin for easy scoring but this could perhaps have been accomplished even with a different layout.

Purpose

The preamble to the Manuals makes clear that this series of tests is designed to assess attainment of children in junior school classes. 'The testing of number and accuracy in computation has been a prime consideration. Children's failures to reach numerically correct answers even when they understand principles is surely one of the causes of their rejection of mathematics' (e.g. Manual for Y1, p. 3). Although the items are largely free from material which relates to a particular curriculum the Y1 and Y2 oral tests contain a few items which employ metric measure and would, therefore, be restricted mainly to Britain among the English-speaking cultures.

In the case of Y2, because its oral and computation sections cater for children of low reading ability, it has been standardized for use with backward children in secondary schools up to age 14:10. For this application a special standardization table is provided which is to be used with the total score from the oral and computation sections only.

Item preparation

'All the items have passed through at least two analyses to establish discriminating power and facility levels' (e.g. Manual for Y2, p. 21). We are not told any detail about item selection or screening but that the 'Y' tests are based on a 'succession of earlier versions' about which teachers' comments have been received and incorporated. Within the present series 50 papers were received for each form of the test over each of the ability levels and these returns were drawn from 77 schools in all. 'The analyses enabled the items to be distributed between the two forms so that any minor inequalities between the pairs at one level of difficulty were counter-balanced in the allocation of the next pair. The equivalence of the two forms was confirmed by testing 99 pupils first by A then by B, and a further 96 pupils by B and A in turn. Comparison of the cumulative percentage frequencies of the A and B scores showed differences of less than one point over the range effectively covered by the samples' (e.g. Manual for Y1, p. 18).

Such close agreement is hardly surprising considering the nature of the parallel forms. In most cases the two forms differ only with respect to the numbers or letters relating to an item so that at first glance, although they are of different colour, they appear to contain the same information. This applies both to the oral section, where the material is largely pictorial, and to the numerical section where different numbers have been applied to the same pattern of operators and layout. The problem sections of these forms are most different from one another because the problems relate to different contexts and may, therefore, be more or less plausible or familiar to the child's own experience.

Administration

The tests are administered as group tests requiring a Manual for the teacher and one expendable test form for each pupil. It is recommended that children sitting next to one another should have different forms of the test, where it exists, but to do this will largely preempt the use of the alternate form for retest purposes without a great deal of care in seating and form distribution.

All the tests are timed and in the case of Y1 and Y2 will be expected to take the time of the oral section plus 25 minutes. This may be as much as 50 minutes. In the case of Y3 and Y4 the time allowed is 30 minutes. In all tests children make their responses on the test form.

Administrative instructions are clear and in a form which enables them to be consulted during the running of the test. Questions for the oral section are clearly set out to be read directly to the pupil, every instruction being repeated twice. The tester is advised that seven seconds should be left between the end of one oral question and the beginning of the next but no indication of reading pace is given.

Scoring

Scoring requires the tester to mark each of four pages and then to total the correct responses. The correct answers are reasonably set out by pages and item numbers in the Manuals but no form of scoring mask is provided, so that scoring is an extremely laborious process. Although the oral sections of Y1 and Y2 involve many questions in which the child must identify a component of the picture, this is done by writing a response code at the margin which may create, for some children, a significant difficulty in performing the task.

Raw scores are converted to standardized scores (or 'quotients' as the Manual calls them) by a table which uses raw score and age as entry points but not sex. There is only one table for both forms of Tests Y1 and Y2.

Standardization

Each of the four tests in the 'Y' series was standardized in a group of 12 schools known to the author to be representative of the national pattern of general ability because of their record on NFER and Moray House tests. Which NFER tests is not stated nor are the geographical locations of the schools but it is encouraging to know that a fair number of schools were involved and that the author was at some pains to ensure the representative character of them. The standardization was based on responses from well over a thousand pupils for each of the four tests divided almost equally into boys and girls.

In the case of Y2, a second standardization took place which called for a sample at secondary level. This was formed of well over a thousand pupils split equally between the two sexes and drawn from six schools. As a cross check on this exercise 140 pupils were tested first on the Y3 and then 8 months later on the Y4 and Y2. The median quotients on these three tests were 108, 106 and 108 (X) respectively where (X) refers to the Y2 test without the problem section. These results were used to construct conversion tables yielding a 'quotient' with a mean of 100 and a standard deviation of 15. Although the samples were balanced by sex there is no indication as to whether separate standardizations were attempted prior to the compilation of the mixed sex tables which are printed. Nor is there any indication of the date of the standardization.

Reliability

In the cases of Y1 and Y2 the reliability of the tests was evaluated by testing pupils on one of the two alternate forms and then retesting them two or three weeks later on the other form. For each test approximately 200 pupils were used, divided into six groups by age and the reliability coefficients quoted all lie within the range of 0.88–0.96. For the Y3 and Y4 which have no alternate form reliability is estimated by KR-20 using approximately 650 papers on each test. It is not stated whether these were divided by age group but the reliability coefficients are reported as 0.96 and 0.97 respectively.

Based upon these reliability coefficients the standard error of measurement is given for each test as 2.5, 2.8, 2.2 and 2.1 respectively in terms of the raw score. The somewhat lower figures in the case of Y3 and Y4 undoubtedly arise from the use of KR-20 as opposed to test-retest. The test then interprets these standard errors in terms of the likely misplacement of one pupil in 20.

Validity

Although the tests in the series of four overlap, a correlation is reported for only one pair of tests taken by children in an overlapping age group. This is a pity because such comparisons would shed additional light on the validity of the test as one of problem-solving skill with the emphasis on computation.

For each of the four tests a sample of pupils (109 for Y1, 152 for Y2 and unstated for Y3 and Y4) was given the relevant 'Y' series test and then the Graded Arithmetic-Mathematics Test (GA-MT) (Vernon, P. E. and Miller, K. M., Hodder & Stoughton, 1977). In each case the median score on the GA-MT was elevated by about three points which the author attributes to practice effects. The correlations in the four cases were 0.87, 0.88, 0.88 and 0.94. This implies, for a value of 0.88, that 23 per cent of the variance is not accounted for by the other test and that for pupils taking one of these tests the standard error of prediction is slightly less than half the standard deviation. Thus for a pupil taking the GA-MT prior to the Y1 the standard error of his score on the Y1 as predicted by the GA-MT would be 5.3 points of raw score as against 11.1 points knowing only his age. For the GA-MT and the Y4 the equivalent prediction would entail a standard error of 3.9 points compared with a standard deviation of 11.4.

These test comparisons are really quite favourable in terms of inter-test correlations in general. The force of the result is that, recognising the screening processes which operate within a school system to remove from opportunist samples the very bright and the very backward children, then formal testing offers very little more in terms of measures which are stable and transferable.

Further comparisons have been made between the Y2 (X) scores and the SPAR reading and spelling tests, the Oral Verbal Intelligence Test and the NFER Non-Verbal Test DH. These comparisons were made with 130 pupils aged 11:06 with a reading age less than 9:05 and 131 pupils aged 14:02. The highest correlations quoted is 0.63 for the older age group between Y2 (X) and the NFER Non-Verbal Test DH. In terms of predictive validity these figures are extremely low and it is difficult to see what this information adds to our knowledge of the test series beyond the fact that it responds in the expected way to a factor of general intelligence.

A very important detail which is missing from all of the above comparisons is any statement of whether the correlations described above were carried out upon raw scores or age corrected standardized scores. The implication of the text is that standardized scores were used but if this is not the case then the correlations will be inflated by a common maturational factor and the predictive validity of the test then becomes rather poor.

Interpretation

The Manuals offer some guidance to teachers in relation to the comparison of scores with their own judgements and expectations, and particularly mentions the problem of the reading difficulties that may arise for some of the questions.

General evaluation

In terms of the avowed aims of the test series this has all the indications of being very carefully and thoroughly compiled. The opening comments in the test Manual about interest in mathematics being related to the ability to yield a correct numerical result has more than a ring of truth but the test user must question whether the availability of a published test based upon this precept is the best way to further the cause. The test is narrow and as shown by comparison with the GA–MT its predictive validity is no higher than can be expected from the general nature of achievement testing.

Like so many tests of this kind, although the author is at pains to spell out the cautionary message of the standard error, the mechanism of deriving standard scores gives an impression of accuracy which is unwarranted. In terms of emphasizing this message to teachers it might be better to standardize in terms of centile groups only or to include conversion graphs rather than tables, showing the margin of standard error. These should be drawn to such a scale that conversion of unwarranted accuracy is impossible.

'Y' Mathematics Series

Review (2) by P. Coxhead

Author: D. Young
Publisher: Hodder & Stoughton
Distributor: Hodder & Stoughton
Age ranges: 7:05– 8:10 (Y1: Forms A and B)
                8:05– 9:10 (Y2: Forms A and B)
                9:05–10:10 (Y3)
               10:05–11:10 (Y4)
                8:05–14:10 (Y2X, poor readers and slow learners).
1979 (M, T); S not stated
Group tests

Test content

'The Y Mathematics Series includes questions on number, measuring (using a ruler), clocks, timetables, the calendar, symmetry, area, factors and prime numbers, fractions, decimals, money, squares and square roots, volume, proportion, percentages, graphs and maps' (all Manuals, various pages). Tests Y1 (Forms A and B) and Y2 (Forms A and B) consist of three sections: Oral, Computation and Written. In the Oral Section, the administrator reads the 20 questions, for which necessary diagrammatic or other information is provided in the pupil test booklet, and the pupil writes down the appropriate answer. The Computation and Written Sections consist of completion-type items, the former having 20 items presented non-verbally, and the latter 15 items presented verbally. In Tests Y3 and Y4 the Oral Section is omitted and there are 20 Computation items and 30 Written items.

The Computation sections consist of use of the four arithmetic operations in problems stated entirely in number-symbolic form. The Written sections consist of verbally stated arithmetic problems, often about money and time.

Purpose

The 'Y' Mathematics Series tests are 'designed to give a firm basis to consecutive assessment as pupils progress through the Junior School'. The mode of presentation is particularly designed to help to 'ensure that the assessment of mathematical ability is not distorted by poor reading ability'. The tests are not intended to be either criterion referenced or diagnostic but rather to 'sample a wide variety of skills and topics'.

Item preparation

The Manuals note that the 'Y tests are based on a succession of earlier versions, so that teachers' comments have helped to determine the present content' (Manual, p. 3). The Manual for Y3 and Y4 states that the 'questions are derived from "banks" formed from material used in a series of tests provided for use in schools over a period of ten years'. Some general criteria for the choice of item content are given in the Manuals but there is very little on which to base an evaluation of the adequacy of the content in relation to the curriculum, for example. Similarly, it is difficult to judge the quality of the processes through which the final versions emerged, other than to note that for all tests, items 'have passed through at least two analyses to establish discriminating power and facility levels'.

Administration

The three Manuals accompanying the tests (Y1, Y2, Y3 and Y4) are each termed a 'Manual of Instructions' and, true to this title, there are very clear directions as to the administration of the tests. Pupils answer directly onto the pupil test booklet in pencil. The tests are timed and should fit within a single class period. A special feature of the administration is the Oral Section in tests Y1 and Y2.

The target ages for normal mixed-ability classes are given at the head of this review; the labels Y1 to Y4 correspond to 1st to 4th years of junior school. Y2 can also be used with backward pupils from 10:05–14:10 and in particular by omitting the Written Section can be used with pupils of poor reading ability.

Standardization

For all the tests, the standardizations are 'based on the scores of pupils in a group of twelve schools known, collectively, to be representative of the national pattern of general ability and achievement because of their records on NFER and Moray House tests' (e.g. Y1 Manual, p. 19). Further, it is claimed that 'relatively small samples may warrant confidence in the norms if they have been calibrated by means of nationally standardized tests'. Close to 1200 pupils were used in the standardization of each test; presumably there were about 600 for each form of Y1 and Y2 although this is not made clear.

This standardization procedure can be severely criticised. Even supposing that 12 schools can be representative in both central tendency and dispersion of the national pattern on certain tests of general ability and achievement, this provides weak grounds for belief that these schools are necessarily representative with regard to a specific set of tests of mathematics ability.

The standardization is used to construct 'Quotients', age-related standard scores with (presumably) mean 100, standard deviation 15. There are no separate sex norms. For test Y2, separate norms are given for scores omitting the Written Section so that the test may be used with pupils of poor reading ability.

Considerable stress is placed on the consistency of median standard scores obtainable by repeated testing of the same group of pupils over a period of time with different tests in the series. For example, for a group of 152 8 year-olds, use of tests Y1 and Y2 with an 8-month interval between gave median standard scores of 104 and 102 respectively.

Scoring

Correct answers are provided for all tests. Generally only one answer is regarded as acceptable but, where appropriate, alternatives are clearly indicated. The tables for conversion of raw scores to 'Quotients' are clear and space is allowed on the answer booklet for totals and quotients.

Reliability

For tests Y1 and Y2, reliability was established by administering the parallel Forms A and B, at 2 to 3 week intervals. Six separate groups of pupils were used for each test. For Y1, parallel form reliabilities ranged from 0.90–0.96 (average $n = 33$); for Y2, the values ranged from 0.88–0.93. For tests Y3 and Y4, internal consistency reliabilities were obtained (KR-20) on single samples, giving coefficients of 0.96 ($n = 637$) and 0.97 ($n = 657$) respectively.

Validity

For all four tests, concurrent validity is considered via correlations with the Vernon-Miller Graded Arithmetic-Mathematics Test. The correlations are given as: Y1, 0.87 ($n = 109$); Y2, 0.88 ($n = 152$); Y3, 0.88 (n unstated); Y4, 0.94 (n unstated). The Manuals note that another approach to validity is for the user to examine the content of the tests. However, it is argued that the specific content is not of great concern since 'the general factor that runs through the test items would almost certainly be found in other possible inclusions'. No factor-analysis evidence is presented for this assertion.

Test Y2 can be used in a shorter form excluding the Written Section to control for poor reading ability in pupils. Evidence of discriminant validity is provided for this version, e.g. for 13 pupils aged 14:02 the correlation with the author's SPAR reading score was 0.24 whereas for the NFER Non-Verbal Test DH the correlation was 0.63.

Interpretation

The major purpose of the 'Y' Mathematics Series is to produce individual age-standardized assessments. The Manuals explain clearly how to achieve this although more prominence should be given to the standard error of measurement of the assessment. Little guidance is given as to the further use of the age-standardized scores, once obtained, other than to compare with quotients for attainments in other fields, when it is suggested that a discrepancy of 10 points or more is 'interesting (and worrying)'. A limited amount of information can be obtained by comparing scores in the different sections of the test and the Manuals do provide some guidance in this area. Compared to the detailed instructions for administration, the advice on interpretation is very limited.

General evaluation

The complete series of tests is designed to produce age-standardized mathematics quotients, with each test so standardized that closely comparable results are obtained whichever is used (provided the level is appropriate). The comparability between tests appears to have been achieved at the expense of true nationally-representative norming so that some doubt must exist as to how accurate the standardization is relative to the target population. Otherwise the tests appear simple and straightforward to use and the Y2 test in particular has some attractive features when reading skill might be a problem. The user must also be willing to accept a rather offhand attitude to content validity.

Composite attainments

List of reviews

Basic Skills Assessment Program   435
Bristol Achievement Tests: 437
   English   437
   Mathematics   442
   Study Skills   445
   General Evaluation of the Bristol Achievement Tests   448
Richmond Tests of Basic Skills   449
SRA Reading and Arithmetic Indexes   455

See also:

Applied Knowledge Test★   612
Peabody Individual Achievement Test★   80

★ Brief report only.

Basic Skills Assessment Program

Reviewed by Ian Plewis

Authors: Educational Testing Service (ETS), Princeton, NJ, USA
Publisher: Addison Wesley
Distributor: Addison Wesley
Age range: 13–18 years; USA Grades 7–12
1977★
Group test

Test content

There are three sets of multiple-choice items: 'Reading' (65 items), 'A Writer's Skills' (75 items) and 'Mathematics' (70 items). There are four choices for each item. In addition, there is a separate, direct measure of student writing—'The Writing Sample'. The Reading items are essentially measuring comprehension of written passages although there are items which use maps, charts, time-tables, loan agreements, tax forms and cartoons. The writing items cover spelling, punctuation, word use and word substitution. The Mathematics items deals with basic operations, simple equations, measurement, charts and simple interest. The Writing Sample consists of four items: writing a job application letter, completing a form, conveying information or directions, writing creatively.

Purpose

'To establish minimum competencies in reading, writing and mathematics'. 'Measures academic and life skills needed for functioning in modern society'. 'Used for early warning system to alert teachers to students' deficiencies'.

Item preparation

The assessment was developed by ETS with 4000 school districts over a 2-year period and drew on the experience of the National Assessment of Educational Progress and other federal and state projects.

★ A specimen set only is reviewed here.

Administration

The assessment is suitable for all secondary school pupils. Each multiple-choice test requires about 45 minutes but all students should be given enough time to finish. Each pupil needs a pencil and rubber, and answers are marked on a separate, computer-read sheet. The marks on the answer sheet have to be made in a particular way.

Standardization

'The national norming sample involved 7700 students drawn from 203 schools in 53 districts'. No details about sample design are given nor is there any information about how norms were calculated.

Scoring

No instructions about scoring are provided. Scoring is carried out centrally at ETS and various measures are sent back to the schools. Local scoring is possible for The Writing Sample but instructions are not in the Manual.

Reliability

No information is given.

Validity

No information is given.

Interpretation

No information is given.

General evaluation

The assessment is designed for USA pupils and would need *substantial* revision before it could be considered suitable for use in this country. Detailed instructions for administration are provided but otherwise so little information is provided about the tests in the specimen set available for review that an overall assessment cannot be offered.

Bristol Achievement Tests

English: *Reviewed by* Desmond L. Nuttall

Mathematics: *Reviewed by* John K. Backhouse

Study Skills: *Reviewed by* R. J. Riding

General evaluation: *By* Desmond L. Nuttall

Authors: Alan Brimer and Herbert Gross
Publisher: NFER-Nelson
Distributors: NFER-Nelson; Educational Evaluation Enterprises
Age ranges: *

Level	S Group	Tables	Schooling
1	8:09– 9:08	8:00– 9:11	3+
2	9:09–10:08	9:00–10:11	4+
3	10:09–11:08	10:00–11:11	5+
4	11:09–12:08	11:00–12:11	6+
5	12:09–13:08	12:00–13:11	7+

1969 (Administrative Manual, Interpretative Manual, Tests); S not stated
1982 (Admin. M, T) (revised)
Group tests

Bristol Achievement Tests: English

Test content

For each level there are two parallel forms of the test, A and B. 'The skills represented in the English Language Tests have been chosen for their critical function in comprehension, composition and expression. Part 1 measures the understanding of words in context. Part 2 measures active reading comprehension of continuous prose. Part 3 measures sentence construction and organiza-

---

* The ages given under 'S Group' show for each Level the age-range represented in the standardization group. Those given under 'Tables' show the ranges accommodated by the conversion tables. 'Schooling' refers to years of education; for example, '3+' means 'at least 3 but not more than 4 years of schooling'.

tion. Part 4 measures composition and flexibility of ideas. Part 5 measures punctuation and spelling' (Administrative Manual, p. 1).

Across the levels, the numbers of items in Parts 3 and 4 slowly increase while the numbers of items in Parts 1 and 2 decrease. A few items are common to adjacent levels. Responses are given in a variety of ways, by underlining, by deleting words and, in the majority of cases, by writing words (or punctuation marks) into the booklet.

Purpose

Little is said in the Manuals about the purpose of the tests. They 'produce balanced measures of basic skills and concepts in school achievement' (Administrative Manual, p. 1); a careful reading of the Interpretative Manual discloses possible uses in curriculum evaluation and diagnosis, for the latter, though, only to the extent 'that a case for further study has been made out and that an appropriate diagnostic test might reveal where teaching could be more profitably placed' (Interpretative Manual, p. 13).

Item preparation

'The theoretical basis for the sampling of achievement was the product of an investigation of the psychological, pedagogical and curriculum literature. The particular form in which the subtests express their probing of a subject area is largely a function of the general editor's personal selection in consultation with the contributors' (Interpretative Manual, p. 21). The principles underlying each subtest are given in sufficient detail to allow other items to be written, and the early trials (of nearly 1300 items) checked not only the conventional item statistics but also the expected progression of easiness with age.

Administration

The tests are designed to be administered by teachers and the instructions for administration and the 'script' itself are crisp. Little is said about establishing rapport or encouraging children to do their best. Each of the five parts is separately timed, but accuracy of timing is not stressed as much as might be expected given an average of only 10 minutes per part.

The age bands for each level overlap, but careful instructions are given to ensure that the appropriate test, defined by 'length of schooling', is administered. What is not made clear in the Administrative Manual (and not very clear in the Interpretative Manual) is that Form A should *always* be given before Form B, whose norms reflect a practice effect on Form A.

Standardization

The standardization procedure is inadequately described. The year is not mentioned (probably 1968), nor is the month (probably May), nor the number of schools. The sample was a national one and employed schools of various types; the samples of children in each type were weighted to conform to the 1966 national distribution. There were between 1072 and 1265 children in the standardization sample who took all tests at any one level, roughly evenly split between the sexes except at Level 3 where there were nearly twice as many boys as girls. As the norms are given for the sexes combined but the Interpretative Manual reveals significant sex differences at Level 3, this deficiency of girls is rather serious.

Lawley's age standardization method was used (see Introduction) and the scores extrapolated at either end (for example at Level 1 the actual age range in the standardization sample was from 8:09–9:08 but norms are provided from 8:00–9:11). The main norm tables provide standardized scores with a mean of 100 and a standard deviation of 15 for two-month intervals. Deciles (without age allowance) are provided for the part scores.

The regression coefficients of raw score upon age are reported. Curiously, at Level 5 for English, no age adjustment is made for Form B on the stated grounds that the age regression was 'not significant'. An adjustment though is made for Form A. Yet, based on the same sample, the regression coefficient is 0.04 for Form B and only 0.02 for Form A.

Scoring

Marking English Language tests can rarely avoid subjectivity and the Bristol tests constitute no exception, though every effort has been made to minimize the exercise of subjective judgement and clarify where spelling is or is not at issue. Few teachers would be in any doubt on most of the items, but it is unfortunate that a misprint in the Level 3 Administrative Manual (revised edition) has made a nonsense of the instructions for ten of the most difficult questions to mark, though for another ten questions the revised instructions are much clearer. The revised edition has abolished the old separate scoring keys that were admittedly somewhat cumbersome, and simply prints the marking instructions in the Administrative Manual which could give rise to some transfer problems.

Clearly labelled boxes for scores are provided at the foot of each page and at the end of each part, and the front page provides a panel just below the personal details of the child (including the all important age) for the part raw scores and deciles, and the total score, standardized score and percentile equivalent. The separate profile sheet to which these results may then be transferred is discussed below.

Reliability

The Manuals are commendably open about the existence of error in measurement and the profile sheet encourages the use of score-bands four standard errors of measurement wide. (The Interpretative Manual also explains the gains and losses that might accrue if the band was only two standard errors wide and proceeds to give incomprehensible advice about how to create such smaller bands if the user wishes). The alternate-form reliability coefficients (two-week interval) vary between 0.93 and 0.95 for the total scores. Across the five levels, the median coefficients for each of the five component parts are 0.84, 0.86, 0.85, 0.65 and 0.79.

Validity

In an Interpretative Manual, 84 pages long and packed with good advice and much information, it is disappointing to find less than 250 words on the subject of validity. Quite appropriately with achievement tests, the Manual relies principally upon content validity (called rational validity) and refers to the rationale of curriculum sampling and test construction. This rationale plus careful analysis of the tests themselves would enable teachers to satisfy themselves about how well the test content reflected the aims and objectives of their own courses.

The Manual mentions data such as the inter-correlations of the tests and subtests and the score-on-age regression coefficients that appear in an Appendix but offers no interpretation, stating baldly that they 'represent positive and necessary support for the validity of the tests' (Interpretative Manual, p. 28). It continues: 'More is needed in the form of correlations with external criteria which can only be obtained later. It was judged better not to delay publication and it is intended that such data will be added to the Manual as it becomes available'. Thirteen years later a revised edition was published but no such data were added.

Interpretation

The Interpretative Manual gives a very full account of different kinds of scores and of unreliability, and provides much guidance about comparison of individuals and groups with the national norms. With a little care and experience (and with the help of the worked example in the Interpretative Manual) the profile sheet can be readily completed if one is prepared to tolerate rounding percentiles to the nearest ten and reliability coefficients to the nearest 0.05 (and if one is not, the Manual instructs one how to do things exactly). The final chart, with error bands clearly shown, is not likely to tempt the user into reading too much into the profile.

One feature of the procedure is not, however, explained fully enough. The profile sheet also provides a table giving decile scores expected on the basis of level of reading skill (i.e. the Part 1 score). The Interpretative Manual implies that this gives useful diagnostic information, especially when a score falls below the expected value. It makes no comment upon the equal number of cases when a score falls above the expected value (over-achievers always compensate for under-achievers). Moreover, while the concept of the standard error of estimate is briefly explained, it would appear that no warning is made about the compounding of errors of estimate with errors of measurement. There are also some discrepancies between the correlations reported in Table L and the supposedly identical ones in Table 3 of the profile sheet.

General evaluation

As the Interpretative Manual has so little to say about validity, the potential user must inspect the tests themselves very carefully and make up his or her own mind about the extent to which the items and subtests reflect the balance of content, aims, objectives and skills fostered in his or her English language curriculum or in language across the curriculum. The user should note that the balance within the tests changes only slightly over levels, whereas one might expect dramatic changes in curricular emphasis and development over the years 8–14.

My own opinion is that, while these tests are more varied and imaginative than many, and gain by not adopting the multiple-choice format that makes much language testing so artificial, their approach is now somewhat dated, not fully reflecting the developments in language teaching and testing, post-Bullock and post-APU. Tests of reference skills and comprehension questions on a passage to analyse character and motives, as well as the author's tone and intentions, are all missing.

There is also evidence of insensitivity to language in some of the items that shakes one's faith in the tests' rationale. For example, 'pounce' in the sentence 'he pounced on the bird' does *not* mean the same as 'sprang' in the sentence 'he sprang across the stream', nor 'reward' the same as 'recompense' except in the curious sentence 'The ministry offered to recompense him for his achievements'.

More general issues, such as the validity and interpretation of the profile, are considered in the evaluation of the whole Bristol Achievement Tests battery.

Bristol Achievement Tests: Mathematics*

Test content

'The Mathematics Tests include those skills which are emphasized in most modern curriculum development programmes. Part 1 examines the understanding of number from the stage of conservation to the level of binary and directional number. Part 2 is concerned with sets and series, and with inductive and deductive reasoning. Part 3 examines spatial discrimination and judgement, and overlaps to some extent with Part 4 which is primarily concerned with measurement and measuring units. Part 5 concedes the need to examine knowledge of conventions and arithmetic laws and processes, but avoids becoming tied to computational accuracy' (Manual, p. 2).

The numbers of items devoted to the five Parts in the five Levels are as follows:

	Part 1	Part 2	Part 3	Part 4	Part 5
Level 1	25	25	15	15	15
Level 2	20	25	15	20	20
Level 3	20	30	15	25	10
Level 4	20	20	30	15	15
Level 5	25	25	20	15	15

Purpose

'The Bristol Achievement Tests have been constructed together and matched to produce balanced measures of basic skills and concepts in school achievement' (Manual, p. 2).

Item preparation

No information is given on item preparation (in the Administrative Manual).

Administration

The Manual emphasizes the importance of mental and physical well-being of the children to be tested by including a special section Conditions for Testing

---

* This review is based only upon the Administrative Manuals and test forms. The Interpretative Manual was not supplied to this reviewer. Separate Administrative Manuals are available for each of the five levels. Their contents are so similar, making changes appropriate to each level, that the tests are reviewed together. It may be assumed that comments apply to all Levels unless explicitly stated otherwise.

in the Manual. This section points out that time control is an essential aspect of the test performance, particularly for the profile of part scores.

The section on the administration of the test gives instructions about reading aloud from the front page of the test. It also gives the times for each part, together with instructions to be given to the children at the end of each testing period.

Standardization

'These (standardized) scores use the achievements of a very large sample of children drawn from schools in England and Wales as a standard . . .' (Manual, p. 2). No further particulars about the sample are given.

Scoring

There are carefully designed scoring keys for each form at each level. They may appear rather complicated but the Manual recommends that one double page should be taken at a time and that all scripts should be marked on those pages. If this is done, the user should not find the keys difficult to use. There appears to be no check built in against answers being missed by the marker since it is recommended that for both incorrect and missing answers the scoring ring is left blank.

Reliability

The reported reliability coefficients are based on parallel forms administered to a number of children within a two-week period. This form of reliability coefficient may be expected to include more sources of error than others and the reader should bear this in mind in making comparisons with other tests. Data are given at each Level for the whole test and for each Part. Samples of over 1000 at each Level were used. Reliability coefficients and standard errors of measurement (s.e.m. below) for the whole test and for the Parts ranged over the following intervals:

	Reliabilities	s.e.m.
Part 1	0.77–0.85	5.8–7.2
Part 2	0.71–0.89	5.0–8.1
Part 3	0.78–0.86	5.7–7.0
Part 4	0.63–0.88	5.2–9.4
Part 5	0.77–0.88	5.4–7.3
Test	0.92–0.94	3.7–4.2

Validity

No mention is made of validity in the Administrative Manual.

Interpretation

A section in the Manual is devoted to the standard error of measurement. The values reported above refer to standardized score equivalents of the Tests and Parts. The examples given in the Manual use confidence levels of twice the standard error and an example on one Part points out that fine discrimination between Part scores is not justified.

The Manual was accompanied by an example of a 'profile sheet'. The intention is that such a sheet should be completed for each pupil tested on the Bristol Achievement Tests. There are spaces for recording results from the English, Mathematics and Study Skills tests and the five Parts of each. The standardized scores, percentile scores and decile scores are first transferred to the sheet from the front pages of the test booklets. A table enables the user to find error limits for each Part. (There is a system of Code Numbers which are reliability coefficients rounded to the nearest 5 in the second decimal place). Then another table allows the user to find the decile score expected for the child on the basis of level of reading skill. Having found all these values, the user is invited to fold back the edge of the card, marking in the obtained scores and its error limits in black and the expected scores in red on the appropriate scale.

The reviewer found that he had to read the instructions very carefully and even so he did not find an indication of how to find the error limits for the decile score on the complete test from the tables on the card. This could have been done and it appears to be an oversight. However, there is a reference back to the Manual on how to calculate exact error limits. Another omission appears to be some guidance on the interpretation of scores expected on the basis of level of reading skill.

General evaluation

The Bristol Achievement Tests in Mathematics have the advantage of a uniform presentation and similar subscales for the five Levels. The Profile Sheet offers the user a more sophisticated service than the other mathematics tests reviewed by the writer. This would be more helpful to the class teacher, or others who have responsibility for supervising a pupil's overall progress, than to the mathematics subject teacher.

It is regretted that there is no account of the way in which the content of the tests was chosen. The tests are expected to measure mathematics achievement but parts of them are highly verbal and might well be measuring verbal reasoning. Other parts may be better measures of spatial ability than of mathematics. The test constructor may have good reasons for these inclusions (or he may be measuring mathematical ability rather than mathematical achievement) but the reviewer found that his mathematical colleagues shared his doubts. It is also questionable whether arithmetic in number bases other than ten should be so prominent. It was noticeable, too, that certain types of item were replicated several times in a test. This replication may be expected to increase the test-retest (or parallel forms) reliability of the scales. However, the content validity of the test may be expected to be lower because content will be less effectively covered.

Since the test constructor has provided five subscales, it is unfortunate that no consideration is given to their validity.

The test constructor was clearly aware of the variety of mathematics courses being followed when the tests were constructed. The course a school is following may be expected to affect the test results. It might, therefore, have been desirable to know more about the course content of the schools in the standardizing sample. Also with changing courses, the date of standardization is desirable—one can only conjecture 1968 or earlier. The reviewer recommends users to examine the content of these tests very carefully before ordering: they cannot be expected to satisfy teachers on all the mathematics courses currently being taught.

It appears that an unfamiliar notation is used for recurring decimals: the value of 3×0.66 is taken to be 2, and the digit in the third decimal place of 5.33 is given as 3.

Bristol Achievement Tests: Study Skills*

Test content

On each Level there are two parallel forms of the test, A and B. Each test booklet consists of five parts with 15 items in each. The content of the items is mostly elementary science (e.g. levers, temperature, properties of materials, plants, animals), maps (usually with contours), geometry (area, volume and shape) and graphs. A variety of responses is required to items: multiple choice, ordering, supplying information to fill in blanks and marking diagrams.

'Part 1 sets out to reveal the children's awareness of the properties of materials and situations . . . Part 2 examines judgements of structures in which there is an interdependence of parts. Part 3 measures the children's ability to

---

* This review is based only upon the Administrative Manuals and test forms for Levels 4 and 5. The Interpretative Manual was not supplied to this reviewer.

deal with processes and sequences in which a concept of serial, ordinal or physical arrangement enables extrapolation and interpolation to be carried out. Part 4 focuses on explanations and on the level of concept-making through which explanation is generalized. Part 5 is concerned with the interpretation of symbolically and graphically presented data and their relationship to observations' (Manual, p. 2).

Purpose

'The Bristol Achievement Tests have been constructed together and matched to produce balanced measures of basic skills and concepts in school achievement. The Study Skills Tests, like those of English Language and Mathematics, each have five parts yielding separate measures. This test covers the social and scientific studies area of the curriculum. It attempts to represent the underlying skills and understandings without prescribing the curriculum's form or content' (Manual, p. 2).

Item preparation

Apart from what has been quoted above, the Manual does not indicate how or why the items were selected.

Administration

This is a group test for which each child needs a test booklet. The Manuals give clear indications of which Level of the test to use for a particular age and of how the test should be administered, together with the precise instructions to be given to the children and the times at which they should be made. Ten minutes is allowed for the completion of each part, and hence the whole test takes 50 minutes.

Standardization

The details of the standardization are very vague. The Manual (p. 2) speaks of, '. . . a very large sample of children drawn from schools in England and Wales', but does not indicate their number, distribution, sex or how they were chosen nor who did the testing. The Reliability section does mention 1098 and 1072 as the numbers for intercorrelation of the Forms A and B at Levels 4 and 5, respectively, but it is not clear whether this was the whole sample. Tables are provided to convert raw scores into standardized scores (mean 100, standard deviation 15). The tables apply to the test as a whole and not to the five parts separately.

Scoring

A marking key is provided for each test and the Manual gives clear instructions on the scoring of items. Profile record sheets are available for the Bristol Achievement Tests.

Reliability

The only measures of reliability given in the Manual are the correlations between the scores of the same sample of children on the parallel forms A and B of the test at each Level. These were 0.88 for Level 4 ($n = 1098$) and 0.83 for Level 5 ($n = 1072$) for the total scores. Correlations for the parts are also given and these range from 0.58–0.97 and from 0.56–0.86, respectively, for the two Levels. As noted above, information about the sample and details of the testing are not given.

Validity

No information about validity is given in the Manual. Although the purpose of the test is stated, there is no indication of the evidence used to select items during the construction of the tests nor of any follow-up studies which show that the items assess what is claimed.

Interpretation

Little guidance is given concerning the interpretation of the scores other than conversion to a standardized score and a decile, and the plotting of the results on a profile sheet.

General evaluation

This test is nicely produced and the Manual gives very clear instructions on how it should be administered and scored. It does, however, lack indication of how it should be interpreted psychologically and educationally. No evidence is produced to justify the selection of the items nor is the psychological rationale behind the construction of the test given. It is very questionable whether the test really does assess 'study skills' as its title claims. In order to answer the majority of the questions children would need a reasonable attainment in the subject matter areas covered, despite the claim in the Manual that the test is curriculum free. To be of practical use this test needs a much clearer justification and documentation.

Bristol Achievement Tests: General Evaluation

In 1982, the Bristol Tests were issued in a new edition. The test booklets have been redesigned and look much more attractive. A very small number of items have been altered, and some appear on different pages from the old edition but the order of items remains unchanged. Each level now has a single Administrative Manual (in place of three, one for each major area). As far as I can see the Interpretative Manual remains unchanged (though the publisher's 1983 catalogue indicates that it incorporates new data).

In the Administrative Manuals, there is the following note: 'This version was trialled alongside the original (1969) edition in 50 schools, utilizing 7500 pupils, during March and April, 1982. A comparison of the results from both versions revealed very high correlations and as a result no amendments have been made to the original statistical information'. This is an extraordinary statement. The high correlations are to be expected (but would have given useful further information about reliability, if reported); what high correlations do not ensure is that the level of performance, crucial to the norms, has not changed. The means and standard deviations of the raw scores of the 1982 sample (weighted, if necessary) should be published so that the user can be assured that the 1969 norms (for which the raw scores are also given) are still valid. The opportunity might also be taken to allay any fears over the sex imbalance in the original Level 3 standardization sample and the Level 5 regression-on-age coefficients (mentioned in the review of the Bristol English Tests). Despite the promise in the Interpretative Manual that more data about validity would be added, the new edition provides none. To have gone to the lengths of reprinting the Administrative Manuals and the tests, administering new and old version to 7500 children, and then to provide no data on norms, validity or reliability is nothing short of dereliction of duty on behalf of the publisher.

The reviews of the individual sections of the Bristol battery (English Language, Mathematics and Study Skills) comment on their coverage. Here I look at features of the battery as a whole and the interpretation of the profile. The plotting of the profile is well illustrated through an example and the error bands are clearly shown, but the interpretation of that profile is rather overdone with comments offered on differences that are manifestly not statistically significant. There is also the possibility of confusion with the other type of comparison suggested, the scores expected on the basis of level of reading skill (subtest 1 of the English Language tests); the example in the Interpretative Manual does not mention these expected scores even though the instructions on the profile chart require the expected scores to be plotted. It would have been particularly instructive in the example since the girl's English Part 1 score is at the first decile while the remainder of her scores are nearer the median; in other words she is a very considerable 'over-achiever'.

The Interpretative Manual gives the intercorrelations of the subtests within each area and the correlations between English Part 1 scores and all other subtests, but not the whole intercorrelation matrix. The median value of these 400 coefficients is 0.65, which suggests that there is a substantial general factor running through the battery. There is, perhaps, slightly more differentiation than in the Richmond Tests, but the remarks about profiles and the general factor in my review of the Richmond Tests apply equally to the Bristol Tests (as do the comments about cross-sectional standardization).

In summary, the new Bristol battery looks attractive and deserves consideration alongside the Richmond battery. Only three hours' testing is required (in contrast to five for the Richmond) and the information gained may be comparable, though the conceptualization of the basic skills is quite different especially in English. But in technical support, the user has been let down badly with the second edition.

Richmond Tests of Basic Skills

Reviewed by Desmond L. Nuttall

Authors: A. N. Hieronymus, E. F. Lindquist and N. France
Publisher: NFER-Nelson
Distributor: NFER-Nelson
Age ranges*:

Level	Age range	School year
1	8:01– 9:00	2nd junior
2	9:01–10:00	3rd junior
3	10:01–11:00	4th junior
4	11:01–12:00	1st secondary
5	12:01–13:00	2nd secondary
6	13:01–14:00	3rd secondary

1974 (S); 1975 (M, T)†
1979–1981 (M, T) printings reviewed

---

* Assumes primary–secondary transfer at 11+. The ages quoted refer to age at 30 September.
† The Richmond Tests are Anglicized and adapted versions of the Iowa Tests of Basic Skills (ITBS).

Test content

'The Richmond Tests of Basic Skills are eleven separate tests, covering a wide range of skills development . . . organized as follows:

Test V: Vocabulary
Test R: Reading Comprehension
Test L: Language Skills
       L-1: Spelling
       L-2: Use of Capital Letters
       L-3: Punctuation
       L-4: Usage
Test W: Work-Study Skills
       W-1: Map Reading
       W-2: Reading Graphs and Tables
       W-3: Knowledge and Use of Reference Materials
Test M: Mathematical Skills
       M-1: Mathematical Concepts
       M-2: Mathematics Problem Solving'

(Teacher's Guide, p. 5).

One 96-page booklet covers all levels (ages 8–14 years) and within each test the levels overlap. For example, in Test R, Level 1 starts at item 1 and finishes with item 60, Level 2 goes from item 12 to item 79, Level 3 from 25 to 98 and so on. Twenty-four pages of the Teacher's Guide are devoted to a detailed breakdown of the skills and content tested. The items are varied and often interesting and imaginative with well-drawn maps, diagrams and graphs in Tests W and M.

All items are multiple choice, and a machine-scoreable version of the answer sheet is available. Alternate forms of the tests are not provided.

Purpose

The principal purpose is to 'provide for the comprehensive and continuous measurement of the growth of an individual child in the fundamental skills' (Teacher's Guide, p. 5) but there are many suggestions for other direct and indirect uses (e.g. as an accounting to the parent, and as an aid to better instruction) which suggests that the authors ambitiously see the Tests as multipurpose, principally for monitoring, diagnosis and curriculum evaluation. Nothing is said about their use in selection and placement, though they are widely used by LEAs and schools for this purpose (see Open University, 1982).

Item preparation

The Tests are adaptations of the well-tried and popular Iowa Tests of Basic Skills (ITBS) which were first developed in the USA in 1955. In the American tradition, the Tests are conceived more as primary mental abilities than as a composite measure of general ability yet, surprisingly, the ITBS allow the formation of composite scores while the Richmond Tests discourage it and provide normative information only for the separate tests.

The Richmond Tests have the same basic structure as the ITBS but no justification is offered for its appropriateness to the British educational system and curriculum. Nor is it clear how the system of item classification (spelt out in great detail) was developed. In fairness, though, it can be said that there would probably be a wide consensus that the skills measured are fundamental in British education (though not, of course, the only fundamental skills since writing, listening and speaking skills are not tested).

The items were not simply Anglicized: 'the content of the tests was first very carefully modified to represent the British environment and current curriculum practice, and then printed in a validation (*sic*) edition for administration, in July 1974, to a sample of 700 ordinary primary and secondary children' (Teacher's Guide, p. 5).

Administration

The tests are designed to be administered under normal classroom conditions by the teacher, and very clear and comprehensive instructions are given for preparing for test administration and the administration itself.

A total of 5 hours is needed for the whole battery, in four sessions of about 80 minutes each. Each session should take place on consecutive days (though younger children can be allowed a clear day between sessions), and the Teacher's Guide makes it clear that under no circumstances should the tests be given in a single day.

A separate, rather cramped, answer sheet is provided, and the practice test is very short. The Pupil's Book, while attractive, could be very daunting to a young child: 96 pages long, A4 size, with no fewer than 1232 items (mercifully not numbered sequentially). No instructions are given early on to reassure children that they are not obliged to work through the whole book, and the atmosphere created is certainly one of competitive testing.

Standardization

The standardization was carried out in October and November 1974 and involved over 12 000 children (Tables of Norms, p. 7; the Teacher's Guide says 17 000) from maintained schools in the UK. The secondary schools were chosen from national lists by essentially random sampling; the junior schools were the feeder schools of the secondary schools in the sample. The sample was reweighted to conform to the population distributions by region and by type of school, yielding adjusted samples varying between 1700 and 2300 for each level and year group, plus similar samples from junior 1 for Level 1 and from secondary 4 for Level 6. Standardized scores (normalized to a mean of 100 and a standard deviation of 15) are provided for six-monthly age groups (i.e. four groups per level except at Levels 1 and 6) thus covering the range 6:09–15:08, though some warnings are made about use at either extreme. The procedure is not described adequately; it is not made clear, for example, how standardized scores were derived for children aged between 12:03 and 12:08 on Level 4 tests (there being an expectation of virtually no children of that age in first-year secondary by October/November). Some basic tables showing how to convert standard age scores (SASs, as they are described) to percentiles and stanines are provided.

Norms are provided for each test separately, but not for any higher level of aggregation. 'No attempt should be made to find the average of the 11 SASs for each pupil. It is impossible to sum up the varied strengths and weaknesses shown by individuals into one single *quotient*. In any case, the basis for true educational guidance is a knowledge of the *range* of scores achieved by each pupil' (Tables of Norms, p. 4).

Much is made of the possibility of monitoring an individual's development over six years, but the norms are *not* longitudinal but cross-sectional. No mention is made of possible sex differences and the composition of the standardization sample by sex is not given.

Scoring

Very clear scoring instructions, using a transparent perspex guide, are provided. Because of the system of levels, raw scores (number of items correct) have to be converted to basic scores before the Tables of Norms are used but again clear instructions are given. A class record sheet with space for basic scores and SASs for up to 20 pupils is provided, as is a pupil profile chart with space just for SASs but for five testing occasions.

Reliability

From the standardization exercise, KR-21 reliability coefficients are provided (an even more inappropriate measure for speeded tests than KR-20). Values are very similar across levels and range from about 0.92 for the Reading Comprehension Test to 0.73 for the Punctuation Test.

Validity

The uses suggested for the Richmond Tests are varied, and the evidence that might be sought on validity equally varied. For curriculum evaluation and diagnosis, content validity is likely to be crucial, and the Teacher's Guide provides a very full statement of the skills and content covered by each of the 11 tests enabling the teacher to judge their appropriateness to his or her curriculum. No information about criterion-related validity is given, nor are the intercorrelations of the tests provided. A duplicated Technical Manual available from the publisher does, however, provide such information. Concurrent validity coefficients with similar tests (e.g. of reading) have values in the range 0.5–0.7 and the median correlation between tests is about 0.75 (very near the median test-retest reliability coefficient over one year of 0.77) with a small sample of pupils from a middle school.

Interpretation

Although guidance is given about how to construct a score band two or four standard errors of measurement wide, this *follows* the discussion about score and profile interpretation. This discussion is clear and well illustrated with potted case histories, but tends to exaggerate the significance of discrepancies for diagnostic and remedial purposes. Within any one of the 11 areas, the advice about improving performance varies from the useful and detailed to the vague and unhelpful: 'Provide variety in method. There is no substitute for ingenious, resourceful teaching' (Teacher's Guide, p. 28).

Test use

An approved shortened version of the Tests (excluding those of Study Skills) was used in:

Galton, M. and Simon, B. (Eds) (1980). "Progress and Performance in the Primary Classroom". London: Routledge and Kegan Paul.
There are 162 references to studies using the ITBS listed in the "Eighth Mental Measurements Yearbook" (Buros, 1978).

General evaluation

The Richmond Tests are of a high quality and well supported technically by the Manuals and the publisher. Their definition of the basic skills will appeal to many, now as in 1975 when they were first produced, and there are a number of features (e.g. the testing of varied aspects of reading comprehension and of reference skills) which make the Tests compare favourably with alternatives.

On the other hand, a whole test devoted to Punctuation and another to the Use of Capitals may be too basic for some teachers. The content validity and the interpretation of the scores can be evaluated only in relation to a particular curriculum.

One major use of the test is in the diagnosis of individuals' strengths and weaknesses, and much is made of the *profile* of scores across the eleven tests. But as Levy points out

> 'Profile interpretation is normative at root rather than truly intra-individual: we are tempted to say that a person is better at A than he is at B; what we really mean is that the person is higher on scale A relative to the population than he is on scale B relative to the population. No doubt the latter statement has some value, but its meaning is more limited than we would like for some purposes. Looking at bumps and hollows in profiles has become a new phrenology' (Levy, 1974, pp. 33–34).

In addition, errors of measurement in the scores to be contrasted, coupled with the non-zero correlations between the tests, make the interpretation of profiles notoriously difficult. Any test battery that emphasizes profiles should, therefore, accept the responsibility of explaining very carefully their interpretation and limitations. The Manuals do not serve the user well in this respect, but the duplicated 'White Papers' available from the publisher (but not well advertised) make up for their deficiencies in some measures. Nevertheless, it is difficult to determine, from the information provided, what range of SASs across the 11 tests is normal and what should be cause for concern (45 is suggested at one point, with 25–30 being normal). Moreover, the Richmond and Bristol Manuals are both wrong in suggesting that the significance of the difference between standardized scores on two different tests should be tested with the standard error of estimate (arising from the regression of one on the other); the standard error of estimate is not the same as the standard error of the difference between the scores.

There is, however, an even more fundamental issue, namely the amount of information contained in the profile when the tests intercorrelate so highly. Both in Britain and the USA (Open University, 1982; and see Technical Manual) there is no doubt that a general factor pervades performance on the tests: the amount of valid information that remains after that general factor is removed is very small. Five hours' testing may yield a small payoff.

One other issue deserves mention. The limitations of the cross-sectional standardization method have been noted above in connection with an annual testing programme, but the month of testing is also important. The tests were standardized in October/November, and from the norms one can deduce that the difference in basic scores between a median child aged 12:00 and one aged 11:06 is 2 on the Vocabulary Test. There is no evidence, and no reason to suppose, that six months later, in May, the second child (now aged 12:00) has improved her score by exactly that amount. In other words the October/November norms may well be inappropriate for a May testing programme (see Introduction).

In conclusion, I would say that a user aware of some of these points and clear about intended use could find much of value in the Richmond Tests and their supporting materials, but a less sophisticated user could easily be tempted to misuse them. A potential user would be well advised to look as well at the Bristol Achievement Tests and to assess the relative strengths and weaknesses of the two batteries, particularly in terms of coverage and definition of the basic skills.

References

Buros, O. K. (Ed.) (1978) "The Eighth Mental Measurement Yearbook". Highland Park, New Jersey: Gryphon Press.

France, N. (1968). A technique for producing and verifying a normal distribution of items. *British Journal of Educational Psychology* **38**, 21–26.

Levy, P. (1974). On the relation between test theory and psychology. *In* "New Approaches in Psychological Measurement" (P. Kline, Ed.). London: Wiley.

Open University (1982). "E364: Curriculum Evaluation and Assessment in Educational Institutions, Case Study 5, Great Barr School". Milton Keynes: The Open University Press.

SRA Reading and Arithmetic Indexes

Reviewed by Tessa Roberts

Author: SRA Industrial Test Development Staff. Manual by Bruce A. Campbell

Publisher: Science Research Associates

Distributor: Science Research Associates

Age range: Adults and young people over 14 years of age

1968 (M, T); 1974 (M) (revision); S not stated

Group test

Test content

The test consists of a Reading Index and an Arithmetic Index accompanied by a Manual. Both Indexes progress through what are claimed to be distinct levels of development. In the Reading Index, these are picture-word association; word decoding; comprehension of phrases; comprehension of sentences; and comprehension of paragraphs. In the Arithmetic Index, the levels are the addition and subtraction of whole numbers; multiplication and division of whole numbers; fractions; and decimals and percentages. Both Indexes are composed of multiple-choice items, the candidate being required to mark with a cross one selected answer from four in the Reading Index and one from five in the Arithmetic Index. The Reading Index requires the completion of sentences and the Arithmetic Index, computation of numbers.

Purpose

'The SRA Reading and Arithmetic Indexes are tests of general reading and computational achievement for adults and for young people over fourteen years of age. They were designed to use with applicants for entry-level jobs and special training programs, where the basic skills of the applicants are often too low to be reliably evaluated by typical selection tests . . . The employer . . . needs a method of evaluating the basic skill levels at which they can function effectively so that they can be placed in appropriate jobs. Similarly, the training supervisor working to upgrade the basic skills of members of this group needs a means of classifying trainees by functional level in order to make the teaching sessions most effective' (Manual, p. 1). The test is said to be particularly relevant to 'members of minority groups' but who these might be is left to the imagination of the reader.

Item preparation

Reading Index

One hundred and eighty-six items, spanning the five levels of reading performance and screened for appropriateness of language and content by the language department of a Job Corps Centre, were tried out with 675 males and females enrolled in American special and adult education programmes. The items were divided into three experimental forms, each of which contained a set of common items to provide a comparative basis for individual items. Each subject received one of these forms and a test of general ability, the SRA Pictorial Reasoning Test. No statistical information is given but items were selected to maximize within-level consistency and to minimize between-level overlap and correlation with the PRT score.

Arithmetic Index

Two hundred and twenty-six items were devised to measure basic skill areas assumed to underlie the applications required in various occupations. The items corresponded to the four developmental levels of arithmetic achievement and were divided into '18 pre-test units with overlapping items'. Each unit was given to a group of from 125–218 pupils from grades 2, 4, 6, 8 and 10. It is not clear to what extent the composition of the groups varied nor whether individual groups received more than one test unit. Items were finally selected to 'maximize reliability of measurement within skill level and to provide at least a 15-point difference in the mean proportion of students passing the items at each successive level' (Manual, p. 3).

Administration

The tests are for use with adults and young people with a low level of basic skills. Each candidate needs the test booklets, pencils and extra paper for the Arithmetic Index since he will be required to work out the answers away from the booklet using the page simply to mark his chosen answer, a practice which incidentally may present difficulties. The booklets are clearly set out and each page is sealed with a carbon backing which transfers the response to a scoring key. Instructions and practice items are included on the first page but there is also a detailed script for the examiner by means of which he ensures that the candidates understand what is required and receive feedback about the practice items. He also checks that they are marking the booklets properly as the test proceeds. Instructions are given separately for each test. The tests are designed to be untimed but if a time limit is administratively necessary an allowance of 25 minutes is recommended.

Standardization

Two sets of norms in the form of percentiles are provided for the Indexes as a whole. One set relates to special education. For the Reading Index this is based on the performance of only 87 trainees undergoing a course of basic education and on-the-job training whose scores show a tendency to cluster at the upper end of the scale. The Arithmetic Index norms are based on 57 similar trainees and 419 students in special and adult education programmes.

The other set of norms relates to occupational groups and figures are given separately for whites and non-whites. The number of non-whites in the sample is comparatively small, however, and the basis for the categorization is not made explicit. A wide variety of occupations have been classified as Unskilled (sample size 322 for the Reading Index; 323 for the Arithmetic Index); Semi-skilled (1426 for the Reading Index; 699 for the Arithmetic Index); Skilled (855 for the Reading Index; 447 for the Arithmetic Index) and Office and Technical (671 for the Reading Index; 1320 for the Arithmetic Index). In all occupational groups the majority 'pass' the Reading Index according to the 80 per cent 'proficiency criterion' proposed and 'fail' the Arithmetic Index.

Scoring

This is a simple matter of tearing the sealing strip from the edge of the pages and counting responses on the marking grid inside. For each different level there is a chain of boxes which makes it easy to arrive at a total. There is no scope for judgement on the part of the marker; a correct response appears as a mark in a box.

Level totals are transferred to the front page of the booklet where they can be compared with a proficiency score set at 80 per cent. The justification for this is stated to be that this criterion requires correct answers for at least 50 per cent more of the items within a level than would be expected by chance.

Reliability

Various internal tests of reliability were carried out but for the most part these involved samples which were extremely small for this purpose. A split-half reliability coefficient (KR-20) of 0.87 is reported for the Reading Index after testing with the 87 trainees. An indication of meaningfulness of the different levels is claimed from the fact that only 4 of this sample failed at one level but passed at a higher one, using the 80 per cent proficiency criterion. For the Arithmetic Index a KR-20 coefficient of 0.91 was obtained with 47 trainees and of 0.95 with 419 special education students. Only 4 of the 57 failed at one level but passed at a higher one. The Raju-Guttman Index of Homogeneity, an indication of the degree to which subjects who have passed an item are likely to have passed all previous items, was found to be 0.93 for the Reading Index with the 87 trainees and 0.95 for the Arithmetic Index with the 57 trainees.

Validity

The Reading and Arithmetic Indexes were intercorrelated with a number of other tests using a variety of occupational groups and trainees. Particular attention is drawn to the fact that correlations with the Pictorial Reasoning Test are low, suggesting that the Indexes are measuring specific rather than general abilities.

The Indexes were also correlated with overall job ranking in a variety of industries and an uneven picture emerged of significant relationships in some jobs and not in others where it might have been expected. This is interpreted not as challenging the validity of the test but as indicating, on the basis of high means and low standard deviations, that employers are currently tending to play safe and employ only those who have clearly adequate skills for the job in question.

Interpretation

The test is designed for use in employee selection and proficiency scores are indicated for each level of both Indexes. Its effectiveness, however, is largely dependent on an accurate analysis of the minimum proficiency levels required for satisfactory performance of a job. It can also be used to determine starting points on basic skills training programmes and, it is claimed, if used in conjunction with a test of general ability may help to indicate those most likely to benefit from such training.

General evaluation

This is a fairly recent test which has been developed to perform a useful function and which has all the virtues of clarity and simplicity in administration and marking. Unfortunately, it is difficult to be sure that it does perform this function adequately because, in spite of many pages of figures, there is a paucity of information about some areas of test development, sample sizes throughout the study are often small and results as a whole do not present a coherent picture. Moreover, the simplicity of the test may have been bought at too high a price: the Reading Index, for example, is based on the doubtful assumption that there is a simple hierarchical relationship between word decoding and phrase comprehension.

For UK use it would be, in any case, necessary to adapt the Reading Index as the influence of American culture and language appears in the text from time to time. Even if the Indexes were without flaws, there would still be the problem that their effectiveness depends on accurate job analysis. The test may have a use for careers advisers and employers, although since a major aim is to detect those who have the necessary skills for a job but might normally be rejected on the basis of general performance, it is only likely to be relevant in periods of full employment.

General abilities

List of reviews

AH1, X and Y	462
AH2/AH3	464
AH4 Group Test of General Intelligence	473
AH5 Group Test of High-Grade Intelligence	477
AH6 Group Tests of High-Level Intelligence	480
AH Vocabulary Scale	483
APU Vocabulary Test	490
British Ability Scales	494
British Picture Vocabulary Scale★	500
Cognitive Abilities Test★	501
Culture Fair Intelligence Tests	502
Deeside Picture Test	506
Differential Aptitude Tests	508
English Picture Vocabulary Test	517
The Essential Intelligence Test	521
Kulhmann-Anderson Test	525
The Listening for Meaning Test	528
Moray House Junior Reasoning Test 2	532
Moray House Junior Reasoning Test 4	535
Moray House Verbal Reasoning Tests	538
Non-Readers Intelligence Test	542
Non-Verbal Test BD	545
Non-Verbal Test DH	548
Oral Verbal Intelligence Test	552
Otis-Lennon Mental Ability Test	556
Picture Test A	561
School and College Ability Tests	565
Torrance Test of Creative Thinking	567
Verbal Test BC	573
Verbal Test C	576
Verbal Test CD	582

★ Brief report only.

Verbal Test D   585
Verbal Test EF   593
Verbal Test GH   596
Watson-Glaser Critical Thinking Appraisal   599
Wide Range Vocabulary Tests   602
Williams Intelligence Test for Children with Defective Vision   604

See also:

Boehm Test of Basic Concepts   19
First Grade Screening Test   41

AH1, X and Y

Reviewed by A. P. Lonton

Authors: A. W. Heim, K. P. Watts and V. Simmonds
Publisher: NFER-Nelson
Distributor: NFER-Nelson
Age range: 6–10 years
1977 (M, T); S not stated
1977 (M, T-Y); 1979 (T-X) printings reviewed
Group test

Test content

AH1, X and Y are parallel group tests of perceptual reasoning. Both tests comprise four subtests:

Series: 'Which one comes next?'
Likes: 'Which of the six lower pictures is like the two at the top?
Analogies: A is to B as X is to _____?
Differents: 'Which of the six lower pictures is different from the two at the top?'

Each subtest contains 12 multiple choice questions, half diagrammatic and half pictorial. Each subtest is preceded by a page of examples. The tests are non-verbal in the sense that the child needs no words in which to express an answer. Slow readers or non-readers can therefore attempt the items, provided that the preliminary examples are fully understood. A reasonably steep gradient of question difficulty is used in order to attempt to cover the widely diverging abilities of children in this age range. The authors suggest, however, that the tests may be difficult for the average 5 year-old and too easy for a bright 10 year-old. The ideal range of ages for the tests is stated as 6–9 years (Manual, p. 5).

Purpose

The tests aim to assess perceptual reasoning in young children without penalizing non-readers. Parallel versions X and Y can be used to prevent collaboration between children, and also for retesting purposes.

Item preparation

The authors constructed a large bank of test items. Less satisfactory items were eliminated until two tests were obtained with a balanced set of questions and similar means and standard deviations.

Administration

The tests are mainly intended for group use. In this case, Forms X and Y can be distributed alternately so that no child sits next to another who is doing the same version. Each child needs a response booklet and a pencil, and the tester a Manual and stop-watch. After establishing rapport, the children are instructed to do the Series examples. When every child has done them correctly, they then proceed to the test proper for three minutes. This procedure is then repeated for the next three sections of the test, taken in order. Very useful and detailed instructions are given to the tester. It is suggested that for children aged 8–10 years, it would be unwise to have more than 15 children in the group. Smaller groups are appropriate with younger children. The total testing time is usually 35–45 minutes.

Standardization

Information is given on what is claimed to be a representative sample of 2106 children. Norms are given for ages from 5–10 years in the form of raw score ranges for five percentile bands: (A) top 10 per cent; (B) next 20; (C) middle 40; (D) next 20; and (E) lowest 10 per cent.

Scoring

Scoring is carried out by copying the child's answers onto the scoring grid on the front page of the answer booklet. Only one answer is correct for each question, and hence all omissions, errors and multiple answers are not credited. The scoring procedure is both simple and rapid.

Reliability

A number of studies are reported for different age groups and for sample sizes ranging from 62–200. Test-retest correlations for tests X and Y and for X and Y combined varied from 0.71–0.81 over intervals of 7–11 months. Split-half correlations for X and Y and X and Y combined varied from 0.72 (Y at 9 years) to 0.84 (Y at 7 years). Curiously, the correlations between the diagrammatic and pictorial sections of the tests are as high, if not higher than, the split-half correlations. Correlations between the two forms ranged between 0.67 and 0.76. Standard errors of measurement are quoted as 3.12 at 6 years, 3.35 at 8 years and 3.13 at 10 years, but these values appear to be based upon Spearman rank correlation coefficients. The Manual warns that differences of up to three points may have little meaning.

Validity

Validation studies were done on 383 children taken from five junior schools. AH1 correlated well with tests of non-verbal reasoning, verbal reasoning, mathematics attainment and English progress. The authors conclude that AH1 is, therefore, testing something basic which is common to all or most cognitive tasks for young children.

Interpretation

The Manual suggests that scores should be taken as indicators of general levels of ability rather than as precise information on how one child compares with another.

General evaluation

The test comes from an excellent stable: it builds on the experience acquired from many years of use of AH2 and AH3. It is technically competent, easy to use and comparable to the best non-verbal tests for children of this age range. It has the advantage that it can be used with non-reading children. It could be used by not only teachers, but also clinicians and researchers. AH1 would be more suitable than Raven's Progressive Matrices for non-verbal assessment of junior school children, because of the wider range of skills sampled.

AH2/AH3

Reviewed by Robert Wood

Authors: A. W. Heim, K. P. Watts and V. Simmonds
Publisher: NFER-Nelson
Distributor: NFER-Nelson
Age range: 10:00–Adult

1974 (M); 1975 (T): S not stated*
1978 (M) (2nd edition); 1982 (T)† printings reviewed
Group test

Test content

Tests from the AH (Alice Heim) stable are so well known that the publisher does not see any reason to state on the Manual or test covers what AH2/AH3 are tests of. In fact, the authors, in their own citation of the Manual (Heim *et al.*, 1974) refer to the AH2 and AH3 'Group Tests of Reasoning'. (Note that the Manual contains an error in the citation of this article. It should read Vol. **65**, 493–504).

'AH2 and AH3 are parallel tests of general reasoning'. So begins the Manual. Later on (p. 24), the authors explain, 'It was our aim when devising the test to concentrate on the assessment of *reasoning*, including as much variety as possible: the three parts employ differing media'. The media are verbal, numerical and perceptual (V, N and P). 'Perceptual' is used in preference to the customary psychometric term 'non-verbal', since the latter often signifies 'diagrammatic (or performance)' as opposed to 'verbal-and-numerical', thus giving rise to occasional misconceptions. 'Perceptual' here denotes material which is either diagrammatic or pictorial.

Whereas with a distressingly large number of tests no clear psychological principles seem to be followed in devising and allocating items in terms of numbers, with AH2/AH3 the principles are named (and defended) and items are allocated to each in equal numbers (10) and in a systematic fashion (cyclically). It is noteworthy that Heim and her co-authors should criticise their earlier test, AH4, for its 'arbitrarily differing numbers of verbal and numerical questions' (Manual, p. 8).

About the verbal items it is stated that: 'The four principles in V are (i) analogies, (ii) problems, (iii) sames/opposites, (iv) features in common. These four occur cyclically in this order, throughout V, each principle thus appearing 10 times' (Manual, p. 8). There follows an extended justification of this format. Likewise for N four principles are adumbrated: (i) series, (ii) problems, (iii) analogies and (iv) the four basic arithmetical rules, which the authors note are implicitly included in (i), (ii), (iii). For Perceptual the four principles are (i) features in common, (ii) analogies, (iii) features in common, *differing*

---

* The norms for the 9+ to 15+ groups were evidently derived in a year before the school-leaving age was raised beyond 15 (Manual, p. 29).
† Date apparent from the fact that the Question Books and the Answer Sheets are printed under the mark of the recently formed NFER-Nelson Publishing Company.

from, and (iv) series. Here pictorial and diagrammatic items are alternated according to a formula. It can be seen that one operation, analogies, runs through the three media and others are present in two. The emphasis on analogies is justified on the grounds that it has 'proved itself, for some psychometrists, an excellent and *sufficient* measure of intelligence' (Manual, p. 12). Note the use of 'some'. The Manual goes on to explain that four principles are used rather than one (analogies) 'partly because this seems to be more enjoyable for the subject'. Moreover, it 'samples' the subject more thoroughly, yielding more illuminating data from the viewpoint of the subject's abilities and interests. The rigid separation of these two aspects of personality is thought to be 'undesirable'. Perhaps, like this reviewer, readers will think that these extra justifications smack a little too much of the *ad hoc*, coming as they do after the bold statement of the four principles, and also will puzzle over the last sentence. Allowing that 'personality' is being used in its non-technical sense, how will these tests of reasoning throw light on 'interests', or indeed 'abilities' other than 'reasoning'? No attempt is made later in the Manual to sustain these claims. Other claims (p. 37) to the effect that independent measures of V, N and P may be useful in the study of such problems as brain injury, handedness, thought-processes and type of imagery, seem altogether more plausible.

AH2 and AH3 are parallel tests; they differ from each other both in the position of the correct answers, and in the actual items. The advantage of being able to give neighbours different tests in situations of close confinement is brought out. Unusually, the tests are intended for a cross-section of the adult population and for children aged 10+ upwards. There is a suspicion that the term 'cross-section' is being used loosely. Norms are presented for several adult subpopulations, e.g. health visitors in training, but it is not clear whether these subpopulations together constitute the 'cross-section' (see, however, the penultimate paragraph of this review). It is also claimed that the tests differentiate meaningfully among 'bright' nine year-olds, but the data presented for nine year-olds as a whole suggest it might be wise to avoid using the tests on any members of this age group.

How is such a wide range of age coverage achieved? By establishing a steep gradient of difficulty and by using two different time limits. 'The duller members of literate groups (aged 10 and over) manage, in the longer time, to gain a total score above chance; and the most able (such as university students) fail, in the shorter time, to obtain 100 per cent on total score' (p. 7). The long time limits are recommended for all school children, 15 minutes each for V and B, and 12 minutes for P. With 40 items to each part these are still speeded tests although the authors argue that the unusually steep gradient of difficulty will serve to reduce the speed element *per se* by arresting the quick but inaccurate at items 'requiring a degree of concentration and of close reasoning which eludes them' (p. 12). If this device works, and data presented suggest that it does, then the information yield from 45 minutes testing is impressive.

Item preparation

All items are multiple choice and all, unusually, offer six responses from which to choose. During trialling, verbal items were offered with a sevenfold choice, after which the least frequently selected response was discarded. Numerical questions, by contrast, were presented in open-ended form in order to obtain plausible wrong answers. The perceptual test was more problematic, as the authors admit. Open-ended presentation would have involved subjects in making drawings, which would have been time consuming; nor did they find it feasible to present the items in the form of a sevenfold choice, having already experienced difficulty in providing 'five indefensible but plausible distractors for each question'. It is not clear what solution was adopted, but in their final form the perceptual tests contain 6 choices per item. Pictorial tests are notoriously difficult to pull off because of clumsy artwork which confuses respondents. These tests pass muster pretty well; only item 27 of AH2 gives difficulty and unfortunately, there, the (for this reviewer) unidentifiable object corresponds to the correct answer. Elsewhere item 14 of AH2 seems pointless and slightly tricky (A is to B as A is to B) but these are small criticisms.

A total of 380 items were trialled to produce 240 items (120 × 2) for the final forms. Two stages of item analysis were required; the first to discard the less satisfactory items and the second to achieve the requisite gradient and equivalence of difficulty between the two tests.

Administration

The material on administration is first-class; even exemplary, especially Section IV on the use of preliminary examples (practice items) regarded, rightly, as very important by the authors. 'Supervising the completion of the illustrative example is the most skilled part of administering tests AH2 and AH3' (Manual, p. 13). Why is this? Because the practice session is the administrator's opportunity to put the subjects at ease with a view to coaxing the best out of them. 'In order to obtain good results with a group test, rapport should be cultivated as sedulously as it is in individual testing . . . It is far easier to antagonise a few members of a group than it is to gladden every member' (p. 14).

Every subject requires a question book, an answer sheet and a pencil. There is adequate space for rough work on the answer sheet. Subjects are expected to enter numbers (of their choice) onto the answer sheets. Mistakes are to be corrected by striking out the mistake and writing the new answer clearly beside it. The three parts—V, N, P—are administered separately. Each has 8 practice items. There is provision in the instructions for subjects whose first language is not English to record that fact. The instructions are comprehensive and clear.

Standardization

Norms are presented for five groups of subjects: comprehensive school children, technical college students, colleges of education students, the armed forces and health visitors in training. There is no information about the representativeness of these samples; for schoolchildren the Manual confines itself to reporting that 'the norms are based on comprehensive co-educational schools drawn from urban and rural areas in England (including Greater London, Merseyside and East Anglia) and in Scotland (Stirling and Clackmannanshire)' (p. 35). This passage seems to be saying that of the areas sampled in England, Greater London, Merseyside and East Anglia were certainly included, plus other unspecified areas. The impression given is that the norming samples are based on 'grab groups'—three colleges of education, 103 soldiers and 85 naval ratings and so on. For the schoolchildren the numbers for the different age groups are: 9+, 178; 10+, 400; 11+, 629; 12+, 577; 13+, 508; 14+, 576; 15+, 383; where 9+ denotes children who are between their 9th and 10th birthdays, etc.

The reason for the lack of 16+ norms is given (p. 29) as being due to the fact that the school-leaving age was 15 at the time AH2/AH3 was being developed, which incidentally gives an indication of the age of these tests (pre-1974). The Manual invites submission of 16+ norming data and it may be that by now such norms are available from Dr Heim. One would hope, also, that the numbers for the other age groups have been augmented, for they are a little slight as they stand, given the claims made for these tests and their likely popularity.

The norms are presented in straight raw score form, and no attempt has been made to supply month by month adjustments. That would have been silly given the numbers involved and anyway the ambitious wide range scope of the test renders monthly figures largely irrelevant. Separate tables are provided for short and long time limits. Each table contains, for each age group, means and standard deviations for V, N, P and total, plus score ranges for five grades, A–E, representing 10, 20, 40, 20 and 10% of the samples respectively. These grades serve to adjust for differences in mean scores between parts and over different age and groups.

On the matter of *sex differences* the Manual is not altogether satisfactory. It observes (p. 37) that the 'usual tendency' is found for males to do better on N and females to do better on V at all schools, and adds that schoolgirls tend to do better than schoolboys on P. In addition standard deviations are higher for males than for females for all three parts of the test. But, the Manual continues, 'Despite the male/female differences listed above, the two sexes produce in general very similar mean total scores. For this reason, males and females share the same norms, in each age-group'. And that is that. But turn to the article (Heim *et al.*, 1974) and you will find a quite extensive section on sex differences. It reports, for instance, as the Manual does not, that no items were deleted or altered because they appeared to be 'unfair' to either sex. Again, it supplies a graph, as the Manual does not, to illustrate that on total score the difference between the sexes is small, and is not consistent. This last observation is surely the crucial one; the absolute difference could always be greater on a larger, more representative sample but if the differences are not consistent you do no quite know where you are. And why are the differences not consistent? Because the aggregation masks sex-related interactions at the subtest level. I would have said that the difference in standard deviations alone was enough to warrant separate tables. What I find hard to reconcile with the decision taken on sex differences are the various claims made that this test will reveal abilities and interests, useful in studies of brain damage, handedness, etc., all of which are likely, or are known to be sex related. Granted, the user can always treat the sexes separately in exploratory work but that is not the same as having separate norms.

Those who like norms presented in diagrammatic and graphical form will be pleased by the Manual. Percentage bar charts, organized in terms of age, the five grades, and the various subpopulations, are presented along with frequency distribution curves for AH2/AH3 raw scores so that readers can evaluate the parallelism of the instruments for themselves (they are parallel). Incidentally, and this is a bit of a carp, the page layout in the Manual can be confusing. With each page divided into two columns and tables inserted across the two columns, the text is forced or rather made to run from one column to the next *between* tables. Page 20 is particularly confusing. Perhaps the publisher could look at this.

Scoring

Scoring is not absolutely straightforward and care is required. While the answer sheets are cunningly laid out to permit the use of ingenious marking keys, care must be taken to ensure that each key strip is laid precisely alongside the answers and also that respondents have not inadvertently written their answers one place out of sequence. 'An experienced marker should explain the system of scoring to any new assistant and check his first few papers' (p. 18).

Reliability

The reader will seek in vain for a section in the Manual with this title. Instead the authors refer to the 'Parallelism' and 'Consistency' of tests, and elsewhere to 'split-half correlations'. This usage is to be welcomed in that it obliges users to think about the different aspects of reliability, as conventionally defined; what they mean and what they themselves are most interested in. But the novice user, looking at the Contents of the Manual, might be perplexed and then unnerved at being unable to find *reliability*.

The various reliability estimates are based on bits and pieces of samples—90 for test-retest, 86 for parallel forms, 100 for split-half correlations—none of which inspires great trust. More data on reliability ought to be supplied. One finding which turns up consistently is that Perceptual appears to be the least reliable of the three parts. This, coupled with other signs, does raise a question mark against this subtest, as the authors concede (p. 37). They end up defending its inclusion on grounds which, again, are not altogether convincing; gives balance, fun to do, discrepant scores may say something (but not if there is something wrong with the test), and, most tendentious, 'it is, after all, not so long since exclusively "non-verbal" intelligence tests were being lauded as the best "measure of g"'.

Validity

The Manual contains a very strong and extensive section on validation. Together with the previous section this is an exemplary presentation which other manuals could copy with profit, e.g. NFER Verbal Test D. The seven tables contain a wealth of correlational data which users will benefit from studying. There are correlations between AH2/AH3 and other tests (verbal, non-verbal, mathematics, reading) and also examination grades including HNC2 for Medical Laboratory Technicians. Table 16 comprises mean scores of streamed comprehensive school children in their second year, according to stream. True, it is only one school, and the numbers in the streams are small but the good intention is there. It is only from a variety of data like these that the user can begin to check the claims made for tests regarding purpose which some manuals so blithely throw out. Given the strongest claim made for these tests—that they can be used to test a wide age range—the percentage bar charts on pp. 39–41 of the Manual are of central importance since they show scores rising consistently with age from 9–15 years. After that the trend is not so clear. There is only one quibble about the tables in this section and elsewhere. Standard deviations should always be given alongside correlations (and means too) so that the reader can make some interpretational adjustment for restriction of range on either or both of the variables, and/or skewness.

The previous section 'Relationship between Parts of the Test' presents intercorrelations between the parts, and these, of course, bear on the validity of the tests for most purposes. It is good to have them by age for they are liable to vary and when they do correlations based on age aggregation will deceive (Goldstein, 1981). Note the bloomer in Table 8 where it looks as if 1 year-olds and 95 year-olds were tested (really 9 year-olds and 15 year-olds)! Actually, patterns of correlation sizes do not differ over the years, the order is uniform and always as follows: (a) V with N, highest; (b) V with P, next; and (c) N with P, lowest. Given the decision to employ three differing media, the authors hoped that the intercorrelations between the parts would be positive and significant but not too high. They believe this is the case; with one exception (N for 9 year-olds which can be discounted) the inter-part correlations lie between 0.64 and 0.79. One could argue about whether this level is right, and whether more specific predictions regarding the correlations between particular pairs of parts should have been imposed, but by and large the authors' claim seems to be upheld. The test has good prospects of validity in differing circumstances, providing a view is taken about P.

Interpretation

The Manual concludes: 'The overall assessment of the individual's general ability is determined by the grade obtained in his total score. Since each part yields its own grade, a three-point profile is produced for each Subject. It is thus possible to gauge his relative strengths and weaknesses on Verbal, Numerical and Perceptual reasoning' (p. 37). Naturally, the value of the profile—vocationally, clinically and theoretically—is a matter of empirical experience. Given the question mark against the reliability of P and indeed the bitty nature of all the reliability estimates, users would be wise not to push too hard any differences observed between V, N, and P, especially those involving P, until they come to understand for themselves the properties of these tests.

Test use

The authors report their own earlier investigations but other work using AH2/AH3 has not come to light. It must be there, however, or if it is not, one imagines that studies using these tests will be reported before long.

General evaluation

AH2/AH3 is the product of over 30 years of research and development work by Dr Alice Heim and her colleagues. That labour must be respected and its fruits show up in many places. The Manual, in its scope and sweep, is a model for others and it contains sections, notably those on administration, which can stand as yardsticks of good practice. There is a gem of a section (x) on time limits and the effects of giving extra time which is interesting in its own right. Indeed the Manual is a 'good read' throughout and the blank page at the end for notes is evidence of the thoughtfulness which is characteristic of these authors' work.

Curiously, given all their experience, the authors' touch is less sure when it comes to psychometric matters. Perhaps they have lost their theoretical bearings a bit. Their rationale for building the test on four principles, enunciated so firmly and winningly, is struck by uncertainty and ends up ringing not quite true. Likewise, their defence of the Perceptual test gives the impression of a rather desperate searching around for justifications. '. . . it is, after all, not so long since exclusively "non-verbal" tests were being lauded as the best "measure of g"'. This may be good knocking copy, directed at old enemies, but it does not seem a basis on which to build a test.

The norms are not as firmly based, either in terms of numbers or representativeness, as one might wish. The validation data are more impressive than the reliability data which, if you have to make a choice, is the way it ought to be. All could do with building up, which is a comment you can make about most, if not all tests. The point is that this Manual has a structure into which fresh data can readily be accommodated.

The Manual is least convincing on the subject of sex differences. While it is certainly true that there are many users who will not give a jot for sex differences, indeed will disapprove of the subject being brought up at all, there are many others who are sensitive to sex differences and who will, at the very least, wish to get to the bottom of what the test has to say about them. Fortunately, the Manual has given enough information to alert these people to likely effects.

The claims for a wide age range coverage hold up, at least for the age range 10+ to 15+, and that is a considerable achievement. Whether you would want to use AH2/AH3 with young adults is debatable; as Heim *et al.* (1974) themselves point out, 'it is, in fact, difficult if not impossible to obtain a random sample of young adults—and to know in exactly what respect one is failing to do so'.

The user who is looking for a *quality* test of reasoning or general ability or intelligence—I am afraid these terms are all used in the Manual—need look no further than this test, or rather these tests for they are parallel, and that is a rare thing. There is no doubt that the V-N-P profile could prove valuable but users will have to determine that for themselves. This reviewer has appreciated the opportunity to study these tests and the Manual, for they are pleasing in so many ways. The criticisms which have been made are, by and large, criticisms which could be made of many other tests, either singly or collectively. I hope that Dr Heim and her colleagues will go on to improve the Manual and make it truly exemplary.

References

Goldstein, H. (1981). The effects of age grouping on the estimate of a correlation coefficient. *Annals of Human Biology* **14**, 181–183.

Heim, A. W., Watts, K. P. and Simmonds, V. (1974). AH2 and AH3: parallel tests of reasoning. *British Journal of Psychology* **65**, 493–504.

AH4 Group Test of General Intelligence

Reviewed by Don Labon

Author: Alice W. Heim
Publisher: NFER-Nelson
Distributor: NFER-Nelson
Age range: 11:00 to adult
1945★
1970 (M); 1968 (T)†
1981 (M, T) printings reviewed

Test content

Part I consists of 65 items, some verbal, some numerical: directions, opposites, series, analogies, computations and synonyms. Part II also has 65 items, involving similar principles, but presented in diagrammatic form: analogies, sames, subtractions, series and superimpositions. In both parts of the test, the principles are presented cyclically, in the order given here. In general, the items representing each principle appear in ascending order of difficulty. Most items are multiple choice, involving selection of the correct answer from 5 possibles. The overall measure is largely one of deductive reasoning.

Purpose

To provide single norm-referenced measures of general intelligence across the English population aged from 11 years to adulthood, and across selected adult groups of below average intelligence.

★ The test is referred to in a paper by Heim, published in January, 1947.
† Dates of standardization not given: see review Group test.

Item preparation

The Manual does not provide details.

Administration

As a preliminary to each part of the test, the teacher administering it goes through a set of practice examples. These preliminary procedures, and the reasons for them, are presented in some detail in the Manual. Whilst the Manual makes these phases clear, they are not simple. They require both an understanding of basic principles of assessment and the possession of class teaching skills. Administration of the test itself is straightforward; the Manual provides the necessary instructions clearly and in sufficient detail. The test is highly speeded. Completion of each part within the allotted time of 10 minutes, even amongst intelligent adults, is likely to be rare. The reusable test booklet has a clear format, as does the answer sheet.

Standardization

The standardization samples described in the Manual fall short of being adequate for national norm-referencing purposes. Adult norms are based on the scores of 1183 male naval ratings, whose unrepresentativeness is acknowledged. Samples from different secondary-school age groups are presented with virtually no information beyond that of the numbers involved. Information concerning tertiary education samples (students on craft, technical and secretarial courses, air company apprentices and university students) is similarly limited. Group sample sizes range from 81–1137. The Manual gives little indication as to when these samples were tested. It may have been some thirty or so years ago.

Scoring

Answers are all in the form of written numbers and all responses are made on one side of a single answer sheet. Hand-scoring, assisted by a marking key which lines up beside the responses, is easy and moderately quick. Also included in the Specimen Set are a machine-scorable answer sheet and a corresponding template. These, however, are not mentioned in the Manual and in any case do not fit the format of the question book supplied.

For each of the reference groups contributing to the Manual's sets of norms, total scores have been classified within an A to E scale, with A and E each representing an extreme 10% and C representing the middle 40%. This classification has also been undertaken for the two separate parts of the test.

Total scores are not presented in the form of quotients, though it would be possible for a knowledgeable teacher to work them out for herself on the basis of supplied values of the mean and standard deviation for raw scores.

Reliability

This appears to be satisfactory, at least as far as adults are concerned. A test-retest reliability study, with an interval of a month, yielded a product-moment correlation of 0.92. The test appears to be fairly consistent internally with correlations between its two parts being generally between 0.7 and 0.8. Factor analysis using Thurstone's centroid method demonstrated a strong general factor running through the whole test.

Validity

Content validity is fairly acceptable, as the items generally are of a kind conventionally found amongst intelligence tests. Validation studies reported in the Manual are moderately supportive but limited in scope. Subsequent studies, however, reported here under Test Use, are more substantial and provide broad confirmation of the Manual's claims. Measures of concurrent validity have yielded correlations of between 0.6 and 0.8 with other intelligence tests. A reported correlation of 0.6 with scholastic achievement is of the order one might expect. The Manual also refers to sources of evidence of predictive validity, in relation to class of university degree and to occupational proficiency, but only in very general terms.

Interpretation

Reliability and validity are sufficient to warrant reasonable confidence in a rank ordering of total test scores as providing a rough rank ordering of general intelligence in a secondary-school year group but, even here, one would need to make some slight subjective allowance for different chronological ages within the sample. Standardization of the test is so weak that one could not be justified in making anything more than the broadest reference to national norms through the norms provided in the Manual. The same limitations apply to interpretation of scores of subgroups in tertiary education, even if they happen to be in exactly the categories identified in the Manual, and of adults in the general population.

The fact that the test is highly speeded also needs to be taken into account in interpreting its results, particularly in the case of high scorers. As is pointed out in the Manual, the items themselves do not present much of a challenge for highly intelligent adults, so differences in their scores are likely to reflect differences in rates of working rather than differences in thinking power.

Test use

The wide use of the test in educational research has provided incidental evidence concerning its validity, broadly confirming the level indicated in the Manual. From this point of view perhaps the most significant of more recent studies is that of Hindley and Owen (1978). Using the AH4 in an extensive longitudinal study of the intelligence of some hundred children, they found that its correlations with the Terman-Merrill test held, at the 0.7 level, even when intervals between administrations of the two tests were of up to 9 years. Other correlational studies have demonstrated relationships between scores on the AH4 and scores on measures of vocabulary (Heim and Watts, 1967), visual and auditory perception and memory (Beard, 1965), English and mathematics achievement (Beard, 1965; Poppleton, 1968; Glossop *et al.*, 1979), judgemental ability (Ellis, 1977), listening comprehension (Wilkinson and Stratta, 1970), ability to discuss problems (Michell and Lambourne, 1979) and reasoning ability (Hartley and Holt, 1971).

General evaluation

This group test can be quickly and fairly easily administered and scored, though some teaching skills are involved in its administration. As a measure of deductive reasoning ability amongst the adolescent and adult sectors of the general population, it has been substantiated as being reasonably reliable and of fair validity. Within highly intelligent groups, however, it probably differentiates more in terms of speed than of intelligence.

The glaring weakness of this test lies in its standardization, which is inadequate with respect both to adolescents and to adults. Because of this weakness, comparisons with reference to national norms can only be made in extremely broad terms, and in this sense the test fails to serve its main stated purposes. Administered to the members of a particular age group it is suitable for purposes of general within-group comparison, though it is not necessarily free from cultural or sex bias.

References

Beard, R. M. (1965). The structure of perception: a factorial study. *British Journal of Educational Psychology* **35**, 210–222.

Ellis, J. I. (1977). Adolescent awareness of stability and change in literature. *Educational Review* **29**, 241–253.

Glossop, J. A., Appleyard, R. and Roberts, C. (1979). Achievement relative to a measure of general intelligence. *British Journal of Educational Psychology* **49**, 249–257.

Hartley, J. and Holt, J. (1971). The validity of a simplified version of Baddeley's three-minute reasoning test. *Educational Research* **14**, 70–76.

Heim, A. W. (1947). An attempt to test high-grade intelligence. *British Journal of Psychology* **37**, 70–81.

Heim, A. W. and Watts, K. P. (1967). An experiment on multiple-choice versus open-ended answering in a vocabulary test. *British Journal of Educational Psychology* **37**, 339–346.

Hindley, C. B. and Owen, C. F. (1978). The extent of individual changes in IQ for ages between 6 months and 17 years in a British longitudinal sample. *Journal Child Psychology and Psychiatry* **19**, 329–356.

Michell, L. and Lambourne, R. D. (1979). An association between high intellectual ability and an imaginative and analytical approach to the discussion of open questions. *British Journal of Educational Psychology* **49**, 60–72.

Poppleton, P. K. (1968). Puberty, family size and the education of girls. *British Journal of Educational Psychology* **38**, 286–292.

Wilkinson, A. and Stratta, L. (1970). Listening comprehension at 13 plus. *Educational Review* **2**, 228–242.

AH5 Group Test of High-Grade Intelligence

Reviewed by Jack Wrigley

Author: A. W. Heim
Publisher: NFER-Nelson
Distributor: NFER-Nelson
Age: 13+, selected highly intelligent adults
1956; revised edition, 1968
Group test (restricted use)

Test content

The test consists of two parts, the first comprising verbal and numerical problems, the second comprising problems in diagrammatic form. There are 36 items in each part. In Part 1, four types of principle are included—directions (some verbal, some numerical), verbal analogies, numerical series, and 'similar relationships', the latter being a more complicated variant of the same-opposite type of question. Part II consists of 36 diagrammatic items, exemplifying four types of principle—analogies, series, 'directions' (requiring mirror imagery and shape construction) and 'feature in common'.

Purpose

The test was devised to discriminate between highly intelligent subjects, adults such as students and research workers. It is therefore not appropriate for groups of below average intelligence or less than 13 years of age. The author claims that qualities needed for success in AH5 include accurate observation, meticulous attention to instructions and ability to appreciate shades of meaning.

Item preparation

The author states that in devising the test items the aim was to raise the level of difficulty by increasing the complexity and closeness of the reasoning involved whilst losing nothing of its cogency. An item analysis based on 767 university students was carried out by K. P. Watts when the test was well established but no details are given of early item analysis at the stage of item preparation.

Administration

Although the test is not highly speeded, a stop-watch is nevertheless required and 20-minute time limits are imposed on both parts of the test. Separate answer sheets are provided and so the question books can be reused. Groups of 20–25 can be tested by one person. The total testing period is between 1 hour and 70 minutes.

Standardization

Although tentative norms are given for various groups such as university students, high-grade apprentice applicants, grammar school children, etc., it is clear that the selection of the groups in the first place is highly subjective and fortuitous even though the samples are sometimes quite large. As the author states 'Given that only the "upper end" of the total population is under consideration what *proportion* should be accepted? . . . In the standardizing of AH5 an empirical approach has been adopted. All the groups (tested) have in common two points: they consist of subjects all of whom are well above the average intelligence of the total population and in no case was their selection solely on a psychometric criterion' (Manual, pp. 17–18).

Scoring

One mark is scored for each correct answer using an answer key which conveniently matches the design of the testee's response sheet.

Reliability

Reliability coefficients derived from repeated testing are not high, varying from 0.68 at age 12+ to 0.89 at 16+. No internal consistency tests appear to be carried out except for the calculation of correlations between the two parts of the test. Here the author claims that correlations of the order of 0.50 are satisfactory since the two parts measure separate qualities. It is difficult, in view of the homogeneous nature of the various samples, to judge whether these correlations are satisfactory or not. It certainly seems likely that the two parts of the test do measure separate qualities and therefore the use of an overall score is somewhat dubious.

Validity

A large number of positive correlations have been found with other tests (Moray House, NIIP Group Test 33, AH4, Progressive Matrices, etc.) and with other criteria (GCE marks, First MB, Theory mark in Education, etc.). Correlations range from 0.24–0.80. As the author states 'Interpretation . . . is not easy'. Some evidence is given to suggest that AH5 is able to discriminate between students with differing degree classes so that AH5 effects relevant discrimination at the *top* end of the scale with subjects already selected for intelligence.

Interpretation

Despite the large number of studies conducted on AH5 the interpretation of test score remains speculative and difficult. This is perhaps inevitable with an ageing test, standardized some years ago, on highly selective groups. In such circumstances, the division of scores into groups A, B, C, D and E corresponding to the top 10%, the next 20%, the middle 40%, the next 20% and the bottom 10%, for the various samples is perhaps all that could be achieved.

General evaluation

AH5 (like its companion AH4) is a well-known highly respected test, designed many years ago. It has retained some of its popularity and usefulness for those who need a high-grade test of intelligence, not too heavily loaded with verbal ability. Many careful empirical studies have been carried out on the test. In spite of this there is a need for a more thorough revision of the test to check the present-day functioning of the items. Discrimination at these high levels of ability is notoriously difficult. This test has made a brave contribution to the task but this reviewer finds it difficult to see very many people willing to use the test except in special circumstances. It could be used alongside other tests in a battery designed to select a few talented individuals. It has the claim to uniqueness in its use of high-grade non-verbal items. But this reviewer sometimes found it difficult to understand the rationale in a whole sequence of items of a similar kind even with the benefit of an answer key. Time has perhaps not dealt kindly with this kind of test and a major revision is now necessary for it to be recommended whole-heartedly.

AH6 Group Tests of High-Level Intelligence

Reviewed by Deborah R. Gooch

Authors: A. W. Heim, K. P. Watts and V. Simmonds
Publisher: NFER-Nelson
Distributor: NFER-Nelson
Age: 'selected, highly intelligent Subjects'. Test SEM for 'Scientists, Engineers and Mathematicians'. Test AG for 'Arts and General'
1970 (M, T); S not stated
Group test

Test content

The AH6 group tests (Forms AG and SEM) include verbal, numerical and diagrammatic problems. *Test AG* consists of 60 items, half of which are designated 'verbal', one quarter 'numerical' and one quarter 'diagrammatic', and give rise to a verbal score (V) and a numerical plus diagrammatic score (N + D). *Test SEM* consists of 72 problems of which an equal number are verbal, numerical and diagrammatic. For this test a V, N and D score are available. Both AG and SEM have questions in common and are of the same difficulty. The types of items are arranged cyclically with a gradient of item difficulty.

The AH6 group tests are the revised versions of the AH4 and AH5 which are mixed tests composed of numerical, diagrammatic and verbal questions. In AH6 the number of diagrammatic questions is decreased. Responses are recorded on an answer sheet, in the form of letters or numbers depending on the type of item.

Purpose

'They are designed for use with selected highly intelligent subjects such as candidates for and students at university and colleges of education, potential entrants to professions, senior pupils at Grammar, Public and Technical schools and colleges . . . The tests were devised in order to effect discrimination among such people, since intelligence tests which differentiate satisfactorily among cross-sections of the total population fail to do so among members of selected, intelligent groups' (Manual, p. 5).

Item preparation

There is a paucity of information on the construction of the questions. There is no indication of an item analysis in the Manual and no criteria for the retention or omission of items.

Administration

The Manual states that 'supervising the completion of the illustrative examples is the most skilled part of administering the AH6 tests'. The examples (there are 18) are of the same difficulty as the first few items in the test and subjects are required to work them out correctly themselves. The different types of problems are equally represented as examples. There is no time limit for the examples, but for tests AG and SEM it is 35 minutes and 45 minutes respectively. Subjects may attempt the questions in any order and are encouraged to work at their own pace. Invigilators are asked to discourage a 'beat the clock' attitude.

Standardization

The norms are presented in tables and as frequency (score) distribution curves, with little accompanying descriptive text. For test AG the norms are based on 1710 school and college students with separate norms for V and N + D. Test SEM has norms for V, N and D separately based on 1189 university science students. The author claims that sex differences are 'sufficiently slight' for the same norms to be used with each sex. The norms allow 5 broad categorizations of the subjects, from group A (top 10 per cent) to E (bottom 10 per cent).

Scoring

The scoring procedure is very simple and marking keys are provided. One mark is scored for each correct answer.

On the answer sheet provided, items of the same type are arranged such that scores in each row and column can be totalled then subtotalled to give a score on V, N + D for test AG and on V, N and D for SEM. Explicit instructions are given for scoring ambiguous responses.

Reliability

The Manual gives precise information on validity and reliability. For AG total score the test-retest reliability coefficient was 0.83 on a sample of 198 school children, of whom 112 were available 5 months later for the retest. This is lower than the test-retest reliability for AH4 and AH5 which were designed for selected groups. Split-half correlations on 100 school children from the above sample, with equal numbers of each sex, are given with adequate descriptions of item selection for these correlations. The rather low split-half reliabilities (V1 with V2, 0.59; N1 + D1 with N2 + D2, 0.65) are put down to the small number of items and the fact that they may be taken in any order.

For SEM, the split-half reliability (odds versus evens) calculated for 100 university students was 0.70. As a measure of internal consistency each type of question was correlated with the other two types since there is an equal number of each type of question. The estimates were as follows: V with N, 0.61; V with D, 0.54; N with D, 0.56. These are low enough, the authors claim, to indicate that three different intellectual qualities are being measured. The authors give no information on the age of the subjects sampled, which, although not as important in this test as in many, could still play a role in test performance.

Validity

Validation is represented in the form of correlations with comparable tests of academic performance, and correlations with non-test criteria such as academic examinations.

Most of the concurrent validation correlations are significant at the 5 per cent level or better. However, the correlation of AH6 SEM diagrammatic score with Ravens Progressive Matrices was effectively zero. For AG the samples consisted of university or college students and for SEM university student scientists. In some of the validation studies the sample size is as small as 34.

The non-test criteria use number and grade of 'O' and 'A' Level passes of 5th and 6th formers. AH6 correlated significantly with Physics (0.57), Chemistry (0.57) and Ordinary Mathematics (0.37), which, the authors argue, tap similar abilities to those required in AH6, namely deductive reasoning. The verbal items of AG correlate significantly with the grade of 'O' Level English attained. The rationale, however, for the inclusion of numeric and diagrammatic items in the test for the Arts and General groups is not upheld due to the much higher predictive capacity of the V over the N + D score and also over the *total score*. Even for science-based subjects the need for the inclusion of diagrammatic items as a measure of scholastic aptitude is not very convincing.

Mean scores on SEM and AG are compared against the class of degree obtained at Oxford and Cambridge. The authors note that 'AH6 appears to effect better differentiation from the viewpoint of selection at the lower than at the top end of the scale'. A variety of 'non-cognitive' explanations such as the person's motivation and interest are given for this. It may be, however, that a 'ceiling effect' is operating whereby the test itself is not discriminating amongst the high scorers. Detailed information of item difficulty would be useful in discerning this point.

Interpretation

The primary purpose of this test is the selection of students for higher education. However, apart from the rather crude classification of an individual into grades A to E there is no further interpretation of the score.

General evaluation

The AH6 tests are simple to administer and score; the Manual is generally clear and concise. It should be noted that some of the items are now rather dated and need to be converted into metric measurement.

A full item analysis would be very useful as would more extensive standardization. A factor analysis would also be helpful for examining the credibility of the D score. Caution is advised if the separate score categories are used because of the small number of items from which the subtest scores are derived. Moreover, comparison of SEM and AG would be based on an even smaller number of common items.

AH Vocabulary Scale

Reviewed by N. C. Graham

Authors: A. W. Heim, K. P. Watts and V. Simmons
Publisher: NFER-Nelson
Distributor: NFER-Nelson
Age: 9–16; university graduates, etc.
1978 (M); 1979 (T); S not stated
Group test

Test content

The AH Vocabulary Scale is a paper and pencil group test of word knowledge. Multiple-choice response format is used throughout, though provisions for an 'open ended' modification by varying the instructions given to subjects is claimed. Subjects select one of the alternatives and write its number (1–6) in the space provided on the answer sheet. A word similar in meaning to the test words has to be selected from six plausible alternatives. The scale is divided into six 40-word sets named P, Q, R, S, T and U. The sets may be given in pairs, P and Q for school children aged 9–11 year-olds; Q and R for 12–14 year-olds; R and S for 15–16 year-olds and sixth formers; ST is suitable for students at university or college of education; whilst TU is intended mainly for university graduates. Use of the 80-word sets is advised for sixth formers and older people but for younger and less highly educated people one of the 40-word sets may be adequate.

Purpose

The test is offered as an adjunct to verbal and non-verbal tests of reasoning as well as specifically as a test of word knowledge. It is claimed to be particularly useful in the assessment of shy or reticent junior school children; in the assessment of teenagers for guiding them in subject choice at school; for estimating the general capacity of psychiatric patients whose other abilities may be impaired, and for the assessment of post-school pupils generally. The authors specifically exclude the notion that the test is intended as a substitute for the assessment of reading. The Introduction in the Manual considers the justification for vocabulary tests in general and for the production of this one in particular which is said to update these and overcome some of the problems associated with previously published and older tests. The test is essentially normative in its application and is claimed to give valuable additional information about a person's range of abilities in relation to specific norm groups.

Item preparation

Care and thought has been given to the selection of the word lists comprising the test. Representativeness and suitability to the purpose was the guiding principle rather than random sampling. Words with a scientific connotation which, nevertheless, are in fairly general use have not been excluded. For similar reasons words with roots in a wide variety of Classical, Western Oriental and African cultures have been included so as to avoid too much culture specificity both in respect to ethnic origin and to the arts/science divide. Crucial information about the principles of the selection of incorrect alternatives is also given. In particular it is claimed that ambiguity has been avoided while the level of difficulty of the correct alternative has been deliberately kept below that of the stimulus word in each item.

Administration

No specific class of user is named but the obvious implication is that it is suitable for responsible use by anyone professionally involved in education, guidance, psychological assessment of any kind including psychiatric settings. Materials, which are well produced, consist of separate question booklets for each subscale or pair of subscales. These are reusable after checking and erasure of any markings. Corresponding answer sheets for each item set are given. Instructions to subjects are clearly printed on the front of the question booklet. Space for personal identification information is provided on the answer sheet. Detailed sequential instructions for the tester are given in the Manual. Subjects complete three example items under supervision with whatever guidance is necessary.

Standardization

Extensive standardization appears to have been carried out by the authors in the five years prior to publication. Norms for seven very specific reference groups are given as the range of scores in each of five bands—top 10 per cent; next 20 per cent; middle 40 per cent; next 20 per cent and bottom 10 per cent. Means, numbers and standard deviations for each reference group as a whole are given. Different reference groups took different combinations of the subscales. The school pupil reference group 9+to 15+ is divided into year groups and a sixth form sample is treated separately but is also divided into year groups.

Sampling information given is as follows for each of the groups.

1. School pupils aged 9+ to 10+

This group was tested only on the easiest subscale (P) and no information is given about the origins of the sample of 894 pupils.

2. School pupils 11+ to 15+

This group was tested on three 40-item subscales (PQR) and two 80-item combined subscales (PQ and QR). The range of scores on each subscale for each of the five bands mentioned above are presented for each year group with omissions of P scores for the 14+ and P and PQ scores for the 15+ group. It is not made clear whether the samples on which each of the subscale norms are based are independent of one another. If they are, sample sizes at each year level range from 595 to 1112 with two deviant samples (11+ R scores, $n = 175$ and 13+ P scores, $n = 128$). The samples were drawn from 13 urban, suburban and rural schools in unspecified geographical areas but involving five local education authorities.

3. Sixth form pupils aged 16+ to 18+

Only 'reasonable' representativeness is claimed for the sample obtained from three comprehensive schools, three grammar schools, one direct grant school and two sixth form colleges at 'different times of the year'. Norms are presented on subscales R, S and RS for three year-groups. Again, it is not made clear whether or not the samples for each of the subscale norms are independent of one another. Sample sizes are given as:

Subscale	R	S	RS
16+	433	341	344
17+	623	470	481
18+	278	208	208

4. College of education students

Ranges of raw scores in the five 'ability' bandwidths are given on the S, T and ST subscales with sample size 809 in each case, suggesting that these are not independent samples but the same people performing on all three scales. Details of sampling are not given beyond the information that five colleges took part, all four years were represented and that the ratio of males to females in the sample was 7 to 3 reflecting the distribution characteristics of colleges.

5. University students

The sampling here appears to have been largely opportunistic due to the practical difficulties involved in more principled procedures. From the opportunity sample obtained from 'various universities' and university candidates (pre-entrants), cross classification of subjects was carried out on the basis of sex by university category by subject of study. Post-test selection of scores from the subgroup categories was made according to ratios derived from the DES's Education Statistics for the United Kingdom. Only data from the ST subscale were used. Sample size was 702.

6. Graduates

It was not possible for the authors to obtain a fully representative sample of graduates. The profession of education is heavily over-represented and caution is therefore counselled. Norms are given on the S, T, U, ST and TU subscales with slightly different sample sizes for each ranging from 303–390 with no explicit information given about their independence or overlap.

7. Miscellaneous adults

With no claim to representativeness norms are presented for this sample to which subscales Q, R, S, QR and RS were given. The sample of 152 subjects aged 20 + to 60 + was drawn from a wide variety of backgrounds and comprised equal numbers of men and women from five age groups. The mean scores and sample size of each of these age groups is given separately from the usual norms and is shown to increase with successive decades of advancing age. These subjects from a variety of occupations were paid volunteers.

8. *Naval ratings*

A group of 300 of these subjects is claimed by the authors to be possibly representative of the majority of young males in 16–25 age range who left school at 15 or 16 and whose interests and abilities are likely to be in the physical world rather than the verbal/intellectual. Norms are given in the usual bandwidths for subscales Q, R, S, QR and RS.

Scoring

Scoring is in terms of right or wrong against a check list of correct answers. The instructions are clear and straightforward for scoring and obtaining separate totals for 40-word and 80-word sets. Instructions are also given when the open-ended modification has been introduced during administration. A subjective element in judging the acceptability of 'free responses' is necessarily present. Copious examples of scored items are given but it is likely that some interference with the objectivity seems bound to occur in this case. Raw scores are entered on the answer sheet and the appropriate grade (A, B, C, D or E) is read off from the norms of the relevant reference group given in the Manual— instructions to do, or for doing, this are not explicitly given.

Reliability

Four types of data are presented, based on samples of 100 in each category/year group drawn from the total body of scores.

(1) Split-half correlations: coefficients are given for each 40-word and each 80-word set on the 11, 14 and 17 year-old age groups and for university students and graduates. All the correlations are in the range 0.54–0.90.
(2) Inter-set correlations: on the same subgroup samples of adjacent 40-word sets the correlations ranged from 0.67–0.82.
(3) KR-21: this analysis was carried out on the results of all groups and gave correlation coefficients for the P scale in the range 0.90–0.94 with a decline in successive 40-word scales to a range of 0.90 down to 0.50 in the T scale. The coefficients for the longer, 80-word sets, as might be expected, were all in the range 0.83–0.94.
(4) Standard errors of measurement were found to be acceptably low and interpreted to mean that the accuracy of scores was such that differences of

3 marks on a 40-word set or 4 marks on an 80-word set may have little meaning. Thus scores at or near the borders of grades should be interpreted with caution.

Validity

There are 13 pages of information about validity studies in the Manual. These studies relate to schoolchildren (11–16 years), sixth formers in schools and colleges, university and college of education students. Comparisons are made with various other psychometric measures, with CSE and GCE subjects taken and results achieved and with subjects taken at university and college, though not with final degree results.

At school level concurrent validity tests were carried out with the following tests: Reading Comprehension (Schonell, Burt, NFER Comprehension); English Progress (NFER Test D2); Verbal Reasoning (NFER Test 15A); Mathematics (NFER, unspecified test); Non-Verbal (NFER Test BD); and AH Verbal/Numerical/Diagrammatic Tests (AH2/3, AH4). Tables of results for all these against different subscales and whole tests in the AH Vocabulary Test are given together with summaries showing the mean correlations over several measures. The results indicate that the AH Vocabulary Test is measuring, to a high degree, abilities which are displayed in tests of verbal and numerical comprehension and reasoning.

Testing on Set R words was found to differentiate significantly between school English groupings of pupils for GCE, CSE and non-examination. Vocabulary scores on three subscales (Q, R, S) and two tests (QR and RS) are listed in descending order against subjects taken in GCE and the correlations of scores against grade gained in each subject are provided. The higher the mean score of GCE/CSE subject groups the higher the correlation with AH Vocabulary tended to be.

Validity studies with students were carried out against several psychometric measures: Mill Hill Vocabulary; Vernon Graph Test; Committee of V-C's Experimental Test of Academic Aptitude; Morrisby DTB Verbal Test. The correlations were much lower but still statistically significant except for the Morrisby test. A separate section deals with comparisons with the AH5 and AH6. The results indicate significantly high correlations with the verbal and numerical subscale of these tests of high grade intelligence with science and arts students separately and together.

In another study, various Oxbridge University disciplines are rank-ordered by the mean scores of students on AH Vocabulary. Oriental Studies comes at the top of the list and Metallurgy lowest. The rank-ordering has some plausibility. It should be noted, however, that the numbers in some discipline groups were very low compared with others. Similarly, the main subjects taken by students in colleges of education are rank-ordered in terms of Vocabulary scores. Here Psychology/Sociology tops the list with Physical Education at the bottom.

Finally, evidence is presented which shows in all groups a tendency for vocabulary score to rise with age up to the fifth decade which constituted the oldest group tested.

It can be tentatively concluded that the AH Vocabulary Test measures abilities which are correlated with verbal and numerical reasoning scores though not with visuo-spatial abilities. It is reasonably predictive of school achievement in public examinations and differentiates between groups of students taking different subjects at college and university.

Interpretation

The test is intended to be used to assess the standing of an individual against an appropriate peer group in terms of age and placing in the educational spectrum. Separate norms are given for each of the groups and grades are easily read off from the raw scores on the appropriate tests and subscales. Caution about the limitation of the sampling of university students, graduates and miscellaneous adults are given. Emphasis is placed on the primary usefulness of the test in the guidance of teenagers in their choice of subjects at the next level of the educational ladder. Specific advice about how to employ the results of the test in this or any other field is not given. The norms and validity studies are left to speak for themselves in a fairly straightforward way.

Test use

Only one major study in which the test has been used after its publication has appeared:

Heim, A. W., Watts, K. D. and Simmonds, V. (1978). Auditory versus visual stimuli in vocabulary testing. *Research in Education* **18**, 13–24.

General evaluation

This is a well constructed, nicely produced test with evident face validity which can be easily administered by teachers and career guidance professionals. The norms are clearly set out and readily interpretable to assess an individual's status against an actual or potential peer group. Although lacking in any theoretical analysis of what sort of a cognitive task word recognition and synonym matching is, the copious validity studies suggest that it calls upon similar abilities to those used in verbal/numerical tests of comprehension and reasoning. The sampling procedures were a little haphazard and governed as much by opportunity as principle and varied as to numerical balance. To this extent the norms are a little suspect in some groups but, generally, the numbers are large enough and the supporting studies sufficiently numerous as to give modest but firm support to the claims made by the authors. The consideration given by the authors to the selection and assembly of items in respect of current trends in vocabulary usage ensures that the norms are up-to-date and likely to remain appropriate for a number of years.

APU Vocabulary Test

Reviewed by N. C. Graham

Authors: S. J. Closs and M. J. Hutchings
Publisher: Hodder & Stoughton
Distributor: Hodder & Stoughton
Age: school leavers and 13–18 in general
1972–73 (S); 1976 (M, T)
177 (M) printing reviewed
Group test

Test content

There are 75 multiple-choice items in which a stimulus word has to be matched to a synonym from five alternatives. Responses are made by marking a numbered box for each item on a separate answer sheet.

Purpose

The test was originally designed in conjunction with the APU Occupational Interests Guide (also by Closs; see also APU Arithmetic Test). It is offered for normative use primarily with school leavers in mind but also in 'a wide range of situations' (unspecified) where 'an overall indication of understanding of words is required'. The instrument is not designed for 'precise diagnosis of verbal fluency'. The context is likely to be careers guidance and personnel selection but need not be confined to these situations. The test is not recommended for less able subjects and is of doubtful validity for high ability pupils.

Item preparation

The test words were culled originally from a selection of national newspapers and magazines with the intention of excluding archaic, over-specialized and little-used words. No reference is made to their appearance in published word-frequency counts and no information is provided as to how the particular words used were selected from the larger pool. Nothing is said about the synonyms chosen as the correct item or about the way the incorrect alternatives were selected.

Administration

The test may be given on an individual basis or administered to groups of any number. Materials consist of a question booklet which is reusable, separate answer sheets and a scoring key besides the Manual. The correct answers are also given in the Manual. Instructions to subjects are printed plainly on the answer sheet and appear to be so straightforward that only simple guidance and reinforcement from the tester are necessary. This is a speeded test and the Manual strongly emphasizes the necessity of keeping strictly to the 15 minutes allowed. Provision is made on the answer sheet for personal details and the date of testing to be entered.

Standardization

Standardization was carried out by the author of the test in 1972–73. The target population was the 13–18 year age range and this was taken to be coterminous with the school population. A representative sample of the total population in the age range was envisioned. In practice, sampling was carried out by schools. Schools were arbitrarily categorized as small (less than 400), medium (400–800) and large (more than 800). Approximately equal numbers of each were drawn from the pages of the Educational Authorities Yearbook, of 1972, by random selection of one category of school in cycles, from successive pages. It is not said whether the entries in the Yearbook were arranged alphabetically, regionally or otherwise. It is difficult therefore to check on the representativeness of the sampling. Because of administrative difficulties (straight refusals and failures to respond) only 14 of the 30 selected schools took part. Presumably (though this is not explicitly stated) every pupil in those schools was tested, giving a total sample of 6234. This included only a few 11 year-olds who are heavily under-represented. The author also notes that the sampling procedure adopted resulted in a very serious under-representation of the 16–18 year-old age group. While there is something to be said for the assumption that the school population is highly representative of the total population in the age range

11–15+, the pupils still in school after that age cannot be said to be other than highly *un*representative of the 16–18 year-old population. The author acknowledges that the use of the test with this age group must therefore be regarded as suspect.

The standardization procedures did not differentiate between male and female subjects.

Scoring

Scoring of the responses is straightforward, using the acetate key provided, which is placed over the answer sheet. The scorer simply counts the number of Xs appearing in the 'windows'.

Reliability

Two very limited studies of reliability were carried out. Internal consistency of the scores of 175 pupils in the 15–16 age range based on item-total score correlations was found to be 0.95. This can be regarded as satisfactory for the age-group but tells us little about the reliability of scores for groups outside that range.

A study of test-retest reliability was also carried out with a group of 142 13 year-old pupils with a one-week interval between the two occasions of testing. The obtained correlation was 0.83 which can again be regarded as satisfactory for this age group only. This study also enabled the author to claim a virtually zero practice effect of the first testing on the second. The obvious face validity and homogeneity of the test may be held to be reason for regarding these studies as indicating the general reliability of the test but this is not wholly demonstrated.

Validity

The test is directly testing vocabulary knowledge so its validity can be judged by inspection of the items. However, statistical evidence is also presented in respect of concurrent and predictive validity. On a limited sample of 142 pupils in the 13 years age range, correlation of scores with Mill Hill Vocabulary Test scores (revised 1965) was found to be of the order of 0.78—clearly a highly significant result which can again only be assumed to be indicative of concurrent validity over the whole of the age range because of the apparent homogeneity of the content.

A larger scale study of predictive validity was undertaken on a sample of 3000 pupils of 14 years and over which produced 2486 usable scores. The subsequent results of these pupils on the School Leaving Certificate were obtained. Correlation with results in Arts subjects are given for Ordinary and Higher Level examinations. All of these are low positive values, ranging from 0.20–0.46 and all but two are highly significant. The exceptions are German and Latin in which the number of pupils was much lower (49 and 47 respectively). It should also be noted that the pupils who complete both Ordinary and Higher Level examinations are likely to be a highly selected group.

No studies are reported which would have a bearing on one of the primary stated uses of the test—namely for career guidance.

Interpretation

Guidance that raw scores mean little themselves and must be interpreted in relation to age group norms is given. Percentile rankings of scores for each year group are provided and simple explanations are given. Care is taken to emphasize the caution which must be displayed in the case of 16–17 year-olds. The rankings for these two year-groups are only appropriate for pupils still at school. As a crude alternative for those who have had no further schooling after the age of 16 a comparison with the 16 year-old age group is suggested as being appropriate.

Statistical information about the shapes of the distribution of scores in each age group is provided. Measures of skewness and kurtosis are given, indicating bias in the upper and lower age ranges. In addition, warning is given about the margin of error to be expected in any test score. Standard errors of measurement are given for each year-group.

General evaluation

The test has obvious face validity as a general-purpose indicator of word knowledge in pupils of average ability in the 13–16 age range. In particular it is suitable for use by responsible teachers and managers without specialist training in the use of tests provided they observe the instructions about range of application, administration and interpretation spelled out in the Manual. It is likely to be of most use in the fields of vocational guidance and personnel selection.

The standardization procedures and the reliability and validity studies, though technically correct in intention, are somewhat limited in scope and inconclusive in practice. These shortcomings are bound to impair somewhat the effectiveness of the test and make accurate interpretation of scores difficult. Further studies relating the test to its primary purpose, namely vocational guidance and personnel selection, need to be done.

British Ability Scales

Reviewed by S. F. Blinkhorn

Authors: Colin D. Elliott, David J. Murray and Lea S. Pearson
Publisher: NFER-Nelson
Distributor: NFER-Nelson
Age range: 2:06–17:10
1975–76 (S); 1979 (T); 1983 (Manuals 1 and 2; Manuals 3 and 4 revised)
Individual test: restricted availability

Test content

The newest, and in many ways the most complex and flexible, individual test of mental ability, the British Ability Scales (BAS) consists of 23 separate scales which are formally part of the battery, plus a 24th which is provided but relegated to an appendix. The set of scales is intended as a toolkit for professional psychologists, and is aimed at an age range of 2:06–17:06 years. The scales cover a range of perceptual and cognitive skills, classified by stimulus mode (visual or verbal), process (reasoning, spatial imagery, perceptual matching, short-term memory, retrieval and application of knowledge) response mode (motor or verbal). Further subclassifications of process provide for 40 possible subscales, so that the classification system appears to be *post hoc* rather than a schema for generating the scales. Short-form and general IQ scores may also be derived from scores on the subscales. Needless to say, given the target age range, not all subscales are appropriate to all age groups. The scales are named and grouped as follows:

	Items	Ages
Speed		
speed of information processing	40	8–17
Reasoning		
formal operational thinking	13	8–17
matrices	28	5–17
similarities	21	5–17
social reasoning	7	5–17
Spatial imagery		
block design: level and power	16	4–17
rotation of letter-like forms	10	8–14
visualisation of cubes	18	8–17

	Items	*Ages*
Perceptual matching		
copying	19	4–8
matching letter-like forms	10	5–9
verbal-tactile matching	19	2.5–8
Short-term memory		
visual recall: immediate and delayed	19	5–17
recall of designs	19	5–17
recall of digits	36	2.5–17
visual recognition	17	2.5–8
Retrieval and application of knowledge		
basic number skills	68	2.5–14.5
naming vocabulary	20	2.5–8
verbal comprehension	27	2.5–8
verbal fluency	6	4–17
word definitions	37	5–17
word reading	90	5–14

Much of the item content is reasonably familiar from earlier measures of mental ability: block design tasks, matrices, vocabulary, number skills, digit span and others have been staples of intelligence testing. The BAS also contains, however, a small number of scales whose design has been directly inspired by theoretical work in developmental psychology, notably by Piaget and Kohlberg. But the novelty of the BAS lies not so much in the item content as in the central role of the Rasch item analysis and scaling procedures used, with the implications and claimed advantages of this model, which are discussed at length in the supporting manuals.

The scales come with four separate manuals. The introductory handbook (Manual 1) alone runs to 10 chapters and 157 pages. The technical handbook (Manual 2) at 193 pages is crucial but scarcely light reading. Manual 3 contains instructions for administration and scoring, and Manual 4 contains the requisite tables for converting raw scores into interpretable standard scores.

Purpose

'. . . the main aim of the authors of the scales has been to provide a more sophisticated and flexible test resource than is provided by previously published intelligence test batteries. As well as enabling global IQ figures to be calculated, the BAS also enables profiles of cognitive strengths and weaknesses to be obtained and evaluated' (Manual 1, p. 2).

'The BAS provides a flexible test resource for test users. As well as having a large number of scales to choose from, users may also select short-form tests within many of the scales, thus reducing the amount of time required for test administration. As well as obtaining ability estimates for each scale, a wide range of measurement facilities are offered, enabling users to: compare discrepancies in scores between scales; estimate predicted scores; calculate various IQ estimates; identify unusual response patterns to the items in a scale; and measure change or growth in abilities over time' (Manual 1, p. 2).

Item preparation

The preparation of these scales took place over a long period from 1965 onwards and included a preliminary but unpublished version. Manual 1 describes how the BAS grew out of existing instruments and psychological theory; the reader is referred to the Introductory Handbook for details.

Administration

Other than paper, pencils, eraser and stop-watch, the BAS comes as a complete kit in a carrying case thoughtfully provided with a cushioned handle—a feature which becomes quite salient at times given the considerable weight involved. Administration instructions are clear and detailed.

Scoring

Scoring procedures are adequate and range from the provisions of straightforward right/wrong marking keys to judgemental procedures based upon lists of alternative acceptable responses.

Standardization

In principle, norms play a less crucial role in the use of the BAS than with more conventional tests; a consequence of the adoption of the Rasch model and associated item selection procedures. This approach assumes that items in a scale differ only in terms of their difficulty, and that subjects' performance on items differs only on account of differences in a single ability. If the model 'fits' then difficulty estimates can be assigned to items which are independent of the ability range of the sample of respondents used to establish them, and ability estimates can be assigned to individuals which are independent of the particular items used. In practice, there is an assumption of unidimensionality, in that the model presupposes, and item selection procedures are designed to identify, items which differ from one another only in terms of their difficulty level.

The principal impact of this approach from the point of view of the user of the BAS is that raw scores are converted first to 'ability' scores and thence, if desired, to standard scores of the more conventional normative variety. The 'ability' scores are, on the assumptions of the Rasch model, on an equal interval scale, and have a natural interpretation in terms of the odds of success an individual has on any given item. Again, if the assumptions of the Rasch model are accepted, most of the scales can be administered as several distinct non-overlapping sets of items but with a common score scale, with obvious advantage for the monitoring of change and development.

Some 3435 children formed the national sample yielding the data on which tables of ability score scales and norms are based, the sampling and testing procedure being described rather fully in the Technical Handbook (Manual 2) and more briefly in the Introductory Handbook (Manual 1). The sample was arranged in six age-bands, each band two to four years wide, with a subsample size of 500–600. Analysed by year cohorts, sample sizes range from 84–405. The representativeness of the standardization sample was studied by region and socio-economic variables, is presented in the Technical Handbook and appears to be satisfactory. There are tables to convert raw scores to Rasch ability scores, and tables for converting these to percentile values and T-scores (mean 50, standard deviation 10) for each scale. In addition there is a table to convert T-scores to IQ scores.

Reliability

Reliability estimation has an important role in conventional tests in yielding standard errors of measurement, which enable estimates of likely error in obtained scores to be made. Conventional internal consistency reliability estimates and associated standard errors of measurement are provided for each subscale arranged by age, based on the standardization sample; in addition for 13 scales, test-retest and alternate form reliability coefficients were calculated based on alternate forms administered one week apart to 60 children aged 9.

By and large the reliability estimates are satisfactory by conventional standards, with the exception of the two Visual Recall scales which show consistently low reliability across all age ranges. The possibility that this is the result of low variance in scores on these scales is raised in the Technical Handbook.

Rasch item analysis procedures yield standard errors of ability estimates which are different in general for each estimated ability. Scores at the extremes of the range for a given test are less secure, since they are based on the passing or failing of very few items. These standard errors are incorporated into the raw scores conversion tables in such a way that there is no excuse for not noting the standard error along with the score.

Validity

Such information as is provided concerning the validity of the scales falls into two categories: the results of principal components analyses of correlations amongst the scales of the BAS, and correlations between various BAS scales and other tests. The latter are generally based on small samples, are heavily dependent on postgraduate student labour and are not capable of bearing much interpretative load. The former indicate that, overall, one or two components reach the conventional Kaiser-Guttman criterion of significance. Averaging correlations across adjacent age groups yields one very large principal component, but rotation of the first two suggests a breakdown into visual and verbal subscales.

Inspection of norm tables provides another kind of evidence of validity: to no-one's surprise, average ability rises consistently with age across all the scales.

Interpretation

Manual 4 gives a brief summary of how to use the standardization tables provided. Manual 1 describes what is meant by the various derived scales, discusses differences between subscale scores and gives illustrative examples to aid interpretation.

General evaluation

The analogy of a toolkit is particularly apt in the case of the BAS. Consider that the value of a toolkit lies not merely in the quality of each individual tool, but in the appropriateness of the particular mix of tools and their capacity for use in combination. Accordingly, evaluation of the BAS must encompass more than an assessment of the technical merits of the subscales.

Plainly these scales were not designed as standard-bearers of a specific psychological theory concerning the genesis, structure and organization of human mental abilities. Indeed, so little space is given to considering contrasts amongst different theoretical positions as compared with the acreage of print detailing the basis of the Rasch model and the steps involved in its computational implementation that one might almost believe Spearman, Thurstone, Guilford, Piaget, Cattell, Eysenck, Jensen, Hunt and Sternberg to be, mutually and severally, uncritical admirers. For this reviewer's taste, a design matrix of stimulus modes, response modes and processes of which only 57.5 per cent is represented in actual test scales smacks a little too much of compromise and *post-hoccery*. This, perhaps, reflects more on the poverty of psychological theory in providing testable distinctions amongst various notional positions than on the acumen of the authors of the battery. But one wonders why no example of a test of spatial imagery using visual stimuli and verbal responses, or verbal stimuli and motor responses, appears. Is this kind of cross-modal transfer irrelevant? Impossible? Psychometrically intractable?

Indeed one wonders quite where many of the scales come from. We are told that almost all of the scales in the kit meet the demands of the Rasch model, but not which scales were tried at length and discarded (with one exception). Maybe none were. Of course, it could well be that Rasch scaling is peculiarly suited to the assessment of the kinds of skills traditionally represented in individual tests of mental ability, and insofar as information is provided to enable informed judgements to be made, the fit of the scales to the model is good overall. However, the goodness of fit criterion adopted specifically excludes those responses where the difference between an individual's estimated ability and the difficulty of an item is so large as to yield 95 per cent probability of either success or failure, on the grounds that their inclusion makes the fit look poor.

There is a nice circularity here: responses are discarded if they look implausible on the assumptions of the model; the fit of the model is tested with implausible responses removed; hey presto! the model fits the data. What would be more impressive would be a test of fit against more general models, with fewer assumptions, rather than against the alternative hypothesis of an unconstrained item-person response matrix.

Merely a side issue is the adoption of the regrettable practice of omitting altogether from the tables of fit for item statistics those probabilities which are held to be satisfactory. It saves only a very little ink, since asterisks are printed instead, whilst raising the suspicion that maybe the missing figures look too good with the use of the modified test of fit.

The adoption of the Rasch model is nearly, but not quite, whole-hearted. The social reasoning and verbal fluency scales were not constructed with Rasch scaling in view. Further, a 'conservation' scale, reflecting the considerable amount of research effort devoted to the study of conservation of volume, number, etc. in the tradition deriving from Piaget, appears as an appendix, although the word 'scale' is studiously avoided; demotion was because of poor fit to the Rasch model.

Perhaps the most widely canvassed unique property of Rasch-fitting scales— the fact that scores of different individuals on different items can nonetheless be compared—is cautioned against. Indeed comparisons across individuals are discouraged altogether. Comparisons across scales for a single individual can only be made on the basis of normative information, leaving only the common scaling of different sets of items within a scale, with implications for the monitoring of change in an individual, as a fundamental advantage of the scaling method used.

Given the strong emphasis placed on Rasch scaling, it came as a surprise to this reviewer that IQ scoring procedures are proposed to provide a measure of 'overall' ability. The procedures proposed, viewed from the purest Rasch position, correspond to adding height, weight and head circumference to get a measure of the overall size of a person, being in effect weighted sums of subscale scores. IQ is cheerfully identified as the first principal component of subscale intercorrelations. There would be cause to quarrel with this identification even were not the subscales pre-screened by the rejection of items failing to fit the model. In the absence of a large-scale study to locate BAS IQs *vis-à-vis* a range of other IQ measures it might be unwise to assume that they are very strongly connected with IQ otherwise measured.

Indeed the most disconcerting aspect of the BAS supporting material is the lack of cross-validation. As far as can be gleaned there exists a single large data base on which numerous analyses have been conducted. On the basis of these data, some items were rejected, yet internal consistency estimates of the reliability of the scales were based on the same data after their removal. Much of the residual unease which lies behind this review can be traced to such features. Nothing would be quite so impressive as an independent data set, analysed and found to yield essentially the same difficulty estimates, the same reliability estimates and the same scale intercorrelations. Without such a data set the suspicion must always remain that the procedures used in estimating difficulty and ability parameters and rejecting non-fitting items have yielded results which are sample-specific. For the sample-free quality of Rasch item difficulty estimates rests on the assumption that the individual's passing or failing an item depends only on his ability and its difficulty. Rejecting non-fitting items in a given sample is highly prone to capitalization on chance.

It is to be anticipated that now the BAS are in use data will become available which will allow rigorous examination of the assumptions of Rasch scaling, and it would indeed be most gratifying to see evidence of robustness of difficulty parameters, especially across groups of subjects with different social and other characteristics. There is a danger that the user community will take the extensive, if sometimes less than readable, documentation in the Manuals as being definitive. The senior author exhorts continuing research, and one can only endorse his call.

Overall, we have here a major effort towards a diversified approach to the assessment of mental abilities. It is too soon to judge how successful it has been, and there are deficiencies in the supporting documentation which may or may not prove to have long-term consequences. But there is much in the way of sound advice and wisdom in the recommendations concerning the appropriate use of ability tests, which, were they followed widely, might dispose of the notion that testing is just about a single IQ figure, fixed for the life of the child.

British Picture Vocabulary Scale

Brief report

Authors: Lloyd M. Dunn, Leota M. Dunn and Chris Whetton with David Pintillie

Publisher: NFER-Nelson
Distributor: NFER-Nelson
Age range: 3–18+
1980–81 (S); 1982 (M, T)
Individual test

Based on the revised version (1981) of the Peabody Picture Vocabulary Scale, there are 156 plates (items) in the Long Form and 38 in the Short Form. Both sets include 6 practice plates. The plates are held in a ring binder which can be set up to form an 'easel' for administration. Each plate consists of four line drawings; the tester says a word and the testee's task is to point to the 'picture of the word' or to the 'best picture of it'. Procedures are described for limiting the number of items presented to a 'critical range'. A wide range of uses are claimed: a measure of receptive (hearing) vocabulary for preschool use; a screening test for new school entrants; a general measure of scholastic aptitude; and assessment of special cases, e.g. speech-impaired children.

The Short Form was standardized on 3334 children. The Long Form was 'calibrated' (Rasch model) using overlapping subsets of items alongside the Short Form and given to smaller samples of each of four age bands. Standardized scores and percentile ranks are given for both Forms at three-month age intervals. Age equivalents are also given.

Cognitive Abilities Test

Brief report

Author: R. L. Thorndike and E. Hagen
Publisher: NFER-Nelson
Distributor: NFER-Nelson
Age ranges: 9–16 (Levels A to G), 16+ (Level H: sixth form and college)
1973 (M, T); S (British adaptation)
No revisions apparent
1980 (M, T) printings reviewed
Group tests

The CAT assesses three areas of ability. The *Verbal Battery* has four subtests: vocabulary (60 items), sentence completion (60), verbal classification (60) and verbal analogies (60). The *Quantitative Battery* has three subtests: quantitative relations (60 items), number series (60) and equation building (36). The

Non-Verbal Battery has three subtests: figure classification (60 items), figure analysis (60) and figure synthesis (65). All subtests are bound into a single, reusable booklet: separate answer sheets for either hand scoring (by keys) or computer scoring are available. Items are all of multiple-choice type. Practice items precede each subtest.

The items of each subtest are marked off to show the start and finish points for Levels A to H, which correspond to age/ability points. Each testee attempts only a subset of the items in any subtest. For example, as the answer sheet for Level F shows, testees assigned to that Level attempt only items 26 to 50 in subtest 1 of the Verbal Battery. Each Battery requires 50–60 minutes to administer including time for instructions.

The multi-level CAT was developed in the USA, in the period 1971–74, as a revision and extension of the Lorge-Thorndike Intelligence Tests. The British adaptation employed a standardization sample of over 16 000 children. Only the Teacher's Book (procedures and administrative manual) is supplied with the specimen set; norms and other interpretative data are given in a separate manual.

Culture Fair Intelligence Tests

Reviewed by Marten Shipman

Authors: R. B. Cattell and A. K. S. Cattell
Publisher: Institute for Personality and Ability Testing
Distributor: NFER-Nelson
Ages: 8+ (Scale 2); 13+ (Scale 3)
Scale 2: 1949, 1960, 1961 (S, T, M) (Forms A and B)
Scale 3: 1950, 1959, 1963 (S, T, M) (Forms A and B)
Group test

Test content

There are Forms A and B for both Scale 2 and Scale 3. The two scales share the same Manual. Each scale and form consists of four tests comprising between 8 and 14 items. All items are perceptual, consisting of series, classifications, topology or matrices that require no more than simple oral instructions. Each scale is allocated 12.5 minutes for completion.

There is no necessity to translate the items with non-English-speaking people but editions of the test are available in 23 foreign countries. Work on the scales was started in the late 1920s by Cattell, inspired by Spearman's work on the nature and assessment of intelligence. Cattell's efforts produced his Group and Individual Intelligence Tests, in 1930, and non-verbal versions of these tests later in the decade. The scales have been continually revised, and since 1949 have been in their present, four-test format. There have been four major revisions since the original 1930 version, each involving item analysis and improvements in the norms.

The two forms A and B are provided for administrative convenience. The complete test consists of Form A and Form B but they can be taken at separate times. Form A can be used by itself and norms are provided for this, but precision is lost if the Form A + Form B test is not used. Given the brief time allocated to each test this division hardly seems necessary for English schools.

Purpose

'The Culture Fair Intelligence Tests measure individual intelligence in a manner designed to reduce, as much as possible, the influence of verbal fluency, cultural climate, and educational level. The tests, which may be administered individually or in a group, are non-verbal and require only that examinees be able to perceive relationships in shapes and figures' (Manual, p. 5). Thus the test is designed to uncover the 'secretly intelligent'. In the introduction to the test these are defined as Blacks, American Indians, Spanish Americans, foreigners in America, culturally deprived and anyone who does not have the upper-class headstart on traditional, verbal tests of intelligence.

The thinking behind the design of the tests was that the bias in the measurement of intelligence was carried by language and scholastic skills. But non-verbal tests can also reflect experiences and abilities in addition to intelligence. The IPAT Culture Fair Tests, still being developed after 40 years, are an attempt to reduce cultural influences to a minimum.

If the Scales are culture fair they should be fair across national boundaries. But the norms for Scale 3 are American and for Scale 2 American and British. Furthermore, the revisions to the test still leave the basic concept of intelligence dating back to the 1930s unchanged. The claims that the test is culture fair are based on extensive revisions. The Manual also suggests that there have been some revisions in the conceptualization of intelligence. 'From our current vantage point, we now recognise that intelligence, though important, is only one element of a larger set of individual attributes that need to be considered when we attempt to understand and predict human behaviour comprehensively' (Manual, p. 5). This, however, is the only reference to this rethinking and makes it difficult to assess the claim that the influence of culture is minimized. There is no discussion of factors such as differential motivation which may reduce the fairness of even the perceptual items in the tests.

Item preparation

The items in the current version reviewed here have been developed over four revisions. At each revision new pools of items were developed and tested to leave only those with high reliability and validity. The current four-subtest format has survived since 1949.

Administration

The tests can be used for individuals or for groups. The tests can be answered on separate sheets thus permitting reuse of the booklets. There is no rigid age-range for the Scales 2 and 3 reviewed here. The test administrator is advised to evaluate the 'potential ability level' of those to be tested. If ceiling effects are anticipated Scale 3 should be used. The norms for Scale 2 stretch from 7:05–14 and Scale 3 from 13–16. However, both scales are usable with adults, when 14 and 16 respectively would be used as age entry points to the norms.

Standardization

Norms for both scales were produced in 1961. Scale 2 was standardized on 4328 males and females 'sampled from varied regions of the United States and Britain'. Scale 3 norms are based on 3140 cases, all American high school students or young adults. Details of the sampling are not given.

The tables of norms yield a standardized IQ score of mean 100 and standard deviation of 16. A Technical Supplement available from IPAT gives a larger spread of IQs than in the tables in the Manual. There are tables for total scores from the full test (Forms A + B) or for Form A only on Scale 2. The same table is used for full or short versions of Scale 3. There is also a table for converting the standardized IQ score into a percentile equivalent.

Scoring

Tests may be hand or computer scored. Answer sheets are designed for the convenient use of a scoring key. There is little scope for ambiguity in answers and the Manual contains instructions for checking the possibility of patterned responses resulting from misunderstood instructions.

Reliability

Test-retest, internal and parallel test form evaluations of reliability are presented for both Scales. These give measures of consistency over time, over items and over parts. Sample sizes vary from 402 to 3999. The correlations for the full test vary from 0.80–0.87 and from 0.67–0.76 for the short version. Given the constitution of the samples based on ability rather than age it is difficult to interpret these reliability correlations for specific ages. For example, the sample of 3999 includes 'elementary, junior high, and high school students, job corps groups, and other adults through age to 60' (Manual, p. 10).

Validity

Validity is expressed in two ways for each scale. 'Concrete' validity (concurrent) of 0.77 and 0.69 for Scales A and B are given for correlations with other individual and group intelligence tests. 'Concept' validity is also reported as 'direct correlations with the pure intelligence factor' (Manual, p. 11). These correlations with 'g' were based upon factor analyses but no details are given. Coefficients of 0.85 and 0.92 are given for Scales 2 and 3 respectively in their full test form.

The key question of validity is whether the Scales are really culture fair. The concept validity coefficient has been calculated through the use of cross-cultural samples, and independent research on this issue is reported (Manual, p. 9). The research reported concludes that mean scores between different cultural groups are similar or that the Scales have construct validity in non-English-speaking populations.

Interpretation

The scores are unambiguously referred to as measuring intelligence. Reference is made to Cattell's early work and to Spearman's work on 'g' factor. But there is no detail of this 1920's model or of its later adaptations. Thus the scores cannot be referred to a theoretical model that could give them meaning. There is then a danger of interpretation without context.

General evaluation

The care and continuity in the construction of these tests means that they are probably among the most culture free of intelligence tests. The norms presented would still provide a reliable guide to relative IQ. The difficulty in using the test is that conceptions of intelligence have changed since its last revision in 1961. 'g' factor intelligence remains the basis for the construction of the test and for the estimates of validity.

Deeside Picture Test

Reviewed by R. A. Davies

Author: W. G. Emmett
Publisher: Harrap
Distributors: Harrap; the Test Agency
Age range: 7:03–8:02★
1957–1961 (S); 1956 (T); 1957 (M)
1964 (M) (3rd edition); no restandardization apparent
1978 (M); 1982 (T) printings reviewed
Group test

Test content

There are seven Sections containing 100 items in all. One item involves the spelling of monosyllabic words; 8 items involve handling letters; 15 items involve handling numbers (nearly all single digits); 5 items involve handling letters and numbers. The remaining items are pictorial in line with the name of the test.

The contents of the Sections are: (1) choice from five examples following orally presented instructions (e.g. 'Put a cross on the number that is 2 less than 7'); (2) choose the odd one out from five or six examples; (3) mentally sequencing five or six examples and marking the first and the last; (4) pairing of related pictures; (5) selecting mirror images; (6) pictorial representations of analogies; (7) creating one or two next letters or numbers in series.

Purpose

The test 'has been designed to measure the general ability of children aged from 6:06–8:06 . . .' (Manual, p. 1).

Item preparation

Two hundred and fifty items were given to 428 children; 100 items were selected on the basis of analyses of item difficulty and discrimination.

★ The age-range of the standardization sample at the date of testing is given above. Conversion tables allow for the much wider range 6:06–8:06.

Administration

Very detailed instructions are given. Each Section is timed separately and is preceded by two or three practice items. The total time required for the test is 65 minutes (plus a break of not less than 10 minutes after Section 4), though the total working time is only 25.5 minutes. The test booklets are not reusable.

In Section 1 and in some of the practice items it is assumed that all the children know that counting along a row proceeds from left to right. The results for a child working from right to left would be invalidated. The instructions could have been extended to cover this.

Standardization

Standardization is based on 10 000 children forming a complete year group (7:03–8:02) tested in Cheshire in 1957. The tables used to convert to standardized scores are based on adjustments, it is said, 'to compensate for the difference between the level of intelligence in Cheshire and that of the whole country'. The tables of norms give extrapolation to the age range 6:06–8:06.

Scoring

The marking key and instructions are clear. Each item carries one mark.

Reliability

The reliability was calculated from a random sample of 200 scripts from the standardizing group and KR-20 appears to have been used. The value obtained was 0.97.

Validity

The validity of the test is assessed on the basis of correlation coefficients between the scores of 450 children from 11 'representative' schools and 'quotients from Moray House tests given in *1959* and *1961*'. The correlations range from 0.74–0.85. The thinking behind claims for validity based on correlations between the Deeside test and tests of English and Arithmetic would not gain universal support.

Interpretation

There is a claim in the Manual (p. 17) that the Intelligence Quotients given are 'not to be confused with IQs from Binet or Terman-Merrill individual tests obtained by dividing mental age by chronological age'. In fact, the 3rd Revision of the Stanford-Binet Intelligence Scale published in Britain in 1961 (before this 3rd edition of the Deeside Test) does use derived IQs.

There is one puzzling point related to interpretation. The testee's chronological age is to be entered on the front of the test booklet. The Manual (p. 1) says 'Ages should be given in years and *completed* months at the date of the test or at some other stipulated date'. If a testee's chronological age were reckoned at a date other than the date of testing would not this produce an additional error?

General evaluation

According to the publisher's imprint on the test booklet, this test has been reprinted 26 times—the latest in 1982. Somewhere there is a demand for a test which is mainly non-verbal for children from 6:06–8:06 years of age and which is relatively expensive as the test booklets cannot be reused.

Differential Aptitude Tests

Reviewed by David Satterly

Authors: G. K. Bennett, H. G. Seashore and A. G. Wesman
Publisher: The Psychological Corporation; NFER-Nelson (British Edition)
Distributor: NFER-Nelson
Age: 11–18; adults
1947; 1962 (Forms L and M); 1972 (Forms S and T)
1979 (M); 1975 (T) (British editions, S and T)*
Group test (restricted)†

Test content

There are eight tests each available in two Forms, S and T, with a booklet of 62 pages for each Form. The tests are:

---

* USA Manual (5th edition), copyright 1974. *British Manual*, first published 1979 (author: J. Hodgkiss). Both are being used in this review together with *Directions for Administration and Norms* (c. 1973) and *Your Aptitudes as measured by the Differential Aptitudes Test* (c. 1973): published by The Psychological Corporation, New York.
† For use by educational psychologists and 'qualified counsellors or teachers and careers service personnel who have undergone specific DAT training'.

Test	Authors' description
Verbal Reasoning (VR)	understanding, thinking and reasoning in and with words
Numerical Ability (NA)	understanding, thinking and reasoning in and with numbers
Abstract Reasoning (AR)	understanding and reasoning with ideas not in words or numbers
Clerical Speed and Accuracy (CSA)	speed at processing work important in all offices and wherever records are made
Mechanical Reasoning (MR)	grasping the common principles of physics
Space Relations (SR)	visualizing from flat paper plans and thinking in 3 dimensions
Spelling (Sp)	recognizing correct and incorrect spellings of common English words
Language Usage (LU)	use of English language and competence in punctuation and choice of words

The Form S booklet is printed in red and black and the T booklet in blue and black. Test booklets are reusable and answers on separate sheets can be scored by hand or machine. Where DAT is used in conjunction with the *Career Planning Questionnaire* machine scoring is essential. Contents and directions for the planning questionnaire are available on request.

VR

This consists of 50 items preceded by 3 demonstrations items. Each item is a sentence with first and last word omitted. Subjects are required to choose from among five pairs of words, the pair which makes the sentence 'true and sensible'. These items are verbal analogies.

NA

This contains 40 items principally of basic arithmetic with 2 demonstration items. Respondents are required to choose the correct answer from five alternatives the last of which is 'none of these' in all cases.

AR

This consists of 50 items with 2 demonstration items. Every item is of the series type in which the respondent must select from 5 figures the one to continue the series of 4 figures which precedes it.

CSA

This is designed to see how quickly and accurately respondents can compare letter and number combinations. The test is divided into two parts each containing 100 items. Each item consists of five combinations of letters and/or numbers. In each item one of the five is underlined. Respondents are to 'look at the one combination which is underlined, find the same one after that item number on the Answer Sheet and fill in the space under it' (Directions, p. 21).

MR

The 70 items which make up this test consist of pictures and questions about them. Two demonstration items with explanations are provided. Three possible answers are provided for each item.

SR

This test consists of 60 items each of which is a pattern which can be folded into a figure. Respondents must choose from four figures to the right of this pattern which one can be made from the 'opened-out' pattern. Two examples with explanations are provided.

Sp

One hundred words are provided, some of which are incorrectly spelled. Respondents are required to indicate whether each word is correctly or incorrectly spelled. Four examples are provided.

LU

Sixty sentences are presented, each of which is divided into 4 parts lettered A, B, C and D. 'In many of the sentences, one part has an error in punctuation, grammar or capital letter'. Respondents are set to identify which part if any is wrong. Three examples with explanations precede the test paper.

Purpose

The original forms of DAT were developed 'to provide an integrated, scientific and well-standardized procedure for measuring the abilities of boys and girls . . . for purposes of educational and vocational guidance' (USA Manual, p. 1). They were designed to meet the 'expressed needs of guidance counsellors and counselling psychologists' (p. 1). A section of the Manual is devoted to a definition of aptitudes: 'The total concept can perhaps be summarized by regarding aptitude as a capacity to learn' (USA Manual, p. 3). The chief purpose appears to be to obtain differential measurement and multiple scores of several abilities which, if several tests are used, produce a profile of individuals' strengths and weaknesses.

Item preparation

Little detail is provided in either the USA or British Manual concerning the specifics of original item preparation. Items were devised 'to avoid as much as possible dependence on particular school subjects' (USA Manual, p. 6). For NA, Sp and LU the aim was to use materials 'common in elementary school in the US' (p. 6). Items are 'not esoteric' (p. 6). Some anglicizing has been undertaken. Sixty-five items in Form S and 49 in Form T were altered and 6 instruction pages amended. 'Many alterations were relatively minor (e.g. spelling) but some of the units in NA and MR were changed to metric'. The method of item analysis in the anglicized version was principally by biserial correlations for item discriminations. No cut-off value is reported but it is claimed that 'the overall level and distribution of item difficulty were both satisfactory for all tests and for both sexes and forms' (British Manual, p. 9).

The principles governing the original item pool appear to have been derived from theoretical conceptions of the aptitudes/abilities mentioned. Thus, for example, VA is 'the ability to abstract or generalize . . . rather than simple fluency or vocabulary recognition' (USA Manual, p. 7) and double-ended analogies are stated as being particularly suitable to measure this ability. No details of the empirical testing of the original 1947 items are provided nor pilot studies reported, though experimental try-outs and modifications are briefly mentioned.

Administration

Recommended users have been mentioned in the paragraph on Purpose above. Instructions for administration are extremely detailed. Basic materials required are the reusable test booklets, separate answer sheets (scorable by hand or machine). The British version uses the Opscan system. 'For the forseeable future this will be the only answer sheet available in a British version' (British Manual, p. 9). (A machine scoring service is available by contact with the NFER Publishing Company). It is not clear whether the *Career Planning Questionnaire*, for which a special answer sheet is needed, is available in the UK.

Each respondent requires two pencils and the administrator needs a timing device. Times allowed for Forms S and T (excluding demonstration items):

VR		30 minutes
NA		30 minutes
AR		25 minutes
CSA:	Part 1	3 minutes
	Part 2	3 minutes
MR		30 minutes
SR		25 minutes
Sp		10 minutes
LU		25 minutes

It is emphasized that timing the speeded test (CSA) must be accurate to the second. Extremely detailed instructions are given for all aspects of administration before, during and after testing. It is essential that supervisors use the specific directions for the answer sheet being used. It will take some time and considerable study for the administrator to master the instructions.

Standardization

Details of standardization will be confined to the British version. All tests used 3rd, 4th, 5th, lower and upper 6th form pupils attending local authority maintained schools. School-based sampling was employed and testing carried out by teachers and career officers over the period October, 1975, to February, 1976. The sample was subsequently stratified by school type, sex, regional distribution and source of school finance (13 per cent of schools eventually used were described as 'voluntary financed'). Tables are presented to show percentages of children in each year group in the standardization sample and the UK as well as by region, and a sample/UK comparison for pupil-teacher ratio. Only in the last named is the discrepancy large, schools in the sample being much larger than in the UK as a whole.

A very thorough effort seems to have been made to ensure a fairly representative sample of the UK secondary school population, but it is not at all clear how successful this has been. The Manual is commendably frank on the sources of bias which exist (schools largely self-selected with the possible under-representation of schools with below average attainment levels, for example). 'It is hoped that when the validity information is available then it will be possible also to check the sample for representativeness' (Manual, p. 12). Nevertheless, more schools volunteered than were needed and some randomization within the self-selected sample was possible. During testing pupils were allocated at random to Form S and Form T. Data are provided enabling the equivalence of the two Forms to be examined. 'Overall, the results of these comparisons were satisfactory, with little difference between means and standard deviations'

(Manual, p. 13). The number of pupils actually involved in standardization was 'about 10 000', but it appears from the acknowledgements that 19 schools took part. Further data on representativeness is awaited with interest. The norms presented are in percentile form, the same norms being held applicable for both Forms S and T. They are presented by year group for boys and girls separately and combined. Presentation is inconsistent since although there are raw score equivalents to the 99th percentile for most tests in most year groups these do not extend beyond the 95th percentile in the older age (e.g. in VR, NA, AR) groups because of the ceiling effects of the test. Users are advised to use the combined sex norms wherever possible.

Scoring

No guidance about scoring methods is given in the British Manual and users will have, for the foreseeable future, to rely on the USA Manual for information. The specimen set supplied for this review contains examples of many types of answer sheet (each with its specific scoring procedure) available in the USA. However, the list of right answers supplied permits hand scoring of responses made on the OpScan answer sheet. Hints are provided in the USA Manual to increase efficiency of hand-scoring procedures.

The score for each test is the number of right answers with no correction for guessing. The CSA test is scored for Part II only. Identical procedures are followed for both forms of test. (Chapter 3 of the USA Manual offers some limited guidance on the interpretation of the percentile norms and emphasizes that they should be treated as values representing 'zones of ability' rather than precise points. Users will need to purchase both USA and British Manuals to use this test since all information regarding scoring procedures is contained in the former).

Reliability

High reliability is claimed for the British versions of the test. Split-half reliabilities (odd and even items) after adjustment using the Spearman Brown formula are presented for both Forms of each test for each year group and for the sexes separately and combined. Alternate-form testing was adopted for CSA, the only speed test in the battery, over a period of from 1–8 weeks. These have been calculated from what are inevitably very variable numbers of scripts (almost 1500 for 5th-year boys and girls but only 140 7th-year girls). Corresponding standard errors of measurement are supplied. The median reliability coefficient for the UK standardization is reported as 0.83. Those for tests recommended in the prediction of scholastic aptitude (tests VR and NA) are higher than this, however. Reliabilities were obtained from subsamples (method of selection not stated) 'corrected for the different variability of scores in the same way as the USA standardization' (Manual, p. 14). 'Users are advised to consider both British and USA reliability data when interpreting the result of this test' (Manual, p. 14). A small amount of repeat testing with alternate forms of the test has been undertaken. This involved a sample of 3rd-year pupils (50–80 pupils) over periods of from 1–4 weeks. The average coefficient for males was 0.81 and for females 0.82. Reliability of CSA was fairly low and highest for the combined VR and NA scores.

Validity

'Until such time as the UK validity evidence is available users are advised to follow the guidelines set out in the USA Manual' (British Manual, p. 21).

The USA Manual contains information about three aspects of validity: (1) the validity of claims that the tests in the battery provide *differential* information about the relative standing of pupils; (2) the predictive validity of differential scores for the prediction of school grades and achievement tests; and (3) the relationship of DAT tests to other published tests. The USA Manual presents over 30 pages of the three kinds of information given below summarizing details of DAT performance over 30 years' use with forms L, M, S and T:

(1) Chapter 7 provides tables of inter-test correlations for Forms S and T for samples of boys and girls separately (with samples of at least 1200 in all cases). Substantial correlations are reported especially between VR and NA, VR and AR, NA and AR, VR and LU, NA and LU (all within the range 0.68–0.80). Clearly these tests and SR measure substantially the same variance among individuals (see General Evaluation section).

(2) A large amount of data extending over 30 pages of the USA Manual are presented to show the relationship of DAT scores to school grades and achievement tests. These data are difficult to summarize but in general VR, NA, SR and LU are the best predictors for most school subjects. Small improvements in prediction are made from VR + NA scores (median correlation is 0.51 and 0.56 for boys and girls respectively in English and English Literature; 0.48 and 0.51 respectively in mathematics; 0.54 and 0.53 in science; 0.56 and 0.58 in social studies and history; 0.42 and 0.56 in business skills). Clearly these are fairly substantial correlations but no higher than those usually found with traditional intelligence tests.

(3) Substantial correlations were found between the relevant DAT test and similar tests available on the USA market. Sample sizes were generally in the range 100–200. 'Of course, there are limits to the applicability of this

USA data to UK use . . . the USA data are based on the grade point system . . . this is not properly comparable with the UK system of regional boards setting public examinations. Accordingly, UK examination results and other information has been collected. When this has been analysed it will be presented in a special Validity Supplement with interpretative comments' (British Manual, p. 20). This Supplement is not yet available.

Interpretation

The main interpretation of DAT test scores is in the preparation of pupil profiles to identify the relative strength of a pupil's abilities when counselling individuals and 'in making administrative decisions about individuals or groups'. Scores are transformed to percentile bands and users are appropriately cautioned that these are not exact figures (Manual, p. 18). The USA Manual contains full information on the presentation of personal profiles for individual description and career guidance (however, the lack of career-relevant detail for British subjects should be borne in mind). 'While slight differences in percentile scores for two specific tests of the battery are of little consequence, large differences should be considered meaningful' (USA Manual, p. 70).

No guidance is given in the Manual as to how big a discrepancy is educationally meaningful. However, a booklet entitled *Your Aptitudes as Measured by the Differential Aptitude Tests* offers some guidance on this by inviting respondents to consider the degree of overlap between a range of half an inch on the chart provided above and below the percentile attained. Even here, subjects are recommended to interpret this in the light of 'other things you know about yourself'. Moreover, the interpretation of the norms for British pupils is made more problematic by the recommendation that users develop their own local norms since 'local factors are important in determining pupil's job opportunities' (p. 21).

General evaluation

The tests are based on Thurstone's model of intelligence, being divided into a number of relatively independent Primary Mental Abilities, and the consequent belief is that the tests permit a more detailed study of intra-individual differences than do tests designed to measure general ability. No particularly clear distinction between 'aptitude' and 'ability' is sustained. The DAT represents considerable technical competence and the evidence of its usefulness has been carefully compiled over many years. Nevertheless, there are serious doubts about its differential ability. Not only do the tests overlap considerably (thus yielding substantially similar information about pupils) but the correlations presented in the USA Manual offer little support for the theory of intelligence from which they were derived. The degree of overlap is particularly marked for NR, Sp and LU (those of most interest to educators) and NA is as effective (in some cases more effective) in the prediction of verbally based subjects such as English language and literature and social studies as VR. Although the authors argue against the usefulness of intelligence type tests they do present separate norms for a combined VR + NA score which—among the USA sample—have correlated very highly indeed with a number of other 'mental ability tests'. The combination VR + NA is described as a measure of scholastic ability.

Effort has been made to update the test material and norms (however, AR and SR tests are very similar to the 1962 version). In spite of this, interest in MR items is biased toward boys. In Form S every picture which contains the human figure shows males with the single exception of a female—in a wheel chair! This criticism applies equally to Form T where the only recognizable female is using a vacuum cleaner. The use of this test to measure MR in females cannot, therefore, be recommended. NA will clearly favour pupils taught 'traditional' rather than 'modern mathematics' though this may be inevitable if the test is to be accurately named. Linn (1978) has written of the limited validity of DAT for occupational criteria in the USA. Although the British Manual is limited and must be read in conjunction with its USA counterpart the question of the occupational usefulness of the tests must remain open until British information has been made available. At present, validity coefficients for the prediction of career performance in British samples seem to vary considerably between samples.

It seems likely that the DAT's usefulness to teachers is confined to those tests more closely resembling school attainment tests, though it is not clear that they can learn more for educational guidance using them than by the use of their own test if carefully constructed, nor about the nature of 'scholastic ability' (VR and NA) than is conveyed by many other 'reasoning type' tests. However, it must be re-emphasized that there are no reported studies of the DAT's validity among British subjects at the time of writing and the above evaluation has been compiled—as the British Manual recommends—using apparently comparable data from USA investigations.

References

Cooper, M. (1974). *Journal of Experimental Education* **42**, 7–10.

Hakstian, A. R. and Bennett, R. W. (1978). *Educational and Psychological Measurement* **38**, 1003–1015.

Hanna, G. S. (1974). *Journal of Educational Measurement* **11**, 145–149.

Omizo, M. (1980). *Educational and Psychological Measurement* **40**, 197–203.

Linn, R. L. (1978). Review of DAT (review no. 485; pp. 658–659). *In* "Eighth Mental Measurements Yearbook". New Jersey: Gryphon Press.

English Picture Vocabulary Test*

Reviewed by J. P. Ryan

Authors: M. A. Brimer and L. M. Dunn
Publisher: Educational Evaluation Enterprises
Distributor: Educational Evaluation Enterprises
Age range: 3:00–18+
1973 (T); S not stated†
Individual test

Test content

Up to 125 items are available for use. Each item requires that one drawing of a set of four be identified in response to a single word stimulus that refers to a noun, adjective or verb appropriate to only one of the drawings. The child is not required to read or write anything, and may respond simply by pointing.

The Full Range version is a 1973 condensation of various smaller tests published between 1962 and 1970. The Full Range edition covers the age range from 3:00–18+ and advice is given as to the appropriate entry point into the item list for the age of the child being tested. It is unlikely that many children would have to respond to as many as half the items.

All of the items are fairly simple black and white line drawings. As the test is a derivation of the Peabody Picture-Vocabulary Test, there is a decided North American flavour to many of the items, but this is likely to have only a minimal effect on responses. (The Listening for Meaning Test (q.v.), produced in 1981 as a development from and intended successor to the EPVT, has an unmistakable British flavour).

Purpose

The purpose of the EPVT is not entirely clear. The Administrative Manual states that 'it is a measure of listening vocabulary and . . . because of its high correlation with more general measures of intelligence it may be employed as

---

* The 'Full Range Edition' is reviewed here. Other versions are: EPVT 1 (Infant school range), 1962; EPVT 2 (Primary range), 1962; Pre-school version, 1968; EPVT 3 (11–18 year-olds), 1970. The EPVT is based upon the Peabody Picture-Vocabulary Test originally published by L. M. Dunn in 1959.
† The Interpretative Manual was not available at the time of preparing this review.

an indicator of academic aptitude . . . it is not a measure of range of vocabulary nor of pictorial comprehension. The resulting test score is perhaps most accurately described as a measure of the level of semantic reference which a child is capable of comprehending' (p. 2).

Item preparation

The Full Range Edition has incorporated items of the four previous tests (EPVT 1 for infants; EPVT 2 for primary age; pre-school version; EPVT 3 for 11–18 year-olds), but fresh items were tried and a restandardization was carried out. These procedures are not described in the Administrative Manual but it was apparently intended to present this information in an Interpretative Manual. The items are, however, derived from the Peabody Picture-Vocabulary Test for which an extensive literature exists.

Administration

Vision and hearing should be adequate but the test can be given to children whose only response ability is to indicate clearly 'Yes' or 'No' in some way. Preferred response modes are either by giving the number of the alternative drawing chosen, or by pointing to it. In cases of doubt the tester can query the response by pointing to the pictures in turn and eliciting a yes/no response. This permits the use of the test with the severely handicapped.

Pronunciation of the stimulus words is based upon the "Concise Oxford Dictionary" (1972 edn, 2nd revision), but it is permissible to use local variants *in addition to* the standard pronunciation. Stimulus words may be given more than once.

In general the starting points are given by the following:

For 3:00–6:11 children, begin at item 1
For 7:00–10:11 children, begin at item 15
For 11:00–18+ children, begin at item 55
For 14:00–18+ above average children, begin at item 90.

The same three practice cards are used with all subjects but the stimulus words used with them vary depending upon age.

Standardization

The Administrative Manual gives no details of the standardization procedure, but states that 'A full description of the standardization procedure will be given in an Interpretative Manual for the complete EPVT range when an attempt will be made to gather together the considerable literature describing users' experience of the test in surveys and extensive screening procedures' (p. 2).

Tables are given to convert raw scores to standardized scores with means of 100 and standard deviations of 15. Ages from 2:11–18:00 are covered and the standardized scores can range from 60–140. The standard scores can be converted to percentile equivalents using a further table and guidance is also given on how to derive vocabulary-age norms if these are required. These other scores are of course only transformation and add no further information. As there are no subtests (in the IQ scale sense) or any other component or derived scores, no further analysis by the user is possible.

Scoring

On first reading, the scoring seems a little complicated, but the process itself is simpler than the description of it.

Correctness of response is indicated on the score sheet which is also the source of the stimulus words. Capitalization of one of the first four letters of the stimulus word indicates the number of the correct picture. A base item score has to be established. If Item 1 is the starting point, it becomes the base item score, but for any other starting point, if the child makes 5 correct responses in the first 8 items, the base score is the number of the first item attempted. If this criterion is not reached, then a reverse order of presentation is used until it is. The ceiling is similarly established when a child makes 5 errors within the space of 8 consecutive items. The score is then calculated by counting all errors between the base and ceiling items and subtracting them from the item number of the ceiling. It is assumed that no errors would have occurred below the base item.

It is also suggested that the time taken to complete the test is recorded, and that a 'rate of test performance' (items per unit time) be derived. The purpose of this is not stated and no data are given to permit its evaluation. Moreover, except in cases of extremely slow performance, the rate of presentation by the tester would be a crucial factor and would invalidate any norms even if they were available. It is probably better to omit any attention to time.

Reliability

No data are given in the Administrative Manual.

Validity

No data are given in the Administrative Manual.

Interpretation

Beyond the score conversions noted above, we await the Interpretative Manual.

General evaluation

This test is easy both to use and to score, and is extremely useful as the source of an IQ estimate for children with restricted or no speech or with a limited ability to respond. Provided that caution is used, the test can be regarded as equivalent to an IQ subtest, and the standardized score as a rough IQ *estimate*.

The test has several faults, however, and the Listening for Meaning Test (LMT) is intended to rectify some of them, but it is a slightly more complicated test to use.

On the EPVT there are 3 rather ambiguous items (Numbers 65, 90, 95) although their overall effect would be small. More important are problems associated with the type of response given. An oral response, giving the number (1 to 4) of the chosen picture on each card, is based on an assumption that children can use the numbers correctly and consistently, especially when under the pressure of making a difficult choice. This would probably work against the lower ability child. On the other hand, the pointing response can easily lead to stab-pointing and the consequent marking of the cards. As this would occur presumably with children of lower ability, various effects might lead to disadvantage a child of about average ability.

The mechanical presentation of the pictures is more difficult than it should be and requires that some makeshift support be used.

The test package consists of three parts—Manual, booklet and score sheet. The Manual is clear with regard to both administration and scoring, but within the booklet of test cards the instructions are a little confusing. Instead of each age group being dealt with separately, they are mixed up in the three presentations of 1st Picture, Practice and Beginning Item. Because the booklet is not tab-indexed there is no easy way to find the beginning item. The layout of the score sheet is rather poor. It is difficult to see why all 125 items could not have been placed on the one page and in strict sequential order.

The score sheet also contains a fair number of items of background information to be filled in. At first glance this seems impressive but on reflection one would wish to know which of these items would be of any use. Much of the information would already be available on any child being tested, and the relevance of other items is undetermined. (This extra information has been omitted from the newer version, the Listening for Meaning Test).

The Administrative Manual does not list any references, and the proposed Interpretative Manual does not appear to have been published.

The Essential Intelligence Test

Reviewed by Andrew Sutton

Authors: Fred J. Schonell and R. H. Adams
Publisher: Oliver & Boyd
Distributor: Oliver & Boyd
Age range: '8 to 12+'★
1940
Revisions not discussed; S not stated
1977 (M); 1979 (T: A); 1982 (T: B) printings reviewed†
Group test

Test content

The test comprises disposable test booklets and separate Manuals for Forms A and B. There are 100 questions in each booklet, of the traditional written 'verbal reasoning' type, grouped into subjects of increasing difficulty (e.g. Missing Words, Synonyms, Analogies, Classification, Opposites), and including arithmetical items. The front cover of the test booklet bears written instructions to the examiner, the rear cover a series of practice questions to be filled in with the help of the teacher. No guidance is given on the upper limits ('12+') of the test's applicability. On the lower limits: '*It cannot be too strongly emphasized, however, that the Essential Junior (sic) Intelligence Tests should be given only to pupils with Reading Ages of eight years and above*' (Manual B, p. 3, publisher's italics).

Purpose

'The purpose of the Essential Intelligence Test is to provide a measure of general intelligence for children between the ages of 8 and 12+' (Manuals, p. 3). Alternative Forms A and B are recommended both for routine annual testing for school record-card purposes, the Forms to be alternated year by year, and for research purposes where reassessment is required after an interval.

★ The ages of the standardization group ranged from 6 years to 14+ (Manual, Form A, p. 4) and 7 years to 15 (Manual, Form B, p. 4); but see text.
† The test booklets show 'Copyright 1940'. Form A is 'Thirty-Third Impression, 1979' and Form B is 'Twenty-Fourth Impression, 1982'. The Manuals are simply dated 1977.

Item preparation

For Form A, 'several hundred questions were prepared and carefully examined by a number of adults in order to eliminate unsatisfactory items' (Manual A, p. 3). The 217 questions were tried on 300 pupils and 100 selected on the basis of discriminating power and spread of difficulty. Form B subscales were selected to correspond closely to those in Form A. Details of this stage of test construction are not given, however, in the Manual for Form B. *There is an especial cause for concern* over the lack of mention in the Manuals of changes made due to decimalization and metrication. This matter will be returned to below.

Administration

General instructions include the somewhat contradictory requirement that the examiner should 'create an atmosphere of enjoyment' and that 'invigilation should be rigid' (Manual, p. 5). Each child requires a test booklet and something to write with. Maximum time for completion is 45 minutes and examiners are cautioned to make arrangements to keep pupils who finish within that time occupied, so as not to disturb the others. Pupils should not be allowed to mark their own tests, see their marked test papers or be given any indication that there might be a retest in 6 or 12 months' time.

Detailed instructions for the teacher include distributing the booklets face downwards and working through the practice sheet on the rear cover. After these procedures are completed the pupils turn over the booklets and fill in their names and other details on the cover, the teacher reads aloud the front-cover instructions and the test begins. There is a time warning 10 minutes before the pupils have to stop. The teacher's 'script' is clearly presented and has to be strictly adhered to.

Standardization

The information on standardization given in Manual B reads in full as follows: 'The test has been standardized on 7759 pupils aged 7 years to 15 years inclusive, by methods similar to those used for Form A' (p. 4). The Manual for Form A ('3200 pupils aged 6 to 14+') only adds that 'careful consideration of the groups chosen made up for limitations, so that the distribution of Intelligence Quotients obtained followed the normal curve very closely' (p. 4). The distribution of IQs is illustrated for 1709 junior school children.

No indication is given as to when these data were procured. Here it must be noted that the same publisher used to produce the Essential Junior Intelligence

Test, also by Schonell and Adams, 'for pupils ages 7+ to 12+', which with certain exceptions to be noted below appears to have been identical to the test reviewed here. The Manuals for Forms B of the two tests are identical, except that the present test is recommended for a slightly curtailed age range, grants much greater emphasis to not testing children with reading ages under eight and avoids Imperial measures in the answers to six of its questions. *The standardization data remain unaltered.*

Scoring

Examiners are invited to complete the test themselves to provide 'an answer pattern for speedy marking' (Manual B, p. 4). Only unequivocal responses merit a point. Correct responses are listed in the rear of the Manual.

Reliability

The entry on reliability in Manual B reads in full as follows: 'A retest with a group of pupils after an interval of three months gave a correlation ratio of 0.92 ± 0.01' (p. 4). Parallel-form reliability is reported from a study of 225 pupils 'between the ages of 9 and 10', which 'gave the high correlation index of 0.953 ± 0.004' (p. 4).

Form A is reported to have an uncorrected split-half of 0.92 ($n = 66$, 11 year-olds); and a 12-month repeat test correlation of 0.92 (sample size and ages unstated). Again, no information is given on when these studies were done: both of the quotations from Manual B repeat *verbatim* the corresponding entries in the earlier 'junior' test.

Validity

The same entry on validity appears in both the earlier and later tests (note that it refers to Form A and to the 'junior' age range): 'Essential Test Form A has since its publication proved to be a most valid and reliable measure of good general intelligence for the age range 7 to 11. In comparison with other group tests (Moray House and Simplex) it has yielded correlation ratios of 0.91 and 0.90. With the Terman Merrill Test (an individual intelligence test) the correspondence was $r = 0.89$' (Manual B, p. 4). No other details are given. Manual A gives even less information: 'Comparison with other valid tests of intelligence gave correlation coefficients of the order 0.91 ± 0.01. (63 pupils, 11 years of age.)' (p. 4).

Interpretation

Raw scores are converted from a table in the Manuals into mental ages in years and months, ranging from 6:05 (A) and 6:06 (B) to '16 y 6 m at least' (A) and '16 y 8 m at least' (B). The Manuals recommend that a ratio IQ should be calculated from this mental age. There is no mention of possible variations in the standard deviations of these ratio IQs at different ages, of possible baseline or ceiling effects or of the possibility of chronological age adjustments being needed at higher ages to maintain comparability. These omissions are particularly unfortunate in view of the test's recommended use in regular reviews of children's IQ.

In Manual B the table of norms is headed 'REVISED SCORES AND EQUIVALENT MENTAL AGES FOR THE ESSENTIAL INTELLIGENCE FORM B CANCELLING ALL PREVIOUS NORMS' which the reader might be excused for thinking referred to some recent update. The previous 'junior' version of this test, however, had the same table, with the same heading *verbatim* at the top and identical mental-age values for every raw score—*even though six of its questions have now been changed to accommodate decimalization.*

Test use

The test does not appear to have attracted the amount of research use hoped for, at least in recent years. The review copies of the test booklets, however, are marked 'Thirty-Third Impression, 1979' and 'Twenty-Fourth Impression, 1982' for A and B respectively. Presumably, therefore, the test has been a considerable commercial success, selling to school teachers, and possibly also to parents, right up to the present day.

General evaluation

The Essential Intelligence Test dates back over forty years. It is quite impossible from the Manuals to see what substantial changes, if any, have been made to the test over that time. It seems at least likely that the normative base may have been rendered out of date by changes in educational level over the long span of time involved, while advances in psychometric theory certainly render the nature of the norms quite obsolete. The Manuals give a superficial impression of an authoritative instrument—and must certainly look familiar and reassuring, tested and true, to many schoolteachers—but so fudges the changes in the world of psychometrics and even in certain of its own test questions as to be actively misleading. Why routinely test children's intelligence six-monthly or yearly anyway for record-card purposes—even with a well constructed and relevant instrument? This provides the teacher at best with a ritual 'IQ' and, in a test so inadequately constructed that many older children will show an inevitable decline in ratio IQ at '12+', may actually produce misunderstandings and anxieties that are positively harmful. There is no way in which even the most skilful psychometrician could interpret a sequence of ratio IQs, gathered as recommended in the Manuals. Nor is there any way in which the test could be restandardized or reconstructed without a very substantial financial investment or with much semblance to its present form in the final result. There seems no alternative to suggesting that this test, whatever its history, ought now to be withdrawn from sale. If it is not, then routine and regular group testing of children on this test will presumably continue to satisfy both the publisher and teachers—with no corresponding positive effect either for the children tested or upon their education.

Kuhlmann-Anderson Test*

Reviewed by Charles F. Owen

Author: R. G. Anderson
Publisher: Personnel Press
Distributor: NFER-Nelson
Age ranges: 12–14 (USA grades 7–9) (Test G)
14–17 (USA grades 9–12) (Test H)
1939
1960 (7th edition)
1963 (Revised) (Booklets G and H)
Group test

Test content

The Kuhlmann-Anderson tests consist of eight booklets covering the age range from Kindergarten to 12th grade: booklet G covers grades 7–9 (approximately ages 12–14) and H covers 9–12 (14–17). Each booklet contains eight tests, four verbal and four quantitative; five of the tests are common between G and H. Each test has between 20 and 25 items.

Verbal tests include tasks such as finding the first and last words of a jumbled sentence, finding words which are alike, finding the middle term in a group of words (one of the examples is American currency). Quantitative tests include

---

* Sub-title: 'Measure of Academic Potential'.

finding the odd member in a series, adding terms to a series, finding the mathematical symbols to complete an equation, solving equations given in words (e.g. 'This No. added to 8 makes 3 less than 15').

All items are multiple choice.

Purpose

The Kuhlmann-Anderson test 'is designed to measure mental growth, especially those mental characteristics which are important in school learning' (Technical Manual, p. 1).

Administration and Scoring

This is a group test which can be administered by a teacher. The tester has a booklet with detailed instructions, and specific directions to be read out to the pupils for each test: these instructions are not reproduced in the pupils' booklet. Pupils fill in their own answers on a multiple-choice response blank: these are machine readable. There are also cardboard masks to lay over the answer sheets for scoring by hand.

Before each of the eight subtests the tester reads the directions aloud, and then takes the pupils through the examples (from two to four) before proceeding. Each section is timed (2 or 3 minutes). Total working time is 23 minutes for G booklet and 24 for H booklet. The Manual suggests that total testing time will rarely exceed an hour.

Standardization

The standardization sample was drawn from 18 schools in 10 states of the USA. 'Three variables were considered in selecting schools to be used in the norm sample: (1) socio-economic level of the community; (2) size of the community; and (3) geographic location' (Technical Manual, p. 6). The sample schools did not form a probability sample, but were drawn so as to be 'representative' of the population: 'Representativeness was ranked high in importance as a sampling goal' (Technical Manual, p. 6). No other information is given about the sampling frame or how the choices were made.

The standardization sample was approximately 20 000 with about 700–800 in each three-month interval between 11:11 and 18:01 (fewer at the extremes). Both G and H Forms were administered to all pupils in grades 6–12. 'In the course of reviewing the tentative norms for the Seventh Edition tests, some linear adjustments were found to be advisable to bring them into closer agreement with those of the Sixth Edition' (Technical Manual, p. 7). No other explanation of these 'adjustments' is given.

There is a small sex difference in favour of girls for the Verbal score, but no difference for the Quantitative score. Tables present norms for girls and boys combined and convert scores to Grade Percentile Ranks for the Verbal, Quantitative and Total scores, and to Deviation IQs for the Total scores (previous editions used IQs based on mental ages).

Reliability

Two subsets of pupils from the standardization sample were used to estimate reliability. These were pupils aged 13:05–13:07 ($n = 699$) for Form G and those aged 15:05–15:07 ($n = 785$) for Form H. Reliabilities were derived from factor analyses of the four Verbal tests and the four Quantitative tests separately. Reliabilities for the subtests range between 0.46 and 0.74 and are generally higher for H than for G.

Reliabilities for the summary scores were based on error variance estimates derived from the factor analyses and are, for V, Q and Total scores respectively, 0.83, 0.84 and 0.91 for Form G and 0.89, 0.85 and 0.93 for Form H. 'For the deviation IQ, the reliability was taken to be the same as that of the Total Score' (Technical Manual, p. 25).

A smaller number of children in the 8th and 9th grades were retested one or two years later: the test-retest correlations were between 0.83 and 0.92.

Validity

Data on the validity of the Sixth Edition have been published elsewhere (Kuhlmann and Anderson, 1952) and items for this Seventh Edition were chosen using Mental Age on the Sixth Edition test as a criterion. In this way, the Manual claims 'The validity of the Sixth Edition tests was built into the Seventh Edition tests' (Technical Manual, p. 18). Apart from this claim, tables present a range of correlations with other tests and with academic grades: these range from 0.49–0.90, with sample sizes from 23–382. Otherwise no information is given about who these pupils were, how they were selected, their ability levels, etc. More studies on well defined samples will be needed to establish both the concurrent and predictive validity of this test.

Interpretation

The Norms Manual gives some guidance on the interpretation of both the Grade Percentile Ranks (GPR) and the IQs. It also discusses the interpretation of the Verbal minus Quantitative difference scores, but the reliability for these are so low (0.19 for G and 0.37 for H, Technical Manual, p. 27) that they should be treated with caution. Tables are also given to relate GPR to expected scores on the Scholastic Aptitude test.

Test use

The Manual recommends the test for use in individual guidance. As the use of the test is unrestricted it can be used by non-psychologists, and the Norms Manual contains some guidance for non-professional users. These include discussions of the use of the different scores, but also such things as to use the scores in conjunction with other information, not to rely on just one test if the results seem odd, and so on.

General evaluation

The Kuhlmann-Anderson tests have a long history, going back to 1939, and have been widely used. They have also undergone extensive revision. Nevertheless, they may have outlived their usefulness. The Grade Percentile Ranks will probably be of little use to non-USA users and otherwise the test only gives an IQ. The only diagnostic information it provides therefore is whether or not a child is doing well for its age (and, less reliably, whether their performance on the Verbal and Quantitative tests is equivalent). This information may be of little use in education.

The Manual suggests that scores might assist a student counsellor in 'matching the student's potentialities with the likelihood of entrance acceptance and survival in certain colleges' (Norms Manual, p. 11), but again, outside the USA this may be of little use.

Reference

Kuhlman, F. and Anderson, R. G. (1952). "Kuhlmann-Anderson Intelligence Tests (Sixth Edition) Master Manual". Princeton: Personnel Press.

The Listening for Meaning Test

Reviewed by J. P. Ryan

Author: M. A. Brimer
Publisher: Educational Evaluation Enterprises
Distributor: Educational Evaluation Enterprises
Age range: 3–18+

1981 (M, T); S not stated
1982 (M) (revised)*
Individual test

Test content

In each item the child is asked to indicate which if any of the two pictures offered indicates a given word, and then is asked if the *other* picture (or both in turn) indicates the word. There are 10 scales (A to J) of 12 items each, plus 4 demonstration items and 12 'focusing' items. The purpose of the latter is to determine a starting point among scales A to J.

While the general technique is derived from the English Picture Vocabulary Test (EPVT) there are specific differences. This test contains only two pictures per item, and the child must respond to each of them. Moreover, neither of the pictures is an exemplar of the stimulus word for some items (between 1 and 4) for each scale. The drawings are simpler than in the EPVT and the flavour is definitely British, whereas the EPVT was unmistakably North American in origin.

Purpose

'The Listening for Meaning Test like its predecessor the English Picture Vocabulary Test is a measure of the understanding of spoken English words through the recognition of pictures that represent their meaning' (Manual, p. 1). The test is said to correlate well with intelligence scales and with comprehension measures. It is a specific aim of the LMT to try to overcome some of the deficiencies of the EPVT, particularly with regard to the uncertainty of the starting point within the test, and in the nature of the response task, especially with less able children.

Item preparation

A random sample of 1002 words was drawn from the 3rd Edition of the "Shorter Oxford English Dictionary", and the sample was screened by 'educated native English speakers to eliminate those words considered not to fit the domain of listening vocabulary' (Manual, p. 11). Thus archaic, esoteric, and literary words unlikely to be found in spoken dialogue, and words without

---

* 'M' refers to the Administrative Manual. The Interpretative Manual was not available at the time of the review.

lexical meaning were excluded, but simple uncommonness was not a criterion for exclusion. These methods removed 327 of the sample words, and of the 675 remaining, others were eliminated because of the constraints implied by the need to supply drawings. Of the 576 words that could have been represented by a drawing, some could also have been removed because of the proposed conditions of presentation. However, it was left to the standardization programme to identify these, and their pictures were eventually used as distractors for many of the items.

Administration

The only response skills required are the ability to attend and to clearly signify 'yes' or 'no' in some way, not necessarily verbal. The tester is required to be painstaking over the four demonstration items to ensure that the task is understood and rapport established. For these initial items two levels of difficulty are available, the lower being used for children under 11 years old, and also for those older than 11 if their understanding is suspect. Pronunciation of the stimulus words should follow that given in the "Shorter Oxford English Dictionary" (1973) and a second, local or dialect, form may be used, but as a follow-up. No contextual cues whatsoever may be offered with any stimulus word. Variation of the instructions is permitted when necessary provided that clues to the solution of the task are not conveyed.

Following the demonstration there are 12 'focusing' items (Scale P). The score on the 'focusing' items determines which scale should be used as a starting point, but do not count toward the total score. Each stimulus word is printed on the score sheet having either the first, last or no letter capitalized. This coding indicates whether the left-hand, right-hand, or neither picture is being the exemplar. The child is asked to indicate which if any of the two pictures indicates the stimulus word, and then is asked if the *other* picture (or both in turn) indicates the stimulus. If responses to both pictures are correct a '1' is placed on the right of the stimulus word on the score sheet; otherwise a '1' is placed to the left of the stimulus word (presumably, the latter coding is used if only one, or if neither of the answers is correct; the instructions are not explicit on this point). Thus, answers marked in the right-hand columns form the score.

No fewer than 12 items of a single scale (A to J scales) must be used if a score is to be obtained. The user is advised that, if possible, at least three consecutive scales should be given in order to ensure a reliable score.

All the test cards plus the operating instructions are on moderately heavy card in a comb binding and can be easily presented.

Standardization

Standardization was carried out by regular users of the EPVT who supplied data on EPVT score, sex, age and a rough estimate of socio-economic status, together with the raw scores on the proposed LMT material. Using 16 EPVT levels, the scores were then scaled using a Rasch technique. Because of an age-related bias in this sample a further testing of 100 each of 6, 10 and 14 year-olds was carried out with several checks to provide the tables in the 1981 Manual, but it is stated that 'there must remain some doubt over their dependability' (Manual, p. 12). The standardization procedure yielded standardized scores (mean 100, standard deviation 15) at each year level from 3–18.

Reliability

Reliabilities and standard errors of measurement are given for testing that commences at each of the scales A to J, and for the situations in which only 1, 2 or 3 consecutive scales were administered. Excluding testing commencing at scales I and J, the reliabilities for one-scale situations ranged from 0.85–0.89, for two-scale situations from 0.92–0.93, and for the three-scale situations from 0.95–0.96. These values have been estimated from inter-item correlations and are hence internal measures. No information is given on test-retest or inter-tester reliabilities, although these would be expected to be lower.

Validity

As with the EPVT, validity remains an unresolved matter. Concurrent validity is said to be high (with 'intelligence scales and with measures of comprehension') but neither the actual criteria nor the data are given. Construct validity is not discussed.

Interpretation

Finding the standardized score from the raw score is a simple procedure but the derivation of this score is almost as far as the interpretation goes. The score is treated in much the same way as an IQ quotient or deviation score, and should be read in conjunction with the relevant standard error. As there are no subtests or any other component scores, no further analysis is possible.

General evaluation

This test is easy to use and score, although not quite as easy as the EPVT. It does have some advantages over the latter, although both suffer from a lack of support information in their Manuals. Both of the tests are invaluable instruments for use with children having restricted or no speech, or otherwise having limited ability to respond. In such cases the standardized score can, with caution, be used as an estimate of IQ. It does seem that the LMT is a possible subtest of an IQ scale, and could be treated in much the same way. But just what it specifically measures, in addition to the IQ component, has not been determined. Further research may throw some light on this. No references are given in the Administrative Manual.

The test material has one small fault. The letter-tabs used on the booklet to indicate the pages of the scales are very flimsy and need immediate reinforcement before use.

Moray House Junior Reasoning Test 2

Reviewed by E. P. Duggan

Author: The Godfrey Thomson Unit, University of Edinburgh
Publisher: Hodder & Stoughton
Distributor: Hodder & Stoughton
Age range: 8:06–10:06
1952–58 (S); 1952 (T)
Revisions (unspecified) 1969
1979 (T) printing reviewed
Group test (restricted)★

Test content

The items consist of numerical and verbal problems, codes, sequences, similarities and differences, selections, sequences, matching words and shapes and word/letter completions. The test is graded in difficulty throughout. The responses required are generally straightforward: filling in blanks, entering response in bracket spaces, underlining words or shapes. The content is somewhat unevenly distributed, e.g. the last 40 items are all connected with shapes (cp. JRT4).

Purpose

JRT2 is used for primary school classification and record cards. The Manual claims (p. 15) that 11 LEAs in England have used the test. It is clearly a verbal/non-verbal test.

★ Available to schools with the permission of the local Chief Education Officer.

Item preparation

No indication is given of this, nor of the sampling frame of items, nor of pilot studies, nor of the intentions of the author.

Administration

Moray House (MH) style of general instructions in relation to numbers of supervisors, their duties, timing devices and materials, and the wording of instructions are given. The test consists of 14 parts—groups of 5–7 items—each part separately timed. The timing of each group of items varies from 1.5–4.5 minutes. Each group has two worked examples. The test is organized into two sections. Section 1 of the test takes a total of 60 minutes, including instructions and examples. Thus after every few items the children are stopped, two examples of the next group are given, the test questions are answered, another stop, and so on, *ad nauseam*. This mode of test administration is open to very serious question. Section 2 is similarly administered, taking a total time of 44 minutes including 23 minutes of instruction. Between sections there is a break for the children of 15–30 minutes, so some 11 pages of testing material can take a minimum of 2 hours, for the purposes of classification and grading only, for nine year-old children.

Standardization

Scores of 36 217 children (19 211 boys, 17 006 girls) in seven LEAs were analysed to produce the conversion tables in order to produce Reasoning Quotients for children aged between 8:10 and 10:04. The results were accumulated from smaller groups of children in each of the areas in the years 1952, 1953, 1956 and 1958. It is interesting to note that in Table 2 (Manual, p. 15) the main Reasoning Quotients ranged from 101.8 in one local education authority in 1952 to 95.9 in another in 1958. No explanation is offered for this. Altogether, eleven LEAs had used the test in various parts of England. Complete year-groups were used for the standardization. The Manual claims that using this procedure, 'the resulting data (were) free from errors due to unrepresentative sampling'—a claim which may reasonably apply to the 11 LEAs used. The point, however, is whether the data are representative of the child population in the whole country, and the Manual is silent on this point. The method used for the standardization was essentially that due to Lawley (see Introduction), giving a mean of 100 and standard deviation of 15. Sex differences varied from area to area, but differences were small overall.

Scoring

By MH standards, the instructions for marking JRT2 are neither as clear nor as well presented as in other MH Tests (e.g. JRT4). However, the scoring keys are clear and the correct answers are well-spaced to match responses. Marking one page at a time throughout the tested group is recommended. The keys also give helpful notes on those items requiring correct spelling and the allowable alternatives. Each page of the test carries a score column for items on that page. The front page acts as a summary sheet for the page scores, reasoning quotient (RQ) and age.

Reliability

A random sample of 200 scripts was drawn from the complete year-group of 14 654 children in one area. The coefficient calculated would appear to be KR-20. The Manual makes the somewhat enigmatic statement that this 'has been shown to yield a slight underestimate'. The value for the whole test is quoted as 0.98 after controlling for the effect of age. For Section 1 (verbal), the value quoted is 0.96 and for Section 2 (non-verbal) is 0.95. Corrected for attenuation, these values become 0.98 and 0.97 respectively. The correlation between Sections 1 and 2 is given as 0.84.

Validity

Correlations between the test and two other MH tests for the scores of 1820 children in Area G are quoted as follows: (a) with MH English Junior 2 (two-day interval), $r = 0.83$; (b) with MH Arithmetic Junior 2 (three days), $r = 0.84$. No other studies are reported.

Interpretation

This is standard for MH Tests. The user is warned against undue extrapolation, above 10:09 or below 8:06 years. The user is also warned (Manual, p. 19) that RQ values of less than 100 for children aged 9:00 and below are likely to be underestimates.

General evaluation

The test is well-graded, appropriate to the age groups concerned, and the format is clear. The administrative instructions are highly cumbersome, and it is somewhat surprising that the quoted internal consistency was so high. On reflection, early criticism of the test in this review may have been caused by the frustration over the repetitious breaks in the instructions in the Manual; but reading of the instructions for each group of related items shows such instructions to be clear. Nevertheless, the Manual is almost twice as long as other MH Manuals. Separate sets of instructions for Sections 1 and 2 of the test are clearly desirable, and these could be placed appropriately before each section since there is a break between them. Neither standardization method, as outlined in the Manuals, is completely satisfactory. More evidence seems desirable, for instance, why the mean RQs determined from the 7 areas varied so widely over 7 years, as commented on above.

The reliability, both for the whole test and for the verbal and non-verbal sections, are satisfactorily high, as are the correlations with other MH tests. The selection of a random sample of 200 scripts from one area only (out of 7 possible), albeit the group size was 14 654, on which to base the reliability of the test may reduce confidence that the values quoted could be uniformly applied to the total sample in the 7 areas, or for that matter, over the whole country. It is suggested that the Manual needs revision to be more informative and discursive on a number of points.

Moray House Junior Reasoning Test 4

Reviewed by E. P. Duggan

Author: The Godfrey Thomson Unit, University of Edinburgh
Publisher: Hodder & Stoughton
Distributor: Hodder & Stoughton
Age range: 8:06–10:06
1966 (S); 1970 (M, T)
No revisions apparent
1977 (M) printing reviewed
Group test (restricted)★

Test content

The items consist of numerical and verbal problems, codes, similarities and differences, sequences, matching words, analogies, comprehension and classification. The test is graded in difficulty throughout. The responses required are generally straightforward: filling in blanks, entering response in bracket

---

★ Available to schools with the permission of the local Chief Education Officer.

spaces, underlining words, and so on. Unlike JRT2 (q.v.) JRT4 has no items related to shapes. (Despite the similarity of the test names, JRT2 and JRT4 differ in several respects).

Purposes

The test is said to be used for grading or streaming in junior schools and is apparently similar in construction and administration to JRT's 3, 5, 6 and 7.

Item preparation

No indication is given of this, nor of the sampling frame of items, nor of pilot studies, nor of the intentions of the author.

Administration

JRT4 is a timed test consisting of 9 practice items and 90 items in the test proper. This follows the more normal format of instruction for administration of the Moray House (MH) Tests, i.e. one set covers the whole test without interruption (cf. JRT2). The practice test lasts 15–20 minutes, then there is a break of 10–15 minutes before the test proper is given which lasts for 40 minutes exactly. The practice test requires examples to be placed on a blackboard and left for the children to see during the main test, presumably to show them how to record their answers, but no specific instructions are given to the children regarding this 'prompt'. The script given in the Manual is satisfactory.

Standardization

A complete year-group (12 294 children) in one large County Authority was used for the standardization. No details of the method of producing the conversion table are given. In the standardization sample, the number of boys and girls is not quoted, but there was a mean sex difference of 6.4 points of raw score in favour of girls, equivalent to about 4 standardized score points of RQ. This was clearly puzzling and not thought to be due to sampling error, the explanation offered being the usual one of the performance superiority of girls over boys up to about 11 years. It may be conjectured that random sampling over a wider area may have given different values. The opportunity sampling used for standardizing the JRT2 (q.v.) in 7 County Authorities gave closer values for the sex mean scores, which may be of some significance in comparing the two tests. It should be noted again that the JRT2 also contains a number of perceptual items.

Scoring

The scoring key is clear and correct answers are well-spaced to match response positions in the test booklet. Marking one page at a time throughout the tested group is recommended. The keys also give helpful notes on items requiring correct spelling, or on acceptable alternatives. Each page of the test has a score column for items on that page. The front page acts as a summary sheet for the page scores, reasoning quotient and age.

Reliability

There is no reference whatsoever to the internal consistency of the test.

Validity

No studies are reported.

Interpretation

This is standard for MH Tests. The user is warned against undue extrapolation above 10:09 or below 8:06 years. The user is also warned that quotients estimated by extrapolation are 'relatively insecure'.

General evaluation

The test is intrinsically good, commensurate with its purpose. The test is well-graded, appropriate to the age groups concerned, and the format is clearly presented. The test booklet seems dated in format, but this may have been an old copy.

The standardization method is not adequately described in the Manual. One year-group was used, which although large and undoubtedly representative of the age group in that County Authority, is certainly of doubtful generalizability to the nine-year-old population in Britain. The absence of any information on reliability is curious. Such an omission, coupled with the unexplained significant difference between the sexes, does call into question how useful this test is in assessing children's abilities at an important stage in their educational development.

Moray House Verbal Reasoning Tests

Reviewed by E. P. Duggan

Author: The Godfrey Thomson Unit, University of Edinburgh
Publisher: Hodder & Stoughton
Distributor: Hodder & Stoughton
Age ranges: 10:00–12:00, 'Juniors' (Tests 82 and 89); 11:00–13:00, 'Pupils'
  (Test 12/1)
Test 82:   1966–1967 (S)
       Revised, 1969 (M, T)
       1979 (M), 1977 (T) printings reviewed
Test 89:   1971–72 (S), 1972 (M), 1970 (T)
       No revisions apparent
       1980 (M, T) printings reviewed
Test 12/1: 1973 (S), 1976 (M), 1973 (T)
       No revisions apparent
Group test (restricted)*

Test content

Each test has 100 items grouped into short subtests of which some examples of
the item types are: code selection; odd word(s) out; sequences; problems;
sentence matching; similarities; use of tabular data; mapping; coded
sequences; and so on. Each test is graded, items increasing in difficulty
throughout. Versions 82 and 89 appear to be very similar in degree of difficulty,
and 12/1, as expected, presents a more difficult version for the older children.
The responses required are simple: entering letters, words or figures in spaces
provided, or underlining letters, words, phrases or sentences in the multiple-
choice questions. The balance of content is good. There is a steady progression
in the degree of reasoning required throughout each test, with the last few
items really testing the brighter children. The variety in the items and
approaches ensures that each item has to be thought through with careful
reference to the rubric given at the head of each group of items.

Purposes

These three versions of the Moray House Verbal Reasoning Tests have all been
used by local education authorities for 10 or more years. Tests 82 and 89 have
been used for 11+ examinations and to 'control promotion to other post-pri-

---

* Available to schools with the permission of the local Chief Education Officer.

mary courses' (Manual, p. 8). Test 12/1 was used to test whole age groups from 11:00–13:00 in five LEAs.

Item preparation

No indication is given of the origin of the items, nor of an original item sampling frame, nor of pilot studies.

Administration

Recommended users of all three tests are schoolteachers in all cases under the aegis of local education authority officers. The instructions in the Manuals for preparation for testing, supervision, administration and marking are identical in every way for all three tests. Apart from the test papers, the materials required by the children are either pencils or ball-point pens, all other desk material to be removed. Supervisors need a watch or clock with second hands, or a stop-watch. Where pencils are used, a reserve supply is to be available. There should, preferably, be two supervisors to each room, one administering the tests, the other to move about the room, checking on copying and that children use the correct method of answering questions. Otherwise, no assistance whatever is to be given. Preceding each test a preliminary test is given to serve as a preparation for the type of question to be answered. These last 15 minutes each and are not marked, nor are the children told that the results do not count. Test 82 has a preliminary test (PT) 21 (not given to reviewer); Test 84 has PT24 (ditto); Test 12/1 has PT25 (ditto).

The time required for the main Tests is, in each case, 45 minutes exactly, and no questions are to be asked or answered during the tests. The script provided for administration and the instructions for marking are satisfactory.

Standardization

Test 82 was standardized in 1966/67 using 57 319 children (28 746 boys, 28 573 girls) aged 9:10–11:09 in eleven LEAs. Test 89 was standardized in 1971/2 using 38 736 children (20 182 boys, 18 554 girls) aged 9:09–12:00 in three LEAs. Test 12/1 was used by five LEAs in 1973 to test whole year-groups within the areas. The standardization sample contained 14 343 children between the ages of 11:00 and 13:00 years. Breakdown of the number by sex is not quoted, but the Manual says: 'Separate scores were available for 3586 boys and 3605 girls in the standardization group' (p. 8).

The sample, in each case, was of the opportunity type, dictated by the requirements of the 11+ examination or by the testing of whole year-groups in given areas. LEA areas were not identified, except by code. Test 82 had a very large sample (62 482) in 11 areas which may or may not have been local, say, in

Scotland. The other two tests covered fewer children in fewer areas. Hence the representativeness of all the samples must be in question, and the norms established for the standardization samples may not be applicable to children elsewhere in Britain. Nevertheless, it may be that for children in other areas of Britain modification of the conversion tables could reasonably be obtained by use of a relatively small restandardization sample in those areas. The conversion tables, give 'Reasoning Quotients' (RQs; mean 100, standard deviation 15) which are found from test scores and ages in completed years and months. Lawley's method of standardization was used (see Introduction). RQs are not related specifically to mental age, and users are warned against so interpreting them. In all three Manuals, clear guidance is given for using conversion tables.

In each test, the results showed that girls had higher scores than boys. For Test 82 the difference was 3.6 points, equivalent to about 2 points of RQ; for Test 89 the difference was 0.7 points, or about 1 point of RQ; for test 12/1 the difference was of 2.9 points, or about 2 points of RQ. The Manuals also suggest that where these tests are used for the purposes of selection for secondary education, boys and girls should be considered separately in determining their RQs unless no sex differences are found. No instructions are given, however, as to how or in what manner the separated scores should be interpreted, or, for that matter, what different procedure should be followed to ascertain the 'true' scores of boys and girls separately from the conversion tables. For Tests 82 and 12/1, average boy/girl differences could be quite large and in the case of 11+ selection could be significant for a child's future education. For Test 89, the sex difference within any LEA was apparently never greater than 2.3 points of raw score, so in this case, separate consideration of the sexes might have less significance (but see Introduction on treatment of sex differences).

Scoring

Instructions for scoring were identical in all three test Manuals. They are detailed, very clear, and unequivocally stated. The scoring key is so spaced that the marker, by folding the key, can align testee's responses and correct answers. Scores for each page of questions are totalled and transferred to the front page of the response booklet, which is signed by the marker(s) on completion, the age of the child is recorded accurately, and the deduced RQ placed at the bottom of the summary sheet. Hence all relevant information about the child is gathered together on the front of the test booklet.

Reliability

MHT 82

The coefficient of internal consistency was calculated using a random sample of 201 scripts from the whole year-group of 4163 children in area CD. After controlling for age effect, the reliability coefficient was found to be 0.97—a satisfactorily high value. The complete year-group in area BQ ($n = 2146$) was used to estimate the equivalence and stability of MHT 82 by giving MHT 80 (presumably a similar or parallel test) to the same children after an interval of 14 days. The value found was 0.94.

MHT 89

The KR-20 for HMT 82, using 201 scripts sampled from 6982 children in area B, was 0.96.

MHT 12/1

Again using a sample of 201 scripts, KR-20 was 0.94.

Validity

Correlations of MHT 82 with other tests at an interval of 14 days were, again using complete year-groups in area BQ: with English MHE 40, $r = 0.91$; with Arithmetic MHA 40, $r = 0.90$. For MHT 89 intercorrelations with other Moray House Tests were obtained from the same subsample of children in area B used to compute KR-20 who took three tests on the same day, were as follows: MHT 89 and MHE 42, $r = 0.90$; MHT 89 and MHM 8, $r = 0.90$; and, MHE 42 and MHM 8, $r = 0.85$. The Manual states (p. 8) that correlations between test 12/1 and other tests were not available but 'expected' it to correlate at the order of 0.9 with either an English or Mathematics test. Perhaps as this appeared to be a largely diagnostic test, it was not thought necessary to give further evidence of validity.

Interpretation

This has been largely dealt with above under Standardization and Reliability, but there are a few additional points. Where no entries appear in the conversion tables it means that no data were available for calculating a reliable RQ. In such cases it is recommended that the RQ of a child in the blank areas at the beginning and end of the tables should be recorded as 70− or 140+ respectively. Users are cautioned that an RQ of 70− does not imply mental deficiency (nor presumably that those of 140+ are 'gifted'). Users are given guidance in relation to children whose ages exceed the upper and lower limits for which the test was designed, while being warned of the limits of such extrapolation. For MHT 82 and 89 the extrapolated age limits were 9:6–12:06 years. For MHT 12/1 they were 10:06–13:06.

General evaluation

Commensurate with their purpose, these three tests are well-designed, progressively graded in difficulty, have face validity, and cover a broad spectrum of reasoning abilities. They are technically competent within the evidence educed from the tests themselves and the accompanying Manuals. There is a uniformity about the Manual content suggesting that a master blue-print exists somewhere containing a great deal of tantalizingly relevant information and evidence on item selection and analysis, reliability and validity, pilot testing and graded question banks not to be revealed to lay users. In terms of the testing procedure, this is no doubt a good thing for the ordinary user, as the excellence of the tests and accompanying Manuals could well be clouded by extraneous and prolix information.

Attempts have been made, with some success, to make item content contemporaneous for the age groups concerned. Indeed, in appropriate cases, it would be simple to modify and update the wording of items from year to year. In view of the stated target populations and the actual samples employed the question of general use of the tests without restandardization in other areas of Britain must remain open, but in view of the test construction, wording and grading, such a question is probably unnecessary but should be tested against similar age-groups elsewhere.

Non-Readers Intelligence Test

Reviewed by P. S. Clift

Author: D. Young
Publisher: Hodder & Stoughton
Distributors: Hodder & Stoughton; The Test Agency
Age ranges: 6:05–8:09; lower ability juniors and secondary school children, 9:00–13:11; children of 10+ years in ESN (M) schools, 9:00–16:02
1964
1978 (S, M, T) 3rd edition
1979 (M), 1980 (T) printings reviewed
Group test

Test content

The Non-Readers Intelligence Test (NRIT) consists of four orally administered subtests, labelled A to D, each consisting of 20 verbal items and preceded by 3 practice items. Subtest A: practice item 1 is 'what has a handle and is used for cooking' (water, tea, meat, pan). Subtest B: which of four items is not like the others? Subtest C is an analogies task. Subtest D is an opposites task. The test as a whole follows a multiple-choice objective format (4 choices).

Purpose

The test is intended to enable teachers to 'sample a wider background of experience and ability and so provide a corrective for assessments of children which have been too strongly influenced by knowledge of their attainments'. The author claims that since intelligence test results generally tend to confirm teachers' judgements about pupils, they are most useful when there is a discrepancy between them, thus 'throwing new light on some children' (Manual, p. 4).

Item preparation

No information about the production of the original set of items is given in the Manual. There is, however, a brief note to the effect that some were in danger of becoming outmoded, i.e. words less frequently used in recent times: 'poker, nib, cocoa, mutton, jersey'. Substitutions of appropriate difficulty have been made for these for the present (3rd) edition.

Administration

Teachers are advised to present the tests in two sessions, for example A and B before mid-morning break and C and D afterwards. The tests are presented orally. Each is in two parts, an explanation which includes three practice items, and the test proper. A 'script' for the teacher to follow is given for each subtest. The author stresses the importance, not of strict adherence to the script, but rather that the teachers should ensure that all pupils understand the task and the method of recording answers, which involves drawing a circle round one of four letters beside each item on the answer sheet. The letters are the initial letters of the alternatives, e.g. k (Kangaroo), h (Horse), etc. The tests are untimed, but times for both the explanations and the tests are suggested, and the importance of developing a deliberate, slow rhythm in presentation is stressed.

Standardization

The tests were standardized in two stages. In the first instance in a local (presumably to Barnsley, where the author was Principal Educational Psychologist) set of schools, '. . . selected to simulate representation of the national balance of socio-economic groups' (Manual, p. 34). Local samples included children from primary, secondary and ESN (M) schools. Subsequently, the data from 23 000 7 and 8 year-old children tested in 7 other local authorities were used to 'slightly modify' the standardization.

Scoring

The tests are marked using a template, and the raw scores converted to intelligence quotients by reference to three tables in the Manual. These tables apply to children aged 6:05–7:11, 7:00–8:11 and 8:00–13:11 respectively.

Reliability

A coefficient of internal consistency derived from data on 350 children is offered: KR-20 value 0.97. The author discusses this in terms of the standard error of measurement it implies: 3.12 points of standardization score for pupils aged 7.5 years, but draws attention to the fact that this standard error does not apply equally to pupils of all ages. Standard errors of measurement (also for pupils aged 7.5 years) but derived from test-retest data, are given in an Appendix (Manual, p. 39). Different administrators were used on the separate occasions, and intervals ranged from 1–13 weeks. These standard errors of measurement ranged from 4.48 to 4.68 points of standardized score. These are all satisfactory.

Validity

Measures of the concurrent validity of the tests with various other well known intelligence tests are offered. For example: for 8 year-olds ($n = 55$), NRIT and Stanford Binet (SB) Form L gave $r = 0.84$; backward 9 year-olds ($n = 84$), NRIT and SB gave $r = 0.88$; ESN (M) children ($n = 81$), NRIT and SB gave $r = 0.86$; NRIT at 8 years and Moray House Verbal Reasoning at 11 years ($n = 297$) gave $r = 0.82$. These are all satisfactory.

Interpretation

The Manual includes a two-page section on 'Examining the Results' which discusses the developmental nature of *ability* as measured by tests such as this (e.g. cautioning that younger less able pupils may have unexpectedly high quotients, as compared with their older classmates: a function of scores standardized by age), and its relationship with *attainment*. In particular, the value is cited of noting discrepancies between ability and attainment in considering the education of some pupils.

General evaluation

The Section on 'Examining the Results' speaks of the familiar, now rather passé, notion of under-achievement as defined by standardized scores derived from tests of ability (such as this) and of attainment (e.g. reading, mathematics), viz. '. . . if two children have low reading quotients, and IQs higher by a considerable margin, . . .' etc. (Manual, p. 20). The problem with this approach occurs when such a discrepancy is reversed, leading to the nonsense of '*over*-achievement'. There are circumstances, however, when a teacher's hunch that a child is either rather dull (but socially plausible) or alternatively rather brighter than superficially seems to be the case, can usefully be confirmed, or denied. Any subsequent action still has to be made in the light of the teacher's own professional judgement of course. The dictum that 'objective' information, such as IQ, is invariably a 'good thing' is dubious however. Intelligence Quotients can lead to false expectations of both a positive and a negative kind, on the part of teachers and parents. Progress will depend also (very much) on the circumstances and other characteristics of pupils, a point made but perhaps not sufficiently stressed in the Manual.

Non-Verbal Test BD

Reviewed by John Nisbet

Author: D. A. Pidgeon
Publisher: NFER-Nelson
Distributor: NFER-Nelson
Age range: 8:00–11:00
1951 (S); 1953 (T, as Non-Verbal Test 5)
1955 (S)
1964–65 (S); 1970 (M, T)
1979 (M); 1981 (T) printings reviewed
Group test

Test content

There are four subtests, separately timed, each preceded by a short practice test: Cypher (substitution), Similarities, Analogies and Series (all based on diagrams). Together they add to a single score for the whole test of 100 items. The cypher test requires the writing of digits corresponding to the code symbols, while the other three subtests are multiple choice, requiring underlining of two diagrams from a choice of seven, or of one from a choice of five.

Purpose

The Manual refers to the purpose of the test briefly and in general terms only: 'This test has been designed to give a measure of the non-verbal ability of children in the age range 8:00–11:00' (Manual, p. 2). At the times of the three standardizations of the test, 1951, 1955 and 1964–65, this kind of test was used by some LEAs as part of the 11+ selection for secondary education and in primary schools for streaming by 'ability'. The belief was that a non-verbal test of this kind was nearer to being culture free, or at least was less influenced by the quality of teaching received by a pupil, and perhaps also less influenced by social and family disadvantage (see General Evaluation, below). Consequently, the Manual explains, 'Care has been taken to provide detailed oral explanations and practice items before the commencement of each of the four subtests, so that all children will be familiar with the type of item they will encounter in working the subtests and poor readers will not be handicapped' (p. 2).

Item preparation

No information is given in the Manual. One might assume from the fact that NFER has continued to issue the test over a 30-year period, that it must have been soundly based on an item analysis procedure. The extensive subsequent use of the test (norms in 1964–5 were based on 30 000 scores) surely could have provided ample opportunity for rescrutiny of items. Some tests were constructed with minimal checks around the period 1951 when purchasers were not discriminating and a quick profit was there to be made. The lack of published evidence about construction of this test is therefore disturbing.

Administration

The test appears to be designed essentially for teachers, but no indication is given of recommended users or use. The test booklet is not reusable, and two pencils (one as a spare) are all that a pupil requires. Each of the subtests is speeded, apparently on quite a tight time limit, adding up to 20 minutes of test time in all. With the practice tests and the fairly detailed instructions, administration of the whole test takes about 40 minutes. The procedure and instructions follow the standard pattern for this type of test.

Standardization

The calculation of norms and age allowance has apparently been based on very substantial numbers, the Manual quoting 14 650 children aged 8–9 years tested in 1964 and 16 737 children aged 9.5–11 years tested in 1965. The

1964–65 standardizations superseded earlier standardizations in 1951 and 1955. The figures seem impressive, but the actual calculations may have been done on samples of these vast numbers: the precise wording of the Manual is: 'The following table gives the statistics of the authorities whose scores were used for the standardization' (p. 2). These children were the complete age groups in two County Councils, 'which were considered representative of the country as a whole'. No other information is given: the use of the term 'County Councils' suggests that metropolitan areas were not covered.

Lawley's method of standardization was used for age allowances to produce quotients with a mean of 100 and a standard deviation of 15. The mean score of girls is 1.5 points or more above that of boys. 'It is therefore recommended that the scores of boys and girls be considered separately' (Manual, p. 3). However, there is only a single table of norms, for both sexes combined, on the grounds that the age allowance is the same for both sexes.

Scoring

Each item within each subtest counts the same; scoring is 1 or 0; the total for subtest 1 (four codings in each of 25 items) is divided by 4; the other subtests add to 25 each; the maximim raw score is thus 100. No separate norms for the subtests, no indication of expected levels of difficulty or patterns of score and no data on the intercorrelations among the subtests are given.

Reliability

The Manual reports a KR-20 reliability coefficient of 0.98 for subtest 1, and 0.94 for the rest together, giving a standard error of measurement between 3.5 and 3.6. This is derived from analysis of the scores of '313 children in six schools representative of the 8:01–9:00 standardization sample'. No details beyond this are given. The Manual mentions, in a sentence, a test re-test correlation of 0.91 (with two weeks' interval), from the data for 56 children with a mean age of 8:11.

Validity

No information of any kind on validity is given.

Interpretation

No information or advice is given.

General evaluation

This test is probably quite a sound specimen of its kind, but the NFER has shown an inexcusable reluctance to publish some of the technical evidence by which it might be judged. In the "Fifth Mental Measurements Yearbook", issued in 1959, the reviewer of the set of NFER Non-Verbal Tests (of which this test was then No. 5) wrote: 'It is surprising that the National Foundation for Educational Research is willing to publish tests with so little information about their construction, reliability, validity, norming, and limitations. Although some of this information can be gleaned from other sources, it is essential that it be included in the Manuals to the tests. As they stand, it is difficult to conceive of Manuals which could be less complete. Until the information is readily available, these non-verbal tests cannot be recommended for general use in schools'. Twenty years and more later, this comment needs still to be strongly affirmed.

The test suffers from attempting to cover rather a wide age range. There is rather poor differentiation in low scores at age 8 (where a raw score of 10 out of 100 wins a quotient of 80) and in high scores at age 11 (where 10 points of raw score between 87 and 97 raises the quotient from 116 to 138). In general, the test must be regarded as a fairly blunt instrument.

The claim to measure the non-verbal ability of children is perhaps questionable. Answering a test of this kind necessarily involves verbal skills, in understanding the oral instructions. A more appropriate title might be 'non-written' or 'non-reading'. Clumsy as these titles are, they correct the false assumption which some users may be tempted to make, that this style of test is somehow more 'pure'.

Non-Verbal Test DH

Reviewed by David Satterly

Author: B. Calvert (T) and I. Macfarlane Smith (M, 1st edition)
Publisher: NFER-Nelson
Distributor: NFER-Nelson
Age ranges: 10:08–12:06; 14:02–15:01 (see below)
1953 (S, M, T) (as Non-Verbal Test 3)
1970, 1974 (S, M)
Group test

Test content

The test consists of 96 items preceded by 8 practice items. Items are arranged four to a page and consist of two basic types. 'The first type consists of a large square with the lower right-hand corner missing, and several smaller squares from which the appropriate one must be selected to complete the large square. The second consists of a sequence of three or four drawings with the next one missing, and a group of five more from which the appropriate one must be chosen to continue the sequence' (Manual, p. 3). It is claimed that in neither of these should pupils have any difficulty in understanding what they have to do. Test booklets are reusable and answers are recorded on a separate answer sheet, the children being required to respond using the number of the drawing chosen to complete the pattern or series. The Manual cites experiments which have been carried out with a short (64-item) version of the test.

Purpose

The purpose is to provide a measure of 'non-verbal reasoning ability' but no purpose to which this information can in turn be put is stated. This test—like others in the series—is correctly described in the publisher's catalogue as not indicative of capacity for learning. Some indications of the inferences about children that are permitted by the test and of its use in educational practice and guidance are called for if the impression that the test has outlived its historical usefulness is to be avoided (see Validity).

Item preparation

No information as to the principles involved in the generation of the original items is provided. Some are similar to those in other non-verbal tests (e.g. Raven's Matrices). When the original item pool of 300 items had been drawn up 'trials were conducted with a representative sample of 60 boys and 60 girls, whose average age was 11 years' (Manual, p. 3). The Manual does not state what population these 120 children represented. It seems unlikely that this was the entire age range for which the Manual recommends the test can be used. Ninety-six items were selected for the final form and arranged in approximate order of difficulty using an Index of Difficulty (Manual, p. 3). Item discriminations were also calculated using the difference in item facility between upper and lower thirds of the score distribution.

Administration

The test is unrestricted but its chief use is probably by qualified teachers and members of the Schools Psychological Service. Each testee requires an answer sheet and a non-expendable test booklet. The time allowed for the 8 items in the practice test is not specified. Explanations of items 1–4 are given to the children but the tester is instructed to allow 'nearly everyone' to have finished before giving the answers to items 5–8. Fifty minutes are allowed for the full

96-item version and the children are told when 25 minutes remain. The shortened 64-item version takes 35 minutes. During testing supervisors are required to ensure that pupils are recording responses in the appropriate spaces as soon as the test has started and to take this precaution again after the first 25 minutes have elapsed. Instructions for administration are clear and concise.

Standardization

Four standardizations are reported in the current Manual. For the age range 10:06–12:00 years a 'fully representative sample' of children aged 10:08–11:10 consisting of 3415 pupils was used. The method of standardization was the NFER's customary use of Lawley's method. The year of standardization is not given. For the construction of norms for use with children aged 11:03–12:09 the test was given in March, 1974, to a total of 9785 children aged 11:06–12:06. This sample was made up of children in the home counties and a northern urban area. Conversion tables may be extrapolated with caution outside the age range sampled. The test has also been tried out on groups of children up to 15 years of age. 'The test was in fact given to a sample of children fully representative of all children in England and Wales aged between 14:02 and 15:01 as part of a national survey' (Manual, p. 4). The date of this study is not given in the Manual and, strangely, the size of the sample is not mentioned nor the survey named. The Manual claims that it was possible to fit together the first and last standardizations and to estimate expected scores in the intervening year groups. It emphasizes that these are approximate only. Where 'full representativeness' is claimed for the standardization sample the test user may reasonably enquire why geographical details, number of schools, etc., are not given. The lack of comparability between norms based on a fully representative sample of over 3000 pupils and one drawn from only two regions yet consisting of nearly 10 000 pupils will be noted. It is not clear why the presentation of information on three separate samples used is not consistent.

For the shortened form of 64 items, standardization (again with a 'fully representative' sample of children) was carried out on 3179 pupils aged between 10:08 and 11:07 years.

Scoring

Scoring is clear and objective using the marking key and stencil provided. Each correct answer receives one mark but the marker is allowed to award the mark if an incorrect method of answering is adopted provided the child's intention is clear and correct. Some subjectivity is, therefore, involved. Standardized scores have a mean of 100 and standard deviation of 15.

Reliability

Data are presented for the 10:06–12:00 sample and for that from the 1974 standardization among children aged 11:03–12:09. For the first standardization sample 210 random scripts provided a KR-20 estimate of 0.95 (standard error of measurement 3.4) but the number of scripts from the 1974 sample, which yielded corresponding values of 0.94 and 3.6, is not given.

Validity

This is a long-established test which has changed comparatively little in almost 30 years. Interest in the measurement of non-verbal reasoning ability was then considerable and the validity of such tests accepted during the years of the 11 + selection examination. There is now far greater scepticism concerning the validity of such tests and the only information provided by the Manual is a correlation between this test and Raven's Progressive Matrices of 0.81, but this value was obtained using only 86 pupils. The catalogue reminds users that the test does not indicate potential for learning but the Manual offers no guidance as to the meaning of 'non-verbal reasoning' nor of its relationship with the performances taught in schools. Clearly non-verbal reasoning is a classification of the test *content* not a description of mental processes, since it is well known that verbal strategies are often used in the solution of such tests. In general, the guidance as to the validity of this test is very meagre.

Interpretation

No guidance is given on how to interpret the scores beyond the familiar norm-referenced statement that each child is assessed by comparing him with a sample of exactly the same age. The only caution is given in the publisher's catalogue (see above). There the emphasis is on what scores do *not* mean than on what inferences they permit.

Test use

Of two reported studies using test DH, one (Twine, 1975) employed it as a 'measure of ability' in experimental design and the other (Harvey and Cooper, 1978) 'as a measure of non-verbal ability'. Interestingly, this test showed exceptionally high correlation with a *written* concept test about electrical circuits ($r = 0.86$) in the latter investigation.

General evaluation

The test is typical of those historically believed to offer an objective measure of ability independent of differences in verbal competence and of opportunities for specific learning. It is well produced and easy to use and score. But serious reservations must be restated concerning the continued use of these types of test in educational practice and guidance. First, they do not elucidate the nature of the processes involved in so-called non-verbal reasoning. Secondly, it is not clear what help they provide teachers in the many teaching decisions that must be taken and, despite the warnings in the publisher's catalogue, use of the test may still lead to the setting of unjustifiably low expectations of low-scoring pupils. Thirdly, their relationship with educationally relevant intellectual processes is not clear and no information is provided in the Manual that might clarify this. Finally, the use of such tests in grouping pupils has almost entirely disappeared in primary schools in this country and the test is probably best reserved for researchers with interest in a quick method of controlling for the 'general ability' thought to be relatively uninfluenced by specific learning opportunities.

References

Harvey, T. and Cooper, C. (1978). *Educational Studies* **4**, 149–155.
Twine, D. (1975). *Educational Studies* **1**, 209–217.

Oral Verbal Intelligence Test

Reviewed by Roger Murphy

Author: D. Young
Publisher: Hodder & Stoughton
Distributor: Hodder & Stoughton
Age ranges: 7:09–10:08; 11:00–13:11 (backward children)
1973 (M, T); S not stated
No revisions apparent
1979 (M, T) printings reviewed
Group test

Test content

Four subtests are orally administered and children record their responses by circling letters on a single page answer sheet. Each of the subtests consists of 23 items including 3 practice items which do not count towards the final test score. *Subtest A* provides the children with four single word alternative answers to a short question (e.g. Which never stops?—bus, time, cough, watch). *Subtest B* invites the children to choose one of four words which is different or which is not like the others (e.g. robin, crow, swallow, worm). *Subtest C* invites the children to complete an unfinished sentence with one of four words. In each case the word that is chosen complements another word in the sentence to reflect the relationship between another pair of words (e.g. Flying is to birds as swimming is to . . . beach, fish, landing, pebbles). *Subtest D* invites the children to choose two words that are opposites out of a group of four (e.g. over, bridge, stile, under).

It would seem that the four subtests test similar skills, but their inclusion is justified partly 'on the grounds of the need for variety in presentation, the desirability of four fresh starts to sustain interest and to lessen the risk of complete misunderstanding' (Manual, p. 33). As the examples given above will have indicated, the test items are fairly straightforward and would be quite unsuitable for use with average or above average ability children older than about 10.5 years. The level of difficulty appears to be fairly constant throughout the test.

Purpose

The test appears to have been designed specifically to be used by teachers. Because it is orally administered, it can be used with groups of children, including some who may not be able to read, as a measure of general intelligence. It can be used to place a class in an order of ability, but the test constructor urges a fuller use of the results than this. The Manual warns, however, of the dangers of over-interpreting the results of tests, which may be subject to error and which should, where possible, be interpreted alongside the results of other tests and other relevant information.

The results of the test should, generally speaking, lead to a greater understanding of children but this 'is likely to be most productive when the teacher can relate the tentative findings to other observations, i.e. to the characteristics and circumstances of the children' (Manual, p. 23). Thus the tester is not claiming any more for this test than that it may provide some additional information about children's general ability in a way that is not influenced by how well they have learned to read at the time. More specifically the test constructor does claim at one point that the test has 'some special advantages in the assessment of backward children and in surveys to ascertain educationally subnormal children' (Manual, p. 33).

Item preparation

No information is given about how the test items were constructed. The Manual merely explains that the test is similar to Young's, previously published, Non-Readers Intelligence Test 'but the questions are more difficult' (Manual, p. 4).

Administration

The Manual outlines the types of groups of children for whom the test is designed (see Ages at head of review). Similar information is given for Young's Non-Readers Intelligence Test (NRIT) and it is recommended that when 'both tests are suitable, the NRIT should be used first' (Manual, p. 4).

The teacher or whoever is to conduct the test session is given very full instructions about what to do. These need to be read in advance and the Manual advises that a practice run through the presentation will help to keep the speed of delivery within the suggested limits. The test does not have a fixed time limit but guidelines are given both for reading and for delivering the items in each of the four subtests. Two half-hour sessions are thought to be ample for the administration of the complete test.

The clear instructions for the tester and the children should ensure that few problems arise in the administration of the test, and the practice items allow for the tester to check that all of the children have understood what they have to do. One possible difficulty that can sometimes arise in the administration is that the tester has to remember to repeat each item once a few seconds after it has been read out the first time. After reading out a number of items it can become difficult for a tester to remember whether an item has been repeated or not. This difficulty can of course be overcome, for example, by putting a pencil mark against each item after the first reading and after the repetition.

Standardization

The main standardization of the test was carried out on two 'local (urban) samples' of children. One of these included 7058 children (aged 7:9–10:8) representing a full range of ability and the other 1610 children (aged 11:0–13:11) who were classified (on unspecified grounds) as being 'backward children'. No information is given about when, where or by whom these trials were carried out.

The conversion tables, which are included in the Manual and which allow raw scores on the test to be converted into Intelligence Quotients, are based on a number of different standardizations of the test. The two samples mentioned above provided much of the information, but other samples were tested as well in order to widen the age range, to test assumptions about the local school population, and to examine the influence of practice effects. The Manual gives the impression that a good deal of effort was put into providing standardization tables for the test, but not enough detail is given about the exact methods that were used for these efforts to be evaluated.

All of the norms relate to global scores and subtest score variations are only expected on rare occasions and even then are thought to be most likely to reflect 'difficulty with the instructions for that subtest or with the type of question' (Manual, p. 20).

The Manual implies that the test is equally suitable for boys and girls, and no separate norms are provided for these or any other subgroups. The assumption about the absence of sex bias is based on the similar median scores that were obtained by boys and girls at three age levels in the first of the two major standardization samples.

The Manual singles out immigrant children as one group for whom the test would probably not be suitable as an accurate measure of intelligence, but the anticipated cultural and language difficulties that they would be expected to encounter are not considered to be a problem for other subgroups (e.g. social class or ethnic) in the population.

Scoring

Detailed instructions are provided for scoring the answer sheets. Basically one mark is awarded for each item correctly answered, and a template may be used to speed up the marking process.

Reliability

Some rather sketchy details are given about various parallel forms and test-retest estimates of the test's reliability. No information, for example, is given about the samples used other than the number of children in them and the median age of the group. A range of standard errors of measurement from 2.9–4.4 are provided for raw scores on the test, and from 2.6–4.6 for Intelligence Quotients derived from these scores, but it is impossible to evaluate the worth of these estimates in the absence of necessary details about the samples used.

Validity

Five tables of results are presented showing the results of correlations and factor analysis carried out in order to explore the relationship of the test with other tests. Several of these other tests are somewhat anonymous unpublished tests and no details are given about their contents. Once again details about the samples used are somewhat sparse and no rationale is presented for the validity testing procedures that were used. Bearing in mind the previous criticisms, there are some results within the correctional and factor analytic data that indicate a reasonable relationship between the test and other published verbal reasoning, verbal and non-verbal tests.

Interpretation

The conversion tables that are supplied allow the raw scores of some children (depending on their age and score on the test) to be converted into intelligence quotients. The Manual contains many warnings about the tentative nature of the results of the test and outlines a number of reasons why they should not be treated as absolute measures of intelligence. There is not all that much guidance about how the results might be interpreted other than that 'Failure to reach an IQ of 70 is usually taken as a rough guide to the need for education in a school for the educationally subnormal . . .' (Manual, p. 22).

General evaluation

This is a fairly straightforward short test that could be picked up by a teacher and used after a fairly brief look at the Manual. The instructions are clear and the test is easy to administer. Apart from these points it is hard to think of reasons why anyone might choose to use this test in favour of other similar intelligence tests. The results of the various attempts that were made to validate the test reveal that, roughly speaking, it measures the same sort of thing as a number of other verbal and non-verbal intelligence tests. Furthermore, the details of the attempts that were made to standardize the test and to estimate its reliability and validity contain insufficient details for them to engender any real confidence in the particular worth of the test.

One positive thing that can be said about the test is that it both claims, and in terms of face validity appears to measure, verbal intelligence without requiring any more than minimal literacy skills from the test takers. This feature sets it apart from many other tests of verbal intelligence.

Otis-Lennon Mental Ability Test

Reviewed by John Nisbet

Authors: Arthur S. Otis and Roger T. Lennon
Publisher: Harcourt Brace Jovanovich
Distributors: NFER-Nelson; The Test Agency
Age ranges: Kindergarten (Primary 1)
　　　　　　Grade 1, age 6 (Primary 2★)
　　　　　　Grades 1–4, ages 6–10 (Elementary 1)

★ Test booklets for Primary 1 and 2 are identical. Forms J and K are reviewed.

Grades 4–6, ages 10–12 (Elementary 2)
Grades 7–9, ages 13–15 (Intermediate)
Grades 10–12, ages 16+ (Advanced)
1966–67 (S); 1966–68 (M, T)†
Group tests

Test content

The pedigree of this test battery can be traced back to the Army Alpha Examination of World War I, which Otis helped to construct. Consequently the tests cover the full range of types of item used in the development of intelligence testing. In the Primary 1 and 2 and Elementary 1 tests, the mental processes samples are 'classification (or eduction of relations), following of directions, quantitative reasoning, and comprehension of verbal concepts' (Manual, p. 5). The tests are pictorial, and no reading is required (even the item 'numbers' are in picture form); but some of the items are strongly verbal nevertheless. The illustrations are clear, though rather unattractive; occasional items have a possible American bias, for example, baseball, basketball and garden sprinklers. The other three levels of the test battery, Elementary 2, Intermediate and Advanced, use a mixture of verbal and non-verbal items, 'arranged in a a spiral omnibus form, sampling fourteen different mental processes' (cover blurb): in short, analogies, opposites, series, etc. are all mixed together, roughly half verbal, half either diagrammatic or numerical. There is some overlap between tests in the form of items common to two levels.

Purpose

The aim is to 'provide for comprehensive, carefully articulated assessment of the general mental ability, or scholastic aptitude, of pupils in American schools' (Manual, p. 4), by means of a test battery which yields comparable scores throughout the whole period of school attendance, from Kindergarten through Grade 12, from age 5–18. By sampling a broad range of cognitive abilities, 'measuring the pupil's facility in reasoning and in dealing abstractly with verbal, symbolic and figural test content' (Manual, p. 4), the tests are designed to 'yield a dependable measurement of the "g" or general intellective ability factor' (Manual, p. 40). Other functions suggested in the Manual

---

† The test batteries derived from the Otis Group Intelligence Scale (pre-1920), the Otis Self-Administering Tests (1927–9) and the Otis Quick-Scoring Tests of Mental Ability (mid-1930s, revised mid-1950s); but 80 per cent of the items are new and have not been used previously in earlier versions.

include guidance on courses of study or career, selection for special programmes for the mentally gifted or retarded, classroom grouping and research. Twice in the Manual, it is emphasized that the tests are not to be considered as measures of innate ability (see below, Interpretation). However, they are claimed as measures of a general level of attained ability, and as such, it is suggested that they can be used for 'comparing level of achievement with measures of aptitude for learning' (Manual, p. 19).

Item preparation

Selection of items was based on results from three studies involving more than 20 000 pupils, with item analysis to balance content and difficulty and to maximize discrimination. No details of the procedure adopted are given.

Administration

Teachers, counsellors and other school personnel are the recommended users. The tests are applied in the usual classroom setting, only the booklets and pencils (with spares) being required by the children (unless special machine-scoring cards are used, see below Scoring). The tests are speeded, but the time limits are reasonably generous. For Primary 1 and 2 levels (55 items) and Elementary 1 (slightly longer), the children are paced by the oral instructions: 'about 15 seconds' is the time allowed for each item. Instructions are laborious, repeated in full for each item throughout a series of similar items. With practice items, these tests take between 30 and 40 minutes. For Elementary 2, Intermediate and Advanced levels, the format is multiple choice, instructions are printed and clear, and 40 minutes is the time limit for the 80 items at each level.

Standardization

National norms are based on testing (autumn and winter, 1966–67) of 200 000 pupils in 117 school systems from all 50 states of USA. Selection of participating schools was done by a stratified random-cluster sampling procedure (with socio-economic status as one of the stratifying variables) to ensure a representative standardization group. A detailed account (55 lines of text) is given in the Manual, and 'full details' are recorded in the 'Technical Handbook' for the series (presumably available from the publisher, though this is not stated). Special care was taken to ensure that the norms are exactly comparable at all six levels.

Representativeness is thus well guaranteed; but as the norms for each test cover a fairly wide age range (Elementary 2 from 8:00–13:05, for example), the number of items which discriminate at any one age level is limited, and the precision of the resulting quotients is limited in turn. No data on sex differences are given.

Both age and grade norms are supplied, ages being grouped within three-month intervals. How age allowances were calculated is not stated in the Manual. The scores which result are in the form of deviation quotients, with a mean of 100 and a standard deviation of 16. Norms are also given in percentile and stanine form.

Scoring

Hand scoring follows the standard procedure, but it is also possible to use Answer Cards (which allow reuse of the test booklets or Machine-Scoring Sheets (IBM 805, IBM 1230, Digitek)). All items are multiple-choice and scoring is objective 1 or 0, according to the scoring key.

Reliability

Extensive data (2.5 double-column pages) are given on reliability. Both split-half and KR-20 coefficients are reported, based on 120 000 tests; they range from 0.93–0.96. Alternative forms reliability, with two weeks' interval, based on 8500 cases, ranges from 0.89–0.94. The standard error of measurement ranges from 3.9–5.4 for Elementary 2, Intermediate and Advanced (derived from the alternate forms calculation).

Validity

The Manual does not offer evidence on validity. A list is given of the procedures adopted to test the validity of the battery—content analysis, predictive validity, correlations with other tests; but for further information the user is referred to the 'Technical Handbook' (no information given on how it is available).

Interpretation

The meaning and use of the test scores are explained clearly and persuasively at two points in the Manual (p. 14 and again at p. 18):

> 'The tests . . . measure broad reasoning abilities . . . Performance on tasks measuring these abilities reflects, to some extent, the experiences that the pupil has had in dealing with abstract relationships among words, numbers, or other types of symbols. Inferences about a pupil's performance on these measures should be based upon proper use and interpretation of the normative data accompanying the

test, as well as a consideration of various social, economic, and other background factors which may affect his performance . . . The assessment . . . rests upon the basic assumptions that (1) all pupils have had substantially equal opportunity to learn the types of things included in the test and (2) all pupils are equally motivated to do their best on the test. If these assumptions cannot be met for a given pupil, then any judgement made concerning his test performance should be tempered by taking account of these factors . . . It must be emphasized once again that these ability tests do not measure native endowment, nor should the notion of constancy, of fixity, of ability level be associated with the test results.'

Test use

Use of the older versions of this test (the Otis Quick-Scoring Test) is frequently recorded in the journals, but usually only as a control measure in a survey and seldom involving analysis of what the test measures. Thus mention of the test in British publications in the past fifteen years refers to the old version, not Otis-Lennon, in this restricted role.

General evaluation

This test battery is the latest edition of a very old and respected group intelligence test. Its survival and its constant refinement over a period of more than 60 years is evidence of its basic soundness and wide usefulness. The background information given in the Manual on construction, standardization, reliability and interpretation, is a model which might with advantage be followed by many test publishers in Britain, if only they had gathered such extensive data. Part of its content is a short essay on the nature of ability and the meaning of a test score, which would do credit to a psychology textbook. The layout of both test and Manual is clear and efficient, well 'polished' after many revisions.

Two reservations which may limit use of the test are its wide age range and the single global score which the test provides. Coverage from Kindergarten to age 18 is an attractive feature of the battery, but it is questionable whether the abilities measured in the three younger levels are the same as those measured in the three senior levels. Within any one level, when test items have to cover four or five age groups, the resulting score is derived from a restricted number of items, and consequently the score is less precise than one from a test designed for a narrower age range. The global IQ which the Otis-Lennon provides is less sought after nowadays than formerly, except as a general background measure in research studies—and this research use seems likely to be the continuing value of this fine old specimen of testing, well matured, still active, nearing retirement age perhaps, but not to be despised even so.

Picture Test A

Reviewed by David Satterly

Author: Joan E. Stuart
Publisher: NFER-Nelson
Distributor: NFER-Nelson
Age range: 7:00–8:06
1955 (as Picture Intelligence Test 1)
1977 (S, M, T)
1978 (M), 1980 (T) printings reviewed
Group test

Test content

The test consists of three subtests, each preceded by a practice test. The first subtest (Section I) consists of 15 items, each comprising five pictures (line drawings), four of which belong together in a particular way. The child's task is to identify the principle of 'sameness' in four of the pictures and to underline the one picture that 'does not belong' (Manual, p. 4). Section II consists of 20 items. Each item has a stem of four pictures which make up 'a pattern or a story' (Manual, p. 4). The child is required to examine the sequence, decide which picture comes next and pick the appropriate picture from the row of five alternatives provided.

Section III is a non-verbal analogies test. It contains 25 items introduced as a task in which 'we have to think of the ways in which things go with one another' (Manual, p. 5). The first two pictures in each row bear a relationship to one another (e.g. car and numberplate; tin and tin opener). A third picture is presented and children required to select from five alternatives that picture which 'goes with it' in the same way as the other two pictures went together.

In all items the pupil's response is by underlining the choice made. The items appear to be of increasing difficulty within sections. In arriving at an overall score greatest weight is given to Section III both in terms of time allotted and number of items set. No details of the factorial structure of the test are provided in the Manual but the sections correspond *prima facie* to similarities, series and analogies respectively.

Purpose

No information is provided in the Manual as to the purpose of this test. However, the publisher's catalogue introduces this test as providing a measure of non-verbal reasoning ability which 'should not be taken to indicate capacity for learning'.

Item preparation

Little concrete information is provided and no detail of the origins of the items is provided. 'Three successive try-outs' of preliminary drafts were undertaken but using an unspecified number of children. Following these try-outs the items were subject to 'careful scrutiny' and item analysed 'for efficiency, difficulty and wrong answer distraction' (the methods adopted are not stated). In order to arrive at a satisfactory method of administration the test was used both individually and with groups. 'Further adjustments' were made to the items 'following adult criticism of certain pictures' (Manual, p. 2). So far as can be ascertained from the rather meagre information contained in the Manual, items were deleted where they presented problems of recognition but it is not clear whether this was because of cultural context or because of poor drawings. Criteria for selection and methods of item analysis have, therefore, to be inferred from little detail. The author does not appear to have entirely overcome the difficulty of providing plausible alternatives for the multiple-choice items. Some drawings have been updated (e.g. the car numberplate is for a recent year) and none should present perceptual difficulties.

Administration

The test is for use with children aged 7.00–8.06 years by teachers and members of the Schools Psychological Service interested in obtaining a measure of 'non-verbal reasoning ability'. No reading skills are required and the only response mode is that of underlining. The supervisor requires a watch with a second hand, disposable copies of the test, a supply of spare pencils and the help of an invigilator to patrol the room. 'The total working time, including the time for the practice tests, is approximately 45 minutes' (Manual, p. 3) with subtests lasting 4, 8 and 10 minutes respectively.

Supervisors are advised to use a blackboard example to show how the test form is to be completed. Each section (subtest) has its own practice and test instructions and each practice item is explained with particular emphasis paid to the understanding of what is required. It is recommended that reasons for some answers being wrong are also discussed.

Standardization

The standardization sample reported in the Manual under discussion consisted of 4024 children in 128 schools drawn from 10 LEAs. The standardization was carried out during March–April, 1977, and was 'selected according to a stratified technique designed to make it representative of the population in England and Wales' (Manual, p. 2). Scores were normalized using Lawley's method. A single conversion table for use with all pupils in the target population (7:00–8:06 years) is provided. It is not possible to tell which regions of England and Wales were sampled.

Scoring

Scoring is straightforward. One point is awarded for each item correctly answered and summed over the entire test. Where the pupil has responded in a wrong way (e.g. by crossing out instead of underlining) the mark should be awarded provided the intention was correct. A similar judgement is to be made where a pupil has changed the answer. No marks are awarded if more than one answer is given. Raw scores are converted into standardized scores arranged to have a mean of 100 and a standard deviation of 15.

The author recommends that the first pages of all scripts are marked, then the second pages and so on, to enable the answers to be more easily memorized with only occasional reference to the marking key. Multiple markers are advised to work in pairs marking and checking page 1 only before passing the papers to a second pair for page 2, and so on.

Reliability

Reliability studies were carried out on a one-in-ten random sample of the standardization sample. The internal consistency of the entire test (KR-20) was calculated at 0.93. The corresponding value for the standard error of measurement is 4.0.

Validity

The Manual contains no information on the validity of the test. There is no indication of the relationship between this test and school performance nor with other published tests of 'non-verbal reasoning'. This concept is not clarified in the Manual and is in any case a somewhat dated one. The only truly non-verbal attribute is that of the material; the idea that children do not employ verbal strategies when solving these problems is naive. In adhering to this difference between non-verbal and verbal *reasoning*, test publishers are perpetuating a distinction that has little validity in contemporary cognitive psychology.

Interpretation

If desired the test enables the user to obtain a norm-referenced measure of 'non-verbal reasoning ability' quickly and easily. However, the Manual offers no suggestions as to the use of this information to teachers nor what the user can learn beyond an assessment which compares each child 'with a representative sample of children of exactly the same age' (Manual, p. 2). The publisher's catalogue correctly cautions that scores are not measures of learning capacity. No detail is provided of any predictive power they possess nor how results throw any light on the nature of 'non-verbal reasoning'. Using such scores will enable the teacher to make comparisons between children as to their current standing in the forms of reasoning the test requires but no advice is offered as to the potential usefulness of such information in the educational context. Given that practices of classifying pupils using reasoning tests among this age-group have never been widespread and 'grouping by ability' is declining in primary schools, the use of this test is probably restricted to those teachers who wish to obtain a quick measure of reasoning ability for research purposes.

General evaluation

The test is easy to administer and clearly designed. More detail about test development including the number of children involved in the preliminary trials would be helpful. Reservations must, however, be entered concerning the validity and usefulness of this test in education. This is not only because of the almost complete absence of information in the Manual but also because of increasing uncertainty about the nature of intelligence and the status of reasoning tests in general. The absence from the Manual of any demonstration of relationship between this or other published reasoning tests and of its usefulness in education is a serious drawback. The Manual states that scores are 'similar to Intelligence Quotients in their numerical distribution, (p. 2) which is, of course, correct. But teachers relying on the Manual for interpretation of scores may be unwittingly led to infer other similarities with intelligence tests and, in particular, some of the mistaken ideas associated with this concept, especially about the limited potential of children with low scores. Interestingly, early versions of this test were called Picture Intelligence Tests but this has been dropped in favour of the no-more explicit notion of non-verbal reasoning used in the publisher's catalogue. The test, though easy to administer and score, is inevitably dated in its theoretical foundation. It is difficult to see what value it has outside a research context, particularly in the light of the weak validity of non-verbal tests for the prediction of the long term prospects for a child's intellectual functioning.

School and College Ability Tests*

Reviewed by David Satterly

Author: Not stated
Publisher: Addison-Wesley Testing Service, Addison-Wesley Publishing
   Company (Copyright held by Educational Testing Service)
Distributor: Addison-Wesley
Age range: 9–19 (USA Grades 3–12)
1966 (as SCAT II); revised 1970, 1979 (SCAT III)
Group test

Test content

'Tests in SCAT Series III have two separately-timed parts. Part I, Verbal, uses verbal analogy items to measure a student's understanding of words. Part II, Quantitative, tests a student's understanding of fundamental number operations through quantitative comparison items' (Notes, p. 1). Each item in Part I consists of pairs of words which go together in a certain way. Beneath them are four other pairs of words lettered A, B, C and D. The respondent's task is to identify which lettered pair of words bear the same relationship to one another as the first pair of words. Response is made on separate answer sheets by marking the same letter as the pair of words chosen. Part I consists of 50 such items. Part II also consists of 50 items. Each item contains two parts, Column A and Column B. The respondent's task is to find if the number that is implied in the one part is greater than the other or the parts are equal and, on separate answer sheet, mark 'A if the part in column A is greater, B if the part in column B is greater, C if the parts are equal'. In the intermediate and advanced levels of the test a fourth choice, 'D if not enough information is given for you to decide', is included. Series III thus includes tests at three levels of difficulty.

Purpose

The test is designed to measure 'understanding of words' and of 'fundamental number operations' with minimum emphasis on the ability to read. The

---

* Series III. The Specimen set reviewed consisted of 'Elementary Level Form X' 'Intermediate Level Form X' and 'Advanced Level Form X' of the test. This review is based entirely on information provided by the publishers in undated manuscript No. 84995. No manual, norms or reliability and validity data are included in these notes.

questions 'require more resourcefulness and insight than traditional computation items' (p. 1). They are designed as power rather than speed tests. The overall purpose of the test is to 'furnish reliable and valid measurement of the scholastic promise of . . . school pupils in grades 9 through 12' (p. 2).

Item preparation

The test was prepared at the request of the USA Educational Records Bureau and involved a review of the types of items expected to estimate verbal and quantitative abilities as well as an estimate of 'total academic aptitude'. Nine item types were experimented with prior to 1957. Results suggested the suitability of verbal analogies for part of the test and subsequent work indicated the advantages of the quantitative comparison type for part II. It is claimed that this latter item type is 'an effective measure and valid predictor' (p. 3) and 'answered more quickly than other types of quantitative items' (p. 3). Two forms of the test were issued as the co-operative Academic Ability Test in 1964 and additional test forms were pre-tested in 1965. The fourth choice in the quantitative items (D, above) was found to cause confusion among children in the lower grades and was eliminated for them. The version reviewed (SCAT III) contains items from the earlier version but between 5 and 10% of items were revised largely on the basis of changes in curricula. No information about the discrimination or difficulty values of the items is presented in the information provided with this specimen set.

Administration

No instructions for administration were provided in the specimen set. Nevertheless it seems straightforward. Total working time for the test is 40 minutes—20 minutes for each part. Timing and directions for administering the tests are the same for all levels.

Standardization

Norms for the SCAT were obtained from 'large samples of students representative of the national population who were tested in the fall and spring from the end of grades 3 through 12' (p. 4). Sample sizes are not given.

Scoring

No details are provided as to the mechanics of scoring but it assumed that one point is given for every correct answer. Scores are reported in raw score, standard scores and percentile ranks. Three scores are obtained: verbal, quantitative and total.

Reliability

Reliability is claimed but not demonstrated in the literature accompanying the specimen test set under review.

Validity

No evidence of validity for the purposes described is provided in the information supplied. However, the test has come in for considerable criticism in the USA in recent years. There appear to be no published results of its use in Britain.

Interpretation

Users will receive very little help from the literature supplied with the specimen set under review. Reference is made in the notes to a comparison that can be made between SCAT scores and the results of a parallel series of tests known as the Sequential Tests of Educational Progress (STEP III) which provide measurement of educational outcomes from pre-kindergarten through grade 12. Additionally, SCAT performance can be used to estimate scores on the Scholastic Aptitude Test (SAT) which is used in the USA by College Entrance Examination Boards. It is claimed that when this estimate is used in combination with the high-school record it 'will lead to a more informed decision than will review of the high-school record alone' (p. 6).

General evaluation

This test is USA orientated in aim and construction. Several of the items in Part I (verbal) would need to be modified to make them suitable for use in Britain. Part II requires less modification, however. The test does not appear to have been used in Britain and, given that the test has recently come under critical scrutiny in the USA, no application in this country is envisaged by this reviewer.

Torrance Tests of Creative Thinking

Reviewed by Desmond L. Nuttall

Author: E. Paul Torrance
Publisher: Scholastic Testing Service, Inc.*

---

* The Norms-Technical Manual (1974) is published by Personnel Press/Ginn and Co. (Xerox Education Company). Copyrights in other materials (Tests, Directions Manual and Scoring Guide) are also held by one or other of this group of companies.

Distributor: NFER-Nelson
Age ranges: 5–10 (USA kindergarten to third grade)
10–adult (USA 4th grade to adult)
1966 (M, T) ('research edition')
1974 (Manuals)
Group tests (at age 10)
Individual tests (younger testees)

Test content

The Verbal Tests, in Forms A and B, comprise seven activities each separately timed: 'asking questions about a drawing, making guesses about the causes of the event pictured, making guesses about the possible consequences of the event, producing ideas for improving a toy . . . thinking of unusual uses of tin cans or cardboard boxes, asking provocative questions, and thinking of the various possible ramifications of an improbable event' (Norms-Technical Manual, p. 4). Up to third grade, the responses are given orally, in other cases responses are written in the test booklet where ample space is provided (usually 50 numbered lines).

The Figural Tests, also having Forms A and B, include three activities each allowed 10 minutes. 'The first task, Picture Construction, is designed to stimulate originality and elaboration. The two succeeding tasks, Incomplete Figures and Repeated Figures, elicit increasingly greater variability in fluency, flexibility, originality and elaboration' (Norms-Technical Manual, p. 5). All ages make their responses by drawing in the test booklets.

Purpose

'This edition of the (Tests) is being made available for more general use in research and experimentation after about 15 years of sustained research and development by the author . . . and by investigators throughout the world' (Norms-Technical Manual, p. 4). More specifically but ambitiously, the Manual suggests five uses: to understand the human mind more completely, to discover effective bases for individualizing instruction, to discover clues for remedial and psychotherapeutic programmes, for evaluating curricular or training programmes and as a means of becoming aware of potentialities that might otherwise go unnoticed.

Item preparation

Torrance's rationale of the test activities is spelt out in some detail in the Manual, following a more general discussion of creativity and his own definition: 'a process of becoming sensitive to problems, deficiencies, gaps in knowledge, missing elements, disharmonies, and so on; identifying the difficulty; searching for solutions, making guesses, or formulating hypotheses about the deficiencies: testing and retesting those hypotheses and possibly modifying and retesting them; and finally communicating the results' (Norms-Technical Manual, p. 8). Elsewhere (p. 21) he claims that the tasks in the test 'sample a rather wide range of the abilities' in the universe of creative thinking abilities but 'he would be the first to admit, however, that these tests do not sample the entire universe'. Rarely is any justification given for the choice of specific tasks, or any reference made to studies using other stimuli (though earlier developmental work is no doubt described in the many publications of Torrance and his co-workers cited in the Manual).

Administration

Full details of the administrative procedure, including a long script that adult subjects might find condescending, are provided in the Directions Manuals and the importance of creating the right atmosphere (no groups larger than a normal class, avoiding the use of the word 'test'—the booklets have titles such as 'Thinking Creatively with Words'—plenty of non-threatening encouragement) is stressed. Each activity has a rigid time limit. The Verbal Tests require the test administrator to display a toy provided in the test kit (an elephant in Form A, a monkey in Form B). The script has not been Anglicized: for example, the toy is the kind 'you can buy in most dime stores for about one to two dollars' (Directions Manual, Verbal Test Booklet A, p. 6).

Standardization

As the tests are designed for research purposes, full norms are not provided. Means and standard deviations of booklet scores are provided for groups of between 200 and 1900 in most school grades and for college undergraduates and graduates, but no information is given about the sampling except that the groups are American, and multi-racial and multi-ethnic, 'are intended to be representative of the mid-range of most school populations' and (somewhat surprisingly) exclude 'samples having special characteristics that might be expected to influence performance on the tests' (e.g. the gifted and the physically handicapped) (Norms-Technical Manual, p. 48). Means and standard deviations of scores on each activity are given for a sample of 112 fifth graders. T-score conversion tables are provided for booklet scores for the same sample and for a combined sample of college graduates and undergraduates. The user is invited to use the first for any sample of children and the second for any sample of college students or adults. No defence of this strange practice is offered, but it must be pointed out that for most score categories, scores do not increase with age, nor is there any discernible developmental pattern.

Scoring

Scoring the tests is a major undertaking and the scoring guide for the Verbal Tests (Form A) runs to 38 pages. A scoring worksheet is provided and is highly desirable. Most activities give rise to four scores—fluency, flexibility, originality and elaboration—and fluency and flexibility scoring is fairly straightforward though some subjective judgement is required. Much more subjective judgement is required for originality and elaboration (to the extent that Torrance now frowns on the use of the latter in the Verbal Tests), in the many cases not listed in the examples. The highest score of 2 for originality is to be given if the responses show 'creative strength (that is, require intellectual energy beyond what is learned, practised, and habitual, and result in responses that are away from the obvious and commonplace)' (Directions Manual, Verbal Test Booklet A, p. 14). The Manuals report a number of studies of scorer reliability which show high reliabilities (in excess of 0.95) even with inexperienced scorers for fluency and flexibility but lower values (down to 0.85) for originality. A scoring service is available (at $2.10 per booklet in 1980–81).

Reliability

In addition to the studies of scoring reliability mentioned above, the Norms-Technical Manual includes a description of a number of reliability studies of alternate forms and test-retest. Both the conditions (e.g. the time interval) and the results are very variable with figures between 0.7 and 0.8 the most common in alternate form studies of single activities, usually with higher correlations for the fluency scores than for other scores. The number of studies involving the whole battery is quite small, and the samples themselves are small and possibly unrepresentative. Coefficients of around 0.8 are most common but some drop much lower (e.g. for figural flexibility, coefficients of 0.73, 0.63 and 0.64 are reported). No mention is made of the standard error of measurement.

Validity

The section of the Norms-Technical Manual devoted to validity is very full and refers to dozens of published studies. Content, construct, concurrent and predictive validity are considered in turn and an impressive amount of evidence is assembled about the relationship between performance on the tests and IQ, achievement, teacher estimates of creative potential, creative achievements and personality. Follow-up studies over periods as long as 12 years show correlations typically of 0.5 between test scores and the quantity and quality of creative achievements, while the median correlation between test scores and teacher estimates of creative potential in 40 studies is 0.20.

Interpretation

The section of the Manual entitled 'Interpreting Scores' is the least satisfactory. Users are again warned that the tests cannot tap all the abilities involved in creative behaviour and are advised to devise seven scores (verbal and figural fluency, flexibility and originality plus figural elaboration). Each of these scores is considered in turn, with virtually no reference to creativity and no warnings about unreliability, with the main emphasis upon either obvious descriptions ('Verbal fluency. This score reflects the test taker's ability to produce a large number of ideas with words', Norms-Technical Manual, p. 57) or quite obstruse quotients or profiles (e.g. delinquent youngsters may score high on unusual uses and quite poorly on guessing causes and consequences). Two new indicators (synthesis and unusual visual perspective) are introduced, and cross-cultural differences are mentioned. Nothing is said about sex differences though in considering verbal-figural score discrepancies the subject's sex might be important.

Test use

As indicated above, the tests have been widely used throughout the world and "The Eighth Mental Measurements Yearbook" (Buros, 1978) lists no fewer than 560 references in which the tests have been employed. Among the more important and relevant to the UK are:

Akhurst, R. A. (1978). Creative thought in children. *Educational Review* 30, 195–207.
Child, D. and Croucher, A. (1977). Divergent thinking and ability: is there a threshold? *Educational Studies* 3, 101–110.
Cropley, A. J. (1972). A five-year longitudinal study of the validity of creativity tests. *Developmental Psychology* 6, 119–124.
Lang, R. J. and Ryba, K. A. (1976). The identification of some creative thinking parameters common to the artistic and musical personality. *British Journal of Educational Psychology* 46, 267–79.
Starr, J. W. and Nicholl, C. (1975). Creativity and achievement in Nuffield physics. *British Journal of Educational Psychology* 45, 322–6.
Torrance, E. P. (1962). "Guiding Creative Talent". Englewood Cliffs, NJ: Prentice-Hall.
Torrance, E. P. (1967). The Minnesota studies of creative behaviour: national and international extensions. *Journal of Creative Behavior* 1, 137–154.

General evaluation

Creativity testing was a bandwagon in the 1960s and 1970s, but there is no doubt that Torrance has made one of the most enduring and thoughtful contributions to the field. The use of his tests has been central to this contribution, and the amount of evidence accumulated is impressive. In this respect, the Norms-Technical Manual is exemplary.

In other respects, though, the Manual and the tests can be criticized. The Manual veers between treating the tests as experimental (hence obviating the need for adequate standardization) and treating them as clinical instruments of proven worth. Its tone often resembles the advertiser's rather than the scientist's, and the test title (Creative Thinking) promises something that the Manual is rightly cautious about delivering.

These comments are best exemplified in the section on Interpreting Scores. Here far too little evidence is offered to support far-reaching clinical interpretations, moreover without due cautionary remarks about the modest reliabilities of many of the scores (let alone of the profiles and quotients suggested).

While the importance of creating the right testing conditions is continually stressed, the degree to which scores on this kind of test can be manipulated is not adequately acknowledged (see, for example, Hudson, 1968; Vernon, 1971; Nuttall, 1973). This aspect of reliability has something important to contribute to the topic of validity: is creativity a stable trait, or a context-specific quality influenced by a constellation of intellectual and affective factors?

Despite the variety of evidence adduced, the Manual fails to address itself convincingly to the issue of whether the tests do measure creative abilities in such a way as to identify individuals with creative potential. It also fails to explore the underlying structure of the seven test scores (though intercorrelations are reported); a composite score might not only be entirely justified but also have greater reliability and validity (and not invite over-interpretation of subscore differences). Finally, as Wallach (1968) points out, the inter-relationships of intelligence, creativity and various criteria of creative achievement (problems with which are in any case not discussed) are not simultaneously explored. Discriminant validation (as so often) is ignored.

References

Buros, O. K. (Ed.) (1978). "The Eighth Mental Measurement Yearbook". Highland Park, New Jersey: Gryphon Press.

Hudson, L. (1968). "Frames of Mind". London, Methuen.

Nuttall, D. L. (1973). Convergent and divergent thinking. *In* "Educational Research in Britain 3" (Butcher, H. J. and Pont, H. B. Eds). London: University of London Press.

Vernon, P. E. (1971). Effects of administration and scoring on divergent thinking tests. *British Journal of Educational Psychology* **41**, 245–57.

Wallach, M. A. (1968). Review of the Torrance Tests of Creative Thinking. *American Educational Research Journal* **5**, 272–81.

Verbal Test BC

Reviewed by E. P. Duggan

Author: D. A. Pidgeon
Publisher: NFER-Nelson
Distributor: NFER-Nelson
Age range: 8:00–10:06
1960 (S, T) (inferred) (as Test 34); 1965 (S?)
1970 (M, T); (re-standardized) S not stated
No revisions apparent
1979 (M); 1980 (T) printings reviewed
Group test

Test content

The 85 items in the test all require single-word answers to be written into the spaces provided. The items are varied; analogies (*x* is to *y* as *a* is to ?); similar meanings; definitions; alphabetic codes; and verbal reasoning problems. Item difficulty increases as the test progresses. Eleven practice items covering each type of item format precede the test itself.

Purpose

The test was designed to give teachers an up-to-date measure of verbal intelligence covering the age range 8:00–11:00 although the conversion table covers only the range 8:00–10:06.

Item preparation

According to the Manual (p. 2) most of the test items were taken from the Junior Intelligence Tests (A and B) of the Australian Council for Educational Research. The items from the two tests were tried out on a representative group of English children and the 71 items thought to be the most suitable were included together with 14 original items. No indication is given of the 'representativeness' of this group either numerically or otherwise. Presumably the 'original' items means 'new' for no explanation is offered, nor are these items identified. It is inferred from a footnote (Manual, p. 2) that the original test was devised *c.* 1960.

Administration

By implication, the test is for the use of class teachers in schools having the appropriate age range of children. General directions for administration of the test are clear and precise: no deviation from oral instructions is allowed, correct timing by watch or clock with second hands is required: the children are to write in pencil, preferably having reserves of pencils available; two invigilators—a 'reader' and a 'surveyor'—are necessary; no assistance is given except to ensure the correct methods of answering and turning of pages; and adequate separation between children is required to prevent copying. The actual test lasts exactly 30 minutes, but the total working time, including that for practice items, is approximately 40 minutes. How approximate is not defined (but see below).

Standardization

The test author considered that in the 10 years elapsing since the original standardization, there was a possibility of error arising from 'non-representativeness' of present-day samples and those of 10 years ago which may be due to observation in recent years of an increase in 'test sophistication'. Hence the need for restandardization.

Verbal Test BC was given to a complete year-group in one large county authority, consisting of 27 142 children (13 467 girls, 13 675 boys) aged 9:05–10:04 years. Apparently, some 6419 younger children were in 'the original sample' and their results were combined with those of the larger group to produce the revised conversion table. No date was given for this restandardization but the Manual states that: 'In 1970 further data were collected to check the accuracy of these norms. The test was administered to 4178 children (2160 boys, 2018 girls) in one LEA. These results confirmed the *1965* data, so no change has been made in the conversion table' (p. 2). It is not clear whether or not the 'original sample' constituted the '1965 data'. The table enables the children's standardized scores (mean 100, standard deviation 15) to be found from test scores and ages to the nearest month. Each child is thus assessed by comparing him with a representative sample of children of exactly the same age. Just how representative the samples were of all English (or for that matter, Scottish or Welsh) children is a matter for conjecture, and perhaps requires a warning note to teachers. In preparing the conversion tables using Lawley's method (see Introduction), the age range of the sample on which the test was standardized was from 8:03–10:04, so the author found it necessary to extrapolate the lower limit down to 8:00 and upwards to 10:06. The method employed was not explained. The present tables supersede any earlier tables supplied for the test.

Scoring

Each correct answer scores 1 point. Credit may be given for correct intention, e.g. if underlining is used instead of writing a response in the space provided. Detailed and clear instructions are given for use of the marking key, including numerical checks, and procedures for the use of either one or several markers. Since exact age is important only years and *completed* months to be used. All relevant scoring information including converted score is entered on the front cover of the test. No record sheets or summary sheets are provided.

Reliability

By implication (Manual, p. 2) some item analyses were carried out, probably in 1965. Some 330 scripts were drawn from the original standardization sample, and from these a reliability coefficient of 0.97 (KR-20) was calculated. This gave a standard error of measurement of 2.5 for the test.

Validity

Although not explicitly stated, the test is said to have been 'given in one school to a group of 92 children who also completed Schonell's Essential Intelligence Test'. The two sets of scores so obtained had a correlation coefficient of 0.91. In another school 72 children were given both tests and additionally Sleight's Non-Verbal Test. The latter correlated 0.71 with Schonell and 0.67 with Verbal Test BC. If the above was a pilot study, it scarcely seemed adequate. No indication was given of the representativeness of the groups of 92 and 72, of a sampling frame or of what principles underlie the test.

Interpretation

It is indicated that a 95 per cent confidence interval should be used based on 2 standard errors either side of the mean. It is suggested (Manual, p. 3) that a standard error of measurement value of 2.6 is appropriate at age 8:01 and 10:00 and 2.9 at age 10:06.

General evaluation

An adequate test for the intended purpose, i.e. comparison of children's verbal intelligence within the specified age range with perhaps some doubts about the extremes of the age range. For the intended user, the class teacher, administration is simple and the scoring and tabular interpolation are also simple. One query is whether such a test should be considered generally applicable to all

British children: the standardization sample was selected from only one local authority. Another query is: for what purpose should it be used?

Verbal Test C

Reviewed by C. D. Elliott

Author: not stated
Publisher: NFER-Nelson
Distributor: NFER-Nelson
Age range: 9:08–10:08
1966 (S); 1971 (M); 1970 (T)
No revisions apparent
'19th impression' (no date) (T) reviewed
Group test

Test content

Following 14 practice examples, there are 85 scored items in the test. These consist of a general mixture of verbal problems such as analogies, similarities, vocabulary knowledge, sentence comprehension, basic arithmetic, letter codes, verbal reasoning and letter and number series. These problems are generally given in a randomized order, the practice examples covering the broad types of problems encountered in the scored items. The responses required of the child are written. The child is required to insert in appropriate spaces either single letters, numbers or words. The items are intended to be suitable for children in the last two years of primary school.

Purpose

The test is normative. The Manual says: 'Verbal Test C has been constructed to provide a measure of general scholastic ability among children in the last two years of the primary school. Scores derived from Verbal Test C may be used to give a general indication of the level of ability of a particular child or class, but should *not* be regarded as providing in any way a measure of capacity for learning' (p. 2). This statement of the purpose of the test is the only one given in the Manual and raises a number of issues which will be considered in the General evaluation of the test, given at the end of this review.

Item preparation

No information is given in the Manual on either the origins of the items or on whether any early prestandardization trials of items were carried out.

Administration

The test is intended for use by teachers with pupils in the age range of 9:04–11:00 years, i.e. in the last two years of normal primary schools. Because the test items present the problems in written form, *it is essential that children should be able to read to a reasonable level before they can hope to answer the questions.*

Each child requires a test booklet (8 pages) on which he or she writes the answers to the test problems. In addition, of course, the child requires a pen or pencil. A time limit of 35 minutes is set for the scored items. The total working time, including the time required for the practice items, is stated to be approximately 45–50 minutes. In the instructions to pupils on the first page of the test booklet it is stated 'No-one is expected to do everything. Just do as much as you can'.

Administration of the test is fairly standard for a group-administered verbal reasoning test. The instructions for administration given in the Manual are clear and satisfactory.

Standardization

'Verbal Test C has been standardized provisionally on 7547 children (3866 boys and 3681 girls) and adjusted by calibration with a fully standardized test, to approximate to national standards . . . The age range of the sample on which the test was standardized extended from 9:08 to 10:08 years. Thus, in preparing the conversion table on pages 8 and 9, it was necessary to extrapolate upwards to 11:00 and downwards to 9:04' (Manual, p. 2).

The above information is the sum total of information given in the Manual on the standardization of Verbal Test C. We can infer, because this was a test developed by NFER, that the test forms were sent out to a number of schools and that the administration of the tests for standardization was done by school teachers. The date of standardization is not given although the NFER Publishing Company's 1978 catalogue gives the date as 1966. No information is given about the sample design or about the method of adjusting the norms by calibration with what is called a fully standardized test to approximate to national standards. Again, it can be inferred that this calibration comparison was done with another of the NFER verbal tests.

No information is given about the representativeness of the sample or the problem of what to do with children who cannot read. The Manual does not say whether such children were excluded from the standardization sample or whether they were included and their zero, or near zero, raw scores included in the normative data.

A table of norms is provided in the Manual enabling raw scores on the test to be converted to standardized scores with a mean of 100 and a standard deviation of 15. The Manual states: 'These scores are similar to Intelligence Quotients in their numerical distribution but they differ in that they are not derived from consideration of mental age' (Manual, p. 2). It does seem to be very extraordinary that, in 1971, the NFER should have been under the misapprehension that Intelligence Quotients were still being derived from mental ages!

The norms given in the Manual, which go in a one-month age-progression, are for boys and girls combined. This is despite the following statement given in the Manual: 'With the children in the standardization sample, the superiority of girls over boys amounted to 3.4 points of standardized score with a standard error of 0.37 points. The difference between the scores is therefore significant and it is recommended that the two sexes be considered independently of each other' (p. 2). *The Manual offers no further suggestions as to how the two sexes could be considered independently of each other.*

Scoring

The Manual contains clear and detailed instructions for scoring. Each correct item receives 1 point, with incorrect or partially correct answers receiving no credit. For 10 of the items (the code questions) the answer must be spelt correctly. In other items there is no penalty for misspelling, with scorers being recommended to allow anything which is a phonetic or otherwise recognizable spelling of the word required. A marking key is provided in the Manual.

Once a raw score has been obtained this is converted to a standardized score. This is a simple process and is clearly described in the Manual. The child's raw scores on each page and his or her standardized score are recorded on the front page of the test booklet which he or she completed. Once again, this is a simple process, and the space for putting this information one the record form is clear and satisfactory.

Reliability

'The reliability coefficient of the test was calculated from an answer pattern drawn from a sample of 245 scripts. The value was found to be 0.98' (Manual, p. 2). The KR-20 coefficient used here is, of course, an internal consistency coefficient. Such methods must not be used with speeded tests, as virtually all technical works on reliability make abundantly clear (e.g. Stanley, 1971, pp. 415–416). *In the absence of evidence to the contrary, it must be assumed that the reliability coefficient quoted in the Manual is spuriously high.* Furthermore, the Manual gives no reason for the use of a sample of 245 scripts for the calculation of this reliability coefficient. This is a small number of individuals on which to estimate the reliability of the test, particularly since it was standardized on 7500 children. What the test constructor should have done and what is not reported, are test-retest or parallel form reliability studies.

A small amount of discussion is given in the Manual regarding the standard error of measurement of the test of 2.13 points. This has been calculated from the reliability coefficient which, if it is spuriously high, will lead to a *spuriously low standard error of measurement*. Test users will therefore need to treat all figures in the Manual given under the heading of 'Reliability' with extreme caution, if not outright scepticism.

Validity

No validity studies are presented in the Manual. In other words, there are no concurrent or predictive correlational studies with other tests, no factor analyses or studies of any other kind. The test user is, therefore, forced into some evaluation of the content validity of Verbal Test C, in order to decide on the likely meaning of any test scores which might be obtained from the test and any likely useful purpose to which it may be put. This is further discussed in General evaluation below.

Interpretation

One or two small hints are given to test users about the interpretation of scores. The first of these is quoted under the heading Purpose given above in this review. Here, we are told that scores provide a general indication of level of ability but in no way provide a measure of capacity for learning. The user is left to his own devices in interpreting this statement.

The second small piece of help is given in the discussion of the distribution of standardized scores given under the heading 'Standardization' in the Manual. Here, users are told that standardized scores of 75, 90, 110 and 125 are obtained by children who do better than approximately the bottom 5, 25, 75 and 95 per cent respectively of children of their own age in the standardization sample.

Other than a few other comments on the interpretation of the (possibly spuriously low) standard error of measurement, the Manual contains no other help to the test user in interpreting the scores.

Test use

The reviewer knows of no important studies in which this test has been used, although it seems likely that it has been used extensively in schools over the years.

General evaluation

The Manual provides clear instructions for the administration and scoring of the test. Everything else—the description of the rationale of the test, the methods of standardization, the handling of sex differences, reliability and validity—are all woefully inadequate.

What are the consequences of this? One of these is that a test has been produced whose Manual is easy to read and follow for teachers, which is reasonably attractive in format to average or above-average children in the 9 and 10 years age groups, and which can be administered in the space of about one lesson. Tables of standardized scores are produced which, when used with the remarkably low standard error of measurement quoted in the Manual, will give teachers a comfortable feeling of precision of measurement of their pupils. As has been noted above, in the absence of further information, this level of precision of measurement may well be spurious.

Having got a list of scores on the test for a class of children, what does the teacher then do with them? This reviewer hopes that the teacher will not compare scores on this test with scores on tests of reading and other scholastic attainments. It is most important that test users should be aware that children who have difficulty in reading may have considerable difficulty in performing on this test. If this is what the authors mean by their statement that the test should *not* be regarded as providing in any way a measure of capacity for learning, this reviewer feels bound to agree with them. Children who score low on this test are not necessarily of low intelligence or even of low verbal ability in tasks that do not involve writing. If there is cause for concern about their performance either on this or on other tests of scholastic attainment, their problems should be investigated using tests, preferably individually adminis-tered, which do not involve reading and writing skills.

So little technical information is given in the Manual that it is impossible to assess the technical competence of the test construction exercise. There is a serious lack of information on the nature of the standardization sample and on the nature of the procedure by which this test was calibrated with another test in order to approximate national standards. A number of technical issues have been avoided, such as any consideration of the fairness or unfairness of having separate norms for the sexes, particularly as girls tend to have slightly higher mean scores than boys. Given the amount of error of measurement which exists in all tests, the difference of three points in the means of boys and girls is of little practical importance for the assessment of any individual, *unless* the test is to be used for purposes of selection in which some cut-off score is to be used as a strict criterion for that selection. The issues are complex but that is no reason to dodge them (see Introduction). In the absence of further information, the data on reliability leads this reviewer seriously to suspect that the reliability coefficient which is quoted in the Manual is far too high and the standard error of measurement is far too low.

Finally in the case of this test, and most other tests of similar type produced for teachers, the test authors have a responsibility to test users in helping them to interpret scores better. Much fuller guidance needs to be given on: (1) how scores from the test may be interpreted; (2) on how they may be compared to scores from other tests; and (3) on how the test authors envisaged that the test may be of practical usefulness. With regard to the first of these points, test authors need to make clear what they consider to be the educational or psychological dimension which the test is measuring. In the case of Verbal Test C, there are clearly a large number of items such as similarities and analogies, which over the years have come to be accepted as good measures of Spearman's 'g'. So this test to some extent contains items measuring general reasoning ability, albeit in a verbal context, with the child being required to read to a reasonable level in order to understand the problems. Additionally, however, the test contains items measuring, to a greater extent, acquired information such as word knowledge and basic arithmetical skills. These perhaps are more likely to have been acquired directly as a result of school learning. What is it, then, that the test is measuring? To say that it is 'general scholastic ability' is to beg the question, and the authors need to make their theoretical intentions much clearer.

With regard to the second point, it is important that authors of tests such as Verbal Test C should report on how that test relates to other tests, either tests measuring similar skills and abilities, or tests measuring other attainments with which scores on this test may be compared. For example, in order to interpret the meaning of scores on Verbal Test C, it would be helpful to know how scores on this test correlate with scores on similar verbal tests, and with scores on non-verbal tests. It would be most important to know the minimum reading-age level which would be necessary to enable a child to perform on Verbal Test C. Furthermore, since test users will often use tests in combination with others, and will compare children's scores on various tests, it would be of considerable value to know the correlation between scores on Verbal Test C and, say, tests of reading, mathematics or other scholastic attainments. Knowing such correlations, and knowing the standard error of measurement of the other scales, would enable the test authors to report standard errors of differences between scores and to report regression equations enabling test users to predict scores on another scale given a particular score on Verbal Test C. It is only by using methods of this sort that scores on different tests may properly be compared and interpreted.

With regard to the third point, it is essential that the test authors address themselves to the uses of Verbal Test C which they envisage. Do they anticipate that it will be used for purposes of selection of children for schools or classes, or their selection for streams or sets within a school? If so, considerable guidance needs to be given to test users on how the test might appropriately be used for such purposes, giving due cautionary warnings about error of measurement and so on. Is it envisaged that the test would be used for diagnostic purposes? If so, it would probably be used in the context of comparisons with scores on other tests. Once again, the test authors need to provide the test user with relevant information and with cautionary advice.

Much higher standards of technical information and reporting are required, and until this is provided, users should treat this test with extreme caution. Until the author and publisher rectify the faults given in this review, it is difficult to see the value of the test.

Reference

Stanley, J. C. (1971). Reliability. *In* "Educational Measurement" (R. L. Thorndike Ed.) (2nd edn). Washington DC: American Council on Education.

Verbal Test CD

Reviewed by E. P. Duggan

Author: Valerie Land
Publisher: NFER-Nelson
Distributor: NFER-Nelson
Age ranges: 9:00–10:07; 10:00–11:07; (3rd- and 4th-year juniors)
1971 (M); 1970 (T); S not stated
1977 (S) (restandardized)
'20th impression' (T) reviewed
Group test

Test content

This test is very similar to Verbal Test BC (q.v.). There are 85 items consisting of: semantic groupings, similarities, differences, missing words or letters, completing series, missing numbers, word interchanges, opposites, codes, sequences. There are 12 practice items sufficiently representative of the variety of forms found among the test items themselves.

Purpose

'Verbal Test CD has been constructed in the light of research findings, to provide a measure of general scholastic ability among children in the last two years of primary school' (Manual, p. 3). Which 'research findings' generated the stimulus for the test are not specified. The case for the verbal test is further justified in the next sentence: 'Scores yielded by verbal tests have been found to correlate most highly with *all other subjects* and are therefore the most useful indication of "streams" where it is not possible to give an attainment test in each subject' (my italics). Strong claims on little evidence provided.

Item preparation

No discussion of the origins of the items or of the item analysis is given but the close relationship of this test with Verbal Test BC suggests that it may be a revised version of that test, extended to 11:00 years.

Administration

The time allotted for the whole test, including the practice items, is 45–50 minutes. The time specified for the actual test is 35 minutes exactly. Apart from this, the general directions and procedure for administering the test are identical with those for Verbal Test BC. As before, they are clear and precise. Again, by implication only, users appear to be class teachers.

Standardization

The Manual states: 'Verbal Test CD was administered for the purpose of *restandardization* to a sample of 10 970 children, selected according to a stratified random sample technique designed to make it representative of the population in England and Wales . . .' (p. 3, my italics). As no mention had been made of the test origin or of previous standardization, the use of the word "restandardization" is puzzling. The sample tested in March and April, of 1977, was 5247 3rd-year and 5723 4th-year junior school children (note that the columns in the table given in the Manual are incorrectly labelled '2nd-year Junior' and '3rd-year Junior').

The data were used to compile conversion tables, employing Lawley's method (see Introduction), giving a mean 100 and standard deviation 15.

Scores were extrapolated to include ages not tested: 'to make them suitable for testing at any time during the year' (*sic*) (p. 3). The user is, however, cautioned that these scores are likely to contain a higher degree of error and that care is needed in interpreting the results.

Mean scores for boys and girls were calculated separately from the standardization data: some superiority for girls was found, but a combined conversion table was presented.

Scoring

The general principles, with one exception, and the use of the marking key are identical with those for Verbal Test BC and need not be repeated since these are also clear and unequivocal. The exception referred to is that there is no penalty for misspelling in 8 of the items, a phonetic or otherwise recognizable spelling being acceptable. The marking key is adequate and clear, including permitted alternatives.

Reliability

KR-20 was used to calculate the reliability coefficient for the 3rd- and 4th-year juniors separately using approximately 10 per cent and 5 per cent samples, respectively, giving values of 0.97 and 0.98. The corresponding standard errors of measurement are 2.43 and 2.30.

Validity

Nothing is reported on validity.

Interpretation

'These scores are similar to Intelligence Quotients in their numerical distribution, but they differ in that they are not arrived at through consideration of Mental Age. Each child is assessed by comparing him with a representative sample of children of exactly the same age' (Manual, p. 3). It is a matter for conjecture whether the normal class teacher will fully understand this.

General evaluation

A useful test for what it purports to do. It is probably applicable to most English children in the age groups suggested. Minor modifications in wording may be necessary for Scottish, Welsh and Ulster children. It is a well-graded test, supported by a clear and adequate Manual; it can, with certain exceptions noted above, be used readily by unsophisticated personnel and adequate precautions in interpretation of results are given.

Since no indication or reference to previous research is given, it is difficult to assess its value. Its obvious connection in rubric, content and scoring with Verbal Test BC suggest the origins might lie in Australian research testing, but beyond that it is not possible to go.

Verbal Test D

Reviewed by Robert Wood

Author: T. N. Postlethwaite
Publisher: NFER-Nelson
Distributor: NFER-Nelson
Age range: 10:04–11:05
1970 (T); 1971 (M)
1976 (S) (restandardized); no revisions apparent
1979 (M); 1980 (T) printings reviewed
Group test

Test content

All the Manual has to say about the rationale behind the test is that it is meant to 'measure those aspects of intelligent behaviour relevant to a verbally biased education; thus most items deal with words; some, however, deal with numbers' (p. 2). The reader will immediately wonder, 'why do *some* deal with numbers; *how* do they deal with numbers; what does *some* amount to, and why that many?' In fact, 'some' means 13 out of 84 items (but not one in the last 20); of these 8 are pure sums while the other 5 are items of the 'missing number in a series' type. These last might (*might*) be justified on the grounds that the test also contains items of the 'missing letter in a series' type but it is a mystery why the 8 sums are there. If the test had been called an intelligence test one might have let the matter go but it is called a verbal test and that must mean something. The only other reference in the Manual to what the test is supposed to be about is on p. 3 where it says that the test is meant to provide a 'general measure of scholastic ability'. So that must be what it is, if you know what that is.

Of the test content dealing with words, the tasks set are the staples of intelligence tests, antonyms/synonyms, missing words/letters, word swaps, codes using letters and numbers (but as symbols only). The distribution of items across these types is not even. There is a powerful smell of 11+ about this test. Evidently the items do tap intelligent behaviour—which items do not?—but one would be hard pressed to *describe* what performance on the test means, or does not mean.

A few items are written in such a way as to give cause for concern. In items 21 and 53 the word 'series' should have been used instead of 'order', which has no meaning as it stands. The wording of item 60 shows that the author knew what was wanted. Item 14 may be out-of-date in the sense that through eating Chinese food children are becoming accustomed to linking sweet and sour, rather than juxtaposing them (even if the contrast in taste is intended). Two other answers seem just as sound. Item 33 calls for a very subtle discrimination which verges on trickery. Again two other answers seem just as acceptable. Curiously one item (58) is considered so potentially obscure that the author has taken the trouble, in a footnote to the marking key, to show the marker how the correct answer is arrived at.

Purpose

According to the Manual (p. 3):

'Scores yielded by Verbal Tests have been found to correlate highly with criteria for academic success and can therefore be used by class teachers as a guide in:
(1) giving an estimate of the expected degree of success should any particular pupil follow an academic course of study;
(2) streaming or banding;
(3) vocational and educational guidance'.

It is therefore seen as an all-purpose test. However, since the test is intended for pupils aged 10–12 years, it is hard to imagine how it could ever be used for vocational guidance, and the absence of a profile feature probably makes it inadequate for educational guidance, even if one were happier about the content. As for the test's predictive value, the Validity section of this review has some comments to make. Here, perhaps it is sufficient to note the unpleasant whiff of determinism about the first purpose, although goodness knows this is a common enough claim by test makers. To imply that a prediction *for a particular individual* is likely to be at all accurate is, of course, misleading.

Item preparation

Two hundred and seven items were administered in three drafts of 69 items each to groups of between 100 and 169 pupils considered to be representative of the 9:06–11:00 year-old population. A second draft of 89 items was administered to two further groups and the item analysis repeated, resulting in the final form of 84 items. Items were arranged in order of difficulty to form a rectangular distribution so that a rank-ordering of pupils would be obtained with approximately equal precision over all parts of the range, and the reliability of discrimination would be maximized. That is what the Manual says.

Now the matter of producing tests with particular distributional forms is a difficult business, especially where the rectangular distribution is concerned (Scott, 1972), but it is certain that success in achieving a targetted distribution depends crucially on the intercorrelation of the items. It is generally agreed (see, for example, Henrysson, 1971) that where item intercorrelations are low (of the order of 0.10), as they generally are with achievement tests, maximum discrimination is most likely to be achieved by choosing items which are all at, or around, the 50% difficulty level. As the average intercorrelation rises, and particularly when it exceeds 0.33, it becomes necessary to spread the item difficulties over the range to avoid the middle of the distribution thinning out too much.

Just what the appropriate prescription should have been in this case is impossible to say, with authority, from the data provided. Probably the intercorrelations are closer to 0.33 than to 0.10. Even so, it may be that Stanley (1971) is right when he argues that 'for most ability, aptitude and achievement tests in many situations it will be best if all items are of equal (and middle) difficulty. Such a test is likely to be better than other-difficulty tests of the same content for discriminating among all except 1 or 2 per cent of the examinees in each test, unless the group is exceptionally heterogeneous'. Scott (1972) says essentially the same thing. For this test, which wants to serve so many purposes, that was probably the right advice. But it is understandable that the test maker should have distributed his item difficulties uniformly. Doubtless he was following his intuition. Beware of intuition in this area.

What do the data provided in the Manual actually tell us? They tell us that the standardization sample, mean age 11 years 0.21 months, had a mean raw score of 37.75 and a standard deviation of 20.99. So the sample was not rectangularly distributed; there is evidence of flattening but also of downward skew. Perhaps the number items pulled down the intercorrelations. All the same it looks to be at least as close to a rectangular distribution as to a normal distribution (a rectangular distribution would have had a standard deviation of 24; with a normal distribution the figure would have been more like 14), so that the transformation to a normal distribution requires a fairly considerable stretching of the raw score distribution.

Sex differences

The Manual takes the trouble to point out (p. 2) that 'care was taken in writing the items (and in the subsequent analysis) to avoid the inclusion of those that might favour one sex more than the other'. This policy does not meet with my approval. The absurdity of selecting items just because they show no sex differences was pointed out long ago by Lorge (1952). He took the view, which I share, that genuine differences should be allowed to reveal themselves, the important thing being to have a convincing rationale for including items in a test. That is what this test does not have and the policy on sex differences only increases the impression of arbitrariness. It also plants doubt in the mind of the reader concerning the credibility of what *has* found its way into the test.

If the object of such a policy is to produce identical score distributions for boys and girls, or at least, approximately the same means, then it did not succeed in this case because girls out-scored boys, on average, to the tune of 4.26 raw score points or 3.08 standard score points. This must be the result of small margins at the item level accumulating to produce a significant difference. Separate conversion tables for the sexes are provided even though the Manual points that this was not strictly necessary because the difference is constant over age. So, presumably, what has been produced is a test where the girls are not as superior as they would have been but are still superior. It would have been interesting to look at an item analysis for each sex, especially for the number items.

Administration

The administration of this test is straightforward and the Manual provides instructions which are clear and uncluttered. There are no unusual features. Answers are written in pencil, sometimes by underlining and sometimes by supplying words, letters or numbers. Erasers are banned and the instructions say nothing about changing answers although the marking principles which follow do anticipate that answers will be changed. The total working time, including the time required for the practice items (of which there are 9), is approximately 45–50 minutes, with 40 minutes exactly for the test. The Manual provides no evidence on whether this degree of speediness (84 items in 40 minutes) is reasonable for all age groups of the target population (10–12 years), although one would have said it was not particularly severe.

Standardization

The test was standardized in the spring term of 1976, on a sample of 10 345 children (5223 boys and 5122 girls). Authorities and schools were selected at random, the Manual notes, in an attempt to obtain a sample which is representative of the national population. No further details are given about any attention paid to LEA and school size so the authority of the sample rests on its size, which is more than adequate.

The raw scores have been standardized to have a mean of 100 and a standard deviation of 15 and, of course, are constrained to follow a normal distribution. Adjustments for age, on a monthly basis, have been incorporated into the conversion tables. This may seem a thoroughly conventional thing to do but there are hidden assumptions which need exposing. The conversion method used is by Lawley (1950). In defence of his method, he offers the following: 'Errors of estimation arising from the construction of the conversion table are in most cases negligible compared with the errors of measurement of any mental test, however good' (p. 86). Let us turn Lawley's argument on its head and see what happens. If conversions were available at each raw score for 10:06 and 11:06 only, which I suppose we would call 10+ and 11+ following other usage, e.g. AH2/AH3, then the maximum 'error' incurred by taking the 10+ figure for 10:00 or the 11+ figure for 11:00 or 12:00 is consistently 2 or 3 points, and most often 2, standardized score points that is. That margin is strictly comparable with the standard error of measurement, given in the Manual as 2.7 raw score points (at age 11) which, in standardized score terms, would be about two points. I do not say that the effects of the error of measurement and the 'error' of reading will cancel out but since the first is more powerful than the second, as Lawley said, it will still be dominant even if the errors operate in different directions.

Lawley felt obliged to defend his method because he had to rest it on several questionable assumptions, of which his assumption concerning the nature of increases in 'intelligence' over time (strictly linear throughout the age span) is the most dubious. Also, by using the cross-sectional method of adjusting for age, which was customary then as now (and in any case was forced on him by the method of data collection), he was unable to take into account *seasonal* effects, which can only be detected by measuring individuals over a given period (e.g. 1 year: see Goldstein and Fogelman, 1974, for more on the distinction between cross-sectional and longitudinal age standardizations). Lawley, as I say, was not to blame for that, nor did he make exaggerated claims for his method. He simply said it was workable. And, anyway, why quibble when all we are talking about is distributing 2 or 3 points across 6 months? I believe there is every reason to quibble. The point about monthly calibrations is that they give an impression of accuracy which is almost always spurious. That impression extends to the whole test and can easily be instrumental in persuading the potential user to choose the test, especially when it is thought that audiences 'back home' will be even more impressed with the accuracy of the test. It would have been better in this case to report conversions for 10:06 and 11:06 and 12 years exactly and invite the user to interpolate or better still, provide separate tables for 10+ and 11+, as other test Manuals do. As a matter of fact, these particular tables could not have been compiled without some interpolation *and* extrapolation; interpolation because Lawley's method requires it, and extrapolation because data collection was restricted to the range 10:04–11:05, necessitating extrapolation over nearly half of the range! One has to conclude that, on their own, neither the data nor the method support such elaborate conversion tables, and certainly not together.

Scoring

The scoring is straightforward with the usual provisos such as where the pupil has changed an answer, credit is to be given if it is clear that the final intention was correct. Where appropriate, phonetic or otherwise recognizable spelling of words is accepted. As noted before, there are no part scores.

Reliability

The Manual reports that the reliability coefficient was calculated 'from an answer pattern drawn up from a sample of 400 scripts from the standardization sample'. The value was found to be 0.97 (by KR-20). The language used here is rather curious, 'answer pattern', 'drawn up', and it seems a pity that only 4 per cent of the sample should have been utilized. With such a large sample there ought to have been an opportunity to run a test-retest exercise, if not other checks on reliability. We are not told how heterogeneous the 4 per cent sample was in terms of the age range tested. Naturally, that affects the size of the reliability estimate. Although the Manual is no doubt trying to be helpful, it is debatable whether the following sentence on its own actually helps the reader who is not quite on terms with educational measurement theory: 'The Kuder-Richardson formula is accepted for comparison of tests, being associated with (although distinct from) the test-retest correlation' (p. 3). Let us not beat about the bush. High values of KR-20 are so common that after a time the experienced reader ceases to pay any attention to them. It is the rare test which is rejected on reliability grounds although it is almost certain that more would be if only we could get a purchase on those aspects of reliability concerning which KR-20, being a measure of internal consistency, is dumb. In any case, it is likely that the practice of reporting reliabilities will decline in favour of the kind of information about an instrument which generalizability studies can provide (see, Thorndike, 1982).

Validity

The validity section of the Manual is disappointing, to put it mildly. This is the 7th impression of the Manual, printed in 1979, the test is in its 21st impression and has been sold since 1970, yet all the Manual can offer is one correlation ($r = 0.90$) between the test and 'an NFER closed verbal test (12A)' on a group of 100, yes 100, pupils! Other than that, it harks back to studies carried out in the 11+ era or precomprehensive school era referring, in an allusive way, to 'evidence on the predictive value of verbal tests for success in future academic courses'. This is pretty pathetic. Now that it is conventional wisdom that the validity of a test varies according to the purpose to which it is put, it is quite improper for a Manual to propose, as this one does, several very different purposes, from streaming to guidance, without offering supportive data against which the user can evaluate these claims.

Interpretation

The interpretation section is the most useful in the Manual because it is full of the sort of cautions and qualifications the user needs to be made aware of, or reminded of. There is also a short bibliography of mental measurement texts which, like the term mental measurement, could do with up-dating. But what, one wonders, is the likely effect of laying down this good advice alongside a poor test? Will it not persuade users to overcome any qualms they might have about the content of the test, and the absence of back-up data, and lull them into thinking that as long as they observe the warnings they will come to no harm? Or else be sufficiently impressed by the Manual's candour to swallow their doubts? I fear so. The point is that these warnings are necessary enough for a good test; for a good test they cease to be relevant, because they no longer protect.

Test use

Verbal Test D was used by Child and Croucher (1977) in their investigation of the relationship between divergent thinking and ability (intelligence) in the upper ranges of ability. They describe the test as a 'standardized test of intelligence' but say nothing about it other than that the range of scores runs from 70 upwards. Nothing is said about reliability; perhaps they thought that, being a published test, everyone would think the reliability OK. For their divergent thinking tests, however, which were modifications of other tests, they did report reliability estimates (test-retest) and these were 0.45, 0.44 and 0.42. Now these are *lousy* reliabilities, albeit over the period of a year, but they do not appear to have concerned the authors one bit. They press on regardless. The cavalier attitude to test desiderata shown by these authors is typical, I would say. The analysis in the remainder of the paper proceeds as if the various measures were impeccable, whereas from what we know of Verbal Test D and what is said about the divergent thinking tests the likelihood of divining anything trustworthy concerning the relationship between 'divergent thinking' and 'ability' from these tests is negligible.

General evaluation

If a test is meant to be an intelligence test it should be labelled as such. Why shelter behind the code 'Verbal', except to avoid accusations of peddling 11+ tests? It is sad that Vernon, of all people, should hail the replacement of 'intelligence' by other labels as a smart idea. 'There is likely to be much less criticism by educationists and parents of instruments called Verbal or Non-Verbal Reasoning Tests—that is the name which Moray House adopted many years ago' (Vernon, 1979, p. 19). Vernon is hinting at what Guterman (1979) comes straight out with. 'If we were to eschew the term "intelligence" and instead use "scholastic aptitude" for IQ tests, such a finding would arouse less resistance and there could be a more enlightened discussion about the education of disadvantaged children' (p. 164). But is anyone so naive as to believe this? I suggest that Gillham (1975) is nearer the truth when he writes 'What does seem likely to happen is that the old ideas will be given new names, will not be presented in the form of "intelligence" tests and will not have their results expressed as single figure IQ scores; and yet will continue to fulfil traditional functions—the presumed measurement of "underlying abilities" or "latent traits", and predictions based on these' (p. 435). One thing is clear. To call a test 'Verbal' when it contains 8 sums is to debase the meaning of language. What we have here is a test with a preponderance of verbal items, as have most intelligence tests, chosen so that sex differences will not show up, except that they do.

Since the test is in its 21st impression it must have sold well. With the booklet comprising 7 pages and the manual 11 pages, and no fancy marking keys, and no part scores to worry about, the test is cheap, uncomplicated and easy to administer. There is no denying the selling power of that constellation of characteristics. However, the discerning user who is prepared to pay a little more will avoid this test, preferring instead tests which are founded on principles, educational or psychological, and which offer data bearing on how they might serve different measurement purposes, or even a single purpose.

If it is the case that some users are liable to be swayed in their choice of test by the norms provided, or rather by the provision of month-by-month figures, then they should realize that neither the data collected during standardization nor the method of conversion used, warrant the elaborate month-by-month conversions of which the tables consist.

Pupils could consider themselves unfortunate were they to be streamed or banded or even given guidance on the basis of the results of this test.

References

Child, D. and Croucher, A. (1977). Divergent thinking and ability: Is there a threshold? *Educational Studies* 3, 101–110.

Gillham, W. E. C. (1975). Intelligence: the persistent myth. *New Behaviour* 1, 433–435.

Goldstein, H. and Fogelman, K. (1974). Age standardization and season effects in mental testing. *British Journal of Educational Psychology* 44, 109–115.

Guterman, S. S. (1979). IQ tests in research on social stratification; the cross-validity of the tests as measures of scholastic aptitude. *Sociology of Education* 52, 163–173.

Henrysson, S. (1971). Gathering, analyzing and using data on test items. *In* "Educational Measurement" (R. L. Thorndike, Ed.) (2nd edn). Washington DC: American Council on Education.

Lawley, D. N. (1950). A method of standardizing group tests. *British Journal of Psychology (Statistical Section)* 3, 86–89.

Lorge, I. (1952). Difference or bias in tests of intelligence. *In* "Testing Problems in Perspective" (A. Anastasi, ed.). Washington DC: American Council on Education, 1966.

Scott, W. A. (1972). The distribution of test scores. *Educational and Psychological Measurement* 32, 725–735.

Stanley, J. C. (1971). Reliability. *In* "Educational Measurement" (R. L. Thorndike Ed.) (2nd edn). Washington DC: American Council on Education.

Thorndike, R. L. (1982). "Applied Psychometrics". Boston: Houghton Mifflin Inc.

Vernon, P. E. (1979). "Intelligence Testing 1928–1978: What Next?". Edinburgh: Scottish Council for Research in Education.

Verbal Test EF

Reviewed by Marten Shipman

Authors: Olive Woods and Valerie Land
Publisher: NFER-Nelson
Distributor: NFER-Nelson
Age range: 11:03–13:02
1971 (M); 1970 (T); S not stated
No revisions apparent
1979 (M); 1980 (T) printings reviewed
Group test

Test content

The 90 questions are presented on seven pages in a continuous layout similar to other conventional verbal reasoning tests. The questions refer to similarities, opposites, rhyming word and alphabetic series, semantic and symbolic analogies, and so on. Each question requires pupils to write letters, words or numbers in a bracket or to underline correct responses. Since some 13 items involve number series or simple computations and 9 items involve letter codings or letter series it is not clear why the title is 'Verbal Test'.

Purpose

'Verbal Test EF has been constructed in the light of research findings, to provide a measure of general scholastic ability among children in the first two years of the secondary school. Scores derived from Verbal Test EF may be used to give a general indication of the level of ability of a particular child or class, but should *not* be regarded as providing in any way a measure of capacity for learning' (Manual, p. 2).

The test is designed to give an indication of the stream in which a pupil should be placed given the difficulty of giving an attainment test in each subject. The basis of this surrogate purpose is given as the relation between scores on verbal tests and subject attainments.

Item preparation

No details are given.

Administration

There are very detailed instructions for administration. Each child needs the seven-page test booklet. The written instructions repeated by the supervisor and spaces for pupil particulars form the front page with six pages of questions. Tests are not reusable. The total working time for the test is 40 minutes and a watch or clock with second hands is recommended. Starting and finishing instructions are included in the Manual. It is stressed that 'No deviation, however slight, should be made from the oral instructions, since *any* alteration may have the effect of making the test easier or more difficult than the form for which standardized scores were obtained' (Manual, p. 2).

The children need two sharpened pencils with a reserve supply available. The procedures to be followed by the two invigilators that are required are also spelled out in fine detail.

Standardization

The test was administered for standardization to a 'fully representative sample of children between 11:03 and 13:02 in a selected area. The scores of 4155 children were collected and the data used to construct the conversion table on pages 6 and 7' (Manual, p. 2). No details are given of the area selected or of the way the sample was chosen. The claim to representativeness is not substantiated.

The technique used in constructing the conversion table was an adaptation of that devised by Lawley (see Introduction). The raw scores are converted into standardized scores arranged to have a mean of 100 and a standard deviation of

15. Scores between 11:3 and 11:0, and 13:2 and 13:6 have been obtained by extrapolation.

Scoring

Items are marked right or wrong with no ambiguity or fractional marks. A marking key is provided. Clear instructions are given for deciding on whether responses that are difficult to interpret are to be judged correct and items are indicated for which misspelling is allowed. The numbers of right and wrong answers are taken from each page and transferred to a table on the front cover of the test and totalled.

Reliability

Reliability is given as 0.97 (KR-20), calculated from a sample of 250 scripts, presumably drawn from the sample of 4155 used for standardization, although this is not confirmed. Standard error for the test is given as 2.8. Compared with this measure for the mean age of 12:02, the Manual makes some obscure remark about a value of 3.2 for age 11:00 and 3.3 for age 13:06 as being due to 'sampling errors of the estimation of the age allowance' (Manual, p. 2). No measures other than internal consistency are given.

Validity

There is no discussion of validity in the Manual except a warning that while the standardized scores on the test are similar to Intelligence Quotients they differ in not having been calculated by reference to mental age. There is a warning that the test does not provide a measure of capacity for learning.

The absence of detail on validity arises from the obscure nature of 'verbal tests'. The Verbal Test EF is designed to provide a measure of 'general scholastic ability'. It would be difficult to assess associative validity unless there were a range of attainment test results available for school subjects. No relationships with actual scholastic performance are reported in the Manual. The absence of measures of predictive validity is regrettable given the recommended use of the test for streaming.

Interpretation

Apart from a reference in the Manual to 'general scholastic ability' the meaning of 'verbal ability' is not spelled out. Hence scores are related to uses such as streaming but not to any underlying psychological attribute. Thus interpretation of scores is difficult and generalization from an operational definition would be hazardous.

General evaluation

The test is one of many verbal reasoning tests designed for this age group. It seems to have been constructed to facilitate streaming. With the declining use of verbal reasoning tests for selection for secondary schooling there is a demand for such tests after entry at 11:00. There is a danger, however, that scores could be interpreted as measuring intelligence or capacity to learn or to have meaning beyond the ability to solve verbal puzzles despite the warnings given.

If it is to be used, then the controls built into the test design and administration and the size of the sample used in standardization suggest that it could be used with confidence.

Verbal Test GH

Reviewed by John Nisbet

Author: Valerie Land
Publisher: NFER-Nelson
Distributor: NFER-Nelson
Age range: 13:10–14:10 (3rd- and 4th-year English secondary)
1965–66 (S); 1961 (as Test 157)
Revisions not apparent
1976 (M); 1980 (T) printings reviewed
Group test

Test content

There are 90 items of the kinds conventionally used in tests of verbal reasoning, evenly distributed throughout: analogies, series, codes, problems, similarities, synonyms, etc. There are no subscales, though blocks of items are grouped under common sets of instructions. Brief, objectively scored responses are required: a single word or digit, or a few letters, or underlining in multiple-choice items.

Purpose

The function of the test is 'to provide a measure of general scholastic ability among children in the third and fourth years of the secondary school' (in England). Scores are 'useful, when it is not possible to give an attainment test in each subject, as a guide to the grading of pupils, supplemented by teachers' estimates' (Manual, p. 2).

Item preparation

No information is given in the Manual.

Administration

This is a speeded test, with a time limit of 45 minutes. Instructions to the pupils follow the standard pattern commonly used in verbal reasoning tests. There is no practice test, and no practice items at the start; but in the body of the test, five of the most complex instructions are illustrated by a single worked example. The instructions within the test are clearly explained. Lay-out is clear and unambiguous. The Manual does not specify recommended users, but it is implicit that the test will be used by teachers, with pupils who are relatively familiar with the kinds of questions set. Children require only a test booklet (not reusable) and two pencils.

Standardization

The test was standardized in 1965 and 1966 on 3137 boys and girls (approximately equal numbers) aged between 13:10 and 14:10. This standardization sample comprised all the pupils (2074) within this age range in one LEA, plus a 'specially weighted sample of 1063 pupils from a large number of schools in several areas in different parts of the country' (Manual, p. 2). No further details are given, and no data from the use of the test with other possibly representative samples. Consequently, it is not possible to judge the representativeness of these norms. The conversion table provides quotients with a mean of 100 and standard deviation of 15, derived by Lawley's method, with extrapolation to give norms for the range 13:06–15:00. The mean raw score (at the mean age of 14:04) of 25.18 out of 90, standard deviation 14.38, demonstrates that it is a relatively difficult test for this age group. At the lowest age level, only 21 points of raw score cover the range of quotients from 70 to 100.

In the standardization sample, girls scored 1.51 points higher on average than boys; separate norms for girls and boys are not given.

Scoring

Scoring follows the standard pattern for tests of this kind. Markers are provided with a key with only one acceptable answer for each item (except in one case where a badly constructed 'opposites' item has two possible answers). Each correct answer counts one point: addition provides a single total score for the test.

Reliability

The Manual reports a KR-20 reliability coefficient of 0.95 derived from a 'sample of 268 scripts'—whether this is a random sample from the standardization group is not specified. From this coefficient is calculated a standard error of measurement of 3.3 (3.52 at the lowest age range and 3.47 at the highest). No other information on reliability is given.

Validity

No information of any kind on validity is given. Technical information in the Manual is limited to two short paragraphs: Standardization (17 lines) and Reliability (10 lines).

Interpretation

On interpretation of the scores, the Manual is even briefer, offering only 3 lines. 'Scores derived from Verbal Test GH may be used to give a general indication of the level of ability of a particular child or class, but should *not* be regarded as providing in any way a measure of capacity for learning'.

General evaluation

The test belongs to the familiar '11 +' series, now rather out of fashion, at least for the 'grading' suggested in the Manual. (This kind of test may, however, still be useful for scaling teachers' estimates to adjust for differences in mean and standard deviation between schools.) Being designed for an older age group than the old selection tests, it helps to fill a gap in the range of tests available. It has plenty of 'ceiling room': even at age 15, a score of 71 out of 90 gives a quotient of 140. Consequently, its discrimination is greater among the above-average pupils, and it would seem to have been designed mainly for those likely to proceed towards more advanced study. But the Manual is silent on such matters: it is written mainly for a teacher applying the test and marking it, as if to imply that interpretation of results is someone else's concern.

The most serious criticism of the Manual is its lack of information on the construction and validity of the test. One must assume that a test issued by a national test agency was based on a sound item analysis, and that data on validity are available in records somewhere. Indifference to reporting such data is surely inexcusable. In fact, the test itself appears to be a reasonable specimen of its kind, and it contains some imaginative variations on the standard item format. It is all the more regrettable that the absence of technical data is likely to discourage psychologists and researchers from using it in studies which might contribute to a better understanding of what it is measuring and how it might best be used.

Watson-Glaser Critical Thinking Appraisal

Reviewed by J. P. Ryan

Authors: Goodwin Watson and Edward M. Glaser★
Publisher: Harcourt Brace Jovanovich★
Distributors: NFER-Nelson; The Test Agency
Age: 15+; British norms for some adult groups
1963 (S); 1964 (M); 1951–64 (T)†
1970–75 (S); 1976 (M) (British Supplement: Form YM only)

Test content

The five subtests are: Inference (20 items), Recognition of Assumptions (16), Deduction (25), Interpretation (24), Evaluation of Arguments (15). Test 1 consists of a number of short information passages, each followed by several statements. The testee is to indicate whether a statement is 'definitely true', 'probably true', 'insufficient data', 'probably false' or 'definitely false'. In Test 2 a statement is followed by several 'proposed assumptions': the task is to indicate whether each assumption is 'made' or 'not made' in the statement. Similarly, Tests 3 and 4 concern whether conclusions or interpretations do or do not follow from the information given; and in Test 5 whether arguments are 'strong' or 'weak' in relation to a particular question at issue. Considerable reading ability is required to obtain a valid result, although unlimited time can be given to complete.

While the material is mainly of USA origin and reference, this should have only a slight effect on Britain at the level of intended use. While the USA norms go as low as the 9th grade (14 years), the British Supplement to Form YM gives norms, but only for various adult groups.

★ British Supplement for Form YM—norms and other data—by Gillian Nyfield, Peter Saville, Janice Field and John Hodgkiss, are published and distributed by NFER-Nelson.
† Publication data for Forms YM and ZM only. Forms A and B (1980) with USA Manual and tests are also available. The 1983 NFER-Nelson catalogue states that Forms YM and ZM are 'Available only while stocks last'. Forms A and B are available and are revisions (new items, 80 rather than 100 items, shorter administration time). The 1983 catalogue of The Test Agency refers to Forms YM and ZM.

Purpose

According to the Manual (p. 2) the exercises 'require the application of some of the important abilities involved in critical thinking'. 'The Critical Thinking Appraisal calls for responses to two different kinds of item content. In some items the examinee is asked to think critically about problems involving "neutral" topics such as the weather, scientific facts or experiments, and other matters about which people generally do not have strong feelings or prejudices. Other items, approximately parallel in logical structure, pertain to political, economic, and social issues concerning which many people have definite emotional feelings, biases, or prejudices. Inclusion of controversial materials is intended to provide a partial sample of an individual's ability to deal critically with issues which may be surrounded by strong feelings or biases' (Manual, p. 2).

Item preparation

The origins of the scale go back to work by Watson published in 1925 and 1937. Since then the items have been refined through the original (1952) edition of the scale and for the current (1964) edition. Details of the item generation can be found in earlier publications.

Administration

A standard set of directions are read out by the examiner. With an individual, or with a superior 'test-wise' group, the directions can be abbreviated. The test booklets are reusable. Responses are made by marking an IBM answer sheet. There are two parallel forms, YM and ZM. The Manual and answer sheet serves both Forms but separate test booklets and scoring stencils are required.

While the test is a power one, suggested times are given for each of the subtests, and it is recommended that the group is moved onto the next subtest when 95 per cent have completed the current subtest. Slower testees can be allowed to return to unfinished items at the end. The suggested overall test time is 50 minutes for the main group.

Standardization

The USA norms for Form YM and ZM are based upon 15 611 cases, ranging from 9th graders to college seniors. There are British norms (YM only) for a variety of adult groups, tested in the period 1970–1975, covering nearly 3000 cases in all. Several of these studies are based on use of a 50-minute time limit. There are separate norms for 'industrial' and 'educational' groups of 'applicant' and 'established' status. In each case the standardizing group is explicitly an 'opportunity' sample. There was a preponderance of males in the British usage but no separate norms for the sexes are available.

Scoring

Scoring can be done by IBM machine or by an easily used stencil. There is no weighting of items, so that the number correct gives the score. It is suggested that multiply-marked items and unanswered items have a red pencil mark put right across the scoring boxes, and the score is then obtained by counting the number of correct responses through the stencil that have not been so marked. Although the Manual says that subtest scores can be derived, there are no norms, USA or British, available for these.

Reliability

Studies on Form YM in the USA yielded corrected (Spearman-Brown) reliability coefficients from 0.85–0.87 using an odd-even split-half technique and based on samples sized from 200 to over 10 000. The only test-retest study was a British one ($n = 17$) which gave a coefficient of 0.89. Two other British studies have compared the YM and ZM forms and alternate forms correlations of 0.72 were obtained in both instances. No USA test-retest or alternate forms reliabilities are reported in the Manual.

For the subtests, the USA Manual gives corrected split-half values from 0.53–0.74, while the British norms give test-retest values from 0.33–0.52, and alternate forms correlations from -0.08–0.60. Curiously, the lowest alternate forms value was for the Argument subtest with a one-day interval, and in the other alternate forms study, with a six-month interval, the corresponding coefficient was 0.49. Various standard errors of measurement are given for Form YM and its subtests, although only based upon small sample sizes ($n = 17, 21, 28$).

Intercorrelations among subtests and between subtests and the total score are reported for Form YM for both USA and British data. Subtest intercorrelations range from 0.23–0.50 (USA, $n = 2947$), and from 0.13–0.52 (British, $n = 221$). Subtest-total correlations range from 0.62–0.79 (US) and from 0.52–0.78 (British).

Validity

The authors spend some time justifying the test in terms of content validity and give references to research involving 'judgements of qualified persons (which) support the authors' belief . . .' (USA Manual, p. 1). The items do seem to have face validity (but see General Evaluation below). Factor analytic studies (USA) are said to have demonstrated that the test reflects 'a dimension of intellectual functioning . . . independent of that tapped by the (Guilford) structure of intellect system' (USA Manual, p. 13).

Various measures of concurrent validity are reported, both for USA and British data. With intelligence measures, coefficients ranged from 0.40–0.76, although lower figures were obtained for performance scales. For example, one USA study ($n = 49$) found a correlation of only 0.02 with the WAIS Performance Scale. Correlations with other 'thinking type' scales ranged from 0.34–0.54, and with personality scales the coefficients were effectively zero.

Interpretation

Total raw scores are translated into percentiles, with the USA norms giving the option of using stanines. The British norms give full percentile information for each of a number of groups. Interpretative advice is limited, perhaps reflecting the test's use in research or as a selection tool.

General evaluation

For an area with comparatively few tests in it, this test could make a contribution. The major problem concerns its content and construct validities. Does it, for example, represent a sufficient range of thinking in real-life situations which involve judgements, inferences, gambles in decision making and the like. The lack of clear evidence about predictive validity is also a major shortcoming. The test certainly looks different and has only moderate relationships with more conventional intelligence and achievement tests, but it is not clear from the evidence what it has to offer.

Wide Range Vocabulary Tests

Reviewed by Sandra Johnson

Authors: C. R. Atwell and F. L. Wells
Publisher: The Psychological Corporation
Distributor: NFER-Nelson
Age range: 8–21 years
1937 (Form B); unstated (Form C)
1975 (M, copyright date); S not stated
1976 (T: Forms B and C) printings reviewed
Group test

Test content

This is a power test with two parallel forms (B and C), each containing 100 sentence-completion items. Embedded in each incomplete sentence is a 'stimulus word' intended to guide the respondent to the correct selection of missing last word from a choice of five in each case; e.g.

'A *street* is a _____ field hill road stream path',

where the correct choice, to be underlined, is usually a synonym of the stimulus word as in the example. The items in Form B are arranged in order of difficulty, those in Form C being arranged in alphabetical order of stimulus words.

Purpose

In the words of the Manual, tests of vocabulary 'provide rapid and accurate determination of scholastic intelligence for literate individuals'. The test authors offer as justification for this claim references to the work of Terman, Wechsler, 'and others', in the field of the measurement of intelligence. They do not elaborate on the meaning of 'scholastic intelligence', nor on a definition of 'literate individuals'.

Item preparation

According to the authors there was an original Test Form A which 'used as stimulus words the list incorporated in the 1916 edition of the Stanford-Binet scale'; empirical evidence had been obtained by the authors (in 1937) to indicate the equivalence of the 5-choice objective test and the free response oral definition. Form A, however, infringed copyright laws and so was discontinued. Forms B and C were then devised 'with difficulty comparable to the original form'. There is no information given in the Manual on the way in which items were constructed or pretested for these alternative forms.

Administration

The test can be administered as an individual or a group test. In either case the test administrator is required to work through one example item with the respondents, who then proceed to underline from a selection of five words listed to the right of each sentence that which they consider satisfactorily completes it. When Form B is administered as an individual test, the authors suggest that testing 'may be stopped when several words (6 or 8) in succession are failed, as the words are arranged in order of difficulty'. There is no further comment on this criterion; neither is any justification offered.

Standardization

Little information is contained in the Manual about the method by which the test was standardized. American age norms are provided in the form of average scores for each year of age for 8–21 year-olds. There is no indication that sampling was by a random procedure. There *is* a comment to the effect that respondents over the age of 13 (i.e. high school and college students) were a highly selected group.

Scoring

Scoring keys are included in the Manual; correct word-choices attract one mark each, incorrect choices or multiple selections gain no marks.

Reliability

No reliability information is given in the test Manual.

Validity

No direct comment is offered on the validity of the test, though there is the reference to the fact that the original form and its successors were modelled on the Stanford-Binet scale.

Interpretation

No guidance is given to the test user on the possible meaning of particular test scores, save that they lie above or below the median score obtained by the 'standardization' sample of American children in the same year group.

General evaluation

In view of the age of this test, its inadequate standardization and its out-dated *American* age norms, it is difficult to see what value it can have for present-day test users in Britain.

Williams Intelligence Test for Children with Defective Vision

Reviewed by C. D. Elliott

Author: M. Williams
Publisher: NFER-Nelson

Distributor: NFER-Nelson
Age range: 3:06–16:00 (blind or partially sighted children)
1956; no revisions apparent
Individual test (restricted)★

Test content

'In order to effect a saving of time in the try-out of items, it was decided to select material from tests already standardized on large groups of seeing children. Several intelligence test scales were reviewed, material being sought that would be suitable for an age range from 3.5 to 15 years. The verbal type of item was selected predominantly because in an earlier research the performance type had been found to be rather too much biased in favour of the child possessing some sight. The final choice included a considerable number from the Terman-Merrill (Stanford-Binet) 1937 version, chiefly from Form M, a number from Valentine's Intelligence Test for Children, some from Burt's Reasoning Tests, a few from group tests, modified slightly for individual testing, and the Vocabulary Test from Wechsler's Children's Scale.

'In order to furnish variety in the nature of tasks to be required from the younger subjects it did seem essential, however, to include a small number of items of the performance type in the lower part of the scale. Items were adapted so that they could be given to both blind and sighted; for instance, mutilated objects in place of pictures, solid wooden shapes in place of pictorial representations, etc. . . . It seemed advisable not to require reading or writing in any of the test items. Testing was of necessity, then, to be of individual and oral' (Manual, p. 7).

With the majority of the items coming from the Stanford-Binet Intelligence Scale, the items are very heterogeneous, and do not form any separate subscales. There are 100 items in the Williams Test altogether, and among them are items involving verbal comprehension; word knowledge; verbal reasoning (analogies and similarities); memory for numbers, sentences and objects; and at the top end, quite a number of items involving problem-solving of various kinds. The original edition of the Wechsler Intelligence Scale for Children (WISC) vocabulary test is included as a separate test, but it is scored in a rather different manner to the scoring system in the WISC itself.

Apart from one or two items involving the child pointing or indicating objects, these items being intended for young children at the start of the test, virtually all of the items require a verbal response from the child. All of them are individually presented to the child by the tester.

Purpose

The title of the test clearly states it to be a test of intelligence for children with defective vision. The test is therefore normative. Its practical purpose is

---

★ As well as being available to qualified educational psychologists the test is available to teachers of the blind and partially sighted, who have attended suitable courses of training.

summarized by the author: 'If the test is given soon after a child's admission to school, a teacher is able to gain some general idea of how much can be expected from a pupil. It is important to remember that no single testing should be regarded as final; the first testing, particularly in the case of an apparently dull child, should be regarded as only a possible indicator of his mental ability. It is also important to remember that children gaining similar IQ scores may have very varying types of ability; for this reason, a summary of a child's particular successes and failures on the test is much more relevant to the teaching programme than the IQ score itself' (Manual, p. 5).

Item preparation

The origins of the items are as described above under Test Content. A prestandardization trial of the items was carried out upon a small sample of 120 children from three schools in the Midlands: a nursery school, an all-age school, and a grammar school (all for the blind and partially sighted). This confirmed that little change needed to be made in the original placement of the items in their order of difficulty or in terms of their content and suitability for blind and partially sighted children.

Administration

Recommended users of the Williams Test are qualified psychologists or teachers of the blind and partially sighted who have attended advanced courses of training. The materials for the test come in a large box which contains the Manual, record forms and the toys and other objects which are used in the presentation of the test items.

There is no set time limit specified for the administration of this test. The tester proceeds at the optimum pace for the child, and no timing is required on any of the items. The Manual does not state the average amount of time required to administer the Williams Test, but this reviewer would estimate it to be on average about 45 minutes. This, however, will vary very much according to the age, ability and temperament of the child.

The instructions for the administration for the test are clearly stated in the Manual. The author takes particular care in stressing the importance of the establishment of good rapport between the examiner and subject. Helpful suggestions about establishing good rapport with blind children are given in this section of the Manual.

All necessary rules for administering the scale, including the establishment of basal and ceiling levels of testing, are clearly described, although the standard of presentation and layout now appears to be somewhat dated in a test which is over 25 years old. Nevertheless, test users are urged in the Manual to familiarize themselves with the directions to such an extent that only a quick glance at them from time to time during the testing will be necessary.

Standardization

The items which had been previously assembled, as described above, were given to samples of blind and partially sighted children. In the partially sighted category were placed children whose visual acuity, when corrected, did not amount to more than 6/36 according to the Snellen Chart. Twenty-two schools for the blind throughout Britain were visited and the test was given to 678 pupils, 299 of whom were blind and 379 partially sighted. Twenty-one schools for the partially sighted were visited and items were given to 241 pupils, with additionally 20 pre-school children being visited in their own homes. 'Every type of school was represented—nursery, primary, all-age, modern secondary, special, technical and grammar' (Manual, p. 8). The age distribution was reasonably even, with between 71 and 90 children being tested within each year group between the ages of 6 and 15 years. Additionally, 51 children aged between 15:05 and 16:00 years were tested and 33 four year-old and 53 five year-old children were tested. The Manual does not state who did the testing.

When all the data had been collected, item analyses were conducted and the test was reduced to 100 items. The aim of the item analyses had been to ensure that no unsuitable items were included in the test and that the test, when given to blind and partially sighted pupils, produced similar mean scores for both groups.

Having done these item analyses, normalized IQ score tables were constructed, enabling raw scores to be converted to IQ with a mean of 100 and a standard deviation of 15. The standardization procedure is described reasonably carefully in the Manual, and clearly enabled the author to obtain a representative sample of blind and partially sighted pupils from all regions of the UK.

Scoring

The scoring instructions are clearly given in the Manual, which is laid out in a very similar manner to the Stanford-Binet test manual. For each item the procedure for test administration is given, together with scoring instructions. For many items, but not for all of them, samples of satisfactory and unsatisfactory responses are given. Many of the test items in the Williams Test require open-ended verbal responses which require some discretion in scoring on the part of the test user. For some tests, notably the Vocabulary Test which is given and scored separately, only general scoring rules are given with no examples of passing and failing responses. Common sense would indicate that this would increase the measurement error of any such test item because of scorer unreliability. To repeat, however, most of the items do have clear scoring instructions.

Having scored each item as a pass or a failure, the total number of correct items obtained from the test is added up for the child who has been tested. This yields a raw score, and the test user turns to tables in the back of the Manual, in order to convert the child's raw score into an IQ. This is done by finding the child's age in years and months down a column at the side of the table, finding the child's raw score in a row at the top of the page, and reading off the IQ at the intersection of the chronological age and raw score. This is a simple process described in the Manual, which also gives a certain minimal amount of information to test users on the interpretation of intelligence quotients.

The record form lists each item with summary scoring criteria in a clear and helpful way.

Reliability

No information whatsoever on the reliability of the Williams Test is given in the Manual. To this reviewer's knowledge, no studies have subsequently been published indicating the reliability of the test, other than a brief note in a paper by Tobin (1978). In this article, Tobin reported a study on a group of 99 children who were given the Williams Test in a test-retest design. This yielded an overall test-retest reliability coefficient of 0.89.

Validity

No validity studies are reported in the Manual. Insofar as the author has spent considerable effort in trying to ensure that all the items in the test are suitable for blind and partially sighted children, the test has a reasonable degree of content validity. Many of the items in the test also have a well established history as part of other well known intelligence scales, and this adds to the content validity of the test. As far as the vocabulary test is concerned, although this test is scored differently to the scoring system in the original version of the WISC, with the Williams Test scoring one for a correct response and zero otherwise, and the WISC having a 0, 1, 2 type of scoring system, if one divides the raw scores on the vocabulary test in the WISC Manual by two, the norms of the WISC and the Williams Tests turn out to be very similar for each age group.

Interpretation

Some minimal help is given to test users in interpreting IQ scores. Users are told that scores below 50 and above 150 are not likely to occur frequently. In addition, test users are told the proportions of children who score below IQ levels of 75, 90, 100, 110 and 125. Apart from that, no other guidance is given. Other than warning the test user that a single-shot assessment, particularly of a dull child, should be regarded as only a possible indicator of his mental ability, the author gives little other cautionary advice. Because no reliabilities were calculated, no errors of measurement could be calculated either, and so the test user is left unaware of the confidence limits of test scores.

The Manual also gives no advice on the practical implications of test scores, or any illustrative case studies. It must be said, however, that this has been the general rule for such test manuals and so the Williams Test is not particularly exceptional in this respect.

Test use

Although the Williams Test is regularly used in the UK in the assessment of blind children, there seem to be few published studies on its use. Zahran (1965) used the Williams Test as a means of matching groups of blind and sighted children, in terms of IQ, in a study of personality differences between blind and sighted children. No data on the Williams Test were reported in this paper, although 100 children were initially tested. In a smaller-scale study Carroll and Hibbert (1973) used the Williams Test in order to assess the IQ of a group of 13 children in a special class for the partially sighted. Six of them were of junior-school age. The means and standard deviations of the IQs were 111.8 (11.7) for the infants and 85.7 (7.3) for the juniors. The children were given the Frostig Developmental Test of Visual Perception, from which perceptual quotients were calculated for each child. A correlation was found between perceptual quotient and IQ of 0.83. More recently, Tobin (1978) has reviewed aspects of the psychological and educational assessment of blind and partially sighted children. He notes that the Williams Test continues to be regularly used in the UK with both pre-school and school-age blind children. He notes that the author herself states that the scale is most reliable within the age range of 7–13 years, and states that it is clear that its use with very young children is likely to give rise to difficulties of administration and interpretation. He also notes that, despite the fact that the test has now been in use for over 20 years, little information is available about its validity and reliability.

General evaluation

The Williams test has been in regular use for over 25 years with children having visual handicaps. It is the only test standardized on blind and partially sighted children in the UK which covers such a wide age range, from 3:05–16:00 years. It is quite evident from the Manual that the author took considerable pains in assembling an appropriate set of items which would be suitable for use with visually handicapped children. The author herself makes the point that 'It is likely that a test result from this standardization would be more reliable (*sic*) than a result from a test standardized on a fully sighted group in the case of a child at a partially sighted school, whose vision is such that he cannot see with ease an Intelligence Test devised for the fully sighted' (Manual, p. 10). The point is well taken, apart from the word 'valid' being probably a better word than 'reliable' in the passage just quoted.

This leads us to the question of the interpretation of IQ scores derived from the Williams Test. An IQ on this test, assuming the standardization to have been a good and representative one, and also assuming that it continues to be representative of the blind and partially sighted population, tells us a child's standing in terms of general intelligence in relation to other blind and partially sighted children of his or her own age. It does not tell us how the child stands in relation to sighted children of his or her own age. For such a purpose, a verbally administered test from a battery standardized on the normal sighted population would be necessary. IQs derived from the Williams Test are, therefore, not necessarily comparable with IQs derived from tests standardized on a representative sighted population.

As well as the point made above, potential test users also need to be reasonably satisfied that the blind and partially sighted population has not changed significantly since 1956. In the space of 25 years many advances have been made in the prevention and treatment of visual handicaps. The number of children receiving education in schools for blind and partially sighted children has decreased. The possibility exists, therefore, that the norms are now unrepresentative of the present-day blind and partially sighted child population.

While the test undoubtedly is a valuable resource for a psychologist or teacher in the assessment of a blind pupil, it seems that scores on the test should be, if anything, interpreted more cautiously than they should have been when the test was first published. There seems to be a case, if money and manpower were available, for a revision of this test to bring the items up-to-date, to make the norms more up-to-date and interpretable, and to apply the kind of technical standards regarding reliability and validity to this test which we would expect from any test published in more recent times.

References

Carroll, H. C. M. and Hibbert, F. G. (1973). The perceptual ability of a class of partially sighted children. *Journal of the Association of Educational Psychologists* 3, 17–21.
Tobin, M. (1978). An introduction to the psychological and educational assessment of blind and partially sighted children. *Occasional Papers*. Division of Educational and Child Psychology of the British Psychological Society 2, 9–17.
Zahran, H. A. S. (1965). A study of personality differences between blind and sighted children. *British Journal of Educational Psychology* 35, 329–338.

Personality and counselling

List of reviews

Applied Knowledge Test★	612
Bristol Social Adjustment Guides	612
Children's Personality Questionnaire★	617
Crowley Occupational Interests Blank★	617
High School Personality Questionnaire	618
JIIG-CAL Occupational Interests Guide★	622
Junior Eysenck Personality Inventory	623
Lewis Counselling Inventory	631
Manchester Scales of Social Adaptation	635
Minnesota Counseling Inventory	641
Mooney Problem Check List	646
Occupational Check List (Advanced)★	649
Occupational Interest Rating Scale★	650
Rutter's Behaviour Questionnaires	650
Sixteen Personality Factor Questionnaire	655
Study Habits Inventory	661
Study of Values	663

★ Brief report only.

Applied Knowledge Test

Brief Report

Author: M. A. Brimer
Publisher: Educational Evaluation Enterprises
Distributor: Educational Evaluation Enterprises
Age range: 14–18+
Undated (M, T), but post-1977 indicated; S not stated
Group test

The four subtests of the AKT are: Mathematics, English, Science and Space. Each of the Tests 1–3 contains 25 items and 15 minutes are allowed. Test 4—a search for mirror-image pairs under rotation—has 30 scorable answers and 10 minutes is allowed. A partner to the Occupational Interest Rating Scale, the aim of the AKT is 'to meet some of the assessment needs of secondary schools for the vocational guidance of young people' and to 'provide measures of availability for use of knowledge in mathematics, English, science and spatial relationship'. 'Rapid appraisal' is another aim of the tests; about one hour in total is required. The test is supplied as an 8-page consumable booklet scored by keys. Rasch scaling is employed to convert raw scores to scale scores.

Bristol Social Adjustment Guides*

Reviewed by Deborah R. Gooch

Author: D. H. Stott
Publisher: Hodder & Stoughton
Distributor: Hodder & Stoughton
Age range: 5:00–16:00
1956 (S); 1974 (M, T)†
1970 (S); 1974 (M, T) (5th edition: '1970 edition')
1980 printing reviewed‡
Group test

---

* Guides: BG1 The Child in School (Boys); BG2 The Child in School (Girls); BG3 The Child in Residential Care; BG4 The Child in the Family; with Diagnostic Apparatus (templates) and Diagnostic Forms.
† Changes between first (1958) and current (1974) editions are not detailed in this brief summary.
‡ In the review below, 'Manual' refers to Stott (1974).

Test content

The BSAG consists of scrambled items in paragraphed statements, from which a teacher well acquainted with the child selects those which best describe the behaviour of the child. The phrases in each paragraph are various responses that a child may make in defined situations. Two main scales represent the under- and over-reacting modes of maladjustment (Unract and Ovract). Neurological items, representing behaviours that cannot be motivated, appear in a third scale. The items are further subgrouped into 5 core syndromes which the author describes as 'impairments of temperament'. These are Unforthcomingness, Withdrawal, Depression (Unract) plus Inconsequence, Hostility (Ovract). A certain number of items are classified as Associated Groupings. These are not specific to a syndrome but are good indicators of maladjustment (Unract, Ovract).

Purpose

The instrument provides a means of detecting and assessing behaviour disturbances in children aged 5–16 years in a school setting. It is aimed at teachers, and clinicians, as a means of diagnosis of maladjustment. It is claimed that a quantitative assessment of the child's adjustment in school is possible.

Item preparation

A competent and careful revision of all sample items is described in the Manual (pp. 13–17). More items were included in the 1970 version and of 195, 133 items achieved significance in discriminating between maladjusted and normal groups. Teachers completed the BSAG on 2527 children born on 15th or 16th day of any month aged from 5–14 years from a population attending school in Ontario. The items were first validated by the criteria of their incidence among children scoring 20 or more , 'the maladjusted', compared with that among the 'stable' scoring 9 or less. Items were rejected if they occurred frequently among the stable. Items which required interpretation or attitudinal bias were also rejected leaving 110 items.

It was from the validation of the 1956 version that the main scales and syndromes were identified. The consistency of the classification at different age levels and between sexes was tested. The associated groupings emerged after repeated clustering of the items.

Administration

There are no specific instructions for teachers completing the test given in the Manual. The teacher underlines the phrases which apply to the child being assessed. It is assumed that the teacher has been in contact with the child for at least one month. The Manual suggests 15 minutes as the maximum time required to complete the Guide with only a small number of subjects being assessed on one occasion. It is emphasized that the behaviour assessed is symptomatic of maladjustment, not personal traits.

Standardization

The most recent norms for the 1970 version are based on the findings of the study mentioned above on the defined sample of 2527 children. Readers are referred to "Taxonomy of Behavior Disturbance" by Stott *et al.* (1975) for a full account of the validation and normative data. These norms provide percentile rank estimates for each age and score combination. There are norms for the two main scales and five core syndromes, for each sex. The severity of the Unract and Ovract syndromes for each sex can be assessed from the norms. Useful statistics are given within the tables.

Despite the comprehensive standardization information provided it would be useful to have norms based on a large British random sample. There are, however, some data available on a random sample of 7–8 year-olds in Liverpool.

Scoring

Items are checked by means of a transparent key in the form of a template fitted over each page of the schedule which allocates a pair of code letters and a numeral to each pair of items describing the behaviour. The number of coded items are summed, and totals for each of the syndromes, associated groups and Ovract and Unract scales are obtained. The author suggests that the overall total is a 'reflection of the child's emotional and social adjustment in school', but this seems rather artificial. The grouping of scores proposed by Stott and used by the National Child Development Study (Davie, Butler and Goldstein, 1972) into 3 main groups seems more appropriate. A child scoring 0 to 9 is designated 'stable', 10 to 19 as 'unsettled' and 20 or more as 'maladjusted'. These are described as 'standard categories' and were derived from a study by NFER where 88 pairs of teachers completed BSAG independently. Correlations were 0.76 and 0.78 for the maladjusted and unsettled group respectively, which are high in this field.

It would be extremely useful to have the various guides, diagnostic forms and templates included in the Manual.

Reliability

Internal and test-retest reliabilities are reported. Scores tended to be lower on repeat testing, probably due to the therapy applied by the teacher after the first assessment. The test-retest reliability was 0.80.

There was a higher correlation among the over-reacting than among the under-reacting scales. Constancy of type of maladjustment indicated that the syndromes Withdrawal and Depression were not as reliable as the Ovract syndromes.

Internal reliability was assessed by means of Coefficient Alpha, a generalized form of KR-20 which is based on the average correlation among items. Once more, the Ovract syndromes appeared uniformly more homogeneous than Unract. Coefficients for the two main scales were 0.8 and 0.9 for Unract and Ovract respectively.

Validity

Many studies on a variety of samples are quoted in the first edition. Various external tests and criteria were employed because of the difficulty of finding an appropriate validating measure, e.g. independent teacher assessments, sociometric status, educational attainment. Of course, the validity and indeed the generality of findings depends on the degree to which the items are respresentative of maladjustment and the extent to which the validating groups are representative. Full details of all the validation studies, with the techniques employed are given in the Manual, so that the reader does not have to resort to references.

Interpretation

The authors state that 'the interpretation of the scores depend on the purpose for which they are intended'. It is suggested that scores for the syndromes and associated groups are given for diagnostic reports. These subtotals can be translated into verbal descriptions of the degree of severity of behaviour which are easily comprehended. Use of an overall BSAG score is not advised because of its heterogeneity. However, for most uses the most meaningful results, arise from the scores for Unract and Ovract, and the core syndromes.

Test use

The most important study which employed this instrument is probably the National Child Development Study (Davie, Butler and Goldstein, 1972) since it used a large British sample of 15 496 children born in one week in 1958. There were 72 per cent more males than females in the maladjustment category, and a strong relationship was found between maladjustment and social class. This study also examined the effects of social adjustment of some physiological and familial factors. The BSAG scores tended to be statistically sensitive to congenital factors.

General evaluation

The Manual contains concise but substantial information on the development, evaluation and purpose of BSAG. For all users, however, it will require careful reading and, for some, it may be too technical.

With reference to the construction of the test and the identification of the subgroups the author's own clinical knowledge will have played a large part. In order to confirm the grouping of the items and suggest possible weightings some form of scaling might have been useful. Any user should bear in mind the subjectivity involved in the construction and completion of a test of this type, and the consequent limitations. The test is, however, based on a pragmatic approach to maladjustment and is useful for teachers as a diagnostic instrument in obtaining judgements of a child's behaviour.

It has also proved an important tool in epidemiological research, and many other psychological studies (Whitehead, 1979; Lambert *et al.* 1977). McDermott (1980) examined whether the two main scales have sufficient factorial integrity to be a valid dichotomy. With a random sample of 2527 children, a principal components factor analysis supported this. Also significant syndrome specificity was established for the majority of the 5 core syndromes. These findings support the claim that the BSAG reflects a complex of identifiable and specific dimensions of social maladjustment.

References

Chazan, M. (1965). *British Journal of Educational Psychology* 35, 63–68.

Davie, R., Butler, N. and Goldstein, H. (1972). "From Birth to Seven: A Report of the National Child Development Study". London: Longmans and National Children's Bureau.

Eaves, J. (1976). *Educational Review* 29, 163–177.

Lambert, L. (1979). Variations in behaviour ratings of children who have been in care. *Journal of Child Psychology and Psychiatry* 18, 335–346.

McDermott, P. A. (1979). *British Journal of Educational Psychology* 50, 223–228.

Stott, D. H. (1974). "Bristol Social Adjustment Guides: Manual". (5th edn). Sevenoaks: Hodder & Stoughton.

Whitehead, L. (1979). Sex differences in children responding to family stress. *Journal of Child Psychology and Psychiatry* 20, 247–254.

Children's Personality Questionnaire

Brief Report

Authors: Rutherford B. Porter and Raymond B. Cattell
Publisher: Institute for Personality and Ability Testing, Inc.
Distributor: NFER-Nelson
Age range: 8–12
1968, 1975 (M); 1959, 1963, 1973 (T); S not stated★
'1975 Edition' reviewed
Group test (training needed)

Four Forms A to D each contain 140 items which assess personality on 14 'distinct dimensions'. Apart from the multiple-choice items which contribute to the 'Dull *vs* Bright' dimension, items require a forced choice between two questions, e.g. 'Does your mother say you are too slow? *or* Do you do things quickly and well?'. The 'dimensions' include: emotional stability, social stability, dominance, dependability and tension. Scores can also be obtained for extraversion, anxiety, tough poise and independence. One Form may take 50 minutes or more to complete, especially with younger children. Use of more than one Form is recommended. Scoring by key or by machine. USA norms are available by age and sex.

The Manual claims, 'it is possible to obtain predictions of school-related criteria such as academic achievement, especially under-achievement, the tendency towards delinquency, the likelihood of leadership potential, and the possible need for clinical help to avoid excessive emotional disturbance . . . It can broaden a teacher's understanding of the need for personality development in each child, give greater reliability to that understanding, and help to interpret various aspects of the child's school adjustment' (Manual, p. 5).

Crowley Occupational Interests Blank

Brief Report

Author: A. D. Crowley
Publisher: CRAC/Hobsons Press

★ The Manual supplied with the specimen set urges users to seek further information in the technical *Handbook*.

Distributor: CRAC/Hobsons Press
Age range: 13+; average and less able pupils
1966–70 (S); 1970 (M, T)
1976 (M, T) (2nd edition)
Group administration

The 4-page Blank has two parts. In Part 1 pupils are asked to indicate their preferences among job titles. Scores are derived to assess interest in the following five areas of occupational activity: Active/Outdoor, Office, Social, Practical and Artistic. In Part 2 the pupils choose one from each of 20 pairs of statements which represent five sources of satisfaction, namely, Financial Gain, Stability/Security, Companionship, Working Conditions and Interest (intrinsic).

The COIB takes about 30 minutes to administer to a group, including the time needed for the pupils to be led through the scoring procedures. Scores on Part 1 and Part 2 are graded A to E according to percentile norms. These are 'based on a sample of over 1200 pupils with average to below-average abilities from different parts of the country—their average age was 15' (Manual, p. 10). Lists of jobs related to the score categories of Part 1 are given. These and the sources of satisfaction scored in Part 2 are intended to form the basis of discussion with a group or with an individual.

High School Personality Questionnaire

Reviewed by S. F. Blinkhorn

Authors: R. B. Cattell and M. D. Cattell
Publisher: Institute for Personality and Ability Testing; British supplements (by permission of IPAT) by NFER-Nelson*
Distributor: NFER-Nelson
Age range: high school pupils; British standardization sample aged 13–15
1958; revised 1968
British editions: 1971 (S); 1971 (M, T) (derived from 1968 USA edition)
Further S indicated
1973 (M); 1981 (British supplements); undated printing of 1968 edition (T) reviewed
Group test

---

* Authors of 'British Supplement to the High School Personality Questionnaire (Form A): Anglicized 1968/69 Edition' are Peter Saville and Laura Finlayson.

Test content

The High School Personality Questionnaire (HSPQ) has four forms (A, B, C and D). Each form has 142 items, of which the first and last are not scored. The remaining 140 items are scored on 14 scales of 10 items each, each scale yielding a measure of one of the 'primary factors of personality' according to the personality theory of R. B. Cattell. Like the Sixteen Personality Factor Questionnaire (16PF) (q.v.) of which it is a downward age extension, the HSPQ is composed of items presenting self-descriptions, hypothetical generalized situations and choices of preferred behaviours. Three response categories are provided of which the second is generally 'uncertain', 'perhaps', 'in between' or similar. An intelligence scale forms part of the test: these items involve vocabulary, verbal analogies and simple logic.

Purpose

Essentially this test is part of a grand system: it is the measure of personality appropriate to high school age (11–18 years) for those who adopt Cattell's theoretical approach to personality. According to the Manual, using the HSPQ the psychologist can '. . . obtain predictions of school achievement, of vocational fitness, of danger of delinquency, of likelihood of leadership qualities, of need for clinical help in avoiding neurotic conditions, etc'. It gives an 'objective analysis of the individual personality to supplement the teacher's personal evaluation'.

Item preparation

As with the 16PF, the Manual gives no details on the origins of the items, which are in a long programme of research begun by Cattell in the 1940s. The justification for the assignment of particular items to particular scales lies in factor analytic methodology, but it is nowhere stated that the criteria adopted and methods employed are controversial and not universally accepted.

The scales of the HSPQ, although from the same stable as the 16PF, are not identical. Factors L, M, N and Q, are not present; factors D and J appear in the HSPQ, but not in the 16PF. These differences are attributed to changes in the salience, and hence measurability, of factors with age. No indications are given in the Manual which would allow the user to judge the appropriateness of the assignment of items to scales, nor is the fact that the research literature is equivocal anywhere mentioned.

Administration

The test is designed to be completed 'by all but the slowest readers' in 40–50 minutes per form. A script is provided for test administrators, and full instructions are also printed on the front of test booklets. The test is virtually self-administering, though care should be taken to ensure correct matching of items in the questionnaire with the appropriate response boxes on the separate answer sheet.

Standardization

American norms are provided, based on average age 14:06 years. The Manual and associated supplement of norms give no details of the sampling and derivations of these norms; however, given the sample sizes (from 1000 to more than 7500) it is reasonable to infer that a wider age range formed the sample, and that the norms were adjusted for linear trends in scores with age, given Cattell's practice elsewhere.

A British supplement of norms for Form A of the HSPQ is supplied. This is based on a sample of 2429 third-year secondary-school pupils from 27 schools, collected in collaboration with the Department of Educational Studies, University of Oxford. The sample is described as stratified by type of school, by region and by urban/rural children. The availability of these norms makes Form A more attractive in the UK. However, differences between American and British norms for Form A are slight (although frequently statistically significant on account of the large samples involved). The inference to the utility of American norms for the other Forms is reasonable. Sex differences far outweigh cross-national differences.

Scoring

Scoring is by stencil. Scores on each scale are sums of integer weights of 0, 1, or 2 for each item. The procedure is routine and straightforward.

Reliability and validity

The Manual for the HSPQ contains a section running to all of 300 words grandly entitled 'Reliability, homogeneity and validity, considered in relation to test purpose', which is a minefield of misinformation. Very properly it begins with a reference to a more comprehensive source (the HSPQ Handbook—not part of the specimen set), but then presents two tables with unreconciled differences.

The first, of test-retest reliabilities, gives figures based on Forms A and B of the test, for retest immediately, one day later, six months later and one year later. The second purports to give equivalence (i.e. alternate form) coefficients, Form A with Form B and Form C with Form D.

Some remarkable inferences may be drawn from these tables. For instance, Factor B (intelligence), surely the subject of more psychometric attention than any other variable, is less reliably measured than any other trait over a one-year interval and is always amongst the least well measured. Factor E, with alternate form correlations between 0.18 and 0.35, has test-retest correlations (on a comparable basis) between 0.61 and 0.85—the scales are clearly not as well matched across forms and they are stable over time.

The figures for alternate form correlations should be treated with suspicion: they are described as 'corrected to full test length'. It is not stated whether 'full test length' is two or four Forms (i.e. 20 or 40 items per scale). Such laxity in specifying the origins of reliability indices is unacceptable.

The Manual gives an idiosyncratic variety of validity coefficient: 'direct concept validities . . . by . . . computer synthesis'. Such coefficients are only calculable by successfully identifying the HSPQ factors in a factor analysis—an enterprise in which independent investigators have been less than successful. The indices are high—misleadingly so—and should be treated as the square roots of internal consistency reliability coefficients, the nearest analogue outside factor analytic methodology.

The British supplement tells a less sanguine story. Alternate form coefficients run as low as 0.02 and peak at 0.56 for Forms A and B. Factor E manages correlations of 0.02 for boys and 0.15 for girls; combining the sexes hoists the correlation to a (still miserable) 0.23 by dint of a substantial sex difference in mean scores. Indeed it is true that a multiscale battery such as the HSPQ must sacrifice reliability for breadth of coverage to some extent; but when retest reliabilities over a period of months are substantially higher than alternate form correlations from scores obtained on the same day, one must seriously question the right of the test to proclaim its ability to provide an objective analysis of the fundamental variables of personality.

The British supplement also presents correlations amongst the scales. From these it is clear that 9 of the scales, viz. factors C, D, E, G, J, O, Q2 and Q3 and Q4, are involved in patterns of correlation within and across Forms which cast doubt on the discriminant validity of the scales.

Interpretation

The Manual provided in the specimen set gives only abbreviated information on the interpretation of test scores—essentially only a list of adjectives applying to individuals scoring high and low on each scale is provided. The Technical Handbook (sold separately) gives more information, including details of how to derive a number of scores on composite variables such as extraversion, leadership potential, etc. Despite an overall cautious tone, the Manual makes some dubious recommendations. For instance, a high score on Factor J, interpreted as 'obstructive' is suggested as a 'clue to watch for' in anticipating delinquency—this when the alternate form correlation corrected to 'full test length' runs as low as 0.28.

General evaluation

The HSPQ is of a piece with its companion inventory the 16PF. Intending users should consult the critical literature on the latter as part of the familiarization process, since it has received more detailed critical attention.

Overall, the supporting material for the HSPQ is excessively sanguine and strives to give the impression that the test represents the outcome of a wholly successful research enterprise. '. . . it is *known* . . . how well a boy with say, high score on Factor E (dominance) will do as a salesman, an executive, a democratic group leader . . .', one is asked to believe. Such triumphalism appears fatuous when alternate form reliability for the self-same Factor E turns out to be 0.002 in a British schoolboy sample. Quite how it is possible with a straight face to claim predictive validity for a scale which falls so disastrously short of even the most minimal standards of psychometric adequacy beggars the imagination.

Undoubtedly, with skill, and liberal sprinklings of psychometric salt applied to the more grandiose claims of the authors it is possible to use the HSPQ effectively. But no-one should under-estimate the magnitude of the task. Multi-factor batteries are almost inevitably curate's eggs; in the case of the HPSQ, however, unevenness of quality reaches its apotheosis.

JIIG-CAL Occupational Interests Guide*

Brief Report

Author: S. J. Closs
Publisher: Hodder & Stoughton
Distributor: Hodder & Stoughton
Age: 14+
1980 (various materials)
Group administration (restricted)†

---

* 'JIIG' stands for 'Job Ideas and Information Generator'; 'CAL' for 'Computer Assisted Learning'.
† Attendance at 'an appropriate training course' required; details 'from the careers service of each LEA'.

The Guide is 'a revised and extended unisex version of the APU Occupational Interests Guide' (which itself is unlikely to stay in print). 'It may be used on its own as a conventional interest test', and scored by hand or machine. 'It also forms an integral part of the JIIG-CAL System for Computer Assisted Career Guidance' (program available under licence).

Children make choices among activities, rate likes and dislikes, etc. Six general interest types are identified: working with hands; working with living things; clerical and sales work; handicraft work; practical work helping people; meeting and talking to people.

Junior Eysenck Personality Inventory

Reviewed by M. B. Youngman

Author: Sybil B. G. Eysenck
Publisher: Hodder & Stoughton
Distributor: Hodder & Stoughton
Age range: 7–16 years
1965 (M, T); S not stated
No revisions apparent
1978 (M, T) printings reviewed
Group test (restricted)★

Test content

The Junior Eysenck Personality Inventory (usually abbreviated to JEPI) consists of 60 items forming three scales. Two of these are fundamental and they measure the personality dimensions of neuroticism-stability and extraversion-introversion. The third scale offers a social-desirability measure although it is referred to as the Lie Scale. The relative importance of the first two scales is also reflected in the number of items since the main scales each contain 24 items leaving 12 for the Lie Scale. Response requirements are a simple YES or NO to each item. Most of the questions refer to personal feelings, or to perceptions of other people's feelings. Less than a quarter are about actual behaviour and, therefore, the tenor is predominantly introspective. This may be important in view of the wide age range claimed for the test. Another feature of the items that could determine effectiveness is the fact that on the Lie Scale

---

★ Orders to be signed by 'a suitably qualified senior member of staff of any recognised educational or medical institution . . .' (Publisher's catalogue).

items are defined logically rather than empirically. This is expressed by insertion of one of the qualifications 'sometimes', 'ever', 'always', 'every' or 'everything' into an otherwise variable behaviour. For example: 'Do you always eat *everything* you are given at meals' (Item 44, my italics). A consequence of this is that the crucial meaning of the item is located within a single word, whereas the other items would not require such close attention to detail for their meaning to be grasped.

Purpose

Apart from an introductory description of the personality theory on which the test is based, the only indication of intended purpose appears towards the end of the Manual where validity and applications are discussed. These comments imply (and it is suggested) that the major purpose envisaged is in experimentation. It is also suggested that 'the scale may be valid in connection with clinical investigations' (p. 13). Since even the supplied norms are only listed in terms of means and standard deviations by age, it is not possible to infer any other intended purpose for the scale.

Item preparation

To quote from the Manual: 'Construction of the 108-item Junior EPI was begun by carefully selecting, adapting or rewriting some items contained in the adult version of the EPI and adding some others' (p. 3). There is no further indication of the basis on which the item selection was made, but it becomes evident later that only the extraversion and neuroticism scales are represented in the 108-item trial version.

This initial version of the scale was piloted on samples spanning the ages from 7–16 years although the top age group was very small and possibly unrepresentative. Most of the sample was from the Rotherham area, with some additional testing being carried out in London. Each of the nine age groups, up to 15 years, were analysed separately yet the sample sizes are still reasonably large, ranging from 491 (age 7)–989 (age 11); 6760 in all. In all instances the principal component analysis isolated extraversion and neuroticism as the two dominant factors but the only empirical evidence offered is the associated latent roots (eigenvalues). These range from 8.3–9.6 for Neuroticism, and from 3.6–6.6 for Extraversion. From these values it is almost certain that other factors had eigenvalues greater than unity but no mention is made of their nature or stability.

The Lie Scale was developed in a similar fashion except that only 16 items were piloted and smaller samples were used, totalling 2777 across the nine age groups. In this respect the table of latent roots is misleading since the Lie Scale results are incorporated even though they derive from different analyses on considerably smaller samples. Furthermore, since the trial version of the Lie Scale contained no extraversion or neuroticism items, the latent root is of the first principal component and is therefore not directly comparable to the E and N latent roots as implied.

The final selection of items 'was based on the loadings of the items on their respective factors, and their lack of loadings on other factors' (Manual, p. 5). The 60 accepted items comprised 24 from each of the E and N scales, and 12 for the Lie Scale. Since the trial Lie Scale only contained 16 items there does seem to be some question as to how comprehensive the piloting was.

Administration

The Manual contains no information on how the test should be administered although the test forms carry a brief instruction for the person completing the test. There is a request not to spend too much time over any question but no estimate is given regarding typical completion times. Responses are recorded in the form of a cross in circles indicating YES or NO to each question. This may require a comment from the administrator since for most children a cross has the opposite connotation to the one intended. The complete absence of any guidance for potential users, or of any indication of the qualifications or experience expected, is a serious omission.

Standardization

Even though JEPI comprises the three scales E, N and L, it will be necessary to follow the Manual structure and treat the L scale independently. The E and N scales were standardized on samples of similar constitution to those used in pilot trials, but of a slightly larger size. Since the pilot and standardization samples are not the same size it must be assumed that they derive from different applications of the instruments although no dates are mentioned. The Manual implies that the sample should represent the general population except at the 15–16 year level. It is not possible to test this assumption without further details of the schools and localities, but there is likely to be some doubt about acceptability outside urban areas.

The account given of the Lie Scale is even less informative since there is no indication of the nature of the sample other than that it excludes children used in the E and N samples. However, if the standardization age-group sizes are totalled the result is 2777, the same as the total sample for the trial analysis. It is, therefore, almost certain that the pilot sample was also used to provide norms. The limitations of this expediency are well known; more general comments appear under General evaluation below.

The standardization data are presented as a series of tables of means and standard deviations for each age 7–16. Boys' and girls' results are separated, as are the norms for the Rotherham and London samples on the E and N scales. The precise definition of each age level is not given and presumably it is assumed that '12 years' includes all children aged from 12:00 to 12:11 years. In view of the emphasis placed on variations with age, this point should have been explained. Profiles showing scale scores for the different ages are presented but no smoothing across ages has been attempted.

Scoring

Scoring instructions are printed on the scoring template supplied with the test. These indicate that a score is achieved by counting the number of crosses that appear in the appropriate holes for each of the three scales. There is no further guidance, for example, on the treatment of ambiguous responses (crossing YES and NO), or of missing responses. There is also no procedure available to check that the counting is correct, or that the total is correct and valid. In view of the fact that pupils record their own responses there does seem to be a risk of introducing error and bias by virtue of differences in the treatment of indefinite responses. The Manual refers to a computer scoring procedure but no details are given.

Reliability

The reliability estimates offered are split-half values (corrected for length) and test-retest results, both forms being computed for each age level, and separately for boys and girls. The split-half sample is the same as that used for standardization, whilst a new sample of just over 1000 boys and 1000 girls is the basis of the test-retest exercise. Neuroticism reliabilities are highest for both forms, the split-half results being rather higher than test-retest. Ranges across the ages are as follows:

Boys	E	N	L
Split-half	0.58–0.86	0.79–0.85	0.61–0.77
Test-retest	0.59–0.92*	0.63–0.87	0.54–0.74

* Second highest value was 0.77

Girls	E	N	L
Split-half	0.63–0.87	0.80–0.89	0.41–0.76*
Test-retest	0.51–0.90	0.53–0.86	0.41–0.89

* Second lowest value was 0.64

Generally there is improved reliability for older children. Overall the results for Neuroticism do seem acceptable, but some reservations do arise from the low reliabilities for Extraversion obtained with the youngest age groups. The Lie Scale also incurs doubt about its reliability for children under 9, and certain inconsistencies in the results at other age levels suggest that further consideration may be needed.

Validity

The Manual is honest in its admission that 'too little is known about the validity of the Junior EPI as yet, to make any claims for use, other than as an instrument for experimentation' (Manual, p. 13). The brief validity section concludes: 'It seems probable therefore that the scale may be valid in connection with clinical investigations and it is to be hoped that in future editions of this Manual further evidence will be available along other lines indicating validity for the three scales' (Manual, p. 13). In view of this avoidance of the validity issue it is extremely regrettable that subsequent reprints of the Manual do not include any further validity evidence, in spite of an interval of 17 years.

There is a section relating intelligence to the scales but this can hardly be said to constitute validity. Rather more evidence can be collated from the numerous studies which have employed the JEPI. Particularly relevant is a study by Eysenck and Cookson (1969b) where teachers' ratings of personality were correlated with JEPI scores. The boys' results (almost identical to those for girls) were as follows:

Teacher ratings	JEPI Scores		
	E	N	L
Emotional stability	0.12	−0.09	−0.04
Perseverance	0.13	−0.06	−0.09
Sociability	0.22	−0.02	−0.15
Impulsiveness	0.06	0.05	−0.04

Even where correlations are in the expected direction (for example Extraversion with Sociability, $r = 0.22$) the values are very small. Some are possibly contradictory since one might reasonably expect Perseverance to be associated with Introversion, not Extraversion as the positive correlation indicates. The same study used oblique factor analysis to investigate scale structures and the authors concluded that 'The results of this study do not require extensive discussion because they are essentially clear-cut and obvious, as can be seen by considering the factors which emerge from the factor analysis—ability/achievement, family size, emotional instability, introversion, neuroticism, and occupational status. The only problem raised by this analysis is the apparent separation between neuroticism and emotional instability as two separate factors' (Eysenck and Cookson, 1969b, p. 129). They suggest that the separation problem requires further research. Is the strength of this assertion justified?

The relevant section of the results can be summarized as follows:

	Interpreted Factors and Loadings*					
	Emotional instability		Neuroticism		Introversion	
	Boys	Girls	Boys	Girls	Boys	Girls
Extraversion (E)	−30		−29	−26	−58	−64
Neuroticism (N)			81	81		20
Lie Scale (L)			−76	−77	25	
Emotional instability	74	81			36	25
Lack of perseverance	58	63			21	
Lack of sociability		23			81	82
Lack of impulsiveness	−85	−82			27	41

* Decimal points omitted; loadings below 0.20 omitted.

Without prolonging the discussion the results do not seem as 'clear-cut and obvious' as is suggested, nor do they readily validate the JEPI scale structure. The factor labelled 'Introversion' is more akin to unsociability, particularly as the extraversion variable is distributed across all three factors. This suggests poor convergent validity. Similarly the 'Neuroticism' factor could not be taken to validate the N scale as it records no substantial loadings on relevant teacher ratings. Rather it reflects a JEPI factor, just as Factor 3: Emotional Instability is effectively a Teacher Rating factor. Indeed the authors themselves refer to a halo effect in the teacher ratings.

A final point in considering validity concerns the Lie Scale. The Manual refers to a relatively high relationship between L and N (borne out by the above analysis). Mention is also made of a relationship between intelligence and IQ. Probably more significant is the link between the Lie Scale and academic achievement. The L scale does load moderately on the academic factor (-0.20 and -0.17). Eysenck and Cookson (1969a) in a separate article record correlations of -0.16 with Reading and -0.15 with English scores. Jensen (1973) reports a correlation of -0.32 between the Lie Scale and Reading at Grade 4. Taken together these results support the earlier suggestion that the Lie Scale may include Reading Ability, as well as Social Desirability, particularly at younger ages where differences in reading ability are more marked.

There does seem to be room for more direct attention to the validation of the JEPI dimensions. Without the improved definition resulting from such analyses, findings reporting correlations of around 0.2 are extremely difficult to interpret or apply.

Interpretation

No guidance is provided on the interpretation of the two main scales, E and N. There is an aside (Manual, p. 12) suggesting that high Lie Scale scores may reflect conscious attempts at faking.

Test use

It would be difficult to find a test that has had more use in British educational studies and therefore only a taste can be offered here. The starting point should be Entwistle (1972) since that source consists of a review of usage to that point. Two major applications by Eysenck and Cookson have already been referenced under Validity, above, as has one by Jensen. Entwistle and Cunningham (1968) is an important early reference since there the authors started the sequence of studies investigating non-linearity in relationships involving Extraversion and Neuroticism. Studies by Crookes *et al.* (1981) and Anthony (1982) confirm that this line of investigation is still very active today. A study by Roberts (1978) is doubly interesting; not only does it use the JEPI in an educational context, but it also provides a certain amount of validation evidence since the main theme, outdoor play, could reasonably be assumed to represent a real-life perspective on extraversion. Unfortunately the evidence does not support the relationship as far as the JEPI measure is concerned. Another study incorporating two strands of interest is Bennett's (1973) re-evaluation of JEPI (see General evaluation below).

Having identified applications which specifically seek to assess or demonstrate characteristics of the JEPI scales, it is difficult to pinpoint other uses which may be of particular interest to potential users. Usually the area of application will itself lead to a number of studies which have employed the JEPI. The Manual's closing comment that 'there are few areas of performance or behaviour where personality is not likely to be an important variable' (p. 15) is possibly rather more optimistic than reality permits. Rarely do correlations between JEPI scores and intellectual measures exceed 0.2 or 0.3, indicating the best that can be claimed is a contributory role in educational determination.

General evaluation

In view of the wealth of comment available, in the numerous studies which have used the JEPI, it is not easy to isolate an evaluation of the test from an assessment of its place in psychological research. Nevertheless the two issues are different and a distinction must be made. Here the concern is the test. Anyone wishing to ascertain the applicability of the JEPI must follow the usual strategy and peruse the pertinent research literature.

Normally the global evaluation of a test would be based on the Manual and supporting documentation, but in the case of JEPI the inadequacy of the supplied material has already been mentioned. Since there are at least two articles which are directly relevant to a discussion of the psychometric properties of the test it seems sensible to include them as part of the complementary evidence. The Manual itself is predominantly a record of the development of the test, or more accurately its adaptation from the adult EPI. At first glance the reliability evidence seems acceptable, particularly for the Neuroticism scale. Bennett (1973) and Roberts (1978) both suggest that the reliability of Extraversion may be undermined by the clear attenuation effect in this scale (evident in items and totals) but this is partly refuted by the fact that reliability and mean scores both increase with age. The reliability estimates for the lower age levels are barely adequate but for older ages moderate levels are achieved. The strongest reservations hold for the Lie Scale since the youngest age levels do record unacceptable reliability estimates. All of these comments, however, do carry the qualification that the method by which the results were obtained was not standard. The Lie Scale data were generated completely separately from those for the E and N scales; and the reliability sample was not independent of the development sample.

Regardless of how acceptable the reliability estimates might be, the major emphasis must be placed on validity, and here the evidence available is not encouraging. Bennett (1973) mentions the low relationship between JEPI dimensions and teacher ratings. One of the studies he refers to (Eysenck and Cookson, 1969b) has already been discussed at length. It had to be concluded that the evidence there was not sufficient to support factorial, convergent or discriminant validity. The absence of any of those forms of validity raises real problems for the researcher because obtained correlations rarely exceed 0.3. It is interesting that many studies which employ the JEPI also use between-groups significance testing. This is not a particularly informative procedure since a weak effect may be sufficient to produce statistical significance (especially with large n) but be virtually impossible to interpret in educational terms.

Bennett (1973) suggests that interpretability is further confounded by the apparent interrelatedness of the scales. Whilst this is not in itself prohibitive, there is a strong indication that some of the communality may be due to the presence of an achievement component, especially at the younger age levels. This is almost certainly so for the Lie Scale, as the marked shift in the mode of the scale's distribution (see Manual, pp. 9–10) indicates.

Other points regarding guidance for users have been sufficiently well aired to need no further comment. The most disconcerting feature of the test in its currently published form is the likelihood that much of the additional information needed for a proper evaluation of the test is available. If the author could fulfil the promise made in the present version of the Manual to update the supplied information, the task of the potential user would be considerably easier.

References

Anthony, W. S. (1982). Extraversion and intelligence: Re-analysis of data of Crookes *et al. British Journal of Educational Psychology* 52, 119–120.

Bennett, S. N. (1973). A re-evaluation of the Junior Eysenck Personality Inventory. *British Journal of Educational Psychology* 43, 131–139.

Crookes, T. G., Pearson, P. R., Francis, L. J. and Carter, M. (1981). Extraversion and performance on Raven's Matrices in 15–16 year old children: An examination of Anthony's Theory of the development of extraversion. *British Journal of Educational Psychology* 51, 109–111.

Entwistle, N. J. (1972). A review of research on personality and academic attainment. *British Journal of Educational Psychology* 42, 137–151.

Entwistle, N. J. and Cunningham, S. (1968). Neuroticism and School Attainment—A linear relationship? *British Journal of Educational Psychology* 38, 123–132.

Eysenck, H. J. and Cookson, D. (1969a). Personality in Primary School children: 1—Ability and Achievement. *British Journal of Educational Psychology* 39, 109–122.

Eysenck, H. J. and Cookson, D. (1969b). Personality in Primary School children: 2—Teachers' Ratings. *British Journal of Educational Psychology* 39, 123–130.

Jensen, A. R. (1973). Personality and scholastic achievement in three ethnic groups. *British Journal of Educational Psychology* 43, 115–125.

Roberts, A. (1978). Extraversion and outdoor play in middle childhood. *Educational Research* 21, 37–42.

Lewis Counselling Inventory

Reviewed by S. F. Blinkhorn

Authors: D. G. Lewis and P. D. Pumfrey
Publisher: NFER-Nelson
Distributor: NFER-Nelson
Age: 3rd-year secondary-school pupils
1973
1978 (M, T) (revised); S not stated
Group test

Test content

Forty-six short sentences, mostly couched in first-person terms are presented, to each of which the subject responds 'agree' or 'disagree'. Item content is rather typical of personality-type measures: minor somatic symptoms, attitudes to family, peers and teachers, self-report of temperament, etc.

Items are drawn from six areas: Irritability, Social Confidence, Health and Relationships with Teachers, Peers and Family. Six to eight items are drawn from each area. In addition there is a six-item Lie Scale.

An optional supplementary free response questionnaire 'allows the client to expand on particular aspects of his self-perceived problems'. The inventory is targeted on 3rd-year pupils: reading age is stated at 'about the 10 and a half year-old level'.

Purpose

'. . . to provide teachers in secondary schools with a convenient instrument for identifying those pupils most in need of guidance and counselling'. And possibly '. . . to provide clues as to the kind of help that is needed'.

Item preparation

The published form of the inventory consists of items selected from a larger set of items 'designed to probe a possible counselling need' in one of the six areas mentioned above, and balanced between positively and negatively worded statements. The complete set of 113 statements were administered to 1477 3rd-year secondary-school pupils from 13 schools in the North-West of England, all pupils present on the day of testing taking part. Item scores were then intercorrelated, and the correlation matrix subjected to a principal component analysis. For want of detail in the Manual, one must assume that product-moment coefficients were used. Insufficient information is given to allow a proper evaluation of this analysis. However, it is stated that eight second-order factors, including six clearly identifiable as the target problem areas, accounted for 27 per cent of all the variance. Eighteen principal components (eigenvalues > 1) accounted for nearly 48 per cent of the variance, but the discussion suggests that a good deal of fragmentation results from rotating so many components.

No information is given on item difficulties, or indeed on any within-scale psychometric indices. Correlations between 'area' subscale scores are given, and also correlations between area scores and total score. Inter-area correlations are low, reaching 0.32 at maximum. According to the Manual, these figures show that 'we may quite properly summate across areas to obtain a total score . . .'. The logic of this statement is neither transparent nor compelling, nor is it supported by argument. No information is given on the construction of the Lie Scale.

Administration

Instructions are given on the front page of the inventory, and are simple and straightforward. Ten to fifteen minutes is suggested as adequate time to allow, plus a further 15 minutes or so for the optional free response supplementary questionnaire. The Manual suggests that for younger or more backward pupils the inventory may be administered orally, but no investigation of the effects of such a procedure on scores, reliability, validity, etc. appears to have been conducted.

Standardization

Only the means and standard deviations for the original sample used in the construction of the inventory are given.

Scoring

Six scoring keys are available (one for each area). No key is provided for the Lie Scale. Scores are sums of response weights of 1 or 3, omitted or doubly marked items being scored 2. The table which passes for normative information states 'These data are based on a 0–4 score system—See Scoring Section, p. 11'. The said page 11 refers to a 0–4 scoring system only for the Lie Scale. This issue remains unresolved.

Reliability

A test-retest coefficient of 0.87 ($n = 139$) with a 3-day interval is reported. 'Internal consistency reliability coefficients' are presented based on the same data used in the principal component analysis used for item selection. No further detail on the method of computation (coefficient alpha, split-half, etc.) is given. Coefficients range from 0.27–0.75.

These figures are unacceptable as indications of the reliability of the scales, since the process of item selection using principal component analysis maximizes internal consistency estimates. Substantial shrinkage may be expected on an independent sample. The practice of quoting internal consistency reliability estimates derived from data used in item selection has very properly been the subject of trenchant criticism in technical journals. To find a Manual published in 1978 falling into this elementary trap is disheartening.

Other reliability coefficients are quoted based on a previous version of the inventory: a split-half (each area being split at random) analysis gave a correlation of 0.78 on a sample of 120, and a test-retest coefficient of 0.81 is reported, based on a 'random sample' of 64 pupils over a three-week time interval. The relevance of these (and other) results to the present version of the inventory is posited on the claimed high correlation between old and new versions (0.82 is quoted), based on a sample of 1476. This sample size is sufficiently close to the 1477 given as the basis for the principal component analysis used in item selection to raise suspicions. Just how closely related in terms of common items, are the old and new versions? The Manual does not say.

Validity

So far as correlations with other tests are concerned the Manual reports a correlation of 0.62 between an earlier version, and the IPAT Anxiety Scale. A study is also referred to which showed associations between higher scores on the present version and introversion and neuroticism scores on the Junior Eysenck Personality Inventory.

Substantial correlations are reported between scores on three areas of the previous form of inventory and teacher ratings, although it is unclear from the description whether all results are reported or only those favourable to the test.

Tables comparing correlations between subscores on this inventory and similar correlations for the Mooney Problem Check-List Junior High School Form (q.v.) are presented. There is a clear and substantial difference—Mooney area scores intercorrelated more highly. These results are presented as support- ing the construct validity of the Lewis Counselling Inventory, but in particular since the Mooney Problem Check-List Manual makes very explicit that it is not intended or constructed as a scored test, the relevance of these tables is obscure.

General evaluation

So far as can be judged from the Manual, this test may well be yet another alternate form for the many measures of extraversion and neuroticism/anxiety available. The item content is very redolent of such measures, and what little concurrent validity information is presented supports this view.

The Manual itself is a very poor example of the genre. At times confusing and inconsistent, parts assume a capacity to follow a discussion of a principal component analysis, yet an account of the calculation of the standard error of measurement assumes no knowledge at all. Rather than being a clear, easily accessible account of the information needed to understand how the test was constructed, for what purpose, and with what success, it presents a poorly organized narrative of dubious technical merit. Relying heavily on diploma dissertation material, the Manual would be barely acceptable as a preliminary report on a scale available for research purposes only. Nowhere is the construct 'need for guidance and/or counselling' established and related to test content. The information provided about this test, and not least the manner of its presentation, leaves serious doubts about the adequacy of its construction and its fitness for purpose.

Manchester Scales of Social Adaptation

Reviewed by M. B. Youngman

Author: E. A. Lunzer
Publisher: NFER-Nelson
Distributor: NFER-Nelson
Age range: 6–15
1958–59 (S); 1966 (M, T)
No revisions apparent
Individual assessment

Test content

The complete 88-item test comprises two main scales, each of which is made up of five subscales, as follows:

(1) *Social Perspective:* general social perspective; knowledge of sport; knowledge of current affairs; cultural or aesthetic knowledge; and, scientific knowledge.
(2) *Self-Direction:* socialization of leisure and play activities; self-help; exercise of responsibility in the home; freedom of movement; and, exercise of financial responsibility.

The scales are predominantly a development of Doll's Vineland Social Maturity Scale. There is considerable overlap between these scales and Doll's, with a certain amount of re-allocation of items. Doll's occupation scale is, however, omitted because of the reduced age range of the Manchester scales. Apart from the translation into the British context, certain differences are identified in the Manual. These include the separation of subscales, particularly in the intellectual and personal areas, together with some modifications in scoring and interpretation.

All scales contain at least 8 items except Self-Direction: Home (3 items) and Self-Direction: Financial (5 items). Individual items are not verbatim questions to be asked of the child, but instead they indicate information to be elicited. The interviewer can if necessary modify the form of the question, or follow-up with prompts in the event of an inconclusive reply. There is also a facility in some of the scales, mostly the Self-Direction ones, to grade responses, rather than to operate a simple right-wrong criterion.

There is a clear stylistic difference between the items contributing to the two main scales: the Social Perspective items are essentially factual, whereas the Self-Direction items assess behaviour and understanding of social behaviour. Inevitably any construct as broad as social adaptation is likely to raise problems in domain sampling. A more detailed consideration of this aspect appears below under General evaluation. At this point it may be worth noting the possibility of a sampling inadequacy. For example, the Social Perspective: General scale comprises 13 items. Five of these test knowledge of personal details of name, address, neighbourhood, birthday and year of birth. Three are about time, and three are about correspondence. This does seem to represent a highly selective definition of social perspective.

Purpose

In the author's words the instrument constitutes a 'direct assessment of social competence; less directly it may be taken as a measure of social adaptation' (Manual, p. 4). 'It is expected that the scale will be used more frequently in the assessment of sub-normals than of normals' (p. 8). This is reiterated in the introduction where it is stated that the test attempts 'to measure sub-normal degrees of social adaptation' (p. 2). Nevertheless, it is emphasized that the underlying philosophy implies an interaction between environmental and hereditary factors. There is relatively little indication of the intended manner of use, but is is made clear that whilst Doll's scale generated Social Ages, the Manchester Scales do not. Apart from the provision of a normative profile little guidance is given on interpretation or use, leaving possible applications very much in the hands of the user.

Item preparation

Having its origins in Doll's Vineland Scale this particular instrument does not require a detailed account of the theoretical basis of the items and, accordingly, the Manual does not concern itself with the derivation of individual items. The separation of intellectual and personal aspects of social adaptation has already been mentioned. The other main issue tackled in the Manual is that of the criteria for item selection. The developmental nature of the items is mentioned; that is, achievement increases with age. The universality of items is also highlighted. This requirement means that everyone should achieve success on the item eventually, unless some 'genuine defect' prevents it. It also implies that an item should not discriminate against any large section of the population. For that reason references to telephones were excluded since it was felt that they did not meet the criterion of universal availability.

Administration

The administration procedure consists of a standardized interview, the structure of which is determined by the scoring criteria. The Manual lists a question for each item which is open to variation so that alternatives may be pursued or prompts may be offered. The questions really serve to indicate what information is required to permit scoring. Alongside most of the questions comments are provided on administration and scoring criteria. Many of the items incorporate levels of achievement so that a series of criteria are offered to decide the award of 0, 1, 2, 3 or even 4 points.

There is no explicit indication of the qualifications required of intended users, but guidance is given on the manner of use. The interviewer must be familiar with the test and a supportive, interested style is prescribed. Further guidance for the interviewer is offered in the form of continuation criteria for each subscale, and a suggestion that the interviewer may return to earlier items if failure on them was considered a temporary lapse.

The estimated time required is 30 minutes or less for younger children and 35–40 minutes for older pupils, 'but some are more talkative'.

Standardization

All development and standardization was performed on the basis of two administrations of the scales. The first, in 1958, was to a sample of 194 children representing all ages 6–15 years, with equal proportions of boys and girls. The sample was designed to represent the school population; it consisted of a stratified sampling of schools, five types being identified by socio-economic characteristics, with random selection of pupils within schools. For pupils the pseudo-random criterion was to take the two boys and two girls closest to the ages of 6:06 years, 7:06 years, and so on. The schools were either in the Manchester area or from the surrounding rural region. The second administration, in 1959, to children in the Macclesfield area and in Cheshire, used a similar sampling strategy. It is pointed out that since the five types of schools did not include special schools, there are no sub-normals in the sample, unless they happen to be present in the normal schools sampled. Interviews were conducted by the test author and full-time Educational Psychology students.

Test development was based on the 1958 sample. Only the Social Perspective scales suffered any major revision following the pilot trial and therefore the standardization data relate to both samples for Self-Direction, but only to the 1959 sample for the Social Perspective scales. Age standardization was an intrinsic feature of the sample design since all sample members were approximately at the mid-point of their year range.

The Manual gives standardization tables for the total score, the two main scales, and for all the subscales except Responsibility in the Home. This one is omitted because its scoring procedures were modified after the 1959 administration. The norms themselves were generated by plotting graphs of the results obtained, and then drawing in smooth curves fitted by visual inspection. For each age the tables give scores associated with all nine 10th percentiles for the overall and main score totals, but only the quartiles, and the 10th and 90th percentiles are offered for subscales.

Scoring

Considerable variations exist between the scores awarded for items in different subscales and therefore separate, detailed instructions are provided. These cover the criteria for the award of points at each level where more than one level exists. The adequacy of these instructions is likely to vary with the question. For all items the absence of any definite correct or acceptable answer means that some interviewer discretion is required. A particularly difficult item is that requiring the pupil to draw a map of where he lives. The item, comments and scoring instructions cover almost half the page. Not only is interpretation of the four score levels (0–3) likely to be subjective, but a further requirement is that the interviewer should have sufficient information of the local area to be able to judge the accuracy of the map. The Social Perspective items are similarly demanding; although they relate to factual information, no correct answers are listed, often because many acceptable responses exist. A scoring form is supplied to record item scores and to facilitate scale and subscale totalling. The form also includes a profile chart which records raw scores and percentile scores.

Reliability

The author acknowledges the problem of heterogeneity of items in estimating the reliability of developmental tests, but also points out that the individual age group samples would be too small to produce acceptable statistics. As a compromise three overlapping age bands—6–9, 9–12 and 12–15—are used as a basis for the estimates. The bands are claimed to be theoretically sound since they correspond with the Piagetian stages of cognitive development. This strategy results in sample sizes of 80 for Social Perspective (1959 data only) and 160 for Self-Direction (1958 and 1959 data).

Item-scale correlations, derived by what would now seem to be a rather old-fashioned method, were used to obtain reliability estimates and some very high values are reported. The Self-Direction and Social Perception scale totals register 0.94 and 0.96, respectively, across the three age bands. Self-Direction subscale values vary from 0.73–0.88 except for money (0.65 at 9–12 and 0.66 at 12–15) and self-help (0.53 at 12–15). The range for Social Perception is

0.70–0.93 with two exceptions at 6–9 (0.65 for aesthetic and 0.66 for scientific). A small test-retest exercise was also conducted using two samples, one of 40 children aged 8–9 years and one of 43 13 year-olds. The time interval is not indicated but it is emphasized that since different testers were involved on the two occasions, the estimates incorporate an inter-rater consistency check. The reported values are 0.75 for Social Perspective and 0.86 for Self-Direction. Total scale results are 0.87 for the younger group and 0.90 at 13 years. Some or all of these reliability coefficients are likely to have inflated values due to the width of the age groups used.

Validity

A discussion of validity in the Manual argues that comparison with similar measures is not possible because the only one available was the Vineland Scale on which the Manchester Scales are based. Comparison with an external estimate of social competence is offered as a possible approach (based on interviews, observation, etc.) but that it had not been attempted. This left construct validation as the main approach. Construct validity is claimed to be explicitly present in that the 'items bear directly on aspects of social competence, and do not merely provide clues from which social competence may be inferred' (p. 12).

The only quantitative validity data are derived from the two small samples used for test-retest reliability estimation. Correlations with IQ are as follows:

	Age 8 ($n = 40$)	Age 13 ($n = 43$)
Total Scale	0.26	0.48
Self-Direction	0.20	0.24
Social Perception	0.25	0.60

The conclusion drawn is that Self-Direction 'is relatively independent of IQ', and that Social Perception is 'only partly a function of intelligence even at the age of 12(*sic*), when the measure is heavily weighted with items on general knowledge' (Manual, p. 13).

Earlier discussion of the nature of social competence did isolate cognitive and non-cognitive components and these results do support that expectation at the 13 year-old level, even though the quotation, given above, is ambivalent on whether a high or low correlation is desirable. But in seeking a broader base for validation it would be necessary to supplement the information supplied. Intelligence as a criterion can only have secondary relevance, and even that requirement is not met at the younger age level. Without much more evidence on the relationship between scores on these scales and associated constructs in the area of attitude and social adjustment it is not possible to be confident about the extent to which these scales represent a valid measure of social adaptation.

Interpretation

If the term 'sub-normal' is interpreted as an aspect of score distributions then one of the expressed purposes is met since the Manual provides percentile tables for each age, and median achievement ages for each item. These would enable individuals who fail to achieve at levels associated with specified norms to be identified. There is also the facility for drawing norm-based profiles, allowing an overall picture of adaptation to be evaluated. Any further interpretation of obtained results would be largely at the discretion of the user since the Manual does not include guidance on diagnosis or action. There is limited guidance (one sentence) for use with severely retarded children, but given the initial assertion that the scales are likely to be used more often with sub-normals, this is hardly sufficient.

General evaluation

The starting point for the evaluation of any test has to be the extent to which it meets the purpose for which it is intended. Clearly, there is insufficient quantitative evidence to accept that such validity has yet been established. How far does other information presented overcome or confirm this inadequacy?

Since over 20 years has elapsed since the construction of the scale, it is reasonable to inspect the items to test the claim of qualitative construct validity. The first problem is that some of the items are no longer correct.

Q21: What kinds of sporting event take place at the White City? Presumably athletics is expected, but that is no longer true.
Q28: What are the *three* main political parties in this country?
Q30: What do the letters UNO stand for? (current usage is UN).

Then there is the strong likelihood that present difficulty levels are quite different from those of 1958. This is particularly likely in sport where fame is so temporary. So almost everyone could name at least one boxer, and very few would not be able to name one athlete.

More fundamental reservations arise in relation to item sampling. The highly selective definition of social perspective (general) has already been mentioned. The same must be said of the sport scale which has a very middle-class content; athletics, cricket and rowing are included, but not darts, snooker or motor racing. It would be very difficult to justify the selection of any

10 items in such a varied area as sport. Alongside the sampling of items, the sampling of respondents does raise questions. Social adaptation must depend on cultural expectations to some extent, and the use of schools only in the North-West of England may be unsatisfactory. Certainly children's games do show regional variations and the name 'Tig' is not necessarily universal. Similarly the exclusion of sub-normals does appear rather expedient in view of the expressed purpose of the scale. It may not be legitimate to assume (by extrapolation) that sub-normals (whoever they are defined as) can be superimposed on the distributions obtained from a normal sample. This is particularly important in diagnostic applications.

Bearing in mind the discussion of validity, and other more specific features, it is difficult to be confident that these scales will provide acceptable results with modern samples. The original standardization was carried out in what amounted to a 'pre-television' society. The intense social exposure that is now available to children, even if it is vicarious, must have implications for the Social Perspective scales. And even from the evidence given in the Manual the support for the Self-Direction scales is not strong. Some concerted modernization and reassessment must be attempted before widespread usage can be recommended.

Minnesota Counseling Inventory*

Reviewed by Stephen Sharp

Author: R. F. Berdie and W. L. Layton
Publisher: The Psychological Corporation
Distributor: NFER-Nelson
Age range: 15–18 (USA High School, grades 9–12 and first-year college)
1953 (S); 1957 (M, T)
No revisions apparent
Group test

Test content

The Minnesota Counseling Inventory (MCI) contains 355 items each of which is a statement, the task being for each student to decide whether each statement is true or false as it applies to him. The responses are placed on a separate answer sheet which enables the MCI booklet itself to be reusable. Nine scale

---

* Reported to have been declared 'out of print'. Some stocks may remain.

scores are obtained from the responses. The first is simply the number of items omitted which, if too large, invalidates the whole inventory. The second is a validity scale which assesses the student's tendency to present socially acceptable characteristics. The inventory scales themselves are: Family Relationships, Social Relationships and Emotional Stability, which assess the extent of adjustment in these areas; and Conformity, Adjustment to Reality, Mood and Leadership, which probe the mechanisms whereby this adjustment is reached. The MCI also contains 44 items not currently scored whose inclusion relates to future scale development with this test.

Purpose

Four purposes are given for the inventory: '1. To sensitise teachers and counselors to relevant personality characteristics differentiating students. 2. To identify students in need of therapeutic attention. 3. To assist in understanding students as they attempt to achieve a more mature self-understanding and integration between themselves and their environment. 4. To provide a means of determining the effects of educational experiences upon relevant personality characteristics' (Manual, p. 3).

The test is not designed for use in selection programmes or with students of less than eighth-grade reading ability or 'major psychological disturbances'. Rather, it aims to provide diagnostic information about personality structure and problems of use to teachers and advisers working with adolescents in 9–12 grade age range, either inside or outside schools.

Item preparation

The scales of the MCI were developed from two previous tools, the Minnesota Personality Scale (MPS) and the Minnesota Multiphasic Personality Inventory (MMPI). Items were taken from three of the MPS scales and five MMPI scales. These items were rewritten to simplify the wording and reviewed by 'a selected group' of parents, teachers and clergymen. The 415 resulting items were submitted to a group (no size given) of high-school students. A resulting inventory form containing 413 items was then pretested on 24 000 students from ten States in the spring of 1953. Following 'a series of item analyses' (of which no results are given), the items were reduced to 355 and some of these scripts were rescored and used as standardization data.

Administration

The MCI can be administered by 'almost any teacher' although the Manual recommends some knowledge of the technical aspects of tests and of the personality theory of the adolescent for interpreting scores. Some knowledge of education, statistics and the psychology of individual differences is the sort of experience required.

No materials are needed other than the answer sheet and reusable booklet. The test takes around 50 minutes on average though this is not a limit—students are given as long as they need to respond to all items even if more than one session is necessary, though the Manual advises that this should be avoided if possible. Verbatim instructions for the tester are given: they are straightforward as no questions can be answered during the test session and the tester is mainly concerned to ensure that the testee completes personal details on the front of the answer sheet, etc.

Standardization

Four normative groups are used, i.e. boys and girls in grades 9–10 and grades 11–12. Each group contains between 1200 and 1600 pupils drawn from 25 schools in Iowa and Minnesota. No date is given. Means and standard deviations are presented for each group and each scale and they are compared with samples of size 200 drawn (presumably at random) from the larger and more geographically-scattered pretesting group mentioned above and rescored on the reduced number of items. While the resulting profiles are very similar, some of the differences would reach statistical significance, though no comment on this is made in the Manual.

Norms are presented for each of the four groups and each of the eight scales (the exception being the number of items omitted which is not in general considered to be a scale) in such a way that each of the 32 standardized variables has a mean of 50 and a standard deviation of 10. But the distributional characteristics are unaltered—no attempt at normalization was made.

Full details are provided of the standardization group even down to the names of the schools used and, in general, every effort has been made to base standardized scores on data of sufficient size and representativeness (but see comments under General evaluation below). Such efforts are clearly necessary when the significance of test scores, as in this case, is evaluated purely by reference to the norms of a standardization group.

Scoring

Before each sheet is scored, the number of items omitted is counted. If there are more than 25 of these, the MCI is not scored, though efforts should be made to get the student to supply the missing answers. Hand scoring is carried out by placing a stencil over the answer sheet and counting the number of marks visible. There is a stencil for each scale. The sheets can also be machine scored in which case electrographic pencils must be used and should be added to the necessary materials. The raw score for each scale is transformed into a standardized score by referring to one of four tables for the four normative groups. By circling appropriate raw score entries in the tables, an individual test profile is built up.

Reliability

The split-half reliability of each scale is assessed on samples of size 200 in each of the four normative groups. After Spearman-Brown 'correction', coefficients range from 0.56–0.95, falling mainly within the range 0.75–0.90. Higher coefficients are found for Family Relationships, Social Relationships and Emotional Stability, i.e. the 'adjustment' scales, than for the 'mechanism' scales named above.

Test-retest reliability used four groups of size 107–121 of which two had a one-month inter-test gap and two had a three-month gap. Coefficients range from 0.56–0.93. Again, 'adjustment' scales have greater reliability than 'mechanism' scales but the difference is not so marked in this case. The validity scale was assessed separately and has a test-retest reliability of 0.67 for boys and 0.64 for girls. This is lower than the other scales and may indicate the smaller number of items on which it is based on shifting attitudes towards taking the inventory.

Validity

The Manual warns that no information exists concerning the validity of *combinations* of MCI scale scores. Therefore the use of general test profiles and of differences between scale scores must be with appropriate caution.

The validity of individual scales was assessed by constructing rating forms which carried descriptions of behaviour characteristics typical of students scoring high or low on each of the seven diagnostic scales of the MCI, e.g. students who are natural leaders or who have particular family problems. These forms were issued to 'teachers . . . school nurses, counselors and principals' (no numbers or selection details given) who were asked to nominate students fitting closely the given profiles of high or low scorers. Then, for each of the four normative groups and each of the seven scales, the 'high' and 'low' groups were compared with each other or with random samples of size 200 from the overall standardization data. The nominated groups varied widely in size from 9–317 averaging around 120. Most of the scales yielded highly significant differences between high and low groups for most of the comparisons, the major exceptions being Mood, for which only 15 out of 24 reached the 1 per cent level, and Adjustment to Reality, for which one in eight reached this level. These findings are compatible with the data on reliability, which indicated a better performance from 'adjustment' scales than 'mechanism' scales.

Validity is also investigated through the subscale intercorrelation matrices from samples of size 200 for each of the four normative groups. A consistent pattern was found with the strongest relationships being between Social Relations and Leadership and between Emotional Stability and Adjustment to Reality. These are intuitively plausible as are instances of low coefficients between scales not so clearly related. However, there is no proper discussion of the implications of the intercorrelations and it is left to the test user to study the matrices for himself.

Interpretation

The meaning of each subscale score is heavily dependent on the behaviour profiles used in the validation work. Research articles and supporting literature for the MMPI and MPS, from which the MCI was derived (see above), were used to construct these profiles. The section in the Manual on interpretation consists of descriptions of idealized high and low scorers used for validation, the idea being that high and low scores are indicative of the personality types described. The Manual does not place enough stress on the imperfection of the relationship involved: while commenting that 'extensive overlapping is found among groups when the distributions themselves are compared' (p. 14), it does not explore the variability of personality types within a group of high or low scorers or comment directly on how accurate the descriptions are as a guide.

Test use

Since the test is published in the USA, it is perhaps useful to give at least one reference to its British context:

Zahran, H. (1967). The self-concept in the psychological guidance of adolescents. *British Journal of Educational Psychology* 37, 225–240.

General evaluation

The main difficulties of the MCI relate to time and space. The derivation of its present form happened around thirty years ago and it is to be expected that the properties of such socially-relevant scales as Family Relationships and Conformity will change markedly over such a period. Similarly, the standardization and validation were carried out in the USA. No British norms appear to exist and there are obvious dangers in generalizing àcross cultures. Although the scales themselves are diagnostic, the evaluation of raw scores is normative and the test will have more appeal to an American user of the 1950s than a British one of the 1980s.

The other weakness concerns the validation. This was approached by selecting for personality types and comparing corresponding scores. In practice it happens the other way round, i.e. the scores come first, so it would have been better to have selected for high and low scale scores and looked at the range of personality assessments within each group. This would have provided information on the accuracy of the scales, which is currently missing.

In general, the MCI was a competent, adequately documented test at the time and place of its construction. The modern British user, however, would be well advised to consider carefully the problems he will face in implementing its results in what will be a very different context, especially for a tool of this type which is heavily dependent on social and cultural values which are likely to vary significantly.

Mooney Problem Check List

Reviewed by S. F. Blinkhorn

Authors: R. L. Mooney and L. V. Gordon
Publisher: The Psychological Corporation
Distributor: NFER-Nelson
Age: Junior High School (J); High School (H); College (C); Adults (A)
1950 versions reviewed
Group test

Test content

Four forms are available, Junior High School, High School, College and Adult, the last being intended principally for those no longer in education. Each form consists of a list of phrases expressing a problem: the Junior High School form offers 210 problems, High School and College forms contain 330 problems each, and the Adult form offers 288. The problems range widely across sources of human misery: the possibilities of divine retribution, sinus trouble, not being allowed to use the family car and 'having considerable trouble with my teeth' get equal billing with anxieties about schoolwork, sex, social relationships and self doubt.

The appropriateness and completeness of the item content of each form is not easy to judge. Drugs other than tobacco are not mentioned. Girls in junior high school are not offered 'menstrual disorders' as a problem, but may worry about not being allowed to use the family car (by the time they reach college the situation is reversed); some terminology is American to the point of being opaque in the UK ('grade' is used in the sense of both 'mark', as in 'worried about grades' and 'year' or 'form' as in 'being a grade behind').

The problems are grouped in sets of five (six in the adult form), according to 'problem areas', so that the check-list appears to consist of a sequence of short blocks. Cunningly, the blocks are arranged so that they fall into a horizontal pattern, allowing an easy scan of density of problems acknowledged by broad topic. The Junior High School form has 7 problem areas, the Adult 9 and the High School and College 11.

Purpose

The Manual for the 'educational' forms suggests five uses:

(1) to facilitate counselling interviews;
(2) as a survey tool, to locate students in need of help and the most prevalent problems current in the student body;
(3) as a basis for discussion and group work;
(4) 'to increase teacher understanding in regular classroom teaching'; and,
(5) as a research tool.

Fundamentally the check-lists are intended as an aid to help students express their personal problems. The Manual emphasizes that they are not intended as tests, that scores or counts of problems are of very limited use, and that the *numbers* of problems checked are limited by the respondent's awareness, and his willingness to reveal problems.

Item preparation

The 'educational' forms of the check-list are drawn from an initial list of over 5000 items from a variety of sources. The criteria for selection of items included considerations of phrasing, prevalence of problems, seriousness of problems, gradation of seriousness, judicious vagueness where appropriate and personal rather than general social orientation. No detail is given as to how specifically these criteria were implemented, although a number of trial versions are reported as having been used.

Administration

The check-lists are described as self-administering. Respondents first under-line problems they experience, then circle the numbers of problems which trouble them most. The Manual suggests that 'practically all' of a group will finish a check-list in 50 minutes.

Standardization

None.

Scoring

Scoring, in the usual sense of deriving a number which stands as a measure of some trait or attribute, is inappropriate with these check-lists. Counts of the total number of problems marked, either overall or within problem areas, may have some limited utility, but only with reference to local conditions and resources.

Reliability

Conventional assessment of reliability is stated to be inappropriate for an instrument of this type.

Validity

The validity of a check-list must primarily be assessed in terms of its adequacy in covering relevant material and its efficacy in encouraging respondents to respond freely. Both of these considerations are covered in the Manual, and it is clear that the authors took pains in these respects. However, they must be assessed in the context in which the check-list is used: sensitivity to local conditions is likely to be the rule rather than the exception.

Interpretation

There are no scores to interpret, and the authors maintain that the check-lists are neutral with respect to competing counselling orientations. Hence the Manual is concerned to dissuade the user from treating them as scored personality inventories.

General evaluation

Problem check-lists fall at the boundary of what can be classified as a 'test', and hence a fit subject for review in this volume. Only in the sense that they impose a structure, a system, on collecting information about an individual and indeed sample his responses, do they have anything in common with the ordinary run of tests. Rather, they are a source of raw material for counselling or survey work, and it is of course entirely possible to construct scales out of check-list items. However they are used, the usual questions of reliability and validity should be asked of the mode of employment, rather than the list of problems. One would expect a good deal of context sensitivity.

There are, however, two further questions which prospective users should consider. First, is the selection of problems adequate, comprehensive, up-to-date and plausible in the context in which it will be used? It is more than 30 years since the Mooney Problem Check-Lists were last revised, and there are clear Americanisms in the item content. The fact that the majority of the items seem, to this reviewer, to be relevant in contemporary Britain may reflect the unchanging nature of the human predicament. But it may well be that changes in society since the date of last revision have thrown up significant new problems which a prudent counsellor would wish his clients to have the opportunity of expressing—concern about drugs, nuclear war, imminent ecological disaster or third-world poverty, for instance, which are perhaps closer to school-age populations nowadays, and more personally felt. Secondly, is the problem-oriented approach enshrined in these check-lists appropriate? A scored personality inventory with such unremittingly negative items would draw criticism on grounds of response bias or susceptibility to acquiescence response set. One wonders to what extent the format of the check-lists encourages over-response (or under-response for that matter). Could it be that the check-lists could foster problems, suggesting new possibilities for worry? What is lacking is a comparison with alternative means of acquiring the same information, which would offer some empirical basis for evaluating the check-lists. One would hate to think they are merely antidotes to contentment.

'Having no problems' does not appear as a problem.

Occupational Check List (Advanced)

Brief Report

Author: A. D. Crowley
Publisher: CRAC/Hobsons Press
Distributor: CRAC/Hobsons Press
Age: 14+; pupils of above-average ability
1972 (M, T)
1976 (M) (revised)
Group administration

The 2-page check-list has two parts. In Part 1, the pupil underlines those of 108 occupational activities he/she would like. The activities represent the following six vocational interest categories: practical, enterprising, scientific, clerical, artistic and social. In Part II, pupils rate the importance to them of 15 aspects of a career (e.g. good salary, using one's initiative).

Although the check-list can be scored and some reliability and validity data are given, it is suggested that the main purpose of the OCL is to provide a basis for discussion in the light of lists of occupations, interest groupings, specific likes and dislikes, and so on.

Occupational Interest Rating Scale

Brief Report

Author: M. A. Brimer
Publisher: Educational Evaluation Enterprises
Distributor: Educational Evaluation Enterprises
Age: 14+
Undated (M, T), but post-1977 (M) indicated; S not stated
Group administration

A reusable booklet contains two parallel forms, Forms 1 and 2. Each Form consists of a list of activities presented in 53 pairs. For any pair the pupil rates both activities on a scale of one ('very disinterested') to five ('very interested'), the pair merely providing a temporary frame or focus for judgement. About 35 minutes are required.

Scores are obtained by scoring key for seven occupational areas—Business, Technical, Care, Aesthetic, Scientific, Numerical and Field—and for five types of interaction or 'directions of involvement'—Persuasive, Operational, Empathic, Making ('goal directed') and Intellectual. To obtain scores for the latter groups of scales, responses from both Forms must be used.

Raw scores are converted to scale scores which assume a Rasch model. Interpretation is by use of 'highs' and 'lows' in the profile of interests (and directions of involvement).

Rutter's Behaviour Questionnaires

Reviewed by D. R. Gooch

Authors: M. Rutter and W. Yule
Publisher: Department of Adolescent and Child Psychiatry, Institute of
  Psychiatry, Maudsley Hospital

Distributor: Department of Adolescent and Child Psychiatry, Institute of
 Psychiatry, Maudsley Hospital
Age range: 7–13 years (for both Scale A(2)–Parents, and Scale B(2)–Teachers)
1968 (report forms)
Individual reports

Test content

The questionnaire for parents (to report upon or rate a child) was developed in parallel with the similar questionnaire for teachers (Rutter, 1967). The parents' scale consists of 3 sections, the first relating to a child's health problems, the second to habits and the third to behaviour. There are 8 questions in the first section, e.g. 'Complains of headaches', to which the parent marks a cross in the box indicating the frequency with which the child manifests the problem. The ratings in this section are either 'never in the last year', 'at least once per week' or 'occasionally but not as often as once per week'. The second section relating to habits, e.g. 'Does he/she have any eating difficulty' is rated by parents as 'No', 'Yes—mild' or 'Yes—severe'. The third section presents 18 descriptions of behaviours to which the parent responds by signifying whether the statement 'certainly applies', 'applies—somewhat' or 'does not apply' to the child.

The teachers' scale consists of 26 statements concerning the child's behaviour, 18 of which are identical to the questions in the third section of the parents' scale. The teacher is required to check whether the statement 'certainly applies', 'applies—somewhat' or 'does not apply'.

Purpose

The purpose of both scales as quoted by Rutter (1967) is to 'fulfil a need for a reliable and valid short questionnaire suitable to be used with children in the middle range, and which could be used to discriminate between different types of behavioural or emotional disorder as well as discriminate between children who show a disorder and those who do not'. Rutter also states that 'when the teachers' questionnaire and the parents' questionnaire are used in combination they provide a very efficient screening procedure provided the correct cut-off points have been used'. The scales were designed to discriminate between an anti-social and a neurotic disorder.

Item preparation

There is paucity of detailed information on the origins of the items used in both scales, although pilot investigations on samples of children were carried out 'to establish the questions and the method of scoring'.

For the teachers' questionnaire children aged 7–13 years from 8 schools were rated on the 3 point scale by 2 or more teachers (sample size not given). The teachers were also interviewed. From the preliminary study ambiguous and loaded items were eliminated. Items used to produce neurotic and anti-social subscores were based on the proportion of neurotic and anti-social and control children scoring 1 or 2 on each item during the pilot study. The items chosen all reliably discriminated between those designated as anti-social and neurotic of both sexes except for item 23 ('has had tears on arrival at school or has refused to come into the building in the past 12 months') whose discrimination was less than 5 per cent for males.

As for the Parents' Questionnaire (PQ) the case notes of all new referrals to the Maudsley Hospital Children's Department (for whom a parent's questionnaire had been obtained) were examined and a diagnosis of a neurotic, anti-social or other condition was made. The items used to produce a neurotic or anti-social subscore were selected as for the Teachers' Questionnaire (TQ). The item 'biliousness' (now 'Asthma or Wheezing Attacks') was not significant at 5 per cent level for girls. In this investigation the general population consisted of 198 children (99 boys and 99 girls) while the clinical sample consisted of 120 children (72 boys and 48 girls).

Administration

There is no Manual provided with either questionnaire. Instructions on completion are, however, given before each section, and are simple and explicit. The time taken to complete each questionnaire, in practice, is about five minutes.

Standardization

There are no norms provided or available in the literature.

Scoring

The scoring of each questionnaire is simple and is shown below:

PQ. Section 1: Never in last year (0 points); Occasionally (1); At least once per week (2).
Section 2: No (0); Yes—mildly (1); Yes—severely (2).
Section 3: Does not apply (0); Applies somewhat (1); Certainly applies (2).
TQ. Does not apply (0); Applies somewhat (1); Certainly applies (2).

The individual item scores are then summed to produce a total score with a range of 0–62 for PQ and 0–52 for TQ. The scoring is a two-stage procedure. For the PQ a score of 13 or more indicates a disorder. A 'neurotic' subscore is obtained by summing the scores on items C, G, V, 6 and 16. An 'anti-social' subscore is obtained by summing the scores on items III, 3, 13, 17 and 18. Those scoring more on the neurotic items than on the anti-social items are designated as 'neurotic' while those with an 'anti-social' score exceeding the neurotic score are designated as 'anti-social'. Children with equal neurotic and anti-social subscores remain undifferentiated.

For the TQ a score of 8 or more indicates a behavioural disorder. A 'neurotic' subscore is calculated by summing the scores on items 7, 10, 17 and 23 while the 'anti-social' subscore is obtained by summing the scores on items 4, 5, 15, 19, 20 and 26. Designation of an anti-social or neurotic disorder is made in a similar way to the PQ. If the scores on both are equal the child is designated as 'undifferentiated' or as having a 'mixed' disorder.

Reliability

Reliability was tested in a variety of ways for both questionnaires. For the PQ, retest reliability was studied by getting 83 mothers to rate their 9–13 year-old children twice with a two-month interval between. The mothers were not told of the retest. The product-moment correlation between the total scores on the two occasions was 0.74. Inter-rater reliability was tested by asking the mother and father of each of 35 children aged 9–13 to complete the PQ simultaneously but independently. This yielded a correlation of 0.64. Inter-rater reliability was further assessed by comparing the total scores on the questionnaires completed by the fathers, with the total scores on those completed by the mothers, two months earlier. The correlation in this case was 0.63.

The retest reliability for the TQ was assessed by asking 4 teachers to rate 80 blind 7 year-old children on two occasions separated by a two-month interval. The correlation between total scores on both occasions was 0.89. Inter-rater reliability was tested by asking four teachers to rate 70 children (35 girls, 35 boys) who were in the last term of infant school. Two to three months later 4 other teachers rated the same children; the correlation between the two total scores was 0.72.

Validity

Discriminative power of the PQ was tested by comparing the score of children in a geographically restricted population (a random sample of 99 boys and 99 girls, aged 9–13, from Aberdeen) with the scores of 72 boys and 48 girls attending the Maudsley Hospital with emotional or behavioural disorders. The best discrimination was obtained with a total score of 13 or more; 15.1 per cent of males and 8.1 per cent of girls in the population sample obtained scores of 13 or more compared with 70.8 per cent of boys and 66.6 per cent of girls in the criterion group. A further test of validity was carried out on 75 children referred to the Maudsley Hospital. A diagnosis of 'neurotic' or 'anti-social' was made from an examination of the case notes. The diagnosis based on the scale subscores was then compared with the clinical diagnosis made previously from the case notes of children scoring 13 or more on the questionnaire. The agreement between the clinical and questionnaire diagnosis was about 80 per cent for both 'anti-social' and 'neurotic' children.

Rutter's survey carried out between 1964 and 1965 of the health, education and behaviour of 9–12 year-old children, living on the Isle of Wight, provided another source of data for validation studies (Rutter, Tizard, Whitmore, 1970). The total population of 10–11 year-olds ($n = 2199$) screened with both the PQ and TQ yielded 271 children with a psychiatric disorder. The children were further assessed by interview and school information. On this assessment 50.4 per cent of children scoring 13 or more on the PQ were rated as having a definite psychiatric disorder compared with 6.8 per cent of the population as a whole. In addition, when the questionnaire designation of 'neurotic', or 'anti-social' was compared with the final psychiatric diagnosis made on the basis of the interviews, there was 78 per cent agreement.

The discriminative power of the TQ was tested by comparing scores of a random sample of 55 boys and 31 girls aged 9–13 years with 2 clinic samples of the same age range. It was found that a total test score of 9 or more was the most discriminative. It was found that 11 per cent of boys and 3.5 per cent of girls of the general population scored 9 or more compared with 80 per cent of boys and 60 per cent of girls in the psychiatric sample. There are similar results from other cross-validation studies.

In order to test discrimination between neurotic and anti-social disorders teachers rated all children diagnosed as either anti-social or neurotic from clinical notes. When compared to the clinical diagnosis, for all those scoring 9 or more there was 90 per cent agreement for anti-social and 80 per cent for neurotic disorders. It was also found that the TQ was more efficient for differentiating between anti-social and neurotic disorders than the interview techniques.

Rutter concludes from these results that although the TQ is about as likely as the PQ to identify the neurotic cases, the PQ tended to under-represent anti-social males. However, when the questionnaires are used in combination Rutter claims that only one in five of the total number of children with a psychiatric disorder is missed. On the other hand, it was found that a personal interview with the parents was the 'single most useful method of gathering evidence for the final diagnosis of psychiatric disorder'.

General evaluation

The Rutter Behaviour Questionnaires offer a quick, easy to administer, reliable and valid instrument for the diagnosis of behaviour disorders. There is an abundance of information available on the studies carried out to establish reliability and validation, but because there is no manual provided, users must search the relevant literature for themselves.

It is claimed that neither questionnaire is likely to diagnose monosymptomatic and less common disorders, e.g. obsessional disorders. Also the TQ will not select children with symptoms manifest outside school, and the PQ is unlikely to select cases with symptoms manifest inside school. The lack of overlap between the two scales, is in part, therefore, due to behaviours being context or situation specific. For this reason, the two should be used together for efficient screening.

On closer inspection of the items in the questionnaires some appear to be loaded. For example, the item 'not much liked by other children' (appearing on both questionnaires) may encourage negation.

On the PQ the behaviours concerned in questions C and D in Section 1 (Bedwetting, Asthma or Wheezing) may be the effect of a behaviour disorder rather than the 'cause' or indication of it. These problems may also be hereditary. Both questionnaires appear to be rather heavily loaded on the 'anti-social' or 'hyperactive' type questions. In particular, item 3 on TQ (item 2 on PQ) 'squirmy, fidgety child' is rather similar to item 16 (item 14 in PQ) ('cannot settle to anything for more than a few moments'). More information on the selection of the items would be useful to explain the initial construction of the scales.

References

Rutter, M. (1967). A children's behaviour questionnaire, for completion by teachers; preliminary findings. *Journal of Child Psychology and Psychiatry* **8**, 1–11.

Rutter, M., Tizard, J. and Whitmore, K. (1970). "Education, Health and Behaviour". London: Longmans.

Sixteen Personality Factor Questionnaire*

Reviewed by S. F. Blinkhorn

Authors: R. B. Cattell *et al.*
Publisher: Institute for Personality and Ability Testing; British Undergraduate Norms published by NFER-Nelson†

---

* Forms C and D reviewed.
† Authors: Peter Saville and Stephen Blinkhorn.

Distributor: NFER-Nelson
Age: High School students and above; norms for British university
   undergraduates
1954; 1969 (T); 1972, 1979 (M); 1972 (Tabular Supplement No. 2)
British editions: 1973 (S); 1976 (M)
1979 (M) copyright edition reviewed
Group test

Test content

As its name implies the 16PF consists of 16 scales, each designed to measure a
'primary factor' of personality. In brief, these are as follows:

A Reserved v. warmhearted
B Less v. more intelligent
C Affected by feelings v. emotionally stable
E* Humble v. assertive
F Sober v. happy-go-lucky
G Expedient v. conscientious
H Shy v. venturesome
I Tough-minded v. tender-minded
L Trusting v. suspicious
M Practical v. imaginative
N Forthright v. shrewd
O Unperturbed v. apprehensive
Q1 Conservative v. experimenting
Q2 Group-oriented v. self-sufficient
Q3 Undisciplined self-conflict v. controlled
Q4 Relaxed v. tense

In addition, Forms C and D contain a 'motivational distortion' scale, intended
to be used in the detection of non-typical response patterns in situations such
as occupational selection, where respondents may be inclined to intentional or
unintentional faking.

Each scale in Forms C and D contains 6 to 8 items. Each item (except for
those in the intelligence scale) is a statement or question presenting and/or
contrasting self-descriptions, a choice of preferred behaviours or hypothetical
generalized social situations. Three response categories are provided of which
the second is generally an 'uncertain', 'in between' or 'sometimes' category.
Item content ranges from reports of mild somatic symptoms ('I have occasionally had a brief touch of faintness, dizziness . . .'), through occupational

---

* No D.

preferences to opinions on social mores ('I think most people take their duties to the community seriously enough'). Items in the British editions conform to English (rather than American) orthography, and minor cultural adjustments (cricket for baseball, etc.) have also been made.

Forms C and D contain a total of 105 items each, items from the various scales being intermixed in a rough cyclic order.

Purpose

The 16PF, along with the High School Personality Questionnaire (q.v.) was developed in intimate connection with the personality theory of the principal author, R. B. Cattell, and is intended as a general-purpose measure of what, in his view, are the fundamental variables of human personality. Thus it is applicable in clinical, counselling, employment, educational, marriage guidance and research settings, to name only some areas which have received specific attention.

Item preparation

The history of the 16PF is long and not a little controversial. Its origins lie in research conducted in the 1940s and it was originally seen by its authors as a temporary expedient, doomed to extinction as better, more objective, personality measures, not involving self-report, were developed. Such better measures proved more elusive than anticipated, and the 16PF has been successively revised and updated. There are at present five forms of the test: Forms A and B contain 187 items each, C and D 105; Form E is intended for adult subjects of low reading attainment. But since the questionnaire is embedded in a specific detailed theory of personality, the origins of each of the Forms and the stages in item selection are buried somewhat in a long, and sometimes impenetrable, series of research publications.

The general strategy of development involved:

(1) item selection by use of factor analytic techniques.
(2) attempts at factor matching between questionnaire scales and other personality assessment methods.
(3) refinement of the scales in successive research studies, iterating where possible (1) and (2).

The extent to which elements of this strategy have been successfully implemented remains controversial, and is the subject of a continuing and occasionally acerbic research literature. No comprehensive, complete or easily accessible account of the origins of the current forms of the questionnaire is available from a single source. Even an exhaustive literature search leaves some questions unanswered.

Generalized, and usually bland or not unsympathetic, accounts of the origins of the 16PF are given in many general textbooks of psychology and personality theory. However, the gap between a textbook account and actuality should not be underestimated.

Administration

Full details on completing the questionnaire are printed on the cover of the test booklet. The usual exhortations common to most personality tests ('answer what is true for *you*', etc.) are present, but high ability subjects may feel a little patronized by the tone of the instructions. The test is untimed, though the Manual suggests 25–35 minutes is required to complete each of Forms C and D. Apart from the need to establish good rapport with the subject, the administration of the test gets only brief attention in the Manual. In practice it is virtually self-administering, although occasionally individuals have difficulty in correctly matching items in the questionnaire to the appropriate response boxes on the separate answer sheet.

Standardization

American norms for Forms C and D of the 16PF are based on a sample of 'nearly 5000' stratified by community size, socio-economic status, geographical location, and race and matched to USA census data. Norm tables are presented for high-school students, college students and general population, age-corrected to 17, 20 and 30 years respectively. Note, however, that age was not a stratifying variable in the sampling. More than half of the total sample comes from school and college groups so far as can be judged. The 'nearly 5000' subjects in the test of the description of the sampling procedure become 5077 and 5040 in the norm tables themselves. The norm supplement describes a simple method of age-correcting scores based on linear trends, but does not detail the derivation of the age-correction factors provided.

Roughly 700–800 subjects of school age form the basis of the high-school norms, numbers varying across forms of the test.

British undergraduate norms, based on a volunteer sample of 1259 drawn from most of the universities in the country, and roughly equally split by sex and arts/science discipline are provided in a separate supplement. The Handbook to the 16PF, a separate publication, additionally gives statistical data on scores from various occupational groups, etc.

Scoring

Two stencils are required to score the test, assuming that machine scoring services are unavailable. Scores on each scale are sums of integer weights of 0, 1 or 2 for each item. The procedure is routine and straightforward.

Reliability

The Manual distinguishes two forms of test-retest reliability: 'dependability' (short time interval between test occasions) and 'stability' (long time interval), and admits these and 'equivalence—that is, parallel (alternate) form reliability—as relevant to 'consistency' of the test with itself. So far as Forms C and D are concerned the only test-retest indices provided are 'dependability' coefficients for Forms C and D combined based on 150 American undergraduates. Coefficients range from 0.67–0.86. Correlations between Forms C and D versions of the scales range from 0.16–0.61, discounting one value given as 0.15 as an almost certain misprint. This discrepancy between two approaches to the estimation of reliability, test-retest values being rather higher in general and much higher for certain scales, is disturbing, has implications for the construct validity of the scales, and is discussed further below.

Internal consistency measures are not provided in the Manual, although they are reported in the research literature, being in general close to the 'equivalence' coefficients in the Manual.

Validity

The Manual presents only what are referred to as 'concept validities' for Forms C and D combined. Concept validity is defined as the correlation between the scale in question and the 'pure' factor it represents. To calculate such a correlation it is first necessary to conduct a factor analysis and succeed in identifying the appropriate 'pure' factor. To date, only Cattell and his co-workers have reported success in this enterprise for the full set of scales, and this approach to assessing the validity of the test remains a matter of controversy. It certainly yields large correlation coefficients: 0.45–0.91 is the range reported for Forms C and D combined. Such figures should, however, be considered as analogous to the square-roots of internal consistency estimates of reliability rather than as validity coefficients in the more conventional sense. Correlations between the scales and external criterion variables are alluded to in the Manual. Various such correlations are to be found in the Handbook, and very many have appeared in the research literature.

Interpretation

Guidance on interpretation is given in terms of descriptions of typical behaviour for high and low scorers on each scale. The 'motivational distortion' scale may be used to detect distortion of an individual's true scores by specific situationally related factors (e.g. attempts at 'faking good' when applying for employment). The Manual supports a combination of actuarial methods and 'knowledge of the psychological nature of the factors' as the basis of interpretation. Much emphasis is placed on the primacy of the 16 factors as the fundamental variables of personality, and the importance of developing knowledge and clinical judgement. However, the Manual also provides a means of deriving four 'second-order factor scores', by weighting and summing the scores on the 16 scales, thus providing broader, and effectively more reliable measures. The Handbook provides yet more ways of deriving additional scores.

General evaluation

The quality of the 16PF is most uneven. The psychometric adequacy of the scales, by conventional standards, varies from excellent to abysmal. Proper evaluation, even by an experienced and sophisticated user, is constantly hampered by the idiosyncrasies of terminology and incompleteness of detail in the supporting Manual and Handbook. These documents mix apologia for Cattell's theory and methods, argument for use of certain terminology and rather laboured instruction in the use of correction factors and the like, with the essential reporting of detail and provision of guidelines for interpreting the scores obtained. The appearance of abundant detail is deceptive, since there are issues of importance which get no attention at all.

Principal amongst these is the question of the extent to which the 16 personality scales may properly be regarded as having discriminant validity. That is to say, do the scales each measure a different attribute, and is it the same attribute for nominally equivalent scales in different forms? Whatever the facts concerning the research underpinning the 16PF, and the reality or otherwise of the factors, a scale such as N in Form A of the 16PF which is reported as having test-retest reliability as high as 0.78 yet an alternate form correlation of 0.21 cannot be used with any confidence. In a number of cases, correlations amongst scales are excessive in view of the alternate form reliabilities. Seven of the scales (C, G, L, N, O, Q3, Q4) are involved in patterns of correlation which cast doubt on the empirical distinctness of various scales.

A second issue—the trade-off of bandwidth against reliability—does receive attention, but its treatment is inadequate. A test such as the 16PF gains in scope, i.e. measures many distinct variables, at the expense of measuring less accurately, having few items per scale. The implications of the low reliability of some of the scales, or indeed of the very considerable variation in reliability estimates across scales, is nowhere made clear. Some scales—such as L, M and N—have standard errors of measurement which are truly spectacular, and quite generally there should be a warning to users of the test that scores on individual scales will not bear much interpretation.

On the other hand, when used actuarially, combining scores on various scales to predict some criterion using an equation based on empirical research, the 16PF has shown a good deal of utility. It is one of the two most widely used personality measures in the UK, *faute de mieux* rather than because of intrinsic merit.

Any prospective user will have to attempt to cope with a rationale, a set of methods and a point of view which are presented as intimately bound up in the use of the test, and which (quite inaccurately) are represented as being central in modern psychology. Yet the very controversy surrounding Cattell's work has led to an extensive literature in which almost all the relevant issues have been aired. In this sense the 16PF is one of the best-documented tests available. However, its use as a source of interpretable 'facts' about the personality of individuals has considerable potential for harm except in the most skilled, experienced and prudent hands.

Intending users should acquaint themselves in detail with the research literature: they may find their enthusiasm for the test inversely proportional to the extent of their reading.

Study Habits Inventory

Reviewed by S. F. Blinkhorn

Author: C. Gilbert Wrenn
Publisher: Stanford University Press
Distributor: NFER-Nelson
Age: high school seniors, college students
1934
Revised edition, 1941 reviewed
Group test

Test content

The inventory consists in four sections: 'Reading and Note-taking Techniques' (5 items); 'Habits of Concentration' (4); 'Distribution of Time and Social Relationships in Study' (8); 'General Habits and Attitudes of Work' (11).

Items are statements couched in the first person singular. Three responses are allowed for: 'rarely or never', 'sometimes', 'often or always'. No attempt appears to have been made to balance the apparent desirability of affirmative responses to the items either within or across the four sections. The instructions emphasize reporting of actual habits of study, that is to say respondents are invited to describe their behaviour in terms of the items in the inventory.

Purpose

The Manual emphasizes the use of the inventory as an aid to counselling and/or self improvement, to 'assist students to recognise the particular habits which may be keeping them from attaining their best scholastic achievement'.

Item preparation

From an initial pool, items were selected which discriminated within pairs of university students matched for intelligence but exhibiting contrasting extremes of scholastic achievement. Roughly one in three items were retained after a two-stage development process. Essentially the method of scale construction was empirical criterion keying explicitly modelled after the development of the Strong Vocational Interest Blank.

Administration

As a self report inventory without special design features which might require carefully controlled administration, no special procedures are recommended for this test. The Manual suggests that twenty minutes be allowed for completion. The test booklet is disposable.

Standardization

None.

Scoring

Scoring is by stencil scoring key. Integer scoring weights in the range -13 to $+10$ are assigned to each response, and response weights summed. No indication whatever is given in the Manual as to how scores should be evaluated.

Reliability

No indices are reported in the Manual.

Validity

Correlations between total score on the inventory and grade-point-averages for unspecified groups of unknown size of 'students' lie in the range 0.24–0.58. These results appear to have been obtained between 1935 and 1940 in the USA.

Interpretation

No specific interpretive guidelines are provided.

General evaluation

This inventory has little to offer other than a list of 28 study-related behaviour tendencies. From a modern perspective it appears astonishingly naive in construction (and appallingly documented to boot). So little detail is given in the pamphlet that passes for a Manual, that it takes a careful comparison of scoring key and test form, to discover that 10 of the 28 items have response weights which defy logic. For instance, *never* missing important points in lectures while copying notes on something which has gone before scores +10. *Sometimes* missing such points scores −9 while *often or always* missing them scores 0. Thus the student who always misses important points has better study habits than the merely occasionally preoccupied. Were some theoretical or practical account of this oddity presented, one might feel easier with what appears to be the outcome of uncritical acceptance of the results of a radically empirical scale construction technique. Since one in three of the items are scored unaccountedly oddly, it may be assumed that the other two-thirds have been subject to no more critical scrutiny. Inadequate sample sizes may well be to blame. An inventory whose Manual has not been revised in 40 years, and which fails dismally to meet minimal standards of documentation and technical reporting, can scarcely be considered usable in any serious sense. This test requires urgent technical support, or it should be withdrawn from publication forthwith.

Study of Values

Reviewed by M. B. Youngman

Author: adapted by Sylvia Richardson from 3rd edition, 1960, by Gordon W. Allport, Philip E. Vernon and Gardner Lindzey
Publisher: NFER-Nelson (by arrangement with Houghton Mifflin Company, USA)
Distributor: NFER-Nelson

Age: College students (or adults with equivalent education)
1931 (USA edition); S not stated; Revised 1951, 1960 (USA)
1965 (British edition)
Group test

Test content

The Study of Values is a two-part inventory containing six value dimensions. These correspond to the six types identified by Spranger, the *Theoretical*, the *Economic*, the *Aesthetic*, the *Social*, the *Political* and the *Religious*. Part 1 comprises 30 items in the form of questions for which two possible answers are offered. For example: 'Which of the following would you be most likely to listen to on the radio: (a) a party political broadcast; (b) a religious service?' (Item 6). The testee is asked to respond in one of four specified styles ranging from complete agreement with one answer (representing one of the six dimensions) to complete agreement with the other (representing a different dimension). For the 15 questions of Part 2 a four-option ranking structure is used. Each hypothetical question has four response situations which represent four of the six dimensions. The testee has to rank these in order of preference. The result of this test structure is that each of the six dimensions is tapped by 20 questions, 10 in each part. Since items define two or four dimensions the structure also implies inter-related dimensions.

The version supplied is described as the first British version. It depends on earlier American versions for its overall content, but all individual items have been rewritten. The author admits that this may have slightly changed the nature of some of the dimensions, especially the *Social* value where the original altruistic emphasis has been broadened.

Purpose

'The Study of Values aims to measure the relative importance of six basic interests or motives in personality' (p. 3). The concentration on an educated adult population and the provision of self-scoring facilities could suggest a purely personal use, but the author does stress that the test 'should be used only when there is supervision and guidance in the interpretation of results by people who have had considerable experience in psychological testing and personality theory' (p. 3). The final section of the Manual lists a variety of possible uses for the test. One area of use covers the usual counselling, vocational guidance and selection associated with tests for adults. However, almost as much attention is paid to the educational nature of the test. It is suggested that students in the behavioural disciplines are likely to benefit by completing the test and then discussing their results because of the practical demonstration such an application offers. Even on personal grounds it is suggested that the kind of self-analysis afforded by the test is a valuable opportunity for an individual provided appropriate interpretation and discussion is also made available. There is also a summary of various findings resulting from many research applications of the test, although only one reference concerns a British application.

Item preparation

No information is given on the derivation and evaluation of individual items, beyond the general expectations of the British version as already referred to under Purpose above. This seems particularly regrettable in view of the admission that all items were rewritten (p. 9).

Administration

Limiting application of the test to educated adults simplifies many aspects of administration. Even so the Manual is very comprehensive on the method of administration and on the kind of guidance that should be given to testees. Responses are recorded in the test booklet, but completion can be individual, or in groups, or even in absentia since testees are allowed to fill in the booklet at home so long as the supervision conditions are met.

Various time requirements are recommended, depending on the mode of administration. In the simplest situation where completion only is required, it is suggested that most subjects complete the booklet in about 20 minutes. Where discussion or interpretation is also required a further hour should be allowed. This is considered particularly important if the test is completed at home.

There are several suggestions for familiarizing testees with the test and with the response procedures. The typical reassurance that the test is not an ability measure and that there are no right or wrong answers is mentioned. The tester's attention is also drawn to the slightly unusual response methods the test employs. Overall the administration instructions seem clearly presented, pertinent yet succinct.

Standardization

Standardization of the British version was carried out on a sample of 324 men and 326 women. Its detailed composition is given as: university students (64 men, 52 women); training college students and secondary-modern teachers (118, 111); adult students (41, 79); sixth form (40, 54); miscellaneous (61, 30);

totalling 324 men and 326 women. No representativeness is specified or claimed for this sample and it is difficult to identify any population it could represent. There is a clear bias towards students of education and any generalization beyond that interest group is likely to be suspect.

The results of the standardization are presented as a table of averages for men and women (Manual, p. 15), as a profile chart (Test Booklet, p. 12) and as a table giving the scores associated with various percentile ranges (Test Booklet, p. 12). There is no further subdivision, for example, by age or by occupation. The very limited nature of the standardization data may be partly compensated by the demonstration of similarity between results for the British and American versions. Accepting this comparability would allow American results to be referred to for more specific subsamples. However, the evidence offered for comparison is too sparse for any confident conclusion to be drawn.

Scoring

Anyone using the test should have little or no difficulty over scoring. The Manual provides detailed step-by-step instructions on all aspects of scoring, including those important inevitabilities of missing responses and verification of totals. There is a slight inconsistency in the timings offered since although an earlier comment estimated completion time as 20 minutes, and scoring is estimated as 5 minutes per test, there is a global estimate suggesting one hour for taking and scoring.

The scoring procedures are incorporated in the Test Booklet and, therefore, anyone completing the test should be able to obtain personal scores with the minimum of bother. As with the administration instructions the scoring details are carefully presented. The scores obtained are raw scores with a maximum of 60 for each value. There is no attempt to incorporate any correction or standardization in the British version, and consequently variations between the different value scores need not necessarily be indicative of any personal bias. Sample average profiles themselves exhibit variation in value levels.

Reliability

Item analyses were performed on two samples ($n = 198$ and 256) of a similar constitution to the standardization samples reported earlier. The Manual reports various statistics based on the second sample but it is not clear how accurate these results are because of certain confusions in the reporting. KR-20 reliabilities are said to be calculated from 'means' representing only the accepted items, whilst 'totals' include all items. It is not clear whether 'means' refers to 'mean biserial correlations' or to some other mean. Either way, the reported values are likely to be inflated by virtue of being derived from simultaneous item rejection and validation. The quoted reliabilities range from 0.78 for *Theoretical* to 0.95 for *Religious*, although the latter value is 0.11 higher than any other. All the quoted values are within 0.05 of the 1951 American results. Compared with values typically achieved for personality scales the reliabilities reported here do seem acceptable.

Validity

The Manual heading 'Some Evidence Relating to the Validity of the British Form' is not immediately encouraging and indeed the evidence presented is not particularly relevant. There is a long deliberation over the apparently greater variability between scores for the six values for the British Form, but no direct examination of whether the value scores reflect actual values. This discussion does include a table comparing scores for 205 'Teachers' and 237 'Non-teachers' but the differences are very small (all less than 1.3 on averages of around 30). The only statistical significant difference shows Non-teachers to score higher on the *Political* value (1.29 points) which in itself is difficult to interpret.

Indirect evidence is offered in the form of tables of occupational profiles for various American samples. A wide range of occupations is represented and males and females are listed separately. However, of the 29 categories presented only 7 involve samples of over 200. A major reservation would attach to the assumption that one could expect similar value profiles for comparable British occupational groups. An even more serious limitation is the absence of any attempt to relate obtained value scores to other criteria of personal values.

Interpretation

There is regular reference to the importance of expert guidance and interpretation, but the underlying assumption seems to be that such guidance should mainly concentrate on the limited personal interpretability of psychometric instruments. The more detailed information on interpretation is given in the form of suggestions for possible uses, and particularly in psychological research. Even here, though, the Manual is more a list of sources for further study since only the briefest of comments is offered in each category of use.

Test use

Only one reference is given for the British version and that to an unpublished thesis held by the University of London.

An extensive bibliography lists numerous references to applications of the American version. Unfortunately none of these is dated after the 1960 revision.

Accordingly, potential users are advised to bear in mind the substantial differences between the British version and the version used in the researches referred to in the Manual.

General evaluation

It is usually desirable for research measures to exhibit a theoretical relationship with the problem area and the Study of Values does satisfy that need with its derivation from Spranger's types. Even if some other theoretical standpoint is preferred, there does seem to be sufficient recognizable reality in the value definitions to meet many research interests. The major qualification to this initial appeal must be the difficulty of establishing any acceptable empirical validity. Commendable though the quoted reliability figures might be, the prerequisite for confident use of an instrument must be demonstrated validity. It may be that the American evidence (such as that emanating from the various research applications) is sufficient to fulfil this requirement, but without that any general recommendation must be withheld.

On practical grounds the instrument has many virtues. The administration and scoring procedures are well presented, and they appear straightforward and effective. The overall presentation of the test is tidy, and its content is likely to be interesting. The content areas should be reasonably stable over time, but in view of the distant date of publication, and assuming that the British trials were conducted several years earlier still, it would be desirable for an updating of the standardization information to be pursued.

There are certain limitations (over and above the substantial problem of validation) which do need to be borne in mind. Under the appropriate sections above, comments have drawn attention to the limited information and guidance offered on interpretation. This would preclude any diagnostic use of the instrument and it would question any normative use, in the area of vocational selection for example. Probably the most likely type of use would be in research and the emphasis of much of the discussion in the Manual does support that suggestion. Not only would such applications benefit from the explicit theoretical basis of the instrument, but they would also be assisted by the ease of administration and scoring. If such applications can substantiate the value of the British version, it should then be possible for someone to collate the findings from these researchers to produce the validation evidence still needed.

Other topics

List of reviews

CSMS Science Reasoning Tasks 670
Comprehension Test for College of Education Students 680
Garnett College Test 683
Maitland Graves Design Judgement Test 685
The Meier Art Tests 688
Modern Language Aptitude Test 692
Seashore Measure of Musical Talents 696
Wing Standardized Tests of Musical Intelligence 701

CSMS Science Reasoning Tasks

Reviewed by J. R. Hartley

Authors:	Michael Shayer	(Tasks 1 and 2)
	Dietmar Kuchemann	(Task 3)
	Hugh Wylam and Michael Shayer	(Task 4)
	Michael Shayer and Hugh Wylam	(Task 5)
	Philip Adey	(Task 6)
	Hugh Wylam	(Task 7)

Publisher: NFER-Nelson
Distributor: NFER-Nelson
Age ranges: 10–16 years (Set 1; complete)*
10–14 years (Set 2)
13–16 years of USA college students (Set 3)
1973–78 (Preparation and trials)
1977; 1979 (Copyright dates on materials)
1980 (Version 1); 1982 (M‡, T)
Group test†

Test content and purpose

The seven tasks which form the CSMS Science Reasoning Test were developed during 1974–80 by a research team based at Chelsea College, University of London, and funded by the Social Science Research Council. The overall purpose was to provide materials, suitable for group administration, which would determine the Piagetian level of operational thinking which a pupil has reached. Original Piaget and Inhelder data and research contexts were used as a basis for this development work. Of particular interest is 'the relationship

---

* The tasks can be used individually or a group of them chosen. (Using more than three carefully chosen tasks is not likely to increase the validity of the performance estimates). However, the tasks are being arranged in three new package sets. Set 1 (which includes all the seven tasks), Set 2 (which covers the concrete and formal Piagetian stages of development), and Set 3 (which spans the mature concrete to formal operational stages). Additionally, there is a Mini and a Full Specimen Set of the Tasks).

† The authors have adapted experimental tasks which were used by Piaget and Inhelder during individual interviews when the pupils themselves handled apparatus. The CSMS Science Reasoning Tasks are designed for use with *groups* but are based on demonstrations by the tester together with diagrams and written questions. The tasks can be used for individual testing, but are more restrictive and attract a less varied response than the original Piaget/Inhelder interviews. On the other hand, the tasks do not require as much experience to administer.

‡ As well as booklets which accompany the tasks, NFER publish "A General Guide" (*Authors:* Wylam, H. and Shayer, M.) which should be read by all intending users. The version used in this review was published in 1980.

between the optimum Piagetian level at which a pupil can function and the understanding of science which he or she can achieve'. It is maintained that the data provided by the individual's task performances 'assist in deciding a suitable (science) curriculum to follow'. The tasks can assist in decision making and guide curriculum planning and the choice of curriculum materials. Within a research team the tasks can become a tool to aid the formative evaluation of curriculum developments.

The tasks, each occupying 35–50 minutes, use simple equipment which 'should be available in every school'. These seven tasks are set in different contexts so that their administrative requirements, their demands on the pupils, and the specific purposes they assume have some variation. Accordingly, in this review, the headings of test content and purposes are taken together for each of the seven tasks.

Task I: Spatial Relationships

This task is based on Piaget and Inhelder (1956). It contains four questions, and tests co-ordination of spatial relationships through drawing. Two items concern the sketching of jam jars with water levels, and then with plumb-line, as they are imagined to be tilted and placed on their sides. Other questions ask pupils to draw a mountain/houses scene and the view when looking down a long straight road lined with trees. The direction of the water surface and plumb-line, and points of perspective, determine the pupil's conceptual level, which on this task can range from pre-conceptual through pre-operational (1), early concrete operational (2A) to late concrete (2B) or above (2B+). The questions should occupy about 30 minutes.

Task II: Volume and Heaviness

Based on Piaget and Inhelder (1974), the task includes: concentration of liquids poured from one cylinder to another, substance-conservation, intuitions of displacement following immersions of plasticine in a measuring cylinder full of water, flotation/displacement using solids (metal and plasticine) in block and then in disc form, notions of density following the flotation of one box containing fluid inside another, and, finally, a version of Archimedes' principle. The pupil is not only asked for conclusions but for reasons and explanations of his methods.

From these data the pupil's conceptual levels are assessed. The rationale is that, initially, the child does not differentiate aspects of 'size', i.e. mass, weight, volume and density. Following conservation of substance (early concrete operational Stage 2A) and, a little later, weight (middle concrete Stage 2A/2B), volume is conserved and distinguished from mass and weight (mature concrete Stage 2B/3A). This paves the way for an analytical concept of density through weight/volume ratio (early formal operational thinking 3A) and for the concept of flotation through the ratio of weight of the same volume of water. The task is hierarchical and takes about 50 minutes to complete.

Task III: The Pendulum

This is based on Piaget and Inhelder (1958, Chapter 4). The pupil has to determine the effects of the length of pendulum (long/short), the weight of bob (light/heavy) and the strength of push (gentle/hard) on the time of swing. After predicting the effects, demonstrations are given, and from these data, the pupil develops his conclusions. (Only length is an important influence, but he has to overcome strong intuitions in order to realize this). He is also required to suggest experiments to test the effects, and a series of questions examine control of variables (this requires formal levels of thinking). The task takes approximately 45 minutes to complete and categorizes pupils from late concrete (2B) to late formal (3B) operational thinking.

Task IV: Equilibrium in the Balance

The exercise is based on Piaget and Inhelder (1958, Chapter 11). The pupil is required to recognize and use inverse proportions when a pivoted metre rule functions as a simple beam balance. As well as making predictions, the pupil sees a demonstration and is asked to set down his explanations of the data. A series of items manipulate additional weights and positions, and the task concludes with a question testing understanding of the beam principle in terms of virtual work. The questions range from late concrete (2B) to early formal (3A) and, for the virtual work item, to late formal operational stage of thinking (3B). The task should be completed in approximately 35 minutes.

Task V: The Inclined Plane

This is an extension of Task IV. It requires the pupil to recognize and use inverse proportions for a truck model held on an inclined plane by a weight hung over a pulley. The variables are the weight of the truck, the hanging weight and the angle of the inclined plane. The questions use concrete reasoning for the effects of changing variables singly, but for explaining the connection between truck and hanging weights at different angles of incline, the variables have to be integrated and considered as one system. The question also uses the principle of virtual work through consideration of the weights and the vertical distances they move. This requires proportional reasoning (late formal Stage 3B) and a rejection of angle incline as the most important variable.

The task is based on Inhelder and Piaget (1958, Chapter 12) and takes approximately 45 minutes to complete.

Task VI: Chemical Combinations

The mixing of unknown liquids is demonstrated; from the observed colour changes, the pupils have to infer combinational rules and give reasons for their answers. Other items require the planning of experiments to test related hypotheses. Two experimental contexts form the complete task. The first, taking 20 minutes uses phenolphthalein as an acid-alkali indicator; the second, which is more complex, uses the oxidation of potassium iodide and the reduction of iodine by sodium thiosulphate, to provide the reactions and colour changes. This second task requires a 40 minute working session. Appreciating that it is the combination of liquids which determine colour changes, requires formal reasoning and so the range of answers taken during the task distinguishes between the concrete (2B− and 2B) and formal (3A and 3B) stages of cognitive development. The task is based on Inhelder and Piaget (1958, Chapter 7).

Task VII: Flexible Rods

Based on Inhelder and Piaget (1958, Chapter 3), the task is concerned with variables (length, weight, shape, thickness, metal material) affecting the bending of metal rods. Experiments are demonstrated and pupils provide conclusions and deductions together with explanations of their answers. The effects of some of the variables, e.g. thickness and length, are intuitable, but those of cross-sections and type of metal less so. Some items test control of variables and experimental strategy, and in later questions some of the variables act in a compensatory manner. The test grades pupils from late concrete operational (2B) to the formal (3A and 3B) stages of thinking, and requires about 50 minutes for completion.

Thus all the tasks primarily assess pupils on a criterion, namely their optimum level of operational thinking following the Piagetian framework, and not in relation to other representatives of a standardized pupil population.

Item preparation

The principal aim was to develop Piagetian-type tasks which could be used to assess levels of operational thinking, when they were administered to a pupil-group or a class, by an experienced teacher. The authors have tried to retain many of the advantages of the individual interview; thus the administrator demonstrates phenomena, provides data to set against pupil predictions, and makes sure the group fully understands what it is being asked. At the same time the tester must ensure objectivity in administration and in marking.

Each task was derived from the original Piagetian description with the marking instructions distinguishing between several levels of reasoning. Trials were based on up to eight versions, 'each piloted with at least one class of pupils of appropriate age and ability'. A final version, to settle instructions and scoring rules, was given to over 200 pupils. The sample of schools taking part in these items and scale developments was not chosen from a strict sampling frame, but contained sufficient variety in pupil age, ability and background. There was a mix of rural and urban comprehensives, some middle schools and some selective schools. The age range of 10–16 years with a wide spread of ability within these years was provided by a total test sample of over 1000 children.

An estimate of the level of operational thinking of a subject was obtained from his performance on the tasks overall (see section on Scoring below).

A plot of the percentages of subjects succeeding on an item, against the assigned Piagetian levels of the subjects, showed the discrimination level of that item. If an item showed poor discrimination it was eliminated, and where the discrimination gave a stage level different from the initially assigned trial level, the marking instructions were altered to account for this (interested readers are referred to Shayer, 1978). Sufficient items were included to cover the range and partition on a seven-point scale, from pre-operational to late-formal operational stages of thinking (General Guide, p. 8).

Administration

Clearly, great stress is placed on the proper administration of the seven tasks; general principles are discussed in the accompanying Guide, and each task has its own Manual containing explicit and detailed guidance. The type of administration lies between that of a conventional test and that of a lesson. Thus 'although the response sheets have the basic questions printed, each problem should be talked through in a way which seems appropriate to communicate it to the particular class' (General Guide, p. 12). If pupils do not understand what is required, 'they should be encouraged to say so'. Another important feature of the administration, and one which is central to the pupil's answering of the questions, is the demonstrations which provide phenomena/data to stimulate explanation, and/or feedback to set against pupils' predictions. Thus, 'it is important that the administrator is fluent with the moves described in the Task Manuals. A practice run is recommended, with some pupils if possible'. The apparatus used is readily available within schools. Note that the administration makes a deliberate use of the skills possessed by the experienced teacher. Also he must have discipline and control ('pupils must be seated to minimize copying yet be able to see the demonstrations') and must judge the pacing of the tasks ('the class should have enough time to become involved, but . . . without gaps in time which allow their attention to wander').

Standardization

The tasks allow an estimate of a pupil's level of operational thinking with respect to the Piagetian criteria. This estimate is made without reference to the performance of other pupils. However, age norms have been obtained by the authors for the CSMS Tasks I, II and III. A sample of approximately 10 000 schoolchildren was used, though numbers within a Task/Age Cell varied from 400 to 2000. The General Guide contains tables and graphs showing the percentage of children (total and by scores) at differing stages of reasoning by age. The age range spans 10:00–15:09. The Calvert Non-Verbal Reasoning Test was used to check the representativeness of the chosen sample and to permit generalization to the pupil population as a whole. The data from each school were combined and plotted using the school's Calvert data to provide a reference mean. The Piagetian percentage corresponding to a Calvert mean of 100 was taken as the value for a representative sample. Pupil samples of at least several hundreds were used and the pupil proportions/percentages at the various levels of operational thinking are reported with confidence intervals. The Guide provides two references to the details of this work which were used to comment on Piagetian notions of the Pupil-Age v. Thinking-Stage relationship. A general finding was that the 'spread of ability was much wider than had been previously thought'. Some small but significant sex differences are recorded.

Since the principal use is likely to be as a criterion-reference test, these procedures seem adequate. The age norms also provide some data of interest but the sampling and analysis restriction/procedures should be clearly borne in mind, and the results used for general background guidance.

Scoring

The Manual provided with each task contains detailed notes on acceptable answers to each item. However, since the questions require a constructed free response, the marker must interpret particular forms of words which are used and 'should seek to maximize the understanding of the teacher thinking about the reasoning strategies of his pupils' (General Guide, p. 12). Within a task some items are not scored since they serve as an introduction or as a focus for pupils' attention. For those which are assessed, each pupil scores 1 if he or she gives an appropriate response, i.e. meets the criterion of the stage of reasoning given to that item. All other responses score zero. The marks are entered on a class assessment sheet which is clearly labelled for each task. Apart from Task 1, a total score is not computed; instead the assessor applies rules to determine the operational thinking level generally followed by the pupil for that task. The rules follow a two-thirds success principle, judging that pupils should be categorized within a stage if they succeed on two-thirds of the items which characterize that stage.

Reliability

For each of the Tasks II to VII, an internal consistency coefficient (KR-20) was calculated using sample sizes of 240 pupils for Task II and 560 for the remainder. (The method of sample-drawing was outlined in the Item preparation section). The reliability coefficients ranged from 0.76 for Tasks V and VI containing 14 and 16 item respectively, to 0.86 for Task VII (Flexible Rods) with 17 items. For Task I, an alternative method resulted in an internal consistency coefficient of 0.82 (Shayer, 1978, p. 139 *et seq.*).

A test-retest reliability was also calculated, but the sample sizes were extremely small, ranging from 24 for Task III to 38 for Task VII. The time gap between testing occasions was 3–4 months; the calculated coefficients were adjusted to correspond to the range of the internal consistency sample, but in general the test-retest values were lower (varying from 0.64 for Task VI to 0.85 for Task VII). This might be expected because of the fluctuations of an individual from one occasion to another. Having regard to the relative sample sizes, it is clear that the internal consistency measure is the more precise.

Since each of the Tasks gives an assessment of the pupil's level of operational thinking, the between-task estimates can be compared. Such correlations were calculated for a sample of 481 children who completed all of the Tasks IV, V, VI, and VII (Equilibrium in the Balance, Inclined Plane, Chemical Combinations, and Flexible Rods, respectively). The coefficients ranged from 0.49–0.69 (average 0.58).

The reliability data showed that 'from the use of one of the Tasks, on a single occasion, there is a 95 per cent probability that the individual's true mean lies within ±1.1 levels' (General Guide, p. 14) (but note that this estimate, and the coefficients above, are based on the assumption that the stages lie on a seven-point equal-interval scale). It is claimed that this error of estimate can be narrowed to ±0.7 levels approximately if an appropriate pair of tasks is chosen. This would require a testing time of 85–95 minutes and the reliability may then be raised to 0.91. The General Guide counsels against using more than two tasks to raise the reliability higher—'formal operational thinking is a sufficiently unitary theory for any test beyond two to be giving a redundant signal' (p. 14).

Validity

The science reasoning tasks are based on the developmental theory of Piaget and performances are classified in accordance with his qualitative stages of intellectual growth. It is argued that because this assessment derives from pupils' mental processing, the CSMS test can be used equally well to match curriculum demands to pupils' reasoning capabilities, and also serve curriculum evaluation studies.

It is not our concern to comment on the validity of the Piagetian model for cognitive development. There are ample references in the literature (some supplied by the General Guide, p. 6) for the teacher and research worker to determine if the model (and hence the CSMS test) is appropriate for their work.

It is necessary, though, (1) to consider the agreement between data provided by the CSMS Group Test, and those obtained by Piagetian interviews (concurrent validity); (2) to establish if the notion of operational thinking underpinning observed levels of performance has sufficient coherence and explanatory power (construct validity); and (3) to determine if science curricula can be analysed in Piagetian terms which show their intellectual requirements, and hence if the matching curricula decisions based on the CSMS tests are justified, and if they contain information which could not be obtained from more conventional classroom tests.

Before reviewing evidence, it should be noted that the teacher can select tasks from any of the seven provided within the CSMS Test, and that validity can be increased 'by pairing tasks which involve different schemes'. For example, Tasks II and IV which 'tap different aspects of scientific thinking over and above the general organization of thinking which they both estimate' (General Guide, p. 14).

Comparisons were made between Science Reasoning Test data (for Tasks III to VII), and the assessment on these tasks conducted through individual interviews. The numbers of pupils involved were small (between 15 and 24 per task); the group test always preceded the interview by a period of one week to one month. The mean differences (assuming the stages are placed on a seven-point equal-interval scale) were approximately one-fifth of a stage on average and showed no systematic variation. The mean of the Group/Interview correlations was 0.67—lower than the Group Test/Retest correlation of 0.77. This is taken to support the comparability of the Science Reasoning Test with the Piagetian Interview technique, but 'there is some extra source of variation when subjects are interviewed over and above the variability found when giving the group-test'. However, the small numbers of pupils involved limit the authority of these conclusions.

A sample of 647 14 year-old pupils were tested on Tasks III–VII. The estimates (based on a sample of about 550) they each provided, of reasoning level profiles, were compared; there was little difference in the overall mean levels on the different tasks (3.28–3.47 using the seven-point scale for the stages), but a greater variation in the proportions of pupils occupying the different substages (on average about 6 per cent). The average of the inter-task correlation matrix (with a sample of 481) was 0.58 and when the coefficients were factor analysed, one factor explained 59 per cent of the variance. Over the five tasks, the common factor variance was 2–3 times greater than the specific variance attributable to each task. It is maintained that these data 'confirm the presence of a strong unitary construct underlying the five tasks'. Note that the samples were confined to one age group, but the task data supplied by that age group show a consistency of view. However, the experiments did not use other independent measures of the reasoning construct or other related constructs by way of comparison or contrast; neither did they investigate the explanatory power of the construct outside the actual reasoning tasks themselves.

Finally, the General Guide (p. 24) refers to a study in which Tasks II and III were used to check that science curricula could be analysed in terms of the levels of thinking required for their understanding. Samples of 26 and 86 12–13 year-old pupils completed the Reasoning Tasks following a two-month section of work taken from the Nuffield Combined Science Curriculum. Also a 50–60 item test assessed course objectives 'which laid emphasis on the understanding of concepts rather than recall'. The correlations between the Science Reasoning performance data and the achievement post-tests were 0.77 ($n = 26$) and 0.78 ($n = 86$).

In this experiment sample sizes were relatively small and concerned only one area of application. The data give support for the predictive validity of the reasoning tasks, though they were not set against other measures which the teacher might employ for prediction. More extensive work is needed to enable these results to be generalized, and to give more precise data on how sensitive is the understanding of classroom curricula materials (and teaching approach) to the stage of operational thinking of pupils.

These concerns also require tools for the Piagetian analysis of curricula which can be used by teachers without specialized training. The CSMS team has been further engaged on this task.

Interpretation

Detailed guidance is given on the classification of pupil performances for each task in terms of the criterion levels of operational thinking. For a deeper understanding of the tasks and the interpretation of responses, those not conversant with the Piagetian framework are referred to Inhelder and Piaget (1958). Useful advice is given in the General Manual (p. 14) on the choosing of task combinations to ensure a balanced assessment, and on the ways the tasks can be used for curriculum development, for decision making, and for curriculum evaluation (pp. 14–15). Various matching policies between test results and the cognitive demands of teaching materials are also outlined.

General evaluation

The CSMS team has produced reasoning tasks which assess level of operational thinking. The tasks are adaptations of Piaget's experiments to allow group administration and, given the nature of the task, supporting data show them to have adequate reliability (internal consistency). The sample sizes of pupils used in the validity studies were usually small, and the results must be given a cautious interpretation. The data, though, show agreement with levels of reasoning assessments obtained from Piagetian-type interviews.

To suit particular purposes, teachers and research workers are able to make selections from seven independent tasks. The composite test is seen as an efficient research tool in its own right, particularly useful when individual Piagetian interviews are unnecessary or impracticable (e.g. when a stage assessment is needed for a group of pupils and limited time is available). It can be administered, without specialist training, by the experienced teacher.

A primary purpose of the CSMS test is to assist the researcher in curriculum evaluation, and the teacher in curriculum decision making by allowing materials to be chosen whose demands match the reasoning levels of the pupils. This claim raises interesting questions, for example, to what extent is success-ful classroom achievement dependent on the logical structure of the curriculum tasks irrespective of their content or the teaching approach? Is the accuracy of estimate of the test (about ± 1 stage level) sufficiently precise for hard curriculum decisions, or should the matching exercise be more loose and the CSMS test information supplemented by that from diagnostic tests? These are matters of theoretical as well as practical interest. The validation data provided by the team could not be comprehensive enough to address these questions adequately; they are issues raised by the tests themselves which, through experiment, can be used to provide some answers. During the next few years, the experience of using the CSMS tasks should permit a truer judgement of their worth both to educational research and to educational practice.

References

Inhelder, B. and Piaget, J. (1958). "The Growth of Logical Thinking". London, Routledge and Kegan Paul.

Lawson, A. E. and Renner, J. W. (1975). Relationships of science subject matter and developmental levels of learners. *Journal of Research in Science Teaching* 12, 347–358.

Piaget, J. and Inhelder, B. (1956). "The Child's Conception of Space". London: Routledge.

Piaget, J. and Inhelder, B. (1974). "The Child's Construction of Quantities". London: Routledge.

Shayer, M. (1978a). A test of the validity of Piaget's construct of formal operational thinking. Unpublished PhD thesis, University of London.

Shayer, M. (1978b). The analysis of science curricula for Piagetian level of any demand. *Studies of Science Education (Leeds)* 5, 115–130.

Shayer, M. (1979a). Has Piaget's construct of formal operational thinking utility? *British Journal of Educational Psychology* **49**, 265–276.

Shayer, M. (1979b). The match of science curriculum to the learner in the middle and secondary school. (Together with the response by Driver, R.). *In* "Cognitive Development Research in Science and Mathematics", pp. 62–86. Centre for Studies in Science Education, University of Leeds.

Comprehension Test for College of Education Students

Reviewed by Stephen Sharp

Author: E. L. Black
Publisher: NFER-Nelson
Distributor: NFER-Nelson
Age: Candidates for entry to training college and first-year training college students
1962 (M, T); S in early 1950s (?)
No revisions apparent
Group test

Test content

The test consists of seven comprehension passages which are not placed in any particular order. Each passage is followed by a number (between seven and ten) of items relating to the content of the passage. There are 60 items in all. Response requirements vary from underlining one out of a number (usually five) of alternative answers to supplying a missing word of which some letters are provided. The subjects of the passages are mainly political with some history and some ethics.

Purpose

Seven aims are given. The test '. . . . could be used to help and supplement other methods of selecting students for entry to college . . . to throw some light on their individual difficulties in understanding what they read . . . to show whether students are suited to certain alternative or advanced courses . . . the test should be helpful in comparing different groups of students . . . in furthering research on comprehension . . . in answering this test students should learn more about the uses of other objective tests . . . the results of the test will help to show the need for a planned approach by a united college staff to the general problem of students' reading' (Manual, p. 9).

Item preparation

The seven passages and 60 items were selected from 30 passages and 517 items. The aim was to isolate a general comprehension ability, as the criterion for the selection of the final items was that they should test 'as briefly as possible, and with as sharp discrimination as possible, the general ability tested by the whole of the experimental version . . . This was ensured by making each experimental version, as a whole, the criterion on which the item analysis was based' (Manual, p. 10). However, the Manual says nothing more detailed than this, so it is not possible to discover how varied the original passages were, how the items in the final version performed on item analysis, how many students were involved in the pretesting and how they were selected or, in general, how the final version was arrived at.

Administration

Emphasis is placed on accurate timing of the test. The students are given 45 minutes, some indication of the strictness of this limit being given by the fact that only 33 out of a sample of 100 students reached the last two items. Other aspects of the administration are very scanty. Apart from the booklet itself, students need only a pencil and, apart from starting and finishing the test, the supervisor speaks only to tell the students that 15 and 30 minutes have elapsed.

Standardization

The standardization group consisted of 679 male and 911 female first-year college students. They were arrived at by using random numbers to select a sample of training colleges of which all 'except one entered virtually a complete first year'. The number of colleges is not given nor are any details about that one college but it is stated that the random procedure was modified so as to ensure a close correspondence between the proportions of students of various types in the standardization group and in the total student population. The types of student used are those at 'normal' colleges, those at colleges established since 1945, those training to be technical teachers and those training to be art teachers. Appropriate figures are given and the profile of the standardization group over these categories is shown to correspond well to that of the general student population of 1952 which is presumably the date of standardization.

The standardization data yielded considerable evidence of sex differences and so separate norms are given for men and women. The norms convert raw scores into percentile ranks in bivariate tables with no reference to age.

Scoring

A scoring key is given and, as marking for each item is dichotomous, there should be no scope for differences between markers, although the Manual stresses the importance of an independent marking check. In cases where there are several methods of designating a response, the scoring key indicates which ones are acceptable, by using both specific instances for appropriate items and general guidelines to cover other cases.

Subject to the answers given in the key, marking appears straightforward and waterproof. However, the uniqueness of some of the answers is open to dispute; the fact that many of them involve the completion of a word of which some letters are missing inevitably introduces the possibility of candidates giving answers just as suitable as those in the key, yet no marks can be given for them.

Reliability

This was estimated from a sample of 127 male and 113 female first-year students 'drawn' (the Manual does not say how) from four colleges. The index used was 'the Kuder-Richardson formula' (presumably KR-20) which yielded a value of 0.94. As the ages of the students are not included in any of the calculations reported, there is no distinction in this case between fixed-age and variable-age estimates. No details of item analysis are given.

Validity

A validity study employed 79 male and 65 female students comprising the complete 1953 intake of two colleges. They were given the test during their first term in college and the marks were correlated with the students' performances after a two-year course in English Language ($r = 0.48$), Principles of Education ($r = 0.21$), Practice of Education ($r = 0.33$), Crafts ($r = 0.20$) and English Literature ($r = 0.18$). The fact that the first of these figures is higher than the others provides evidence of associative validity while its absolute value (accounting for 23 per cent of total variance) is a measure of its predictive validity for English Language performance.

Interpretation

As the test has such a limited aim, there is little to add to the list of purposes of the test given earlier. However, the Manual does provide some examples of groups of items with a common theme such as the ability to detect irony or the ability to recognize an author's intended meaning. There is no attempt to formulate these groups into proper subscales and their use seems to depend more on the test user's intuitive reading of the items than any information given in the Manual.

General evaluation

The objective of the test is very straightforward, i.e. to provide a measure of a fairly specific ability (English language comprehension) within a tightly-defined target population (first-year training college students). In pursuit of this rather narrow aim, the information provided by the Manual is competent but very brief. In particular, discussions of validity, reliability and test purpose are terse in the extreme. In practice, the test would presumably be used as part of a combination of tests to assess students' strengths and weaknesses and so the lack of supporting discussion may not be so damaging.

The main problem with this test lies in its age. The validity and other studies were carried out in the period 1952–55. The Manual is dated 1962, but no published uses of the test are reported for the intervening years, neither has the Manual been updated. This may be important since many of the comprehension passages are taken from books and newspapers current to the period. Topics covered include the Dean of Canterbury's view of Soviet communism in 1950, Molotov's personality and Hungarian Communist culture also of 1950. As such matters will clearly be less familiar to 1982 students than 1954 students, there must be some doubt cast on the norms reported. So much so that it seems safer to leave any serious use of this test until after a restandardization has been carried out, although it could also be argued that in this case it would be better to modernize some of the passages anyway, or in short to produce a new test. Along with the lack of research support in the case of this test, these drawbacks do not make this instrument a strong candidate for anyone interested in the comprehension ability of training college students.

Garnett College Test

Reviewed by R. Driver

Author: I. Macfarlane Smith
Publisher: NFER-Nelson

Distributor: NFER-Nelson
Age: students taking general course in Engineering Science in College of
  Further Education
1964–65 (S); 1966 (M, T)
1971 (M, T) (revised edition)
Group test

Test content

The test contains 110 items on the topics Mechanics (50 items), Heat (13) and
Electricity and Magnetism (47). The test is divided into two parts. Each part
includes matching pairs, true-false, sentence completion and multiple-choice
types of items. At least two-thirds of the items test simple recall of facts, the
other third assess the ability to apply simple laws in qualitative problems. SI
units are used.

Purpose

The test was originally constructed for use as an attainment test for students
taking the General Course in Engineering Science in Technical Colleges and in
Colleges of Further Education. It was designed to cover the published syllabus
for that course and the level of difficulty was intended to be appropriate for
students taking the one-year course (G*) and for those who were in the second
year of the two-year course (G2).

Administration

The test is designed to take one hour, 30 minutes for each part. Answers are
written on the test booklet. A marking key is given in the Manual as are
instructions for the test administration.

Standardization

This was undertaken in 1964–65 on 862 students in 27 Colleges of Further
Education in various parts of England who were on the G* and G2 courses. A
table of norms for converting raw scores to percentiles is given for the two parts
of the test separately and combined, and for students on the two courses G* and
G2.

Reliability

Two measures of reliability are given. The test-retest correlation for a sample
of 42 students was found to be 0.87, with an interval of six weeks between

testing. An estimate of reliability, or internal consistency of 0.92 was obtained from 110 scripts using a Kuder-Richardson formula (unspecified).

Validity

The test was designed as an attainment test for a particular Engineering course and its usefulness depends on the content of the course remaining stable. With the current changes taking place in FE courses and the introduction of TEC courses at this level this is not likely.

General evaluation

Since the syllabuses of Engineering courses are changing it is possible that this test may not now be appropriate to the content or methods of assessment of new courses in use in Technical Colleges and Further Education Institutions.

Maitland Graves Design Judgement Test

Reviewed by David O'Hare

Author: M. Graves
Publisher: The Psychological Corporation
Distributor: NFER-Nelson
Age: not specified; norms for USA college and high-school groups
1948 (M); 1946 (T); S not stated
Copyright renewed 1948; no revisions apparent
Self-administered

Test content

There are 90 items consisting of either two or three abstract designs. The final ten items consist of photographs of three-dimensional abstract or non-representational works. Each design within a pair or triad utilizes similar (though not always identical) elements. One of the designs in each item 'was organized in accordance with the fundamental principles of art structure' (described below), 'while the other design or designs violated one or more of these principles'. No specific examples are given to illustrate how the items reflect the 'fundamental principles' nor whether particular items have been constructed to reflect particular principles.

Purpose

The test was devised to 'measure certain components of aptitude for the appreciation or production of art structure'. This is held to involve 'evaluating the degree to which a subject perceives and responds to the basic principles of aesthetic order—unity, dominance, variety, balance, continuity, symmetry, proportion and rhythm'. The intention appears to be that the test should be used for selection purposes where 'aptitude for art' might be important.

Item preparation

One hundred and fifty items were originally prepared. All were non-representational, consisting of pairs or triads of abstract designs. These items were given to groups of art teachers, art students, and non-art students. There were three criteria for item selection, although it is not specified whether items had to pass all three criteria in order to be retained. These were: (1) agreement among art teachers as to the better design, (2) greater preference by art students than by non-art students, (3) an unspecified measure of internal consistency.

Administration

The test is self-administered. Subjects require the test booklet and an answer sheet. Subjects are requested to 'look at each page and decide which design you prefer'. There is no time limit.

Standardization

Groups of art and non-art students at 14 institutions (with a total of 1306 subjects) were used to provide separate norms for art and non-art students in college and high school. The high-school norms were based on only 150 students and likewise those for each institution were mostly based on very small numbers. The representativeness of these groups is clearly open to question and the additional fact that they are North American should make the British user view them with caution.

Scoring

The score is simply the number of items correctly endorsed with a maximum possible score, therefore, of 90.

Reliability

The only reported reliabilities are a split-half correlation coefficients (with Spearman-Brown corrections). These are given for each of several separate groups (art students, art teachers and non-art students) and range from 0.81–0.93. The sample sizes for each of these groups ranged from 36–246 totalling 1306 subjects.

Validity

No predictive validity was established. The author hoped that such evidence would subsequently be provided by users of the test. The only evidence of validity supplied in the Manual is provided by a comparison of the mean scores of art students and non-art students. These are 74.3 (standard deviation 8.45) and 49.4 (standard deviation 14.42), respectively, based on sample sizes of 673 and 410 students.

General evaluation

The test has not been widely used as an empirical tool. Millman and Chang (1967) administered the Maitland-Graves test together with the Meier Art Judgement Test and the Welsh Figure Preference Test to a group of 32 non-art students and found a low but significant correlation between the Maitland-Graves and the Welsh Test, but the Maitland-Graves and the Meier were quite uncorrelated (Spearman's rho = 0.19). The most detailed evaluation of the Maitland-Graves test has been conducted by Eysenck (1967, 1970). Eysenck (1967) carried out a principal components study of the intercorrelations between the 90 items. The first five components were obliquely rotated and the loadings of the items inspected. The first component was interpreted as a symmetry factor, the second was correlated with all the three-dimensional designs and the third seemed to be highly correlated with complex designs. The remaining two factors were not easy to interpret from the loadings. Since 'symmetry' was the only one of the 'aesthetic principles' used to guide item construction to emerge from this analysis the status of the other principles remains obscure. Eysenck (1980) administered the test to 50 students and staff at the Royal College of Art. The mean score of the artists was 50 (standard deviation 9.12) which is virtually identical to the mean score of the non-art groups reported by Graves. Since many of the items in the test contrast a symmetrical with an asymmetrical design (with preference for the asymmetrical being scored 'correct' in the test) Eysenck's result could be used to suggest that a general change in artistic taste has occurred since the 1940s characterized by a new preference for the symmetrical. Whether taste in the arts is principally governed by changing fashions or whether it is based on incontrovertible principles is an issue which could only be addressed by repeated testing using tests which are well designed to measure a clearly defined aspect of the aesthetic. The Maitland-Graves in its original form clearly does not meet these requirements. Interestingly, however, a subset of the original items were used by Eysenck (1972) to measure the development of aesthetic sensitivity in children. Although not labelled as such in the study it is clear that all 22 of these items reflect the symmetrical-asymmetrical distinction found to feature prominently in Eysenck's (1967) factor study. The use of this subtest might provide interesting data on the issues mentioned. As an aptitude or selection measure it would clearly be quite dangerous to use this test as published.

References

Eysenck, H. J. (1967). Factor-analytic study of the Maitland-Graves Design Judgement Test. *Perceptual and Motor Skills* 24, 73–74.

Eysenck, H. J. (1970). An application of the Maitland-Graves Design Judgement Test to professional artists. *Perceptual and Motor Skills* 30, 589–590.

Eysenck, J. H. (1972). The development of aesthetic sensitivity in children. *Journal of Child Psychology and Psychiatry* 13, 1–10.

Millman, M. and Chang, T. (1966). Inter-correlations among three widely used art tests. *Perceptual and Motor Skills* 23, 1002.

The Meier Art Tests*

Reviewed by David O'Hare

Author: Norman Charles Meier
Publisher: Bureau of Educational Research and Service, University of Iowa
Distributor: NFER-Nelson
Age: not specified; norms for USA college and high-school groups
1961 (experimental form); 1963 (copyrighted); S not stated
1967 (M, T) (revised)
Preliminary Manual 1967 used in this review
Self-administered

Test content

The test consists of 50 items. Each item comprises four slightly different versions of a work of art. 'The test items are constructions adapted from works

---

* II—Aesthetic Perception.

representative generally of world art from ancient to contemporary, selected in each instance for aesthetic excellence'. The items consist therefore of attempts to mimic works by well known artists such as Modigliani, Kandinsky, El Greco and Moore as well as examples of Chinese, Japanese and Persian works. The differences between the four versions are generally very slight and vary from tonal changes to changes in composition.

Purpose

The test was designed to 'provide a fuller, more complete and varied measure of the art-ability complex'. This is defined as 'the greater ability or capacity as observed in artists . . . to observe phenomena with considerably greater adequacy than will be experienced by the non-art person' (Manual, p. 1). This ability is conceived of in terms of sensitivity to the 'aesthetic character' of a work, for example, 'how unity was attained by a complex balance of designed proportions and possibly other subtleties of good construction'.

Item preparation

The original test comprised 70 items, produced by 'competent young artists' which were 'tried out' with a number of artists and non-artists. No details are given of this nor of how the original 70 items were reduced to the final 50, save that 23 were 'eliminated' 15 more 'improved by revision' and three new items added.

Administration

The test is self-administered without time limit. The instructions direct subjects to '. . . study the organization of the composition or sculpture or design, noting how the versions differ, and perceive what makes one the best aesthetically of the four, the next best, the third best and the poorest'. The subject's sheet consists of four rows of numbered boxes for each item so that rank-order judgements can be recorded.

Standardization

A set of 'preliminary norms' are reported, obtained from 360 'high-school students taking art' and 340 'college-adult subjects'. The mean scores for these two groups are reported as '72–76' and '77–85' respectively. This is related to a mean of 90 obtained from 'groups, such as artists' but no further details are supplied.

Scoring

The scoring key provided simply counts the number of 'correct' rankings. The maximum possible score would, therefore, be 200. The actual range of scores obtained is very much restricted—the Manual gives a range of 41–108 for a sample of 360 high-school students. The scoring system of 'adding up' correctly ranked items is of course a particularly crude and inaccurate method of estimating subject's deviations from the 'correct' rank order. For example, a subject who 'correctly' placed the two best and two worst versions but who reversed the order within each of these pairs would score zero whereas a subject who incorrectly placed three out of four versions but correctly placed the fourth would score one. No information is given as to how the 'correct' rank-orderings were arrived at.

Reliability

Nothing is reported on reliability.

Validity

The test has a greater degree of 'face validity' than comparable tests. Most of the items are of reasonable artistic quality and the variations are subtle enough to provoke interest. There is, however, no reported evidence for any form of validity for this test in the Manual. No data relating the Meier test of Aesthetic Perception to other tests has been reported. There are, however, some findings concerning the Meier test of Aesthetic Judgement (Meier Art Test: I) which is considered 'complementary' to the present test and is similarly constructed. Bolton (1955) reported a correlation of 0.35 between the Meier Test: I and the Maitland Graves Test which was interpreted as indicating that the tests are not measuring the same factors of aesthetic judgement, despite similar claims made by the two tests. Bolton also reports correlations (presumably product-moment) of between 0.36–0.43 between the Meier Test: I and an intelligence test (the Otis Quick-Scoring Test of Mental Ability). The sample size on which these relations were based consisted of 102 female college students. Millman and Chang's (1967) finding of a low (0.19) correlation between the Meier Test: I and the Maitland Graves further supports Bolton's views.

General evaluation

The Meier Art Test: II is a woefully documented test of undemonstrated reliability and validity based on the most dubious of theoretical assumptions.

In common with the Maitland Graves test, the Meier test is predicated on the assumption that *agreement* with 'expert' choices or judgements can be used to assess artistic aptitude or potential. Many artists and educators, however, have strongly argued that *disagreement* with experts might be a much more important characteristic for artistic success '. . . the strength to resist what is normally imposed is almost a prerequisite of the successful artist' (Creedy, 1976). There is nothing in the Meier test (nor indeed in any other test of aesthetic judgement) to suggest that a proper basis of underlying aesthetic principles has been consensually established. Even the author seems to be in two minds about this, claiming first that 'In some versions the variation is so subtle that even competent artists will differ in their rankings' whilst in the next line stating that '. . . the final rank order for each item can be established only by consensus of competent persons in the field'! The test can therefore be regarded as inadequate on both psychometric and conceptual grounds. The materials used in the test might, however, have some usefulness as research materials (rather than as an aptitude test). For example, Pronko, Ebert, Greenberg and Havlicek (1965) and Gordon and Gardner (1974) have used the technique of presenting alternative versions of the same work to study detection and preference judgements. In both cases an existing work was altered in some way (e.g. by lateral reversal or by changing the position of elements within the composition). O'Hare and Westwood (1984) have used a similar technique to Meier in creating a dozen slightly different versions of the same scene to obtain judgements of aesthetic sensitivity from children. All these studies have been oriented towards an understanding of the underlying processes of aesthetic sensitivity and preference and this is where tests such as the Meier Test: II are most obviously unhelpful.

References

Bolton, E. B. (1955). Brief evaluation of two tests of aesthetic judgement. *Peabody Journal of Education* 32, 211–223.

Creedy, J. (1976). *In* "Beyond Aesthetics" (Brothwell, D., ed.). London: Thames & Hudson.

Gordon, I. E. and Gardner, C. (1974). Responses to altered pictures. *British Journal of Psychology* 65, 243–254.

Millman, M. and Chang, T. (1966). Inter-correlations among three widely used art tests. *Perceptual and Motor Skills* 23, 1002.

O'Hare, D. and Westwood, H. (1984). Features of style classification: A multivariate experimental analysis of children's responses to drawings. *Developmental Psychology* (in press).

Pronko, N. H., Ebert, R., Greenberg, G. and Havlicek, L. L. (1965). A psychological examination of one-best-wayism in art: An exploratory study. *Psychological Record* 15, 89–96.

Modern Language Aptitude Test

Reviewed by Don Labon

Authors: J. B. Carroll and S. M. Sapon
Publisher: The Psychological Corporation
Distributor: NFER-Nelson
Age range: 15+ to university undergraduate
1955
1958 (S); 1959 (M) (revised edition)
Group test

Test content

This review is of the shortened form, which consists of the last three parts of a five-part test. (Administration of the first two parts requires a pre-recorded tape, which is not included in the specimen set). Each item is of a multiple-choice type, involving selection of the correct response from 5 possibilities.

Part III, *Spelling Clues*, contains 50 items. In each item, the written stimulus is a word of unorthodox but not illogical spelling. The response choice is from conventionally spelt possible synonyms. The measure, partly dependent on English vocabulary knowledge, reflects sound-symbol association ability.

Part IV, *Words in Sentences*, containing 45 items, is thought to measure sensitivity to grammatical structure. Typically, a word in a sentence is underlined and the testee is asked to decide which of the underlined words in a subsequent sentence serves the same function.

Part V, *Paired Associates*, serves to measure the rote memory aspect of the learning of foreign languages. Two minutes are allowed for the memorizing of 24 supposedly Kurdish words and their English equivalents. Following a practice phase, the key lists are removed, the written 'Kurdish' words are re-presented and the testee has the task of selecting each correct English equivalent from an array of possibles.

Purpose

The test's main purpose is to indicate likelihood of success in learning a foreign language. 'It is particularly useful in predicting success in learning to speak and understand a foreign language, but it is also useful in learning to read, write and translate a foreign language' (Manual, p. 3). Total scores are norm referenced, thus serving as general predictors. In addition, scores on the different parts of the test are seen to have diagnostic value, providing indications of specific strengths and weaknesses in sound-symbol association, sensitivity to grammatical structure and rote memory.

Item preparation

The Manual states that the subtests presented were selected from a much larger array of tests devised and tried out during a five-year Harvard University research study. They emerged from factor analysis as being relatively uncorrelated and they demonstrated relatively good predictive value in foreign language learning. (In the long form of the test, Part I items were thought to reflect 'auditory alertness' and Part II, to an extent greater than Part III, was considered to measure sound-symbol association). The experimental tests were administered to some 5000 people.

Administration

The Manual provides teachers with instructions which are sufficiently clear and detailed to ensure reasonably standard administration. This requires about 30 minutes (for the complete 70 minute test, nearly all the instructions, together with pauses allowing for item completion, are on the pre-recorded tape). Part III is highly speeded; few testees will complete all its items in the time available.

Standardization

For teachers wishing to make use of the test with classes in the UK, this is its weakest aspect. In the autumn of 1958, the complete test was administered to some 1900 students, in the 14–17 years age range, beginning the study of foreign language. Some students were enrolled for French, some for Spanish and some for Latin. Altogether, the students attended 14 high schools, scattered across the USA. A further 1300 or so students, attending 10 colleges and universities, were also tested. There were, in addition, three adult groups, mostly people in the armed forces.

The Manual does not indicate that steps were taken to ensure that samples were representative of the populations of the different age groups concerned. Given the curriculum constraints determining the sampling, it seems unlikely that they were. As translation of norms to British samples adds further uncertainties, particularly in the case of tertiary education students, interpretation of norms can only be undertaken with considerable caution.

Raw scores are converted to percentiles and presented separately for the total test and for the short form, and with respect to males and females. Secondary school norms are also presented separately for the 14+, 15+ and 16+ age groups. Neither standard scores nor quotients are presented as such, though the data included are sufficient to enable teachers to calculate these for themselves. In the presentation of percentiles, there is no age differentiation within year groups.

Scoring

Scoring is straightforward, facilitated by the fact that the test items are of multiple-choice type. The expendable answer sheets are designed for either machine-scoring or hand-scoring. Hand-scoring is quick and simple. Responses are recorded on a single answer sheet and the short form of the test requires only one template. The accumulated raw score is easily converted to a percentile score through reference to a table.

Reliability

Outcomes of the reliability studies are, in general, satisfactory. Odd-even reliability coefficients, using the Spearman-Brown formula correction, were calculated for data collected from three schools ($n = 734$), two universities and two adult groups. Due allowance was made for the speededness of Part III. Reliability coefficients for the short form of the test averaged 0.90, falling only slightly below those for the total test. Coefficients for Part III were of the order of 0.7, those for Part IV generally exceeded 0.8 and those for Part V approached 0.9. Standard errors of measurement were of the order of 3 points of raw score for Parts III and IV, and about 2 points for Part V. Correlations between the different parts of the test, scattered around the 0.3 level, suggested that they were measuring somewhat different aspects of foreign language aptitude.

Validity

In keeping with the main purpose of the test, the validity studies reported in the Manual focused on assessing its success in predicting students' foreign language achievements. In these terms, the test's predictive validity emerged as moderate to fair. The criterion measures of achievement were usually the grades assigned by teachers after a period of training, e.g. of one or two terms. The Manual does not indicate whether the teachers knew the students' initial test scores or how they assigned grades.

Validity testing was extensive. At secondary-school level, for example, it involved almost a thousand students. Correlations between initial language aptitude scores and later performance estimates were generally of the order of 0.5, with the short form demonstrating itself to be as effective a predictor as the total test and a better predictor than conventional intelligence tests. There were no indications that the test might be a consistently better predictor of achievement in one foreign language than in another.

Interpretation

The no more than crude applicability of the norm-referenced scores to British samples has already been mentioned. Reliability and validity, however, are sufficient to justify a teacher having some confidence in using the test to make within-school comparisons, e.g. for 'setting' purposes. Another envisaged use of the test is in selection. This could be undertaken on a criterion-referenced basis. The Manual refers to the possibility of establishing a minimum score (a 'cutting' score), below which the progress is not likely to be sufficient to have made entry to the course worthwhile. It is left to the teacher, though, to work out—perhaps on a trial and error basis—the cutting score appropriate to a particular course.

A further use of the test is in differential diagnosis. The standard errors of the subtests are such that one would usually be unjustified in attempting to differentiate, between levels of specific skills of individuals taking the same subtest, on the basis of raw score differences of less than about 6 points.

Test use

Wilkins (1972, p. 179) points out that the Modern Language Aptitude Test ignores motivational factors. He also refers to evidence indicating that it provides no better a predictor of foreign language learning than do measures of general school achievement. When linguistic measures are combined with ratings of motivation for foreign language learning and with estimates of achievement in other school subjects, as is the case with Pimsleur's Language Aptitude Battery (also distributed by NFER-Nelson), their predictive validity coefficients can be raised from the 0.5 level to the 0.7 level.

General evaluation

The construction of this easily administered test was carried out with care, and the fact that this was done more than a quarter of a century ago is probably not to its disadvantage. The different parts of the test measure fairly well defined facets of linguistic competence, each having some relevance to foreign language learning. In a very broad sense, subtest scores could be used as bases for differential diagnosis and possible remediation.

Whilst the American norms have only very approximate applicability in British settings, the test could be used as a moderately successful predictor of students' relative successes in learning a foreign language, particularly at 14–16 year level in secondary schools. It may be no better a predictor than a general measure of scholastic achievement, though the two in combination would probably be more effective than either in isolation, and could be enhanced further if motivational factors were also taken into account.

Reference

Wilkins, D. A. (1972). "Linguistics in Language Teaching". London: Edward Arnold.

Seashore Measure of Musical Talents

Reviewed by John Sloboda

Authors: C. E. Seashore, D. Lewis and J. G. Saetvit
Publisher: The Psychological Corporation
Distributor: NFER-Nelson
Age: 8+ (USA Grades 4–16)
1919
1939 (revision, Series A; Series B, discontinued); 1960 (2nd revision):
   S not stated
Group test

Test content

There are six separate tests; pitch, loudness, rhythm, time, timbre and tonal memory. Each test contains 50 items of increasing difficulty (excepting the tonal memory test which contains only 30 items). Each item comprises a pair of notes or note sequences which differ in one respect. The subject listens to the pair and then makes a judgement about the difference, recording his answer on a multiple-choice answer sheet. For instance, in the pitch test the subject is required to say whether the second pure tone presented is higher or lower in pitch than the first.

The version of the tests supplied to this reviewer are pre-recorded on reel-to-reel tape, although the Manual states that the tests 'are presented on a single 33.5 rpm long playing record' (Manual, p. 3). It is not clear whether such a record is still available.

Purpose

'Some uses of a musical aptitude test are: educational and vocational counselling, admission to music instruction in schools, and selection for membership in bands and other musical organizations' (Manual, p. 3). The Manual makes no detailed case for any particular use, although by providing tables of age group norms it suggests that a normative use is envisaged.

Item preparation

The sound parameters of all the tests are given detailed specification in the Manual, and the items have been machine generated for complete precision. No details of the rationale for test or item construction are given in the Manual, although the reader is told that 'a detailed account of the content, construction, and analysis of the tests may be found in a report by Saetvit, Lewis and Seashore (1940)' (Manual, p. 3). The reference quoted is unlikely to be easily available to most users.

Administration

The test is for use with any child who is capable of understanding the instructions. Although these instructions require some concentration to grasp they should not be too difficult for the eight year-old of normal ability.

'Each subject needs to be supplied with a copy of the special IBM answer sheet on which to record his responses. He also needs at least one pencil and eraser'.

'The actual testing time for the six parts of the measures is about 30 minutes, but an hour should be allowed for the whole procedure, including instructions, demonstration, etc. It is recommended that younger subjects be tested in at least two sessions'.

'With younger subjects it is possible to limit testing to three parts only: pitch, rhythm and tonal memory' (Manual, p. 4).

The instructions for administration contained in the Manual are clear and detailed. There is an adequate 'script' to be read by the examiner, who is encouraged to spend time demonstrating how the answer sheet should be filled in, and making sure that the subjects understand what is required of them on each test. A shortcoming is that all the instructions refer to a long-playing record, and not the tape actually supplied. It is essential for the successful administration of the tests that high-fidelity playback equipment be used and the testing room should be fairly non-reverberant and free from extraneous noises. These conditions are not fulfilled by the average classroom. If group testing procedures are used, the positioning of a subject with respect to the loudspeaker can materially affect his score. Although the Manual states that one examiner can satisfactorily test up to 25 subjects simultaneously, the reviewer's experience is that more reliable results will be obtained with much smaller groups. Ideally, each subject should hear the test through individual headphones.

'Whenever time and opportunity permit, giving a second trial of the test is a wise procedure . . . It is particularly important that subjects making a poor or doubtful score be retested. When retesting a subject who has made a poor score, the examiner should exercise considerable patience in explaining the test, allowing adequate practice, and making certain that the subject knows what he is to do' (Manual, p. 4).

Standardization

'Norms for the Seashore Measures of Musical Talents are presented for three educational levels' (Grades 4–5, ages 8–9; Grades 6–8, ages 10–12; and Grades 9–16, ages 13–20). 'These levels were selected after study of score distribution for single grades; differences among adjacent grades were generally too small to warrant presentation of norms for every grade. The combinations chosen represent the groups whose distributions differed sufficiently from those of other groups to justify separate treatment' (Manual, p. 7).

The number of subjects used to provide norms for each test varies from about 5600 for the timbre test to 10 000 for the pitch test. This represents an average of about 600 children for each test at each grade level. Norms are presented for each test separately. Neither the date nor the subject selection procedure for the standardization is given, although the schools from which the population was drawn are listed (all in the USA).

The norms are presented as percentile levels for each possible score on a given test. Sex differences 'were found to be very small and inconsistent from one level to another. Combined sex norms were therefore formulated' (Manual, p. 7).

Scoring

There is a 'scoring stencil' supplied which may be placed over a subject's answer sheet. Holes correspond with the positions of the correct answers. 'Before scoring, the answer sheets must be inspected to determine whether more than one choice has been marked for any item. Where such multiple marking occurs, the item should be omitted from the scoring' (Manual, p. 6).

Each answer sheet provides a space for a 'percentile profile' to be drawn on the basis of the test scores. There is no opportunity to derive a total score for all the tests, and the author implies that such a score would have little meaning.

Reliability

'The reliability . . . was estimated by means of internal consistency coefficients (KR-21). This formula has the value of producing conservative estimates, since its use is more likely to under-estimate than over-estimate reliability' (Manual, p. 7). The coefficients given range from 0.55–0.85 according to age group and test. The most reliable tests are pitch, loudness and tonal memory (all above 0.80). These reliability scores are based on results of the standardization sample.

'Those coefficients which are relatively low emphasize the importance of interpreting scores in broad categories only. Where important decisions are to be made with respect to doubtful performance, retesting of the individual is imperative' (Manual, p. 7).

Validity

The tests all have high content validity. They directly measure ability to notice and remember changes in the dimension specified by the title of each test. It is argued, further by the authors, that each ability is manifestly necessary to a high degree of musical accomplishment. The authors disbelieve in the existence of 'general musicality', preferring to hold the notion that musical ability is made up from specific and logically independent subskills, such as the ones tested here.

The Manual supplies no details of associative validity, although the reader is referred to Bienstock (1942) and Lundin (1953) for details of validation studies. A recent review (Shuter-Dyson and Gabriel, 1981) reports that the Seashore tests achieve low positive correlation with a variety of direct measures of musical achievement and with other tests of musical ability.

Interpretation

The Manual offers little positive guidance on how scores should be interpreted, what various types of test profile might indicate, or what action a given score might suggest. The general tenor of the Manual is one of extreme caution. For instance: 'It is easy to show that we cannot find a good violinist who does not have a good sense of pitch; or a good pianist who does not have a good sense of intensity . . . But it does not follow that goodness in these capacities alone will make a good artist' (Manual, p. 7).

The authors state that the tests are not designed for refined discriminations, especially in the upper percentiles of the older age groups. In such cases 'small differences in score are associated with large differences in percentile equivalent'. It is recommended that 'a high score earned by a college student may be interpreted as placing him in the upper half or top quarter, but no more precise ranking should be attempted' (Manual, p. 7).

According to the title, these are tests of musical *talent*, a word which suggests a stable inborn trait which does not arise from particular training. The authors present no evidence to support this view. All the abilities tested could equally well arise from specific training. In this reviewer's view, there can be no necessary implication that someone who performs badly on these tests is unsuited for musical training.

Test use

The bibliography appended to the Manual contains no published work more recent than 1958. Only a few of the 41 references are mentioned in the text of the Manual, and it is not said in what way the majority of them relate to the Seashore tests. Seashore's own book (1938) provides the most accessible account of the theoretical and empirical concerns from which the tests arose.

Shuter-Dyson and Gabriel (1981) supply details of more recent research using the Seashore Tests. They also provide a comprehensive list of studies which have tested the associative validity of the Tests.

General evaluation

These tests are easy to administer and score. The test materials have been constructed with a high degree of precision, although some subjects find the 'electronic' quality of the machine-generated stimuli somewhat aversive. The complete battery takes a long time to administer, and subjects may experience concentration difficulties. For this reason, and because test results are not to be summed into a 'total score', it is always permissible, and often advisable, to use a selection from the total battery. This selection should normally include the pitch, rhythm and tonal memory tests.

The Manual is sorely lacking in guidance concerning the way the scores might be used in an educational context. There is a general lack of discussion of the rationale behind the tests. This makes it hard to recommend their use other than by those who have available expert sources of both psychological and musical advice.

The principal advantage of the tests is that they do not presuppose specific training in music performance or analysis, and so can be administered at a fairly early educational stage to children who have no special musical background. The best consequences of this could be that previously unnoticed high scorers will obtain a chance to embark on specialist music teaching that might otherwise not have come their way.

References

Bienstock, S. F. (1942). A review of recent studies on musical aptitude. *Journal of Educational Psychology* **33**, 427–442.
Lundin, R. W. (1953). "An Objective Psychology of Music". New York: Ronald Press.
Saetvit, J. G., Lewis, D. and Seashore, C. E. (1940). Revision of the Seashore Measures of Musical Talents. "University of Iowa Study Aims Program Research". No. 65. Iowa City: University of Iowa Press.
Seashore, C. E. (1938). "The Psychology of Music". New York: McGraw Hill.
Shuter-Dyson, R. and Gabriel, C. (1981). "The Psychology of Musical Ability" (2nd edn.). London: Methuen.

Wing Standardized Tests of Musical Intelligence

Reviewed by John Sloboda

Author: H. D. Wing
Publisher: NFER-Nelson
Distributor: NFER-Nelson
Age range: 8–17
1948; revised 1957
Revised 1962; S not stated; M undated
Group test

Test content

There are seven separate tests in the complete battery:

'1. Analysis of chords. Stating the number of notes in a chord. 20 items.
2. Pitch discrimination. Stating the direction of movement of a note when only one is changed in two consecutive chords. 30 items.
3. Memory for pitch. Stating in which note a replayed tune differs from the original. 30 items.
4. Harmony appreciation. Choice between a good and a bad harmonization. 14 items.
5. Intensity appreciation. Choice between good and bad use of graduation in intensity. 14 items.
6. Rhythm appreciation. Choice between a balanced and an unbalanced rhythm. 14 items.
7. Phrasing appreciation. Choice between a balanced and an unbalanced phrasing. 14 items.' (Manual, p. 1).

The Manual supplies no details about the nature of the items, their length, sound parameters, or method of recording. In fact the items are played on a piano, and to this reviewer's ear, the recording quality is unsatisfactory and the total effect somewhat unprofessional. The tests are supplied on a pre-recorded cassette tape.

Purpose

'. . . to assess the various capabilities of the 'individual, and to use the results as a basis for advice on the choice of a career or leisure occupation . . . A second use of the results is that, after applying them to wide samples of the population of all ages, an indication will be obtained of the normal stages of growth of the ability with increase of age or advancing study' (Manual, p. 1).

Item preparation

No details of any aspect of item selection and preparation are supplied in the Manual, and the reader is referred to Wing (1948) for further details. This reference should be available from a good university library, but the lack of information in the Manual remains unsatisfactory.

Administration

For children of 10 or under it is suggested that only the first three tests are given. Subjects record their answers in a multiple-choice answer booklet which is supplied with the tests. The first three tests take about 25 minutes to administer, and the total test takes about 1 hour. 'There are practice items for Tests 1 to 3, but not for Tests 4 to 7. With the later tests (on appreciation) there should be no explanation, e.g. on what is good or bad harmony' (Manual, p. 2). The instructions for each test are printed in the answer booklets and subjects are required to read these to themselves. They are then read out loud by the examiner, and are finally summarized on the test tape itself.

No directions are given concerning playback equipment, room acoustics, maximum size of group, or positioning of subjects with respect to the speaker. Since all these factors can materially affect a subject's score, this lack of direction is a major failing of the Manual.

Standardization

The tests were standardized on 8789 children. No details are given of how the sample was selected and distributed between the different ages and tests. Summary norms are provided for each age from 8–17, both for the whole battery, and for the total of tests 1, 2 and 3. Norms for individual tests are not supplied. The norms divide children at each age into five percentile bands: top 10 per cent, next 20 per cent, middle 40 per cent, next 20 per cent and bottom 10 per cent, and the range of test scores corresponding to each band are given.

No details are given concerning the level of musical training achieved by any of the subjects in the standardization sample. This makes it very hard to see how the tests could be capable of their stated purpose of indicating 'the normal stages of growth of the ability with increase of age or advancing study' (Manual, p. 1).

Scoring

A 'scoring stencil' is supplied which may be placed over an answer sheet. Correct answers appear in holes cut in the scoring card. A simple correction formula for missing answers and multiple answers is given.

The total test score can be used in two ways. It can either place a child in the appropriate percentile band for its age, or supply an 'approximate musical age' by insertion into a simple arithmetical formula.

Reliability studies

The Manual gives no detailed information about reliability estimates or how they were arrived at, other than to say that 'reliability coefficients for older children have been of the order of 0.9 and above, but for younger children drop to 0.7' (Manual, p. 4). For further information, the reader is referred in a general way to the 18 appended references, but in particular to Wing (1941, 1954) and Edmunds (1960).

Validity

'An attempt to estimate the validity by comparison of the results of this test with another gave a coefficient of 0.73 with training college students (Wing, 1959). If the figure is corrected for the reliabilities of the tests it would rise to 0.9. With children of 11, however, when compared with teacher estimates the validity dropped to 0.6' (Manual, p. 4). No substantive discussion of validity is given, but the reader is again referred to the references quoted in connection with reliability studies.

The Manual states that advice on reliability, validity, and other problems with specific groups will willingly be given by the author. As far as this reviewer is aware the author died some years ago.

Interpretation

'The tests are suitable for group application within the normal limits of age and conditions for group intelligence tests. They are subject to the same general conditions of application and the same limitations; thus, a high score is a safer indication of high aptitude than a low score of a low aptitude' (Manual, p. 4).

'As the tests are designed to pick out the brighter children, they are not nearly so discriminating at the lower end of the scale. This is because the number of items which is suitable fo the younger, weaker children is not considerable and, therefore, the lowest grades will be guessing for a part of the test; the test must, therefore, lose in reliability as the children get younger' (Manual, p. 3).

Test use

The bibliography supplied in the Manual is now rather dated. Shuter-Dyson and Gabriel (1981) discuss a number of more recent studies that have used the

Wing tests. On the basis of these studies they conclude that the validity of the tests is good. More detailed discussion of the tests themselves is given by Wing (1948, 1962).

General evaluation

It is undoubtedly true that children who can obtain high scores on the Wing tests have a high 'musical intelligence'. If such children are not receiving specialist musical training, then the implication is that they would be ripe for it.

The tests of appreciation (Tests 4–7) require fine multidimensional judgements about style and expression appropriate to melodies taken from the Western classical repertoire. For this reason they are more musically interesting than, say, the Seashore Tests (see this Volume), but for the same reason they also seem to presuppose a more specific set of musical experiences for success. When some of the tests use melodies from the classical repertoire it seems inevitable to conclude that prior knowledge of these melodies will enhance one's score. On these grounds, the Seashore Tests would seem more culturally fair, precisely because they do not relate directly to *particular* types of music.

The presentation of these tests, in the Manual and on tape, is, frankly, poor. The Manual is little more than a set of brief instructions for administering and scoring. Many substantive questions of purpose, validity, interpretation and construction are not dealt with. Such questions may, with effort, be answered through the bibliography supplied; but one is entitled to expect considerably more information in a Manual than is supplied here. A thorough revision is urgently called for.

References

* Edmunds, C. B. (1960). Musical ability, intelligence and attainment of secondary modern and ESN children. Unpublished thesis. University of Leeds.

Shuter-Dyson, R. and Gabriel, C. (1981). "The Psychology of Musical Ability". London: Methuen.

* Wing, H. D. (1941). A factorial study of musical tests. *British Journal of Psychology* **31**, 341–355.

Wing, H. D. (1948). Tests of musical ability and appreciation. *British Journal of Psychology Monograph Supplements* **8**, 27.

* Wing, H. D. (1954). Some applications of test results to education in music. *British Journal of Educational Psychology*. **24**, 161–170.

* Wing, H. D. (1959). Aliferis Music Test, etc. "5th Mental Measurements Yearbook". No. 243.

* Wing, H. D. (1962). A revision of the Wing Musical Aptitude Test. *American Journal of Research in Music* 39–46.

---

* References given in the Manual

Glossary

Age standardization. There are two bases for age standardization as follows:

Cross-sectional. The members of the standardizing group, typically a school year-group, are all measured at the same time and test scores are 'corrected' or 'adjusted' for different ages, leading to an estimate of average change in score for a given age difference (e.g. 1 year).

Longitudinal. An age adjustment is based on the average change in test score experienced by individuals over a given time period (e.g. 1 year).

Cloze technique (or procedure). The test content is a prose passage from which selected words have been omitted. The task for the testee is to insert suitable words in the gaps in the passage.

Factor analysis. A set of statistical procedures which assume that the observed measurements on a set of variables (e.g. tests) are related in a simple fashion to a small number (sometimes only one) of underlying variables or 'factors'. The factor analysis attempts to uncover these factors, to estimate their relationships with the observed variables (factor loadings) and sometimes to provide estimates of the value of the factor for each individual (factor scores).

Item. The basic unit of a test to which a score is given, typically either correct (score 1) or incorrect (score 0).

Item analysis. The name given to the set of procedures involved in studying the statistical properties of the items in a test, their difficulties, discriminating powers and their interrelationships. Item analysis is typically carried out on pilot data to assist in item selection for the final test form.

Item discrimination. A measure of how quickly the item difficulty changes over groups of individuals as ability or attainment increases.

Item facility. The proportion of individuals who answer the item correctly.

Latent trait theory. A form of factor analysis which is concerned principally with binary, i.e. correct/incorrect, observed variables rather than variables measured on a continuous scale.

Normal score distribution. A distribution of scores following the Gaussian or normal distribution curve. Often, mental test scores are transformed during standardization, so that the sample scores have—approximately—a normal distribution with a mean of 100 and standard deviation of 15. Given this, approximate percentile ranks can be assigned to standardized scores; for example, a standardization score of 115 is one standard deviation above the mean of 100, which by reference to tables of the normal distribution, indicates a percentile rank of 84.

Percentile rank. A score has a percentile rank of x, if x per cent of scores are estimated to fall at or below that score.

Profile. Tests which give rise to multiple subtest or scale scores often offer the test user a graphic display of the several scores so that the pattern or profile of performance (e.g. peaks and troughs) may readily be observed.

Reliability. An observed test score is assumed to be composed of a 'true' underlying score plus 'measurement error'. The ratio of the (between individuals) variance of true score to the variance of observed scores is known as the reliability. Several methods are employed for evaluating reliability:

Internal. These use the interrelationships between items within a test. One of the most common measures is the Kuder-Richardson Formula 20 (KR-20), which applies to items scored 1—or 0 (correct/incorrect). A generalization of KR-20 for multi-graded items (or other test units) is known as coefficient alpha. Both KR-20 and coefficient alpha are related to the Spearman-Brown formula for estimating the reliability of a test from the reliabilities of its sub-units (e.g. items or groups of items).

External. This type of reliability concerns the relationships between whole tests which by one criterion or another purport to measure the same true score. Typically, the correlation between parallel tests (e.g. Forms A and B) is used. Test-retest procedures are also sometimes used.

Sampling. Several forms of sampling are referred to in the reviews.

Cluster sampling. See Multi-stage sampling.

Complex sampling. Any mixture of stratified and cluster sampling procedures.

Multi-stage sampling. Sampling carried out in several stages, but at each stage aggregated units (e.g. schools, classrooms) are sampled randomly. At the final stage individuals are sampled within each aggregate unit, or all individuals within the units are chosen (cluster sampling).

Opportunistic sampling. A euphemistic expression for non-random sampling; that is, the use of a readily available group of individuals.

Purposive sampling. A non-random method which uses particular criteria to select individuals, e.g. using physical or social characteristics to attempt to obtain a sample which is 'representative' of the total population with respect to these characteristics.

Random sampling. A selection of units taken from a sampling frame by a random procedure, e.g. by using a table of random numbers.

Sample design effect. In complex sampling, the estimates of population mean scores have a sampling variance which in general is not the same as that obtained from a simple random sample of the same number of individuals. The ratio of the complex sample variance to the simple random sample variance is called the design effect. Thus a large design effect (e.g. say about 4.0) may result in estimates with large sampling errors despite a relatively large number of individuals tested. In general large design effects do not lead to serious biases in estimating standard deviations of test scores or percentiles.

Sampling frame. A list of the units in the population to be sampled. The unit may be individuals or schools (e.g. cluster sampling above).

Stratified sampling. The population is first divided into well defined 'strata' (e.g. geographical regions) prior to random selection within strata.

Standard error of measurement. When used in connection with reliability estimates this refers to the standard deviation of the random measurement error of the test.

Test. The term 'test' most commonly refers to a collection of items which are developed, administered and scored together. Use of the expression 'subtest' usually indicates that what has been labelled 'test' by the author and publisher does in fact contain separately evaluated groups of items. The term 'scales' often refers to a similar test structure although here it is possible that performance on one set of items may be evaluated in more than one way (e.g. speed and accuracy of performance).

Group test. A test designed to be administered to several testees at the same time and not requiring detailed interaction, e.g. prompting, between tester and testee.

Individual test. A test designed to be administered to a single testee at a time and requiring communication with tester during completion.

Parallel tests. Tests which are deemed to have identical statistical characteristics, i.e. estimating the same true score and measurement error variance.

Power test. A test having items graded in difficulty which, in principle, requires no time limit since testees begin to fail items beyond their ability level. In practice many such tests are partially speeded since some testees may not reach their 'ceiling' within a reasonable time.

Practice test. A short preliminary test which is not scored and is designed to familiarize the subject with the test format.

Speed test. A timed test designed so that not all items can be completed within the available time. In principal, it is a test composed of items having zero difficulty such that only the imposition of a time limit creates differences in performance. In practice, many time-limited tests have some gradient of difficulty from early to later items.

Target population. The group of individuals with whom the test is designed to be used; for example, children aged 5:00–6:00 years in Scottish Schools.

Validity. In general, the 'value' or 'meaning' of a test; the extent to which it fulfils its purposes.

Associative validity. Includes predictive and concurrent validity. A justification on the basis of a test's strength of association with other measures.

Concurrent validity. A measure of the strength of association with other current tests.

Construct validity. The overall 'value' or 'meaning' of a test, having regard to all the evidence, especially that of its relationships to other tests.

Content validity. A justification of a test in terms of test item content, involving meaning and relevance for purpose.

Convergent validity. A set of tests which purport to measure the same thing are said to have high convergent validity if their intercorrelations are high or they are strongly related to a well identified factor.

Predictive validity. A measure of the strength of prediction of a subsequent criterion. For example, for an attainment test the prediction of career success.

Publishers and Distributors

Academic Press Inc. (London) Ltd, 24–28 Oval Road, London, NW1 7DX

Addison-Wesley Publishers Ltd, 53 Bedford Square, London, WC1B 3DZ. (Stocks held by A. W. Publishing Co., Inc., Reading, Massachussetts 01867, USA)

American Guidance Service, Inc., Publishers' Building, Circle Pines, Minnesota 55014, USA

Bureau of Educational Research and Services, The University of Iowa, Iowa City, Iowa, USA

Careers Research and Advisory Centre (CRAC). Material published under licence by Hobsons (*see* Hobsons)

Consulting Psychologists Press, 577 College Avenue, Palo Alto, California 94306, USA

Educational Evaluation Enterprises, Awre, Newnham, Gloucestershire, GL14 1ET

Educational and Industrial Test Services Ltd, 83 High Street, Hemel Hempstead, Hertfordshire, HP1 3AH

Evans Brothers Limited, Montague House, Russell Square, London, WC1B 5BX

Guidance Centre, Faculty of Education, University of Toronto, Ontario, Canada

Grune & Stratton Inc. (*see* Harcourt Brace Jovanovich, Inc.)

Harcourt Brace Jovanovich, Inc., Orlando, Florida 32887, USA. Also 24–28 Oval Road, London, NW1

Harrap Limited, 19–23 Ludgate Hill, London, EC4M 7PD
  Australia: The Australasian Publishing Co., Pty Ltd, Cnr Bridge Road and Jersey Street, Hornsby, NSW, 2077, Australia
  New Zealand: Book Reps (New Zealand) Ltd, 48 Lake Road, Northcote, Auckland 9, New Zealand
  Canada: Clarke, Irwin and Co. Ltd., 791 St. Clair Avenue West, Toronto M6C 1B8, Ontario, Canada

Hart-Davis Educational Ltd, Frogmore, St Albans, Hertfordshire

Heinemann Educational Books Ltd, 22 Bedford Square, London, WC1B 3HH
  Australia: Heinemann Publishers Australia Pty Ltd, N. J. Hudson, 85 Abinger Street, Richmond 3121, Victoria. Postal Address: PO Box 133, Richmond 3121, Victoria, Australia
  New Zealand: Heinemann Publishers (NZ) Ltd, D. J. Heap, Cnr. College Road and Kilham Avenue, Box 36064, Auckland 9, New Zealand
  USA: Heinemann Educational Books Inc., John Watson, 4 Front Street, Exeter, New Hampshire 03833, USA
  Canada: Book Society of Canada Ltd, John Irwin, 4386 Sheppard Ave East, PO Box 200, Agincourt, Ontario, Canada M1S 3B6

Hobsons Press (Cambridge) Ltd, Bateman Street, Cambridge, CB2 1LZ

Hodder & Stoughton, Mill Road, Dunton Green, Sevenoaks, Kent, TN13 2YA

Australia: Hodder & Stoughton (Australia) Pty Ltd, Apollo Place, Lane Cove, NSW 2066

Canada: Dominie Press Ltd, 345 Nugget Avenue, Unit 15, Agincourt, Ontario, M1S 4J4

New Zealand: Hodder & Stoughton Ltd, PO Box 3858, Auckland 1 (44–46 View Road, Glenfield, Auckland 10)

Republic of Ireland and Northern Ireland: Cannon J. Ltd, VAT 9/F/21834, Clones Road, Monaghan, Co Monaghan

USA: Educational and Industrial Testing Services, Post Box 7234, San Diego, California 97107, USA

Also: The Psychological Corporation (see below) for a few Hodder & Stoughton tests

Houghton Mifflin Company, Test Editorial Offices, Iowa City, Iowa, USA

Inner London Education Authority, The County Hall, London, SE1 7BB

The Institute for Personality and Ability Testing, Inc., 1602–04 Coronado Drive, Champaign, Illinois 61820, USA

H. K. Lewis & Co. Ltd, PO Box 66, 136 Gower Street, London, WC1E 6BS

Macmillan Education, Houndmills, Basingstoke, Hampshire, RG21 2XS

Australia: The Macmillan Company of Australia Pty Ltd, 17 Moray Street, PO Box 440, South Melbourne 3205, Victoria, Australia

Sydney Office and Showroom: 6–8 George Place, Artarmon 2064

Canada: Gage Publishing, 164 Commander Boulevard, Agincourt, Ontario M1S 3C7, Canada

New Zealand: Macmillan Company of New Zealand Ltd, PO Box 33570, 48 Northcote Road, Takapuna, Auckland, New Zealand

Republic of Ireland: Gill and Macmillan Ltd, Goldenbridge, Inchincore, Dublin 8, Eire

USA: Enquiries to Macmillan Education Ltd, UK

The National Foundation for Educational Research in England and Wales (*see* NFER-Nelson)

Nelson: Thomas Nelson and Sons Ltd (*see* NFER-Nelson)

The NFER-Nelson Publishing Company Ltd, Darville House, 2 Oxford Road East, Windsor, Berkshire, SL4 1DF

Australia: Australian Council for Educational Research, PO Box 210, Hawthorn, Victoria, Australia 3122

Canada: Institute of Psychological Research Ins., 34 Fleury Street West, Montreal, Quebec, Canada H3L 1S9

New Zealand: New Zealand Council for Educational Research, Education House, 178 Willis Street, Wellington C2, New Zealand

USA: Humanities Press Inc., Atlantic Highlands, New Jersey, USA

Oliver & Boyd, Robert Stevenson House, 1–3 Baxter's Place, Leith Walk, Edinburgh, EH1 3AF

Australia: Longman Cheshire Pty Ltd, 346 St Kilda Road, Melbourne, Victoria 3004, Australia

Penguin Books (Aust) Ltd, 487–493 Maroondah H/Way, Ringwood, Victoria 3134, Australia

Canada: Academic Press Canada Limited, 55 Barber Greene Road, Don Mills, Ontario, Canada

New Zealand: Longman Paul Ltd, Penguin Books NZ Ltd, 182–190 Wairau Road, PO Box 4019, Auckland 1, New Zealand

USA: Longman Inc., 19 West 44th Street, New York, NY 10036, USA

Personnel Press, 191 Spring Street, Lexington, Mass. 02173, USA
The Psychological Corporation, 757 Third Avenue, New York, NY 10017, USA
Saville & Holdsworth Ltd., North Lodge, 4 Esher Park Avenue, Esher, Surrey KT10 9NP
Scholastic Testing Service, Inc., 480 Meyer Road, Bensenville, Illinois, 60106, USA
Science Research Associates Ltd, Newtown Road, Henley-on-Thames, Oxfordshire, RG9 1EW
Stanford University Press, Stanford, California 94305, USA
Teachers College Press, 1234 Amsterdam Avenue, New York NY10027, USA
The Test Agency, Cournswood House, North Dean, High Wycombe, Bucks
Walsall Education Department (Psychological Services), Civic Centre, Darwell Street, Walsall WS1 1DQ

Indexes

Reviewers

Backhouse, J. K., 351, 359, 390, 437
Bennett, S. N., 215, 279, 282, 401
Blinkhorn, S. F., 494, 618, 631, 646, 655, 661
Chapman, B. L. M., 332, 344, 424
Clift, P. S., 5, 354, 542
Coxhead, P., 380, 394, 406, 430
Davies, R. A., 416, 506
Desforges, C. W., 348, 356, 385
Driver, R., 49, 88, 683
Duggan, E. P., 173, 222, 225, 227, 396, 532, 535, 538, 573, 582
Elliott, C. D., 89, 576, 604
Forrester, A., 59, 190, 263
Gipps, C., 26, 85, 195, 318
Gooch, D. R., 480, 612, 650
Graham, N. C., 111, 147, 483, 490
Gray, J., 152, 154, 255, 314
Hartley, J. R., 341, 387, 670
Hawkins, A. S., 30, 34, 54, 66, 219
Hewison, J., 121, 133, 161, 246
Jesson, D. St. John, 377, 410
Johnson, S., 128, 252, 602
Labon, D., 149, 473, 692
Lee, D. H., 41, 81
Lonton, A. P., 77, 462
Lovell, K., 369, 382
Mabey, C., 117, 304, 310, 323

Murphy, R., 165, 168, 552
Nisbet, J., 545, 556, 596
Nuttall, D. L., 437, 449, 567
O'Hare, D. P. A., 685, 688
Owen, C. F., 70, 156, 525
Phillips, C. J., 100, 185, 286
Plewis, I., 302, 435
Pumfrey, P. D., 230, 235, 243
Quigley, H., 8, 241, 259
Reason, R., 11
Ridgway, J., 336, 362, 373
Riding, R. J., 437
Roberts, T., 142, 455
Ryan, J. P., 517, 528, 599
Satterly, D. J., 508, 548, 561, 565
Sharp, S., 72, 96, 641, 680
Shipman, M., 502, 593
Sloboda, J., 696, 701
Stibbs, A., 159, 210, 267, 271
Stierer, B., 291
Sugden, D. A., 44
Sutton, A., 19, 521
Thurston, M., 175, 179, 181
Tuson, J., 37
Wood, R., 464, 585
Wrigley, J., 404, 419, 422, 477
Youngman, M. B., 623, 635, 663

Tests

* Brief report only.

AH1, X and Y, 462
AH2/AH3, 464
AH4 Group Test of General Intelligence, 473
AH5 Group Test of High-Grade Intelligence, 477
AH6 Group Tests of High-Level Intelligence, 480
AH Vocabulary Scale, 483
Applied Knowledge Test,* 612
APU Arithmetic Test, 332
APU Vocabulary Test, 490
Assessment in Nursery Education, 5
Basic Number Diagnostic Test, 8
Basic Mathematics Test A, 336
Basic Mathematics Test B, 341
Basic Mathematics Test C, 344
Basic Mathematics Test DE, 348
Basic Mathematics Test FG, 351
Basic Number Screening Test, 354
Basic Skills Assessment Program, 435
The Boder Test of Reading-Spelling Patterns, 11
Boehm Test of Basic Concepts, 19
Bowman Test of Reading Competence, 117
Bristol Achievement Tests, 437
   English, 437
   Mathematics, 442
   Study Skills, 445
   General Evaluation, 448
Bristol Social Adjustment Guides, 612
British Ability Scales, 494
British Picture Vocabulary Scale,* 500
The Burt Word Reading Test, 121
Children's Personality Questionnaire,* 617
Classroom Observation Procedure, 26
Cognitive Abilities Test,* 501

CSMS Science Reasoning Tasks, 670
Crowley Occupational Interests Blank,* 617
Comprehension Test for College of Education Students, 680
Culture Fair Intelligence Tests, 502
Deeside Picture Test, 506
Diagnostic Spelling Test,* 127
Differential Aptitude Tests, 508
Domain Phonic Test, 30
Durrell Analysis of Reading Difficulty, . 128
Early Learning: Assessment and Development, 34
Early Mathematical Language, 37
Edinburgh Reading Tests, 133
Edwards' Reading Test, 142
English Picture Vocabulary Test, 517
English Progress Test A, 147
English Progress Test A2, 149
English Progress Test B2, 152
English Progress Test B3, 154
English Progress Test C2, 156
English Progress Test C3, 159
English Progress Test D2, 161
English Progress Test D3, 165
English Progress Test E, 168
English Progress Test E2, 173
English Progress Test F2, 168
English Progress Test F3, 168
English Progress Test G, 168
The Essential Intelligence Test, 521
Essential Mathematics, 356
First-Grade Screening Test, 41
The Frostig Developmental Test of Visual Perception, 44
Gap Reading Comprehension Test, 175
Gapadol Reading Comprehension Test, 179

Garnett College Test, 683
Gates McKillop Reading Diagnostic
    Tests, 181
Graded Arithmetic-Mathematics Test,
    359
Graded Word Spelling Test, 185
Griffiths Mental Development Scales, 49
Group Mathematics Test, 362
High School Personality Questionnaire,
    618
The Harrison-Stroud Reading Readiness
    Profiles,* 53
The Holborn Reading Scale, 190
Hunter-Grundin Literacy Profile, 195
Infant Rating Scale, 54
The Infant Reading Tests, 59
Infant Screening Test, 66
JIIG-CAL Occupational Interests
    Guide,* 622
Junior Eysenck Personality Inventory,
    623
Keele Pre-school Assessment Guide, 70
Kuhlmann-Anderson Test, 525
Language Imitation Test, 72
Learning Through Listening, 210
The Leicester Number Test, 369
Lewis Counselling Inventory, 631
The Listening for Meaning Test, 528
London Reading Test, 215
Look: Visual Perception, 77
Macmillan Diagnostic Reading Pack, 219
Maitland Graves Design Judgement Test,
    685
Manchester Scales of Social Adaptation,
    635
Mathematics Attainment Test A, 373
Mathematics Attainment Test B, 377
Mathematics Attainment Test C1, 380
Mathematics Attainment Test C3, 382
Mathematics Attainment Test DE1, 385
Mathematics Attainment Test DE2, 387
Mathematics Attainment Test EF, 390
Mathematics Topic Tests, 394
The Meier Art Tests, 688
Minnesota Counseling Inventory, 641
Modern Language Aptitude Test, 692
Mooney Problem Check-List, 646
Moray House English Test 41, 225
Moray House English Test (Adv.) 2, 227
Moray House Junior English Test 5, 222

Moray House Junior Reasoning Test 2,
    532
Moray House Junior Reasoning Test 4,
    535
Moray House Mathematics Tests, 396
Moray House Verbal Reasoning Tests,
    538
Neale Analysis of Reading Ability, 230
Neale Analysis of Reading Ability:
    Adapted for use with blind children,
    235
Non-Readers Intelligence Test, 542
Non-Verbal Test BD, 545
Non-Verbal Test DH, 548
The Nottingham Number Test, 401
Number Test DE, 404
Occupational Check-List (Advanced),*
    649
Occupational Interest Rating Scale,* 650
Oral Verbal Intelligence Test, 552
Otis-Lennon Mental Ability Test, 556
Peabody Individual Achievement Test,*
    80
Picture Test A, 561
The Primary Reading Test, 241
Profile of Mathematical Skills, 406
The Pupil Rating Scale Revised, 81
Reading Comprehension Test DE, 243
Reading Level Tests (Experimental
    Version), 246
Reading Readiness Inventory, 85
Reading Test AD, 252
Reading Test BD, 255
Reading Tests EH1, EH2, EH3, 259
The Reading Vocabulary Tests, 263
Reynell-Zinkin Developmental Scales, 88
Richmond Tests of Basic Skills, 449
Rutter's Behaviour Questionnaires, 650
Salford Sentence Reading Test, 267
Schonell Reading Tests, 271
School and College Ability Tests, 565
Seashore Measure of Musical Talents, 696
Secondary Mathematics Item Bank, 410
Senior English Test,* 278
Senior Mathematics Test,* 416
Sentence Comprehension Test, 89
Sixteen Personality Factor Questionnaire,
    655
Southgate Group Reading Tests: Test 1,
    279

Southgate Group Reading Tests: Test 2, 282
SPAR Spelling and Reading Tests, 286
SRA Reading and Arithmetic Indexes, 455
The Staffordshire Test of Computation, 416
The Standard Reading Tests, 291
Study Habits Inventory, 661
Study of Values, 663
Tests of Proficiency in English: Listening, Speaking, Reading, Writing, 302
Thackray Reading Readiness Profiles, 304
Torrance Tests of Creative Thinking, 567
Transitional Assessment: English,* 309
Transitional Assessment: Mathematics, 419
Verbal Test BC, 573
Verbal Test C, 576
Verbal Test CD, 582

Verbal Test D, 585
Verbal Test EF, 593
Verbal Test GH, 596
The Visual Pattern Recognition Test and Diagnostic Schedule, 96
Walsall Infant Screening Procedure, 100
Watson-Glaser Critical Thinking Appraisal, 599
Wide Range Vocabulary Tests, 602
Wide-span Reading Test, 310
Williams Intelligence Test for Children with Defective Vision, 604
Wing Standardized Tests of Musical Intelligence, 701
Woodcock Reading Mastery Tests,* 110
Word Order Comprehension Test, 111
Word Recognition Test, 314
Yardsticks: Criterion-referenced Tests in Mathematics, 422
'Y' Mathematics Series, 424, 430
Young's Group Reading Test, 318, 323